CLINICAL
HYPNOSIS

CLINICAL HYPNOSIS

A Multidisciplinary Approach

WILLIAM C. WESTER, II, *Ed.D.*

Diplomate in Counseling Psychology
American Board of Professional Psychology

Diplomate in Clinical Hypnosis
American Board of Psychological Hypnosis

ALEXANDER H. SMITH, Jr., *Ed.D.*

Diplomate in Counseling Psychology
American Board of Professional Psychology

WITH 29 CONTRIBUTORS

Behavioral Science Center, Inc. Publications
Cincinnati, Ohio

Behavioral Science Center, Inc. Publications
Cincinnati, Ohio

The authors and publisher have exerted every effort to ensure that drug selection and dosage set forth in this text are in accord with current recommendations and practice at the time of publication. However, in view of ongoing research, changes in government regulations, and the constant flow of information relating to drug therapy and drug reactions, the reader is urged to check the package insert for each drug for any change in indications and dosage and for added warnings and precautions. This is particularly important when the recommended agent is a new or infrequently employed drug.

Although great care has been taken to preserve the authenticity and integrity of the clinical data, all patients' names, physical characteristics, and identifying material have been changed.

Copyright © 1991, BSCI Publications. The first edition was published in 1984 by J. B. Lippincott Company under the title CLINICAL HYPNOSIS: A Multidisciplinary Approach. All rights reserved. No part of this book may be used or reproduced in any manner whatsoever without written permission except for brief quotations embodied in critical articles and reviews. Printed in the United States of America. For information write Behavorial Science Center, Inc., Publications, 2522 Highland Avenue, Cincinnati, Ohio 45219.

Library of Congress Cataloging in Publication Data
Main entry under title:

Clinical hypnosis

Bibliography: p.
Includes index.
1. Hypnotism—Therapeutic use—Addresses, essays, lectures. I. Wester, William C. II. Smith, Alexander H. (Alexander Hamilton), 1949–   . [DNLM: 1. Hypnosis. WM 415 C641]
RC495.C53   1984   616.89'162   83-9366
ISBN 0-938-837-06-O

To my wife, **Betty,** and my children, **Chip,
Lori,** and **Scott,** whose love,
encouragement, advice, and support
have given me the inner strength
required to complete this book.

WILLIAM C. WESTER, II

To my wife, **Nonie,** and to my daughters,
Andrea and **Ellen,** may they always be
blessed with self-understanding and
compassion for others.

ALEXANDER H. SMITH, JR.

Contributors

Daniel L. Araoz, Ed.D.
*Professor of Community Mental
Health Counseling
Long Island University at
C.W. Post Center
New York, New York*

Barbara S. Baisden, M.S.W.
Columbus, Ohio

Edgar A. Barnett, M.B.
*Private Practice in Hypnotherapy
and Psychotherapy
Kingston, Ontario
Canada*

Stuart W. Bassman, Ed.D.
*Director of Counseling Services
Friars Club
Cincinnati, Ohio*

Bennett G. Braun, M.D.
*Associated Mental Health Services
Chicago, Illinois*

Peter A. Carich, Ph.D.
*Private Practice
Granite City, Illinois*

Simon W. Chiasson, M.D.
*Assistant Professor of Obstetrics
and Gynecology
Northeastern Ohio Universities
College of Medicine
Youngstown, Ohio
Past President, American Society of
Clinical Hypnosis*

Sheldon B. Cohen, M.D.
*Private Practice
Atlanta, Georgia*

Dabney M. Ewin, M.D.
*Clinical Associate Professor of Surgery
and Psychiatry
Tulane University Medical School
New Orleans, Louisiana*

Selig Finkelstein, D.D.S.
*Guest Lecturer on Hypnosis
Columbia Dental School
New York, New York*

Erika Fromm, Ph.D.
Professor of Behavioral Sciences
University of Chicago
Chicago, Illinois
Past President, Society for Clinical and
Experimental Hypnosis

Manuel I. Gerton, Ph.D.
Mental Health Practice
George Washington University
Health Plan
Washington, D.C.

Melvin A. Gravitz, Ph.D.
Clinical Professor of Psychiatry and
Behavioral Sciences
George Washington University
Medical Center
Washington, D.C.
Past President, American Society of
Clinical Hypnosis

Neil S. Hibler, Ph.D.
Clinical Psychologist
United States Air Force
Office of Special Investigations
Washington, D.C.

Claudia Hoffmann, Ed.D.
Children's Hospital Medical Center
Cincinnati, Ohio

Beata Jencks, Ph.D.
Associate Instructor
University of Utah
Salt Lake City, Utah

Raymond W. Klauber, Ph.D.
Counselor and Adjunct Assistant
Professor
Southern Illinois University
Edwardsville, Illinois

Eric Krenz, Ph.D.
Associate Instructor
University of Utah
Salt Lake City, Utah

William S. Kroger, M.D.
Clinical Professor of Anesthesiology
and Consultant, Pain Management
Clinic
University of California at Los Angeles
School of Medicine
Los Angeles, California

Harry R. Miller, M.D.
Clinical Assistant Professor
Department of Surgery
Medical College of Ohio
Toledo, Ohio

Joan Murray-Jobsis, Ph.D.
Clinical Psychology Practice
Chapel Hill, North Carolina
Past President, American Society of
Clinical Hypnosis

Donald J. O'Grady, Ph.D.
Associate Professor of Clinical
Pediatrics (Psychology)
Department of Pediatrics
University of Cincinnati College
of Medicine
Cincinnati, Ohio

Martin T. Orne, M.D., Ph.D.
Director, Unit for Experimental
Psychiatry
The Institute of Pennsylvania Hospital
and University of Pennsylvania
Philadelphia, Pennsylvania

Judson B. Reaney, M.D.
Behavioral and Developmental
Pediatrics
Lutheran Social Services
Rapid City, South Dakota

Alexander H. Smith, Jr., Ed.D.
Private Practice
Cincinnati, Ohio

Mathias E. Stricherz, Ed.D.
Counseling Center
Texas Tech University
Lubbock, Texas

Kripa S. Thakur, M.B.
Psychiatrist
Saskatoon, Saskatchewan
Canada

Donald J. Tosi, Ph.D.
Ohio State University
Columbus, Ohio

Thomas W. Wall, Ph.D.
Clinical Associate Professor of
Psychiatry and Behavioral Sciences
University of Washington School
of Medicine
Private Practice
Seattle, Washington

Thomas R. Werner, M.D.
Assistant Clinical Professor of
Psychiatry and Environmental Health
University of Cincinnati College
of Medicine
Private Practice
Cincinnati, Ohio

William C. Wester, II, Ed.D.
President and Senior Psychologist
Behavioral Science Center, Inc.
Cincinnati, Ohio

Foreword

Hypnosis has become a well established part of current medical, dental, and psychological practice. Once regarded as a magical and mysterious process, hypnosis is now recognized to involve measurable changes in human physiology. One can now document and begin to understand that hypnotic suggestion can lead to physical alterations; these changes include the ability of the nervous system to control pain or produce anesthesia, to alter the temperature of target areas of the body, or completely to relax muscle groups. Hypnosis may also allow the subject to reach back mentally to remember psychic trauma, and to build mental images as a basis for behavior modification. The practitioner's approach and suggestions during hypnosis can combine with the subject's responses to create various and powerful effects indeed.

Clinical Hypnosis: A Multidisciplinary Approach is a comprehensive treatment of the field of hypnosis. The theoretical and experimental foundations of hypnosis are examined, psychopathological states are explained, various techniques of induction and therapy are presented, and innovations and future trends are explored. Particular emphasis is paid to the clinical relevance of hypnosis in a wide variety of settings. Especially important are the annotated examples of hypnosis in clinical practice; such concepts as planning, timing, key words, repetition, imagery, reassessment, and intervention are explained and illustrated with clarity and insight.

These able descriptions of expertise have their roots in the distant and immediate past. When we read translations of ancient Egyptian papyri in which are mentioned hypnotic techniques, such as a patient staring at the flame of a flickering lamp when an operation was performed, we can begin to appreciate our debt to early experimenters and clinicians. Old medical records reveal healing by priests who induced hypnotic states; miraculous cures by touch and prayer occurred. Expectations of patients were increased by ceremonial rites, belief was enhanced by religious backgrounds, and imagination was stirred by positive creative abilities.

The ancients used indirect suggestion as the catalyst for healing to take place. Braid's experiments with patients in the 1840s elucidated the importance of direct suggestion when hypnosis was effective in treatment. Esdaile's contribution of reducing mortality rates in surgery from the prevailing 50% to 5% during the 1840s to 1850s was another hallmark in acceptance of the effectiveness of hypnosis. Many others have made important contributions to the progress of hypnosis; their work is reviewed in Chapter 1.

This collection not only teaches neophytes about hypnosis and how to use it clinically, but also serves as a ready reference for those who have been practicing hypnotherapy for many years. Many practitioners occasionally have patients who appear to be excellent hypnotic subjects but do not respond to therapy. This volume provides strategies for difficult problems such as these, and every practitioner of hypnosis can benefit from its content.

The authors of this volume have presented their material in such a way as to put hypnosis in its proper perspective in clinical practice. They point out the fact that it is no panacea, but that it, nonetheless, has an important place in patient treatment. For the professional who does not actively use hypnosis in his or her clinical practice, this collection will be a valuable source of information on the use of hypnosis as an adjunct to treatment in specific disease states and other clinical situations. The therapist can then at least know that hypnosis has aided in treatment in the past and, if appropriate, refer his patient or client with confidence to a colleague who uses hypnosis. Both the ill patient and proper professional practice will benefit.

Dr. Wester and Dr. Smith have done an outstanding job in selecting contributors, assembling and editing material, encouraging professionals, and advancing the cause of hypnosis. Those of us in medicine, dentistry, and psychology have much to gain and much to learn from this very welcome addition to the library of hypnosis.

Harold P. Golan, D.M.D.

Assistant Clinical Professor
Department of Oral and Maxillofacial Surgery
Tufts University School of Dental Medicine

Past President
American Society of Clinical Hypnosis

Preface

an intuition remains,
of surrenders to be made,
and of places made different
by the emptiness embraced.

(AUTHOR UNKNOWN)

CLINICAL Hypnosis: A Multidisciplinary Approach is a journeyman's guide to the applications of hypnosis. We have been fortunate in assembling the fruits of the clinical acumen and theoretical depth of many fine authors in the area of clinical hypnosis. The context in which it is presented should be considered first, before further reading.

The practice of hypnosis involves dual modes of thought. It requires each hemisphere to help the other—right brain and left brain, holistic and linear thought, thinking and intuition. It requires some integration of healthy pragmatics with the reserve of scientific caution and parsimony. We know that we seem to help some patients with some disorders some of the time. Beyond that is a great deal of uncertainty, speculation, and lack of clarity. These latter experiences are part of the mystique of hypnosis, and part of the routine murkiness that goes with being a practitioner. It is hoped that we continue to devise better maps of experience, perception, and shifts in behavior. That is presently the best we can do.

Hypnosis in this sense is a way to tinker with the power of the gods. One's effectiveness in using it depends upon the reverence accorded it. Those who pay these dues of frustration, reconceptualizations, questioning, and all that goes with being an advanced beginner—they are the ones from whom we learn. Those who fail in this reverence become inflated with what they do; they fall off the edge of the earth. Only because the gods have deemed it so, does the practitioner have "success." In a word, the therapist participates in a larger plan by which the human psyche may liberate itself from inertia, destructive complexes, discouragements about living, and those perceptions that bind itself to its greatest potential demise—that one's experience must remain the way it is. Like the shaman, the hypnotist must retire first in order to understand the course of things. Intuition and reasoning, observation and past experience are the tools with which suggestion may become the patient's redemption, however minute.

This is what we have attempted to assemble here. An anlage of thinkers and intuiters, observers and experiencers, who may describe, in their respective ways, the process of hypnosis as it unfolds. We have asked them to describe it from theoretical, empirical, and experiential foundations. We wanted to know methods of assessment and intervention, outcome criteria, and limitations in practice.

Some chose the intuitive–experiential route, others that of observations and theory. Each has attempted to respond to the guidelines so that the reader may begin to think with him in the form chosen about how to use hypnosis properly. We think there is some information for most readers in both "how to" as well as "how come." The reader may wish to sample each, experiencing the horse sense and wisdom of the how-to chapters and then returning to the carefully reviewed how-come chapters.

William C. Wester, II, Ed.D.
Alexander H. Smith, Jr., Ed.D.

Acknowledgments

W<small>E</small> have many people to thank for their hidden efforts in helping this work become possible. Certainly, our wives and families deserve medals for their patience and endurances of our absences, frustrations, discouragements, and wounded pride when we found ourselves sputtering. We owe a sincere thanks to our typist, Norma Malecki and to our reader, Helen Hill. The people from J. B. Lippincott Company, particularly Bill Burgower and Darlene Pedersen, have been most cordial and helpful. The business world is blessed to have such fine people. We are privileged to have been chosen by them to publish this work.

William C. Wester, II, Ed.D.
Alexander H. Smith, Jr., Ed.D.

Contents

13 Hypnosis in Surgery and Anesthesia
DABNEY M. EWIN   **210**

14 Hypnosis and Pain Control
STUART W. BASSMAN, WILLIAM C. WESTER, II   **236**

15 Hypnosis in Other Related Medical Conditions
SIMON W. CHIASSON   **288**

16 Hypnosis in the Treatment of Habit Disorders
JUDSON B. REANEY

17 Hypnosis in Family Therapy
BENNETT G. BRAUN

18 Hypnosis and Dentistry
SELIG FINKELSTEIN

UNIT FOUR
Use of Hypnosis With Psychopathological States

19 Hypnosis in Psychiatry
THOMAS R. WERNER

UNIT **FIVE**
Distinctive Innovations for the Practitioner

UNIT ONE
Orientation to the Practice of Hypnosis

1 Hypnosis in the Historical Development of Psychoanalytic Psychotherapy

MELVIN A. GRAVITZ
MANUEL I. GERTON

Under a variety of names, hypnosis has been known and utilized for millenia as a means of influencing human behavior (Ellenberger, 1970; Regnier, 1891; Stoll, 1904). Therapeutic suggestion has been practiced throughout the history of human endeavor, as we have sought to recognize and treat discomfort, disorder, and disease. Only in relatively recent times, however, has our knowledge of this process been enhanced by scientific as well as clinical methods of inquiry.

Foremost among the many who have advanced our understanding in this area is Sigmund Freud (1856–1939), the seminal thinker and insightful clinician who developed psychoanalysis. As is the case with many pioneers, much of his work had been incorporated into the accepted order of things even prior to his death, and he has exerted a significant impact on modern philosophy, literature, and art, as well as on medicine and psychology. While certain of his ideas have been reduced in importance and some have even been discarded, and while there is still dispute over certain of his conclusions, the essence of his teachings has continued to be accepted, and he remains a powerful influence. It is not hyperbole to say that he has been compared to Galileo, Darwin, and Einstein with a vigor more typically reserved for the conflicts surrounding theology and politics than science.

In seeking to appreciate the origins of Freud's monumental contributions, one must recognize the even older influence of another great development in our continuing quest for the understanding of the healing process. This is hypnosis, a variety of suggestion and concentration, which has been utilized for generations as a therapeutic agent.

Zweig (1932) has said that

> it is undeniable that all the psychotherapeutic methods of today derive by one route or another from the discoveries of Franz Anton Mesmer, who not only as a pioneer happened upon the recognition of the power of what we now call suggestion, but, however crudely and however mistakenly, maintained the

practice of the first scientific method of mental healing against the laughter, the scorn, and the contempt of an unduly mechanical science. These facts suffice to give him a place in history.

Yet, without detracting from the recognition that Mesmer rightly merits, the history of hypnosis and therapeutic suggestion can be traced back many centuries before him.

The ancient Egyptians empirically employed incantations, amulets, and the laying on of hands as treatment modalities without awareness of the inherent force of imagination or suggestion. In cultures throughout the world, even to the present day certain stones and metals have been considered to be endowed with healing powers. Temples dedicated to therapeutic trance states were founded in ancient Egypt some 4000 years ago and in ancient Greece and Rome about 2000 years ago. The touch of the mighty, such as a priest or monarch, was also considered to possess curative influence. Perhaps the greatest of these healers was the English king, Charles II, who drew such huge crowds that on one occasion in 1684, six suppliants were trampled to death while seeking to avail themselves of his healing touch.

Long before Mesmer, the use of magnets to effect cure was practiced by Robert Fludd (1574–1637), who believed that each person possessed a magnetic force and that a magnetic field developed when two people met. Fludd's contemporary, Johann Baptist van Helmont (1577–1644), held similar views, as did Agrippa von Nettesheim, Athanasius Kircher, and Paracelsus. The last named, in particular, anticipated many of Mesmer's theories, and he utilized suggestions given in induced trance states for the cure of illnesses. In the 17th century, Valentine Greatrakes, the noted Irish healer, successfully treated his patients by stroking them, as did Mesmer in later years, whereas Maximillian Hell, a contemporary of Mesmer, employed custom-made magnetized metal plates placed over the afflicted portions of the patient's body.

In the medical thesis ("De Planetarum Influxu" ["On the Influence of the Planets"]) which he presented in 1766 to the University of Vienna, Mesmer (1734–1815) drew heavily on the beliefs that had preceded him over the centuries (Mesmer, 1784; Mesmer, 1948). He maintained that the body responded to gravitational forces which he termed "animal magnetism," and he believed that realignment of these magnetic forces could restore health to an ill person. It is a parenthetic fact of history that Mesmer apparently derived his dissertation to a significant extent from Richard Mead's earlier work of 1704 in which was discussed the influence of atmospheric tides on health and sickness (Mead, 1704; Pattie, 1956, pp. 275–287). (That idea, incidentally, was not first conceived by Mead.) Although Mesmer went on to develop a prominent reputation as a physician in Vienna, later circumstances compelled his removal to Paris in 1778.

There, too, his practice flourished until two royal commissions investigated mesmerism and animal magnetism and concluded that there was no such force, but only imagination. Thus, the practice of mesmerism was considered unscientific charlatanism. Those findings, reported in 1784, effectively ended Mesmer's influence (Franklin et al, 1784; Poissonier et al, 1784).

Despite the temporary eclipse of animal magnetism, certain of Mesmer's disciples continued his work. One of the more active of these was Amand de Chastenet, the Marquis de Puysegur, whose innovative experiments included the "magnetizing" of trees in the countryside. He undertook to do that because the heavy demand on his time precluded his treatment of all of the people who came to see him. Interestingly, many of his subjects experienced therapeutic relief from these magnetized trees (Chastenet de Puysegur, 1784).

While commenting on de Puysegur's attribution to a magnetized tree the same therapeutic properties of a magnetized iron rod, General Noizet, a contemporary, insightfully noted, "To me it is obvious that the effect of the tree was non-existent, and [that which occurred] in its shade [was] entirely the result of the confidence that was placed in its magnetic virtues." He also emphasized the importance of mutual feelings of confidence and trust between magnetist and subject. Noizet, in other words, anticipated what today we call "expectancy set" in experimental psychology and "transference" in psychoanalysis (Chertok and De Saussure, 1979).

De Puysegur also discovered that there was a deeper stage of animal magnetism, which became known as somnambulism and which proved to be an effective therapeutic technique. (Mesmer himself had sought to evoke in his patients not sleep but a state of so-called *crisis,* or induced convulsions and agitation. One of de Puysegur's subjects not only became somnambulistic, but also spontaneously began speaking; in this way, the method of autosuggestion became associated with mesmerism. In addition, this experience was the antecedent of the cathartic "talking cure" discovered by Anna O decades later.

Another mesmerist, Louis Charpignon, found that suggestions made during the magnetic trance could influence the patient upon waking and thereby anticipated the later therapeutic technique of posthypnotic suggestion (Charpignon, 1841).

Unfortunately, de Puysegur and others became convinced that clairvoyance, telepathy, and other mystical forces could be demonstrated by the somnambulistic subject. The wild claims of such supernatural powers served to envelope mesmerism within an aura of spiritism and magic that for years inhibited its use by responsible investigators and practitioners.

Other mesmeric healers, however, began to understand that the essential process involved suggestion and was thereby both behaviorally and statistically normal. They held that somnambulism was the result of a process within the subject and was not imposed by the magnetizer. Foremost among these theorists was Jose Custudio da Faria (1906) and Alexandre Bertrand (1823).

In the decades that followed the demise of animal magnetism, the use of therapeutic mesmerism was alternately acceptable and unacceptable. Beset at times with extravagant claims on one hand and infiltration by the mysticists and spiritualists on the other, hypnosis (or hypnotism, as it was named in 1841 by James Braid [1843]) nevertheless managed to survive for one reason: it was undeniably effective in many cases, when utilized by competent professionals.

By the 1870s, hypnosis had reached an important point in its history with the work, described subsequently, of Jean-Martin Charcot, Auguste-Ambroise Liebeault, Hippolyte Bernheim, and finally Freud.

No less an authority than Freud himself subsequently recognized the debt that he and psychoanalysis owed to hypnosis. In 1924, he wrote,

> It is not easy to overestimate the importance of the part played by hypnotism in the history of psychoanalysis. From a theoretical as well as from a therapeutic point of view, psychoanalysis has at its command a legacy which it has inherited from hypnotism (1961).

Freud's introduction to hypnosis occurred when he was a young student (1935). He attended a public demonstration given by the noted Danish magnetizer, Carl Hansen, whose impressive performances throughout Europe encouraged numerous professionals to experiment with the modality. At this demonstration, Freud had observed that one of the volunteers induced by Hansen had become very pale at the onset of cataleptic rigidity and had remained so throughout the period of hypnosis. As he later wrote in his autobiography, it was this response that convinced Freud of the genuineness of hypnosis. Freud's encounter with Hansen may well have been an important factor several years later when Freud traveled to Paris to study at the Salpetriere, where hypnosis was extensively practiced by Charcot and his associates.

Freud was always receptive to new ideas about the unknown. Not only was hypnosis an example of this, but so was his interest in telepathy. In reference to the latter, he wrote in 1921 at the age of 65, "If I were at the beginning rather than the end of a scientific career, as I am today, I might possibly choose just this field of research, in spite of all difficulties" (1922). Paradoxically, he had a somewhat negative attitude toward what he terms the "mystical" character of hypnosis.

Freud had entered the University of Vienna as a medical student in 1873. While there, he was already personally interested in psychology, as shown by the fact that he took 3½ years of elective courses with the noted psychologist, Franz Brentano. During his third year, Freud studied at Ernst Brucke's famed Physiological Institute, acquiring a rigorous training in neuroanatomy. At that time, he did not have a strong interest in medical practice, but when Brucke pointed out to him that he was likely to experience an impecunious future were he to continue with a career as a biological researcher, Freud turned to the practice of medicine with some reluctance. (Another reason for this shift was his love for Martha Bernays [1861–1951] [Sullaway, 1979]. Marriage would have necessitated a more substantial income than that which came from research. The strength of his feelings for Martha may be gauged by the fact that he wrote her some 900 letters prior to their marriage [Ellenberger, 1970].)

After receiving his degree in 1881, Freud was working in Brucke's laboratory the following year when he was introduced to hypnosis as a therapeutic tool by Josef Breuer (1842–1925), a colleague who was later to play a crucial role in the origins of psychoanalysis (Freud, Freud, Grubrich-Simitis, 1978).

In June 1885, Freud was employed for 3 weeks as a *locum tenens* at Heinrich Obersteiner's private sanitarium near Vienna (Obersteiner, 1893). Hypnosis was regularly practiced by the staff, and the resident director, Maximillian Leidesdorf, took a liking to Freud. It is likely that Freud himself used hypnosis during his tenure at this socially prominent hospital, where he was required to wear a silk hat and white gloves as he attended his patients.

Soon after beginning to work at the sanitarium, however, Freud was notified that he had been awarded a government-sponsored traveling grant by the University of Vienna's Medical Faculty, on the basis of a strong and decisive recommendation by his mentor, Brucke. Consequently, Freud left for Paris, taking with him a letter of introduction from the noted neuropathologist, Moritz Benedikt, who had himself been a practitioner of hypnosis for many years (Benedikt, 1894). Freud remained in Paris from October 13, 1885, to February 28, 1886, under the tutelage of Charcot, a giant in French neurology. This charismatic and doctrinaire teacher was especially noted for his remarkable hypnotic cures of hysteria, particularly paralyses.

Influenced by Charles Richet, the brilliant Nobel laureate and physiologist, Charcot had undertaken the use of hypnosis by 1878. This was a courageous move, since the modality had at that time been discredited, largely as a result of the controversy surrounding Mesmer's animal magnetism a century before. In 1882, Charcot strongly supported the use of hypnosis in a historical address before the French Academy of Sciences (Ellenberger, 1970). In that presentation, he described the hypnotic trance as a physiological process occurring in the three successively deeper stages of lethargy, catalepsy, and somnambulism. His paper created a sensation, for it was this same academy that several times before had condemned such practices as unprofessional and unscientific. In being presented as a somatic phenomenon and with Charcot's imprimatur, hypnosis thereby became an appropriate subject for scientific study. Charcot's influence helped to generate a revitalization of officially sanctioned interest in hypnosis by restoring dignity to its use. He also laid the groundwork for two decades of prolific French study and practice of the method (Guillain, 1955; Gravitz, 1981).

Charcot's theoretical position that hypnosis was a physiological variant of hysteria and as such was a form of psychopathology was regularly communicated to the hundreds of visitors who came to the Salpetriere to attend his Tuesday and Friday lectures on nervous and mental disorders. While Charcot's theories on hypnosis were later discredited by the work of the Nancy School of Liebeault and Bernheim, Freud was nonetheless greatly impressed with the "Napoleon of Neurosis," as Charcot was affectionately and respectfully called. Freud subsequently translated into German certain of Charcot's writings, and he named his eldest son after Charcot (Freud, 1958).

During his brief stay at the Salpetriere, where decades earlier Phillippe Pinel had liberated the insane from their chains, Freud frequently attended Charcot's lectures on hypnosis and hysteria with "a sense of astonishment and an inclination to skepticism," according to his own statement (Freud, 1935). The clinical demonstrations that accompanied the lectures revealed to him that several states of consciousness or awareness could coexist in the same individual semi-independently of each other. This and other understandings helped to provide insights into the psychological origins of hysteria and the phenomenon of multiple personality, or double consciousness, as the French termed it. Freud was later to write that these hypnotic demonstrations gave him "the most profound impression of the possibility that there could be powerful mental processes which nevertheless remained hidden from the consciousness of men" (Freud, 1935). Such understanding was later to lead him to the development of psychoanalysis.

Charcot showed that hysterical symptoms could be artificially produced by hypnotic suggestion, with the dysfunction appearing either soon after hypnosis or even weeks later. (Today we call such phenomena posthypnotic suggestions.) In Paris, Freud also learned that hysterically predisposed persons could be placed in hypnosis and could later develop impairments without having been given direct suggestions. In such subjects, the power of direct external hypnotic suggestion was replaced by that of autosuggestion on a subconscious level. Freud subsequently wrote that Charcot "succeeded in proving by an unbroken chain of argument that these paralyses were the result of ideas which had dominated the patient's brain at moments of special disposition." In other words, Charcot had understood and had experimentally demonstrated the previously unknown unconscious mechanism of hysterical symptoms. Freud also recognized that, using hypnosis, "M. Charcot was the first to teach us that to explain hysterical neurosis we must apply to psychology" (Ellenberger, 1970). After observing that hysterical paralyses appeared to fit a lay person's understanding of paralysis and not the laws of neuroanatomy, Freud concluded further that hysteria "behaves as though anatomy did not exist, or as though it had no knowledge of it" (Chertok and De Saussure, 1979).

In addition, Charcot rejected the then-common theory that hysteria was always caused by the female hysteric's disturbed sexual development. He observed that hysteria could occur in prepubertal children and even in males, the latter being somewhat of an astonishing statement in certain circles in those times.

Although acknowledged as a master, Charcot was not without his critics. His experiments had been conducted on only a few dozen patients, most of whom were regular long-term residents of the Salpetriere and many of whom had been coached in advance by certain of Charcot's assistants, unbeknown to Charcot. One such patient, Blanche Wittman, received the title, "Queen of the Hysterics," for her performances. While Freud was impressed by what he saw, others were not. Joseph Delboeuf, a Belgian physician who visited Paris conjointly with Freud, returned home to write a highly critical account of the careless experiments on which Charcot's work was based (Delboeuf, 1889). Delboeuf, incidentally, was a strong supporter of the position that nonmedical hypnotherapists had much to contribute to the treatment process, and in that sense, he anticipated Freud's views on nonmedical psychoanalysts.

After returning to Vienna in April 1886 following a month of study in Berlin, Freud announced the opening of his practice. In May of that year, he delivered two papers on hypnosis at professional meetings. His increasing interest in the modality resulted in his preparation of the German translations of several of Bernheim's books on the subject, which appear to have been Freud's earliest writings in psychology. Then, with his financial base more secure, he finally married Martha Bernays in September of that same year, having become engaged to her in June 1882. Despite his interest in the modality, Freud did not incorporate hypnosis into his regular practice until the end of the following year and then only in the form of direct suggestion, as was typical of that time. Perhaps the delay was influenced by the criticisms of hypnosis by certain authorities, especially Theodor Meynert, a noted neuroanatomist.

While it is conceivable that unconscious resistances were operating, it is a fact that when Freud did finally include hypnosis in his therapeutic armamentarium, he did so with enthusiasm. In his own words,

> . . . there was something positively seductive [an interesting choice of word— M.A.G./M.I.G.] in working with hypnotism. For the first time there was a sense of having overcome one's helplessness; and it was highly flattering to enjoy the reputation of being a miracle-worker.

Even so, Freud found hypnosis to be "a temperamental and, one might almost say, a mystical ally."

Hypnosis was widely practiced throughout Europe during those years. There was a prolific outpouring of books, pamphlets, popular magazines, and scientific journal articles. In the single year of 1887, for example, at least 17 books on hypnosis were published, which was a level of productivity unsurpassed to the present day (Gravitz, 1981). Many respected physicians were employing the modality with success, including Albert Moll, Paul Moebius, Rudolf Heindenhain, and Richard von Krafft-Ebing, all of whom were known to Freud. At the same time there were denunciations of hypnosis from some authorities such as Meynert, who attacked Freud personally with the epithet that he was "only a hypnotist." Meynert also contended that hypnosis was the subjugation of one person by another, which could lead to mental unbalance, and that most hypnotic success was the result of either fraud or self-delusion on the part of the patient and therapist. Meynert further objected that much of the basis for hypnosis was sexual in nature. Freud's considered response was that respect for prominent figures, meaning Meynert, should take second place to the respect for facts. In that rejoinder, he paraphrased Charcot, who had used virtually the same words in replying to his own critics. However, it is possible, nevertheless, that Meynert's objection did affect Freud on some level, as is considered subsequently.

It should be noted that among Meynert's many contributions was his original concept of defense as a basic attitude of the organism. Freud was later to build upon this his own theory of defense mechanisms.

Despite the occasional criticism, Freud continued to employ hypnosis in his practice. Seeking to perfect his deepening techniques, he traveled to the French city of Nancy in the summer of 1889 with a female patient with whom his treatment had not been successful, and he spent several weeks there with Liebeault (Liebeault, 1886) and Bernheim (Bernheim, 1886). (They were not more successful with Freud's patient than he had been.) The Nancy view was that hypnosis was not a pathological condition but was instead a normal mental process related to suggestion, which was a universal phenomenon. It was at the Nancy School that scientific experiments, as performed by Jules Liegeois, showed that conflict could be engendered between the conscious and unconscious by giving subjects a posthypnotic command that was contrary to their moral and ethical values. The creation of an artificial neurosis by this method of conflict was undoubtedly known to Freud.

Also while Freud was in Nancy, Bernheim informed him that patients who had been deeply hypnotized to the level of somnambulism with amnesia could nevertheless be made to remember in a later waking state what they were otherwise unable to recall. This was accomplished by firmly ordering the patient to remember and by simultaneously pressing the hand forcibly upon the patient's forehead. Freud believed that his own patients might be helped to remember the apparently unconscious traumas that were responsible for their hysterical symptoms. From this understanding came the techniques of forced concentration and digital pressure that Freud began to use apart from hypnosis upon his return to

Vienna. He also utilized the method of free association in hypnosis and the practice of requiring the patient to lie down on a couch.

After his stay in Nancy, Freud, together with Bernheim, Liebeault, and numerous other dignitaries, traveled to Paris for the early August 1889 Congress for Experimental and Therapeutic Hypnotism. This important scientific meeting was strongly influenced by the Nancy School, and virtually no one from the Salpetriere participated in it. Paradoxically, in October of that same year, Paris was the setting for an International Congress on Magnetism, which was devoted to Mesmer's teachings and which was largely attended by lay persons. One cannot but compare that latter movement with some of the fringe developments of today.

As Freud continued to conceptualize his own theories, he became increasingly dissatisfied with the limitations of hypnosis as he saw them (Freud, 1891). One concern of his was that even when hypnotherapy remissed the symptoms, they could either return as they had been or in a substitute form. "In the long run," he said, "neither the doctor nor the patient can tolerate the contradiction between the decided denial of the ailment [by hypnosis] and the necessary recognition of it outside [hypnosis]" (Sullaway, 1979).

The years between 1888 and 1893, in particular, were marked by unabated disagreement between the Paris and Nancy Schools, and Freud, of course, was aware of this, especially after his 1889 visit to Nancy. By 1893, the work of Bernheim and others had convinced him that Charcot's theories of the psychopathological and physiological nature of hypnosis were without foundation. By that time, also, it was generally accepted by the scientific community that emotions and memories of a psychologically disturbing nature were forced into the unconscious as a defense mechanism (Murphy, 1949).

Even so, Freud's own understanding of hypnosis remained equivocal, although inclining toward the psychological approach of the Nancy School. Many years later in 1930, he wrote in a letter to A. A. Roback, "Over the question of hypnosis, I sided against Charcot, even if not entirely with Bernheim" (Freud, 1960). It would therefore seem that Freud's views on hypnosis developed through two overlapping stages: while at first he was impressed with Charcot's theories, he later shifted his allegiance to Bernheim. Each of these positions reflected his preference for a dualistic approach, and his beliefs about hypnosis allowed for both neurophysiological and psychological levels of explanation. He evidently never departed from his initial position in 1888 that it "would be just as one-sided to consider only the psychological side of the process [of hypnosis] as to attribute the whole responsibility for the phenomena of hypnosis to the vascular innervation." Many years later, in 1921, he proposed a phylogenetic theory of hypnosis which showed support for the so-called innate disposition view originally discussed by Charcot. Still, Freud's concept of the dualism of mind and body, derived from his study of hypnosis, continued to influence significantly the development of his subsequent psychoanalytic theories (Wetterstrand, 1897; Jones, 1953; Jones, 1954).

The basics of Freud's emerging new system of treatment began to take shape with his departure from the field of hypnosis and with his growing use of urged concentration, digital pressure, and free association. He used the term "psycho-analysis" to describe his new ideas only 9 months after the publication of *Studies in Hysteria.*

There was another practitioner of hypnosis who was to point Freud toward the path of psychoanalysis. This was Josef Breuer, who was 14 years his senior and who had also studied at the University of Vienna under Brucke. Sullaway has noted that Breuer was an accomplished physiologist whose own research in that field provided a conceptual basis for the theory of hysteria which he and Freud subsequently developed. Breuer was well regarded for both his keen and critical intellect and his personal traits of warmth, kindness, and caring. The two men first met while both were engaged in their respective research under Brucke in the late 1870s. While later studying under Charcot, Freud learned hypnotic techniques that were mainly based on direct authoritarian commands for symp-tom remission. However, Breuer taught Freud another style of hypnotherapy in which the modality was used to aid patients in recalling the circumstances at-tendant to the onset of their hysterical symptoms. The origin of Breuer's method was his treatment in the early 1880s of his classic patient, Bertha Pappenheim (1860–1936), who is better known in the psychoanalytic literature as Anna O. Coincidentally, she later became related to Freud through her marriage to a relative of his wife.

In the fall of 1880, Anna O began to manifest signs of severe psychological disturbance, the precipitating event having been the mental and physical ex-haustion that followed a period during which she nursed her ailing father for several months prior to his death. She presented a variety of extraordinary symp-toms, which are detailed in *Studies in Hysteria* (Breuer and Freud, 1937). These included states of confused delirium and hallucinations, for which she later be-came amnesic and which then blended into a state of autohypnosis. She called the latter her "clouds." Breuer discovered that if, when she was in an autohypnotic state, he repeated to her the frightened words for which she was amnesic and which she spoke in her delirium, then she was able to recall the forgotten details and obtain therapeutic relief. Anna O gave this procedure the English terms of "talking cure" and "chimney sweeping," while Breuer called it catharsis. Each symptom proved to be related to certain emotional conflicts associated with the stress of her nursing duties. Parenthetically, but probably not unrelatedly, the development of the cathartic method in hypnosis developed at the same time that Jacob Bernays, who was the uncle of Freud's wife, was publicizing in his own nonpsychological writings the Aristotelian theory of catharsis as a device in theatrical drama. Ellenberger (1970) has noted that, for a time, catharsis was a much discussed topic of conversation in Viennese social and intellectual circles of which Anna O was a member.

Breuer and Freud discussed the treatment of Anna O as early as 1883, and when the latter went to Paris in 1885 he described the case to Charcot. Forty years later, Freud wrote in his autobiography: "But the great man showed no interest in my first outline of the subject, so that I never returned to it and allowed it to pass from my mind" (Freud, 1935).

According to Ellenberger, it was not until 1889 that Freud himself employed the cathartic method with his hysterical patient, Emmy von N, whom he treated with hypnosis. Other hysterical patients were also treated by this method, and their progress is detailed in *Studies in Hysteria,* published in 1895. These cases represented a quantum leap forward in our understanding of emotional disorder and psychotherapy. It was logical and appropriate that hypnosis was the therapeutic medium.

In their joint theory of hysteria, which was summarized by them in the statement that "hysterics suffer mainly from reminisces," Breuer and Freud presented several fundamental assumptions which were derived from the hypnotherapy of their patients. To begin with, as Clarke (1980) and Sullaway (1979) have noted, there are mental forces and energies that operate in a mechanistic manner to produce both normal and disordered behavior. Further, the mental apparatus seeks to maintain an economically constant state of psychic energy. In hysteria, a certain amount of excitation or emotion becomes pathologically "converted" into symbolic somatic symptoms (*e.g.,* functional paralyses). This principle of self-regulated constancy provides the economic underlay for the related "pleasure–unpleasure" principle. Unpleasure may be viewed as mechanistically similar to a sudden rise in the level of excitation within the nervous system, while pleasure is mechanistically equivalent to its discharge through the appropriate reflex mechanism (*e.g.,* the sexual act). In his *Beyond the Pleasure Principle,* Freud held that the two principles of constancy and pleasure–unpleasure represented, in a sense, two aspects of the same process. In economic terms, Sullaway continued, cathartic hypnotherapy aims to facilitate the nervous system's normal but occasionally thwarted tendency to fulfill the requirements of constancy and pleasure. The therapist seeks to achieve this goal by uncovering through hypnosis and other means the major sources of "strangulated affect" within the unconscious and by "abreacting" them along more normal and conscious pathways.

Another of Breuer and Freud's theoretical assumptions maintained that there were three different dynamic mechanisms that could produce the strangulated affect: when a powerful emotion, such as fear, is experienced during either involuntary or self-induced "hypnoid states" (as in the case of Anna O); when a strong emotion is not permitted immediate or adequate conscious expression (as with inexpressible grief over a loss); and when there are thoughts that are intolerable to the ego (as with certain sexual ideas).

The last of Breuer and Freud's assumptions is that there is an unconscious part of the mind in a topographical sense. This concept was first enunciated by Breuer in his discussion of the case of Anna O and was frequently used by Freud in his own later psychoanalytic writings.

In his collaboration with Breuer and subsequent elaboration upon Breuer's work, Freud was indebted to Charcot, who had shown through hypnosis that hysterical behavior followed logical principles, even if these were not immediately evident.

Paradoxically, by the time that the hypnosis-based *Studies in Hysteria* was published in 1895, Freud was already well on the way to abandoning the method of hypnosis, which he publicly did in 1896, the same year in which he first used the term "psychoanalysis." He discontinued use of the modality not because he considered it to be useless as a treatment aid, but owing to a combination of both rationally objective and personally subjective motives. His objective opposition included the contentions that therapeutic hypnosis failed to produce permanent cures and that the results depended on the patient's relationship with the therapist; that hypnosis interfered with the elicitation of psychodynamics; that the patient's resistance to treatment was facilitated by hypnosis; that only a small number of patients could benefit from hypnosis; and that hypnotic techniques gave the patient the impression of a laboratory experiment and, in that respect, negatively influenced the course of treatment. Another factor was Freud's growing belief that analytic resolution of the patient's resistance was a powerful therapeutic tool, while hypnosis was believed to circumvent such analysis.

Of at least equal, if not greater, importance were Freud's subjective and more personal reasons. These included his acknowledged dislike of being stared at by his patients for many hours of the day. It was also significant that he was deeply involved in the development of his own psychoanalytic theories and techniques, bringing to that task intense interest and a sense of possessive discovery. In his hypnotic methods, moreover, he appears to have experienced a sense of personal failure because he was unable to hypnotize his patients as deeply and as frequently as he deemed necessary. One might surmise that if all of Freud's patients had been hypnotizible, then there would not have been any psychoanalysis. In his *Five Lectures on Psychoanalysis* of 1910 (Freud, 1957) he stated, "When I found that, in spite of all my efforts, I could not succeed in bringing more than a fraction of my patients into a hypnotic state, I determined to give up hypnosis," and thereby the development of psychoanalysis was well under way.

Then, too, Freud found hypnosis to be monotonous, boring, and mystical. His knowledge of hypnotic techniques was rather narrow and limited, and he relied heavily, as has already been noted, upon authoritarian commands. Breuer's cathartic method and the uncovering through hypnosis of the circumstances surrounding the origins of a patient's symptoms were noteworthy exceptions to that traditional style. Furthermore, the induction methods *per se* employed by Freud were limited in scope. These included the use of manual passes *a la* Mesmer above the patient's face and body, the placement of digital pressure upon the patient's forehead, grasping the subject's head between his own two hands and then commanding sleep, or holding the index finger sternly before the patient and calling, "Sleep!" as in the famous 1889 case of Emmy von N (Breuer and Freud, 1937). (Several years prior to her consultations with Freud, Frau Emmy had had hypnotic treatment by Auguste Forel [1888] in Switzerland, who in turn had referred her to Otto Wetterstrand in Sweden. The latter was known for his method of prolonged hypnosis-induced sleep which was given at his sanitarium, known as the "Palace of the Sleeping Beauty" [Wessterstrand 1897].)

Another crucial point to be noted is that Freud came to view hypnosis as involving for the patient more sexual meaning and even erotic stimulation than he felt could be comfortably tolerated. While the hypnotic relationship with the therapist was said to depend in part upon the unconscious sexual transferences of the patient, it would seem that Freud's own significant countertransference feelings were also significant, as will be discussed below.

Related to his retreat from hypnosis was Freud's increased understanding of the dynamic forces operating in neurosis. He recognized that in order for treatment to be effective, he needed "to overcome a psychical force in the patient which was opposed to the pathogenic ideas becoming conscious (being remembered)." In this way, Freud was led to the concept of defense, or repression, which was a major turning point and vital to the development of psychoanalysis as an integrated theory (Freud, 1960).

In a few short years, by the turn of the century, the professional use of hypnosis had waned in part, but not entirely, because of Freud's position and the concurrent rise in interest and influence of psychoanalysis. In addition, the reputation of hypnosis in responsible circles had once again become clouded by the contaminating forces of mysticism and charlatanry. (The same kind of contamination may be developing today in the early 1980s.)

Even so, there were a notable few, including Paul Schilder, Wilhelm Stekel, and others, who continued to practice hypnosis as the 20th century unfolded. There was a resurgence of interest during World War I, when "shell shock" and other neuroses were successfully treated by the modality. In fact, the Fifth International Psycho-analytical Congress, an important meeting that focused on those problems, convened in Budapest in September 1918. Freud, who was then 62 years old, made a remarkable statement before the audience:

> It is probable, too, that the application of our therapy to numbers will compel us
> to alloy the pure gold of analysis plentifully with the copper of direct suggestion;

and even hypnotic influence might find a place in it again, as it has in the treatment of war neuroses. (Freud, 1919)

Freud used virtually identical language in 1937 in his *Analysis Terminable and Interminable,* when he commented that "someday the pure gold of psychoanalysis may have to be alloyed with the copper of suggestion" (Freud, 1964).

Prior to the Budapest congress, in 1918, Freud had written, "I myself would reach back for the hypnotic method" in the treatment of certain mental disorders. Thus, it is evident that he continued to have an appreciation for the benefits of the modality, despite his announced abandonment of the hypnotic method in 1896. It would appear that one important factor that may have originally caused him to move away from hypnosis and that continued to keep him from it was his own feeling that erotic influence played a role in the patient–therapist relationship. During a lecture series at the time of the first World War, he discussed hypnosis within the context of a general theory of neurosis and reported the following:

> During the treatment of an especially obstinate attack in a patient whom I had several times relieved of nervous symptoms [by hypnosis], she suddenly threw her arms around my neck. Whether one wished to do so or not, this kind of thing finally made it imperative to inquire into the problem of the nature and source of one's suggestive authority. (Freud, 1922)

In his autobiographical study, which was published several years after the previous report, Freud returned to the same theme:

> One day I had an experience which showed me in the crudest light what I had long suspected. It related to one of my most acquiescent patients, with whom hypnotism had enabled me to bring about the most marvelous results, and whom I was engaged in relieving of her suffering by tracing back her attacks of pain to their origins, as she woke up on one occasion threw her arms round my neck. The unexpected entrance of a servant relieved us from a painful discussion but from that time onwards, there was a tacit understanding between us that the hypnotic treatment should be discontinued. I was modest enough not to attribute the event to my own irresistible personal attraction, and I felt that I had now grasped the nature of the mysterious element that was at work behind hypnotism. In order to exclude it, or at all events to isolate it, it was necessary to abandon hypnotism. (Freud, 1935)

By admitting that his female patient's startling behavior could not be explained by his "personal attraction," Freud began to understand the existence of a force that interposed itself between him and his patients. In this way, the concept of transference began to take shape in his thinking.

While the first patient mentioned suffered "nervous symptoms" and the other had attacks of pain, it cannot be determined if these two reports were of the same or two different patients. Even so, the countertransference dynamics are clearly evident. What is truly remarkable is that Freud appears to have deliberately conveyed to his patient that the event and its meaning were never to be discussed between them, despite the fact that the scrutiny and understanding of resistance, transference, and countertransference formed the very foundation of his psychoanalytic method.

One should note in further reference to the incident just described that Freud had written that he had "long suspected" what he concluded was the erotic nature of hypnosis, which in turn indicates that he "long" had an underlying (unconscious?) feeling that sexuality was involved in hypnosis. One might be inclined to speculate that in the countertransference mode he could have unknowingly and without conscious intent helped precipitate the patient's action by providing subtle cues to her, since we know today that such covert communications are possible.

In any event, Freud's subsequent theory of the sexual etiology of neurosis then began to take shape. As he observed in 1914, in his *History of the Psychoanalytic Movement:*

> The fact of the emergency of the transference in its crudely sexual form, whether affectionate or hostile, in every treatment of a neurosis, although this is neither desired nor induced by either doctor or patient, has always seemed to me the most irrefragable proof that the source of the driving forces of neurosis lies in sexual life. (Freud, 1957)

In fact, the theory of an erotic component in hypnosis may be traced back to the 1784 report of Bailly and others, which followed the original French investigation of animal magnetism chaired by Benjamin Franklin, the first scientific investigator of hypnosis (Franklin et al, 1784).

Freud again returned to the question of hypnosis in 1921 with his *Group Psychology and the Analysis of the Ego* (Freud, 1922). In that work, he compared being hypnotized with being in love. There was, he said, the same subjection, compliance, and absence of criticism toward the hypnotist as toward a love object, and he considered the hypnotic relationship to be a "group of two." Once again, this reflects Freud's continued interest and his feeling that eroticism is involved in hypnosis. Another antecedent of this theory was a view advanced in 1888 by Alfred Binet, the noted French psychologist, who stated, "The magnetized subject is like a passionate lover for whom there exists nothing else in the world but the loved one." It is known that Freud was familiar with Binet's work (Binet and Fere, 1887).

There is a curious account by a Hungarian, Franz Polgar, telling of his service as Freud's personal hypnosis assistant or technician for a half-year period in 1924. However, this otherwise unsubstantiated report that the psychoanalyst was himself again using hypnosis at that time has recently been proved invalid (Gravitz and Gerton, 1981; Gravitz, 1982; Polgar, 1951).

There are other reasons to conclude that Freud continued to have a positive interest in the modality into the 1930s. Joseph Wortis, an American who was in analysis with Freud in 1935, reported that on one occasion Freud spoke favorably and at length about hypnosis (Wortis, 1954). In the paper that was left unfinished at the time of his death in 1939, Freud cited compliance with posthypnotic suggestions as evidence for the existence of the unconscious (Freud, 1964). That was not a new point for him, moreover, since in his *Introductory Lecturers in Psychoanalysis* he had stated that hypnosis proved that one could possess information without being aware of it on a conscious level (Freud, 1922).

In summary, Sigmund Freud's utilization of hypnosis, or therapeutic suggestion, exerted a significant influence on the origins of psychoanalysis and, thereby, on later psychotherapies, including those practiced today. Together with Breuer, who was himself a most perceptive observer of human behavior, Freud developed a dynamic understanding of hysterical neurosis which was facilitated by the use of hypnosis, as well as by the motivation and intelligence of their patients. It was from this hypnotically derived theory of neurosis that the broader outlines of psychoanalysis subsequently evolved. Fueled over the years by a few dogmatists and partisans, the notion that Freud completely rejected the modality is inconsistent with the historical record of his own words. Freud's interest in hypnosis throughout his professional life and the impact of this interest on his psychoanalytic theories and techniques have clearly been significant developments in the larger history of the healing process.

References*

Benedikt M: Hypnotismus und Suggestion: Eine klinisch-psychologische Studie. Leipzig and Vienna, Breitenstein, 1894

Bernheim H: De la suggestion et des applications a la therapeutique. Paris, Doin, 1886

Bertrand A: Traite du somnambulisme. Paris, Dentu, 1823

Binet A, and Fere C: Le magnetisme animal. Paris, Alcan, 1887

Braid J: Neurypnology, or the Rationale of Nervous Sleep Considered in Relation to Animal Magnetism. London, Churchill, 1843

Breuer J, Freud S: (1895) Studies in Hysteria. New York, Nervous and Mental Diseases Publishing Co, 1937

Charpignon J: Physiologie, medecine et metaphysique du magnetisme. Paris, Germer-Bailliere, 1841

Chastenet de Puysegur AMJ: Memoires pour servir a l'histoire et a l'establissement du magnetisme animal. Lyon, n.p., 1784

Chertok L, De Saussure R: (1973) The Therapeutic Revolution: From Mesmer to Freud. New York, Brunner-Mazel, 1979

Clarke RW: Freud: The Man and the Cause. New York, Random House, 1980

da Faria JC: (1819) De la cause du sommeil lucide. Paris, Jouve, 1906

* In the following references, a year-date in parentheses after the author's name indicates the date when first published. The abbreviation S. E. indicates the *Standard Edition of the Complete Psychological Works of Sigmund Freud,* which was edited by James Strachey and published in London by the Hogarth Press in multiple volumes.

Delboeuf JPF: Le magnetisme animal; a propos d'une visite a l'ecole Nancy. Paris, Germer-Bailliere, 1889

Ellenberger H: The Discovery of the Unconscious. New York, Basic Books, 1970

Forel A: Der Hypnotismus und seine strafrechtliche Bedeutung. Berlin and Leipzig, Guttenberg, 1888

Franklin B, Majault, Leroy, Sallin, Bailly, D'Arcet, DeBory, Guillotin, Lavoisier: Rapport des commissaires charges par le roi, de l'examen du magnetisme animal. Paris, Moutard, 1784

Freud EL (ed): Letters of Sigmund Freud 1873-1939. New York, Basic Books, 1960

Freud E, Freud LF, Grubrich-Simitis I (eds): Sigmund Freud. New York, Harcourt Brace Jovanovich, 1978

Freud M: Sigmund Freud: Man and Father. New York, Vanguard, 1958

Freud S: Hypnose. In Bum A (ed): Therapeutisches Lexikon fur praktische Artzte. Vienna, Urban & Schwartzenberg, 1891

Freud S: (1910) Five lectures on Psychoanalysis. S.E., Vol 11, 1957

Freud S: (1914) History of the Psychoanalytic Movement. S.E., Vol 14, 1957

Freud S: (1916-17) Introductory Lectures in Psychoanalysis. London, Allen & Unwin, 1922

Freud S: Wege der psychoanalytischer Therapie. Internationaler Zeitschrift fur Psychoanalyse 5:61-68, 1919

Freud S: (1920) Beyond the Pleasure Principle. London, Hogarth, 1960

Freud S: (1921) Group Psychology and the Analysis of the Ego. London, International Psycho-analytical Press, 1922

Freud S: (1924) A Short Account of Psychoanalysis. S.E., Vol 19, 1961

Freud S: (1925) An Autobiographical Study. London, Hogarth, 1935

Freud S: (1937) Analysis Terminable and Interminable. S.E., Vol 23, 1964

Freud S: (1940) Some Elementary Lessons in Psychoanalysis. S.E., Vol 23, 1964

Gravitz MA: Bibliographic sources of nineteenth century hypnosis literature. Am J Clin Hypnosis 23:217, 1981

Gravitz MA: Polgar as Freud's hypnotist? Contrary evidence. Am J Clin Hypnosis 24:272, 1982

Gravitz MA, Gerton MI: Freud and hypnosis: Report of post-rejection use. J Hist Behav Sci 17:68, 1981

Guillain G: (1955) J. M. Charcot 1835-1893: His Life—His Work. New York, Hoeber, 1959

Jones E: The Life and Work of Sigmund Freud. Vol 1. New York, Basic Books, 1953

Jones E: The Life and Work of Sigmund Freud. Vol 2. New York, Basic Books, 1955

Liebault AA: Du sommeil et des etats analogues, consideres surtout au point de vue de l'action du moral sur le physique. Paris, Masson, 1866

Mead R: De imperio solis ac lunae in corpora humana et morbis inde oriundis. London, Smith, 1704

Mesmer FA: (1779) Mesmerism, by Doctor Mesmer. With an Introductory Monograph by Gilbert Frankau. London, Macdonald, 1948

Mesmer FA: Recueil des pieces les plus interessantes sur le magnetisme animal. Paris, n.p., 1784

Murphy G: Historical Introduction to Modern Psychology. New York, Harcourt Brace, 1949

Obersteiner H: Die Lehre vom Hypnotismus. Leipzig and Vienna, Breitenstein, 1893

Pattie FA: Messmer's medical dissertation and its debt to Mead's De imperio solis ac lunae. J History Med Allied Sci 11:275, 1956

Poissonier, Caille, Mauduyt, Andry: Rapport des commissaires de la Societe Royale de Medicine, nommes par le roi, pour faire l'examen du magnetisme animal. Paris, Moutard, 1784

Polgar F: The Story of a Hypnotist. New York, Hermitage House, 1951

Regnier LR: Hypnotisme et croyances anciennes. Paris, Aux Bureaux du Progres Medical, 1891

Stoll O: Suggestion und Hypnotismus in der Volkerspsychologie. Leipzig, Veit & Comp, 1904

Sullaway FJ: Freud: Biologist of the Mind. New York, Basic Books, 1979

Wetterstrand OG: (1890) Hypnotism and Its Application to Practical Medicine. New York, Putnam, 1897

Wortis J: Fragments of an Analysis with Freud. New York, Simon & Schuster, 1954

Zweig S: (1931) Mental Healers. New York, Viking Press, 1932

2 Preparing the Patient

WILLIAM C. WESTER, II

Preparing the patient is the first and perhaps the most important aspect of the hypnotherapeutic process. Conducting an interview with or taking a history from your patient requires a professional skill backed by your training and experience in medicine, psychology, or dentistry. This screening process is a phase in the hypnotic process that separates the professional from the lay hypnotist. The screening process assists the professional in identifying patients for whom hypnosis might be contraindicated. Suicidal individuals, those suffering from certain forms of psychoses, overly dependent individuals, and borderline patients may exhibit significant psychopathology that would rule out hypnosis as the most appropriate therapeutic modality. The intake interview also allows time for a relationship to develop between the patient and therapist, and this rapport in itself will foster hypnotic susceptibility.

It should be noted that this screening process can begin prior to the patient's ever seeing the therapist. A well-trained staff can be extremely helpful in acquiring basic information which later can be used as part of the interviewing process. For many patients, the first contact is with a nurse or receptionist. It is important for these staff members to be knowledgeable about hypnosis and the hypnotherapeutic process. They are able to obtain information such as identifying data, referral source, and the reason for choosing hypnosis as a treatment procedure even prior to the patient's first visit.

After obtaining a complete history, the therapist can request additional specific information about the purpose and goal of treatment at the time of the first visit. For example, in the case of a patient who is seeking help for obesity, it is important to obtain data such as typical eating patterns, the patient's motivation for change, and other data that may be useful later in treatment. If a patient commits himself to a typical eating day, this information will allow for a base from which to measure any objective changes as a result of intervention.

18

After the therapist obtains the initial data and rapport has begun to develop, it is important to talk about hypnosis and the patient's expectations of this form of treatment. The therapist may elect to have the patient ask questions, or he may provide this information in a more structured form. The therapist can begin by briefly defining hypnosis in terms of available literature and the current state of the art. The patient can be helped to identify with such phrases as an "altered state of awareness or perception," "a highly relaxed state," or "a state other than a state of being fully alert or asleep." Barber and Calverley (1964) have shown that simply labeling the situation as "hypnosis" is sufficient to enhance responsiveness (Barber, Spanos, Chaves, 1974). There is some controversy as to whether the therapist should use the term hypnosis or use a more innocuous term such as relaxation. Why avoid something that may even enhance the suggestibility of the patient? Patients come to treatment with a "mind set" which can be utilized to the therapist's advantage during the prehypnotic procedures. While mechanical devices are unnecessary and infrequently used, if a patient insists on using a pendulum and the use of the pendulum will enhance cooperation and suggestibility, then by all means follow the patient's directives.

Myths and Misconceptions About Hypnosis

Myths such as the belief that hypnosis is identical with sleep can be clarified at this point, by reassuring the patient that he will not fall asleep and will remain in control of himself at all times. The stage I sleep EEG pattern is similar to that of the normal waking state except for the presence of rapid eye movements (REMs). The EEG record of the hypnotic state is consistently similar to that of the waking state. Experiments have shown that if the therapist walks out of the room the patient emerges from hypnosis as soon as he realizes that the therapist has left (Evans and Orne, 1971). You can give a reassuring suggestion, such as, "You will remain in control at all times, and if for any reason at any time you become uncomfortable, you can open your eyes and terminate this state. I have never had a patient who had to do this; however, it is important for you to know that you maintain this control." This suggestion can be helpful in reassuring and relaxing the patient who has little knowledge of hypnosis. Prehypnotic statements can be made about the fact that the patient will hear everything that is going on if he so chooses and will not be unconscious at any time. For example: "You may hear sounds from another office or the traffic outside, but these sounds will just fade away as we proceed." This type of statement can be helpful if such conditions exist. Telling the patient ahead of time that he will know about and hear other sounds helps to keep him from reacting if other sounds do occur (Kroger, 1977).

Some patients are concerned about the power of the hypnotist over the patient. By reassuring the patient about the control issue, you can help him understand that he is not going to do anything against his will. Conn (1981) suggests that hypnosis is not an external force that can be used to overcome a patient's willpower. Hypnosis can be used as an alibi, a folie á deux, a neurotic compromise, or a legitimation or rationalization of behavior, as well as being genuine, involuntary, and automatic. The idea of coercion through hypnosis is a myth that will not disappear as long as it is fostered by uninformed hypnotists who believe that all initiative and self-determination is surrendered by the patient to an all-powerful hypnotist. This issue of doing something against one's will is obviously complex; however, a simple explanation during the initial session is sufficient for your purposes.

Another myth is that of spontaneous talking. The patient needs to be reassured that he will not spontaneously begin talking or revealing information he wishes to keep secret. It is equally important for him to know that he can talk while under hypnosis and that a talking procedure may be appropriate to assist him with his problem.

Udolf (1981) lists several other misconceptions about hypnosis not usually found in the literature. These include the misconception that the therapist must be a charismatic, dynamic, or forceful person; that hypnosis is an unusual or abnormal condition; that hypnosis helps patients develop powers of extrasensory perception; and that hypnosis is harmful to subjects. When employed by a trained therapist, hypnosis is safe.

After you have dealt with the aforementioned misconceptions, it is helpful to ask the patient if he has any additional questions about hypnosis. In most cases, this process will help ensure a good response when the therapist continues with the induction procedure. It is important to realize that the induction procedure begins at the time the patient makes the first contact or appointment.

Assessment of the Patient

There are several other considerations and factors to be evaluated by the therapist prior to the utilization of hypnosis. Therapists who are cognizant of these factors will improve their rapport and therapeutic effectiveness. Crasilneck (1975) identifies seven factors to be considered during the screening assessment:

1. Why does the patient come for treatment at this time?
2. Who sent the patient? Did the patient decide on treatment himself?
3. Is the patient sufficiently motivated to give up his symptom?
4. Is the symptom being used to manipulate others?
5. Is the symptom organic or psychogenic?

6. What is the patient's degree of impulsivity and what is his level of frustration tolerance?

7. What is the patient's general personality or history?

Why Does the Patient Come for Treatment at this Time?

It is important to ascertain the patient's motivation for treatment and whether or not a positive prognosis can be made. Many patients select a therapist who uses hypnosis as a last resort, and they expect magical and rapid results. For example, most obesity patients have tried every possible diet, various weight reduction programs, and diet pills. Some have even gone to the extent of having their mouths wired shut or undergoing stomach stapling or intestinal bypass surgery. Knowledge about the patient's motivation may be of value to the therapist in selecting the most advantageous hypnotherapeutic approach.

Who Sent the Patient?

Who referred the patient to you and whether or not the patient is there because he wants to be are factors related to the issue of motivation. Hypnotherapy is most effective when the patient comes to treatment with a positive mind set about hypnosis. Frequently, referral sources such as physicians or previous patients predispose the patient to be a cooperative subject. For example, it is not uncommon for the patient to travel 100 miles or more because his family doctor has highly recommended the "hypnotist" doctor. This type of patient typically comes highly motivated for treatment, and, in fact, some practitioners feel that the patient is already in a trance-like state when he enters the office. On the other hand, if the patient has a negative set about hypnosis or if he is resentful, he probably will not be a good subject. For example, a person who comes to therapy in order to stop smoking because his spouse wants him to stop may have resentment that interferes with treatment. Professionals who use forensic hypnosis frequently see resistant subjects who may be in their office because a detective has asked them to cooperate in this way. The witness may in fact come to such a session but may be experiencing anxiety and reservations about whether or not he wants to follow through with this procedure. As a result, the subject's resistance affects hypnotizability.

Does the Patient Want to Give Up His Symptom?

Symptoms can serve a very important purpose for a patient, who, in turn, may not be aware that he is resisting all forms of treatment because of the benefits being received from his symptom. For example, an 87-year-old patient did not want to give up the pain symptom in her left foot because she associated pain with living and felt she would die if the pain were gone. This patient was taught a way to reduce the intensity of the pain and instructed not to give up all of the pain. Thus, the patient may not be motivated to give up his symptom until he is able to understand and gain insight into the secondary gain being obtained. In some cases in which the patient is receiving such secondary gain, it may be unwise to attempt to remove the symptom, and a therapeutic approach other than hypnosis may be more appropriate.

Is the Symptom Being Used to Manipulate Others?

People tend to do things for a reason, and the symptom may in fact be used to manipulate other individuals. The Adlerian theory that behavior is purposeful can be valuable to the therapist who is trying to evaluate whether or not a patient is using his symptom to manipulate others (Dreikurs, 1964). Asking the patient directly about the payoff he is getting from his symptom, or making a more subtle statement such as "could it be that you . . ." may be helpful in analyzing what is happening with this patient. The patient's nonverbal response to such a hypothetical statement can provide valuable information about the underlying dynamic process of the symptom and of the individual.

Is the Symptom Organic or Psychogenic?

Nonmedical practitioners must be extremely careful to rule out any organic cause for the presenting symptom. For example, a patient's obesity may be directly related to a thyroid problem or a male patient's erectile dysfunction problem may be related to undiagnosed diabetes. Some states actually deal with this issue in their licensing law, with the incorporation of such statements as, "In order to make provision for the diagnosis and treatment of medical problems, a licensed psychologist engaging in psychological psychotherapy with clients shall maintain a consultative relationship with a physician licensed to practice medicine by this state" (ORC 4732.20, 1972). Many patients are initially referred to a psychologist by a physician; however, if this is not the case and the symptom could be medically related, then the organic causative factor should be ruled out before treatment.

What Is the Patient's Degree of Impulsivity and Level of Frustration Tolerance?

When obtaining a history, the therapist must try to understand the patient's frustration level and degree of impulsivity. If there is evidence pointing to poor impulse control, the patient can be helped to understand how his behavior may interfere with treatment. Many habit behaviors, for example, are "empty" habits (habits no longer having unconscious significance) but still having a strong conditioning element. The smoker who states, "I don't remember picking up that cigarette" would be classified in this category. Fairly simple behavioral techniques can be helpful to make your patient more accountable and cognitively aware of what he is doing. For example, you might say to the dieter, "We have a contract between us, and you must wait 10 minutes before eating something inappropriate to your goal," or to the smoker, "I want you to send me a postcard every day for 7 days indicating that you are a nonsmoker." These suggestions help make the patient with poor impulse control more aware of his behavior.

What Is the Patient's General Personality or History?

Finally, other information obtained when you take the history may be valuable in treating the patient. The individual with migraine headaches may have significant occurrences in his life that contribute to the presenting problem. His home life, work environment, school environment, and even his fantasy life may be playing a role in his problem. It is important to reemphasize that hypnosis is an adjunctive tool to be used to help patients but not at the exclusion of all other appropriate psychotherapeutic procedures.

The First Induction

A fairly straightforward and simple progressive relaxation technique may be the best induction technique to use with a new patient. This procedure allows for an unfolding of natural responses that helps to eliminate the mystique about hypnosis. The therapist can easily move from this nonthreatening induction to a variety of deepending techniques and then to specific therapeutic suggestions. The experienced therapist and hypnotist considers not only the suggestions but the entire process to be therapeutic. Barber (1980), in a discussion of "modern hypnosis," states that more traditional hypnotic procedures should be replaced with an integration of whatever techniques are most appropriate for the patient. Like any other therapeutic approach, the hypnotic approach is only as effective as the therapist.

PROGRESSIVE RELAXATION PROCEDURE	COMMENTS
"Just sit back in the chair now and relax and let yourself be comfortable. Just close your eyes, listen to	Initial relaxation with focus on patient being responsible for relaxation

PROGRESSIVE RELAXATION PROCEDURE	COMMENTS
my voice, focus in on what I am saying, and let yourself relax. One of the best ways to begin to relax is to take a few moments, focus in, and concentrate on your breathing. Get in tune with your entire breathing process . . . think about it, sense it, feel it, experience it. Sense and feel air coming into the body as you inhale; sense and feel some air leaving the body as you exhale; begin to feel the relaxation, particularly in the chest muscles each time you exhale. Also note the nice rhythm produced each time you inhale and exhale . . . a very comfortable, relaxing rhythm . . . much like a metronome . . . just inhaling and exhaling. As this very normal breathing process continues, you will find that you are able to relax more thoroughly and more comfortably, and as I continue to talk with you, your breathing will assist you in relaxing even more deeply . . . even more completely . . . and at the same time I would like you to focus your attention on the top part of your head . . . your scalp . . . much like you did with your breathing, get in tune and in touch with your scalp, feelings in your scalp, sense and feel the muscles, the skin tissue, the hair follicles, and pay particular attention to the muscles of the scalp, allowing those muscles to become just as comfortable and just as relaxed and smooth as you would like. The mind is a very powerful thing, and anything that you need to do to enhance that feeling of smoothness and comfort-	Eye closure and focusing of patient's attention on therapist's voice Deep-breathing exercise Patient begins to be aware of bodily responses and changes. Reassurance that what is happening is normal Reinforcement that the patient's own process will bring about a deeper state of relaxation Transfer of patient's breathing awareness to bodily awareness Use of the phrase "as you would like" continues to reinforce that the patient is in control and can function accordingly

PROGRESSIVE RELAXATION PROCEDURE	COMMENTS

ableness in those muscles is perfectly all right; for example, think of something smooth, like a quiet lake early in the morning . . . not even a ripple on the water, just as smooth as glass, or smooth like a plastic table top . . . just very smooth, and then just let that feeling of smoothness and comfortableness and relaxation just filter through all of the muscles in the scalp, and then just as if you were taking a relaxing shower, let that feeling of comfort and smoothness and relaxation just flow down into the muscles in the forehead. When we frown or get angry we get little wrinkles in our forehead, and just let those muscles smooth out and become relaxed and comfortable . . . flowing, comfortable relaxation . . . now, down into the muscles of the forehead, the temples, the cheeks, down into the chin, around the mouth, just all of the facial muscles now comfortably and thoroughly and more deeply relaxed . . . such a good feeling, and that feeling of comfort and relaxation can continue down into the muscles of the neck . . . the front, the back, the sides of the neck, down at the base of the neck where we get sort of tense or tight at times, flowing, comfortable relaxation across the shoulders, across the shoulders now, and down the arms, down the arms and through the elbows and forearms and the wrists and the hands . . . comfortably, thoroughly relaxed. The hands and sometimes even the scalp may tingle a little, may feel a little warm or a

Permission to relax even further

Introduction of imagery

On-going reinforcement of the relaxation process

Many patients experience a physi-

PROGRESSIVE RELAXATION PROCEDURE	COMMENTS

little cool; that sensation doesn't have to happen, but if it does it's very normal and natural . . . there is nothing to be concerned about . . . just enjoy the deep comfortable relaxation. Your breathing is excellent now, it has slowed down nicely, comfortably, and as that feeling of relaxation and comfortableness continues to flow down through all the muscles in the back and the sides and the chest and down into the waist . . . you can just sense yourself relaxing more deeply and completely, more thoroughly and more deeply relaxed . . . and as that feeling of relaxation and comfort comes into the waist area and down into the hips, you may sense a feeling of heaviness in the entire body, a feeling of heaviness more completely and more thoroughly relaxed, flowing, comfortable relaxation, down through the hips and down into the legs, down through the legs, down into the ankles, and finally into the feet . . . the entire body, all of the muscles in the body, thoroughly comfortable, and deeply relaxed . . . listening to my voice, focusing in on what I am saying, and just letting go . . . complete, total, relaxation."

ological change. This suggestion makes these feelings, if they occur, seem normal and natural.

Therapist continues to watch for nonverbal cues and then reinforces the behavior seen.

More direct suggestion about patient experiencing a deeper level

Deepening experience

The Posthypnotic Talk

Listen and learn from your patients. When the therapist has finished working with a patient it is a good idea to give the patient a few moments to alert himself fully from the hypnotic state. During this phase of treatment, you can ask the patient to tell you what he felt during the hypnotic experience and how he feels at the present time. Your patient will provide you with valuable information. If you listen carefully, you can use this information to assist your patient further by enhancing future hypnotic sessions. For example, analyze the following comments that are frequently given:

"That was the most relaxed I have ever felt."
"I felt the tingling and warm feeling just as you described."
"My favorite place was really beautiful, and the sun was warm."
"I think I may have fallen asleep—I was so relaxed."
"I could not get an image of a favorite place."
"I don't think that I was hypnotized."
"I just could not stop thinking—it is hard for me to let go and give up control."
"My arm felt heavy instead of light, and I could not see a balloon."

The first four statements can give you valuable cues about the degree of relaxation, physiological changes taking place, the patient's ability to utilize imagery, and perhaps even some deeper trance phenomena. The last four statements suggest a problem in developing images, skepticism about hypnosis, analytical compulsive thinking, control issues, and resistance. Whether it is positive or negative, the posthypnotic information should be addressed. The first four positive statements can be reinforced with comments such as the following:

"I could really tell that you were deeply relaxed. I was able to observe your good breathing rate and facial muscular relaxation."
"As I mentioned, during hypnosis, tingling and other physiological changes are natural. You may or may not experience them as we continue to work with hypnosis."
"It's really nice to take a mini-vacation in our mind."
"You were deeply relaxed; however, you fully alerted yourself at the appropriate time."

You should also deal with the negative statements in order to enhance suggestibility during the next session. Appropriate responses to the four negative statements might be as follows:

"That's okay— not everyone responds in the same way. We will do something different next time."
"That's a very common feeling. What *did* you feel and experience?"
"Control is an interesting issue. As you learn more about hypnosis and realize that you are in total control and that this is your 'state,' you will respond just fine."
"Isn't that interesting. Was your arm so heavy that it was immobile?"

As you continue to develop rapport with your patient and obtain additional information, you can begin to map out your next therapeutic strategies.

The Use of Supplemental Information

Many professional organizations have developed literature to educate the public on a variety of professional procedures. I have written a "Questions and Answers about Clinical Hypnosis" brochure that can be sent to the new patient or made available in the waiting room. The brochure contains information on professional training, cost, misconceptions about hypnosis, description of induction, brief history of therapeutic use, length of treatment, and ways to find a qualified hypnotherapist. Such a source of information can be helpful in answering many of the patient's questions in advance of the first appointment (Wester, 1982).

References

Barber T: Self-Suggestions for Personal Growth and the Future of Hypnosis. Presented before the American Psychological Association Annual Convention, Montreal, September 1980

Barber T, Calverley D: Toward a theory of hypnotic behavior: Effects on suggestibility of defining the situation as hypnosis and defining response to suggestions as easy. J Abnorm Soc Psychol 68:585, 1964

Barber T, Spanis N, Chaves J: Hypnosis, Imagination, and Human Potentialities. New York, Pergamon Press, 1974

Conn J: The myth of coercion through hypnosis. Int J Clin Exp Hypn 29:95, 1981

Crasilneck H, Hall J: Clinical Hypnosis: Principles and Applications. New York, Grune & Stratton, 1975

Dreikurs R: Children: The Challenge. New York, Duell, Sloan and Pearce, 1964

Evans F, Orne M: The disappearing hypnotist: The use of simulating subjects to evaluate how subjects perceive experimental procedures. Int J Clin Exp Hypn 19:227, 1971

Kroger W: Clinical and Experimental Hypnosis, ed. 2. Philadelphia, JB Lippincott, 1977

Ohio Revised Code—4732.20, 1972. Ohio Psychology Licensing Law

Udolf R: Handbook of Hypnosis for Professionals. New York, Van Nostrand Reinhold, 1981

Wester W: Questions and Answers About Clinical Hypnosis. Columbus, Ohio Psychology Publishing, 1982

3 Using the Patient's Breathing Rhythm

BEATA JENCKS

The relationship between breathing and altered states of consciousness is self-evident and can be observed in animals that are hypnotized (Ratner, 1967). Any ancient priest or shaman must have known that slow, deep breathing induces restful, sleeplike states of hypnosis, that hyperventilation leads to excited states of altered consciousness, and that purposeful control of inhalations versus exhalations can bring body and mind to different levels of activity.

The terms *hypnosis* and *altered states of consciousness* are used interchangeably in this chapter, although, generally, I prefer the term hypnosis for indicating relaxed and sleeplike states and the term altered states of consciousness for describing actively contemplative or excited states, and for movement hypnosis (Jencks, 1979).

Foundations

Chinese Breathing Theory

The earliest known recorded medical text that is related to breathing therapy, was engraved in China on 12 small jade plates in the 6th century B.C. Indian Buddhist breathing exercises were brought to China by Boddhidharma, probably about 526 A.D. His teachings were later called Zen in Japan. The old theories and their practice have survived ever since in China, and they were lately investigated by the Hungarian expert on Chinese and Tibetan medicine, Stephen Pálos. His book on breathing (Pálos, 1974) is not only an extensive work on present Chinese breathing therapies, but it also compares them to the ancient texts on breathing methods. Pálos remarks that Chinese medicine employs concepts and experiences that differ from those accepted by Western medicine, and that the results of the ancient Chinese treatments are often superior to those achieved by modern West- **29** ern medical treatments. The Chinese treatments include both breathing and hypnosis.

Yogic Breathing

The oldest Indian literary record that related hypnosis with breathing (Der Grosse Brockhaus, 1931) appeared about 200 B.C. in the Hatha Yoga branch of the comprehensive yoga philosophy. Yogic breathing (Vishnudevananda, 1960) makes much use of retention, rhythms, and locks. These exercises are often too strenuous for Westerners who have not undergone previous relaxation training, since their nervous systems are generally not as calm and "parasympathetically oriented" as those of the Indians for whom the yoga system was originally designed. Plokker (Stokvis and Wiesenhütter, 1971) observed yoga masters in India before these practices became fashionable in the West. He noticed in the early 1900s that even Indian disciples of yoga were advised to proceed slowly with breathing exercises, and only according to individual progress, from the simple to the difficult.

Middle East Trends

The Persians as well as the Semites used breathing exercises in their religiosanitary systems. Exercises of the Mazdaznan (Hanish, 1914; Jencks, 1977) reached Europe and the United States in the late 1800s.

Western World Developments

In Grecian medicine, breathing exercises were not important, nor were they in the medicine of the Middle Ages. However, they did play a role in the religious systems of these cultures. The monks of Mount Athos used the breathing rhythm while saying their prayers, and Loyola (1491–1556) advised that each word of a prayer be said during an inhalation, while the attention should be fixed on the meaning of that word during the remainder of the breathing cycle (Schultz, 1932). Pairing inhalations with meditative thoughts increases attention, concentration, and invigoration. Thus, Loyola used the physiologically invigorating effect of inhalations (Jencks, 1974) for keeping his students from drowsiness during their religious exercises.

Contemporary Methods

In continental Europe, many psychotherapies used since the early 1900s have included the use of breathing (Stokvis and Wiesenhütter, 1971). Bonnet allowed his patients to repeat hypnotic formulas in rhythm with breathing. Hirschlaff used a "respiration metronome" for regulating inhalations and exhalations during hypnotic relaxation. Jolowicz ranged Coué's method by having large groups of subjects breathe in unison, starting with a deep inhalation for half a minute, holding the breath, and then releasing it explosively. Upon this, followed relaxation suggestions that induced the hypnotic state. Then followed specific suggestions for individuals while Jolowicz touched their forehead or diseased body parts. Extended exhalations, yawning, and abdominal breathing was advised by many early psychotherapists. Décsi let his patients start their self-hypnosis with close attention to the breathing cycle by feeling the respiratory movements in shoulders, chest, and abdomen. Self-suggestions followed, and the exercise ended with several deep inhalations and exhalations. Wilhelm Reich (Johnsen, 1976) observed his patients' breathing for assaying anxiety and muscle tension. In Norway, some of his early breathing measures survived in the work of Bunkan's (1979) diagnostic and therapeutic method. Schultz (1932) observed that the breathing rhythm becomes irregular during stress responses, and also that persons who visualize easily breathe more regularly. He used the formula, "It breathes me," with passive attention to the breathing, in his Standard Autogenic Training exercises. The passive attention was intended to present conscious interference with autonomic functioning. It resulted in subjects' reports of feeling "being cradled by waves," or "being one with a breathing cosmos."

Fuchs (1949/50) also emphasized that conscious interference with breathing must be avoided. Her patients lay on a couch with closed eyes, while she monitored the respiration with her hand on their chest, suggested relaxation during exhalations, and suggested further during the exhalations loosening of joints, opening of tight body passages, widening of body cavities, and softening of skin and other tissues. Fuchs called her method first "Self-Rhythmization" and later "Functional Relaxation." She maintained that it was not "hypnosis." She also let her patients *re-member* and *experience* insensitive, "disowned" body parts, much as Perls did (1969) later.

In my early work (1970a, b, c; 1971), I adopted much of Fuchs' method. However, soon it became evident that patients were lured by this approach into dependency promoting and deeper than necessary hypnotic states, and that the monitoring hand of the therapist on the body of the patient was unnecessary, since breathing can easily be observed visually. Further, at first in work with healthy theater students and later also with patients, it became evident that the utilization of inhalations was as important as the use of exhalations, and that conscious guidance of the breathing was even more successful for rehabilitative purposes than just "passive attention" (Jencks, 1974).

In the United States, the utilization of breathing in hypnosis has not been as extensive and developed as in the Orient and on the continent of Europe.

Kroger (1977) observed that shallow, diaphragmatic breathing is usually associated with lighter stages of hypnosis, while slow, deep, regular, abdominal breathing is characteristic of the deeper stages of hypnosis. Ratner (1967) had observed that the respiration of hypnotized birds was slow and shallow as compared with control birds. This earlier observation includes two of Kroger's observed aspects. Kroger then suggested the hypnotic deepening instruction "You will go *deeper* and *deeper* with each breath you take." This is not an effective deepening suggestion, since inhalations counteract deepening of *relaxed* hypnotic states, and Kroger probably intended a relaxed, deep state. For "superawake" or active movement hypnotic states, inhalations are an effective means of induction. The wording of instructions for breathing in hypnosis must be carefully chosen, since subjects may either take instructions very literally or they may interpret vague instructions in diverse ways. If a subject is told to "breathe deeply," this may be interpreted as to inhale deeply, to exhale deeply, or to do both deeply. The effects upon hypnotic states will differ drastically. Since relaxation is physiologically promoted by exhalations, instructions for inhalation, while "going deeper" is suggested, are inappropriate unless "counterbreathing" (Jencks, 1977) was intended. Counterbreathing may be used for the purpose of exercising or stressing muscles, or for increasing the vial capacity while doing stretching exercises. It is appropriate in some yoga exercises and for athletes, but not for hypnotic deepening or for hypnotic arousal. For those, exhalations and inhalations, respectively, are appropriate. Kroger's further instruction, that the therapist should breathe deeply in unison with the patient, is a good utilization of teaching by example.

Many good hypnosis practitioners give appropriate instructions for deepening or levitation, or utilize correctly the subject's breathing phases. However, seldom was the appropriate use of breathing pointed out to students of hypnotic methods. During a workshop of the American Society of Clinical Hypnosis in Park City, Utah, in 1970, no mention of the relationship of breathing to hypnosis was made, and yet the following appropriate uses were demonstrated:

R. La Scola— "Take a very deep breath, let it out slowly, and relax."

H. E. Owens— "With every breath that you exhale, think 'relax.' "

R. E. Pearson— "As you take a deep breath, there is a tendency for your hand to rise from your knee."

A. E. St. Amand— "I touched her shoulder, and pressing down on expiration, she went deeper."

Assessment of Subjects

Appropriate utilization of breathing will profit any subject during heterohypnosis or self-hypnosis.

Patients and subjects for whom breathing measures alone or incorporated into more complex hypnotic procedures were useful have been (1) any subject needing muscle tension relief or mental relaxation (Jencks, 1977); (2) psychotherapy patients that needed to learn to cope with the environment and to counteract habituated neurotic responses (Jencks, 1970c, 1976, 1978); (3) patients with asthma and other breathing difficulties (Jencks, 1976, 1978, 1980a, 1981b, 1982); (4) subjects with sleeping difficulties (Jencks, 1980b); (5) patients with aches and pains (Jencks, 1977); (6) children (Jencks, 1980a, 1981, 1982; Jencks and Guertler, 1981); (7) patients with speech difficulties (see below); (8) adjunct measures for medical patients (see below); and (9) athletes (see Chap. 27).

Assessment of subjects' cooperation, amount of anxiety, and capability for entering hypnotic states can be achieved by observing the results of the simple instruction, "Sit back, relax, allow your eyes to close, and *just exhale relaxedly.*" If eyelid fluttering results, the practitioner is assured of a cooperative and good hypnotic subject. If cooperation is lacking or anxiety becomes obvious, anxiety-reducing breathing measures without eye closure (Jencks, 1977) can be introduced prior to subsequent hypnotic procedures.

For patients who "fear hypnosis" or otherwise resist it, breathing measures alone, without additional hypnotic procedures, can be used. Subsequently, relaxation suggestions can be paired with imagery during the appropriate breathing phases.

Children and athletes need continuous challenges for maintaining interest and cooperation. The many possibilities of utilizing the breathing rhythm offer choices for progressively varied programs (see also Chap. 27).

Healthy subjects, such as businessmen, students, housewives, or nurses, greatly appreciate the simple procedures and immediately effective results of utilizing the respiration phases. Since they breathe anyway, they welcome the use of such "mini-hypnoses" without eye closure throughout their daily routine for relaxation, invigoration, and other purposes (Jencks, 1974, 1977).

Such "mini-hypnoses" are also appropriate for anxiety and stress reduction for medical patients during needle insertion, for swallowing medicine, for easing urination after operations, or for bearing with x-ray scanning apparatus that may evoke claustrophobic reactions in apprehensive patients, when it passes over the body closely repeatedly in the darkness of a strange room.

Interventive Processes

Breathing measures can be used by themselves as hetero- or self-"mini-hypnoses," or they can be incorporated into any therapeutic or stress-ameliorating hypnotic procedure. The efficacy of whatever hypnotic method is used, is decreased by *not* utilizing the effect of the breathing phases.

In the following, the expression *breathing rhythm* or *breathing cycle* refers to the sequence of exhalation and inhalation, or vice versa, and the expression *breathing phase* refers to either the exhalation or the inhalation.

Attention to the breathing rhythm induces, by itself, a hypnotic state, but appropriate utilization of the breathing phases (Table 3-1) greatly increases the effectiveness of hypnotic procedures.

Table 3-1. Physical, physiological, and psychological feelings, actions, and images related to the breathing rhythm

Exhalation	Inhalation	Holding the Breath
Physical and Physiological		
Relaxation	Increase of tension	Maintenance or increase of tension
Heaviness	Lightness	Unstable equilibrium
Calmness	Stimulation	Restlessness
Warmth	Coolness	Variability
Darkness	Brightness	Variability
Softness	Hardness	Rigidity
Moisture	Dryness	
Weakness, weariness	Strength, invigoration, refreshment	Momentary conservation of strength
Psychological		
Patience, endurance	Speed, being startled	Anxiety, oppression
Contemplation	Ready attention	Strained attention
Equanimity	Courage	Cowardice
Deep thought, concentration	Openmindedness, creativity	Closedmindedness
Introversion	Extroversion	
Boredom	Excitement	Keen interest
Satisfaction	Curiosity	Uncertainty
Depression	Cheerfulness	Nervous tension
Comfort	Exhilaration	Uneasiness
Generosity	Greed	Stingyness
Actions		
Relax, release, let go, loosen	Tense, bind, tighten, grasp	Hold on
Release pressure, stream, or flow out	Increase pressure, stream, or flow in	Maintain or increase pressure
Liquify	Solidify	Maintain consistency
Expand, widen, open	Contract, narrow, close	Dimension unchanged or congestion
Sink, descend, fall asleep	Ascend, levitate, rise, wake up	Maintain level
Lengthen	Shorten	Maintain length
Move or swing forward, strike, kick, punch, reach out	Move, draw, pull, or swing backward, haul in	Stop, stand, or hold still
Send, give, help, offer	Receive, take, demand	Keep, interrupt
Laugh, sigh, giggle	Sob, gasp	Smile, frown

Observation of a patient's breathing allows the practitioner to measure the subject's anxiety as soon as the patient enters the office. The breathing of an anxious person is usually shallow, with intermittent holding of the breath and sighing. The patient's attention can be drawn to such a pattern, its meaning explained, and relaxation induced by means of relaxed, prolonged exhalations, with or without eye closure. Or, the therapist may observe the patient's respiration and let relaxation suggestions coincide with the subject's exhalations, thus tuning into the patient's breathing phases unnoticed.

A simple demonstration for making the subject aware of the relaxing effect of exhalations and the strengthening effect of inhalations is the following. The subject is instructed to raise one arm to shoulder level and observe how breathing in and out will make the arm move up and down. Then the subject may experiment with moving the arm down during inhalation and up during exhalation and feel which of the two procedures feels more natural.

Levitation suggestions should always be paired with the subject's inhalations, and deepening suggestions with exhalations. Thus, hypnotic deepening may be combined with arm levitation by making use of both inhalations and exhalations alternately during the same procedure.

For deepening hypnosis, instructions may be "Inhale, hold your breath . . . , and now let go of it and go down . . . , deeper . . . , and deeper. . . ." Each "deeper" is timed with the subject's exhalation phase, and his inhalations are allowed to occur during pauses of speech or during irrelevant remarks or diverting guided imagery. If the image of descending stairs is used, each step down is suggested during the exhalation phase, although several breathing cycles may have passed, during intervening suggested imagery, since the last step down. A completely different hypnotic state is induced when climbing a mountain is suggested during the inhalation phases.

With guided imagery, correct timing must be used for suggesting certain feelings, actions, or images into the appropriate breathing phases for best results (see Table 3-1). If this is disregarded, suggestions that are made during the inappropriate breathing phases may counteract the suggested responses. Imagery coupled with the respiratory phases is limitless. For instance, the following sequence can be used, incorporating *in*halations and *ex*halations. "And now you are on a meadow, and you allow yourself to (*ex*) *lie down.* And you start dreaming, and while you dream a (*in*) *cool breeze* passes over your forehead. It is very pleasant, but if an insect bothers you, just (*ex*) *blow it away.* That's right, just (*ex*) *blow away* all your troubles . . . (*ex*) *away* for the moment. . . ."

Occasionally, subjects slip into a deeper level of hypnosis than the practitioner intended. That happens especially in group situations, where one set of instructions must serve many subjects. Then the following suggestion is useful: "And now, all of you who have slipped so deep that you are not really listening to my instructions, *in*hale! *In*hale again, and come with your inhalations to a more attentive level." This proved especially useful in large groups of university students undergoing Standard Autogenic Training, who preferred to pleasantly slip into oblivion rather than concentrate on the consecutive formulas for conditioning the autonomic nervous system.

For children, the most useful breathing interventions have been the direct use of the imagination with exhalations and inhalations, Passive Movements (Michaux et al, 1961; Jencks, 1977; Jencks and Guertler, 1981), and specially designed guided-imagery fairy tales (Jencks, 1980a, 1981). Blowing up imaginary balloons and playing games in which animal sounds and machine noises are mimicked during prolonged exhalations have been invaluable for asthmatic children and those with speech difficulties for extending the exhalations, teaching abdominal breathing, and allowing relaxation to occur. Passive Movements were originally developed in France for inducing hypnotic relaxation in overactive children that were not capable of learning Standard Autogenic Training (Schultz, 1932; Jencks, 1973). The method derives its potent effect from nerve cells in the joints, that evoke by reflex slower, deeper breathing, which in turn results in greater relaxation. The method was made into a game of "Clippy Doll" (Appendix 3-1) by Jencks and Guertler (1981). Appendix 3-2 gives the fourth in a series of therapeutic fairy tales. It specifically offers imagery for more relaxed, deeper breathing and a positive attitude toward chest and lungs. The three earlier tales introduce concentration, eye closure, relaxation, and stress-reducing imagery.

Assessment of Effectiveness

Disorbio (1975) investigated the effect on anxiety reduction of EMG biofeedback, versus Jencks' breathing measures, versus EMG and breathing combined. He obtained statistically significant behavioral speech anxiety decreases for the breathing and the combined training, but not for the EMG biofeedback alone. This is the only research known to me that reported comparative statistical results of my breathing interventions. In a recent workshop for therapists that work with disturbed children, a comparison of the potential effectiveness of Stroebel's Kiddie QR (Stroebel, Stroebel, and Holland, 1980), Cautela's (1978) progressive relaxation, and my breathing measures (1974, 1977) proved the last as the most helpful, simple, and promising of good results.

Beyond these two comparative studies, the following reports are examples, besides those published in my earlier reports, of the efficacy of the described breathing procedures.

A phlebotomist reported from a veterans' hospital consistent anxiety reduction results with intensely nervous and shaky patients from the detoxification unit.* During repeated blood drawings, simple relaxation and diversion inducing instructions were given: "Now take a deep breath, hold it a moment, and let it out slowly while you relax." The needle was inserted during the exhalation, and the patients reacted then calmly to the blood drawing.

Results of the hypnotic relaxation procedures in self-care asthma programs for children, mentioned previously, have been rather successful over the last 2 years. Similar good results are now reported from a speech clinic, using part of the asthma self-care program with kindergarten-age children. The fairy tale part of that program was used independently by an 8-year-old asthmatic girl. Her grandmother had once read the four tales to her at a time when no respiratory stress was evident. The tales apparently made a deep impression on her, since a few weeks later, the child reported:

> I felt an attack coming on in that smoke-filled room, with all the excitement around me. But I just caught Twinkle in those rings between my fingers and thumbs, and I held Twinkle there and thought all the time of Twinkle's beautiful crystal palace in my chest, and I did not have an attack.

A further, somewhat unusual example of the efficacy of the utilization of breathing is the following from a group course at the University of Utah. An alexic 24-year-old female, a very bright and eager student, was instructed to experiment with exhalations for relaxation during her reading assignments for the course. Within 2 days she had reduced her usual time of 20 minutes for reading two short pages to only 8 minutes per two pages. However, she had added by herself "inhalations for concentration and alertness" during her experimenting, after reading about this in her text (Jencks, 1977) for the course assignment.

Finally, a caution about the use of breathing measures with patients that are incapable of coping with reality. I have observed several mental breakdowns when the anxiety level of such patients was raised too high, apparently by the physiologically healthful changes, due to treatment procedures, which overtaxed the mind by forcing it to cope with the reality of the body.

Future Trends

Recent reports of generally superior results from the United States, Canada, and Sweden, due to the incorporation of Jencks' breathing procedures into hypnosis, auger a rather bright future for these ancient measures to be used again in a modern manner.

More specifically, it is hoped that this chapter will stimulate prospective practitioners and teachers of hypnosis to do the following.

* Colton D: Personal communication, 1981

First, that they will incorporate the appropriate phases of the breathing cycle into whatever hypnotic techniques they are using.

Second, that they will learn to reduce their own stress level with momentary "mini-self-hypnoses" by utilizing their own breathing phases.

Third, that they will teach their subjects to couple the imagination with appropriate respiratory phases during guided or free imagery exercises.

Fourth, that by letting patients use simple inhalation and exhalation interventions, paramedical personnel can aid in reducing the patients' stress level during injections, taking of medicine, urinating after abdominal operations, dressing changes, and so on.

Fifth, that this chapter will stimulate future experimenters to design comparative research to investigate the relative efficacies of tranquilizing medication, versus progressive relaxation, versus Standard Autogenic Training, versus biofeedback training, versus breathing procedures, in large groups of hypertensive patients, pre- and postoperative hospitalized patients, subjects with sleeping difficulties, or in the design of programs for natural childbirth and for other stress-reduction courses.

Appendix 3-1

Passive Movements— "Clippy Doll"

Cut in one piece, from light cardboard, the body and head of a doll. Make small holes where hip and shoulder joints would be, and insert into each hole a paper clip as upper limb for arms and legs. Attach onto each paper clip two more, for lower limbs and hands and feet.

Let the child color the body part and play with the paper clip limbs. Let him feel how relaxed those limbs are. Then tell the child that he will now *be* such a "Clippy Doll," and proceed according to the following instructions.

(1) Have the child sit or lie relaxedly. (2) Gently take one of his arms and support it with one hand at the elbow. Use your other hand to move parts of the child's arm freely, but very *slowly* and *gently*. (3) Start with the wrist and fingers, then forearm, then upper arm, then, while gently supporting it, the whole arm. Make slow movements, as wide as the joints allow, but never use any force. The procedure should be as gentle as a lullaby. (4) Encourage the child to hum, purr, or growl during the exercise in order to make sure that he exhales deeply and slowly. (5) After both arms have been thus relaxed, do the same with the neck, moving the head gently, pulling it gently away from the shoulders and trunk. (6) Proceed to the lower limbs if necessary and time allows. (7) Shift the supporting

hand any time as the movements demand, always having the child's limb supported so that he feels no weight or insecurity with respect to the movements.

This exercise, if performed properly with the prolonged exhalations by humming or other noises, is exceedingly functional in relaxing the diaphragm and allowing trapped air to get out of the lungs because of the deepened breathing. It brings about deep physical and mental relaxation and feelings of security and cooperation, and it is extremely useful if a child is too tired or ill to relax by himself.

Appendix 3-2

Twinkle's Magic Crystal Palace and Its Visitors—Therapeutic Imagery for Relaxed Deeper Breathing and a Positive Attitude Toward Chest and Lungs

"Now you will hear about Twinkle's magic crystal palace and its special visitors. Make yourself comfortable . . . , breath in and out deeply . . . , put your arms down, and your hands flat like a landing pad for Twinkle. Close your eyes gently, and make the two magic rings with your thumbs and fingers, and catch and hold Twinkle again in those magic rings.

"Twinkle has been waiting eagerly to show you the beautiful magic crystal place within you. While you breathe deeply, Twinkle takes the little bell, the little light, and the magic wand, and travels up into your chest.

"From the inside, your chest seems like a big building with many rooms and halls, pathways, and little doors. All the walls are so very thin that Twinkle's light can shin right through them, and you can see from room to room. Twinkle takes the magic light and lights many little lamps in the rooms. Every time you breathe, those lanterns glow and burn brighter . . . , and everything becomes light and bright and beautiful, just like a huge crystal palace. Everything becomes light and bright, easy, and happy inside you.

"Each time you breathe, a refreshing, moist, cool wind blows through the halls and brings wonderful air into your crystal palace.

"Now notice that many visitors are coming to and have arrived at the crystal palace. These visitors are all friends of Twinkle, and they are on a long journey. They come from the long journey through all the pathways of your body: from the hands, the feet, the brain, from everywhere. They come to the crystal palace to get some of the wonderfully refreshing air, to become strong, and healthy, and happy, because they are very exhausted and tired from their long journey. They are small and round, and as they roll through the little doors, they do not feel very well. They are ever so tired, and look a little blue. Every time you breathe in and out, in and out, the refreshing breeze, the good fresh air blows through the crystal palace and makes the little lamps glow, and also refreshes Twinkle's little friends. With that good, fresh air the little visitors feel better and better, and more and more refreshed. They are no longer blue, but turn pink and red for joy, because they feel much better each time you breathe in and out. Twinkle is so happy to share the good fresh air of the crystal palace with all the little visitors. The little doors open and close, open and close, and the now refreshed, red, healthy, and happy small round visitors roll out of the little rooms and happily start their journey through your body again. That makes you refreshed and happy, healthy and strong.

"Any time you become tired or out of breath, think of Twinkle's small blue visitors, and breathe deeply to help them become red, and healthy, and strong in that crystal palace. Remember, when you become tired or blue, or out of breath, sit or lie down and catch Twinkle in the magic rings of your fingers. With the magic light or the magic wand, ask Twinkle to chase all those tired small blue beings back to your chest, to that beautiful crystal palace. Breathe deeply to make all the little lamps that glow brightly, and help the little blue beings to become red, and happy and healthy, and that makes you feel so good!

"It is now time for Twinkle to leave the crystal palace and all of its visitors. Breathe or sigh deeply, stretch your arms, and maybe also your legs. Let go of the magic rings and release Twinkle for now. Open your eyes widely, and breathe deeply again, and go back to work or play."

References

Benson H: The Relaxation Response. New York, William Morrow, 1975

Bunkan BH: Underskelsesmethodikk og behandlingsmetoder ved muskulaere spenninger. Oslo, Universitetsforlaget, 1979

Cautela J, Groden J: Relaxation: A comprehensive Manual for Adults, Children, and Children with Special Needs. Champaign, IL, Research Press, 1978

Disorbio JM: The Effects of Three Approaches to Relaxation Training Upon the Reduction of Anxiety Associated With a Real Life Stress. Unpublished thesis, California State University, Chico, 1975

Fuchs M: Über Atemtherapie und entspannende Körperarbeit. Psyche (Stuttg) 3:538, 1949/50

Hanish O: Z.-A. Mazdaznan Health and Breath Culture. Chicago, Mazdaznan Press, 1914

Jencks B: Self-Rhythmization. Part I. Instructing A Person In The Basic Concepts. A teaching film. Salt Lake City, University of Utah, 1970a

Jencks B: Self-Rhythmization. Part II. Instructing a Group in Finding and Adjusting Self-rhythms. A teaching film. Salt Lake City, University of Utah, 1970b

Jencks B: Self-Rhythmization. Part III. Self-Rhythmization Therapy With a Psychosomatic Patient. A teaching film. Salt Lake City, University of Utah, 1970c

Jencks B: Basic Self-Rhythmization Exercises: Instruction Manual for Trainees. Salt Lake City, Jencks, 1971

Jencks B: Respiration for Relaxation, Invigoration, and Special Accomplishment. Manual. Salt Lake City, Jencks, 1974

Jencks B: Utilizing the Phases of the Breathing Rhythm in Hypnosis. Presented at the Seventh International Congress of Hypnosis and Psychosomatic Medicine, Philadelphia, 1976

Jencks B: Your Body: Biofeedback at its Best. Chicago, Nelson-Hall, 1977

Jencks B: Utilizing the phases of the breathing rhythm in hypnosis. In Frankel FH (ed): Hypnosis at its Bicentennial. New York, Plenum Publishing, 1978

Jencks B: Movement Hypnosis: Therapies and Research. Presented at the American Society of Clinical Hypnosis, San Francisco, November 1979. Reprinted in: Svensk tidskrift for hypnos, December 1979

Jencks B: Outline for Preschool Asthma Program for the Utah Lung Association. Unpublished manuscript, 1980a

Jencks B: The Effectiveness of Diverse Hypnotic Procedures for the Amelioration of Sleeping Difficulties. Presented at the American Society of Clinical Hypnosis, November 1980b

Jencks B: Hypnotic Factors in the Design of a Preschool Asthma Family-Education Program. Presented at the American Society of Clinical Hypnosis, November 1981

Jencks B: Simple Exercises to Relieve Breathing Difficulties and Increase Vital Capacity. Submitted for publication, 1982

Jencks B, Guertler M: Psychophysiological Combination Therapy with Children. Presented at the Biofeedback Society of America, Louisville, Kentucky, March 1981

Johnsen L: Muscular tonus and integrated respiration. In Boadella D (ed): In The Wake of Reich. London, Coventure Ltd., 1976

Kroger WS: Clinical and Experimental Hypnosis. Philadelphia, JB Lippincott, 1977

Michaux L, Lelord G, Lauzel JP, Wintrebert H: La relaxation chez l'enfant par le mouvement passif. Etude E. E. G. Revue de Medécine Psychosomatique, 3:53, 1961

Pálos S: Atem und Meditation. München, O. W. Barth Verlag, 1974

Perls FS: Gestalt Therapy Verbatim. Lafayette, Real People Press, 1969

Ratner SC: Comparative aspects of hypnosis. In Gordon JE (ed): Handbook of Clinical and Experimental Hypnosis. New York, Macmillan, 1967

Schultz JH: Das Autogene Training. Leipzig, G. Thieme Verlag, 1932

Stokvis B, Wiesenhütter E: Der Mensch in der Entspannung, ed 3. Stuttgart, Hippokrates Verlag, 1971

Stroebel E, Stroebel CF, Holland M: Kiddie QR. Hartford, QR Institute, 1980

Vishnudevananda S: The Complete Illustrated Book of Yoga. New York, Julian Press, 1960

4 Techniques of Induction and Deepening

ALEXANDER H. SMITH, Jr.
WILLIAM C. WESTER, II

The Context of Induction—The Therapist's Perspective

The process of induction takes on a more complicated clinical picture when the nature of suggestion is explored in the larger context of the patient's total psychological organization. A frequent limitation in the practice, and especially in the teaching of hypnosis, is the neophyte's feeling that he is like either a centipede attempting to keep track of all its legs or a confused mechanic. Neither position is very comfortable for the therapist nor especially helpful to the patient. Those competent in hypnosis seem to draw from a cogwheeling of well-grounded theoretical foundations both of hypnosis and of broader mental functioning, and of some smooth, meaningfully ordered approach to the patient in his/her unique manner of perception and relationship to the therapist.

The former issues, those of the theoretical underpinning can be found, at least in part, throughout this work, particularly in those chapters addressing theory. Also, the reader can intuit the ad hoc formulations about what makes hypnosis seem to work from the practitioner-oriented chapters dealing with specific foci in treatment.

Our attempt here is to pull together basic approaches to induction, and, using a clinical example, to consider major issues directly relevant to conducting a "successful" hypnotic experience. "What to do" once the patient has entered a trance is a matter left to the practitioner within his/her specific area of expertise. Presumably, the trance is utilized within the integrated framework of the specialty and of hypnosis as it relates to broader mental functioning. We advocate the use of hypnosis only in conjunction with a clearly defined specialty and only within the practitioner's range of competence. We discourage the use of hypnosis by those without these backgrounds.

A number of issues of which the practitioner should be aware exist in beginning induction. The entire procedure can be viewed from a number of theoretical perspectives. In this chapter, although we "combine" psychodynamic and behavioral approaches theoretically, we limit our discussion to practical

42

matters and raise theoretical ones only in support of a specific clinical example. The thrust of the chapter is to facilitate the beginning hypnotist with some basic knowledge of how to go about using induction within the patient's frame of reference. Our clinical example does not demonstrate induction *per se,* but rather treats accompanying issues that lead up to induction methods.

Issues in the Therapist's Orientation to the Patient

Basic to our discussion is the unconscious motivation that prompts the patient to seek hypnosis. Within this category the patient's psychological organization may be reflected. Relevant here are three main points that give induction a specific context to the patient. To be sure, there are others we have omitted in the interest of brevity.

First, the patient has some curative fantasy about being helped. The patient does not simply appear requesting hypnosis. Conscious expectations are not the same as unconscious ones. The curative fantasy (Ornstein and Ornstein, 1976) brings into focus those strivings within the patient that remain a part of his/her experience, defenses, and organization of motives that affect productive love and work.

As the therapist intuits this constellation of needs expressed through the request for hypnosis, she/he may employ methods that use the curative fantasy for therapeutic "leverage." The curative fantasy is not the same as transference. Rather, the transference formed reflects the strivings of the patient who expects to feel completed, aided, and "cured." More often than not, the curative fantasy reflects what the patient historically needed but found unavailable, rather than what "did happen."

Secondly, the patient brings to hypnosis all the *cumulative trauma* (Khan, 1964) and disappointment that reflect his/her specific learning history. Most therapists of virtually all persuasions encounter the "attempt" by the patient to generalize these destructive experiences to their current life. To be sure, hypnosis is not excluded. The range of such projections extends from cautious questioning by a prospective patient for anxiety reduction to the blatant avoidant, delusioned, or chaotic response from a psychotic patient. In using induction, the therapist must tailor the approach to this "bad object" system of internally represented destructive experiences. The literature is filled with examples that show how the therapist may craftily attenuate these fears of the patient. We shall not elaborate upon them except to point out that this issue is a major concern in approaching induction.

Finally, a major psychodynamic element in the introduction of hypnosis to the patient is *adaptive regression.* This term refers to the relative capacity by the patient to freely suspend current energies devoted to active, deliberate mediation of drives, needs, and demands of the external world (and of the internal world) and to permit a retreat to "primary process" thought in the service of replenishing the ego with energy for later mastery (Bellak et al, 1973).

Adaptive regression requires a modicum of ego flexibility so that the patient can withdraw energy normally used for adaptation without posing any threat to his/her security and well-being. An example of adaptive regression is listening to a joke and permitting one's attention to daily affairs to be suspended. The instinctual gratification derived from identifying with elements in the joke becomes a replenishment for the ego's further demands and tasks in life.

Fromm (1972) has discussed the relationship of adaptive regression to active and passive mastery and to the receptivity required in hypnosis. In induction, the patient is asked to let go if his usual modes of thought, critical judgment, and so on, and to become receptive to the hypnotist. The stimuli formerly impinging on the patient lose their significance, as the adaptive regression in the service of the patient is asked to let go of his usual modes of thought, critical judgment, and and to the accompanying perceptual changes for therapeutic benefit.

Induction for trance requires some facility by the patient to respond with adaptive regression components. However, many patients have limited capacities for this process owing to their defensive needs and, in particular, to their internal system of "bad objects" or learned, dysfunctional expectations about outcomes with others. Some patients apparently are more suited for trance than others (Speigel and Speigel, 1978). The therapist must therefore consider this in devising an induction. The reader is referred to Chapter 7 for a more theoretical elaboration of the hypnotic relationship.

These three issues—the curative fantasy in requesting hypnosis, the cumulative trauma the patient carries about, and the capacity for adaptive regression—form a model around which the therapist devises an induction. We have considered these as a minimal background against which induction proper must be examined. We turn now to a clinical example of a patient's initial request for hypnosis and to some basic principles that may guide the therapist in the use of the techniques we describe here. It is within a context of the patient's overall ego organization that technique becomes meaningful. We have, therefore, avoided merely listing techniques, and have emphasized the need for a theoretical orientation.

Principles of Induction

Mode of Receptivity

The therapist discerns a mode of receptivity in the patient according to (1) the nature of the request, (2) manifestations of avoidance of the therapist by the patient, and (3) immediate response by the patient to invitation by the therapist for adaptive regression.

It is particularly important for the therapist to assess the manner of the patient's experiential style. Numerous approaches have been described from an "on-site" intuitive position of the therapist. More systematic approaches are available in Erickson and Rossi (1979), Bandler and Grinder (1975, 1977), and Lankton (1980).

The therapist moves into the patient's unconsciously preferred style of experiencing by attending to the prevailing *form* of the patient's verbalization, linguistic use of action words, bodily posture, defensive behavior, and so on. From this information, the therapist may "play with" forms of complementarity and gain some access to the inner world of the patient.

Clinical Example

A male patient, in his forties, sits with a taut bodily posture, his head and neck appearing strained forward. He describes his present life situation with loud, oppressed affect and in passive terms.

Patient: *"I can't get anything done . . . work (sales) is becoming boring . . . I see it as something I should have progressed in, but the company doesn't seem to notice me . . . I've been taking graduate courses at night in management . . . I work out at the "Y" . . . my wife says she's not happy at home . . . all of this and here I am a big zero at 43. . . . I heard about hypnosis—maybe it could help. . . ."*

The therapist already has considerable data about the patient's "life style" and his aspiration to levels of excellence beyond reach. If he is psychodynamic in his approach, the therapist may sense the fear of success based perhaps on problems about becoming a more separate person, or, perhaps one who challenges others. "Mid-life crises" are also implicated. The patient is passive, complaining, and vague, and experiences little self-generated energy.

Before any of these unconscious life issues can be addressed in a therapeutic sense, the therapist must join in with the patient's tension in some meaningful way. If the therapist is a little shrewd, or if he has been "burned" by experience, he knows that this sort of fellow is likely to try to defeat the success of hypnosis, much as he attempts to do this to himself, building more need for succor.

The therapist might use the following tactics.

Therapist: *"I'm not sure; big zeros are difficult to help . . . and, you know, . . . I just seem to be bumping into them all the time . . . I mean guys who, you know, . . . are cast off by their companies . . . sometimes it's just . . . I don't know, tragic."*

Patient: *"Hey . . . Doc . . . wait a minute . . . I thought you were the expert . . . you know . . . I came to you for help and right off the bat—bingo—I'm screwed again . . . maybe I should go to one of those other doctors they gave me names of . . . come on, Doc . . . I thought I could become better in sales—I just want to be good at what I do . . . I want some answers—can this process really help . . .?"*

Therapist: *"With you, I don't know . . ."*

Patient: *(Starts laughing)*

Therapist: *(Calmly smiling) "What's the matter . . .?"*

Patient: *[Laughs harder] "I dunno . . . you're off the wall! You don't even give a damn about your own reputation . . . hell, I could go out of here and tell all my friends—'I just went and saw this guy for hypnosis and the first thing he does is to become uncertain . . .' [laughs again] You're not like in the movies. . . ."*

Therapist: *That's the least you could do . . . Keep me on target . . . We need more patient's like you—who really challenge us . . . It helps us sleep better at night. . . .*

Patient: *[Considerably calmer, sits up, clears throat laughing] "Well, Doc, I guess I'm giving you kind of a hard time here. . . ."*

Therapist: *"No . . . really . . . you never know what'll happen to you when you walk into this line of work . . . You know the feeling . . . sometimes you're up, sometimes you're down—but you always come around and it always works out."*

In this brief, initial exchange between the patient and therapist, the therapist has laid the groundwork for a successful induction in several ways. First, throughout the exchange, the therapist joins in a complementary role play, the patient's negatively charged projection about the therapist and the defended receptivity of the patient. The patient wants help, but fears, for a number of reasons, the intrusion of the hypnotic procedure. The therapist therefore "joins" the defensive process, interspersing waking, indirect suggestions of trust, "We need to be tested," "It helps us sleep at night," and so on. The therapist suggests that the patient increase his defensiveness, and dissociates himself in such a way as to help the patient further attack the therapist.

The effect there is to shift the energy used by the patient to defend himself over to the observing ego. In a word, the therapist has *implanted* himself into the patient's internal system of discouraging introjections and projections (see Chap. 7) by *proxy*. The patient responds with a calmer demeanor and with an interest in hypnosis. The therapist has steered clear of an initial trap of making the hypnotic induction possibility another life task at which the patient can fail. Now further assessment and intervention may begin with the therapist's mindfulness of the transference—the material may be utilized *from within* the patient's ego organization.

Assessment of Patient's Capacity for Adaptive Regression

The therapist makes an ongoing assessment of the patient's capacity for adaptive regression in hypnosis, and chooses an induction approach that complements the form and meaning of the regression, and relates it to the objective in hypnosis.

The use of the hypnotic procedure is necessarily an entrance into the patient's internal self-regulating system of identifications, memories of facilitating, and destructive experiences.

The narrative suggests that the patient has difficulty in modulating the press of his internal demands. Mood swings are implicated although the therapist does not yet have sufficient evidence of this. Adaptive regression capacities initially seem limited, since the patient is highly defensive, bombastic, and demanding. The patient must be able to regress "on the side" and not directly. For this reason the therapist further challenges hypnosis and then casually moves to an indirect form of suggestion: "You never know what will happen when you walk into this line of work . . . sometimes you're up, sometimes you're down" (reflecting the patient's apparent affective style). The groundwork for resolution is then laid: "But you always come around, it always works out." The curative fantasy is at once gratified and brought into the "reality principle." The therapist has bought time.

The above rationale is depicted to give greater context to the meaning of induction techniques. In the example, no specificity about how and what the hypnosis will address exists in any contractual way. The therapist has merely facilitated the patient's joining him in further work. Moreover, the patient's initial comments suggest some rather substantial areas of conflict, requiring any number of psychotherapeutic approaches.

In the example, any number of techniques might be employed once an agreement has been reached about what the hypnosis, at a conscious level, should do. The essential ingredients thus far include the following: (1) to help the patient ward off further conflict and pathological regression; (2) to understand his request for hypnosis as a help in firming his precarious self-esteem in all that this may mean dynamically; (3) to work with him in such a way as to neutralize his attempts to defend himself from being helped; (4) to explore further the nature of his difficulties without disrupting his overall organization. We will stop here with the example and shift to what induction methods might be used. It should be understood that the methods now given are to be integrated with similar tactics discussed in the example. We assert that the methods must be used as guidelines. Understanding the patient's inner makeup is far more important than adhering to style.

Some Induction Techniques

In practice, it is perhaps more important for the therapist to be internally consistent in his formulation about induction than it is to be overprecise with minute details of theory. The patient unconsciously picks up the affect of the therapist about his method. It is more important that the therapist be able to shift flexibly according to the needs of the patient, maintaining the apparent effects of his previous intervention on the patient's subsequent response. It is essential that the therapist find a manner of participating in the patient's experiential process.

In this sense, the techniques we describe are written from a pragmatic point of view. We do not aspire to catalogue exhaustively all possible techniques. We are wary of attempts to do so when the focus on the what the patient is experiencing becomes secondary. We hesitate to give them names in any formal sense if the result is that the practitioner worries about which one to use. We hope, instead, that the reader will digest the descriptions and look for formal characteristics, common denominators, and aspects of structure that appeal to him.

Moreover, the therapist is more likely to be successful in trying methods that reflect his own internal maps of mental functioning. Like well-fitting clothes, they must be chosen according to one's own size, shape, and taste. Though the match between therapist and patient is highly significant, we do not treat this issue here.

The techniques are simply descriptions of apparently successful invitations by the therapist for the patient to regress adaptively, to set aside destructive, fearful experiences, and to allow the hypnotic experience to further enhance his self-realization, mastery, and competence. Why these approaches work *some of the time* is a matter we do not address here.

Coin Technique

The coin technique is an eye-fixation technique that uses natural physiological processes. This technique is especially good for use with the resistant patient. The therapist must be patient and carefully watch for nonverbal cues. The patient is asked to sit comfortably with one arm fully extended and slightly above eye level. The fingers are cupped inward in such a manner as to allow a coin to rest on the tips of the fingers. The patient is then instructed as follows: "Keep your eyes focused on the coin now as I talk with you. Continue to look at the coin as you listen to my voice. In a few moments (I am not certain just how fast), your arm and hand will become heavier and heavier. As your arm and hand becomes heavier and heavier, your arm will begin to come down very slowly. Just keep looking at that coin as your arm and hand become heavier and heavier [assuming some downward movement in the arm and hand]. That's right—heavier and heavier. You will also begin to notice that your arm and hand will act as a lever, and as the arm comes down, your eyelids will begin to close. The further your arm comes down, the more and more the eyelids will want to close. You will know when you are in a completely relaxed state because the coin will fall from your fingers. Isn't that interesting! As your arm and hand have come down, your eyelids have almost closed. Your fingers are so relaxed that the coin is almost ready to fall. Your eyelids are very heavy now, and you may even want to close them before the coin falls from the fingers. That's right—almost totally and completely relaxed. As the coin falls from your fingers, your arm and hand will just come to rest in your lap (or at your side). [Assuming that the coin falls and the eyelids are closed.] Good!—deeply, deeply relaxed—just listening to my voice."

If the patient does not close his eyes or drop the coin, continue to intersperse and reinforce suggestions of relaxation, heaviness of arm, and hand and eye closure. Sooner or later, the patient's arm will move, and when it does, begin to reinforce movement and follow the procedure outlined above.

Eye Fixation

Induction methods become a matter of choice and the skill of the operator. We do not use this method unless a patient has a preconceived set that this is the way to be hypnotized.

Any focal point is appropriate, from a spot on the wall to a face drawn on a child's thumbnail. Some professionals have a predetermined spot just above eye level (to put strain on the eyes) and opposite where the patient usually sits. One colleague wears a mouse tie pin and has the patient fixate on the tail of the mouse. If you like using a pendulum, you can ask the patient to pick a spot of reflection in the pendulum as his focal point. The purpose of using this technique is to fatigue the eyes and eyelids so that they develop a natural heavy feeling and the eyes close. The eye-fixation technique also reinforces the narrowing and focusing of the patient's attention. However, over the years, we have found that it is much easier simply to tell the patient to close his eyes and relax.

An example of the eye-fixation technique follows: "Just get comfortable in the chair and then pick out a spot or anything on that third shelf in the bookcase in front of you. As you concentrate on that spot, your eyelids will become heavier and heavier. Not too fast—just let the feeling come naturally. Continue to look at that spot and now notice that your eyes have started to blink. Your eyelids are much heavier now, and in a moment you will want to close them. Just listen to my voice and look at that spot. Almost closed now. Of course you can close them at any time and when you do, just let yourself—the entire body—relax completely. Very nice." (If eye closure has not occurred, continue reinforcement of suggestions.) Any deepening procedure can be used if needed and treatment suggestion can now be introduced.

Arm Levitation

The arm levitation induction method generally requires patience on the part of the professional. It is important not to rush the patient and therefore, this may be a time-consuming technique. This method is an excellent method to use with the patient who is looking for a "test" that hypnosis "is really working." If a patient is not responsive to arm levitation suggestions, the operator can easily shift to another technique.

An example of that arm levitation technique follows: "Please close your eyes and get comfortable. Focus your breathing and realize how easily and quickly your breathing process can help you to relax. As I talk with you, it will be easy for you to focus on my voice and the relaxation you are feeling. Each time you exhale, you will notice that your muscles will relax more and more. I would also like you to focus your attention on your right arm and hand or on your left arm and hand. It really doesn't matter which one you focus on—just concentrate on one. As your concentrate on that arm and hand, I want you to see a string attached to that arm and hand at about the wrist. Attached to that piece of string is a balloon filled with a special kind of helium gas, and the balloon, any color you wish, is just floating above your wrist. Perhaps you have seen a child with such a balloon when he gets a new pair of shoes or is at the circus. Just keep concentrating on that balloon above your wrist and notice how your hand and arm begins to feel. The arm and hand feel much lighter and in a few moments— not yet—the arm and hand are going to feel so light that the balloon will just help it to float upward very slowly to a comfortable level. You will notice that your fingers begin to move first, and before you know it there will be a space between your fingers and your lap [or arm of chair depending on where the patient is sitting]. [If the hand has not already moved, additional suggestions can be given about not knowing which finger will move first, etc. If the hand begins to move:] Isn't that interesting. That's right. Remember now that the hand will move slowly upward to a comfortable level. Lighter and lighter with a nice feeling of floating, and as the arm and hand gets lighter and lighter, you will find yourself relaxing deeper and deeper. That's right . . . lighter and lighter and deeper and deeper. In just a few moments now we are going to untie the balloon and just let it float away—not yet. When we untie the balloon and let it float away, your arm and hand will become heavier and heavier and will come down slowly to rest on your lap [wherever hand was]. Okay now, let's untie the balloon and just let it float away and notice how much heavier your arm and hand have become. That's right. As your arm and hand begin to come down, just let yourself relax deeper and deeper, and when your arm and hand finally rest in your lap, you will be in a deep, deep state of relaxation . . . just listening to my voice and really enjoying this good feeling. That's right . . . deeply, deeply relaxed."

Visualization (Imagery)

Visualization and imagery techniques can take a variety of forms and can be used as an induction or deepening technique. The following examples will provide a set, but as you will see, you can be just as creative as you wish.

Television/Theater Approach. If used as a deepening procedure, the television/ theater approach could be used after a progressive relaxation or other procedure. Children easily identify with a favorite television show: "Just see in your mind a TV screen [or "see yourself in the front row of a theater"] and as soon as you have that image, let me know by moving one of your fingers. You are in control of all dials and now turn the TV on [have an image appear on the screen] and turn the dial to your favorite program. As soon as you see your program, let me know by moving your finger once again. Just relax and enjoy your program. Watch it carefully now because I am going to ask you what is happening at different times. You can relax deeper and deeper as you continue to enjoy your program [or "show"]." Additional deepening, relaxation, and treatment suggestions can be interspersed at this time.

Imagery Approach. The therapist can allow for a great deal of permissiveness/ creativity with an imagery approach. Most patients can relate to a pleasant or favorite place, except for depressed patients, who are usually not interested in thinking about a favorite place. After a progressive relaxation technique or used directly, the visual imagery approach can be a very pleasant experience for your patient. Here is one example: "As you continue to relax, just allow your mind to get a thought picture or image of a favorite place. This can be someplace you have been or somewhere you might like to go. Let yourself enjoy your favorite place just as much as you would like." For example, some people think of a time when they went to the beach or ocean (this suggestion is given because a high number of patients will visualize a beach scene) and can really get into their image. They can almost hear the waves coming in, feel the warmth of the sun, feel the gentle breeze, smell the salty air, etc. "As you really enjoy your image let yourself relax deeper and deeper. That's right. As you continue to enjoy and relax deeper and deeper, your unconscious mind will hear everything I am saying. Further suggestions and ideomotor signaling can be used as needed to develop a deeper trance site. Therapeutic suggestions can be made as your patient continues to enjoy his favorite place.

Rapid Induction

The experienced therapist may want to use a rapid induction technique in order to use therapeutic time more advantageously. Rapid induction procedures require confidence and skill and are not recommended for beginning hypnotherapists. This procedure can be used with any patient but may be more effective in an ongoing basis with a patient who responds well to suggestion.

An example of the verbalization is as follows: "As we begin today, I want you to remember two things. Don't stop or inhibit anything from happening in terms of your relaxing and becoming comfortable. Just close your eyes now and relax. Let your breathing become very regular and comfortable. [The therapist then lifts the patient's arm by holding the arm very gently at the wrist. A slight bouncing movement gives the patient a nonverbal cue that the arm is lighter and will just want to float as the therapist slowly removes his fingers from the patient's wrist. If the arm remains elevated/cataleptic, then the therapist can continue to deepen the state.] That's right. Now, as I continue to talk with you, just let yourself relax deeper and deeper . . . as deeply as you'd like." Therapeutic suggestions may be given while reinforcing the comfortable, relaxed, hypnotic state.

If the nonverbal approach is uncomfortable for the therapist, then the verbalization could be modified: "If it is all right with you, I am going to lift your arm to about this level. [By using the same procedure described above, you will be able to feel if the arm is light and floating or heavy. If it is light, continue as above—if not:] Let your arm just feel and experience a light and floating feeling. That's right." Let go of the arm and continue as above. In either case, if the patient does not experience the light and floating feeling, then switch to suggestions of heaviness, and as you let the patient's arm down, you can give suggestion of heaviness and deepening.

Deepening Techniques

Elevator Technique

The elevator technique is usually used as a deepening technique following a progressive relaxation technique or other procedure. (Always check to see if your patient has a fear of elevators before using this procedure.)

Following some other procedures, the elevator technique could be employed as follows: "As you remain comfortably relaxed, just imagine in your mind that you are in a store or building with an elevator. See yourself standing in front of the elevator on the tenth floor. Notice the lights above the elevator, and you can see that the elevator is somewhere above the tenth floor—perhaps 11 or 12. [You can use ideomotor signaling to check out the imagery.] Go ahead and push the down button. Let me know by moving the index finger on your right hand when the elevator doors open at the tenth floor. [Positive signal from patient.] Good! Now, step into the elevator and make yourself comfortable. You can stand or even have a chair waiting for you. It's your elevator, and just let yourself be comfortable. As the elevator doors close, the tenth floor light is still on and doesn't go off until the elevator begins to move down very slowly. As the elevator moves down, just let yourself relax deeper and deeper. I will count as the elevator makes its nonstop trip to the first floor. The tenth floor light is out, and the ninth floor light comes on. Deeper and deeper relaxed . . . 8 . . . just really let yourself relax deeper and deeper . . . 7 . . . so comfortable . . . 6. [Notice nonverbal cues and reinforce.] That's right . . . deeper and deeper relaxed . . . 5 . . . when you get to the first floor . . . 4 . . . so relaxed now . . . the door will open . . . 3 . . . and when you get off, you will find yourself . . . 2 . . . in a beautiful garden [or favorite place or a place based on intake information] . . . completely relaxed and just listening to my voice . . . 1 . . . The doors open . . . go ahead . . . just step into the beautiful garden . . . find a comfortable bench or other comfortable spot and just sit down and enjoy the splendor of the garden."

The therapist can continue to heighten the imagery if necessary and then begin treatment suggestions.

Escalator Technique

The escalator technique is much like the elevator technique in that it provides a mechanism to assist the patient in bringing about a deeper state of relaxation. The therapist can use this technique after another technique such as an eye fixation or progressive relaxation or as an initial induction method. (Always check to see if your patient has a fear of escalators before using this procedure.)

One variation of this technique follows: "See yourself standing at the top of an escalator. This is a slow-moving escalator with safe steps and a secure, hard rubber handrail. As you look down the escalator, you will see a soft, plush, comfortable chair—any kind you wish—any fabric, color, texture, with or without pillows. [Ideomotor signaling can be employed if necessary.] In just a moment, I will ask you to get on the escalator, and as you move down slowly, just let yourself become more comfortably and deeply relaxed. Just focus on my voice, since I will be talking with you as you go down the escalator and relax deeper and deeper. When you reach the bottom, I will ask you to just sit in your comfortable chair . . . totally and deeply relaxed. Go ahead now and step on the escalator and feel the movement downward as you relax deeper and deeper. The escalator is moving slowly . . . about one quarter of the way down now as you really begin to feel deeper and deeper relaxed. Almost at the halfway point now, and the shape, color, texture of your chair becomes clearer and clearer as you relax deeper and deeper. [Watch for non-verbal cues of relaxation and reinforce.] Very good! Isn't that nice how much more relaxed you became as you passed the halfway point. Just moving down slowly and deeply . . . three quarters of the way down and almost totally relaxed and really looking forward to sitting in your chair . . . just listening to my voice. Coming to the bottom now and the steps are disappearing into the floor. As you come off the escalator, just position yourself correctly and sit down in your chair . . . totally and deeply relaxed."

The chair at the bottom of the escalator gives the patient a destination and somewhere to remain as the therapist continues with treatment.

Combination—Two Door Technique

After using a professional relaxation technique as described in Chapter 2, instruct the patient as follows: "That deep feeling of relaxation you are experiencing can become even deeper by seeing in your mind a very short set of stairs—just ten steps—and at the bottom of the steps, a landing with two doors. Just raise the index finger on your right or left hand . . . as soon as you have that thought or image in your mind. That's fine. You are at the top or tenth step and as I count off the steps, just let yourself relax even deeper . . . I will tell you more about the two doors as we go. Ten and 9 . . . deeper and deeper relaxed. Eight . . . such a good feeling . . . being able to really let go and relax just as deeply as possible . . . 7 . . . even deeper now and when we get to the landing . . . 6 . . . that's right . . . deeply relaxed . . . I am going to ask you to select one of the two doors . . . 5 . . . deeper and deeper relaxed . . . 4 . . . I am not sure what is behind each door, but I do know that behind each door is a very beautiful, pleasant place . . . 3 . . . when you reach the landing, you will open the door your hand selected . . . 2 . . . that's right . . . almost there . . . deeply, deeply relaxed . . . 1 . . . you will be able to, and now on the landing . . . go ahead and open the door and just enjoy that beautiful, pleasant place . . . just step into that pleasant place and just let yourself enjoy it as much as you would like. You can sit, stand, or lie down—whatever is most comfortable. Just enjoy the sounds, the color—whatever is there in *your* pleasant place."

Therapeutic suggestion can be interspersed at this point.

A Final Caveat—The Limitations of the Therapist and of Techniques

The techniques described generally utilize relaxation, distraction from impinging stimuli, and some creation of "mystique" about the technique. This latter element is perhaps the least understood but most widely embraced as part of the therapeutic armamentarium.

In using hypnosis, the therapist becomes a shaman or a witch doctor. He creates a ritual into which the psyche of the patient blends with that of the therapist. The therapist suggests and the patient produces compliance. The patient turns over his psyche into the relationship in a unique way. The therapist implicitly promises at least to do no harm. The therapist also implicitly promises, like the shaman who sits in his hut before invoking the spirits, to have more or less cleansed himself of "evils" that may conflict with the patient. In a primitive sense, then, the therapist in hypnosis, perhaps more so than any other form of treatment, becomes the "tribe's" trusted healer. This is so because the hypnotist's task is one of invocation.

Hypnosis is probably more dangerous for the therapist than for the patient, in the sense that he can easily become the prey of ego inflation and of identifying with the spirits, so to speak, than with the shaman.

In a word, the work of induction and of hypnosis in general is a "divine" matter, concerned with the most precious gift allotted man—the gift of mind. Technique, therefore, must be understood from a historical perspective—some push within that enables "mind" to cure itself, to pull itself up, and to differentiate itself into myriad forms.

The hypnotist can become part of this history either by becoming technique-oriented, or by allowing the psyche and the nature of suggestion to unfold in an ever-revealing form. To the extent that we are driven to the former, we are sorely limited in what and whom we heal. To the extent that we resist the temptation to "treat" the patient, we become able to "invoke" the latent possibilities of integration. This is the meaning of technique: an ever-present awareness of the limits of what we do, a constant effort to refine models of the mind that broaden the choices available to us, and a willingness to submit our approaches to the scrutiny of the prevailing scientific community. In this sense, we return to our hut with the shaman and humbly purify our thinking and technique over and over again. The rest is the word of the gods.

In order to avoid duplication of induction, deepening and treatment procedures, we provide the following list of other procedures described throughout this book.

References

Bandler R, Grinder J: Patterns of the Hypnotic Techniques of Milton Erickson. Vols. 1 and 2. Capistrano, CA, Meta Publications, 1975–77

Bellak L, Harvich M, Gedeman H: Ego Functions in Schizophrenics, Neurotics and Normals. New York, John Wiley & Sons, 1973

Erickson MH, Rossi EL: Hypnotherapy: An Exploratory Casebook. New York, Irvington Publications, 1979

Fromm E: Ego activity and passivity in hypnosis. Int J Clin Exp Hypn 20:235, 1972

Kahn MM: Ego distortion, cumulative trauma and the role of reconstruction in the analytic situation. Int J Psychoanalysis 45, 1964

Lankton S: Practical Magic. Capistrano, CA, Meta Publication, 1980

Ornstein P, Ornstein A: On the continuing evaluation of psychoanalytic psychotherapy: Reflections and predictions. In Annual of Psychoanalysis, Vol 5, pp 329–355. New York, International Universities Press, 1976

Speigel H, Speigel D: Trance and Treatment: Clinical Use of Hypnosis. New York, Basic Books, 1978

5 Hypnotic Phenomena

THOMAS W. WALL

Hypnotic phenomena can be viewed from two perspectives: the phenomena that result from the application of hypnotic techniques and strategies (*i.e.,* what hypnotized people do), or the phenomena of hypnosis itself (*i.e.,* what hypnotized people experience). The focus of this chapter will be the phenomena we term hypnosis and where appropriate, phenomena used especially in therapeutic interventions will also be discussed. The emphasis in this chapter will be on hypnosis in the clinical setting, because as Haley (1973) has noted, hypnosis in research and hypnosis in therapy are two different orders of phenomena.

This chapter provides the reader with an opportunity to become familiar with the underlying constructs that have been useful to me in my own efforts to understand hypnosis and certain hypnotic phenomena. The lines of inquiry will include several viewpoints. The issue of whether hypnosis requires a special state or trance construct will be used to acquaint the reader with the problems of language in constructing models to explain the phenomena of hypnosis. The examination of trance logic as a phenomenon will be used to exemplify a central hypnotic characteristic and the difficulties in explaining hypnotic phenomena. The concept of dissociation as an alternative to the different models will be used to support the notion that hypnotic phenomena are best explained in process terms. Finally, evidence from hemispheric specialization will be used to support the belief that hypnosis results in the shift from left hemispheric activity to right hemispheric activity.

There is something apparently unique about the process and content of certain verbal and nonverbal communications generated by one person that leads another to exhibit various hypnotic phenomena. Likewise, there seems to be something unusual about what happens to the person who receives these communications when they lead to the experience of hypnosis. The outcome can be as dramatic as that of performing surgery without anesthetic agents that reduce the experience of pain, the control of bleeding, and the promotion of both physical and psychological healing.

Haley (1973), in discussing the work of Milton Erickson, has stated that hypnosis results from a specific style of communication. It is not the state of one person, rather, it is a special type of exchange between people. Something called the *hypnotic response* must happen to allow this type of interpersonal event to occur. To examine this special type of exchange requires a discussion about a problem basic to considerations of all experiential events. Whatever form of language used or explanation constructed to account for the events thought to occur during hypnosis will be found inadequate. That is, any linguistic description of an experience will not represent the same thing as the experience, particularly if the mode of experiencing is non-language–based. Language can create models about hypnosis and hypnotic events, but language about the experience is never the experience itself. Reality is represented as a neurological construction and from that a model or conceptual framework is evolved. That is, we are using an explanatory model, or meta model, to explain another model presumed to exist as a neurological system. This is the position proposed by Bandler and Grinder (1975).

There are many levels at which we can describe the same thing. For instance, the auditory experience of electrically produced or amplified music can be described in terms of body sensations, rhythm, beat, and tonal quality; or in language peculiar to electricity and the movement of electrons. One must select which language structure works best for the purposes at hand, that is, to explain and appreciate the experience of this type of music, or to build a hi-fidelity amplifier. Numerous and divergent formulations about the phenomena of hypnosis exist in part because different levels of model building or descriptions are possible. I offer the reader a number of model possibilities to better understand and appreciate what happens.

There are a number of basic assumptions that are important to consider when examining the phenomena of hypnosis. The first assumption, mentioned earlier, is that hypnosis is an interpersonal event requiring a reciprocal interpersonal relationship; hypnosis does not require and should not imply a therapist-dominated or controlling relationship with the subject. The hypnotic event is viewed as the result of an interaction whereby one person does or says something that allows another to have an internally generated experience.

The second assumption is that hypnotic capacity is inherent and resides in every individual by virtue of a set of personal resources to generate an induction process. These resources may have to be uncovered, worked with, or even, in particular instances, discovered for the first time but nothing intrapersonal need be added or taken away. The therapist provides the opportunity to explore these capacities or resources if the subject consents.

Third, as Spiegel (1978) has noted, the capacity to be hypnotized is a sign of relatively intact mental functioning. Although more disturbed patients can be hypnotized (Scagnelli, 1976, 1980), in general their capacities for hypnotic trance are somewhat limited.

Fourth, each person experiences hypnosis uniquely and generalizations cannot be made as to what will occur or how a person will become absorbed in his experience of hypnosis. Because each of us has unique patterns of responding and unique patterns of stabilized consciousness (Tarte, 1975), the therapist must discover which methods and which patterning of content best allows the desired hypnotic phenomena to be elicited. Lastly, hypnotic phenomena (*e.g.,* trance) is naturalistic (Erickson, 1958) reflecting capacities within us already. Hypnosis arises from the repatterning of components that constitute our ordinary experiencing in the world.

Consciousness and the Phenomenon of Trance

Hypnosis usually occurs in four phases: preparation, induction, utilization, and conclusion of trance. The phenomenon called the hypnotic state or trance has been the subject of much debate. Haley (1965) has presented a clear account of the confusion in considering the notion of trance. Because his description would be hard to improve, his quote follows:

> The various theoreticians have proposed at least the following descriptions of hypnotic trance. The trance is sleep, but it isn't sleep. It is a conditioned reflex, but it occurs without conditioning. It is a transference relationship involving libidinal and submissive instinctual strivings, but this is because of aggressive and sadistic instinctual strivings. It is a state in which a person is hypersuggestible to another's suggestions, but one where only auto-suggestion is effective since compliance from the subject is required. It is a state of concentrated attention, but it is achieved by dissociation. It is a process of role playing, but the role is subjectively real. It is a neurological change based upon psychological suggestions, but the neurological changes have yet to be measured and the psychological suggestions have yet to be defined. Finally, there is a trance state which exists separately from trance phenomena, such as catalepsy, hallucinations, and so on, but these phenomena are essential to a true trance state.

Trance is a "special-state" construct defined by subjective experience. The arguments for trance or state hypnosis have a set of common assumptions:

1. There exists a special state of consciousness or awareness called hypnotic trance.
2. It is characterized by increased suggestibility, enhanced imagery, and imagination, including the availability of visual memories from one's personal history.

3. It involves a decrease in planning function without any loss in ability to initiate or terminate actions.
4. There is a reduction in reality testing. A variety of reality distortions are reported. These include the acceptance of falsified memories, the production of positive and negative hallucinations (Orne, 1962), revivification of earlier memories with suggestions of age regression, post-hypnotic amnesias, and distortions in the subjective experience of time. Representatives of the existence of the hypnotic trance or state position are Fromm and Shor (1972), Hilgard (1977), Orne (1977), and Erickson (1967).

In opposition to this viewpoint is what Barber has labeled the cognitive–behavioral position (1974). This view argues that responders to test suggestions are having different experiences "not because they are in different states, but because they are receiving different communications" (Barber, 1972). The features of this position are:

1. The proposal of a state difference is unnecessary to account for differences in response to test suggestions.
2. Differences in responsiveness are related to attitudes, motivations, and expectancies toward the communications received.
3. The person responsive to test suggestions has a positive internal relationship toward the communications he is receiving.
4. The person unresponsive to test suggestions has a negative internal relationship toward the communications he is receiving.
5. The three factors of attitude, motivation, and expectancy vary and interact in complex ways to determine responsiveness to suggestion.
6. Concepts taken from abnormal psychology (*e.g.,* trance or dissociation) are misleading and do not explain behavioral and subjective responses. Responsiveness to suggestion is a normal psychological phenomenon.
7. The phenomenon associated with test suggestions are considered to be within the range of normal human capabilities.

Barber and Wilson (1977) have proposed that regardless of whether a trance-induction procedure is used, subjects are responsive to test suggestions for various hypnotic phenomena to the extent that they think along with and imagine the themes as suggested. Josephine Hilgard, in an extensive study in 1979, confirmed the role of imaginative involvement as an important antecedent condition for hypnotic responsiveness; thus, both Barber's and Hilgard's viewpoints acknowledge the capacity for imaginative involvement as playing a significant role in the achievement of phenomena associated with the use of hypnosis.

While the controversy continues, the clinician using hypnosis must make sense of this important area of difference; namely, is there a trance state or not?

The question may be superfluous from a clinical standpoint, since clinicians are more concerned with relief of suffering than with particular theoretical positions. As a way of resolving these differences, I have found the viewpoint of Tart (1975) useful in bridging the gap between theoretical differences and clinical experience. Tart takes a special state position. He distinguishes among discrete states of consciousness (d-SOC), a discrete altered state of consciousness (d-ASC), and a baseline state of consciousness (b-SOC). He defines a d-SOC as a "unique, dynamic pattern of configuration of psychological structures, an active system of psychological substructures." Examples cited are the ordinary waking state, sleep, and dreaming.

A d-ASC refers to a state that is different from some baseline consciousness. A d-ASC is a new system with unique properties that have been generated as a restructuring of consciousness. "Altered" is intended in this sense as a purely descriptive term carrying no values. In other words, the experience of hypnosis (d-ASC) results from an internally generated construction process of attitudes, values, motivations, and expectancies. This is in response to certain explicit communications (inductions) originating in the therapist and transmitted to the subject. By definition, an induction is any activity used to create a d-ASC of hypnosis, which is a repatterning of the existing resources and capacities of a person.

Baseline consciousness is stabilized by a number of processes, including dealing with variability in the environment. It is apparently difficult to process steady stimuli without eventual distortion in neural processing; thus, the construction process is susceptible to confusion under conditions of minimal variability, for example, sensory deprivation. Hypnotic inductions are designed to assist the transition away from baseline consciousness to a d-ASC, or away from external reality, which is the major source of data for stabilization of consciousness.

The term trance as used here is the subjective experience that arises with a shift from external reality to internal reality. The shift is away from *acting* on the world to *experiencing* it more directly. This involves becoming dissociated from ordinary concepts or categories of experience to being involved more directly with experience. Trance states are experiences without language or logical categories; rather, they are effortless and spontaneous responses to internal and external cues. By contrast, baseline consciousness, composed of conceptual representations of the world, is a model of reality maintained by three primary factors (Miller, 1979):

1. Continuous streams of sensory impulses to the sensory cortex, coming through organs of perception
2. The vast network of associative functions continuously interacting in the human cortex and producing the phenomena of wakeful consciousness and awareness of the external world

3. The varying stimuli (*e.g.*, alterations in light, color, sound, form, smell, touch) producing reactions, thus contributing to consciousness and awareness

Returning to an earlier idea, we do not operate directly on the world in which we live. We create a model or map and use this to guide our behavior. This model determines to a large extent how we will perceive the world and what our attitudes, values, and motivations will be; thus, an effective hypnotic intervention implies some change or difference in the way we represent our experience. Baseline consciousness is stabilized as a result of this construction process and related feedback systems. These feedback systems may include cues arising from body sensations as well as changes in the environment.

Bandler and Grinder (1975) have proposed three fundamental processes to account for the necessary difference between the world and the constructed model or representation of the world. These processes are deletion, distortion, and generalization. *Deletion* is the process by which attention is diverted selectively to certain dimensions of experience and excludes others. The model is reduced from the original experience to the extent that this selective inattention process occurs. The result is an impoverished model. Distortion is the process that allows a shift in experience of sensory input. An example would be fantasy, daydreaming, or the creation of positive–negative hallucinations. Generalization is the process by which elements of a person's model become detached from the original experience and come to represent the entire category of which the experience is an example. Bandler and Grinder (1975) cite the example of the person who at some time in his life has been rejected and makes the generalization that he is not worth caring for, thereby deleting caring messages and distorting them as insincere. The implication for the clinician using hypnosis is perhaps obvious; interventions should be directed at providing a fuller, more accurate representation of experience.

To move from a b-SOC to a d-ASC, involves certain principles. The induction process must take into account the pattern of functions and the many stabilizing relationships that maintain consciousness. The reader is reminded of the analogy to music cited earlier and of the various languages that can be used to describe different levels of the experience.

Although the induction, or shift, from the waking state to the hypnotic state has been described by various authors, how the actual transition is accomplished remains a mystery. Tart has specified induction operations as a two-step process: "disruption" and "patterning." Erickson specifies the two-step operation as "accepting" and "utilizing," whereas Bandler and Grinder refer to "pacing" and "leading" as descriptive terms for these operations. Whichever is preferred, all are descriptive terms for a two-stage process that requires the same general operations in principle.

The first stage of induction is the application of a disruptive process that begins by accepting the b-SOC and then gradually begins to disrupt the stabilization elements. This disruption needs to be of sufficient magnitude (although it often begins subtly) to disrupt enough stabilization so that baseline patterns of consciousness cannot maintain their integrity. It should be noted that this cannot happen in the absence of consent and without appropriate motivation, attitude, and expectancy. Simply applying the disruption pattern alone is usually insufficient to produce an altered state of consciousness.

Disruptive forces must be followed by applying patterning forces, the second operation. Disrupted psychological function is now compelled to form a new pattern, resolved as an altered state of consciousness. As Tart notes, these patterning forces also may serve to disrupt the ordinary functioning of the waking state insofar as they are incongruent with the functioning of this state; hence, the same stimuli may serve both disruptive and patterning functions. The process is the disruption in the constructed state (model) of consciousness and a reconstruction into the formation of a new, self-stabilized structure. Reversing this process, or deinduction, works the same way to reinstate the previous baseline state. Examples of disrupting forces are a quiet atmosphere, focusing of attention, accepting the patient's behavior and pacing it, and "being with" the experience elicited by the verbal cues (as opposed to dissociating and thinking about what is said). Other examples of disrupting forces are suggestions that create associative links to previous experiences, dissociation from body cues, and the disappearance of body sensations from consciousness. The suggestions for relaxation and letting-go of tensions (*i.e.,* sitting quietly and immobile in a comfortable position) reduce significantly any cues from the body that might be used to maintain baseline consciousness. A powerful patterning force involves the gradual shift in the locus of control from self-direction to that of allowing the hypnotist's voice and thoughts to take over the role of director. Gill and Brenman (1977) have proposed this as the transference aspect of hypnosis. They emphasize the belief that one should not speak of the "state" of hypnosis, but rather of the "hypnotic relationship."

The phenomenon of hypnosis may be viewed as a process whereby baseline consciousness is disrupted and repatterned. Forming this new, altered state renders consistent apparently diverse viewpoints that describe the same process with different linguistic models. Important factors such as expectancies about hypnotic experience, how hypnotized subjects behave, motivation to experience hypnosis, and attitudes toward the experience are powerful determinants toward understanding the hypnotic induction procedure and the role of consciousness.

Whether one adopts the cognitive–behavioral model or the trance-state model seems less important than understanding and using the common, general principles that both have to offer. Both positions take into account the psychological variables of motivation, expectancy, and attitude that usually involve subject preparation or the establishment of rapport. Barber (1974) has emphasized the role of the subject's willingness to think and imagine with the themes that are suggested. This is itself a disruptive–pattern process that has to alter consciousness and pattern it to another form; thus, how one describes the process is viewed as less important than understanding the outcome to be accomplished and how to achieve it.

Trance Logic

In a paper that has received considerable attention and argument, Orne (1959) discussed the phenomenon of trance logic, that is, the ability of hypnotic subjects to demonstrate logical inconsistencies. Orne (1977) has stated, "What characterizes the hypnotizable subject is not to comply with any and all requests, but rather the specific tendency or ability to respond to suggestions designed to elicit hypnotic phenomena." Specifically, Orne has used the transparent and double hallucination experience reported by subjects as evidence for tolerance of logical inconsistencies.

In transparent hallucination, the deeply hypnotized subject reports seeing a hallucinated person sitting in a chair and, simultaneously, seeing the chair through the hallucinated person. In the double hallucination, the subject sees the actual person standing in the room and, at the same time, sees a hallucination of the same person elsewhere in the room. Orne has noted that trance logic is exhibited by almost all highly suggestible subjects who have been through a hypnotic induction procedure and are judged to be in a hypnotic state. Trance logic is reported by very few subjects asked to simulate hypnosis. Orne has argued that trance logic tends to be a unique feature of hypnosis.

In opposition to this notion that hypnosis has unique characteristics is the work of Barber (1969), and Sarbin and Coe (1972). The work of Johnson, Maher, and Barber (1972) was an attempt to replicate Orne's work. These investigators concluded that trance logic was not found to be a discriminating characteristic of hypnotic subjects. Hilgard (1972), in a critique of the work of Johnson and colleagues, concluded that their data yielded results "largely indeterminant, but with trends all in favor of Orne's findings." In a reply to Hilgard's critique, Johnson (1972) argues that their disagreement reflects more general problems of conducting research in hypnosis. Johnson notes that Orne and Hilgard follow the specific-state paradigm, which postulates that hypnotic induction procedures cause qualitative changes in the organism. Moreover, this special state is instrumental in eliciting certain behaviors such as catalepsy, muscle rigidities, anesthesia, age regression, hallucinations, amnesias, and other phenomena. It is not surprising that researchers using this paradigm observe those phenomena that they predict will occur. If one assumes trance logic, one observes trance logic when the hypnotized person acts differently.

Orne has proposed that research in hypnosis should begin with reasonable operational definitions of the phenomena. The two major ways offered to define hypnosis have been what is done to the subject, and the subject's response. Orne (1977) summarizes his definition by defining hypnosis as that "state or condition in which subjects can respond to appropriate suggestions with distortion of perception or memory." He offers a descriptive rather than an explanatory definition. He notes the most striking characteristic of hypnotized subjects, as opposed to simulators, is their "remarkable willingness to mix the experiences as suggested by the hypnotist with percepts in the real world."

In contrast to this viewpoint, Barber (1969) has proposed a cognitive–behavioral approach, with the following assumptions:

1. The phenomena to be explained are the overt behaviors and subjective reports traditionally associated with suggestions/procedures labeled hypnotic inductions.
2. The most proficient strategy available at present for explaining these "hypnotic" behaviors (*e.g.,* catalepsy, anesthesia, age regression, hallucinations, and amnesia) is to establish lawful relations between the behavior and denotive antecedent and concurrent conditions.
3. As antecedent–consequent relations are established, researchers should proceed to integrate the relations under a few general principles that use concepts that are closely tied to the data.

Relevance of Hemispheric Specialization to Hypnosis

It is clear that the age-old argument of state versus nonstate still persists as a function of viewpoint. How is the clinician able to reconcile these differences and apply the results to an understanding of the phenomena of hypnosis? Investigators have studied the phenomena of transparent hallucinations, "disappearance" of body parts, changes in equilibrium, changes in distance of the experimenter's voice, and other feelings of unreality.

To avoid this repetitive argument, I view hypnosis from a communicational or informational process viewpoint. Research on brain function and hemispheric specialization appears useful in this regard. In the 1960s, Roger Sperry at the California Institute of Technology began studying certain epileptic patients in whom the corpus callosum had been severed, thus separating the major communicational network between the hemispheres (therapeutic commissurotomy or split-brain). His results were both interesting and revealing in elucidating differences in hemispheric specialization. Watzlawick (1978) has summarized these findings:

> The observable consequences of the hemispheric disconnection of the human
> brain show that we actually possess two brains which can function independently

of each other. As a result of this duality, they may not only react in an identical fashion to environmental stimuli, but each of them will respond only to those external influences which fall into the domain of its competence. From this it follows that any attempt to influence either the one or the other brain must be made in that hemisphere's specific 'language' in order for the signal or communication to be received and processed.

Typically, in right-handed people, the left hemisphere appears to process information presented either sequentially or by utilizing abstract language in verbal-receptive and verbal-expressive behavior for analytic reasoning tasks. The right hemisphere appears to process information in a holistic or global pattern, using stimuli that are not readily coded linguistically. The right hemisphere is associated more with intuition, creativity, imagination and spatial-reasoning ability. More simply, the language of the left brain is words and numbers sequentially organized, and the language of the right brain is sensory images or representations.

What characterizes hemispheric differences most critically is not that they are specialized to work with different types of material, that is, the left with words and numbers and the right with spatial relations and forms. Rather, each hemisphere specializes in a different cognitive style; the left for an analytic, logical mode using words and numbers as tools; and the right for a holistic or gestalt mode suitable for spatial relations, whole–part relations and artistic endeavors (Galin, 1974).

Watzlawick (1978) views the translation of perceived reality—that is, model construction, or the synthesis of our experience of the world into an image—as most probably the function of the right brain. Barnett (1981) proposes the view that right-brain activity matches the common concept of the unconscious; thus, an increasing body of scientific thought on cognitive functioning and hemispheric specialization shows that the two cerebral hemispheres each process information in different and specialized ways. For example, activation of the right hemisphere is associated with increased imaginative ability and hypnotizability. In a provocative book, Hilgard (1979), examining many antecedent personality conditions, has shown that the capacity for imaginative involvement is closely related to hypnotizability. Milton Erickson discovered that those patients who deal with problems logically and analytically (left brain) were more difficult to hypnotize; hence the development of the confusion technique, designed to distract the left hemisphere in an effort to shift the communicational pattern to the right hemisphere. Barnett (1981) has commented that the right hemisphere appears to be a parallel yet subordinate consciousness not directly accessible to awareness.

The possibility that hypnosis may interfere selectively with left-hemisphere function has been raised by numerous researchers. Zeig (1977) used bilateral tympanic (eardrum) temperature to explore the relationship between hypnosis and functional brain asymmetry. He reported that suppression of the left-hemisphere function occurred for the highly susceptible group during hypnotic induction. In another study, Fromkin, Ripley, and Cox (1978) used a dichotic listening task to explore the relationship between hypnosis and cerebral lateralization of function. Their results support a change in cerebral laterality accompanying a shift from normal or waking consciousness to hypnotic consciousness. Hypnosis appears to facilitate a shift toward greater participation in the right cerebral hemisphere. Pagano and Frumkin (1977), using dichotic listening, have shown that the practice of transcendental meditation may produce a shift to right-brain function. Graham and Pernicano (1979), studying the relationship of hemispheric dominance to hypnotic susceptibility, have suggested a connection may exist between hypnosis and the nondominant hemisphere. Their results suggest that hypnosis involves greater activation of the right hemisphere for most subjects. Their work also suggests that hypnosis may involve a cognitive change of state, and that many hypnotic phenomena cannot be explained entirely in terms of motivational variables.

In a direct test of cortical functioning, Chen, Dworkin and Bloomquist (1981), using cortical power spectrum (CPS) of brain potentials, report a pattern of laterality shift in CPS occurring at different stages during an oral surgery procedure performed under hypnosis. There was a significant reduction in total cortical power output during hypnosis, and right hemispheric power output became more dominant during all postsurgery hypnosis stages. Prehypnosis-heightened levels of left cortical power were reestablished after hypnosis. These data would appear to confirm that the left cerebral hemisphere dominates (*i.e.,* puts out more power) in normal waking consciousness, and that the right hemisphere was relatively more active in the "altered" state of consciousness.

The relationship between hypnosis and differential hemispheric involvement has been suggested to account for a number of well-known hypnotic phenomena. Hypnosis has frequently been used to induce various emotional states artificially (Levitt and Chapman, 1972). This often results in a more powerful emotional expression than that obtained by direct expression (Hepps and Brady, 1967). The increased participation of the right hemisphere in emotional processing has received clinical and experimental support (Galin, 1974; Dimond et al, 1976) and may account for the heightened intensity of emotional experience in hypnosis.

Memory enhancement is another common phenomenon involving the use of hypnosis. Frumkin, and colleagues (1978), have noted that active, intentional memorization is primarily under the influence of the left hemisphere, and involuntary memory is governed by the right hemisphere. They note that the most dramatic cases of memory enhancement during hypnosis involve involuntary retrieval of information or cases in which no effort was made to memorize the material. Perhaps it is reasonable to conclude that certain forms of memory enhancement (recall) and the ability to respond to certain emotional states (relive) are related to specialization of the right hemisphere's role in the hypnotic process.

A phenomenon that has confounded both clinicians and experimenters and was first described by Hilgard and Hilgard (1975) involves a subject's awareness of stimuli that his behavior indicates is nonexistent. The "hidden observer" was the term used to describe this phenomenon. The findings that hypnosis temporarily reduces left-brain function or dominance and promotes a shift to right-brain informational processing suggests a cerebral lateralization explanation for the split or dissociation in consciousness noted by the Hilgards. Dissociation is a major hypnotic phenomenon that has received considerable attention, especially in the area of brain behavior relationships.

Consciousness and Dissociation

A. R. Luria (1978) has defined *consciousness* as

> the ability to assess sensory information, to respond to it with critical thoughts and actions, and to retain memory traces in order that past traces or actions may be used in the future.

The ability to assess continually and remain responsive simultaneously suggests a dual, dissociative function, a divided consciousness. In a now-famous demonstration, Hilgard (1977) discovered that hypnotized subjects may register and understand information, and yet be unresponsive to it in hypnosis. The information concealed from the hypnotically altered state of consciousness is available to the hidden observer, the part not available to the consciousness of the hypnotized person. The hidden observer is dissociated from the hypnotic experience of the subject. Miller (1979) has proposed that when a strong, focal, nonvarying stimulus is used, as for example with eye fixation, it tends to reduce and inhibit the associative processes in the sensory cortex. This, Miller argues, promotes dissociation and diminished motor activity through an inhibitory effect on the cortex.

A speculation that has been useful in my own work with hypnosis is to consider the hidden-observer phenomenon as a left-hemisphere function dissociated from the right hemisphere. The left-hemisphere function seems congruent with the mode of cognition that psychoanalysts call secondary process thinking, which has a language-based planning function. The right-brain function seems more analogous to what analysts have termed primary process cognition, a form of thought that is characteristic of the unconscious mind. Galin (1974) notes:

1. The right hemisphere primarily uses a nonverbal mode of representation, presumably images; visual, tactile, kinesthetic, and auditory.

2. The right hemisphere reasons by a nonlinear mode of association rather than a syllogistic logic; its solutions to problems are based on multiple converging determinants rather than a single-causal chain. It is much superior to the left in part–whole relations, that is, grasping the concept of the whole from just a part.

3. The right hemisphere is less involved with perception of time and sequence than the left hemisphere.

4. There is considerable evidence that the right hemisphere does process words, but the words are not organized for use in propositions.

Although the right brain may express itself in language, it would be consistent with its mode of cognitive function to use words that reflect holistic processing. That is, to compile complex language patterns simultaneously and relationally rather than individually and sequentially. We can thus speculate that aphorisms, metaphors, humor, puns, double-entendres, and figurative language may be illustrative of the kind of verbal communicational patterns understandable to the right hemisphere. It is well-known that hypnosis often involves metaphors, analogies, and figurative language.

Further evidence linking altered states of consciousness to a dissociation of brain functioning is dreaming. Again, this is an example of the type of mental activity described by analysts as primary processing, a characteristic of the unconscious mind. Davidson (1975) explains that this mode

> may be described as extralogical, independent of formal rules of causality, of spatial and temporal sequence, and uses of nonverbal representation by multimodality images.

These features of primary process functioning are those thought to characterize right-brain function during hypnosis. This is not to deny the presence of left-hemisphere function during hypnosis. The hypnotic experience requires integration of secondary processes so they "make sense" to the subject. Light hypnotic states are often referred to as mixed states, implying a mixture of conscious (in-awareness) and unconscious (out-of-awareness) processes. It is conjectured that continuous integrating function occurs even in deeper, more dissociated states characterized by greater involvement of unconscious processes. The lack of almost any capacity to integrate secondary processing in some individuals may account for why psychotics often appear difficult to hypnotize.

If there is a shift to right-brain functional dominance during hypnosis, then the unavailability of analytic, reasoning language may explain the subjective experience of hypnosis. By definition, trance states would defy the logical structures and rules governing the behavior that underlies analytic language. Davidson (1975), commenting on meditation and other mystical states, makes the point that whether the stress is on departures from logic, independence of space and time, simultaneous (holistic) versus sequential processing, or nonverbalized perceptions, the resemblance to current concepts of right hemisphere functioning is apparent.

Although there is no real disagreement that most formal language function is left hemispheric, most altered states of consciousness that have been studied or practiced are labeled as ineffable, that is, they cannot be described. Our descriptions of hypnotic phenomena are therefore models about our experience and are not the same as the experience. Depending upon one's experience with hypnosis, these descriptive models will vary.

The apparent ability of a hypnotic interview to penetrate the so-called repression barrier may be a function of differences in cognitive modes of the two hemispheres. Even in normal adults, the functional relation of the hemispheres remains a mystery. Galin (1974) has speculated that they may operate in alternation; that is, taking turns, depending on the contextual demands. There may be an inhibiting function of one hemisphere when the other is "on", or the dominant hemisphere makes use of one or more subsystems of the other hemisphere, inhibiting the rest. Another view Galin (1974) presents is that one system dominates over behavior, but it can only disconnect rather than totally inhibit (disrupt) the other hemisphere, which remains independently conscious. This latter view is consistent by analogy with the dissociation view of Hilgard.

In my own model of explaining my experience with hypnotized patients, I have found invoking hemispheric differences a useful explanation in constructing interventions, both using hypnosis and in other therapy modalities. I regard inductions, verbal and nonverbal, as necessarily disrupting communicational strategies to influence left-hemisphere functioning through distraction or dissociation. This results, when followed by repatterning suggestions, in an (hypnotically) altered state of consciousness or shift to right-brain modes of function. The shift varies in its degree throughout the hypnotic experience. To strengthen the probability of a successful and sustained induction requires a continual pattern of communication that reinforces a change to right-brain modes of cognitive style in processing the induction.

In this section I have attempted to suggest that the phenomenon of dissociation in hypnosis results in a shift from predominately left-brain function to right-brain cognitive processing. When one compares generally agreed upon characteristics of hypnosis and hypnotic phenomena with discrete, hemispheric, specialized functions, it is difficult to escape the conclusion that hypnotic phenomena can be described as mental shifts from left brain to right brain. Moreover, such shifts can be described in the language of psychology with the language of physiology.

Conclusion

The focus of this chapter has been on what is thought to occur that results in the phenomena of hypnosis and the nature of the hypnotic experience. Whether hypnosis requires a special state or trance construct was used to acquaint the reader with the problems of language in constructing models to explain the phenomena of hypnosis. The examination of trance logic as a phenomenon was used to exemplify a central hypnotic characteristic and the difficulties in explaining hypnotic phenomena. The concept of dissociation as an alternate to the different models was used to support the notion that hypnotic phenomena are best explained in process terms. The evidence from hemispheric specialization supports the belief that hypnosis results in the shift from left-to right-hemispheric activity. No attempt was made to discuss more specific hypnotic phenomena, such as hypnotic analgesia and anesthesia, hallucinations, post-hypnotic suggestions and age-regression. Although these are the more common clinical phenomena, I chose to familiarize the reader with the underlying constructs that have been important to me in my efforts to understand hypnosis, as well as other clinical phenomena. I hope the reader shares in acquiring new learning and understanding through the process of my own inquiry.

References

Bandler R, Grinder J: The Structure of Magic, Vol 1. Palo Alto, Calif: Science and Behavior Books, 1975

Barber TX: Hypnosis: A Scientific Approach. New York, Van Nostrand–Reinhold, 1969

Barber TX: Suggested ("hypnotic") behavior: The trance paradigm versus the alternative paradigm. In Fromm E, Shor RE (eds): Hypnosis: Research Developments and Perspectives. New York, Aldine–Atherton, 1972

Barber TX: Implications for human capabilities and potentialities. In Barber TW, Spanos NP, Chaves JF (eds): Hypnosis, Imaginations, and Human Potentialities. New York, Pergamon Press, 1974

Barber TX, Wilson SC: Hypnosis, suggestions, and altered states of consciousness: Experimental evaluation of the new cognitive-behavioral theory and the traditional trace-state theory of "hypnosis." In Edmonston WE Jr (ed): Conceptual and Investigative Approaches to Hypnosis and Hypnotic Phenomena. New York, New York Academy of Sciences, 1977

Barnett EA: Analytic Hypnotherapy Principles and Practice. Kingston, Ontario, Junica Publishing, 1981

Chen A, Dworkin S, Bloomquist DS: Cortical power spectrum analysis of hypnotic pain control in surgery. Int J Neurosci 13:127, 1981

Davidson J: The Physiology of Meditation and Mystical States of Consciousness. Presented at the Battelle Seattle Research Center, 1975

Dimond SJ, Farrington L, Johnson P: Differing emotional response from right and left hemispheres. Nature 261:690, 1976

Erickson MH: Naturalistic techniques of hypnosis. Amer J Clin Hypn 1:3, 1958

Erickson MH: Deep hypnosis and its induction. In Haley J (ed): Advanced Techniques of Hypnosis and Therapy-Selected Papers of Milton H. Erickson. New York, Grune & Stratton, 1967

Fromm E, Shor RE: Underlying theoretical issues: An introduction. In Fromm E, Shor RE (eds): Hypnosis: Research Developments and Perspectives. New York, Aldine–Atherton, 1972

Frumkin LR, Ripley HS, Cox GB: Changes in cerebral hemispheric lateralization with hypnosis. Biol Psychiatry 13:6, 741, 1978

Galin D: Implications for psychiatry of left and right cerebral specialization. Arch Gen Psychiatry 31:572, 1974

Gill MM, Brenman M: Hypnosis and Related States. New York, Hallmark Press, 1977

Graham KR, Pernicano K: Laterality, hypnosis, and the autokinetic effect. Amer J Clin Hypn 22:2, 79, 1979

Haley J: An interactional explanation of hypnosis. In Shor RE, Orne MT (eds): The Nature of Hypnosis. New York, Holt, Rinehart & Winston, 1965

Haley J: Uncommon Therapy. New York, WW Norton and Co, 1973

Hepps RB, Brady JP: Hypnotically induced tachycardia: An experiment with stimulating controls. J Nerv Ment Dis 145:131, 1967

Hilgard E: A critique of Johnson, Maher and Barbers' "artifact in the 'essence of hypnosis'": An evaluation of "trance logic," with a compilation of their findings. J Abnor Psychol 79:2, 221, 1972

Hilgard ER: Divided Consciousness. New York, J Wiley & Sons, 1977

Hilgard ER, Hilgard JR: Hypnosis in the Relief of Pain. Los Altos, Calif., William Kaufmann, 1975

Hilgard JR: Personality and Hypnosis. Chicago, The University of Chicago Press, 1979

Johnson RF, Maher BA, Barber TX: Artifact in the "essence of hypnosis": An evaluation of trance logic. J Abnorm Psychol 79:2, 212, 1972

Johnson RF: Trance logic revisited: A reply to Hilgard's critique. J Abnor Psychol 79:2, 234, 1972

Levitt EE, Chapman RH: Hypnosis as a research method. In Fromm E, Shor RE (eds): Hypnosis: Research Development and Perspective. Chicago, Aldine–Atherton, 1972

Luria AR: The human brain and conscious activity. In Schwartz GE, Shapiro D (eds): Consciousness and Self-Regulation, Vol Z. New York, Plenum Press, 1978

Miller M: Therapeutic Hypnosis. New York, Human Science Press, 1979

Orne MT: The nature of hypnosis: Artifact and essence. J Abnorm Psychol 58:277, 1959

Orne MT: Hypnotically induced hallucination. In West LJ (ed): Hallucinations. New York, Grune & Stratton, 1962

Orne MT: The construct of hypnosis: Implications of the definition for research and practice. In Edmonston WE Jr (ed): Conceptual and Investigative Approaches to Hypnosis and Hypnotic Phenomena. New York, Academy of Sciences, 1977

Pagano R, Frumkin L: The effect of transcendental meditation on right hemispheric functioning. Biofeedback Self Regul 2:4, 407, 1977

Sarbin TR, Coe WC: Hypnosis: A Social Psychological Analysis of Influence Communication. New York, Holt, Rinehart & Winston, 1972

Scagnelli J: Hypnotherapy with schizophrenic and borderline patients: Summary of therapy with eight patients. Amer J Clin Hypn 19:1, 28, 1976

Scagnelli J: Hypnotherapy with psychotic and borderline patients. The use of trance by patient and therapist. Amer J Clin Hypn 22:3, 164, 1980

Spiegel H, Spiegel D: Trance and Treatment. New York, Basic Books, 1978

Tart C: States of Consciousness. New York, EP Dutton, 1975

Watzlawick P: The Language of Change. New York, Basic Books, 1978

Zeig JK: Tympanic Temperature, Hypnosis, and Laterality, Ph.D. dissertation, Georgia State University, 1977

6 Tests of Susceptibility/ Hypnotizability

SHELDON B. COHEN

Hypnotizability—Susceptibility to hypnosis
Suggestibility—The quality of state of being
suggestible, susceptibility to suggestion
or influence

WEBSTER'S, 1967

This chapter is written by a clinician and directed toward fellow practitioners. Any references to research aspects of hypnotizability are tangential and designed primarily to further clinical understanding. I shall first briefly discuss tests of hypnotizability, then present data that show how experienced clinicians use measures of hypnotizability, and conclude with ideas that may be relevant to the reader's use of hypnosis.

A test for hypnotizability for patients should be recognized as a unique occurrence in clinical practice. It is generally stated that hypnosis is not a treatment *per se* but merely a technique used to achieve a therapeutic result. There are no tests of psychoanalyzability, of behavioral modification ability, of dental extractability, or surgical operability. These are all techniques employed by the specialist in the context of his practice. Certainly, a judgment and evaluation are made about the applicability of the method to the malady, but there are no standardized measured responses of "susceptibility" or applicability of these clinical measures. The clinician attempts to relieve the patient's problems and is much less interested in measuring method than in achieving a therapeutic goal.

In discussing tests of hypnotizability, one searches in vain for suitable models upon which a framework of understanding can be erected. Certainly, many other tests that measure human potentialities have similar attributes, but from a clinical viewpoint, it must be borne in mind that almost invariably in the 73 clinical use of tests of hypnotizability the tester is also the therapist, making his role ambiguous, to say the least. There is no technician who draws the blood sample, places the electrodes, or performs other procedures and who then does the mechanical and chemical measurements that bring forth concrete physiological data.

The model that seems most appropriate is that of the track coach and the athlete. In many ways, this model fits modern-day views of hypnosis, inasmuch as the therapist–hypnotist is viewed as a facilitator who enables the patient to best use his own basic natural talents. It is within the context of this therapeutic alliance of patient and doctor that clinical testing of hypnotizability occurs. The movie "Chariots of Fire" beautifully illustrates the tale of the superb sprinter who, with the aid of proper coaching, was able to take the gold medal in the 1924 Olympics.

There was once a coach who decided meticulously to test the abilities of each potential member of his team to perform the spectrum of track and field events. He put each individual through a 100-yard dash, a mile run, broad jump, high jump, 440 hurdles, and discus throw and then added several other events to make a total of 10 measures of track–field ability. Not having a stopwatch, he counted off the seconds, and not having a ruler, he judged distances with his eye. Doing this for a period of time, he became fairly adept at measuring relative capacities of his athletes. However, he soon found that it was a terribly tiring process for the athletes and also for himself. Consequently, he began to have the athletes do some of the tests in groups and to keep their own times and distances.

Other coaches modified the tests and the emphasis upon various events and approached the events in novel ways. It also became apparent that the same events were not really indicated for grammar school tykes and Olympic hopefuls, so that further special refinements were made to take age into account. From these tests, coaches could make rough approximations as to which of their athletes were likely to perform best in sprints and which in the weight events. Other coaches would simply have the athlete perform a 50-yard dash initially and then continue with a measured mile run, and would be pleasantly surprised that many of those who were slow starters managed to do quite well. Consequently, they questioned the need for any of the testing. Coaches soon learned that the circumstances of testing, athletes' motivations, general health, and possible external distractions also played a significant role in the scores obtained.

Of such stuff are the clinical measures of hypnotizability made.

Current Tests of Hypnotizability

It should be strongly emphasized that the tests employed by clinicians and researchers are time bound. Thus, several of the tests in use at this writing had not been developed a decade ago, and a decade from now, the listing of tests may be entirely different. However, if we look beyond the terminology and stated theoretical and practical rationale for the tests, common elements can be found in all of the usual tests employed at this time, later tests building upon, elaborating, and modifying earlier ones, which may then be refined and modified themselves.

Hilgard (1978/79) has sketched out the evolution of the concept of hypnotizability, noting that in 19th century studies it was generally reported that 12% to 45% of subjects reached a deep or somnambulistic state. He noted the development of standardized scales using a number of items that were commonly associated with hypnosis:

> . . . suggested eye closure, items of the motor inhibition of challenge type (eye catalepsy, arm immobilization, arm rigidity, finger lock, verbal inhibition), posthypnotic voice hallucination, and a test of posthypnotic amnesia. Any satisfactory test of hypnosis, regardless of its special purposes, can be expected to correlate with a scale based on such samples of hypnotic behavior (pp 68–69).

The Stanford Scales

The first of today's commonly used scales was developed in a psychological laboratory at Stanford University (Weitzenhoffer and Hilgard, 1959). The initial scales were called "Stanford Hypnotic Susceptibility Scale, Form A and B (SHSS:A, SHSS:B)." Table 6-1 shows the original data of the 12 items in this scale. Each item is scored simply as a pass or failure.

Form C (Weitzenhoffer and Hilgard, 1962) was later constructed to include more items of fantasy and cognitive distortion (Table 6-2).

Table 6-1. Contribution of each item within the total, SHSS:A and SHSS:B (standardization sample, N = 124) (Weitzenhoffer and Hilgard, 1959)

Item	Percentage Passing	Reliability: SHSS:A vs. SHSS:B: tetrachoric r's	Correlation with total scale minus this item: biserial r's
1. Postural sway	69	.96	.38
2. Eye closure	58	.78	.57
3. Hand lowering	81	.83	.63
4. Arm immobilization	14	.74	.75
5. Finger lock	32	.83	.72
6. Arm rigidity	32	.88	.83
7. Moving hands	70	.75	.51
8. Verbal inhibition	23	.94	.79
9. Hallucination	35	.71	.55
10. Eye catalepsy	30	.94	.79
11. Posthypnotic suggestion	49	.60	.60
12. Amnesia	32	.77	.69

(Hilgard ER: Am J Clin Hypn 21:69, 1978)

Table 6-2. Contribution of each item within the total, SHSS:C. (Derived chiefly from the standardized sample, [N = 203], with supplementation in reliability tests)
(Weitzenhoffer and Hilgard, 1962; Hilgard, 1965)

Item	Percent Passing	Reliability SHSS:C vs SHSS:A, or Alternate Forms, SHSS:C: tetrachoric r's	Correlation with total score minus this item: biserial r's
1. Hand lowering	92	.77	.60
2. Moving hands apart	88	.65	.49
3. Mosquito hallucination	48	.76	.80
4. Taste hallucination	46	.60	.75
5. Arm rigidity	45	.67	.76
6. Dream	44	.63	.57
7. Age-regression	43	.69	.68
8. Arm immobilization	36	.60	.81
12. Amnesia*	27	.74	.85
9. Anosmia to ammonia	19	.65	.65
10. Hallucinated voice	9	.70†	.63
11. Negative visual hallucination (sees two of three boxes)	9	.60	.87

* Amnesia out of order of difficulty because necessarily at end of administration.
† Estimated on basis of correlation of +.70 with music hallucination.
(Hilgard ER: Am J Clin Hypn 21:71, 1978)

Further refinements of the Stanford Scale have been made, creating the "Stanford Profile Scales" whose goal is to select out individuals with particular hypnotic capacities. The Stanford Group also has developed a "tailored" SHSS:C, which allows investigators to substitute particular items for special research purposes.

The Stanford laboratories have developed a scale for children (Morgan and Hilgard, 1973) to meet the needs of pediatric practice. The Stanford Group later developed an abbreviated test, the Stanford Hypnotic Clinical Scale (SHCS:Adult), containing five items (Hilgard and Hilgard, 1975) (Table 6-3).

Shor and Orne (1962) modified the Stanford Scales for group administration. These modifications minimize the time and effort required of the researcher in administering the tests and scoring the results.

The Barber Scales

Barber and co-workers (Barber and Wilson, 1978/79) have developed two scales whose essence is to measure the capacity to be responsive to suggestions and to imagine creatively. It is the thesis of these tests that the conditions of administration of the tests do not have to be defined as hypnosis and customary induction techniques do not have to be utilized.

Table 6-3. Percent of subjects passing each item of the Stanford Hypnotic Susceptibility Scale Form C (SHSS:C) and of the Stanford Hypnotic Clinical Scale (SHCS:Adult) and contribution of each item to the total score of the clinical scale ($N = 111$)

Item	Percent Passing Each Item		Correlation with Total Score Minus This Item, SHCS:Adult Biserial r's
	SHSS:C	SHCS:Adult	
Moving hands	84	81	.57
Dream	69	60	.77
Age regression	67	66	.54
Posthypnotic suggestion	32*	27	.36
Amnesia	44	40	.61

* The posthypnotic item is from the Harvard Group Scale rather than from the Stanford Scale.
(Hilgard RH: Am J Clin Hypn 21:136, 1978)

A. The Barber Suggestibility Scale (BSS) consists of eight items:
   1. Arm lowering
   2. Arm levitation
   3. Hand lock
   4. Thirst "hallucination"
   5. Verbal inhibition
   6. Body immobility
   7. "Posthypnotic-like" response
   8. Selective amnesia
B. The Creative Imagination Scale (CIS) has 10 items:
   1. Arm heaviness
   2. Hand levitation
   3. Finger anesthesia
   4. Water "hallucination"
   5. Olfactory–gustatory "hallucination"
   6. Music "hallucination"
   7. Temperature "hallucination"
   8. Time distortion
   9. Age regression
   10. Mind–body relaxation

The goals in the development of these two tests were brevity, use without reference to the term "hypnosis," and movement away from what was considered to be an authoritarian manner of administration to a "permissive" clinical atmosphere.

Hypnotic Induction Profile

The Hypnotic Induction Profile (HIP) differs from the other major tests of hypnotizability in that it is the only one developed by a physician. The originator, Herbert Spiegel, is a psychiatrist who originally was trained as a psychoanalyst. The HIP evolved from clinical observations of patients. As the name implies, it is designed as an induction process that can be administered in 5 to 10 minutes with several standardized items. These can then be tabulated to give a rating that is thought to be not only a measure of hypnotizability but an indicator of severe psychopathology and of personality characteristics.

The test consists of two major elements, upward roll of the subject's eyeballs and arm levitation. Hypnotizability is considered to be positively correlated with the amount of sclera seen on upward gaze and with responsivity to the varied suggestions about arm levitation, whether the levitated arm is felt to be dissociated, whether there is a difference between the levitated and nonlevitated arm, and the sensations perceived in the levitated arm. Scoring is somewhat intricate, and the reader should be forewarned (Stern, Spiegel, and Nee, 1978/79).

The HIP requires of the examiner a high degree of familiarity with the testing procedures—the examiner himself is the instrument, and if he is not finely tuned, the HIP will not be valid. Thus, persons new to the test should not expect to be able to master the technique immediately and should be aware that several— perhaps many—practice administrations are the necessary prerequisite to valid administration.

Hypnotizability and Mental Health

Over the years there have been two contrasting notions about hypnotizability and mental health. Some clinicians have considered that the capacity to undergo hypnosis indicates emotional disease, while others considered hypnosis to be a normal psychological function. Recently, Spiegel and associates (1982) have reviewed the literature on the topic and compared the HIP scores of patients with schizophrenia, affective disorders, and generalized anxiety with those of normal controls. They found a direct correlation between degree of psychopathology and resistance to hypnotizability. Specifically, they found that schizophrenics were least hypnotizable and that patients with affective and anxiety disorders tended to be more hypnotizable as their conditions improved. This would support their thesis that hypnotizability requires the capacity to concentrate, and, consequently, disturbed thought processes interfere with this ability.

Spiegel and co-workers present the hypothesis that use of the HIP may, therefore, have diagnostic significance. However, readers should be cautioned that there is no study indicating that use of this test is in any way superior to the clinicians's evaluation obtained through the usual diagnostic interview.

Use of Tests of Hypnotizability by Clinicians

A group of experienced clinicians were queried about their use of tests of hypnotizability (Cohen, 1982). Thirty-seven (82%) of 45 physicians, clinical psychologists, and dentists answered a survey given at a workshop in which they were teaching hypnosis to fellow professionals. Thirty percent reported current usage of tests of hypnotizability, 24% had abandoned them, and 46% had never used tests of hypnotizability. The only test used routinely was the HIP, employed by three (8%) of the clinicians. Another three (8%) used standard tests (one each SHCS: Adult, HIP, BSS) "frequently," with others reporting infrequent use of standardized tests, use of their own personal test, or use of a single item from a standardized test. In the opinion of the majority of these clinicians, the tests were not generally indicated or helpful. Some believe they might even produce an antitherapeutic bias.

The data lead to the conclusion that none of the tests of hypnotizability have yet proved their efficacy to even a significant minority of clinicians.

The Clinical Significance of Hypnotizability

When all is said and done, the clinician ultimately asks himself the question, "How important are the tests of hypnotizability or the need to know about hypnotizability for *my* practice?" In an article entitled "The Clinical Importance of Hypnotizability," published in 1979, Mott notes that there are literature reports of a significant correlation between hypnotizability and pain reduction in the laboratory and that individuals who are more hypnotizable are more likely to gain relief from pain, migraine headaches, posttraumatic headaches, and asthma.

On the other hand, Barber (1977) reported that 99 out of 100 dental patients were able to use hypnosis as the sole anesthetic agent in undergoing dental operative procedures. In a follow-up article (Barber, 1980) he gives examples of patients who scored very poorly on standard scales of hypnotizability, yet responded quite well therapeutically with naturalistic, nonauthoritarian techniques. This would certainly seem to indicate that the most important consideration is the therapeutic alliance, with the technique of therapy being dependent on the therapist's making the necessary emotional contacts with the patient.

Practical Considerations

Since the formal tests are frequently used in research publications, some of a clinical nature, anyone using hypnosis should be familiar with the parameters of each test to be able intelligently to evaluate research reports. Certainly, all readers will want to try out the several clinical tests and decide for themselves what utility they have in their own practices. Beyond that, I suspect that each reader will have his own favorite method of induction and will use the patient's responsivity to the induction process as a rough measure of "hypnotizability."

I employ several different techniques, relying on a "feel" as to what seems right for the patient at a particular time. Most of the time, I use a simple handclasp as an initial induction-testing procedure. I have been using it for so long that I am not sure which of my teachers to credit as my model. It would not surprise me if some enterprising historian found that the technique had been used hundreds of years ago. I ask patients to clasp their outstretched hands tightly together, with palms pressing, and then to stare quite intently at one thumbnail of the outstretched hands. I tell the patient that the hands will be squeezing together tighter and tighter as if they were in a vise, then before they know it, the hands will feel as though they were stuck together and will not come apart even if they try to move them apart. At the appropriate time, I tell the patients that they might try to move them apart, and then I score on the patient's chart, a rough approximation of the response from 0 (no response) to 4+ (hands clasped together so tightly the patient cannot move them at all). With a patient whose hands remain together, I give suggestions for lid heaviness and eye closure and move on with the induction process. I have found this to be simple and effective but certainly would not imply that it is necessarily any better than any other test with which the reader may be familiar. Basically, any of the items listed in the different tests may be used, but most people find that one of the tests involving motor functions will work satisfactorily, and as more experience is gained with that particular item, the clinician may fashion his own rough measure of "hypnotizability."

(Readers interested in more details on measures of hypnotizability are referred to the References and, in particular, the special issue, "Measures of Hypnotizability," of The American Journal of Clinical Hypnosis, Volume 21:2 and 3, 1978/79.)

References

Barber J: Hypnosis and the unhypnotizable. Am J Clin Hypn 23:4, 1980

Barber J, Mayer D: Evaluation of the efficacy and neural mechanism of a hypnotic analgesia procedure in experimental and clinical dental pain. Pain 4:31, 1977

Barber TX, Wilson SC: The Barber suggestibility scale and the creative imagination scale: Experimental and clinical applications. Am J Clin Hypn 21:85, 1978/79

Cohen SB: Clinical uses of measures of hypnotizability. Presented to the American Psychiatric Association, Toronto, 1982

Hilgard ER: The Stanford susceptibility scales as related to other measures of hypnotic responsiveness. Am J Clin Hypn 21:68, 1978/79

Hilgard ER, Hilgard JR: Hypnosis in the Relief of Pain. Los Altos, CA, William Kaufman, 1975

Morgan AH, Hilgard ER: Age differences in susceptibility to hypnosis. Int J Clin Exp Hypn 21:78, 1973

Mott T: The clinical importance of hypnotizability. Am J Clin Hypn 21:263, 1979

Shor RE, Orne EC: The Harvard Group Scale of Hypnotic Susceptibility, Form A. Palo Alto, CA, Consulting Psychologists Press, 1962

Spiegel D, et al: Hypnotizability and psychopathology. Am J Psychiatry 139:431, 1982

Stern D, Spiegel H, Nee J: The hypnotic induction profile: Normative observations, reliability and validity. Am J Clin Hypn 21:109, 1978/79

Webster's Third New International Dictionary. Springfield, MA, G & C Merriam Co., 1967

Weitzenhoffer AM, Hilgard ER: Stanford Hypnotic Susceptibility Scales: Forms A and B. Palo Alto, CA, Consulting Psychologists Press, 1959

Weitzenhoffer AM, Hilgard ER: Stanford Hypnotic Susceptibility Scale, Form C. Palo Alto, CA, Consulting Psychologists Press, 1962

UNIT TWO
Theoretical and Experimental Foundations for the Practitioner

7 Sources of Efficacy in the Hypnotic Relationship— An Object Relations Approach

ALEXANDER H. SMITH, Jr

The scope of studies about the hypnotic experience broadly falls into two categories: the *change process* by way of suggestion in trance behavior and the *relationship* between the patient and the hypnotist. This second element forms the background into which the fabric of change is woven. However, its significance is frequently relegated to a secondary position in clinical studies. Its investigation is less frequently considered than that of technique. Consequently, the qualitative aspects of the hypnotic relationship remain an indirect focus when the nature of hypnosis and its possible clinical applications are considered.

This re-examination of the nature of the hypnotic relationship seeks to clarify, within the psychoanalytic framework, (1) the nature of the unconscious processes occurring within and between the therapist and the patient; (2) the unique contractual aspects between them; (3) means by which the hypnotic relationships permit the incorporation of suggestion and the production of its effect; and (4) the effect of mutually regulating aspects of the patient's self-organization and of the therapist's responsiveness to this organization on the desired outcome. It is hoped that, within this framework, the sources of effectiveness and of limitation may become more apparent and add further explanation to our understanding of hypnosis.

A central feature of this examination is that the unique relationship between the therapist and the patient forms the distinguishing matrix of characteristics, both behavioral and experimental, out of which flows the possibilities of direct and indirect influence. However, for the influence process to proceed in a facilitating manner, the prediction of the effect, of the style of the therapist's interventions, the specific suggestions themselves and of the patient's response to them must be conceptualized along the lines of the patient's overall ego organization (Gill and Brenman, 1959). Without such a systematic understanding, the endeavor becomes a loose array of hit-and-miss attempts.

The inadequate conceptualization and empathic comprehension of the patient's self-organization can result in a stalemate (Saretsky, 1981) or even lead to iatrogenic effects. Further, .the particular significance the patient attaches to the hypnotic relationship affords the therapist a precise range of choices for intervening effectively, according to the prevailing defensive and adaptive features of the ego at the time.

To elaborate this system of interactional effects between the patient's organization and the hypnotic endeavor, the evaluation of psychoanalytic object relations theory and self psychological is considered. This backdrop forms a newer context against which the historical developments about transference in hypnosis may be brought to a more carefully defined nature in the development of the ego.

Psychoanalytic Theories About the Hypnotic Relationship

Older Theories About the Transference

Freud (1905) evolved his understanding of the hypnotic relationship to the point at which he believed that the essential ingredients included a masochisticlike submission to the authority of the therapist, much as an individual submits to the will of a group, merging the will with it. In place of the ego-ideal, the person places the object of the hypnotist.

In his earlier understanding of the hypnotic relationship, Freud seems to have intuited a significance of the developmental process and of the necessity of the therapist "fitting" into that framework with suggestions. His later writings reflect a more disdainful flavor toward the process, as he had subsequently focused on the ego and the process of analysis. Chertok (1977) has discussed this ebb and flow of interest in hypnosis. Ferencizi (1905) also worked within a developmental framework, theorizing that the transference developed along a continuum of "the mother hypnotist," who induces compliance through castration fear. His conceptualization, of course, is fitted into that of the Oedipus complex and, at times, seems to have become procrustean in effort.

Other Freudian theorists of this time appear to have considered the hypnotic relationship mainly within the context of the superego double (Rado, 1925), fusion of ego-ideal with ego (Jones, 1948), and as ego double (Fenichel, 1945). Other contemporaries of Freud have made significant indirect contributions. Adler's (1939) main theoretical construct of life-style was built around mistaken self-perceptions of inferiority and mistaken goals of compensation. Interestingly, he depreciated hypnosis as essentially an indulgence of the patient's tactics of helplessness. Ironically, however, Adler's papers on psychotherapy are filled with what recently have become popularized versions of indirect suggestion such as paradox, prescriptions of symptoms, countermoves against the patient's resistances, foiling of power tactics that defeat social interest, and so on. It was perhaps, an unfortunate turn of events in which Adler did not recognize the interface between hypnotic maneuver and his own methods. Even in hypnosis, Adler's work stands as an undervalued contribution from which theories of intervention have evolved (Munroe, 1955).

Jung does not seem to have been enthusiastic towards hypnosis, though his style was, again, like Adler's, much more pragmatic and often filled with encouragement, suggestion exhortation, and prescription about attitude change. This was particularly true when the analysis and synthesis of unconscious elements were either less relevant or potentially too disorganizing to the patient. Certainly, his explanation of the archetypal influences is an unequalled contribution, only recently appreciated in American psychology (Singer, 1973). His works on psychotherapy and the process of transference (Jung, 1954) are indirect contributions to understanding the hypnotic relationship. In particular, his concept of the transference is a broader one than Freud's. The relationship is viewed in its teleological and proactive aspects in which the therapist and patient blend their unconscious needs toward a resolution of the patient's difficulty. Such a concept is decidedly different from the "blank screen" and offers a greater understanding of the relationship through its open-system quality.

Other major contributors have understood the hypnotic relationship within the ego-analytic framework. One view is that it is an incorporation of the figure of the therapist into the ego and superego of the patient (Kubie and Margolin, 1944). This means that the "boundaries" between the patient and therapist are blurred in such a way that the destructive, introjected parental attitudes are replaced by more benign ones. The nature of introjection, however, as it has come to be understood (Klein, 1948; Schafer, 1968) is more elaborate than the concept that Kubie and Margolin had available at that time. The developmental specificity of interaction between the patient and therapist is implied but not explicated. Further, Kubie and Margolin gave the transference a secondary significance to the psychophysiological changes induced.

Watkins (1954) viewed the transference that developed between patient and therapist as essentially the equivalent of a trance. This concept is interesting in that the distortions by the patient often do, in fact, result in a fixed pattern of perception. The concept is more easily understood within a reductive model in which the interpretations and clarifications that occur are directed toward enabling the patient to distinguish himself from what he is *not*. The constructive, proactive processes are not as easily elaborated within this model.

Gill and Brenman (1959) moved the understanding of the hypnotic relationship more closely to a configurational one. They hypothesized an interaction between the subsystem of the ego apparatuses, primarily automatized and now libidinized and "lent" to the hypnotist (*i.e.,* perception, memory, judgment, etc.), and the intense transference stimulated. Their issue with transference and regression is that the so-called revivification of a previous state is a technically inaccurate term, since regression requires an ego more fully developed to permit the transference experience.

Interestingly, Gill and Brenman state that an adequate development of the ego is necessary to permit lending itself to the hypnotist. Their accent is upon ego functions and less upon the object relational experiences that facilitated their development. The transferences stimulated are seemingly viewed in their historical reductive aspects rather than in the object-relational needs of a still-evolving ego organization.

Gill (1979), after drawing lines of distinction between regressed ego states and altered states of consciousness, points out that the nature of transference in hypnosis is still not well understood. Fromm and Hurt (1980), extending Fromm's (1972, 1979) work on ego processes in hypnosis, emphasize the reciprocal roles of ego activity and passivity in the hypnotic state, and of both roles within a receptivity to the hypnotist. Through this receptivity, the patient may alter cognitive structures about stimulus intensities and thus affect the "automatized" responsiveness in subsequent waking states.

The issue of receptivity within the ego structure is prominent in Fromm's writings. Interestingly, it is contextualized by reference to object relational experience:

> Inner perception replaces cognition as the principal cognitive structure. Memory reverts to genetically earlier modes of organization. Memory traces are imbued with premature drive qualities and *organized in constellation that reveal early object cathexes.* (Fromm and Hurt, 1980, p 21; italics mine)

Elsewhere Fromm (1968) and Grunewald (1972) have discussed the vicissitudes of countertransference and transference within the context of the hypnotic relationship.

This orientation has "tracked" the development of ego processes occurring in the hypnotic relationship within some context of object relational organization. However, the emphases here remain on the outcome of facilitation of ego processes.

Generally, all of these studies have viewed the hypnotic relationship along the traditional dualistic lines: that of the facilitating working alliance that exists between the patient and the therapist and that of the transference phenomena in (by and large) the *classical* sense. This latter set of phenomena refers specifically to the patient's experience of the therapist as a part or whole figure from the patient's past toward whom the patient now reacts in historically consistent fashion.

Limitations of Previous Paradigms of Transference in Hypnosis

The ascription of transference (in the classical sense) to the hypnotic relationship is somewhat troublesome. While the elements of transference are undoubtedly existent in almost all therapeutic and interpersonal relationships, the usage of the term as it frequently appears in the literature tends to have a curtailing and oversimplifying effect on the understanding of the proactive or integrative aspects of the hypnosis.

The use of the transference phenomena as a means of searching for the patient's resources that have been developmentally arrested (Stolorow and Lachman, 1977) and counterpoised within symptomatology becomes less specific in description, if considered at all. It has become necessary to re-examine the hypnotic relationship from a developmental self-organizational and object relational posture in order more accurately to understand the relationship in its uniqueness and thereby understand its potential in facilitating change. Instead of "downward" reductive focus, it has become more useful to approach these phenomena from an "upward" coalescing posture.

A number of issues discussed here become more apparent when the role of object relations in ego development is examined.

Essentially, the ego of Gill and Brenman (1959) and of Fromm (1977), Fromm (1972), Grunewald, Fromm and Oberlander (1979) is one that emphasizes the intrapsychic functional organization of various ego capacities in relation to each other. Other theories, progressively older in nature, become less and less configurational in conceptualization and thus permit less specific understandings of the effects of the defensive and instinctual expressions (one upon the other) within this ego organization.

From within this ego-organization-adaptive-level-achieved paradigm, the role of object relations—that is, the experience of the earliest and most global experiences of the infant in relation to the maternal object, all the way to the current capacities for experiencing distinction from and love toward current others (objects)—does not appear conceptually clear in its effect upon ego organization in the hypnotic relationship.

Secondly, the nature of the regressed ego in its regulational functions has been more extensively studied, than in its object relational capacities. Levin's and Harrison's (1976) study of primary process thinking and adaptive regression, and Lavoie's and Sarbouren's (1976) study of susceptibility among psychotics both concluded that the effect of quality and nature of object relations upon adaptive regression must be more carefully considered.

Adaptive regression in the service of the ego (Kris, 1952; Bellak et al, 1973) must be distinguished from pathological regression. Frequently, this latter concept is described when more dynamic and genetic issues about the patient are examined. To further complicate the matter, the regressed ego of object relations refers to yet another admixture of behavior patterns, percepts, and experiences having to do with the capacities to perceive, seek, and anticipate and love the other object as distinct from itself. In pathological forms, this feature frequently takes the form of paranoid and depressive anxieties (Klein, 1948), with splitting or a blurring of self and object representations (Kernberg, 1975; Jacobson, 1964) and an overall arrest in the development of mature relations.

The hypnotic relationship is an intricate series of interactions based upon conscious and unconscious object-relational capacities of both the patient and the therapist. It is the pivot around which the process of hypnosis works or fails. Therefore, the essentials of hypnosis must be viewed in context of the basic capacity to relate—the capacity to form a relationship, marked by frequent cues of dependency, trust, capacities to tolerate blending with another's self, and capacities to receive without fear and to reemerge, using the experience within the patient's total ego organization. These relational capacities of the ego have received increasing attention and have continued prominence in the understanding of developmental organization. Their relationship (of object-relational organization) to adaptive regression is vital to understanding hypnosis.

Proactive Paradigms of Developmental Arrest

While some attempt has been made to review object relations theory in light of the hypnotic relationship (Smith, 1981), the essential elements of modern metapsychology within psychoanalysis remain, sadly, scattered and without application to hypnosis. A brief overview of current shifts within psychoanalytic systems of theory and intervention permits articulation of differences in emphasis and provides a scaffolding upon which the hypnotic relationship may be further understood.

Three major components of psychoanalytic theory may be said to exist. Admittedly, the lines of distinction are rather arbitrary, but, nevertheless, they do correspond to modes of emphasis in theory and practice.

Classical

The modern "classical" position has continued to exert influence in psychoanalysis. This "sect" has continued to remain more or less within the tripartite structural theory (id, ego, superego) and psychosexual developmental position of fixation and regression. It tends to view psychopathological states as the outcome of drive fixations and defensive organizations occurring within developmental lines of the ego (Glover, 1955; A. Freud, 1963; Hartman, 1958; Schafer, 1968).

Psychotherapy is directed toward appropriate interpretation of the transference elements as they occur and relates them to the genetic–dynamic configurations of introjection and projection processes, identifications, and other defensive organizations within the transference.

Central to this theoretical system is the ubiquitous Oedipus complex, which is optimally "resolved" within the transference (Greenson, 1967; Dewald, 1976). The focus within this dimension is on the integration of the ego through a "downward" working of material of resistance and transference toward the uncovering of affects defended at specific developmental points, and of the instinctual (sexual and aggressive) derivatives that appear within symptomatology, character problems and other dysfunctional behavior. The basic ingredients include a re-learning of adaptation according to more advanced psychosexual maturation, following the relinquishing of infantile modes of behavior. This process occurs within the relationship of patient to therapist (Strupp, 1975). Bellak, Hurvich, and Gediman (1973) have outlined this broad framework of ego functions, along the lines of psychotherapeutic assessment and treatment.

Self Psychology

A second orientational shift has been toward the psychology of the self. This focus examines development of self-organization from within the expansion of Freud's (1914) original papers on narcissism (Kohut, 1971; Ornstein, 1980)—that is, the capacity to direct libidinal energy towards one's self is viewed as a developmental line separate from object love.

The self is viewed as the summative experience of functioning. Kohut and Wolf (1978) write:

> The patterns of ambitions, skills, goals, and the tensions between them, the
> program of action they create, and the activities that strive toward the realization
> of this program are all experienced as continuous in space and time . . . they are
> the self, an independent center of initiative, an independent recipient of
> impression.

Kohut's (1971, 1977, 1980) monumental examination of the treatment of narcissism and his colleague's (Goldberg, 1980, 1978; P. Ornstein, 1980; Ornstein & Ornstein, 1975, 1976) elaboration of this line of development have emphasized a developing self that relies on the needed constellation of responses by "selfobjects," experienced in varying degrees of separateness.

Essentially these concepts case the nascent self into a developmental framework that is based on an empathic observation rather than on an "experience-distant" mode (Kohut, 1980) and that generates an emphasis of understanding from *within* the patient's experiences of development.

The self–self object relations then are ones that form enabling mergers of mirroring and idealization held to be *essential* in the formation of a cohesive self.

Psychopathological states are seen essentially as disintegration products of the failures by the needed self-objects to supply appropriately dosed empathic responses to the self (Kohut, 1977; Stolorow and Lachman, 1977).

The constituents of the developing personality within this framework are grounded in a dual-axial bipolar self in which the ambitions, strivings, and utilization of talents and abilities form one pole, and the ideals and goals of effecting these ambitions form the other. The "tension arc" between them results in a mutually regulating effect. The thrust for these two poles results from the qualitative responsiveness by the needed merger and mirroring object (usually the mother) and by the participation by the idealized object (usually the father) in the merger of strength and esteem accorded the person in the developmental process.

Changes within the personality occur through "transmitting internalizations" and not through the replacement of id with ego. It is noteworthy here that the shift is away from a paradigm of drives that result in ego organization. Instead, the self-object response enables the drive organization to occur (Kohut, 1977).

Within this framework, the Oedipus complex is viewed as a conflict contextualized by the prevailing, previously achieved self-object organization (Tolpin, 1978) and is accorded a major difference in emphasis. The emphasis seeks to understand the effect of the conflict on subsequent self-organization rather than on the defensive identifications and mediation of drives by the ego.

Object Relations Theory

A third point of emphasis is that of object relations. Within the ego, adaptive functions are seen as potentiated according to the prevailing outcome of positively or negatively charged relations to objects experienced during the first 2 to 3 years of life. The shift is toward the primacy of objects as organizers of the infant ego and as the precursors of later object relations (Spitz, 1965; Mendez, Fine, and Guntrip, 1976).

This motivational focus runs on a continuum from instinctually projective-related introjective experienced (Klein, 1948) to that of mutual regulating aspects of these organizing experiences between infant and mother (Jacobson, 1964; Kernberg, 1976; Giovacchinni, 1972; Blank and Blank, 1974, 1979; Winnicott, 1965).

The emphasis here is on understanding the formation of the infant ego through the structuring and accompanying affective response by the mother to the ever progressive differentiation of representations of self from other with the ego (Beres and Joseph, 1970).

Within this context, the omnipotent self-object unit of relations between mother and infant, the idealization of parental figures, the regulation of self-esteem, and the formation of a stable boundary of relations between self and other take place in stepwise progression from states of indifferentiation and fusion to those around separation/undereducation to object constancy (Mahler, 1968, 1972). Each phase in this progression predisposes subsequent outcomes of later phases according to the affective climate that matched fusion and differentiation.

The stability of the self-organization is founded on the specificity of these outcomes, with more primitive defenses being used to ward off the associated unpleasant affects (Mahler and McDevitt, 1968).

Kernberg (1975, 1978), Masterson (1972, 1981), and Rinsley (1977), among others, have elaborated on the developmental arrests resulting from phase-specific thwarting of developmentally appropriate needs. Borderline and narcissistic disorders frequently result from such arrests. Defenses such as splitting good from bad self and object representations, primitive denial of negatively charged object relations, idealization and devaluation cycles with the therapists, condensation of sexual and dependent needs, pseudo-independent facades, or fragmentation-prone personalities with multiple phobias, and acting out proclivities are behavioral styles by which the self-organization settles to defend against abandonment depression (Masterson, 1981).

Changes occur through restructuralization of the ego within the transference, where the previous splitting of good and bad, self and other representations are brought together, permitting an advancement in perceiving objects as whole and constant and having good and bad together (Kernberg, 1978, 1976; Masterson, 1981).

Converging Foci in Developmental Object Relations— Foundations for the Hypnotic Relationship

The three major thrusts in these emphases are, of course, not mutually exclusive in a metapsychological sense. They point to pivot conditions necessary for a smoothly developed means of ego functioning. Their relevance to the hypnotist is particularly important, since frequently the process of hypnosis does not permit a thorough analytic undertaking. Often the therapist is called upon to infer these constellations within the patient, in a relatively short period of time and without bringing them to the consciousness of the patient.

The therapist then must understand, within a broader framework, the relative balance of the patient's psychic organization and the points at which the hypnotic experience converge with it. Five major synthetic issues are described here that may afford a broader foundation for understanding what occurs within the hypnotic relationship:

1. The proactive elements of developmental arrest and symptom formation
2. The capacity to create good self and object representations
3. The facilitating maternal response matrix
4. The nature of transitional object relatedness and the formation of a curative fantasy
5. The regressed ego and the use of bad internal objects as a defense against abandonment

The discussion of these processes may then form a framework for assessment and intervention in the hypnotic relationship.

The Proactive Elements of Developmental Arrest and Symptom Formation

A major feature in the growing body of developmental object relations studies is that the ego's resiliency is implied in its attempt to master the trauma by incorporation of the object connected with it, and its delegation into ego and superego structures.

In other words, it is not that the ego forms itself into structures bearing the stamp of the objects (Freud, 1905), but that it has the capacity for doing this that is relevant here. There is a constant that accompanies the ego throughout its entirety, and that is that it functions always in relation to an object.

Fairbairn's (1954) maxim that the ego is object-seeking rather than drive-discharging is indeed compelling when the issue of symptomatology is considered. The symptom carries with it an attempt by the ego to relate itself to an object or to maintain its economy through a disavowal of the needs for such an object (Kohut, 1977; Ornstein, 1980).

The issue here is that, within hypnosis, a fundamental but not always obvious consideration is that of the patient's search to restore or to set in motion self-organization that has not been attained by himself. In this sense, the concept of a "self-object" that has essentially a "goodness-of-fit" into the missing structures of the self is helpful. (However, this system of Kohut's does not seem adequately to elucidate the impact of good and bad objects within the ego and their regulational aspects in the patient's behavior.) Drive organization occurs only within the context of an object-relational experience. *The therapist then has this first basic principle that the patient seeks him in some attempt to master conflict.*

The dependent nature of this attempt is therefore a felicitous beginning in that it is quite adaptive and fundamentally human. This consideration must accompany the transference phenomena that may occur at higher levels (*i.e.,* oedipal or pre-oedipal replications and distortions). Fenichel's (1945) concept of "passive-mastery," in which active mastery has failed, is relevant here, although it is not cast in a developmental framework.

The Capacity to Form Good Self and Object Representations

Modell (1975) has suggested that these instincts within the ego that are object-seeking aid in representation within the ego of the positive and negative outcomes of the self in relation to objects (Jacobson, 1964). These inner affective and cognitive operations that retain these experiences facilitate or inhibit greater ego capacities and affect the greater differentiation of self from other in good and bad aspects. This capability of holding positive and negative experiences in relative balance, and the use of them for further expectancies, organizational schemes, and outcomes form a sense of identity (Kernberg, 1976) and affect the overall balance of ego organization. Sandler and Rosenblatt (1962) have elaborated on representational formation. In essence, the representations became the fibers of the ego's future.

The hypnotic experience directly affects this organization, although the means for doing so is indirect. The capacity to represent the outcome of experiences, and to form object constancy (Fraiberg, 1969; McDevitt, 1975) are of paramount importance in the hypnotic relationship. The shifting of connecting affects that exist between these structures are also of vital significance. Their benign aspect allows the patient to approach the hypnotist, to idealize the process or the person, and to create the magic expectations.

The Facilitating Maternal Response Matrix

The infant-maternal orbit (Mahler, 1968) consists of a mutually regulating response matrix, out of which follow the ministrations by mother to the primal need of the infant. From within this matrix, the infant's capacities to respond are potentiated. This is achieved through the gradual internalization of the mother's affective–cognitive–behavioral cues not only to the specific behavioral patterns within the infant but also, and perhaps more importantly, to the infant's capacity for integrated, coordinated, whole functioning (Spitz, 1965).

"The presence" or mirroring of the infant's innate readiness for integrated functioning is perhaps the single most significant maternal response internalized by the infant. The use of the word "internalized" is indeed advised, since this potential appears only in its effects and not in any easily measurable way. The maternal mediation of possibilities of responsiveness within the infant and the mother's facilitation of its actuality in the infant's behavior bear a striking parallel to the mediation by the therapist by way of the hypnotic relationship (Kubie and

Margolin, 1944). While this parallel is perhaps overstated, its significance remains central to our present theoretical frameworks and to the manner in which we approach the relationship and the activities within hypnosis. It is the facilitation of ego processes through the maternal response that is crucial to our discussion.

Important synthetic elements that emerge here point to the "ignition" effects of the mothering agent on ego functions, which constitute a crucial reciprocating dynamic seen in hypnosis.

Of interest here are the major activities of the hypnotic process, namely, the capacity to expect, to relinquish boundaries and to fuse with another's experience, to be lead by sensory experiences into a focus (hyper-cathected) of attention, to connect comfort and calmness with the "holding function" (Winnicott, 1965) of the hypnotist's voice, and to allow soothing, through a relational dimension of these processes, so that the repressed or split off "bad objects" do not invade nor damage the newer self and object representations that became implicit in the repairing quality of the relationship (Khan, 1974).

Germane to the patient's symptomatology, for example, are the ego processes of visualization, sensation and perception changes, rehearsals, memory accessing, and so on. These functions are mediated by the survival climate of the maternal object in infant life. Through the mother's initial psychic fusion with the infant's needs, the infant may first passively associate climate with functions and eventually objects with functions (Giovacchini, 1972). The infant is thus able to move from "being" to "doing" in Guntrip's (1969) sense, not simply by a buildup of a reservoir of good object representations but through the tandem relationship of the primal need for participation by an organizing, attachment-capable (Bowlby, 1973), receptive object to the specific competency about to be facilitated. Visual alertness in infants is an example (Korner and Thomas, 1970; Korner and Grobstern, 1966).

There is thus a mutual process inherent in the buildup of the object-relations within—namely, the receptive response by the mothering one to the receptive need by the infant for stimulation, and maintenance of identity processes in motion around that specific phase. The exercise of the ego and the buildup of these hierarchies of processes are of significance to hypnosis.

Crucial to the hypnotic relationship is a comprehension of the quality of needs for and defenses against the hypnotist-as-object and use of introjective and projective systems to disavow or to regulate painful tensions and affects resulting from archaic needs, now revived, that are being thwarted.

Talented therapists often empathically and intuitively find ways to eschew the defensive organization in such a way as to permit the internal object organization to be carried forward outside the conscious awareness of the ego and without an analytic understanding of its process.

The processes of perceptual distortion, change in stimulus salience, use of imagination, heightened sensation, "trance logic," and the like are functions within the domain of the ego. However, any brief consideration of these processes raises the question of how they came about; and the primary organizing function in the maternal environment must be considered as a model. The hypnotic relationship is therefore not a recapitulation of early maternal relations, nor is it primarily a side-by-side reworking of mother or father transferences. These formulations do not leave us with any understanding or developmental tools needed to help the patient move forward.

Instead, the hypnotic relationship is seen essentially as the continuation of self-organization processes visible through the specific "curative fantasy" of the patient.

The Curative Fantasy, and the Use of Transitional Object-Relatedness on Basic Activities in the Hypnotic Relationship

The third constellation of studies synthesized here involves the successful passage into increasingly experienced separate identity states. The vicissitudes of separation–individuation are the subject of several well-known sources (Mahler, 1968, 1972; Kernberg, 1976; McDevitt, 1975).

Within these sequellae the concept of the transitional object (Winnicott, 1958) has been posited as a series of mediating experiences from which the infant achieves the initial phases of separation by the retention of and investment in a comforting object, such as a blanket or teddy bear. Winnicott observed that such objects served as a structuralizing function for the ego, by which the inner reality of omnipotent control of the mother and the outer reality of the separate mother may be comfortably bridged.

Defective availability of the transactional object (here this refers to the maternal "understanding" of the toddler's need for this experience as much as in her aiding in providing the object) has been posited as resulting in numerous psychopathological states such as character disorders (Horton et al, 1974), inability adequately to separate in childhood (Mahler, 1961), capacity to symbolize comforting representations (Modell, 1975), phobias (Appel, 1974), formation of fetishes (Greenacre, 1970), and, in particular, stereotyped action patterns (Winnicott, 1965; Wagner and Fine, 1976) that deny separation. More elaborate reviews of the clinical aspects of transitional objects are in the works of Wagner and Fine (1976) and Kahne (1967).

This function by which the infant creates an illusionary representation of control in response to the gradual failure of omnipotence by the mother is pivotal for the "transmuting internalization" (Kohut, 1971) to occur in appropriate decrements. These are neither too exhausting nor too inhibiting for separation to proceed, but permit a climate by which the exciting and quiet aspects of maternal response may come together, affording an optimal regulation of arousal and stimulation (Kohut and Wolf, 1978).

The transitional object experience affords the infant a staging area for the hatching phenomena of separation (Mahler, 1968). The subsequent phases observed by Mahler and his colleagues are affected in a pyramidlike way. The experience permits a bit-by-bit internalization of maternal regulation (Tolpin, 1971), resulting in a cohesive self-experience. It allows for the optimal use of illusion (Khan, 1974).

The capacity, then, to use hypnosis and to regress in the service of object-relational restructuring experiences immediately suggests that these phenomena are involved in the therapeutic process (Searles, 1976).

Deviation in other ego functions must then be correlated with the outcome of transitional object needs adequately met in phase-appropriate stages.

The use of hypnosis—even the choice of it as a modality—constellates these issues. The fantasy about what the hypnotic relationship will do cannot be understood without consideration to its transitional object quality, that is, one in which the patient retains an omnipotence by way of his request and fantasies of a union with the omnipotent therapist (Gill and Brenman, 1959; Fromm, 1968).

The convergence of expectations (Sacerdote, 1974) leads to a mutually regulating relationship between the patient's capacity for/defense against the idealized and the disappointing aspects of the hypnotist and the hypnotist's countertransferential needs to comply/resist these images, or to compulsively "treat" the patient (Saretsky, 1981).

The therapist's ability to intuit the quality of tolerance for disappointment within the patient is most vital in formulating interventions that neither excite nor thwart the patient's needs. This concept has been described elsewhere as the "curative fantasy" (Kohut, 1971; Ornstein and Ornstein, 1975) and is essential in assessment for hypnotic work. It embodies a developmental line of anticipatory growth by the patient, based on the level and quality of developmental arrest. (It is understood here that we are discussing a range of developmental configurations from "normal" to most pathological.) *As the transitional object relatedness is a prototype for future qualitative whole object and self differentiations, the prevailing outcome of this set of experiences is counterpoised in the curative fantasy about what the hypnosis will do.*

The curative fantasy leads directly to the current level of object relations development and casts other ego functions within its shadow. In essence, the curative fantasy at once ties together the quality of transitional object experiences either integrated or defended against, the missing responsiveness to developmental organization not presently supplied within the ego, the current level of internal object differentiation, and the quality of the subjective psychosomatic unity or psychic cohesiveness within the patient (Kohut, 1977).

This concept provides a tool for the therapist to infer what the patient's overall organization seeks but cannot ask for. The curative fantasy takes the therapist to the doorstep of the "basic fault" (Balint, 1968), the nodal point of frozen relatedness and internal bad-object (exciting or depriving) complexes. It ties ego functions such as executive and synthetic functions (cessation of smoking) with the aims of treatment (*e.g.,* weight reduction), with internal bad objects (depriving, withholding, exciting) in the unconscious needs sought from the therapist (devouring the therapist to ease the transitional trauma and the pressuring emptiness of the loss of magical union). Many other such combinations, of course, exist.

The hypnotic relationship in this sense forms the glue of ego functions within the holding response by the therapist. These functions are outside the awareness of the patient, but, it is hoped, not that of the therapist. This is because the uniqueness of hypnosis often denies the therapist the opportunity for imparting an analytic understanding of these issues to the patient. The patient still proceeds with the balance of ego organization and with the accompanying level of tolerance for shifts away from whatever pathological degree of organization that may exist. This last issue now is considered before discussion of intervention processes.

The Regressed Ego and the Use of Bad Objects as Defense Against Abandonment

Within the personality, the basic ego weakness is that point at which the development of the psychic organization was arrested and at which the attachments were made to the destructive, rejecting, or otherwise toxic experiences of loved figures. It is the point in development of psychic organization at which the "basic fault" in growth occurred and at which the ego splits itself (Freud, 1905; Fairbairn, 1954; Guntrip, 1969) to manage these experiences, while warding off their unpleasant effects.

Guntrip (1969) has written extensively on the nature of this aspect of the self, which he saw in similar ways to Winnicott's (1965) "self in storage." It is where the basic ego relatedness between mother and infant has failed. The process of primary relatedness that has been broken up then contributes to the ego's dramatic turning against itself, fearing and, at times, hating the object. This is so because the ego fears that the craving for basic relatedness will result in either retaliation by the object (persecutory anxiety) or the destruction of the object (depressive anxiety). Thus it fears its weakness because it will lead to abandonment, destruction, or worse—total unrelatedness.

> The struggle to force a weak ego to face life, or, even more fundamentally, the struggle to preserve an ego at all is the root cause of psychotic, psychosomatic and psychoneurotic tensions. (Guntrip, 1969, p 177)

The organization of psychic tensions resulting from the ego split within itself brings about the frozenlike massive characterological patterning we observe in various disorders. The major consideration here is that in the hypnotic relationship this organization may be discerned through the request for hypnosis and by the expectation of its effect.

The patient seeks fundamentally to contract with the hypnotist to remain in the current attachments to destructive introjects and yet to be free of their painful consequences. Alongside these phenomena is fear of shift from within of the frozen ego of development toward a more fluid, open emergence into experience. This may be similar to Kohut's (1977) concept of a disavowed, grandiose self, although the emphasis here is not on the mirroring of needs, but on the patient's learned fear of relating with them to a new, nontoxic object. Guntrip's clarity about this issue is, again, helpful.

> The schizoid person, *to whatever degree he is schizoid,* hovers between two opposite fears, the fear of isolation in independence with his loss of ego in a vacuum of experience, and the fear of bondage to, of imprisonment or absorption in the personality of whomever he wishes to for protection. . . . That is the schizoid dilemma, equal inability either to do with or without the needed protector, the parent-figure whom the insecure child inside will have, but whom the struggling adult conscious self cannot tolerate or admit. This presents the greatest obstacle to psychotherapy. (Guntrip, 1969, p. 291; italics mine)

As we can see, it is the fear that growth will lead to destruction that gives this issue its poignancy. Fundamentally, this continuum of fear of need for the help from another constitutes one significant dimension of the hypnotic relationship that has yet to be elucidated. The expectation/fear of the mergerlike experience creates the balancing of psychic organization to which the hypnotist must attune him. Its manifestations occur in any dependency-avoidant behavior complex. The emphasis here is "person centered" rather than "system centered" (Guntrip, 1971). With this shift in emphasis, the nature of regression itself takes on added meaning in hypnosis. It is the fulcrum on which the activity of suggestion and influence pivot. It is the point at which developmental arrest interfaces with the hypnotic relationship, permitting the possibilities of efficacy in the activity of hypnosis. Understanding these vicissitudes permits the assessment and intervention to proceed in an optimally facilitating manner.

Assessing the Patient's Object-Relational Organization Within the Hypnotic Relationship

The unique problem facing the hypnotist-therapist is that of comprehending in a relatively short time the major characteristics of the patient's total ego organization, including that of object relation. Most assessment procedures in hypnosis have been directed toward capacities for trance rather than capacities to form the hypnotic relationship. Other parameters must therefore be addressed informally. What appear to be higher level adaptive functions, such as independence in object relations, or major subliminatory activities, such as choices of work, interests, and so on, may in fact be defensive or compensatory structures (Kohut, 1971, 1977) for aggravated ruptures in earlier formation responses needs. The therapist must therefore proceed within a framework that permits a glimpse at these issues.

All defenses, conflicts, and introjective and projective systems carry the echo of a major pattern of organization within the patient. In a larger sense, we ask what did not happen as well as what did happen (Guntrip, 1969). I have learned that it is better to err on the side of caution and over pathologizing than to become confluent with the patient's defensive systems in such a way as to become nearsighted. The paradox here seems to be, contrary to other orientations, that a more forward-looking, self-fulfilling prophecy can be implanted into the relationship specifically where the patient's symptoms and defensive needs are understood in their proactive, corrective attempts to remain an organized ego, than when applied in a random fashion (Blank and Blank, 1979).

All symptoms, from mildly neurotic to severely psychotic, contain a germ of movement toward more healthy functioning.

Three Foci for Immediate Assessment

Three main answers are within immediate descriptive possibility that aid in assessing the overall capacity to form a relationship in hypnoses. They are (1) the nature of the request, (2) how the request is verbalized, and (3) the therapist's immediate affective response to the patient. The integration of these data, and their confirmation in further patient-response clusters afford some rapidly working "gyroscopes" in hypnotic work.

The Nature of the Request. The request in itself embodies a complex constellation of conscious and unconscious needs within the patient. As described earlier, the "pull" within the nature of hypnosis constellates transitional-object relational phenomena, even, I believe, in normal persons. Consequently, the request suggests to the therapist the qualities of object relatedness that the patient either defensively resorts to or around which he is developmentally arrested. Immediately, the therapist has one major issue to determine: is this relationship that is to be formed one that is based on fixated problems of separation–individuation or is it a retreat to an earlier, more blissful relational experience in which passive needs are used in the service of mastering other ego functions in the calmness of a temporary merger that poses no particular threat? The distinctions about developmental arrest are indeed crucial (Stolorow and Lachman, 1977).

From the nature of the request, the therapist may also ascertain initial impressions about its symbolic nature. Simple requests for smoking and weight reduction, often embody major object-relational problems of object constancy, internal self-soothing, and other vicissitudes of maternal deprivations. Frequently, these are patients who have been "around" to other therapists or to questionable "fast-results" clinics. The addictive quality of their problems often necessitates a more carefully conducted assessment. The masochistic and yet frequently demanding nature of their requests signal that the relationship will require careful tracking of, in particular, immediate gratification demands.

All requests and expectations must be carefully explored for the developmental level of object relations attained, type and quality of idealization of the therapist, any splitting of hypnosis or of the therapist from previous experiences, the capacity to regulate affects and tensions, and the nature of the anxiety involved in the request. These suggest an unconscious curative fantasy and the role the therapist plays in the patient's object organization. What is the fantasy unconsciously designed to do?

Verbalization of the Request. The verbalization of what the patient wants often gives the therapist an introduction to the *defensive systems* involved. The linguistic style, especially, will shed considerable light on these patterns of functioning. Is the patient primarily active or passive? Does the patient's language suggest a stability in relationships, or is it marked by chaos, impulsivity, and jerkiness? Is the tone the smooth one of a more advanced level of object-relations in which some separateness has been comfortably bridged or is it scratchy, clawing, and desperate like that of a survivor of the Titanic? Does the patient use primarily repressive defenses, suggesting a higher level of organization, or does he manage the ego organization through projective comments about others, or through self-minimalization?

These and other parameters of initial interviewing are important to the hypnotist, in particular, because from the narration given, the therapist has further data to infer what the unconscious posture of the patient will be toward the therapist. At times, particularly with nettlesome, unsoothable patients, it is useful to listen just for verb phrases or just for shifts from one statement to the next to ascertain the current hidden nature of the request. The gyroscopic fix on these types of request can be unified by the therapist's asking himself what maternal, organizing function is missing here that would lead to greater organization of drives, affect differentiation, and so on.

The Therapist's Own Affective Response. The utility of countertransference responses has been discussed, particularly by Searles (1979). Essentially, the therapist seeks to differentiate the response to the patient that originates from within the therapist's own areas of object-relational conflicts, from those induced by the patient's own object-relational organization. Needless to say, a therapy or analysis for the therapist greatly increases his capacities to use this process effectively.

From the climate that the patient creates within the therapist, the therapist may obtain subsequent formulations about the current level of object organization, the prevailing affects accompanying them, and the anticipation of how the hypnosis will proceed from within this matrix.

Again, the "pull" of the hypnotic relationship will be toward the earliest introjective systems and their accompanying ego organization. The therapist may determine these by permitting himself to be temporarily sucked into the ploy of the patient, to become manipulated, or to make him accessible to the climate of pressuring, seduction, uneasy alliance, hatred and disdain, enraging helplessness, wheedling or cajoling, or whatever responses the patient excites. By tasting it, the therapist can begin to determine how he might incorporate this into understanding the patient (Searles, 1976).

Certain countertransference pulls are inherent in hypnosis. Aside from the often-cited Swengali-like complex, these are the more subtle ones, which frequently are stimulated through the interplay between the patient's and the therapist's self-organizations. Most understanding is the need "to do something" for the patient. As hypnosis is often conceived of as a "doing" activity, it often attracts "doers" who can be forced through the patient's pathology into a rescuelike activity. Such responses are ultimately destructive because the unconscious complementary need to steal from, to deprive, or to harm (the wishes against which the "doing" of hypnosis is a reaction formation) will be frequently played out in even the most subtle ways.

The therapist, therefore, must attune to these differentiations in order to provide a holding climate wherein the bad object systems internalized do not overtake the relationship between the therapist and the patient. This single dimension is most prominent in considering the hypnotic relationship. The therapist must stand midway between the bad object systems, the continued need for and yet feared growth of object relatedness, and the regressed ego of growth, which the patient hides with characterological, defensive, and other distracting systems. He must not overstimulate nor neglect any of these features, but use them selectively to address, according to potentially receptive responses, the way in which he can effect within hypnosis, a new form of relatedness that assures the patient freedom from the therapist's destructiveness, hate, or wish to control. This last experience then permits new learning by the patient.

Intervention in the Hypnotic Relationship

We are now in a position to cull the major components of intervention within the hypnotic relationship and to advance a more specific constellation of processes within the ego that "quicken" the learning occurring at the level of suggestion. From the developmental psychoanalytic emphasis upon early object-relational experiences, four major foci emerge when considering the response matrix of the patient and the therapist. These form a scaffolding for intervention:

1. The nature of the curative fantasy as it relates to the symptoms presented
2. The prevailing internal experience of transitional object relatedness that now forms a nucleus of introjective and projective systems around separation–individuation
3. The current nature of the regressed ego and the patient's attitude of defense toward this experience
4. The effect of these systems on the rest of the ego and its current level of functioning

A Definition of the Hypnotic Relationship

The hypnotic relationship here is defined as that quality of unconscious invest-ment by the patient, inferred through the curative expectations, for potential help from the therapist as an enabler of ego processes currently unavailable or un-developed within the patient. It is theorized that it is at this point in the devel-opmental ego organization of the patient at which the separation–individuation processes were arrested and disavowed or to which the patient has regressively retreated in the service of greater reorganization. The hypnotic relationship is seen as constellating the major vicissitudes of, in particular, the transitional object phenomena, that is, that point in development at which the fluid shifting of omnipotent control of the maternal figure occurs through illusionary control of the transitional object.

It is assumed that the specific self-organization of the patient, including pathological forms of object-relational capacities and arrested ego functions, are brought squarely into focus within the patient's capacity to relate to the therapist. In this sense, there will be a range of object relatedness in the transference from higher level, oedipal dominated, whole-object organization to defensive, split, part-object functioning. In the latter case, the therapist functions as a real object, aiding progressive ego formation rather than as an object of transference of past figures (Blank and Blank, 1979).

This shift in paradigm does not in any sense exclude the outstanding con-tributions of Gill and Brenman (1959) and of Grunewald, Fromm, and Ober-lander (1979) about subsystems of the ego and the capacities to regress. Instead, the hypnotic relationship is given more specific points of efficacy by considering how object-relational capacities may affect other ego functions. Thus, the passive and active dimensions of regression (Fromm, 1979) may assume a different sig-nificance developmentally.

Principles of Intervention Within the Hypnotic Relationship

1. The therapist relates to the symptoms and complaints through the curative fantasy that is inferred and allies with the highest level of ego organization, including that of object relatedness.

The initial formation from the patient's curative fantasy leads directly to an understanding of the quality and nature of developmental arrests in the separation–individuation process. He establishes a relationship of holding and concern around the patient's defensive organization. This is done by way of temporarily assuming the posture that is induced by the patient's objective-relational behavior.

The therapist can use indirect means of metaphor, distraction, or increasing awareness both outside and inside the sessions to induce a *latent good-object representation.* Often, this is a fine line to walk because masochistic, paranoid, or similar trends of inner object organization will seek to destroy the "good therapist." Initially, however, the therapist must ally with the attempts by the patient's ego to organize itself around the curative fantasy about hypnosis. Intervention into the highest level of ego organization carries forward the indirect, implicit, but compelling expectations of further growth and autonomy.

2. The therapist attunes to the transitional nature of the patient's illusion in the hypnotic transference inferred through the curative fantasy and symptoms. The nature of suggestions should be given work according to decrements or increments in behavior and experience. In this way, the therapist remains inside, yet outside of the patient's illusory system.

The hypnotic expectation always implies a constellation of transitional-object phenomena in the treatment. This means that, owing to the nature of the hypnotic relationship as we have defined it, the developmental processes by which the patient has come to relinquish the orbit of omnipotent, fusionlike states is implied in the hypnotic process. The patient seeks to control this illusion state through the participation in an ancient activity that "suggests" magic and omnipotent control. Whatever the uniqueness of the current ego organization involved, the means by which ego organization proceeded around the acquisition of self-representational structures, as distinct object representational ones, is brought into play.

The nature of hypnosis, except hypnoanalysis, does not afford an opportunity for working through these issues, if indeed they should require analysis. Instead, these processes must be tracked outside the patient's awareness. Maintenance of an optimal disillusionment is necessary for the patient to avoid traumatic rupture of the now trust-enhanced transitional illusion (which would result in premature termination, and possibly other forms of acting-out). In like fashion, the therapist must carefully avoid implied gratification of this illusory state in such a way that the patient is unable to use the therapist in his reality-based function. The latter process would sooner or later be viewed as an unfulfilled promise with any number of possible effects.

It may well be that the transitional-object incidence of affects, self-representations, and accompanying defenses form a decisive core of prediction-generating data about the effects of suggestion. These issues bear experimental investigation. G. Fromm (1981) has described these vicissitudes in considering impasses in treatment:

> A healthy transitional relatedness facilitates an imaginative mastery of the experience of absence. Pathologic transitional relatedness does not allow absence to be constituted as experience. Rather, the object is totally present (totally possessed by the omnipotence of the patient) and simultaneously nonexistent, as a *distinct* other. There is never absence. It may be that the patient cannot integrate the experience of absence prior to his analyst making a similar integration (p 26).

This process relinquishment of omnipotence of control can be facilitated by the use of graduated increment or decrement in desired experience and behavior, rather than all or none. Such a process permits a distance from the trap of "succeeding" with the patient. It permits also the internal, often masochistic, attachment to internal figures to "go to sleep" and to be outpaced by the cognitive awakening of newer possible behavior systems within the ego. It also permits the patient to use the symptom itself as a transitional object (Searles, 1976; Kahne, 1967), only now under the therapeutic symbiotic nature of the relationship.

3. The therapist steps between the regressed ego and the negatively charged introjects through the following indirect means: (a) introject innoculation, (b) cognitive containment, and (c) subliminal stimulation.

Introject Innoculation. A fascinating body of technique has developed within psychoanalysis that seeks to mediate negatively charged introjects through the metaphoric concept of "a little of the hair of the dog that bit you."

Coleman-Nelson's (1974, 1956), Coleman-Nelson and Nelson's (1975), and Spotnitz's (1981) view of borderline and related states are those problems of fixation and retardation, rather of regression" (Nelson, 1974, p 66). By supporting the conscious or unconscious projections and resistance, the following responses are observed: the patient views the introjects outside himself; he ventilates the evoked affects, strengthening the healthy ego, which seeks to rid itself of these toxicities; and the patient is able to recognize, through the therapist, that these are representative of his own ego. Nelson lists the following possible stances for the therapist:

1. Active mirroring (imitating or joining the resistance)
2. Recapitulating a reported interpersonal experience

3. Assuming the role of the self-image (patient's idealized, hated, or unconscious self)
4. Assuming the role of the introject
5. Assuming the role of a stranger (uncomprehending, distant)
6. Playing along with the fantasy
7. Following the patient's self-dosing indications for these processes

The application of similar approaches has been demonstrated from within other paradigms, such as those of Haley (1974), Erickson (1979). However, here the rationale is within a developmental framework. The application of these methods permits the therapist a wide range of behaviors that still include an adherence to the fears around basis-ego-relatedness. This rationale also enables the therapist to remain systematic and relatively free of impulsive maneuvers that only drive the patient into further defensiveness. It permits the introjects to be there but to lose their virulence. These examples are cited to encourage introduction designs based on a thorough understanding of the possibilities currently within the patient, and not as "techniques" *per se.*

Searles (1976) has reviewed these concepts, adding only that, in his own view, it is not by assuming a play-acting role, but by using the actual feelings of the therapist, that these procedures are effective.

Cognitive Containment. The therapist has available a large body of research within cognitive therapy that may be integrated into the schema outlined (Meichenbaum, 1977; Mahoney, 1974).

These intervention systems permit, within the object-relational schema, a means for the patient establishing self-soothing functions in managing anxiety, reducing arousal to an optimal level, and aiding in the acquisition of more distinct boundaries between self and object representations. The imitative and replicative nature of self-statements may also serve as organizing transitional objects of a higher, more verbal nature. Similar effects can exist in cognitive reappraisals of anxiety-evoking stimuli (see Chap. 11).

The efficacy here is not solely in the effectiveness of cognitive therapies, but in the potential of their uses in a symbolic and developmentally organizing sense. Their appeal is in the verbal "prosthetic" value by which the patient may have the therapist "implanted." The bridge between developmental psychoanalytic theory and cognitive therapy has yet to be crossed, but they offer, in my opinion, a wide range of future integrations.

This cognitive intervention, of course, can be presented in a variety of indirect or direct means, both within trance and outside it. The therapist uses appropriately distancing and indirect metaphoric allusions to contain the destructive aspects of the introjects. The experiencing ego and observing ego may be therapeutically split so that the patient continues to retain the experienced introject, but with increased distance and integration. Assimilation may occur in this way, freeing the ego to experience a different relatedness (Baker, 1981; Scagnelli, Chap. 20). The effect of hypnosis on cognitive structure has been studied by Fromm and Hurt (1980).

Subliminal Stimulation. The unique component of the hypnotic relationship is that its effectiveness lies in the use of indirect stimulation. The use of this process permits the attentional cathexis that goes toward the maintenance of the current ego organization to be freed up and divested towards more growthful mastery of conflict. This can occur in a number of ways. It is through the underlying dimension, which requires constant assessment, that these interventions affect subsequent statements by the patient, indicating what effect has occurred.

Exactly Repeating the Patient's Words. Although exactly repeating the patient's words is part of the regime described under introject innoculation, it also has the effect of stimulating a relationship in which the boundaries around a self-representation may be shifted and directed toward more differentiation. Basic here is the obvious: once the patient's words have been repeated, the patient never repeats them again and elaborates with different words. Within the relationship, the paradox is that of binding the patient and therapist, while enabling greater self-elaboration.

Metaphors and Images of Resolution Related to the Developmental Arrest of the Patient Presented Indirectly. A large body of evidence exists supporting the effects of subliminal stimulation in a therapeutic modality (G. Klein, 1958; Holzman, 1959; Silverman, 1976). The use of imagery, of course, is familiar to many hypnotic orientations. However, its use within a developmental schema has not received a great deal of attention. In particular, its implementation within the psychoanalytic therapies, by nature "analytic" rather than "synthetic," remains a vista to be addressed.

The therapist can implant these images once the nature of the curative fantasy and the elements of the overall ego organization have been ascertained. The implanting can be done in content while the therapist "plays out" the analogue process within the relationship. Thus, the therapist alludes to the satisfaction that comes to mothers whose infants smile back at them in warm, calm, pleasant gazes so that the mother and infant can feel like one person. While so doing the "gazing" behavior he elicits from the *process* of conversation converges with the *content*.

4. The therapist relates to the patient's overall organization through an apperception of joint containment and through the mobilization of healthy responsiveness in both the patient and in himself.

Three issues emerge here that aid our understanding of a coordinated effort between the patient and the therapist, and within each, toward a positive outcome in the hypnotic relationship. They are the activity of suggestion, the utilization of resistance, and the latent ideas of healthy functioning within both the therapist and the patient.

The Activity of Suggestion. Suggestion is a unique process, subtle in nature, and very complex, psychodynamically speaking. Essentially, it is the means by which the therapist creates the idea of healing within the patient in such a way that the patient can either experience it as part of himself or as part of the therapist. This possibility further enables the current ego-organization to proceed toward healthier responsiveness, whether along defensive or more integrated lines.

The therapist's attitude toward the activity of suggestion is indeed crucial, for through its delivery, the therapist communicates his own needs and defenses as they relate to the patient's symptomatology. In other words, the therapist creates peripheral cues in his imparting of suggestion, which have, in their nature, unique resonance to the conflict of the patient.

A personal example of this is my own impatience towards smoking problems. I have found that I transmit a certain disdain or even hatred by being too accommodating to scheduling, through excessive use of aversive stimuli in the hypnotic process, or through wording suggestions to the patient that frequently carry subtle frustrating affects. I have learned that it is better to refer these patients to someone else. The point here is that I came to learn about all of this after several failures with reasonably good subjects. The activity of suggestion is one, I have come to understand, that resides more actively in the admixture of unconscious stimulation between the therapist and the patient, than simply within the patient. In this way, he does not become "technique-ridden" but functions within the created trust within the relationship.

Utilization of Resistance. The nature of resistance is often discussed as a defense (within the context of frustration on the part of the therapist) or, more recently as a kind of ploy by the patient that must be "outfoxed" by the therapist. I find neither concept very useful.

Resistance is often created by the therapist when he does not appreciate the ego-organization of the patient. In that sense, the resistance is a good option for the patient. Resistance to the therapist must be distinguished from defense within the ego, based on the warding off of painful stimuli. Generally, resistance can be understood as an attempt to preserve some level of mastery and ego-organization. It has been stimulated either through bracing against introjects upon the therapist or by the invasiveness of the therapist.

The manifestations of resistance are widely known and are not treated here. The point here is really the attitudes of the therapist himself. While the therapist begins to encounter these behaviors and experiences in the patient, it is more useful to use them in the service of treatment than to butt up against them. Often, this means siding with the resistance *effort,* but not the *content.* In the hypnotic relationship, this might occur, for example, in patients who claim that they cannot enter a trance.

The patient's challenge may really be a fear of loss of control (frequently, it is), but also an attempt to remain stabilized and integrated at the current level of functioning. Supporting the idea of control in a concerned way often enables the trance to proceed. The patient needed to know that the therapist would work "upward" and not dismantle what the patient had already achieved, even though its content (fear of loss of control) was dysfunctional.

The Mobilization of Latent Ideas of Healthy Functioning Within the Therapist and Patient. The blending of the unconscious modes of expectation between the therapist and the patient remain a fascinating area of exploration. Indeed, Jung (1954) compared the work in transference to the nature of the medieval alchemical studies as metaphoric of the necessary steps in individuation. The therapist joined in the mixing of dissociated elements in the psyche to facilitate the production of pure gold (individuation). At times, the therapist would become the container for these substances. At other times, he would work at several levels simultaneously from more distant to mergedlike roles with the patient.

Hidden within, was the *prima materia,* the beginning substance form which transformation of energy would take place. And, of course, implicit was the nature of the process itself. It had a distinct movement that resulted in completion and integration. The way was not random, but marked, much like a map of a buried treasure. Each step was necessary in its unique order. The integration within the psyche was, Jung thought, much the same as the alchemical process.

As the patient and the therapist commit themselves to the undertaking within hypnosis, there is, I think, an orderly, somewhat definable phenomenon that characterizes effective work. I do not have a name for it other than its simple experiential description: it is a mutual recognition, given in increasingly clearer ways, that what each does in the relationship "fits." There is some correspondence between the work and the outcome. The outcome is not random, but follows a path that is what we commonly refer to as "healthy." And by this phrase I do not mean solely those increases or decreases in behavior, nor the reduction in symptomatology, nor isolated behavioral cues. It is, instead, an experience of integration and mastery at increasingly greater levels of success. It is a subjective recognition of a sense of autonomy, of contained and focused energetic function, of a self that contains a history with the therapist. These features, I doubt, are very researchable. Yet they form the boundaries of an experience within the hypnotic relationship that are facilitating and determined, to some extent by nature, much like the initial maternal environment of survival. I suppose I would be sticking my neck out even further to assert that the recognition of this facilitating union of the therapist to patient has some "innate" qualities. Secretly, I think it does, though I doubt it can be demonstrated.

Nevertheless, the restoration of functions within the patient occurs through a relationship. Throughout this chapter, I have generally avoided the enumeration of specific techniques. There are several fine examples throughout this text. The hypnotic relationship transcends technique—it cannot be taught; its features can only be interpreted. Without it, however, the activity of hypnosis becomes only an activity of maneuvers, mechanical in nature. It is hoped that its depth can be further understood. In its uniqueness as a relationship, the work of hypnosis takes on developmental and humanistic dimensions as well as ones that relate specific ego processes. The global aspect of these functions is that they converge around man's basic attempt, in a coherent and meaningful way, to relate to another human being. Upon this rests the possibilities of hypnosis.

References

Adler A: Social Interest. New York, Putnam, 1939

Appel R: Treatment of schizoid phenomena. Psychoanal Q 60, 1974

Baker E: A hypnotherapeutic approach to enhance object relatedness in psychotic patients. Int J Clin Exp Hypn 29:136, 1981

Balint M: The Basic Fault. London, Tavistock Publications, 1968

Bellak L, Hinvick M, Gediman HK: Ego Functions in Schizophrenics, Neurotics and Normals. New York, John Wiley & Sons, 1973

Beres J, Joseph E: The concept of mental representation in psychoanalysis. Int J Psychoanal 51:1-9, 1970

Blank G, Blank R: Ego Psychology: Theory and Practice. New York, Columbia University Press, 1974

Blank G, Blank R: Ego Psychology II: Psychoanalytic Developmental Psychology. New York, Columbia University Press, 1979

Bowlby J: Attachment and Loss: Vol. II, Separation. New York, Basic Books, 1973

Chertok L: Freud and hypnosis: An epistemological appraisal. J Nerv Ment Dis 165:99, 1977

Coleman-Nelson M: Externalization of the toxic introject: A treatment technique for borderline cases. Psychoanal Rev 43:235, 1956

Coleman-Nelson M: Effect of paradigmatic techniques on the psychic economy of borderline patients. In Greenwald H (ed): Active Psychotherapies. New York, Jason Aranson, 1974

Dewald P: Transference regression and real experience in the psychoanalytic process. Psychoanal Q 45:213, 1976

Erickson MH, Rossi EL: Hypnotherapy: An Exploratory Casebook. New York, Irvington Publications, 1979

Fairbairn WRD: An Object-Relations Theory of Personality. New York, Basic Books, 1954

Fenichel O: The Psychoanalytic Theory of Neurosis. New York, Norton, 1945

Ferencizi S: The analysis of comparisons (1915). In Richman J (ed): Further Contributions to the Theory and Technique of Psychoanalysis.

Fraiberg S: Libidinal object constancy and mental representation. Psychoanalytic Study of the Child. New York, International Universities Press, 24:9, 1969

Freud A: The concept of developmental lines. Psychoanalytic Study of the Child. New York, International Universities Press, 18:245, 1963

Freud S: The Standard Edition of the Complete Works of Sigmund Freud. Strachey J (ed). London, Hogarth Press, 1953–66, Vol. VII, 1901–1905

Freud S: 1914a. On Narcissism: An Introduction. The standard edition. London, Hogarth Press, 14:67, 1957

Fromm E: Transference and countertransference in hypnoanalysis. Int J Clin Exp Hypn 16:77, 1968

Fromm E: Ego activity and passivity in hypnosis. Int J Clin Exp Hypn 20:235, 1972

Fromm E: An ego psychological theory of altered states of consciousness. Int J Clin Exp Hypn 25:372, 1979

Fromm E, Hurt S: Ego-psychological parameters of hypnosis and other altered states. In Burrows G, Dennerstein L (eds): Handbook of Hypnosis and Psychosomatic Medicine. New York, Elsevier/North-Holland Biomedical Press, 1980

Fromm MG: Impasse and transitional relatedness. In Saretsky T (ed): Resolving Treatment Impasses. New York, Human Sciences Press, 1981

Gill MM: Hypnosis as an altered and regressed state. Int J Clin Exp Hypn 20:224, 1979

Gill MM, Brenman M: Hypnoses and Related States: Psychoanalytic Studies in Regression. New York, International Universities Press, 1959

Giovacchini P: The symbiotic phase. In Giovacchini P (ed): Tactics and Techniques of Psychoanalytic Therapy. New York, Science House, 1972, pp 137–69

Glover E: The Technique of Psychoanalysis. New York, International Universities Press, 1955

Goldberg A (ed): The Psychology of the Self: A Casebook. New York, International Universities Press, 1978

Goldberg A: Advances in Self Psychology. New York, International Universities Press, 1980

Greenacre P: The transitional object: The fetish with special reference to the role of illusion. Int J Psychoanal 51, 1971

Grunewald D: Transference and countertransference in hypnosis. Int J Clin Exp Hypn 19:71, 1971

Grunewald D, Fromm E, Oberlander M: Hypnoses and adaptive regression: An ego psychological inquiry. In Fromm E, Shor R (eds): Hypnosis: Research Developments and Perspectives. Chicago, Aldine-Atherton, 1972

Grunewald D, Fromm E, Oberlander M: Hypnosis and adaptive regression: An ego psychological inquiry. In Fromm E, Shor RE (eds): Hypnosis: Developments in Research and New Perspectives, rev 2nd ed. New York, Hawthorne, Addine, 1979

Guntrip HJS: Schizoid Phenomena, Object Relations and the Self. New York, International Universities Press, 1969

Guntrip HJS: Psychoanalytic Theory, Therapy and the Self. New York, International Universities Press, 1971

Haley J: Uncommon Therapy: The Psychiatric Techniques of MH Erickson. New York, Ballantine Books, 1974

Hartman H: (1939) Ego Psychology and the Problem of Adaptation. New York, International Universities Press, 1958

Holzman PS: A note on Brener's hynoidal theory of hypnosis. Bull Menninger Clin 23:145, 1959

Horton P, Lovy JW, Coppolilo HP: Personality disorders and transitional relatedness. Arch Gen Psychiatry 30:229, 1974

Jacobson E: The Self and Object World. New York, International Universities Press, 1964

Jones E: The nature of auto-suggestion. Papers on Psychoanalysis, 5th ed. Baltimore, Williams & Wilkins, 1948

Jung CG: The collected works of C.G. Jung, Bollinger Series. Read H, Fordham M, Adler G (eds): The Practice of Psychotherapy, Vol. 16. Princeton/Bollinger Series, 1954

Kahn M: On the persistence of transitional phenomena into adult life. Int J Psychoanal 48:247, 1967

Kernberg O: Borderline Conditions and Pathological Narcissism. New York, Jason Aronson, 1975

Kernberg O: Object Relations Theory and Clinical Psychoanalysis. New York, Aronson, 1976

Kernberg O: Contrasting approaches to the psychotherapy of borderline conditions. In Masterson J (ed): New Perspectives in Psychotherapy of the Borderline Adult. New York, Bruner-Mazel, 1978

Khan MR: The role of illusion in the analytic space and process. In The Privacy of the Self. New York, International Universities Press, 1974

Khan MR: Dread of surrender to resourceless dependence in the analytic situation (1971). In Privacy of the Self. New York, International Universities Press, 1974

Klein GS: Cognition without awareness: Subliminal influences upon conscious thought. J Abnorm Soc Psychol 57:255, 1958

Klein M: Contributions to Psychoanalysis. London, Hogarth Press, 1948

Kohut H: The Analysis of the Self. New York, International Universities Press, 1971

Kohut H: The Restoration of the Self. New York, International Universities Press, 1977

Kohut H: Summarizing reflections. In Goldberg A (ed): Advances in Self Psychology. New York, International Universities Press, 1980

Kohut H, Wolf ES: The disorders of the self and their treatment: An outline. Int J Psychoanalysis 59:413, 1978

Korner AF, Grobstern R: Visual alertness as related to soothing in neonates: Implications for maternal stimulation and early deprivation. Child Dev 37:867, 1966

Korner AF, Thomas EB: Visual alertness in neonates as evoked by early maternal care. J Exp Child Psychol 10:67, 1970

Kris E: Psychoanalytic Explorations in Art. New York, International Universities Press, 1952

Kubie LS, Margolin S: The process of hypnotism and the nature of the hypnotic state. Am J Psychiatry 100:63, 1944

Lavoie G, Sarbouren M: Hypnotizability as a function of adaptive regression among chronic psychotic patients. Int J Clin Exp Hypn 24:238, 1976

Levin LA, Harrison RH: Hypnosis and regression in the service of the ego. Int J Clin Exp Hypn 24:400, 1976

Mahler M: On sadness and grief in infancy and childhood. Psychoanal Study Child, 16:332, 1961

Mahler M: On Human Symbiosis and the Vicissitudes of Individuation. New York, International Universities Press, 1968

Mahler M: On the first three sub-phases of the separation individuation process. Int J Psychoanal 53:333, 1972

Mahler M, McDevitt JB: Observations on adaptation and defense in *statu nascendi:* Developmental precursors in the first two years of life. Psychoanal Q 37:1, 1968

Mahoney MJ: Cognition and Behavior Modification. Cambridge, MA, Ballinger, 1974

Masterson JF: Treatment of the Borderline Adolescent: A Developmental Approach. New York, Bruner-Mazel, 1972

Masterson JF: The Narcissistic and Borderline Disorders. New York, Bruner-Mazel, 1981

McDevitt J: Separation-individuation and object constancy. J Am Psychoanal Assoc 23:713, 1975

Meichenbaum D: Cognitive Behavior Modification: An Integrated Approach. New York, Plenum Press, 1977

Mendez A, Fine H, Guntrip H: A short history of the British school of object relations and ego psychology. Bull Menninger Clin 40:357, 1976

Modell AH: The ego and the id: Fifty years later. Int J Psychoanal 56:57, 1975

Munroe RL: Schools of Psychoanalytic Thought. New York, Holt, Rinehart & Winston, 1955

Ornstein A, Ornstein P: On the interpretive process in psychoanalysis. Int J Psychoanal Psychother 4:219, 1975

Ornstein P: Toward a psychology of health. In Goldberg A (ed): Advances in the Psychology of the Self. New York, International Universities Press, 1980

Ornstein P: Self psychology and the concept of health. In Goldberg A (ed): Advances in Self Psychology. New York, International Universities Press, 1980, pp 136–161

Ornstein P, Ornstein A: On the Continuing Evaluation of Psychoanalytic Psychotherapy: Reflections and Predictions. Annual of Psychoanalysis, Vol 5, pp 329–355. New York, International Universities Press, 1976

Rado S: The economic principle in psychoanalytic technique. Int J Psychoanal 6:35, 1925

Rinsley DB: An object-relations view of the borderline personality. In Hartocollis D (ed): Borderline Personality Disorders. New York, International Universities Press, 1977

Sacerdote B: Convergence of expectations: An essential component for successful hypnotherapy. Int J Clin Exp Hypn 22:95, 1974

Sandler J, Rosenblatt B: The concept of the representational world. Psychoanal Study Child, 17:128, 1962

Saretsky T: Resolving Treatment Impasses. New York, Human Sciences Press, 1981

Schafer R: Aspects of Internalization. New York, International Universities Press, 1968

Schater R: Mothering. Cambridge, Harvard University Press, 1977

Searles H: Transitional phenomena and therapeutic symbiosis (1976). In Countertransference and Related Subjects. New York, International Universities Press, 1979

Silverman LH: "The reports of my death are greatly exaggerated." Am Psychol 31:621, 1976

Singer J: Boundaries of the Soul. New York, Anchor Books, 1973

Smith A: Object relations theory and family systems: Toward a reconceptualization of the hypnotic relationship. Psychotherapy: Theory, Research and Practice 18:54, 1981

Spitz RA: The First Year of Life. New York, International Universities Press, 1965

Spotnitz H: Modern Psychoanalysis of the Schizophrenic Patient. New York, Grune & Stratton, 1981

Stolorow R, Lachman M: The developmental prestages of defenses: Diagnostic and therapeutic implications. Psychoanal Rev 46:73, 1977

Strupp HH: Psychoanalysis, "focal psychotherapy" and the nature of the therapeutic influence. Arch Gen Psychiatry 32:127, 1975

Tolpin M: On the beginnings of a cohesive self. Psychoanalytic Study of the Child, 26:316. New York, Quadrangle/New York Times, 1971

Tolpin M: Self-objects and oedipal objects. Psychoanalytic Study of the Child, Vol. 33, pp. 167–184. New Haven, Yale University Press, 1978

Wagner HW, Fine HJ: A developmental overview of object relations and ego psychology. Unpublished manuscript. University of Tennessee at Knoxville, 1976

Watkins JG: Trance and transference. J Clin Exp Hypn 2:288, 1954

Winnicott DW: (1955) Metapsychological and clinical aspects of regression within the psychoanalytic setting. In Collected Papers: Through Pediatrics to Psychoanalysis. New York, Basic Books, 1958

Winnicott DW: Early ego integration (1962). In The Maturational Processes and the Facilitating Environment. New York, International Universities Press, 1965

Winnicott DW: Transition objects and transitional phenomena (1953). In Collected Papers: Through Pediatrics to Psychoanalysis. New York, International Universities Press, 1975

8 Hypnotherapy and Behavior Modification

WILLIAM S. KROGER

I have used hypnotherapy within a psychodynamic approach for a wide variety of psychosomatic disorders (Kroger and Freed, 1951; Kroger, 1977). The rationale for combining this approach with behavior modification has been explained (Kroger, 1976). More recently, hypnotherapeutic techniques and behavior modification have been integrated with imagery conditioning (Kroger, 1976). I have found use of the latter model, rather than use of other techniques alone, more effective in the treatment of a number of conditions.

Before discussing the innovative hypnobehavioral stratagems involving imagery conditioning, I should like to make some cogent observations based on using hypnosis as a therapeutic modality for almost half a century: Patients are not treated by hypnosis but *in* hypnosis. Hypnosis is not a trance, sleep, nor a state of unconsciousness. Rather, it is a process along the broad, fluctuating continuum of awareness wherein *selective attention to relevant signals or suggestions are attended to with concomitant inattention to irrelevant ones.* As in every other psychotherapeutic modality, there is a ritual wherein expectances, role playing on the part of therapist and patient, and subliminal cues shape expected responses and make contrary responses more improbable—the demand characteristics so well elucidated by Orne (1962).

Thus, in the presence of appropriate motivation, a favorable mental set, ritual or misdirection of attention, belief, confidence, and expectation—catalyzed by the imagination or experiential background (the sum total of an individual's life experiences)—all lead to conviction or programmed faith. The induction of hypnosis is the induction of conviction. No one has a monopoly on faith! This is what differentiates hypnosis from strong and directive suggestion and persuasion. The last two mobilize resistance, whereas hypnosis, in the presence of conviction, allows faith-laden suggestions to be accepted uncritically. Conviction of cure leads to cure, and individuals get cured in the manner by which they expect to be cured. Nothing could be simpler.

In hypnosis, narrowing of the perceptual fields results in a heightened attention span. The resultant hyperacuity increases susceptibility to suggestion and enhances voluntary and involuntary performance. The *raison d'etre* for the adjunctive use of hypnosis in the hypnobehavioral model is that it enables most patients to "tap forgotten assets and hidden potentials so as to transcend their normal volitional capacities" (Lazarus, 1973). Every individual possesses this capacity, but everyone does not know how to use it. If these assumptions are valid, then hypnotic conditioning, even though it may be due to a self-fulfilling prophecy (Lazarus, 1973), should potentiate behavior therapy.

The basis for classical conditioning therapy, the precursor of behavior therapy, was established by Pavlov (1951) and Thorndike (1913). Watson (1919) and Guthrie (1935) made significant contributions to behavior therapy. Recently, Wolpe (1958) used counterconditioning or systematic desensitization, often with hypnosis, for eliminating the anxieties of certain neuroses. About the same time, Skinner (1938) and his disciples demonstrated that they could modify behavior by conditioning and reinforcement learning. The rationale is that whenever a particular behavior is reinforced or rewarded, there is a greater chance that it will be repeated. If the behavior is punished, it will go into extinction.

I (Kroger and Fezler, 1976) reasoned that since both hypnosis and behavior modification make use of sensory imagery conditioning and cross-fertilize in many areas, an "imagogic therapy," involving highly structured images for eliciting specific hypnotic phenomena, should play an important role in the hypnobehavioral approach. Structured images are an effective agent for bringing about behavioral changes, especially if they incorporate all five senses. The Western world is now avidly embracing Eastern philosophical healing methods, especially Zen and Yoga. These rely heavily on hypnotic suggestion, imagery conditioning, and relaxation—all the *betes noires* of anxiety. Since this is the cornerstone of a great deal of hypnosis and behavior modification, it is obvious that what's new is old and what's old is not new.

My best results have been obtained in chronic psychosomatic disorders, such as anxiety neuroses, migraine, asthma, backache, sexual problems, and habit patterns (*e.g.,* obesity and smoking). The poorest responses were in psychotics, those with deep-seated characterologic disorders, chronic alcoholics, and drug addicts. I am well aware that a subtle placebo effect is present in all forms of psychotherapy, including hypnotherapy *per se.* More than 60% of emotionally disturbed persons recover with time—the celebrated cure-all. Hippocrates said, "Healing is a matter of time, but is sometimes a matter of opportunity."

However, the majority of the patients referred to the hypnotist–psychiatrist are the "end-of-the-line patients." These miserable "medical shoppers" invariably have been refractory to conventional psychotherapies. Many are looking for magic and quick results. Therefore, a commitment to stay in therapy should be obtained whenever possible. There is also a definite correlation between an emotional or financial commitment and the prognosis for recovery. Anything that increases motivation greatly enhances the unleashing of the recovery forces.

Program Phases of the Hypnobehavioral Model

Historo-Diagnosis

Taking a careful history, making a diagnosis, and establishing good rapport are essential. Patients sense the psychotherapist's interest and warmth. The strength of the interpersonal relationship is the important vector in any type of psychotherapy.

Hypnotic Induction

After a preliminary discussion to remove the popular misconceptions, I use a standard double-bind induction technic, which has been described elsewhere (Kroger, 1977). Motivation is obtained early because the structured nuances of the induction procedure builds in a *control system* to be used later for attaining greater sensory awareness. For instance, I suggest that development of eyelid heaviness and tightness, lightness of the arm during levitation, rigidity and stiffness of the limb during catalepsy, and relaxation of the entire body will lay the foundation for controlling other feeling states, such as those of the five senses. I state: "The degree to which you can control these simple built-in feeling states will determine how well you will control the more complex ones involved in your problem behavior. You can then take any one or combination of these feelings and put these together for controlling your behavior" (Kroger, 1977).

In this manner, greater control of autonomic system functioning (ANS), as well as control of desired behavioral changes, is instituted early. Thus, words, thoughts, and feelings act as conditioned stimuli for eliciting specific autonomic responses, even though the original stimulus has been forgotten. As Pavlov stated, "Suggestion is the simplest form of a conditioned reflex" (Kroger, 1977).

Usually, two or three sessions are required to induce and deepen the hypnosis. Any one of a number of standard methods, such as the "elevator" or "stairway" technique, can be used. To further deepen the hypnosis, slow, deep, and regular breathing can be employed.

Autohypnosis

I employ autohypnosis with nearly all patients. If full control of simple feedback subsystems (the "how am I doing" error-correcting information-transmission mechanisms) that produce relaxation and other sensory alterations is learned, then more complex and resistant processes become amenable, at least to semi-volitional regulation.

After sufficient practice, autohypnosis is obtained by a triggering cue, such as closing the eyes and letting the eyeballs roll upward for a few seconds. When they roll down, lid closure will follow, and the autohypnotic state will remain until terminated by dehypnotization. I do not use a progressive relaxation technique, since it is too time consuming.

I tell patients that they should learn autohypnosis for the following reasons: (1) They will have a feeling of pride and self-esteem because they have removed the symptom. (2) They will not be dependent on me nor any other therapist. (3) If the original symptom returns, they will use the same autosuggestion that once removed it. (4) Should a substitute-symptom replace the removed one (and this is highly equivocal), they can readily remove it as they did the original symptom. It is highly unlikely that symptom-substitution will occur, especially if the patient himself eliminated the original symptom.

It is obvious that such extraverbal suggestions covertly bypass criticalness and have greater likelihood of being accepted. Furthermore, these auto-suggestions are "woven into the fabric" of the patient's personality structure, and when employed during autohypnosis, they are patient-centered rather than doctor-directed.

Imagery Conditioning

Before any posthypnotic suggestions are given, I employ a standardized image called the beach scene (Kroger and Fezler, 1976). This image was developed by Dr. Fezler and modified by myself for deepening hypnotic relaxation, counter-conditioning anxiety, and allowing what one imagines to better generalize to reality. To make the image stronger, all five senses are employed rather than the customary visual one. This is more effective for inhibiting anxiety.

In good hypnotic patients who practice the beach scene, the anxiety can be converted from a liability to an asset. One can suggest that the anxiety can elicit a profound relaxation response by pairing it with the beach scene in a typical Pavlovian conditioning paradigm.

The verbalization of this specifically structured image is as follows: "Imagine you are walking down a deserted beach. One that you might have visited, seen in a motion picture or travel poster. You can see the miles of gleaming white sand in front of you. To your left, note the palm trees gently swaying in the breeze. There is a blazing sun directly above you. It is high noon. You are wearing a swim suit. You can feel that *hot* noon day sun beating down on your body so that every fiber, every pore of your body is invigorated. Your bare feet are touching the *hot, dry sand.* Feel the *hot, dry* sand. And as you move closer to the water's edge, you can feel the *cool, wet* sand. Look down and see the waves lapping over your feet. Some are sinking into the sand; others are continually going back out. You are now walking by a huge group of rocks on your right. Hear the large waves *crash and smash* against the rocks. *Taste* the spray that comes in your direction, and wipe it off your lips. Inhale that zesty breeze coming off the water. Fill your lungs up with that clear fresh air. Look above you and see the fleecy white clouds above you in an azure blue sky. And as your eyes wander over the sky to the horizon, marked by a hazy violet color, note how it separates the restless ocean from the calmness of the sky. Imagine yourself out there on that horizon. You feel completely relaxed, and because you are so *relaxed,* you concentrate better and as a result you will develop exquisite receptivity to suggestions—your own, and this will lead to greater objectivity. It is here in this altered state of consciousness that you will be able to give yourself positive, constructive and appropriate suggestions to reverse negative, destructive and inappropriate or harmful suggestions."

The similarity between this state and Nirvana (Yoga), Zazen (Zen Buddhism), union with God, cosmic consciousness, transmigration of the soul, ecstasy, and other altered states of consciousness can be discussed later with the patient. It is stressed to the patient that the above suggestions, which are usually taped, be rehearsed again and again. After the image is learned, simply thinking of the beach scene will deepen hypnosis so that conditioning will be stronger and more rapid. As emphasized, anxiety reduction also is more readily achieved.

Other structured images for achieving hypnotic phenomena, such as time expansion and time condensation, glove anesthesia, age regression and dissociation, and other hypnotic phenomena, have been described in detail (Kroger and Fezler, 1976). When used with hypnobehavioral techniques, these images appear to yield better results. They are not presented as a panacea but as an adjunctive method for decreasing anxiety and for developing greater self-control and hypnotic concentration. It should be emphasized that these structured images are to be differentiated from guided affective images and projective ones.

Posthypnotic Suggestions or Affirmations

The affirmations given depend on the nature of the behavior to be changed. These are incorporated in the patient's repertoire. If they are repeated *long enough, strong enough,* and *often enough,* they reinforce desired responses by *interoceptive conditioning.*

As previously mentioned, this is relatively easy if control of the nonlearned, nonconditioned, or involuntary reflexes, such as heaviness and lightness, are first taught. These ideosensory activities are functions of the "instinctual" or primary signaling system described by Pavlov. They are mobilized rapidly, since they are necessary to preserve the integrity of the organism. Because they are "on" or "off," they have been compared to "digital" notions in higher central nervous systems functioning and information processing (Kroger, 1977).

Patients are trained to elicit sensory changes, such as heat or cold, by appropriate images. After these ideosensory mechanisms are perceived as real, more complex ones, such as aversive conditioning used for removing faulty habit patterns, are readily developed by merely recalling the representations of disgusting thoughts, feelings, ideas, and attitudes. Such symbolic activities are learned, conditioned, and voluntary. They are part of the secondary signaling system of higher nervous elaboration. They act by analogy and have therefore been referred to as analogic notions—the latter controls the former (Kroger, 1977). This method is not new but differs from Pavlovian conditioning initially produced by external stimuli—*exteroceptive conditioning.*

My approach is similar to the extraordinary mind–body responses provided by Yoga, Zen, and other Eastern therapies. These indicate that the ANS is not as automatic as believed and that some portions of it can, by appropriate conditioning, come under volitional control. In other words, autogenous biofeedback cues can trigger alterations in sensory states in a manner similar to biofeedback training (BFT). Well-trained Yogins do not need BFT to alter many autonomic functions.

Hypnobehavior Approach

Recent data (Paterson, 1976; Kline, 1976) indicate that conditional reflexes established under hypnosis are more durable and less likely to go into extinction. I (Kroger and Fezler, 1976) have taken this type of conditioning one step further by employing sophisticated hypnotic techniques, learning theory, and imagery conditioning to establish corrective behavioral changes. The punishment and reward alternatives implicit in behavior modification can be incorporated, particularly if the affirmations are oriented around the patient's emotional needs.

Overt (*in vivo*) behavioral techniques, such as systematic desensitization, sensitization or aversion therapy, flooding and implosion therapy, role playing or behavioral rehearsal, assertive training, modeling, or observational learning, as well as token economies and operant conditioning, are enhanced if learned while in hypnosis.

Covert (*in vitro*) behavioral techniques all involve imagery. All the technics mentioned in the preceding paragraph can use imagining, rather than the experiencing of the actual or *in vivo* stimuli. Here, too, hypnosis facilitates the imaginings. For a more detailed discussion of overt and covert behavioral techniques used in the hypnobehavioral model, see Kroger and Fezler, 1976.

Symptom-Manipulation

Most of the techniques that include brief hypnotherapy have been described by Erickson (1959). The first is *symptom-substitution*. Through posthypnotic suggestions, for instance, in treating obesity, one can "trade down" to other eating behaviors, such as chewing gum, or get patients interested in organic or dietetic foods. In *symptom-transformation* the overeating can be transferred by an appropriate posthypnotic suggestion to other behaviors, such as physical exercise, shopping, child raising, attending PTA meetings, and taking an interest in community affairs. Although seemingly similar to symptom-substitution, reduction of excessive eating occurs by transforming the symptom into a less noxious one without directly attacking the character of the symptom itself. In *symptom-amelioration* the overeating is reduced. First, it is deliberately increased by posthypnotic suggestion; if this is done volitionally, it eventually can be decreased. *Symptom-utilization* consists of encouraging, accepting, and redefining cooperative activity of an aversive nature toward the faulty patterns. This differs from symptom removal by direct suggestion. Any one or all can be used in various combinations.

Holistic Approach

The term "holistic," as herein used, refers to a study of total mind–body–environmental interrelationships. The dictum is to treat the personality who has the symptom rather than the symptom *per se*. The significance of the symptom in the *here and now* and *what* it means to the individual often are more important than how the symptom developed. An existential approach directed to aforementioned areas often is more fruitful than uncovering through psychotherapy.

Briefly, the therapeutic design is structured around the following: (1) How much of the symptom do you really need to keep? (2) What are you trying to prove by maintaining the chronicity of the symptom? (3) How rapidly can your personality divest itself of the symptom? (4) How would you feel without the symptom? One should always remember that symptoms belong to human beings—to personalities.

As Conn (1977) has described in detail, there are needs inherent in all anxiety-ridden persons, *i.e.*, the need to talk, the need to be told what to do, the need to be accepted, the need to be ones real self, and the need to emancipate oneself from any undue dependency on the therapist.

There are only three avenues open to the anxiety-ridden patient: (1) He can "develop a thicker skin" and learn to live with his problems. (2) He can walk away or retreat from his life situations to fight another day when stronger. (3) He can come to grips with his difficulties, provided the therapist teaches him the necessary coping mechanisms.

When the hypnobehavioral model is employed, there is "no space between" patient and therapist. Patients sense the therapist's interest and warmth. There is no question that the strength of the interpersonal relationship is the important vector in any type of therapy. Also, it is the empathic therapist who motivates the patient with faulty behavior to effect an adaptive behavioral change, which, in turn, leads to attitudinal change. Successful hypnobehavioral therapy is, therefore, a collaborative and reciprocal effort between therapist and patient—each learning from the other.

Although I have no statistical data to support my contention that hypnobehavioral therapy is more effective than conventional psychotherapy, I believe that it is. Furthermore, it often reaches the "port-of-last-call patient" who has tried nearly everything.

Hypnosis and behavior modification, as well as imagery conditioning, are derivatives of ancient therapies. That they have survived as meaningful therapeutic adjuncts indicates that they will not be hailed as "treatments of the year." There are limitations—not all patients are amenable to hypnotic conditioning. Many are not willing to practice the exact techniques promulgated by the behaviorist. The hypnobehavioral method is a time-consuming process for the therapist. Also, finally, the methods described here are not a panacea. I have had dramatic successes and dramatic failures.

References

Conn JH: In Kroger WS (ed): Clinical and Experimental Hypnosis. Philadelphia, JB Lippincott, 1977, pp 354–357

Erickson MA: Further clinical techniques of hypnosis: Utilization techniques. Am J Clin Hypn 2:3, 1959

Guthrie ER: The Psychology of Learning. New York, Harper & Brothers, 1935

Kline MV: The effect of hypnosis on conditionability. In Dengrove E (ed): Hypnosis and Behavioral Therapy, pp 131–147. Springfield, IL, Charles C Thomas, 1976

Kroger WS: Behavioral modification and hypnotic conditioning in psychotherapy. In Dengrove E (ed): Hypnosis and Behavior Therapy. Springfield, IL, Charles C Thomas, 1976

Kroger WS: Clinical and Experimental Hypnosis. Philadelphia, JB Lippincott, 1977

Kroger WS, Fezler WD: Hypnosis and Behavior Modification: Imagery Conditioning. Philadelphia, JB Lippincott, 1976

Kroger WS, Freed SC: Psychosomatic Gynecology: Including Problems of Obstetrical Care. Philadelphia, WB Saunders, 1951

Lazarus AA: "Hypnosis" as a facilitator in behavior therapy. Int J Clin & Exp Hypn 21:25–32, 1973

Orne MT: Implications for psychotherapy derived from current research on the nature of hypnosis. Am J Psychiatry 118:1097, 1962

Paterson AS et al: Acquisition of voluntary control over automatic nervous functions by conditioning and hypnosis. In Dengrove E (ed): Hypnosis and Behavior Therapy, pp 83–103C. Springfield, IL, Charles C Thomas, 1976

Pavlov IP: Twenty Years of Objective Study of the Higher Nervous Activity Behavior of Animals. Moscow, Medzig Publishing House, 1951

Skinner BF: The Behavior of Organisms. New York, Appleton-Century, 1938

Thorndike EL: The Psychology of Learning. New York, Teachers College, 1913

Watson JB: Psychology from the Standpoint of a Behaviorist. Philadelphia, JB Lippincott, 1919

Wolpe J: Psychotherapy by Reciprocal Inhibition. Stanford, CA, Stanford University Press, 1958

9 Ericksonian Theories of Hypnosis and Induction

MATHIAS E. STRICHERZ

Many aspects of Erickson's genius can be readily learned and adapted by the practitioner in medical, psychological, and scientific fields. This chapter details several of Erickson's techniques, theories, and interactive capabilities with his patients. Erickson's verbal and cognitive strategies in psychotherapy, personality reorganization, symptom relief, and utilization of client resources is presented. You will become acquainted with Ericksonian conceptualizations of the nature of trance, methods of trance inductions, characteristics of trance development, methods of ratifying trance, and specific linguistic tactics used to modify patients within a psychosocial context.

Many have attempted to categorize Erickson's style within various frameworks. Haley (1973) portrays Ericksonian strategic therapy within a communicative interactional system. Ericksonian therapy discussed in Jungian concepts and subconscious motivational patterns were shown by Erickson, Rossi, and Rossi (1976), Erickson and Rossi (1980), and Erickson and Rossi (1979). Zeig (1980a, b) presented Erickson's strategies within both the utilization of the client's subconscious symptoms and the anecdotal style with which Erickson taught novice psychotherapists and patients. Beahrs (1971) masterfully presented Erickson's hypnotic theory within a social influence concept, utilizing both indirect and covert modification of patient functioning.

The following formulations are based on social influence, social interaction, and conceptualizations of strategic psychotherapy. Gillis (1974, 1979) and Festinger (1957) provided conceptual social psychology frameworks that demonstrated how the subconscious mind can be directed to allow the incongruent and ego-dystonic to become congruent and ego-syntonic. Ericksonian strategies of thought and interactions apparently change symptoms by creating positive patient expectancies and meeting these expectancies, while reducing dissonance and allowing movement towards health. Erickson did not have a specific theory of personality, since he believed that personality theory restricted the therapist's conceptualization of the patient's psychological functioning. Thus, Erickson developed a new theory of personality for each patient, congruent with the patient's identity, psychological state, wants, needs, and strengths. Accordingly, it is the therapist's task to assess a patient on each of these levels.

Many patients seeking hypnosis expect therapy to be logically sequenced. They expect to tell problems, experience induction, be treated, receive posthypnotic suggestions, and, finally, have proof of being hypnotized. In an Ericksonian model, since formal inductions are directly used in less than 10% of cases (Beahrs, 1971), these general expectations may not be met. However, Erickson mastered the technique of inducing both clients and their expectations.

The fluidity with which language permeates the strategic psychotherapeutic interaction between operator and subject allows for several principles to be expressed. These principles have been defined in Social Influence Theory. The first is that therapy needs to be an interaction that allows the therapist to "attain a position of ascendency or power over the patient; second, he pushes his client to examine his problems in a new light; third, he convinces his clients that the therapy is definitely working apart from any objective evidence of change" (Gillis, 1974). Beahrs (1971), in defining Ericksonian therapy, indicated that this interaction between therapist and patient can be applied in a simple conceptual framework. This framework is as follows: (1) Observe the patient's communications on all metalevels, attending to his thinking, verbal constructs, nonverbal communication that relate both conscious and other-than-conscious information about the patient. (2) Exist within the patient's level of conscious and unconscious functioning. (3) Modify the patient's cognitions and behavior to continue a one-down complimentary relationship. (4) Use manipulation of behavior so that the resulting change from within the patient's framework will be ego-syntonic as well as interactionally appropriate. (5) Use subconscious strength that exists outside of a patient's awareness. (Inherent within the Ericksonian framework is the concept that the subconscious is more than a depository of negative emotions, feelings, behaviors, and impulses. The subconscious provides the person with the strengths that have grown from the types of pain that a person has encountered. It is capable of creating images of behavior and cognitions that go far beyond the patient's expectations or current capabilities of self. It allows the client the protection needed from unnecessary pain in current functioning that began during earlier development or at primitive autonomic levels.) (6) The synthesis of conscious and subconscious cognitions into a unified gestalt within the person's psychosocial ecology seems to be a guiding principle in Ericksonian interaction. As such, points of demarcation for the specific stages of psychotherapy within Ericksonian theory may be nonexistent. Instead, there is a fluid interaction between induction and posthypnotic suggestion, treatment and cure, greeting and ending.

Often, the patient who desires hypnosis expects to experience age regression to a time of trauma, to be subconsciously questioned (should the answers be negative, to not remember), and to receive posthypnotic suggestions and be cured. For example, a 21-year-old college music major requested hypnosis so that he would enjoy playing and practicing his trumpet so much so that he would continue to study music at Juliard Conservatory of Music following his graduation. This patient expected to be placed in a trance, have the reason for his not wanting to practice his trumpet discovered, have his psyche changed, be dehypnotized, be smiling, and be well on his way to success as another trumpet virtuoso. Simply put, strategic hypnotherapy generally does not entail the use of searching age regression, intrusion upon the subconscious through direct questioning, or direct suggestions for immediate symptom relief and ultimate change in the person's total psychological ecology. Basic to this style of interacting with the patient is the belief that symptoms are formed for a purpose that maintains internal psychic equilibrium. Such symptoms can be modified within the ecological structure through decathexis.

Trance

The nature of therapeutic trance includes several characteristics of cognitions and behaviors that are relevant to scientific paradigms. As the trance state develops, the subject loses a sense of functioning in the external world and maintains contact with the operator as their link. Inner realities are emphasized to the exclusion of external realities. Trance states do not necessarily increase suggestibility. The key to understanding suggestibility within the trance state is found, rather, in the type of suggestion given. A person will not incorporate offensive or dystonic suggestions. Within the therapeutic trance, attuning to the subject's motivation/symptom formation/cognitive style/representative system is fundamental in providing change. This attuning is called *utilization* and is the basis of Ericksonian psychotherapy.

Learning in trance appears to be subconscious learning. The observing of critical ego is acquiesced, while the conscious frame of reference and development with explicit attitudes and *modus operandi* are set aside. Three purposes of trance induction seem appropriate: The major purpose is to encourage foci of attention on inner realities while modifying the patient's consistent habitual patterns of control and finally altering the patient's acceptance of his own inner associations.

Ericksonian trance induction includes several general approaches. A *casual conversation* weaves either suggestions for trance state or suggestions for conscious alterations of functioning. *Confusion* depotentiates the patient's habitual frame of reference. As the patient tries to follow the apparent ramblings of the therapist, the acquisition of right hemispheric functioning provides modifications of images as well as sensory functioning. *Surprise,* although in many cases comparable to the confusion technique, immediately causes functioning outside of the normal habitual frame of reference (*i.e.,* right hemispheric functioning). *Questioning* uses both direct and indirect suggestions to provide expectancies of behavioral change (*i.e.,* yes sets). *Calling to awareness of new senses within the body* requires a person to exclude external realities and focus upon internal realities of the awareness (*i.e.,* "I wonder how much heavier your right hand is feeling than your left.") Within many of the approaches used to induce the hypnotic state *permission to the unconscious mind* either for an *unconscious search* or the utilization of an *unconscious process* creates an internal reality that is amenable to modification using linguistic techniques (Erickson and Rossi, 1979).

Specific approaches to hypnotic inductions found throughout Erickson's writings include an *early learning set:* "When you first went to school, you knew what it was like to follow the teacher, that one and one was two . . ." Additionally, *truisms* have been used: "You knew that this was an A and this was not a B and that sometimes the rules changed, and you learned to adapt and you learned that the letter with one valley was called a U and when it had two, it was called a W. And you learned the letter with one hump was an N and when there were two humps, it was called an M and not a double N and you knew that there were inconsistencies and you learned how to adapt." An additional approach, *not doing,* posits passive acceptance: "And there is no need that you pay attention to my voice. You don't need to pay attention to the sense that your hands are feeling heavy and your eyelids are feeling heavy." *Implications to the subconscious mind* give the patient's subconscious permission not only to enter trance but to begin the process of cognitive change: "Your unconscious mind knows when and where and how you will achieve, and it knows how to bend your elbow and it knows how fast your hand will rise and it knows how fast you will be able to change and soon your conscious mind might begin to understand, too." An additional way of achieving trance is by having the patient *recall* those times at which he was a dreamer or had *previous trance experiences* or the experience of fixedly contemplating either some activity or object. Several other induction approaches that are found in Erickson's work include eye fixations, hand levitations, catalepsies, and nonverbal approaches (Erickson and Rossi, 1979).

The nonverbal approaches to Ericksonian induction include changing voice tones, marking, imbedding indirect commands within, perhaps, an anecdote, changing tempo, pitch, or timbre, changing syntax and grammar as well as modeling appropriate trance behaviors or an approach such as the handshake induction (Erickson, 1964a). For the most part, the characteristics of trance induction that use subconscious functioning have the purpose of depotentiating habitual frames of reference. The ways in which that can be achieved include the use of *boredom* (telling a story, another story, and another story or some seemingly inconsequential and unrelated anecdote), *double binds* ("perhaps you would prefer going into a trance in 5 minutes or 10 minutes"), *involuntary signaling* ("and if you desire to go into trance, perhaps you will discover that your right hand or right index finger raises, or if not, your left."), *partial remarks and dangling phrases* (when left incomplete, these imply that a person needs to achieve a psychological gestalt through right hemispheric functioning), and *yes sets,* which provide, even for the resistant subject, a consistent way in which acceptance and acquiescence to the verbiage of the therapist can take place ("Do you recall the time when you were a little child, perhaps as young as eight or nine, and sitting under a tree and looking at the blue sky," or "and long ago there were times in which you might not have known for sure why you did something. Is that not correct?" "And you recall coming in here today, now?" Through a consistent series of "Yes" responses, the person is taken further and further away from a frame of reference that would also be rigid and resistant to the therapist. Yes sets can be established when the therapist questions about commonly shared childhood experiences. All depotentiating frames of reference techniques are accomplished linquistically with syntactical and vocal impact from the therapist.

While trance is being induced, several indices of trance development can be noted: comfort, relaxation, and literal responding to question; retardation of autonomic responses and blinking; and often spontaneous hypnotic phenomena, such as amnesia, regression, and time distortion. There are a variety of ways of indirectly ratifying trance and, therefore, causing a deepening of trance to take place as well as convincing the patients that they are indeed in a trance. One method is the *double-bind question:* "Do you know you are in a trance?" "A part of you really thinks you are awake, do you not?" *Reversing the count* will ratify trance (*e.g.,* 20, 19, 17, 13, 11, 9, 11, 13, 16, 18, 19, 20). Erickson, Sector, and Hershman (1981) indicated an indirect double-bind question: "What difference does it make whether you think you are wide awake?" Using *ideomotor signaling* for ratifying trance provides the patient's inner reality with congruent proof of altered state. It is apparently more advantageous to provide minute points of trance achievement than to provide a challenge such as "your eyes are tightly closed, glued shut. Try to open them. You can't. Go ahead, try." If such a challenge is given and failed, trance would be ratified. For the resistant subject (all subjects will have resistance on some level of psychic functioning), if the challenge is passed, not only may rapport be threatened, but the termination of trance state may be spontaneously accomplished. Patients who seek hypnosis are motivated to be hypnotized.

Ericksonian Hypnotherapy

The task in interacting with the patient is to allow and encourage enhancement of goal-directed behaviors when those goals are congruent with internal needs, physical well-being, and psychological or social ecology. For the most part, strategic-based psychotherapy is an interactional system achieved by direct and active intervention (Haley, 1973). Strategic therapy includes those therapies in which the therapist takes responsibility for directing people, changing modalities, and succeeding in therapy. Nixon (1979) posits assumptions to be considered in the application of strategic therapy. Included in his assumptions are the following:

1. The therapist needs a reason for everything done with the family and, as such, defines the problems, plans interventions, evaluates outcome, and accepts direct responsibility in the treatment; however, the therapist *denies responsibility for the client's change.*
2. The therapist must identify the patient's style of cognitive functioning, perception of reality, and the multi-level complexities for symptom maintenance. Paramount in this assumption is understanding of the patient's reality. As such, rigid application of personality theory is antithetical to an understanding of the patient's behavior. A new personality theory needs to be established with each new presenting client.
3. Behavior is both circular and repetitive (*e.g.,* marriage to a third alcoholic spouse; vomiting episodes that take place only when the family visits relatives; headaches that recur nightly, 15 minutes before bed.)
4. Patients are motivated to change in psychotherapy; however, the motivation may not be what the patient thinks or says it is.
5. Although the patient may have attempted to resolve his or her problem before seeking assistance, these attempts were unsuccessful. The therapist's encouragement for and understanding of these attempts are appropriate. Some patients need to tell their story. By allowing the patient to relate the story in whatever fashion is necessary, the therapist remains in a one-up complementary position, learns the language system, and hears the linquistic ecology that the patient interacts within and from. Paramount in Ericksonian-based theory is observation of language and behavior for both omissions and comissions.

The Patient's Defensive Structure Breaks Down

Direct therapeutic leads may create a resilience within defense structure that will become or remain resistant to change. Therapeutic interventions offered in an indirect way can circumvent and go beyond ego-defense boundaries and allow a recathecting of energy. A patient seeks respect for the development and maintenance of his or her symptoms. Accordingly, an indirect approach maintains that respect within the patient and offers a congruent interaction with subconscious functioning.

Verbal Tactics Within Ericksonian Therapy

The key to verbal interaction and strategic psychotherapy as practiced by Erickson is indirectness and symptom utilization. In symptom utilization, the therapist meets and modifies a patient's cognition to achieve both a trance state and sought-for goals. Psychiatric models offer many tactics of utilization for which the following conceptualizations of psychic structure seem appropriate both for assessing patients and offering change:

1. Symptoms exist within a language structure.
2. Symptoms exist on conscious and subconscious levels.
3. Subconscious levels are protected by defense mechanisms and psychic processes.
4. Defense mechanisms equal resistance and are relaxed in hypnosis.
5. Defense mechanisms serve an ecological purpose and as such, need to be respected.
6. Defense mechanisms exist within a linguistic framework/structure.
7. Symptoms and defense mechanisms can be placed on separate and related verbal continua (*e.g.,* pain, intensity of pain, secondary gains from pain).
8. Change of symptoms or alterations of defenses can be accomplished linguistically. That is, talking therapy causes change both directly and symbolically.
9. All symptoms have more than one linguistic meaning/component.

The tactics defined in the following section, found in much of Erickson's work, seem to follow a major therapeutic maneuver. This maneuver paradoxically allows a utilization of symptomatology, while simultaneously offering indirect metacommunication that symptomatology will eventually, if not immediately, disappear (Stricherz, 1982). Rapport is established quickly by accepting the patient's definition of the problem. Trust is developed, and the beginning of creating expectations advanced. The tactics to be discussed include symptom alteration, subtle and obvious resistance, and symbolic psychotherapy.

Symptom Alteration Tactics

Utilization

Utilization allows the reality of a patient's symptom, while the therapist secures that symptom in the process of change. With delusional patients, the therapist can battle with a delusion or an hallucination. Erickson, upon meeting a hospitalized patient who believed he was Jesus, quickly engaged him in occupational therapy using carpenter skills. With chronic pain, the patient can be engaged in discussion of the pain, the intensity of the pain, and some of the fear of how bad the pain will be. With utilization tactics, the therapist neither denies the existence of nor the patient's right to have his symptom.

Time Scheduling

In time scheduling, the patient is indirectly given permission to control a symptom that had been uncontrollable. "Mr. King, tomorrow evening after supper, sometime between 8:00 and 9:00, whenever you would like, for whatever ten minutes of that time, the choice is yours . . . I'd like you to have a headache on both sides of your head instead of just one."

Teaching Better Ways of Utilizing a Symptom in Achieving Secondary Gains

This strategy augments an understanding of hidden dynamics surrounding symptom formation. The indirect rather than direct interpretation appears to be appropriate for insight development. A child who is eneuretic may be easily convinced that he no longer need wet his bed except for when he wants to get his mother's goat. A husband may be instructed that pain in his lower back could occur more often than when he does not want to take out the garbage: "Perhaps, you could get a lower backache when your wife wants you to go to PTA, dinner, or a movie, not only when you don't want to take out the garbage or retire to bed at her selected time." Symptoms that require intervention within a relationship often need to have all parties informed of the intervention so that the relationship can be maintained while modifications of symptomatology take place.

Scheduling the Symptom

Hypnotic ploys can be implemented within the conscious and subconscious tactics of scheduling when the symptom will disappear, negotiating for symptom intensity, and moving somatic symptoms to unimportant parts of the body. A patient can schedule, through automatic writing or waking input, symptom duration and termination. Using these tactics within a pain-control paradigm, a patient may decide to move a headache into a little finger or a lower back pain into a hypersensitive knuckle.

Providing a Worse Alternative

This technique utilizes practice of the symptom (an appropriate way to gain control over a subconscious symptom) in such a manner that the patient is left with the illusion that he is consciously eliminating a symptom. While I was working in a state hospital in 1973, one of the patients, who had been hospitalized for schizophrenia for 8 years, had developed a pattern of placing discarded trash in her skirt pockets and purse. The staff was instructed to give her all discarded material by placing it in her pockets or purse. Within 48 hours her symptom had subsided and she declared to all present that she no longer thought it necessary to collect refuse within the unit. If a patient with a sleep disorder is instructed, upon not falling asleep after 15 minutes, to get up and scrub floors, clean the bathroom bowl, or clean the cupboards for an hour, cessation of symptoms takes place before long. Erickson's treatment of a married couple who were both eneuretic is a classic example of providing a worse alternative (Erickson, 1954).

Symptom Prescription

Symptom prescription can be either direct or indirect. Prescribing a symptom serves two purposes: (1) the symptom can be experienced behaviorally without concomitant psychological effects, such as guilt, anxiety depression, and so on, and (2) the symptom can be experienced psychologically without the necessity of behavioral activity. Both depotentiate the client's habitual frame of reference in relation to the symptom. Direct symptom prescription fosters control over subconscious material. Direct prescription includes practicing a symptom that already exists, encouraging the continuation of a symptom that appears to be extinguishing, and desensitizing to learn more from that symptom. "Mrs. Jones, perhaps you need to experience more of your old depression this week so that you can learn something more from it or find out if there is anything else you need to learn by it." Symptom prescription is directing the patient to do what he is already doing (Zeig, 1980a).

Grace, a 54-year-old terminal cancer patient, was expected to live less than 9 months when she entered psychotherapy. Following chemotherapy, she experienced many of the treatment-specific side effects. Grace was instructed to convert her guest bedroom into her symptom room. In that room, she was instructed on the proper way of being depressed and nauseous. Her depression symptoms were completely controlled within 7 days. Within 2 weeks, she discovered that she could isolate nausea to her guest bedroom for less than 15 minutes a day.

Cure Ploy

The cure ploy tactic is to be used in the early stages of hypnotherapy when enough brief insight has been achieved by the patient with good ego strength to allow him the option of eliminating further undesirable behavior. "Mr. Smith, your subconscious has taught you quickly. You now know some things that you did not know before, and your subconscious will reward you (indirect cure ploy)." While working in a community mental health center, I met a delivery man who had entered psychiatric treatment during the latter part of the 1950s, following the Communist scare. This man developed a paranoid schizophrenic ideation following his release from a Veteran's Administration facility and an operation for cancer of the colon. He received outpatient treatment, and one day, "out of the blue my therapist said I was cured and I don't need to come back." Accordingly, this man released from treatment has been doing well since and has had no further problem.

Resistance Techniques

Within strategic therapy further verbal interchanges techniques can be both obvious and subtle. The use of resistance techniques requires a commitment to the power of language and a commitment to establish a meaning for symptoms so the symptom can either change or be integrated.

No-Miss Interpretations/Reframes

The no miss interpretation tactic is employed to let the patient know of underlying reasons for cognitions, behaviors, and emotions. The therapist relates to the patient supportively and offers out-of-awareness interpretations. "And it seems, Mrs. Smith, that underneath that hurt is a lot of anger." "Although you are excited and happy about being engaged, unconsciously you seem rather ambivalent." "It seems that you are willing to sacrifice your physical well-being by keeping your migraines so that your family feels needed." These tactics emphasize the therapist's power, since the patient sees the therapist as incisive and perceptive.

Ingratiation Tactics

Ingratiation tactics provide a bond between therapist and patient either by pointing to similarities or by using flattery in such a way that symptoms are cast in a new light. "Mrs. Jones, it would seem that even though you do weigh 280 pounds, your fat is very sensual fat and not the droopy and ugly fat that just hangs ungracefully from many fat people" (Stricherz, 1982). Quite often, the client will be told a story about the therapist's behavior or psychological structure that shows a similarity between the patient and therapist. When such a story is related indirectly, directives provide solutions to problems that previously had not been considered by the client.

Selling Improvement/Attribution

These strategies provide a basis for the patient to view problems in a new light and to commit to the therapy process. At times when therapy is not going well, these tactics provide an incentive to the client to work harder and view his behavior as actually having been changed. "It seems, Mr. Smith, that you've done much better and are getting better quicker than perhaps even you thought. Why, this week you didn't come home for supper only twice. That's three times better than last week."

Challenging the Subject

When patients present and wish to have symptoms changed and altered, but do not appear to be motivated to do so, a challenge or chastizing technique may create conflict that will motivate the patient. Challenging techniques provide a release of energy away from the old cathexis. "I wonder when you will feel, today, or perhaps tomorrow, finally as you realize that since you are no longer able to touch your wife or kiss her that really, in fact, your fingertips, arms and lips are broken" (Stricherz, 1982).

The Overhearing Strategy

When a patient has been resistant to therapeutic change, arrangement with a secretary or a colleague to call during a session can give the therapist a chance to discuss another patient's problem that has many similarities with that of the current patient.

The patient is provided with direct feedback, given indirectly, for alternate forms of behavior and thinking, and the illusion that new alternatives have come from within his or her own resources rather than from the therapist.

Busy Schedule/Demand by Colleagues

These tactics, suggested by Gillis (1979), enhance expectations of therapy because the patient realizes that the therapist is skilled and in high demand. Occasionally, when "therapy hoppers" present for treatment, the only time available may be Saturday morning at 7:30, Thursday morning at 6:00, or Friday at midnight.

Demanding Intense and Arduous Tasks

Resistant patients or "therapy hoppers" can be challenged indirectly to change and achieve by either providing homework or having patients participate in an exercise to uncover aspects of personality. Patients may be instructed to complete a timeline, starting at present and going back as far as they can remember, placing every detail of their life line including feelings, behaviors, decisions, and outcomes. Such an exercise gives the therapist much information about the patient's *modus vivendi*. Additionally, when an obviously resistant patient presents, it is not uncommon for him to take a Minnesota Multiphasic Personality Inventory three to five times. If the patient continues in therapy, and when instructed by indirect suggestions he generally does, the inciting of drive allows for drive reduction he may not have received in other less active approaches. Intense, arduous, or inconvenient homework assignments do instill and increase drive. The inconvenience of these tasks motivate a patient to change and accept therapy.

Obvious techniques that utilize a patient's symptoms and resistance include the following.

Encouraging a Relapse (Paradoxical Intention)

This technique can be offered if it appears that a patient or family has improved rapidly and that there is a high probability for a relapse. This technique is not a self-fulfilling prophecy and is applied when failure seems imminent or when the therapist wishes to enhance continued elimination of a symptom. "You've not been depressed for several weeks. Perhaps, during the following week you need to take an hour or two and get back into your depression . . . just in case that there's really something else you need to learn from it," or "Your fighting hasn't really improved, it's just an illusion. But if you insist you're better this week, you need to have a bad fight and see if you're really over being so badly hurt by each other." The couple is frequently mystified by this directive and will probably mildly refuse. The therapist would then insist and vigorously encourage them to fight at least once during the coming week (Nixon, 1979). Thus, if a symptom returns, patients experience it in a new light without anxiety, sadness, or guilt, as they had in the past. This is primarily due to the directive of the therapist. Additionally, if the symptom does not return, the patient is substantiating that a behavioral gain has taken place.

Encouraging a Response by Frustrating It

Use of this tactic encourages clients to perform a behavior by providing a metacommunication and injunction against performing the behavior. "I don't think it's right for *me* to *talk you* into taking *your* medicine."

A 28-year-old male had been in treatment for 10 months and, although making progress, exhibited a diffuse anxiety. "Randy, it seems to me that you have made many changes in therapy. You are no longer anxious the way you had been in the past, you no longer feel you have to sleep with your gun under your pillow. You feel as if you can contribute to your family and you've even started dating. And you've told me many things about yourself, and there's something that you've held out. And I don't want you to tell me it until you're ready. And I don't know if that will be next week at the beginning of the session or at the end of the session, or you might want to wait until the beginning of the following week. I don't want you to tell me until you are ready to tell me." In this case, Randy, in the latter part of the next session, indicated to me that as a child he had frequent intercourse with both his brother and animals on the farm. Following that, the remainder of his anxiety subsided. Since most patients do withhold information from the therapist, when this technique can be given at the beginning of therapy, the directive to withhold places the therapist in a one-up yet complementary relationship with the patient.

Symptom Substitution

If a symptom interferes with the patient's psychosocial necessities, the subconscious can often be induced to allow a less debilitating symptom to exist. A doctoral student presented with severe avoidance response for opening books and journals that were needed to complete the dissertation. Negotiation with the subconscious allowed for a catalepsy of the little right finger whenever the person wrote anything on his dissertation. In this case, the need for a symptom was utilized and provided the basis for creating a symptom that was compatible with successfully completing the dissertation.

Symbolic Psychotherapy

The process of fostering changes in a person without a direct discussion of the reasons for certain therapeutic interventions, allows a patient the illusion of control that symptoms are changing under his care and direction. Symbolic psychotherapy entails the use of homework assignments that incorporate indirect reflection of the patient's symptom. The following examples illustrate the use of symbolic therapy.

Jack, a 55-year-old businessman, was assigned the following over a 2-week period: During week 1, he was to list on paper all of the gifts he had given in the last 3 years. His homework indicated that he had given gifts in excess of $16,000 to friends and secretaries. In week 2, Jack was instructed to go to a florist shop and buy a golden barrel cactus. He was then to drive to the community hospital and was to go to a particular floor. As he searched for the room, he would know exactly when the room was right by trusting his intuition. He was to go inside, give the golden barrel cactus to the women he found inside, and indicate to her without giving his name, or saying anything about himself, "This is for you. May you have a long, happy, and healthy life. May your love flourish and sustain in all activities." After giving the cactus to the woman, Jack was to leave the room and to wish her a speedy recovery. He did so, and after exiting the hospital he, for the first time in his life, shed tears and felt a new sense of relief and excitement. This no-strings-attached gift to the elderly black woman offered a realization that he was capable of giving a gift from the heart.

Mary, a 32-year-old medical service professional, experienced extreme pain in urinating and required urethral dilatations once every 2 to 12 months for 8 years. She experienced severe menstrual cramps and diarrhea 2 days before the onset of her cycle. No organic cause was found. Two days prior to her cycle, she would go to the supermarket, buy food for the next five days, move her blanket, pillow, and hot water bottles into the bathroom and spend her nights on the toilet. Mary listened carefully while I talked about her yearnings (urinings). She was instructed that 2 days before her next period she was to purchase a very attractive new red dress, and was to wear that red dress on the first day of her period. She received instructions in exactly how she was to prepare and wear her new dress. She had from that time a complete cessation of menstrual cramps and for 3 years has been symptom free from urinary tract disorders and painful urinations.

A 23-year-old female, once divorced, was experiencing kinesthetic hallucinations four times a week between midnight and 4:00 AM. During those hours, she would be awakened by a pressure on her shoulder or on her breast. This pressure resembled that of the hand "of a man I seem familiar to." After she called me wanting to know if she were "going crazy" or if she had a "ghost," it was agreed that she would be seen for brief hypnotherapy. Her subconscious indicated that there was a man, a relative, in her past who came into her room in the night and, while she supposedly slept, touched her body. Several metaphors were offered about the Oriental practice of honoring deceased ancestors. These metaphors appeared congruent with her studies in anthropology and religious forms. That evening, she was requested to place in an area of the house that was outside of her bedroom the type of food that this person enjoyed. Following that first evening, a complete cessation of the kinesthetic hallucinations was experienced. Her sleep has remained uninterrupted. She has now discussed the incidents relating to her deceased relative with her mother. This case shows the symbolical easing of guilt that came with being victimized. The conflict between not having controlled and having related from a victim stance in her first marriage was set into play with the kinesthetic hallucinations.

Erickson used symbolic psychotherapy frequently in directives to patients who were unsure of decisions. He would have patients climb Squaw Peak and walk through the Phoenix botanical gardens. Both tasks generated subconscious searches.

Concluding Thoughts

The interventions described here provide a utilization of symptoms in discovery of the underlying dynamics, or the abilities to experience the symptom in a socially acceptable way. The sample verbal tactics are not conclusive of those offered in an Ericksonian framework. Because there is no particular therapy that can be classified as Ericksonian, the style of presentation to the patient appears to be the identifying characteristic. Since Erickson's death, works have attempted to define what constitutes Ericksonian therapy. The spirit is more crucial than specific treatments in classifying a style as Ericksonian. Accordingly, many Ericksonian strategies will be developed because they follow the tenets of utilization, indirectness, and respect of the individual; whether these are Ericksonian or neo-Ericksonian is moot. The primary issue is the utilitarian manner in which such techniques may serve the patient's movement toward a positive direction. As Erickson techniques are separated from the man, his charisma, and the demand characteristic felt by those who interacted within his hypnotic milieu, they will be the techniques that exist within the minds of the many therapists who apply that portion of Erickson that exists within each of us. Thus, his work will be carried forward.

The following quotation is offered to illustrate Erickson's belief about psychotherapeutic fact:

> . . . I think about the elaborate schools or theoretical schools of psychotherapy. Freud developed psychoanalysis to apply to all people, male or female, of all ages, in all situations, in all cultures, and he uses the same format on all and developed his school of psychotherapy to apply to all times. He analyzed Moses, Edgar Allen Poe, Winnie the Pooh. I do not think that any school or theoretical school is any more than a religion to which you try to fit the patient. Adlerian schools emphasize masculinity, inferiority, and compensatory reaction. Adler never did any experimental work to prove his concepts of how a right-handed person writes, how a left-handed person writes any better than a right-handed person . . . compensatory inferiority with compelling drive . . . a most compelling thing. And there is Karen Horney with her school of psychoanalysis and Sullivan's school . . . Jungian school . . . Rogerian school . . . all well developed orderly psychotherapeutic schools of thought to which the patient is

fitted. I think the individual is the individual entirely, so therapists should be in accord with the individual's own personality, own life experiences. Nobody can understand anybody else's language. I had you put down whether you came from an urban or rural background because that has big influence on you (referring to an exercise required of participants). And I grew up on the farm. I left it more than 50 years ago. Now on the farm you ate breakfast, *dinner* and *supper*. In the city I learned you eat breakfast, *lunch* and *dinner*, never *supper*. My sister left the farm nearly 50 years ago and lived in the city. I hadn't seen her in a number of years. She made a trip around the world and she was relating her travels within this country and that country and so on. My wife, who grew up in Detroit, happened to hear my sister and me talking about supper. She listened for a while and she added, "How come you are talking about supper?" and we realized that our farm, so long ago, still carried over an old association, no matter how old, has an influence on you. And it is amazing the amount of influence your past has. . . .*

Appendix 9-1

The following case example illustrates the use of symbolic psychotherapy and the manner in which suggestions were embedded within directives to the patients presenting problems of sexual dysfunctions. The couple was a 29-year-old school teacher and husband, third year medical student. Susan was inorgasmic. Greg's sexual functioning was appropriate. The couple had been in family therapy, behavior therapy and had experimented with many different techniques in attempting an appropriate orgasmic response. Religious injunctions were apparent. Susan's father was "large framed, extremely conservative, overbearing, obnoxious and punitive in interactions with her, Greg and the world." The following hypnotic intervention and commentary about technique are offered. This case is reported in greater detail in *The American Journal of Clinical Hypnosis* (Stricherz, 1982).

INTERVENTION
"Before you can do what you need to do and what you have come here to do, you will need to have a conversation with your father and become a separate person."

COMMENTARY
"Before you can do what you need to do and what you have come here to do"—this embedded command presupposes that what has been sought in therapy will take place and builds expectations that the couple will achieve its goal. The directive, "you will need to have a conversation with your father and become a separate person," began both a change of perception of no longer

* This quotation is taken from an unpublished transcript of a weekly teaching seminar that was attended in Dr. Erickson's home during the Fall of 1979.

INTERVENTION

COMMENTARY

being a little girl and a process of demanding an intense task. The task that followed, a Gestalt alter-ego technique, contained a catharsis and a release of blocked psychic energy that Susan had in relation to her father. During the alter-ego process, chastizing for imperfect symptom formation was used (*i.e.,* Susan did not appear to be feeling the anger or resentment that she fostered for her father and was admonished for making only a meager attempt at symbolically showing her father her anger). Her anger was escalated, and Susan utilized a very appropriate and deep rage for the first time in her adult life.

"Your problem is one that is ready to be over with, it is obviously ready to be over with, otherwise you would not have come to see me. Seeing someone who does hypnosis, is obviously for you the *last* resort; you've tried almost every home technique that is available, and now if you agree to follow very specifically and very religiously all of my suggestions and recommendations, your problem will be gone."

In this portion of the intervention, the clients' expectations were enhanced. They were told that the problem was ready to be over with, otherwise they would not have come to see the author. This utilization of their presenting problem fostered the expectations that they have made a final decision. This is built upon by marking the phrase, "the *last* resort." Since symptom formation was related to religious injunctions, the linguistic style of repeating directives, as well as, commanding the patients to specifically and religiously follow the suggestions, paced symbolically Susan's symptom formation. The embedding of commands in the use of *recommendations* served to foster a congruence within Susan's primitive regressive adaptations to her sexual injunctions. This congruence with specific injunctions given by Mom that when Mom was not in the back seat while Susan dated (and she was until Susan was 18), Jesus would be, carried an equal impact subconsciously in Susan's change of sexual functioning.

"You are to go sit on your bed, and both of you are to become naked and just look at each other's body. Do not touch, do not kiss, just look at each other's

The directive for the patients to sit on their bed and have only visual contact created trance. In that trance Susan began a symbolic search that allowed for

INTERVENTION

body. Following this, you are to put your clothes on and you are to go out into either your kitchen or living room, whichever is right for you, and you are to make two signs and get two straight-back, rigid chairs. One of the signs you are to make is to say 'Jesus,' printed in very large letters, and the other sign is to say 'Mom,' printed in very large red letters. You are to take these two signs and the chairs place the chairs alongside your bed with the signs on the seat of each chair, and then on that first night you are to try to have intercourse while Jesus and Mom are with you watching you in your bedroom. On the second night, you are to leave the chairs with the signs of Jesus and Mom in the bedroom, but you are to get a brand new blanket, any color you wish, whichever is right for you, and cover the chairs and the signs and then try to make love on your bed. And on the third night, you are to very religiously spend between 5 and 10 minutes removing the chairs and the signs from your bedroom."

COMMENTARY

a recathecting of energy bound by the primary negative injunctions. The patients were told that all will be well if they do exactly what was directed of them, an indirect specification of time and cure. The process of sitting on the bed and rehearsing the directives for their activity in those next three nights provided a future-paced rehearsal of the embedded directive for an orgasmic reflex within Susan. The directive to find "two straight-back rigid chairs" and make two signs utilized symptomatology on two levels. First, two people were involved in the creating of the sexual dysfunction; second, an ambiguity of the word two (too) defined symptom intensity. This metacommunication was linked with the behavioral directive of removing the signs and rigid chairs. By doing so, the appropriate amount of rigidity is left within the bedroom. Susan's symptom is utilized by placing Jesus and Mom in her bedroom (i.e., they exist in her mind as being present). The directive and symbolic use of "brand new blanket" creates an expectation of change (i.e., something brand new is going to happen). The use of the word blanket entails a symbol for new feelings, here symbolic of a new covering that will exist within the orgasmic response within Susan. During both first and second nights, the couple received an embedded command to fail, "try to make love/try to have intercourse." The second night's directive, to leave the chairs and cover both the chairs and the signs, symbolically separated Susan from her early injunctions. On the third night, the ritualistic behavior of removing the chairs and the signs from the bedroom and at the same time leaving the blanket embedded the symbolism of something different, that is, something "brand new" remains (i.e., orgasm). The ambiguity of the word signs, describing both the object and the representational impact of the symbol, implants permission to eliminate the "sign" of Jesus and Mom, inorgasmia. No direct statement that Susan would be orgasmic was made.

References

Beahrs J: The hypnotic psychotherapy of Milton H. Erickson. Am J Clin Hypn 14:73, 1971

Erickson M: A clinical note on indirect hypnotic therapy. J Clin Exp Hypn 2:171, 1954

Erickson M: The confusion technique in hypnosis. Am J Clin Hypn 6:183, 1964

Erickson M: Pantomime techniques in hypnosis and implications. Am J Clin Hypn 7:64, 1964

Erickson M, Rossi E: Hypnotherapy: An Exploratory Casebook. New York, Irvington, 1979

Erickson M, Rossi E: The Nature of Hypnosis and Suggestion. Vol. I–IV. New York, Irvington, 1980

Erickson M, Rossi E, Rossi S: Hypnotic Realities: The Induction of Clinical Hypnosis and Forms of Indirect Suggestion. New York, Irvington, 1976

Erickson M, Sector I, Hershman S: The Practical Application of Medical and Dental Hypnosis. Chicago, Seminars on Hypnosis Publishing Co, 1981

Festinger L: A Theory of Cognitive Dissonance. New York, Harper & Row, 1957

Gillis J: The therapist as manipulator. Psychol Today 90, December 1974

Gillis J: Social Influence in Psychotherapy: A Description of the Process and Some Tactical Implications. Jonesboro, TN, Pilgrimage Press, 1979

Haley J: Uncommon Therapy: The Psychiatric Techniques of Milton H. Erickson, M.D. New York, Norton, 1973

Nixon G: The Strategic Maneuvers of Psychotherapy. Unpublished manuscript, 1979

Stricherz M: Social influence, Ericksonian strategies and hypnotic phenomena in the treatment of sexual dysfunction. Am J Clin Hypn 1982 (in press)

Zeig J: Symptom prescription and Ericksonian principles of hypnosis and psychotherapy. Am J Clin Hypn 23:16, 1980

Zeig J: Symptom prescription techniques: Clinical applications using elements of communication. Am J Clin Hypn 23:23, 1980

10 The Theory and Practice of Hypnoanalysis

ERIKA FROMM

Gill and Brenman (1959), Fromm, Oberlander, and Gruenewald (1970), Levin and Harrington (1976), and Gruenewald, Fromm, and Oberlander (1979), have pointed out that hypnosis may be considered what Kris (1952) has called a "regression in the service of the ego." Like other regressions in the service of the ego (sleep, reverie, artistic creation, etc.), hypnosis can bring about or facilitate the functioning of the productive, integrative, and coping mechanisms within the personality; and thus lead to healthy solutions of conflict. Hypnotherapy may be practiced in several ways; a particularly useful technique is hypnoanalysis. Hypnoanalysis enables the therapist to talk with the patient's unconscious ego* directly and therefore works much faster than psychoanalysis.

Hypnoanalysts use the same induction and deepening techniques that are employed by other hypnotherapists. After trance has been induced, the methods and techniques of hypnosis and psychoanalysis are skillfully combined. At our disposal as therapists are a number of specific tools with which we can help the patient in the uncovering and working-through processes of hypnoanalysis. I shall discuss here the most important of these tools.

Uncovering the Unconscious Sources of Conflict

Classical psychoanalysis employs mainly four techniques, all of which can be used in hypnoanalysis. They are the following:

---

* The concept "ego" is used throughout this chapter in the psychoanalytic sense, not in the common-usage sense of "selfishness." In psychoanalytic parlance, the ego is that conglomeration of functions that deals with the outside world and that, within the personality, moderates between the demands of the drives and those of the superego (the conscience). These functions comprise perception, motility, cognition, imagery and fantasy, attention, memory, talents, defenses, integrative and coping mechanisms, and the ability to make decisions (free will).

1. Free association
2. Interpretation of defenses and resistances
3. Transference analysis
4. Dream interpretation

Free Association

The discussion of free association is brief because the hypnoanalyst uses free association in a manner very similar to that of the psychoanalyst, except that in the hypnotic state more frequently than in the waking state, associations appear in the form of imagery. The patient is encouraged to become aware of all the different images, thoughts, and associations that go through his mind regardless of whether or not there seems to be a logical connection between successive images and thoughts. Sometimes in hypnosis, the patient is asked just to become aware of these images and associations by himself. More often, as in psychoanalysis, the hypnoanalyst asks the patient to report these. Free association is used in the uncovering process as well as in integrative processes.

Defenses and Resistances

The interpretation of defenses and resistances is an essential part of psychoanalysis. For example, the psychoanalyst points out to the patient that he is late and that there must be some meaning behind this lateness—usually a defensive meaning. By being late, the patient may try to avoid having to spend a full hour in working on his problem, or by consistently being late, he may wish to provoke the analyst into throwing him out of therapy. The psychoanalyst interprets this behavior to the patient. The hypnoanalyst interprets defenses in the same way.

The patient is more vulnerable in hypnosis than in the waking state. Therefore, defenses should be handled more carefully, gently, and respectfully. Defenses should not be pierced too quickly. The following case furnishes an illustration:

A highly sensitive, artistic graduate student, who wanted to become a writer or a musician, came for hypnotherapy because he had difficulty finishing work on his doctorate, and because he wanted to know whether he was a homosexual. He had both homosexual and heterosexual fantasies but never dared to approach either men or women, and consequently led a totally celibate life. He told me in hypnoanalysis about his father, a Midwestern farmer, who wanted his son to step into his footsteps and who objected to the son's professional choice.

It was clear to the patient consciously that his father conceived of his artistic interests as being "feminine." However, I had the feeling that much more was involved in this patient's doubts about his sexual identity and in his need to keep away from any sexual contact. I used the well-known theater technique and suggested to him when he was in a rather deep trance that we would go to a theater, sit down in our seats, and see a play which in some ways was connected with his problem. I described the beautiful red velvet curtain that was now being pulled up. As it was going up, the patient said, "Uh-uh, the rope broke. The curtain has fallen down." Silently, I recognized this as a defense. The patient was not yet ready to look more deeply at his problem. I then explained how he could relax some more while the curtain was being repaired, a process I described in elaborate imaginistic detail. A little later I said that the rope was now repaired, the play could begin, and the curtain was again being pulled up. Again, when the curtain was halfway up, the patient informed me that the rope had broken. Not only that, he said, but now a golden metal curtain had come down, totally shutting the stage off from our vision. Thus, through imagery, the patient told me in unmistakable terms that he still needed to protect himself from finding out more about the roots of his problem, that he was not yet ready for such uncovering. Because it would have been wrong to pierce this defense at that time, I dropped the subject for a while.

A month later, we went through the imagery of going to a theater again. This time no curtain fell. The patient saw on the stage an older man who was sexually attacking a young boy. This brought up a hitherto totally repressed memory of having to sleep in the same bed with his grandfather between the ages of nine and twelve and of his grandfather's attempting to abuse him sexually a number of times. The patient could now see the deeper dynamics of his homosexual fears.

In hypnoanalysis, interpretation of resistances is not necessarily pursued as zealously as in psychoanalysis. At times, the hypnoanalyst should interpret resistances, but more often, it seems to me, he accepts their existence silently and does not draw them into the focus of interpretive activity. He notes the patient's resistances, and he notes *when* the patient resists. Then the hypnoanalyst tries to think of ways to word his therapeutic endeavors so that the patient does not *need* to resist. Only if this does not work does the hypnoanalyst go on to draw the patient's attention to his resistance and analyze it together with him. On the whole, in hypnoanalysis one makes somewhat less of resistances as a cornerstone of therapy than one does in psychoanalysis. Moreover, because the hypnotic subject or patient characteristically often has a strong wish to cooperate with the hypnotist and to please him, resistances are not as frequent in hypnosis as they are in psychoanalysis transacted in the waking state.

Transference

Transference is a term used in psychoanalysis to indicate that the patient unrealistically feels about his therapist as he felt about a significant figure in childhood. He sees his therapist—who is part of his current world—through the colored glasses of the past. These glasses may be rose colored or dark. In either case, the patient tries to re-enact with his therapist an important relationship that he has had earlier in life. In psychoanalysis, one speaks about positive and negative transferences. When a patient is in a positive transference, he feels love for his therapist and idealizes him; in a negative transference, he hates him. Both kinds of transferences have to be worked through.

While transference feelings are very strong in psychoanalysis, they are even stronger in hypnotherapy and hypnoanalysis. Hypnosis tends to bring into focus, more rapidly and more deeply than does any other type of therapy, the patient's conflicts and repressed affect. This occurs because in hypnosis the patient is in closer contact with the unconscious than he is in the waking state (in which psychoanalysis is transacted).

There are three major general categories of transferences: (1) infantile dependency transferences, (2) oedipal transferences, and (3) sibling transferences. Each can occur in hypnoanalysis.

Infantile Dependency Transferences. The hypnotic situation *per se* tends to foster infantile dependency transferences, especially in the beginning. The patient who comes in for hypnotherapy frequently expects the hypnotist to take care of him and to solve all his problems, while he, the patient, is "asleep." The patient wants to be dependent. He unrealistically sees the hypnotist as the omniscient, omnipotent parent. He may fantasize that he is being held in the therapist's arms, nursed, and rocked. Transference feelings are unrealistic; in the transference the patient may overlook such "minor" details as the actual sex of the therapist. He can make a man into a mother figure, a woman into a father figure. In either case, he may want the hypnotist to make decisions for him, as his father or his mother used to do when he was a child. The patient expects to be taken care of, either as he was taken care of in his early childhood by his parents, or as he wishes he had been.

Oedipal Transferences. As the Oedipus complex has two sides—the desire to have a love relationship with the parent of the opposite sex and the desire to win the object of one's love away from the parent of the same sex whose wrath one fears—the oedipal transference in hypnosis can similarly take two forms: seduction (ingratiation) or fierce competition coupled with death wishes. In hypnoanalysis, all of these archaic feelings are transferred to the person of the hypnotherapist. A female patient may fantasize that the male hypnotist lures her to him, holds her in his strong arms, and seduces her. Another may bring a lawsuit against her male hypnotherapist for supposedly having attacked her sexually while she was in a trance. In this latter instance, wish and fear have merged into one fantasy, which has, in turn, become a psychic reality to the patient. Such a woman patient, when she was between the ages of 3 and 6, experienced the normal oedipal wish of every little girl: that her father take the initiative and have a sexual relationship with her. But she has not resolved this oedipal wish; in her Unconscious it keeps throbbing, and later she transfers this wish to the hypnotist. She wishes to be seduced by the hypnotist. In bringing suit, she is unconsciously revenging herself on the therapist/father for *not* having seduced her. She blames the seductive wish on the hypnotist, transferring to him the unfulfilled hope whe had with regard to her father. The fact that she is in trance and passive makes it more possible in her own mind to rid herself of the responsibility.

Sibling Transference. In hypnoanalysis the patient frequently acts out old sibling rivalries in a transference situation. Such a patient becomes very competitive. For example, one of my hypnotherapy patients, who is in an allied profession, never went into more than a very light trance with me. In her first hour, she asked me to teach her autohypnosis, and since then she has told me several times that at home, when practicing autohypnosis, she can get herself into a much deeper stage than I can help her go into. Clearly, sibling rivalry here rears its head: "I can do better than you can."

Would it be helpful to interpret the sibling rivalry to the patient in hypnosis? I do not think so. She would feel uncomfortable, ill-at-ease, and guilty. The competitiveness can become a useful tool, provided the therapist does not feel the need to be the patient's sole savior. If she also can use autohypnosis effectively, why not let her? In ordinary psychoanalysis, one analyzes all transference phenomena. In hypnoanalysis, it is sometimes wiser not to make the patient aware of every transference feeling that comes up (Fromm, 1968). One can do more constructive work at times by *utilizing* transference feelings in hypnoanalysis than by *analyzing* them. In the case of this patient with the need to outshine me, I praised her while she was in heterohypnosis for her competence in autohypnosis. I told her how pleased I was that she was learning to help herself go into trance. I even suggested to her that at home, in the evening, she would put herself into a much deeper trance than I could put her into—and that then memories and images would come to her that would shed new light on her major problems, alcoholism and compulsive overeating. Moreover, what she would bring in during the next hour, would furnish ample material for further hypnoanalysis. Later, I could suggest to her that she would soon find herself as competent in dealing with her problems as she was in putting herself into trance.

In addition to these three general categories, which I have so far discussed, there are, of course, more specific transference feelings and reactions that are worthy of examination. For example, a patient whose mother had suddenly died one night when he was four years old and asleep, had great difficulty in going into anything but the lightest stages of trance. Every once in a while, he exhibited in his light trances a curious minute pulling-up movement of his head and shoulders—as if he wanted to alert himself or prevent himself from going down into deeper sleep. At the end of most of his hypnotic sessions he would become very solicitous about *me*. He would ask me how I felt, wonder whether I was tired, or remark that he must be a strain on me. Since he was my last patient of the day, we often left the building at the same time, and he would always insist on carrying my brief case or my books to my car. At first, I thought that this was an expression of gallantry. But then I recognized that the behavior both in and out of trance was an expression of the same transference reaction: the patient pictured me as weak and was afraid I might die and leave him . . . as his mother had done. Further hypnoanalytic work revealed his unconscious fantasy that his mother had died because she had had to work too hard in caring for him when he was a small child.

When he next made this curious head-and-shoulder movement in trance, I quietly said to him, "You don't need to be afraid of making demands on me. I am strong. I am not going to die." The patient heaved a great sigh, relaxed, and immediately went into much deeper trance. I then interpreted to him his imagined guilt about his mother's death.

Dream Interpretation

The fourth classical psychoanalytic technique is dream interpretation. Freud (1953) called the nocturnal dream "The Royal Road to the Unconscious."

In dream interpretation, one differentiates between the manifest and the latent content of the dream. The manifest content is what the dreamer actually saw or heard or did in the dream. The latent content consists of the unconscious or preconscious thought processes underlying the manifest content. Freud (1900) compared the total dream work to a mountain range partially submerged in the ocean, with the manifest content representing the tops of the highest mountains that stick out as islands above the sea level. The latent content is comparable to that part of the mountain range that is submerged below the ocean's surface. In the dream work, symbolism, condensation, displacement, and substitution are used rather than logical and formally organized thought. Therefore, the meaning of a dream often seems quite unintelligible at first.

The dreams of patients in therapy deal with conflicts—mainly, in Freud's view, with childhood conflicts. According to Freud (1953), dreams represent a "primary wish-fulfilling process" which is interfered with by the "dream censor," that is, the conscience. In Freud's view, the motivating force for the dream is the instincts, which strive for expression and gratification but are in conflict with the conscience.

Thomas French and I (French and Fromm, 1964), utilizing the notion of the dream as conflict, place more emphasis on ego processes in the dream and on the dream's cognitive structure. We conceive of the dream as an ego-function, a problem-solving attempt of the unconscious and the preconscious ego. The dream is a cognitive process. The thoughts closer to consciousness show up in the manifest content; the more deeply unconscious thoughts are hidden under the surface, in the latent content. French and I (French and Fromm, 1964) have also been able to demonstrate that every dream is a reaction to and an expression of a current conflict, a focal conflict, that is, a conflict in which the dreamer is involved in his *present* life situation. The dream may have roots in the past, but people do not dream about the past as such. The past has to be activated in the present, in the interrelationship of the patient with real life figures, *here and now.* It is the Here and Now situation that gives rise to a disturbing wish within the patient. This disturbing wish, in turn, leads to and is in conflict with a reactive motive. The reactive motive may be guilt, fear, pride, shame, or a counterwish. Every dream contains one or more successful or unsuccessful attempts to solve the conflict (Fromm and French, 1962).

In beginning attempts to interpret the dream, the psychoanalyst or hypnoanalyst often finds himself in a situation similar to that of Monsieur Broussard when he discovered the Rosetta Stone. The message of the dream—or parts of it—are written in hieroglyphs (the language of the patient's unconscious). It must be translated faithfully into the language of the waking state (the language of the conscious). How does the interpreter go about this task?

The interpreter should not just decode "symbols." Like the *good* translator of poetry from a foreign language and culture, who faithfully and artistically tries to recreate in the language of the translation the specific poetic atmosphere and quality of the original poem, so the dream interpreter must also recreate the dream's specific, elusive atmosphere in order to make the dream meaningful to the patient's conscious mind.

Dream interpretation—like the understanding of the hypnotic patient's verbal and nonverbal communications—requires intuition. Similarly, it also requires scientific self-discipline and the willingness to evaluate critically and conscientiously the ideas and hypotheses one has arrived at intuitively. The therapist must constantly check and recheck whether his intuitive hypotheses about the meaning of the dream are correct, need modification or refinement, or should be discarded because they are wrong.

In dream interpretation, the hypnoanalyst enjoys a distinct advantage over the psychoanalyst. The psychoanalyst must wait, often for weeks, for the dream reports the patient brings in, and he is constantly faced with the fact that much of the content of dreams—even those that are remembered—has been repressed, forgotten, or distorted. In hypnosis, however, there are a number of tools available to facilitate and improve working with dreams:

1. The hypnoanalyst can hypnotically induce dreams right in the hypnotic session—dreams that the patient reports immediately after they are finished.

2. The hypnoanalyst may suggest to the patient that he dream about a particular conflict or problem that the therapist is trying to help him solve.
3. If the patient has not come to a solution by means of the dream, the hypnoanalyst can ask him to redream the dream and to try again to cope with the same problem, either in a different manner or on a different level. The therapist can encouragingly tell the patient that he will find a better solution in his continuing attempts at redreaming (Sacerdote, 1967).
4. The therapist may also suggest to the patient that he will be able to understand the symbolism and meaning of his dreams better and better as time goes on.

In addition to these four useful tools, the hypnoanalyst has two other valuable techniques at his disposal. First, in hypnoanalysis (in contrast to psychoanalysis, which is done in the waking state) one has recourse to the posthypnotic suggestion. The hypnoanalyst can give the patient a posthypnotic suggestion that at home, during the week to come, he will dream some important dreams at night; and the therapist may tell the patient that, even if he should forget them, the dreams will rise into consciousness and be remembered by him as soon as he steps into the therapist's office next week. Then the therapist can explore with the patient the full dream product and interpret it, rather than being forced to work with the fragments remembered.

Finally, it happens not infrequently in hypnoanalysis that when the patient is asked to dream right there during the hour—particularly the patient who is not in deep trance—he will hypermnestically remember an old nocturnal dream that he had never reported before. This is usually a very important dream that he had earlier repressed. Or he may produce a daydream that also can be gainfully interpreted.

The dream is only one among many roads to the unconscious. In hypnoanalysis, as we have seen, there are a number of others. Modern permissive hypnosis enables the therapist or the investigator to talk with the unconscious directly. The psychoanalyst, whose patient is *not* in hypnosis, talks to the conscious ego, and only in the dream and in slips of the tongue does the patient's unconscious communicate directly with the psychoanalyst. When the patient is in hypnosis, particularly in deep hypnosis, the hypnotist talks directly to the patient's unconscious by using hypermnesia, imagery, age regression and other means; and the patient's unconscious can answer directly. Therefore, hypnosis can bring about improvements or cures more quickly.

Integration, Growth, and Mastery

The hypnoanalytic methods I have described so far are mainly used for uncovering and interpreting unconscious conflict. However, uncovering alone is not enough.

Once the therapist has laid bare the inner recesses of the patient's conflict, he must help the patient to resolve the conflict. The hypnoanalyst must also lead the patient to see where his inner struggles lie and how he can better reorganize his personality and reintegrate it, so that he can build for himself a new, productive, joyful life. The real purpose of hypnoanalysis is to facilitate maturity and continued growth.

Proponents of classical psychoanalysis originally conceived of maturity as a final plateau of growth reached by the healthy person at the end of adolescence. Through Erik Erikson's work (1950), however, psychoanalysts have learned that growth continues throughout the normal life span. It can be facilitated as well as hampered in full adulthood and even in old age.

In the second part of this chapter I show how selected ego-psychoanalytic concepts can be applied in hypnotically facilitating personal growth in healthy persons, as well as in persons who are emotionally ill. I discuss (1) the use of imagery and fantasy, (2) the ego ideal technique, and (3) coping, mastery, and the joy of functioning at one's full level of competence.

The Use of Imagery and Fantasy

The psychoanalyst Heinz Hartmann (1958) pointed out that there are two types of fantasy: (1) symbolic fantasy or imagery, which is the cognitive mode of the unconscious ego, and (2) reality-testing fantasy, the fantasy that one uses to plan ahead for realistic situations, thinking out exactly what one might say or do in a difficult situation that one must face. The hypnotherapist uses both types of fantasy. He makes use of symbolic imagery in hypnotherapy when, for instance, he might symbolize to the patient the process of his movement from illness towards health as a wide and turbulent river that the patient must cross or as a mountain that he must climb. Reality-testing in fantasy may be used in dealing, for example, with flying phobia. The hypnotherapist may describe for the patient step by step the details of his driving to the airport, checking his bags, going through the security check, entering the plane, settling himself down comfortably with a book, and finding that book so engrossing that throughout the whole trip his attention is riveted to it and he is not aware of any discomfort about flying. Or, in hypnosis, the hypnotherapist may put a patient who is afraid of being interviewed for a new job through a rehearsal of that dreaded interview, step by realistic step. By putting him through such a rehearsal several times, that is to say, *by testing reality in fantasy* in the hypnotic state, the therapist can help him to gain mastery in reality. Reality testing in fantasy in the presence of the supportive hypnotherapist leads to the development of coping mechanisms previously not available to the patient (Frankel, 1976). In hypnosis, the patient gains mastery over the imagined situation with greater courage and with a greater sense of confidence about being able to handle it. Thus, the patient transfers the sense of success from the imagined to the real situation on the basis of the simple principle that "nothing succeeds like success" (Frankel, 1976, p 101).

Why and how can fantasy help the patient in hypnoanalysis to find better solutions to his problems? The psychoanalyst Hartmann (1958) correctly pointed out that in the normal course of healthy growing up, a central regulating factor arises: the "inner world," the world of imagery, fantasy, memory, and thinking. He further stated that the "inner world" and its functioning make possible an adaptation process that consists of two steps: temporary withdrawal from the external world and subsequent return to the external world with improved mastery. The inner world allows one to step back, look, and think things over—and then to act with improved mastery. This process is similar to "regression in the service of the ego" (Kris, 1952), a psychoanalytic concept on which Gill and Brenman (1959) based their theory of hypnosis. Hartmann (1958) called the same process an "adaptive regression."

In the ordinary waking state, one must be reality-oriented and must think mostly in the reality-oriented, logical ways. Hypnosis, because it is an altered state rather than the reality-oriented waking state, gives the therapist a better chance to use fantasy (*i.e.*, imaginative thinking in visual, auditory, or other sensory forms) instead of or in addition to logical sequential thought. This is so because in hypnosis the patient functions much more frequently with his unconscious ego than he does in the waking state. Learning self-hypnosis can be compared to learning to snorkel. To the person who begins to snorkel, a whole new world opens up, the brilliant, colorful world of life below the surface of the tropical oceans—an enchanting new world. Similarly, to the person in hypnosis or in self-hypnosis, a totally new world, his own inner world, opens up. If he is healthy, he will get enormous enjoyment from looking at this inner world of his. If he is emotionally sick, the experience may not be so enjoyable, but hypnoanalysis can help him to deal with and to tame his inner-world monsters. It may also help him to become aware of resources and assets within himself, which may previously have lain untapped and unrecognized below the surface.

The Ego Ideal Technique

Another psychoanalytic concept that I have found most useful to work with in hypnoanalysis is that of the ego ideal. Psychoanalytic ego psychology differentiates between the superego (the conscience) and the ego ideal. "The superego's main function is to set boundaries; the ego ideal sets goals" (Stolar and Fromm, 1974, p 301). The ego ideal represents what one hopes to be or strives to be. If one does not reach one's level of aspiration, one feels shame—shame about not being as grown up or as competent or as perfect as he would like to be.

The hypnoanalyst can help a patient learn to cope with something he dreads by literally bringing the ego ideal into the therapy, as if the ego ideal were a real person. For instance, one may suggest to the patient that someone who looks very much like him and who is the person the patient would *like* to be steps into the room, sits down at the other end of the couch, and tells how he has joyfully and competently mastered the goals that the patient would like to reach. For example, Kate, a female medical student, had a fear of blood; she fainted whenever she saw blood. However, she wanted to become a physician. I described an ego ideal, "Melissa," that had come in as a competent young woman physician, able to bandage a child's bleeding wound or to do surgery when needed. I let "Melissa" tell Kate that she had scheduled surgery for a patient and that she must now go over to talk to the patient for a while and see that he is wheeled into the operating room. Then I suggested to Kate that she felt an urge to move into the body of "Melissa" that could not be overcome, and that, safely encased in "Melissa," she was going to watch the surgery that "Melissa" would perform on the patient. In the next therapy hour, I let her feel that she had become so accustomed to seeing blood and so relaxed about it while watching from within "Melissa's" body that she now could step out of "Melissa" in the (imaginary) operating room and assist "Melissa" with the surgery. Still later, I let my patient do the surgery by herself in imagery and then urged her to do it in reality "when the right time comes." Thus, I use the ego ideal in order to help hypnoanalytic patients achieve competence and mastery of fear or conflict.

Coping, Competence, Mastery, and the Joy of Functioning

Ives Hendrick (1943) was the first psychoanalyst to propose that there is an inborn ego drive—the instinct to master the environment. He postulated "an inborn drive to do and to learn how to do." He felt that the human being derives "primary pleasure" when efficient action enables him to control or alter his environment. It is this primary pleasure in competence and mastery that the therapist tries to stimulate in hypnoanalytic patients.

During the last 20 years, therapists and researchers in psychoanalysis and hypnoanalysis have focused more and more frequently on the concepts of coping with challenges and competently and joyfully mastering them. Lois Murphy (1962) has pointed out a new way of thinking about coping: Coping, in her view, refers not only to a person's attempt to deal with conflicts, but also to a person's own manner of dealing with newness, with challenges in his environment, and with novel situations. Coping is the successful meeting of challenges. And challenges are the spice of life.

In supportive therapies, including many types of hypnotherapy, part of the therapist's task consists of helping the patient to alleviate anxiety, tension, and conflict. However, not all tension in life is undesirable. Quite the contrary. Tension can be joyful, as is the tension in foreplay and in the sexual act. And joyful tension is at least part of what one experiences in the creative process, the ecstasy part of the "agony and the ecstasy." Any theory of personality that leaves out the concept of the pleasure of functioning, the joy of being able to do something well, ignores a multitude of processes that are characteristically experienced by children and by dedicated adults. One may teach, do research, climb mountains, ski, play a strenuous and hard game of tennis, or row in a race—not because it is one's job and one is paid to do it, or because one thinks one ought to do it for one's health, but because it is fun, because it is exciting, because one passionately *wants* to do it. There is joy in ego-functioning at increasingly higher levels of competence.

Summary

The hypnoanalyst has several advantages not available to the psychoanalyst. In psychoanalysis, improvement or cure is brought about by a three-fold procedure: uncovering, working through, and new integration. The same basic procedures are employed in hypnoanalysis. In hypnoanalysis, however, the therapist need not necessarily uncover the historical roots of conflict as is done in classical psychoanalysis. The hypnoanalyst can also take a "here-and-now" or a teleological approach and work with contemporary psychoanalytic methods from and with a patient's ego strength.

The hypnoanalytic techniques I have discussed in the second part of this chapter are various uses of imagery, including reality testing in fantasy and reality mastery, the ego ideal, and coping, competence, and the joy of functioning. I have attempted to point out how, by evoking the appropriate imagery in line with these concepts, we can help patients to grow, to use to their best advantage the assets they have, and to build a better life for themselves. In hypnoanalysis many more tools can be employed to bring about cure. The hypnoanalyst attempts to help the patient achieve new harmony within himself, between his drives, his conscience, his ego ideal, and his ego. He also attempts to help the patient develop new methods of coping so that he can master his environment— perhaps even improve it—or adapt to it joyfully.

Acknowledgments

This study was supported in part by the University of Chicago's Biomedical Research Support Grant PHS 2 S07 RR-07029-16.

I wish to thank David Zesmer for his editorial assistance.

References

Erikson E: Childhood and Society. New York, WW Norton, 1950

Frankel FH: Hypnosis: Trance as a Coping Mechanism. New York, Plenum Medical Book, 1976

French TM, Fromm E: Dream Interpretation: A New Approach. New York, Basic Books, 1964

Freud S: (1900) The Interpretation of Dreams. In Strachey F (ed): Standard Edition, Vols. 4 & 5. London, The Hogarth Press, 1953

Fromm E: Transference and countertransference in hypnoanalysis. Int J Clin Exp Hypn 16:77, 1968

Fromm E, French TM: Formation and evaluation of hypotheses in dream interpretation. J Psychol 54:271, 1962

Fromm E, Oberlander M, Gruenewald D: Perceptual and cognitive processes in different states of consciousness: The waking state and hypnosis. J Projective Techniques Personality Assess 5:375, 1970

Gill MM, Brenman M: Hypnosis and Related States: Psychoanalytic Studies in Regression. New York, International Universities Press, 1959

Gruenewald D, Fromm E, Oberlander MI: Hypnosis and adaptive regression: An ego-psychological inquiry. In Fromm E, Shor R (eds): Hypnosis: Developments in Research and New Perspectives. Hawthorne, NY, Aldine Publishing Co, 1979, p 619

Hartmann H: (1939) Ego Psychology and the Problem of Adaptation. New York, International Universities Press, 1958

Hendrick I: The discussion of the instinct to master. Psychoanal Q 12:561, 1943

Kris E: (1934) Psychoanalytic Explorations of Art. New York, International Universities Press, 1952

Levin LA, Harrington RH: Hypnosis and regression in the service of the ego. Int J Clin Exp Hypn 24:400, 1976

Murphy L: The Widening World of the Child. New York, Basic Books, 1962

Sacerdote P: On the psycho-biological effects of hypnosis. Am J Clin Hypn 10:10–14, 1967

Stolar D, Fromm E: Activity and passivity of the ego in relation to the superego. Int Rev Psychoanal 1:297, 1974

11 Cognitive–Experiential Therapy and Hypnosis

DONALD J. TOSI
BARBARA S. BAISDEN

Rational Stage Directed Therapy (RSDH), is a cognitive–experiential therapeutic technique, originated by Tosi (1974) and Tosi and Marzella (1975), which gives priorities to cognitive control over the affective, physiological, and behavioral functions of the person. The restructuring of the cognitive functions occurs by way of skills that are developed, implemented, and reinforced while the client is in a state of deep relaxation or hypnosis. The hypnotic state amplifies and heightens the cognitive restructuring of emotional, physiological, and behavioral processes. In this chapter, the more recent conceptual innovations and research on cognitive–experiential therapy, which we have called RSDH (Tosi, 1980), are presented. Of central importance is the elaborated ABCDE framework of human functioning (Tosi, 1980), which defines the self as a complex set of cognitive, affective, physiological, and behavioral functions occurring within a social environment. Moreover, we assume that the fundamental operations of the self occur along time and awareness continua in terms of pervasive experiential themes. The stages of the therapeutic process through which the hypnotic modality is used to achieve cognitive restructuring along the continua of time and awareness are described. The application of the RSDH technique in treating a group of hypertensives is also illustrated.

An Integrated Model of Human Functioning

The model with which we work assumes that human functioning is both dynamic and integrative. Mooney's (1963) prototypic model of person–environment interaction and Ellis' (1974) ABC model linking emotion to cognition were elaborated by Tosi (1974, 1980) to include points D (physiological concomitants) and E (behavioral responses). As shown in Figure 11-1, the self, or person, depicted in the broken circle, operates as an open system with the environment, labeled **155**

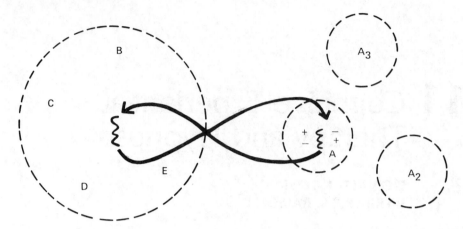

Fig. 11-1. Person and environment interaction

A = Situational conditions (a_1, a_2, a_3, a_4)

B = Cognitive functions (b_1, b_2, b_3, b_4)

C = Affective responses (c_1, c_2, c_3, c_4)

D = Physiological responses (d_1, d_2, d_3, d_4)

E = Behavioral responses (e_1, e_2, e_3, e_4)

A. The self consists of a set of (B) cognitive, (C) affective, (D) physiological, and (E) behavioral operations relative to the social environment or other objects (real or imagined). People also interact with internal conditions such as bodily reactions, sensations, or images, as well as to conditions external to themselves.

Furthermore, the As, Bs, Cs, Ds, and Es operate as a network of relationships. The model suggests that an emotional response cannot make sense unless it is related to some kind of cognitive appraisal, situational event, and change in bodily functioning, with all processes operating together in a unitary fashion.

Humans are uniquely cognitive beings. As conscious animals, we are able to reflect and apply various cognitive operations on past, present, and future experiences. As symbolic animals, we are able to ascribe meaning to our behavior. We are rarely, if ever, passive receivers of environmental events or stimuli.

Consider the situation of one person yelling at another. Rather than the person's yelling causing a particular reaction in the other, it is most likely the manner in which the person being yelled at interprets the situation that gives rise to or sets the stage for his emotional, physiological, and behavioral responses (Lazarus, 1971). If the person doing the yelling is of little importance to the person being yelled at, the response will probably be less intense than if the person yelling is someone of significance. To the extent that a person has some problems with being the target of such verbal attack and evaluates the event negatively, negative emotions such as hostility or frustration may arise.

Recognizing that human beings are not totally cognitive, the model of human functioning being presented additionally requires a definition of emotion that includes behavioral and physiological responses, and environmental conditions. Our view, consistent with that of Magda Arnold (1968), suggests that emotions are felt tendencies to approach or avoid a situation judged to be suitable or unsuitable, which are reinforced by specific bodily changes according to the type of emotion.

Technically, emotional responses involve complex psychobiological operations. Cognitive symbolic events such as judgments, evaluations, and appraisals of stimuli, whether external or internal, involve both higher cortical and subcortical mechanisms (those of the hypothalamus and the limbic system) of the brain. These mechanisms have been found to stimulate the pituitary activating system that regulates, in part, the endocrine system and behavioral motoric actions. With this in mind, consider a further elaboration of the ABCDE presented in Figure 11-1.

Cognitive operations (B) are the individual's interpretations, appraisals, or beliefs about situations or events. B is actually a cognitive set, comprised of four levels, b_1, b_2, b_3, and b_4, any or all of which may occur above or below the threshold of awareness. At b_1, there is an appraisal, a belief, or a judgment about the *situation*. An appraisal of the individual's response to the situation is referred to as b_2 (*i.e.,* a thought, image, cognitive operation, emotion, physiological response, or behavioral response). At b_3, the appraisal or judgment about an environmental event and one's response to that event may be generalized to the entire self. When the entire self system is evaluated, either positively or negatively, this tends to lead to a greater intensification of the emotional state, thus reinforcing other events. Represented by b_4 is a set of learned and well integrated cognitive coping strategies that may be either self-enhancing or self-defeating. Cognitive–symbolic coping strategies include the following:

1. Disassociation–association
2. Selective attention–inattention
3. Denial–repression–suppression–projection
4. Logical–critical–divergent thinking
5. Imaging
6. Distortion*
   a. Mislabelling
   b. Overgeneralizing
   c. Magnification/minimization

* See A. Beck (1976)

      d. Arbitrary inference

      e. Selective abstraction

      f. Cognitive polarization (either-or)

      g. Projection

7. Destructive/constructive behavioral
   approach–avoidance tendencies

The B set gives rise to or becomes associated with a set of affective responses that may be designated as the C set—c_1, c_2, $c_3 \cdots c_n$. When people experience emotions such as anxiety, hostility, and guilt, depression and frustration may be felt.

During emotional arousal, there are physiological concomitants and resultants, that is, the reactions of the body as experienced at that moment or over time. These are designated d_1, d_2, $d_3 \cdots d_n$. Examples are increased heart rate, vasoconstriction, muscle tension, gastric secretions, elevated systolic and diastolic blood pressure, sweating, skin rashes, headache, and backache. When these physiological responses associated with emotions persist over a long period, the body's natural defense system may break down and, as a result, this may lead to various physiological complications, such as viral and infectious diseases and psychosomatic conditions.

Finally, at point E, the previously mentioned cognitive, affective, and physiological activities are translated into action tendencies or behavioral responses e_1, e_2, $e_3 \cdots e_n$, which may be overt or covert, that is, more or less directly observable. Such actions serve either to impact on or to avoid the environment in some way. Behavioral activity (real or imagined) produces positive or negative consequences (reinforcement effect) that increase the likelihood of the behavior occurring or not occurring in the future. Such consequences may be of a social nature occurring in the environment or may be self-administered by way of the cognitive processes.

Note that although the operations of B are somewhat sequential, the components of the C, D, and E sets are seen as response possibilities, with several responses, and with habitual patterns emerging. However, the range of affective responses seems to be smaller and thus more uniform and predictable—possibly because the vocabulary in which we cognize and express fundamental human emotions is relatively limited. Physiological and behavioral response possibilities, respectively, seem more diverse, uniform, and less predictable. The model is not rigidly deterministic. It attempts to describe and predict a process that is common yet at the same time specific to individuals; it generates hypotheses or probabilistic statements about cognitive, affective, physiological, behavioral, and social outcomes. Consider the following example.

THE ELABORATED ABCDE MODEL

A) Event	a_1	John calls Bill a dirty name
B) Cognitive	b_1	"I can't stand to be called dirty names."
responses		(Evaluation of situation)
	b_2	"I can't do anything about it." (Evaluation of response to situation)
	b_3	"I am a weakling." (Evaluation of shelf)
	b_4	"I must either fight or run away—I will run." (Cognitive–symbolic coping strategies)
C) Affective	c_1	Anxiety
responses	c_2	Hostility
	c_3	Self-doubt
D) Physiological	d_1	Peripheral vasoconstriction
responses	d_2	Gastric secretion
	d_3	Increased blood pressure
E) Behavioral	e_1	Avoidance of John
responses	e_2	Unassertiveness
	e_3	Cowardly behavior

Having observed a rather fatalistic view at b_2, Bill may then strongly suggest to himself that he has been a coward in the past, tell himself that he will never be able to do anything about John's behavior, and therefore concludes at b_3 that he is a total weakling and is doomed to remain one. While all this is occurring, Bill may remain unaware of such evaluative thinking, noticing only his anxiety and cowardly behavior. In the event of a meaningful emotional state, as seen here with Bill, organismic arousal occurs and may become the sole focus of attention. Situational, behavioral, and cognitive factors may escape awareness or appear to be unrelated. Dissociation—a type of selective inattention similar to that found in hysterical cognitive maneuvers—may be in operation. Consequently, certain events, thoughts, feelings, and behaviors can occur without a person's cognizance.

Awareness and Time Continua in the Experiential Life Span

Attempts to deal with material that is not available to consciousness have existed since before Freud. Rather than bifurcating the mind into the conscious and unconscious, however, we conceptualize the operation of the mind along two fundamental continua of human experience. Meaningful human experiences are organized along dimensions of time, ranging from the distant past to the projected future, and of awareness, ranging from what is least consciously known to what is fully conscious.

Behavior may not only be a response to characteristics of the immediate situation, but may also be functionally related to how one responded to a similar situation in the past, as well as having ramifications for how one is likely to respond in the future. To the extent that an experience is related to past or future projections, it can be placed along a time continuum. Since a person may not be fully aware of this relationship, or, within the present moment, even be aware of the full range of cognitive, affective, and physiological responses he is making, the experience can also be placed along an awareness continuum.

Any element of an ABCDE sequence occurs within the space defined by these two continua. Recall the A set as referring to an internal or external, real or imagined, event relating to the past, present, or future time, or to an integration of this time dimension. In actuality, we can deal with events only as they occur in the present, but in order to be fully understood, they need to be seen in the context of the past and future. Likewise, the B, C, D, and E response sets all occur somewhere along an awareness continuum and relate to a past, present, or future time. When Bs, Cs, Ds, and Es are viewed thusly, within the field of these two dimensions, they become experiential themes. Such integrated and internalized relationships are not momentary situational responses, but entities have emerged over the developmental span of the person and have endured for relatively long periods of time. Human functioning is characterized and organized by the many such themes that make up the experiential life span.

Cognitive Restructuring Along Time and Awareness Continua by way of Hypnotic Modality

Cognitive distortions of human experience are defensive maneuvers that have been learned, often early in life, to avoid anxiety and other emotional discomfort. The contents of such distortions, often operating below the threshold of awareness, are comprised of belief/disbelief systems that are often likely to be dysfunctional to the person. Psychotherapy seeks to expand awareness, so that both the process and contents of such operations are made available to consciousness, where they can be explored and ultimately modified.

Recently, Shevrin and Dickman (1980) cited research evidence from such diverse topics as selective attention, cortical evoked potentials, and subliminal perception to support their conclusion that "no psychological model that seeks to explain how human beings know, learn or behave can ignore the concept of unconscious psychological processes." Reviews of work on selective attention (Posner, 1973; Sternberg, 1975) suggest that conscious psychological processes are influenced by an initial phase of cognitive activity that occurs outside of awareness. Unconscious processes may determine to a great extent what enters conscious awareness.

Research on subliminal perception (Kostandov and Arzumanov, 1977; Shevrin, 1978) reveals that the specific emotional content of a stimulus can raise the threshold of perception of that stimulus. This too suggests that an emotionally evocative stimulus or event may be subjected to a complex, selective, but *unrecognized* analysis prior to the point at which it enters awareness. Perception of an event is inspired by psychological processes of which an individual is unaware, and the individual's understanding of the exact nature of that event may be distorted because connections to other relevant factors may not have been made. For example, one may experience intense rage for no apparent reason at someone one does not even know very well. One thinks, "Some people just enrage me." The connection jumps from (A) the event to (C) the affect, ignoring (B) the cognitive evaluative component. This occurs perhaps because the cognitive appraisals at b_1, b_2, and b_3, which preceded the emotional state, were so irrational and distorted that the cognitive events themselves were intolerable to the person, and thus were dismissed in order to protect the self-system.

A therapeutic model that seeks to expand awareness should also address cognitive operations occurring at the different levels of brain functioning on psychological content along the time and awareness content. Such functions include the operations of the primitive braiin that involve emotive/imagery content.

Two reasons can be advanced for working with the primitive brain. For one, cognitive functioning below the awareness threshold is not all negative or dysfunctional. Many theorists have observed positive aspects and creative potential. Theoretically, people who are unaware of this source of creativity may not be sensitive to situations that might stimulate it. We know that as people begin to explore new possibilities within themselves and in the world, they begin to behave in ways that earlier they would have considered impossible.

A second reason has to do with the concepts of congruence/incongruence as identified by Carl Rogers and extensive researches in social psychology (Greenwald, 1980). People possess beliefs at a conscious level about themselves, the environment, the present, the past, and the future. Beliefs are associated most often with emotional, physiological, and behavioral states, especially when there is self or ego involvement—that is, cognitive appraisal at b_3. However, below the threshold of awareness, people's beliefs may be inconsistent with what is professed at a conscious level. The conscious belief is supported by distorting reality through a variety of cognitive maneuvers or, simply put, by ignoring or not focusing attention on the contradictory belief. Inconsistencies or incongruities in belief or evaluative systems (b_1, b_2, b_3) may produce tension and thus influence bodily functions and behavior, especially when challenged or exposed as they are in psychotherapy. For example, I say that I am not prejudiced and I can argue intellectually against racism. Behaviorally, however, I may engage in typically racist behavior. Although not apparent to me, this inconsistency may in fact be obvious to others. When challenged by someone on this point, I may become anxious and defensive and attempt to rationalize or otherwise justify my position.

The point being made here is that inconsistencies within the self and in relationship to the environment are predictably human. People are rarely, if ever, consistently consistent, even though psychologically they might be better off if they were so. However, the entire self-system need not be impugned if an inconsistency is discovered—although, unfortunately, some human beings tend to do just that.

Cognitive restructuring of the thought processes seems to be more natural or more easily accomplished at a conscious level of experience. Neurologically, cognitive restructuring initially occurs in the cerebral cortex, the structure that houses memory and logical–critical and evaluative thought. However, the subcortical areas (limbic system) of the brain may not be influenced initially by such activity. These areas of the brain seem to have a more direct role in the production of emotions. As we move into the more primitive functions of the human brain, we find that the organism can tolerate inconsistencies—the logical and the illogical—at the same time. This is evidenced in trance-logic and dreams. If human beings are to experience a greater sense of personality integration, the process of cognitive restructuring that occurs in higher cortical functions needs to operate also on contents of the primitive brain. Ultimately, higher and lower cortical functions need to operate together as does a horse and a rider. The logical and critical operations of the cerebral cortex (by way of the hypnotic modality used in RSDH) are focused and directed to the psychological content of the more primitive areas of the brain to achieve a more comprehensive restructuring of thoughts, feelings, bodily states, and behavior.

Cognitive therapies have tended to ignore the role of unconscious processes (Arieti and Bemporad, 1978; Tosi, 1974, 1980). However, both clinical and experimental findings suggest that events and processes that are not fully conscious can become so once attention is directed to them (Shevrin and Dickman, 1980).

Hypnosis—An Emerging Rational Perspective

Hypnosis maximizes the person's ability to concentrate and direct attention to behavioral processes above or below the awareness threshold, and minimizes distractions that inhibit and interfere with learning. At the same time, hypnosis provides a vehicle whereby cortical and subcortical brain functioning can be integrated (Kroger, 1977; Fromm and Shor, 1979; Tosi, 1980).

Hilgard (1973) identified four major theories of hypnosis. Sarbin and Coe (1972) posit a social–psychological model. Hypnosis is seen as a specialized social situation, suggesting a person's involvement in role-taking activity based on performance expectations for particular situations (*e.g.,* the mother role). Similarly, Barber's (1969) perceptual–cognitive theory bases hypnosis on the beliefs, convictions, and expectations of the hypnotic subject. These theorists, de-emphasizing the role of intrapsychic factors in hypnosis, prefer to demystify the phenomenon by using a more parsimonious social–psychological explanation.

Gill and Brenman's (1959) psychoanalytic theory defines hypnosis as a regressed ego state in which there are changes from conscious perception and awareness to preconscious or unconscious states. In the same vein, Orne (1967), Shor (1959), and Fromm (1978) postulate a trance or altered state of consciousness theory.

Hilgard concluded that each theory accepted basically the same facts, while using different labels, and that the issues could be resolved through debate and by new data as it became available. As this occurs, a more rational model of hypnosis emerges.

When ego psychologists define hypnosis as a regressed ego state, they generally mean that human beings are capable of reflecting on experiences that they become aware of through activation of memories of past experiences recorded in the stream of consciousness. Cognitive processes can then operate on such information that may not have previously been in the person's awareness, if only to explore the relevance of past experiences to some present situation or future projection.

Erika Fromm summarizes the ego-analytic theory of hypnosis:

> In hypnosis, ego activity in the sense of reality perception and the making of choices is diminished, but not fully abolished. There is greater suggestibility. What is suggestibility in ego psychological terms? I conceive of it as a form of ego receptivity. The ego in hypnosis is particularly receptive to stimuli coming from within or from without and it lets them influence imagery, thoughts, behavioral action and feelings even if they do not conform to the laws of secondary process logic. For instance, in an age regression a subject may experience himself as a little boy or girl of five playing. However, because in hypnosis critical-judgemental and reality-oriented faculties of the ego are to a great degree temporarily excluded from functioning, the perceived coexistence of the adult and the child is not judged by the hypnotized subject to be absurd or illogical. The subject operates on the basis of a special logictrance logic (Orne, 1959)— which is comparable to dream logic as described by French and Fromm (1964). No difference exists for him between fantasy, imagery and actual reality. The imagery has reality for him as it does for the young child in the waking state. Cognition for a hypnotized subject is organized much more along the lines of primary process, as in a young child. (Fromm and Schor, 1979, p 93)

In the rational or cognitive view of hypnosis developed in this chapter, the role of higher cortical functions is given priority. These functions operate quite effectively and efficiently while a person is in a hypnotic state. We that believe this permits a person to achieve a more expanded orientation to reality that gives fuller consideration to both objective and subjective facts and their interrelationships. This view will become more evident in the example of cognitive–experiential theory (RSDH) provided later.

The cognitive experiential model (RSDH) views hypnosis as a naturally occurring phenomenon that may be self-induced or other-induced, depending on the degree to which a person is receptive, suggestible, or willing to explore the possibilities of the functions of the mind in either a systematic or a nonsystematic fashion. Hypnosis is largely characterized by concentration, focused awareness, reflective thought, relaxation, and selective attention and inattention. Any of these processes can be directed toward or away from information or facts existing in the person and environment.

Stages of Experience in Psychotherapy

In cognitive–experiential therapy, cognitive restructuring occurs within the framework of six developmental stages. Originally postulated by Quaranta (1971), the stages were modified and operationalized by Tosi (1974, 1980) and Tosi and Marzella (1975) for the RSDH approach. They are awareness, exploration, commitment, implementation, internalization, and behavioral stabilization. Within these stages, experiential themes—those integrated sets of functions associated with points A, B, C, D, and E—are cognitively restructured along the continua of time and awareness. A hypnotic-imagery modality is used, which serves to amplify the cognitive restructuring process and permits an intensification of a person's experience in psychotherapy.

Under hypnosis, the person employs imagery to focus on negative states, while at the same time learning to identify accompanying irrational ideas or cognitive distortions. Next, the individual imagines a more favorable or constructive emotional/physiological/behavioral sequence and concurrently experiences more rational and realistic thoughts associated with the more positive outcome states.

A person's level of experience in psychotherapy needs to be balanced by counterpart experiences in that person's world outside of therapy. However intellectually stimulating and emotionally evocative the therapeutic relationship might be, it should not become a sanctuary for avoiding responsible behavior. Growth experiences that occur within the therapeutic context need to be translated by way of concrete actions to meaningful situations outside the office door.

The six stages of therapeutic experience are outlined as follows (Tosi, 1980).

AWARENESS

In this first stage clients are introduced to healthier conditions which oppose self-defeating thoughts, feelings, physiological responses and behavior. Self-observation and monitoring are given special emphasis, leading the person to discriminate between adaptive and maladaptive behavioral patterns. The focus is upon cognitive functioning. The therapist assists the client: 1) to redirect attention to new information about the self and the behavioral modifying process; 2) to consider interrelationships among cognitive, affective, physiological, behavioral and social processes; and 3) to consider possible courses of action as well as goals.

Awareness may be *passive–reflective* or *active–subjective.* Passive–reflective awareness utilizes the human ability to be conscious of self and to treat the self as object. Essentially, one becomes an observer of one's thoughts, feelings, body responses and behavior. This form of awareness is somewhat dissociative in that one views oneself as a camera might, from a distance, but the attention here is selectively focused on relevant themes as described within the ABCDE framework.

Active awareness, on the other hand, implies a more subjective participation in thought, feelings, and action—a greater involvement with self and environment in the immediate moment. Where passive–reflective awareness is dissociative, active–subjective awareness is associative and integrative. As experienced, it seems to be characterized by an integration of thought, affect, bodily response and behavior analogous to what is referred to as the "gestalt" experience.

Reflective awareness gives perspective to subjective experience. Both serve different purposes and both need to be addressed in a therapeutic learning process.

EXPLORATION

In the second stage clients are encouraged to experiment with ideas derived from therapy. Both in the imagination, via hypnosis/imagery and in "safe" real life situations, cognitive restructuring skills can be applied and consequences experienced and evaluated. Self-exploration reinforces the development and expansion of self-awareness, but in this stage awareness is directed to more realistic and concrete matters.

Cognitively, exploration involves the directing of attention to psychological content occurring in each quadrant of the awareness and time continua. The therapist can guide the client's focus of attention to specific areas of concern, or can suggest free movement within the experiential life space until some ABCD or E event becomes figural and demands its own attention. This type of cognitive operation, termed divergent thinking by Guilford (1967), is heavily emphasized in the exploration stage. It is multi-directional, as opposed to the linear or convergent thinking generally used in problem solving. The hypnotic modality facilitates divergent operations by: 1) maximizing awareness along several levels of brain functioning; 2) maximizing focused attention and concentration; and 3) minimizing distraction and interference from other sources of stimuli.

COMMITMENT

After giving full consideration to new information and skills learned in the first two stages, the client reaches a point of commitment to implement constructive action. This stage is often accomplished by mixed emotions and high anxiety. Commitment implies choice, decision and risk; the decision to change is weighed against the costs and rewards of old but familiar behavior. Some clients may terminate, some may develop psychosomatic symptoms—all require patience and acceptance on the part of the therapist, as well as encouragement to take constructive, positive action.

Decisions made at this stage are, after all, ones that the client has determined to have some probability of success. Furthermore, empirical validation is available in the real life situations. Possibilities only glimpsed in earlier stages come within reach, as individuals sense movement to higher and more integrated levels of functioning. The stage of commitment serves as the threshold for a heightened motivation that tends to be *realized* in the following stage, via the implementation of responsible actions that impact both on the environment and the self. Commitment is an act of the intellect that gives full consideration to emotional, physiological, behavioral and social consequences.

IMPLEMENTATION

Implementation, the fourth stage, implies deliberate and constructive use of cognitive/behavioral skills that are being developed. Commitments need to be translated into situationally appropriate action if they are to be reinforced, maintained, and generalized to other situations. Desirable social consequences are self-reinforcing, and tend to increase further participation in the therapeutic learning both inside and outside the relationship.

While cognitive experiential therapy makes extensive use of imagery and hypnosis, steps need to be taken to ensure that behaviors occurring in the imagination also occur in real life. Implementation of constructive actions often require significant effort.

INTERNALIZATION

The fifth stage, internalization, is characterized by an integration of more constructive thoughts, feelings, bodily responses and behavior into the self-system to the point where they operate more natural to the person. Aronfreed (1968) states "Concepts of internalization . . . rest very heavily on the extraordinary ability of human beings to acquire cognitive structures with which they can process information about their behavior and their environment." While integrated behavioral patterns appear to be internalized under certain stimulus conditions, such as therapy, some form of mediational bridging is required if outcomes of significant value are to be maintained. Luria (1976) suggests that verbal-semantic labels serve as those bridges and later activate responses in a manner that is integrative and natural. Such semantic labeling of affective, physiological and behavioral responses may occur at levels below the threshold of awareness.

The RSDH approach is predicated on the belief that internalization is facilitated when an individual has had extensive opportunity: 1) to become aware of the relationships among the response sets described in the ABCDE framework; 2) to explore these relationships via hypnosis/imagery; 3) to make more conscious choices to discriminate among functional and dysfunctional tendencies; and 4) to implement constructive action. The degree of internalization of what has been learned through these stages is dependent upon the extent to which awareness has been expanded to include material that had previously existed below the threshold of awareness—thus building those mediational and verbal-semantic bridges noted by Aronfreed and Luria.

BEHAVIORAL STABILIZATION

The final stage of experience, behavioral stabilization, is evidenced when behavioral changes realized through the preceding stages become more frequent and permanent. Personal and social development continue, but now are based on new experiential themes and patterns that become the foundation for more constructive actions in the future.

Assessment

Before initiating RSDH, the therapist needs to identify the essential psychological and social aspects of the client's behavior, including functional (healthy) as well as dysfunctional (unhealthy) models of thinking, feeling, bodily responses, and behavior. In addition to the basic clinical interview, a major feature of the behavioral analysis used in RSDH is an assessment battery that emphasizes multiple criterion measures in order to determine both global and specific aspects of personality functioning both before and after treatment.

The Minnesota Multiphasic Personality Inventory (MMPI) and Tennessee Self Concept Scale (TSCS) are used for measures of overall personality functioning. Specific cognitive functioning is measured by the Personal Beliefs Inventory (PBI). The Subjective Units of Disturbance (SUD), the State-trait Anxiety Scale, and Multiple Affective Adjective Checklist (MAACL) are used as measures of affective functioning. The employment of such widely known and used instruments has important benefits for research purposes as well as for clinical assessment.

Another instrument used is the Self-directed Behavioral Changes Instrument (SDBC) (Tosi and Black, 1981), which was developed to assist the client (1) to identify problematic ABCDE processes and (2) to become aware of the cognitive restructuring techniques prior to the initiation of RSDH. It therefore serves as a diagnostic instrument as well as a therapeutic one. The SDBC is routinely included in the assessment battery, serving as a bridge between assessment and treatment.

Specific physiological function can be determined by blood pressure readings, laboratory reports of cholesterol and triglyceride levels, and self-reports of relative health. Functional adaptive and maladaptive behaviors related to assertiveness, work adjustment, speech fluency, academic performance, and social adequacy are assessed through self-reports or reports by supervisors, co-workers, and family. When appropriate, clients are instructed to log the frequency, intensity, and duration of symptoms and behaviors.

As should be obvious by now, assessment is defined broadly, reflecting a holistic orientation whereby human functioning is viewed as an integrated system. Particular target behavior, such as anxiety systems, nonassertiveness, or psychosomatic symptoms, are always placed within the context of more global personality structures.

In addition to using a broad spectrum of assessment instrumentation, structured didactic exercises are used to delineate for the client how each component of behavior (cognition, affect, behavior) functions as part of the dynamics of the presenting problem. It is important that clients clearly understand the relatedness of behaviors, beliefs, and physiological concomitants to the presenting problem. Finally, the relatedness must be understood within a temporal context, with a comprehension of past, present, and future components of ideations and their effect on the overall functioning of a person.

The Intervention Process

The following is an abbreviated example of RSDH derived from current research on hypertension at Riverside Methodist Hospital, Columbus, Ohio (Tosi, Rudy, and Lewis, 1982). The treatment procedure included (1) a thorough behavioral assessment and orientation to RSDH, (2) hypnotic induction, (3) the cognitive restructuring of irrational beliefs previously identified through the Common Beliefs Survey and the SDBC, and (4) the directing of cognitive restructuring through the six experimental stages. Structured "*in vivo*" behavioral tasks were given routinely while subjects were in a hypnotic state or a normal waking state. All subjects were asked to listen to tape recordings of all RSDH sessions over the duration of an 8-week treatment period. Each RSDH session ran about 1½ hours.

Hypnotic Induction

The induction in RSDH is relatively simple, although certain suggestive elements are introduced to set the stage for cognitive restructuring. Hypnosis is initially defined within the RSDH framework in order to allay the anxiety and misconceptions that the hypertensive subjects may have had.

Induction begins with deep rhythmic breathing and the suggestion of the formula: inhale relaxation/exhale tension. Subjects are asked to place this formula in the back of their minds, thereby producing automatic, ongoing deepening. As the process continues, a suggestion is given that the subjects relax and experience a slowing down of internal bodily processes and a similar slow, calm, yet clear mental state. They are asked to observe the contrast between the relaxed heaviness of their bodies and the relaxed alertness of their minds.

The induction continues with progressive muscle relaxation, beginning with the head and working down the trunk to the lower half of the body. When the lower half is fully relaxed, the sensation is deepened by way of backwards counting from 25 to 0. At this point, with the following statement, subjects are further oriented to hypnosis.

> In this state of hypnosis, human beings are capable of thinking clearly about personal issues in their lives. We are capable of imagining things vividly and are very capable of experiencing feelings about present, past, future events. We can also notice that our awareness has expanded to the point where we can get in touch with or even see thoughts and feelings of which we were previously unaware. It is a state of concentration that allows us to expand our mind, a very comfortable relaxed state. We believe hypnosis is one of the ultimate forms of self-control. Because hypnosis is concentration and heightened awareness, it can free the mind to function more efficiently to achieve greater control over thoughts, feelings, bodily responses and behaviors. So, continue to relax and to experience a complete absence of tension. You will begin to notice that your mind and body are operating as one, in a highly integrated fashion.

Awareness Stage (Sessions 1, 2, 3). Work on awareness begins during the first 3 weeks, as subjects become familiar with the induction technique and practice it themselves through use of audio tapes between the weekly sessions. When achieving a hypnotic state, subjects are directed to concentrate on critical points of the ABCDE model. A suggestion is made that in this stage of detached relaxation, they visualize, as on a television screen, any personal event that has been a source of personal discomfort. They are to imagine any emotional response to the event—threat, anger, frustration—that may be inhibited for fear of social disapproval or reprisal. They are then asked to concentrate on any negative thoughts that they might have about themselves for acting unassertively or defensively and to note any accompanying rise in the bodily symptoms of hypertension. Subjects are encouraged merely to reflect passively on situational events, emotional and bodily changes, and behavior. The aim is to be able to visualize a negative ABCDE sequence. A suggestion is made to relax even more deeply, and a minute or so of silence is allowed for this to occur.

At this point, attention is focused on B—the thoughts, ideas, or beliefs the subject holds about the situation, responses to the situation, and the self. Once more they are instructed to concentrate on a specific life event during which they experience fear or personal failure in relation to a significant other and consequent loss of approval or security.

> Focus your attention now on the thoughts you are having in the sequence you are observing. For the most part your thoughts are probably similar to ones you became aware of through listening to tapes and doing the special ABCDE exercises (SDBC). We have hypothesized that when people have disturbing reactions such as rage, hostility, anxiety and guilt, and experience negative bodily reactions such as increased blood pressure, it is certain internalized thoughts or sentences that tend to activate those reactions. Such thoughts may often occur without the person being consciously aware of them.

Typical irrational thoughts or ideas found to be associated with hypertension are then presented. Before doing so, subjects are reassured that they need only consider those ideas that are appropriate to them.

> Concentrate passively on these ideas, as you did earlier.
>
> 1. I must be alert and on guard.
> 2. I have to be ready for anything.
> 3. I cannot let anybody get ahead of me—I must be an effective person and must not fail under any circumstances. I could not cope with failure.
> 4. If I would fail, people would know that I am worthless or inadequate.
> 5. I can't stand being placed in such a situation—I would like to strike out but I had better inhibit my anger.
> 6. I should never feel anger or express it.
> 7. I must compete but it frightens me, because people, especially authorities, can somehow hurt me.
> 8. I need some people to rely on, but this makes me feel so weak and inferior that I get very frustrated and angry, but can't seem to express it. I sometimes hate myself.

After the subjects spend some time in reflective awareness, a suggestion is made that in weeks to come, they will become increasingly aware of how such ideas influence them emotionally, physically, and behaviorally. They will gradually become more accepting of themselves for having such tendencies and at the same time more desirous of exploring new ways of overcoming them.

Finally, following the period of reflective awareness, subjects are asked to experience momentarily the negative ABCDE sequence—to feel some discomfort, particularly the symptoms of rising blood pressure that may often accompany negative or irrational thoughts. They are then instructed to STOP the experience and to relax and let their minds clear. Time is allowed for relaxation before the subjects are to experience a more positive ABCDE experience or rational restructuring.

In this phase, subjects are to imagine alternative thought patterns at point B, and observe the changes in C, D, and E that are associated with them. While subjects are in a state of hypnosis they are instructed to imagine and reflect on the same problematic situation. Now, however, they are to slow down their mental processes and observe themselves formulating a more rational, self-enhancing set of thoughts, for example:

> I don't like what is happening to me in this situation and it is important for me to see clearly what is going on so I can deal more effectively with it. Rarely is any situation a matter of life or death. I can respond calmly to this situation and cope with it. Even if I do not deal effectively with this situation, that hardly makes me a failure as a human being. I can express my feelings in spite of what others may think—although it would be in my best interest to try to act appropriately even if I don't have things exactly the way I would like. I can be concerned about a situation without being overly preoccupied with it. Nor do I have to be terribly preoccupied with what I think may happen in the future. What major catastrophies are really going to happen that I cannot probably cope with? How can anybody really disturb me unless I allow them to?

> In the past I have often depended on others for their approval or disapproval of me, but I don't have to be so dependent on their approval for a sense of personal worth. I am of value to myself because I exist. I certainly have the right to be frustrated at times and also have the right to express my feelings without punishing myself with blame, guilt, anger and fear. Even if people retaliate or disapprove of me, I don't have to personalize their behavior. If someone disapproves of something I do, that doesn't mean they are disapproving of me.

As subjects become increasingly aware of more self-enhancing rational thoughts, they are directed to notice the resulting lessening of tension, anger and anxiety, and physical and behavioral changes.

> Notice how these more rational thoughts become associated with more desirable feelings and bodily states. Observe your body relax—observe your forehead—notice how comfortably cool it becomes. Notice how clear your mind becomes. Notice how your thoughts, feelings and bodily responses set the stage for a more effective way of dealing with uncomfortable situations. You may even notice your blood pressure decreasing as your thoughts become more rational and more appropriate. Now let yourself experience this more rational sequence—to *feel* the difference.

Instructions are given to listen to prepared tapes that reinforce rational thought patterns and to practice cognitive restructuring skills daily in real-life situations. As is frequently done throughout the RSDH treatment, a suggestion is made that practice produces mastery over the procedures.

The Exploration Stage (Sessions 4, 5, 6). The rational or cognitive restructuring procedure in the exploration stage is applied to other situationally relevant events in the subjects' lives. More emphasis is placed on the directing of attention to psychological content existing below the threshold of awareness in the present, past, and future. Subjects are encouraged to experience a deeper state of hypnosis and relaxation while exploring many different ABCDE elements and their connections. "*In vivo*" behavioral tasks are given in the form of posthypnotic suggestions.

Commitment, Implementation, Internalization, and Stabilization (Sessions 7, 8). By the time the subjects approach the stage of commitment, about two weeks later, hypnosis and cognitive restructuring are very familiar and can be employed with more ease and efficiency. The four stages of commitment, implementation, internalization, and stabilization may be handled somewhat differently than the earlier two stages. Rather than devoting a week or more to each stage, in our study, subjects were guided through all four stages during each of the final 2 weeks of treatment. The advantages of the procedure are a better understanding of the developmental nature of therapy and the reinforcement provided by repetition.

Once the state of hypnotic relaxation has been achieved, the therapist reviews for the subjects the work of previous sessions. They are reminded of their new understanding of how thoughts affect their emotions, bodily states, and behavior, and how the process of exploration has deepened their awareness of the benefits of thinking more rationally. They are then asked to concentrate only on the more rational thoughts that they have recently explored. At each session the therapist goes through detailed examples of appropriate thinking and its resulting benefits. The repetition of this material, which is essentially a condensed version of what was covered in the exploration stage, serves to reinforce newly formulated rational thought and behavioral patterns.

Following this, the stages of commitment, implementation, internalization, and stabilization are introduced, largely through suggestion.

> As you concentrate on the more rational ideas that you have explored over the past several weeks, you will find that you have become increasingly committed to implementing and internalizing them. For instance, the idea that "I must be alert and on guard all the time, or else," simply translates into, "if I'm alert, I can be responsive; in an appropriate manner." The idea that "I cannot let anyone get ahead of me, I must be an effective person and must not fail under any circumstances," translates into, "I can achieve a more effective life; failure is not horrible because there is no such thing as total failure, even though I may fail at a task, that hardly makes me a failure as a human being." The idea that "if I would fail, people would know that I'm a worthless human being," translates into "failure can never make me worthless." Notice as you concentrate on the more constructive or rational ideas, you become increasingly committed to implementing these on a day to day basis. You become increasingly committed to not only implementing these ideas, but to internalizing them. You can even begin to see yourself, thinking more rationally in the future, feeling more desirable feelings, being more calm and more effective as a human being over an extended period of time. The thought may produce a feeling of well-being. You will find that our work here will continue even though our sessions will come to an end shortly. You will find that many of the thoughts and ideas that you have

explored, tested, become committed to, and then implemented and internalized, can remain with you over time. You may find that your self-awareness will expand more and more and more. You may realize that human beings while never perfect, can strive for a far more effective life. You will find that self-awareness will expand even further as you study, read, and experiment with more rational thoughts and behaviors. You may wish to continue practicing the simple self-hypnosis exercises and you may find that many of the new skills you have learned here will become more natural to you and more and more automatic. There may be many situations in life that will remind you of the things that we have done here. For instance, when events occur in your life that you thought were the major sources of your personal disturbances, you will almost automatically ask yourself, "What am I telling myself? How am I appraising the situation? How am I appraising myself?" You may find that your ability to discriminate between situations, your responses, and your entire self may become greatly enhanced. You may want to continue to work on yourself, not because you have to, but simply because you know such work serves your best interest as a human being.

Research

Since the inception of rational stage-directed or cognitive–experiential therapy, a number of multivariate research studies have been conducted at the Ohio State University. Research efforts have included experimental, correlational, and single-organism studies. The experimental studies on the effects of rational stage-directed hynotherapy (RSDH) and rational stage-directed imagery (RSDI) employed multiple criterion measures reflecting cognitive, affective, physiological, and behavioral indices of change. Correlational studies attempted to demonstrate associations among these various human functions. Single-organism case studies were designed to develop rational stage-directed methods for a variety of clinical populations and to gather some initial data on the potential effects of the procedure.

Two studies providing evidence of the relationship among combinations of cognitive, affective, physiological, and behavioral functions were conducted by Tosi and Eshbaugh (1978), and Forman, Tosi, and Rudy (1980). Tosi and Eshbaugh performed a hierarchical factor analysis on the Hartmann Personal Beliefs Inventory, which is a measure of irrational beliefs. The analysis yielded several lower order factors comprised of items that were primarily cognitive, affective, and behavioral. Of interest was the highest order factor that emerged—low self-worth, which suggested a general negative appraisal altitude of the self-system. The lower order factors appeared to be variations of low self-worth.

More recently, Forman, Tosi, and Rudy (1980) investigated the relationship between cognitive factors and psychophysiological disorders. The results indicated that medically diagnosed psychosomatic groups (migraine, peptic ulcer, and low-back pain) were more perfectionistic, self-depreciating, and prone to blame others than was a medical control group. Bessai's Common Beliefs Survey III (1977) was used as a measure of irrational belief patterns.

The first in a series of experimental outcome studies on cognitive–experiential therapy was conducted by Moleski and Tosi (1976). Rational–emotive therapy (RET) was compared to systematic desensitization (SD) with the presence and absence of "*in vivo*" behavioral tasks with a group of adult stutterers. RET, the cognitive restructuring therapy, was significantly more effective than SD in reducing speech disfluency, anxiety, and attitude toward stuttering. SD, however, was more effective than the control group and in some cases yielded very positive results. The inclusion of *in vivo* behavioral tasks tended to augment both therapies, although this effect was not consistent along all criterion measures.

A number of experimental investigations on RSDH-I followed the Moleski and Tosi study. Marzella (1975) studied the effects of RSDH, RSDI, Hypnosis only (HO), and a control on the emotional stress of graduate students enrolled in a counseling practicum. The findings yielded conditional support for the RSDH-I treatment. Emotional stress as measured by the clinical scales of the MMPI was reduced for the treatment groups (RSDH, RSDI, and HO) but not for the control group.

Reardon and Tosi (1977) investigated the effects of RSDI on the self-concept and emotional stress of delinquent females. RSDI was found to be significantly more effective than cognitive restructuring alone, placebo, and control groups, with respect to positive changes in self-concept and reduction of emotional stress. Self-concept was measured by the total P score on the TSCS and by the clinical scales of the MAACL. Further improvement of subjects in the RSDI group occurred over a 2-month follow-up period, whereas the other groups showed minimal directional change.

Boutin and Tosi (1982), in a more sophisticated experimental study, examined the effects of RSDH with test-anxious nurses. RSDH, when compared with an HO group, a placebo, and a control group, proved to be the most effective treatment. HO also demonstrated significant results. At a 2-month follow-up, it was found that the RSDH group had experienced still further decreases in test anxiety, whereas levels of anxiety in the HO, placebo, and control conditions remained the same as they had been at the post-test I measure. The findings of the Reardon and Tosi and the Boutin and Tosi studies suggest that subjects who receive RSDH treatment appear better able to internalize the treatment procedure and continue to use what they learn in therapy.

In a nonclinical setting, Howard (1979) investigated the effects of a modified RSDH procedure on neuromuscular performance, the facilitation of muscular growth, the reduction of anxiety, and the enhancement of self-concept with 32 male volunteers from the Ohio State Barbell Club. RSDH was compared to other group treatment using cognitive restructuring, hypnosis, and a nontreatment control. Results demonstrated that the RSDH treatment was significantly effective on all dependent variables. Furthermore, on two dependent variables—the P score on the TSCS and a measurement of arm size—RSDH subjects showed continued significant improvement from posttest I to posttest II. The cognitive restructuring, hypnosis, and control groups yielded no significance on dependent measures.

Recently, Fuller (1981) found RSDH to be an effective treatment for depression in a group of elderly people confined to a nursing home. RSDH was compared to a cognitive-restructuring treatment, HO, and a control. RSDH was significantly more effective in improving self-concept and alleviating depression than either cognitive restructuring or the control. The hypnosis group did just about as well as RSDH immediately following treatment, but the effects of RSDH were maintained over a 2-month follow-up, which was not true for the hypnosis group.

Corley and Tosi (1980) reported a study showing the efficacy of RSDH with underachievers in a university setting. RSDH combined with study skills training (SST) was compared to groups consisting of cognitive restructuring–SST, relaxation–SST, and SST alone. Because of the high risk nature of this population owing to probationary status, classic control groups could not be used. In general, the results favored the RSDH and study skills with respect to positive changes in self-concept, irrational thinking, anxiety, and study habits. The other groups performed about as well as RSDH on some of the criterion measures, however RSDH significantly out-performed the other groups with respect to increases in grade point average. The effects of RSDH once again tended to hold up more than the other groups over time.

Case studies treating guilt (Tosi and Reardon, 1976), depression (Reardon, Tosi, and Gwynne, 1977), test anxiety (Boutin, 1978), nonassertion (Howard and Tosi, 1978), learning disability and hyperactivity (Tosi, Fuller, and Gwynne, 1980), migraine (Howard, Reardon, and Tosi, 1981), crisis intervention (Tosi and Eshbaugh, 1981), anxiety neurosis (Tosi, Howard, and Gwynne, 1982), and hypertension (Rudy, Tosi, and Reardon, 1977) provide clinical support for RSDH as a treatment modality.

A comprehensive multivariate study of the cognitive, affective, physiological–biochemical systems of hypertensives at Riverside Hospital in Columbus, Ohio, is currently in its final stages. One phase of the study that tests the efficacy of RSDH is being completed at the time of preparation of this paper (Tosi, Rudy, and Lewis, 1982). The effects of RSDH on irrational thinking (cognitive), anxiety–anger (affective), renin, catecholamines, and sodium (biochemical), and systolic/diastolic pressure (physiological) are being examined.

Furthermore, although qualified, support of the effectiveness of RSDH is reported by Smith, Glass, and Miller (1980). A meta-analysis of therapy approaches showed that, prior to correcting or controlling for confounding outcome effects, the highest average effect size was produced by the cognitive therapies other than, but similar to, Ellis' rational–emotive psychotherapy. According to Smith and Glass, RSDH is one of the therapies that falls within this highly effective group.

References

Arieti S, Bemporad J: Severe and Mild Depression. Boston, Little Brown & Co, 1978

Arnold M: The Nature of Emotion. Baltimore, Penguin Books, 1968

Aronfreed J: Conduct and Conscious: The Socialization of Internalized Control Over Behavior. New York, Academic Press, 1968

Barber TX: Hypnosis: A Scientific Approach. New York, Van Nostrand-Reinhold Co, 1969

Beck A: Cognitive Therapy and the Emotional Disorders. New York, International Universities Press, 1976

Bessai JL: The Common Beliefs Survey: A Factored Measure of Irrational Beliefs. Presented at the Second National Conference of Rational Psychotherapy, Chicago, Illinois, June 1977

Boutin G: The treatment of test anxiety by rational stage directed hypnotherapy. Am J Clin Hypn 21:52, 1978

Boutin G, Tosi DJ: The treatment of test anxiety by rational stage directed hypnotherapy. J Clin Psych (in press)

Corley D, Tosi DJ: The treatment of academic underachievement through rational stage directive imagery (RSDI): An experimental study. Presented at the Third Annual Conference on Rational Emotive Therapy, New York, June 1980

Forman MA, Tosi DJ, Rudy DR: Cognitive factors in psychosomatic disease. Research paper presented at the Third Annual Conference on Rational Emotive Therapy, New York, 1980

Fromm E: Altered states of consciousness and hypnosis. J Altered States of Consciousness 79:115, 1978

Fromm E, Shor R: Hypnosis: Developments in Research and New Perspectives. New York, Aldine, 1979

Fuller J: Rational Stage Directed Hypnotherapy in the Treatment of Self-Concept and Depression in a Geriatric Nursing Home Population: A Cognitive Experiential Approach. Unpublished doctoral dissertation, Ohio State University, 1981

Gill MM, Brenman M: Hypnosis and Related States: Psychoanalytic Studies in Regression. New York, International University Press, 1959

Greenwald AG: The totalitarian ego: Fabrication and revision of personal history. Am Psychol 35:603, 1980

Guilford JP: The Nature of Human Intelligence. New York, McGraw-Hill, 1967

Gwynne PH, Tosi DJ, Howard L: Treatment of nonassertion through rational stage directed hypnotherapy (RSDH) and behavioral rehearsal. Am J Clin Hypn 20:263, 1978

Hilgard ER: The domain of hypnosis, with some comments on alternative paradigms. Am Psychol 28:972, 1973

Howard L: The Modification of Self-Concept, Anxiety, and Neuro-Muscular Performance Through Rational Stage Directed Hypnotherapy: A Cognitive Experiential Perspective Using Cognitive Restructuring and Hypnosis. Unpublished doctoral dissertation, Ohio State University, 1979

Howard L, Reardon JP, Tosi DJ: Modifying migraine headaches through rational stage directed hypnotherapy (RSDH). Int J Clin Exp Hypn 1982 (in press)

Howard L, Tosi DJ: Effects of rational stage-directed imagery and behavioral rehearsal on assertiveness. Rational Living 13(2):3–7, 1978

Kostandov E, Arzumanov Y: Averaged cortical evoked potentials to recognized and non-recognized verbal stimuli. Acia Neurobiologiac Experimentalis 37:311, 1977

Kroger WS: Clinical and Experimental Hypnosis in Medicine, Dentistry, and Psychology. Philadelphia, JB Lippincott, 1977

Lazarus AA: Behavior Therapy and Beyond. New York, McGraw-Hill, 1971

Luria AR: Cognitive Development: Its Cultural and Social Foundations. Cambridge, MA, Harvard University Press, 1976

Marzella JN: The Effects of Rational Stage Directed Therapy Upon the Reduction of Selected Variables of Psychological Stress: A Comparative Study. Unpublished doctoral dissertation, Ohio State University, 1975

Moleski R, Tosi DJ: Comparative psychotherapy: Rational emotive therapy vs systematic desensitization in the treatment of stuttering. J Clin Consult Psychol 44(2):309–311, 1976

Mooney R: A conceptual model for integrating four approaches to the identification of creative talent. In Taylor C, Barron F (eds): Scientific Creativity: Its Recognition and Development. New York, John Wiley & Sons, 1963

Orne MT: What must a satisfactory theory of hypnosis explain? Int J Psychiatry 3:206, 1967

Posner M: Coordination of internal codes. In Chase W (ed): Visual Information Processing. New York, Academic Press, 1973

Quaranta J: Conceptual framework for career development programming. In McCormick R, J Wigtil (eds): Guidance for Planning and Evaluating Career Development. Project sponsored by the Division of Guidance and Testing. Columbus, Ohio, Ohio Department of Education, 1971

Reardon JP, Tosi DJ: The effects of rational stage directed imagery on self-concept and reduction of psychological stress in adolescent delinquent females. J CLin Psychol 33:1084, 1977

Reardon JP, Tosi DJ, Gwynne PH: The treatment of depression through rational stage directed hypnotherapy (RSDH): A case study. Psychother Theory Res Pract 14:95, 1977

Rudy DR, Tosi DJ, Reardon JP: Holistic Approach to Patients Combining a Medical Model With Direct Cognitive Experiential Psychotherapy. Presented to the American Society of Clinical Hypnosis, October 1977

Sarbin TR, Coe WC: Hypnosis: A Social Psychological Analysis of Influence Communication. New York, Holt Rinehart & Winston, 1972

Shevrin H: Evoked potential evidence for unconscious mental processes: A review of the literature. In Prangishvili AS, Sherozia AE, Bassin FV (eds): The Unconscious: Nature, Functions, Methods of Study. Tbilisi, USSR, Metsniereba, 1978

Shevrin H, Dickman S: The psychologically unconscious American. Am Psychol 5:421, 1980

Shor RE: Hypnosis and the concept of the generalized reality-orientation. Am J Psychother 13:582, 1959

Smith ML, Glass GV, Miller TI: The Benefits of Psychotherapy. Baltimore, Johns Hopkins Press, 1980

Sternberg S: Memory scanning: New findings and current controversies. Q J Exp Psychol 27:1, 1975

Tosi DJ: Conceptual Modes for a Cognitive–Experiential Therapy. Presented at the Annual Convention of the American Society of Clinical Hypnosis, Minneapolis, Minnesota, October 1980

Tosi DJ: Youth Toward Personal Growth: A Rational Emotive Approach. Columbus, Ohio, Charles E. Merrill, 1974

Tosi DJ: The personal beliefs inventory: A factor analytic study. J Clin Psychol 32:322, 1976

Tosi DJ, Black V: Self-directed Behavioral Change in the Cognitive, Affective, Physiological and Behavioral Domains: An Expanded Cognitive–Experiential Perspective Based on Rational Emotive Theory. Unpublished research paper, Ohio State University, 1981

Tosi DJ, Eshbaugh DM: A cognitive–experiential approach to the interpersonal and intrapersonal development of counselors and therapists. J Clin Psychol 34:494, 1978

Tosi DJ, Fuller J, Gwynne P: Case Studies Treating Guilt and Test Anxiety. New York, 1980

Tosi DJ, Fuller J, Gwynne P: The Treatment of Hyperactivity and Learning Disabilities Through RSDH. Presented at the Third Conference on Rational Therapy, New York, 1980

Tosi DJ, Howard L, Gwynne P: The treatment of anxiety neurosis through rational stage directed hypnotherapy: A cognitive experiential perspective. Psychother Theory Res Pract 19(1):95–109, 1982

Tosi DJ, Marzella JN: Rational Stage-Directed Therapy. Presented at the First Conference of Rational Psychotherapy, Chicago, June 1975

Tosi DJ, Reardon JP: The treatment of guilt through rational stage-directed imagery (RSDI). Ration Liv 2:8, 1976

Tosi, DJ, Rudy DR, Lewis J: The Effects of Rational Stage Directed Hypnosis on the Hypertensive Syndrome. An experimental study in progress, 1983

UNIT THREE
Hypnotic Applications in Medicine, Psychology, and Dentistry

12 Hypnosis With Children and Adolescents in the Medical Setting

DONALD J. O'GRADY
CLAUDIA HOFFMANN

Hypnosis is becoming more widely used within medical settings as one of the treatment modalities in the psychosocial care of children. The psychosocial component of pediatric care has typically focused on the feelings associated with the diagnosis and prognosis of physical disorders. Such work continues as we try to help physically ill children and adolescents to cope with the fears and restrictions of being different. However, efforts have been expanded to include use of specific techniques such as hypnosis to reduce the side effects of diagnostic and therapeutic procedures and to alleviate pain directly associated with the disease process, as well as to import a sense of coping or mastery to the children who use it.

The effectiveness of a psychosocial care program, including the use of hypnotherapy, is increased in a context that emphasizes the incorporation of such care into the routine treatment regimen, thus avoiding "last resort" treatment of problems that have become more severe and chronic with time and consequently more difficult to treat (Kellerman, 1980). In many medical settings, however, psychosocial care is not routinely offered to patients, and psychosocial staff called in on a consultant basis may encounter many problems in providing services, including hypnotherapy (Lewis, 1978; Peebles and O'Malley, 1978). For example, although most pediatric nurses and pediatricians surveyed by Gardner (1976) were found to have positive attitudes about child hypnosis, they were not actually knowledgeable about hypnosis and its clinical applications. This situation limits the number of children who might be referred for hypnotherapy and unwittingly sabotages ongoing hypnotherapy. "It is disheartening to give a post-surgical child patient hypnotic suggestions for increased food intake only to discover that someone else has put the emesis basin closer to the child than the dinner tray!" (Gardner and Olness, 1981, p 50) Providing in-service hypnosis education programs has been found to increase awareness of the usefulness of hypnosis by hospital staff and to facilitate the use of hypnotherapy with patients (Olness, 1977).

Our purposes in writing this chapter are first to present the reader with a broad overview of hypnosis with children, including current trends and limitations, uses of hypnotherapy in a medical setting, and correlates of hypnotic responsiveness. Second, we want to share our experience and provide practical information about assessing factors associated with effective hypnotherapy and the use of children's hypnotic responsiveness scales. A six-phase hypnotherapeutic approach is presented, along with brief case illustrations. Finally, we speculate about future trends in hypnosis with children.

Current Trends and Limitations

Hypnotherapy has been used with children for more than 200 years. However, interest has increased significantly in recent years, as reflected in the growing number of publications in the area. A bibliography of hypnotism in pediatrics (Weitzenhoffer, 1959), published more than 20 years ago, contained 86 references spanning the years 1886 to 1969. In contrast, 114 references were cited for the last 25 years in a bibliography published by Gardner in 1980. Acceptance of hypnosis by health professionals has been cyclical in nature, with a decline in the first half of this century. Renewed interest in the field was stimulated by the publication of Ambrose's (1961) book *Hypnotherapy With Children,* which reviews the successful use of hypnotherapy to treat a wide range of children's problems. Gardner and Olness' (1981) recent book on child hypnotherapy surveys the current state of the field, reviewing the literature, practices, and controversies in the field.

Several factors may be contributing to the greater use of hypnotherapy with children, including an increased population of children surviving with serious chronic illnesses who are in need of strategies to cope with the pain and anxiety related to their disease and treatment; the publication of dramatic case presentations describing the successful use of hypnotherapy; and increased training opportunities in hypnotherapy offered in universities, professional schools, and workshops. Although the wider acceptance of hypnotherapy may provide an effective adjunct to current treatments, awareness of limitations of this treatment modality is essential.

First, a health professional should not attempt to treat a problem with hypnotherapy unless he or she is also competent to assess the problem and recommend other therapies if necessary. Expertise in one's primary health profession, knowledge of child development, and the ability to establish good rapport with children are prerequisites to the effective use of hypnotherapy with children.

Second, it is now recognized that hypnotic responsiveness is, to a great degree, a talent that lies within the client and that even those who are highly responsive may not be able to use hypnosis effectively for all purposes (*e.g.*, pain control). Only 1% to 2% of an unselected population are "hypnotic virtuosos" who can experience everything the hypnotist suggests (E.R. Hilgard and J.R. Hilgard, 1975). The hypnotherapist is now viewed in the role of a coach or guide who can aid in the directing of hypnotic abilities toward the accomplishment of therapeutic goals. Accordingly, in contrast to previous authoritarian approaches, the current trend is toward more permissive types of hypnotic inductions, with a special emphasis on teaching clients self-hypnosis (Fromm et al., 1981; Gardner, 1981; Ruch, 1975).

Third, there is a need for a more careful set of diagnostic procedures and a realistic appraisal of the proportions of successes to be expected when using hypnosis for different procedures. A hypnotherapist attempting to use hypnosis may assume that his technique is faulty if he does not succeed in a high enough proportion of cases, when he may in fact be doing as well as can be expected (E.R. Hilgard and J.R. Hilgard, 1975).

Fourth, many of the reports of successful treatment with hypnotherapy have been in the form of individual clinical case reports or quasi-experimental studies. More studies are needed in which subjects are randomly assigned to experimental and control groups drawn from the same population; all subjects are assessed for hypnotic responsiveness; other factors possibly contributing to significant treatment effects are explored; and methodology is presented in sufficient detail to permit replication.

Uses of Hypnotherapy

Hypnotherapy has been used as the primary or adjunctive treatment for a wide range of childhood problems. We limit our review to the uses of hypnotherapy in a medical setting and refer the reader who is interested in the hypnotherapeutic treatment of children with primary emotional and learning problems to Gardner and Olness (1981) and Gardner (1980). In the care of children with medical problems, hypnotherapy has been used in the treatment of pain and anxiety, chronic life-threatening illnesses, psychophysiological disorders, pediatric surgery, and habit disorders. Each problem area is reviewed, with emphasis on the presentation of controlled studies when available.

Pain and Anxiety

Within medical settings, hypnotherapy is frequently requested for the control of anxiety and pain associated with acute and chronic illnesses and related procedures. The relationship between hypnotizability and pain reduction through hypnosis is not perfect; however, there is a 50% greater probability of successful pain reduction for those highly responsive to hypnosis (E.R. Hilgard and J.R. Hilgard, 1975).

The best single predictor of success in pain reduction is the amount by which pain is reduced when such hypnotically suggested reduction is first attempted. Measured hypnotic responsiveness is the next best predictor. The Hilgards' experiments with training in both hypnotic responsiveness and in hypnotic analgesia showed that adults with little talent for hypnosis improve their skills only slightly with training. In contrast, adults with considerable hypnotic ability initially can profit from special training in hypnoanalgesia.

Since children as a group demonstrate greater hypnotic responsiveness than adults, it would be expected that they would be more successful at using hypnotherapy for pain control. In fact, this was the finding in a controlled experimental study of the usefulness of hypnotherapy in the relief of acute pain in burn patients (Wakeman and Kaplan, 1978). Forty-two burn patients, ranging in age from 7 to 70, were matched on the basis of age and extent of total body burns (*i.e.,* 0% to 30% and 31% to 60%) and assigned to hypnotherapy and control groups. The treatment groups received hypnotherapy with an emphasis on self-hypnosis and suggestions for hypnoanalgesia, dissociation, and reduction of anxiety. During equivalent time spent with the control groups, the primary therapists offered general verbal support, but no specific suggestions for pain control. All subjects were allowed an *ad lib* selection of analgesic medication, and the percentage of the maximum allowable medication requested by each patient was calculated. Significantly lower percentages of medication were used by the hypnotherapy groups than by the control groups. In addition, children and adolescents (ages 7 to 18) used significantly less medication than the adult groups (ages 19 to 30 and 31 to 70), suggesting a more effective utilization of hypnotherapy as an adjunct to medication for pain control. This research represents one of the better controlled experimental studies of the effectiveness of hypnotherapy available in the literature owing to its use of a large number of subjects matched on the variables of age, severity of condition, and therapist's attention. It is unclear whether subjects were randomly assigned to treatment and control groups. Although Wakeman and Kaplan concluded that hypnosis was the single most important variable in patient responses, assessment of patient hypnotic responsiveness prior to group assignment would have contributed to even greater confidence in these findings.

Clinical case studies of severely burned children treated with hypnotherapy are reported by Bernstein (1965) and LaBaw (1973). Hypnotherapy has also been successfully used to reduce the pain and anxiety associated with cancer (Dash, 1980; Gardner, 1976; Gardner and Olness, 1981; J.R. Hilgard and Morgan, 1978; Hodel, Hoffmann, and O'Grady, 1982; Hodel, O'Grady, and Steffen, 1982b;

LaBaw et al., 1975; Olness, 1981), sickle cell anemia (Zeltzer, Dash, and Holland, 1979), accidental injury (Jones, 1975), surgical procedures (Bensen, 1971; Cullen, 1958; Jones, 1977), migraine headaches (Gardner and Olness, 1981), and gastrointestinal disorders (Williams and Singh, 1976). Variations in the experience of pain depend on such factors as individual difference in pain tolerance; the context of the pain, including adult expectations that the discomfort is manageable; and the emotional significance of the pain. Currently, there is no research showing which hypnoanalgesic techniques yield the best results with children of different ages, suffering different kinds and degrees of pain.

Investigators (Crasilneck and Hall, 1973; E.R. Hilgard and J.R. Hilgard, 1975; J.R. Hilgard and Morgan, 1978; Shacham and Daut, 1981) emphasize the importance of differentiating the constructs of anxiety and pain, while acknowledging that anxiety can intensify the pain experience and pain can cause anxiety. J.R. Hilgard and Morgan's (1978) experience in treating children with cancer suggests that it is necessary to use methods of anxiety reduction prior to giving suggestions for pain reduction. Once anxiety is reduced, the patient is better able to experience hypnotic analgesia. However, ability to control anxiety was only minimally correlated with hypnotic responsiveness as assessed by the Stanford Hypnotic Scale for Children. In addition, anxiety could be successfully reduced by the use of relaxation and distraction methods without the use of hypnotherapy. Reducing anxiety may be necessary but not sufficient for controlling pain through hypnotherapy (Crasilneck and Hall, 1973).

The relationship between depth of trance and effectiveness of hypnoanalgesia appears to be curvilinear. Although hypnotic depth can vary rapidly within the same subjects, in general, the greater the depth of trance, the more likely that the suggestions for pain relief will be successful (Crasilneck and Hall, 1973). A more profound trance is required to relieve pain than to control anxiety (Hilgard and Hilgard, 1975). However, subjects experiencing extremely deep trances are unlikely to respond to suggestions for pain control.

Although the usefulness of hypnotherapy for pain control has been demonstrated both clinically and experimentally, the theoretical basis for its effectiveness is not yet understood (E.R. Hilgard and J.R. Hilgard, 1975; E.R. Hilgard, 1977). Hilgard proposes a two-component interpretation of pain reduction through suggestion and hypnosis. The first component, involving little alteration of the general state of consciousness, consists of waking suggestions for relaxation and anxiety reduction and can be used by practically all subjects. The second component, available only to the more hypnotizable subjects, involves profound dissociations in the information-processing subsystems related to overt pain and covert pain.

For patients responsive to hypnoanalgesia, indicators of pain that are under voluntary control, such as crying out, grimacing, and catching breath, are consistently found to be reduced more than are relatively involuntary or physiological indicators (*e.g.,* heart rate and blood pressure), suggesting that at some level the body is responding to the signals of painful stress upon it. According to laboratory experiments of hypnoanalgesia, the hypnotized subject is processing the painful stimulation, but it is masked by an amnesialike barrier from conscious awareness. About half of those able to reduce their pain substantially through hypnotically suggested analgesia are able to uncover a concealed experience of pain through the special techniques of automatic writing or talking. Upon inquiry, "another part" of some subjects, dissociated from the hypnotized part of the subject, acknowledged higher pain at the sensory level (covert pain) while the "hypnotized part" reported low levels of overt pain. Hilgard uses the metaphor of a "hidden observer" to characterize the additional information that is reported in a very objective manner by "some part" of the subject that is aware of the covert pain.

Additional theoretical bases for hypnoanalgesia may be provided by investigators of the neurochemical and neurophysiological aspects of pain. Endorphins and enkephalins are endogenous morphinelike peptides, which create an analgesic effect when released into the blood. Olness, Wain, and Ng (1980) and Goldstein and Hilgard (1975), however, have been unsuccessful thus far in establishing a relationship between endorphins and hypnotic analgesia. Further theoretical consideration of hypnoanalgesia are reviewed by Saccerdote (1970) and Dash (1980), and behavioral and neurochemical aspects of pain and reviewed by Varni and his associates (Varni, Katz and Dash, in press).

Chronic and Terminal Illnesses

Children with chronic and life-threatening illnesses often feel little personal control over the course of their disease and treatment, and this contributes to feelings of extreme anxiety, futility, and despondency. The successful use of hypnotherapy, especially self-hypnosis, for ego support as well as to reduce disease and treatment-related symptoms has great potential for the types of mastery experiences that enhance self-efficacy expectations and alleviate anxiety and depression.

Hypnotherapy has been used as an adjunctive treatment in a wide variety of chronic diseases in children including cancer (J.R. Hilgard and Morgan, 1978; LaBaw et al., 1975; Olness, 1981), diabetes (Gardner and Olness, 1981), juvenile rheumatoid arthritis (Cioppa and Thal, 1975), traumatic brain injury (Crasilneck and Hall, 1970), seizures (Gardner and Olness, 1981; Williams, Spiegel, and Mostofsky, 1978), and cerebral palsy (Lazar, 1977).

Cancer. With the considerable improvement in childhood cancer survival rates in the last decade, hypnotherapy has become widely used not only to alleviate symptoms associated with the disease process itself, but to cope with the distressful side effects of repeatedly administered treatment procedures. Many patients experience nausea and vomiting associated with chemotherapy, and pain and anxiety related to bone marrow aspirations, lumbar punctures, and intravenous injections. In a study by Zeltzer (1980), adolescents with cancer, in contrast to other chronically ill adolescents, reported their treatment to be worse than their disease and considered treatment-related symptoms to be their most severe problem.

Individual case studies of the successful use of hypnotherapy to alleviate disease- and treatment-related symptoms in pediatric cancer patients have been reported by Crasilneck and Hall (1973), Gardner (1976), Dash (1980), Miller (1980), and Zeltzer (1980). A case study of a terminally ill adolescent presented by Ellenberg and her colleagues (Ellenberg et al, 1980) is noteworthy in that self-reports of the severity of multiple symptoms were provided prior to and after hypnosis. The results showed that hypnotherapy was most effective in reducing the anxiety and acute pain associated with bone marrow aspirations, headaches, and backache. Heterohypnosis was found to be more effective than self-hypnosis as the illness progressed.

Several large-scale studies present cumulative results collected over years, for a series of pediatric cancer patients. LaBaw and his associates (LaBaw et al., 1975) treated 27 children, ages 4 to 20, over a 2-year period in twice monthly group hypnotherapy sessions. Individual hypnotherapy training sessions were also available for patients; however, the number of patients requiring individual treatment was not reported. The use of self-hypnosis was encouraged and thought to be related to treatment outcome. There was no control group or objective evaluation of results. Results were based on informal observations of patients' functioning subsequent to training and were reported in the form of case reports of 12 patients who represented varying degrees of success, from poor to excellent. Positive outcomes included reduced anxiety, longer sleep periods, more adequate nutritional intake and retention, and greater tolerance of therapeutic procedures.

Olness (1981) more recently reported on her clinical experience with cancer patients consecutively referred for self-hypnosis training for symptom relief at the Minneapolis Children's Health Center. The children, ranging in age from 3 to 18 at time of referral, had been followed from 2 to 5 years, or until death. Training consisted of an average of four practice sessions in the hospital, two or three more individual practice sessions at 2-week intervals following discharge, and participation in an optional twice monthly group session. A tape cassette of individualized exercises was provided for home use. Assessment of relief from pain of procedures and from nausea was based on clinical observations and reduction of need for analgesic or antinausea medication. More substantial symptom relief was associated with referral at time of initial diagnosis and regular practice. All 12 patients referred at the time of initial diagnosis demonstrated substantial symptom relief. Younger children (ages 5 to 11) were able to attain pain and nausea control after an average of two sessions, in contrast to older children (ages 12 to 18) who were able to reduce anxiety and nausea in two sessions, but required four sessions to achieve pain control. Olness attributes the difference to a diminishing in imagery skills after age 11. A success rate of 90% is reported (Gardner and Olness, 1981). However, no objective measures or control group was employed in the study.

A measure of hypnotic responsiveness, The Stanford Hypnotic Clinical Scale (SHCS), was administered to 34 patients, ages 4 to 19 years, in a 3-year study conducted by J.R. Hilgard and Morgan (1978). Approximately 50% of the children experienced substantial symptom relief. Of the 16 children referred for relief of anxiety and pain associated with bone marrow aspirations and spinal punctures, none of the ten younger children (ages 4 to 6) experienced substantial relief. In contrast, four of six older children (ages 7 to 13) were successful in achieving symptom relief. Hilgard attributes this difference to the lack of young children's responsiveness to standard hypnotic procedures. It is suggested that young children are more responsive to "protohypnosis," distraction by external stimulation (*e.g.,* a story) rather than imaginative involvement in their own fantasy, which is characteristic of formal hypnosis. In addition, these children were extremely anxious, as a consequence of previous diagnostic and treatment procedures. In contrast, 12 of the 25 subjects in the Olness study received hypnotherapy prior to undergoing distressful procedures, which may have contributed to her higher rate of success. Hilgard and Morgan note that the anxiety can be reduced by the use of relaxation and distraction methods without formal involvement in hypnosis. Accordingly, these results might be expected to correlate minimally with hypnotic responsiveness. Once anxiety is reduced, hypnotic analgesia can be used to reduce felt pain.

In a controlled study of 35 pediatric cancer patients (ages 7 to 17), Zeltzer and LeBaron (1982) compared the efficacy of hypnotherapy with nonhypnotic behavioral intervention techniques in reducing pain and anxiety during bone marrow aspirations and lumbar punctures. Independent observers and patients themselves rated pain and anxiety during baseline and intervention procedures. Baseline ratings of pain and anxiety experienced during bone marrow aspirations were significantly higher than those for lumbar punctures. Although both types of treatment resulted in significant pain reduction, hypnosis was significantly more effective than nonhypnotic techniques in reducing pain. Anxiety reduction during bone marrow aspirations followed a similar pattern. Both treatment strategies were equally effective in reducing pain and anxiety associated with lumbar punctures, usually a less stressful and painful procedure.

In addition to symptom relief, hypnotherapy has also been used to enable seriously ill children to cope with the terminal stages of their disease (Gardner and Olness, 1981; Gardner, 1976; Zeltzer, 1980). Attempts to modify the disease process itself through the use of self-hypnosis to enhance immunologic responses are described by Olness (1981) and Gardner and Olness (1981). Acknowledging that there is no supporting scientific evidence that imagery techniques affect the course of potentially terminal diseases, they would not discourage a patient from practicing imagery therapy, provided other prescribed treatment was continued.

Hemophilia. For children with hemophilia, hypnotherapy has been used to reduce bleeding episodes as well as to relieve pain and anxiety. In a controlled study by LaBaw (1975), 20 male hemophiliacs, ranging in age from 5 to 48 years, were randomly assigned to hypnotic treatment and nontreatment control groups. Hypnotherapy was provided in twice monthly group sessions over a 30-month period. Participants were encouraged to use self-hypnosis to alleviate pain and reduce the severity of their illness. Results showed that the hypnotic treatment group required significantly fewer units of blood than did the nontreatment control group. The effect of age on treatment outcomes was not reported.

Sickle Cell Anemia. Hypnotic imagery of vasodilation was used to alleviate pain during sickling crises of two 20-year-old men with sickle cell anemia (Zeltzer, Dash, and Holland, 1979). A comparison of pain-related hospital contacts 12 months pre- and 8 months posthypnosis training showed a marked decrease in the frequency of emergency room visits and hospitalizations for pain. In addition, reduced analgesic needs and increased attendance at school and work were demonstrated.

Psychophysiological Problems

Other medical problems with autonomic nervous system components, including asthma (Collision, 1975; Diamond, 1959; Gardner and Olness, 1981), allergies (Perloff and Spielgelman, 1973), and nausea and vomiting (Gardner, 1976; Gardner and Olness, 1981) have been treated by hypnotherapy.

Many case studies attest to the dramatic improvement in asthmatic children treated with a wide variety of hypnotherapeutic techniques, including hypnoanalytic and other insight-oriented methods: suggestions for ego strengthening and symptom relief; relaxation training; and teaching patients to increase and decrease wheezing. However, Gardner and Olness (1981) note that training in biofeedback or relaxation strategies have also resulted in positive outcomes. They suggest that factors contributing to improvement may include enhancement of mastery, reduction of anxiety resulting in physiological changes, relaxation of bronchial smooth muscle, changes in parental attitudes and behavior, and resolution of unconscious conflicts. Asthma attacks may be precipitated by psychological factors (intrinsic asthma) or by external stimuli, such as allergies (extrinsic asthma). It is the intrinsic asthma that is most responsive to hypnotherapeutic interventions. In a review of 121 asthmatic patients treated with hypnotherapy, Collison (1975) found that patients most likely to benefit from treatment were age 20 or younger, demonstrated high hypnotic responsiveness, lacked steroid dependency, and had significant emotional factors in the etiology of their disease (*i.e.,* intrinsic asthma).

Forty of 55 asthmatic children treated by Diamond (1959) achieved complete remission of their symptoms and remained asymptomatic during a 2- to 4-year follow-up period. Hypnoanalytic techniques employed included age regression to the time of the first asthma attack and insight-oriented approaches.

Surgery

Although hypnosis is rarely used as the sole anesthetic in major surgery, it has been used as an adjunct to chemical anesthesia. It is also occasionally used to avoid the use of general anesthesia in minor procedures. The successful use of hypnosis with 35 surgical patients, 14 of whom were children or adolescents, was reviewed by Hoffman (1959). Induction techniques appropriate for patients from infancy through 20 years of age were presented by Cullen (1958). Benson (1971) reported on the use of postanesthetic suggestions with surgical patients in the recovery room. Of the 30 posttonsillectomy children given suggestions for rapid and uncomplicated convalescence, only four required analgesic medication following surgery. According to Gardner and Olness (1981) the use of hypnotherapy in pediatric surgery may result in the reduction or omission of preoperative sedation, easier induction of general anesthesia, and increased postoperative comfort and cooperation. Hypnotherapy can facilitate emergency room procedures by modifying negative expectations and providing anxiety and pain relief.

In a controlled pilot study of the effects of hypnotherapy on expressions of anxiety and pain following surgery (Gaal, Goldsmith, and Needs, 1980), the children, ages 5 to 10, undergoing tonsillectomy were divided into hypnotic treatment and control groups. The hypnotic treatment consisted of a 10-minute induction immediately prior to surgery and tape-recorded suggestions for postoperative feelings of comfort after the induction of anesthesia. The control group interacted socially with the experimenter for 10 minutes immediately prior to surgery and heard a tape-recorded story. After surgery, the hypnotic treatment group was significantly less anxious than the control group, as assessed by independent observers, and experienced significantly less postoperative pain, as assessed by self-reports and their need for chemical analgesics.

Habit Disorders

Among the childhood habit disorders responsive to hypnotherapy are enuresis (Olness, 1975; Olness, 1976; Gardner and Olness, 1981), tics (Gardner and Olness,

1981), hair pulling (Gardner, 1978b), thumb-sucking (Mohlman, 1973; Staples, 1973) nail biting, and habitual drug use (Baumann, 1970).

The effectiveness of hypnotherapy is dependent on the child's motivation for overcoming the habit and his willingness to take the primary responsibility for change. Gardner and Olness (1981) suggest that motivation can be assessed directly by verbal questioning or indirectly through ideomotor signaling while the child is in a state of hypnosis (*i.e.,* raising fingers to indicate "yes" or "no"). It is helpful to explore how the habit inconveniences or embarrasses the child and the child's perceptions of the positive consequences of overcoming the habit. If the child finds the habit more pleasurable than inconvenient and is in treatment owing to parental pressure, hypnotherapy is unlikely to be successful and should be postponed. In contrast, the prognosis is favorable if the hypnotized child indicates a desire to change his behavior. Gardner and Olness used a trial of four to six hypnotherapy sessions to determine whether the child was really ready to overcome the habit. During hypnotherapy, suggestions emphasize the patient's competence, ability for mastery, and images in which the habit disorder has been resolved. Parents are encouraged to express confidence that their child can indeed resolve his problem.

Gardner and Olness (1981) presented a detailed description of the hypnotherapeutic treatment of enuresis and encopresis. Olness (1975) reported that 31 of 40 children, ages 4 to 16 years, with nocturnal enuresis were successfully treated with hypnotherapy. Most of the children were cured within 1 month. According to Stanton (1979), 20 of 28 enuretic children, ages 7 to 18 years, were successfully treated after one to three sessions through a hypnotherapeutic approach that emphasized indirect suggestion, distraction, ego enhancement, and confidence building. Fifteen of the children had maintained their "cure" at a 1-year follow-up.

Detailed behavior modification approaches developed by Azrin and associates (Azrin and Foxx, 1974; Azrin and Nunn, 1973; Azrin and Nunn, 1974; Azrin, Sneed, and Foxx, 1973) have also proved to be effective in treating childhood habit disorders, including enuresis, encopresis, and tics. Comparative studies are needed to indicate which treatment or combinations of treatments may be most effective for different patient populations. Factors such as age, hypnotic responsiveness, and severity and duration of disorder may moderate treatment outcomes.

Hypnotic Responsiveness in Children

Children, as a group, are highly responsive to hypnosis. As with adults, the induction of hypnosis results in an altered state of consciousness characterized by narrowed attention, absorption in the phenomena of the trance, and detachment from the surrounding external environment (Fromm et al, 1981). The adaptive use of hypnosis, both planned and spontaneous, can often be observed in infants and children as they focus on repetitive stimulation (*e.g.,* rocking, thumbsucking) or engage in fantasy. Although hypnosis is a natural phenomenon, there is variability among children in hypnotic responsiveness related to many variables.

In exploring the correlates of children's hypnotizability, Gardner and her colleagues (Gardner, 1974a; Gardner and Hinton, 1980; Gardner and Olness, 1981) suggested that the fact that children, as a group, are more hypnotizable than adults (London, 1965; London, Morgan, and Hilgard, 1973) is possibly attributable to factors in the child's natural waking state (*e.g.,* fantasy play, daydreaming) that are similar to hypnotic behaviors. Cognitively, children routinely engage in the focused concentration, concrete thinking, limited reality testing, and use of fantasy characteristic of the hypnotic state. Emotionally, children's eagerness for new experience, intensity of feeling, desire for mastery, and willingness to experience regressive states contribute to their hypnotizability. On an interpersonal level, children are more likely than adults to be responsive to authority and to acknowledge the need for help. Additional variables that may affect children's hypnotizability include parents' cooperation and involvement, hypnotherapist's skills, and situational constraints (*e.g.,* time limitations, attitude of medical staff).

Despite the face validity of the variables presented, Gardner emphasizes the need for research to indicate which correlates are necessary but not sufficient and to evaluate their relative significance. Studies exploring the relationship of childhood hypnotic responsiveness and the factors of age, genetics and parent–child interactions, cognitive development, and imaginative involvement will be briefly reviewed.

Age

The relationship between age and hypnotic responsivity is complex. Most normative studies have concluded that hypnotizability is limited in young children, achieves its apex during the middle childhood years of 7 to 14, and then decreases somewhat in adolescence, remaining stable through mid-life before decreasing again in the older population (Gardner and Olness, 1981). It should be noted that no significant differences in hypnotic responsivity have been found between boys and girls of any age. London has conducted several normative studies using the Children's Hypnotic Susceptibility Scale (London, 1963). Using data from 59 children, London (1962) found that children were often more successful on almost all of the Children's Hypnotic Susceptibility Scale items when compared with adults on the Stanford Hypnotic Susceptibility Scale. However, London was unable to establish a significant curvilinear relationship between age and susceptibility, although there was a trend in that direction.

In a standardization study with a group of 240 children, London (1965) found a modest curvilinear relationship between age and susceptibility, with the peak in the 9- to 12-year range. Standard deviations were large at all ages. London noted, however: "The extent of susceptibility or lack of it among different children within a single age group is more impressive than are changes across ages" (London, 1965, p 195).

A normative study by Morgan and E.R. Hilgard (1973) of hypnotic susceptibility for 1232 subjects, ranging in age from 5 to 78 years, based on a modified Stanford Hypnotic Susceptibility Scale Form A (Weitzenhoffer and E.R. Hilgard, 1959), also found a peak in susceptibility in the preadolescent years and a gradual decline thereafter. A more recent study based on the Stanford Hypnotic Clinical Scale for Children (Morgan and J.R. Hilgard, 1979) led to similar conclusions about heightened hypnotizability in middle childhood.

Despite the consistency of the studies showing limited hypnotizability in young children, Gardner and Olness (1981) question these conclusions because of clinical data indicating that children of preschool age and younger respond positively to the therapeutic uses of hypnosis. They suggest that the hypnotizability of young children is underestimated owing to the use of inappropriate induction techniques, the uncertain validity of hypnotizability scale items, and the difficulty of assessing hypnotizability in young children. Young, immature children often resist suggestions for eye closure, and accordingly, they score low on hypnotic susceptibility scales based on an eye closure–relaxation induction. In the development of the Stanford Hypnotic Clinical Scale for Children, Morgan and Hilgard (1979) found that 4- to 8-year-old children, using an active imagination induction, passed items reflecting hypnotic phenomenon that they had previously failed with an eye closed–relaxation induction. These results led to the inclusion of a form for children 4 to 6 years of age using an active imagination induction in addition to the form for children 6 to 16 years, using the eye closure–relaxation induction. However, even with the use of appropriate induction techniques, available scales do not show children of 4 to 6 years to be as hypnotizable as older children, and these scales are not applicable to children younger than 4.

Although some infants and preschool children exhibit spontaneous behaviors that are similar to behaviors associated with hypnosis in adults, one can question, as Gardner and Hinton (1980) noted, whether these behaviors in young children are really the equivalent of similar behaviors in older children and adults. The problem of defining hypnosis is especially relevant for the very young age-group. According to J.R. Hilgard and Morgan (1978), children in this age-group respond more readily to what they named "protohypnosis," that is, external distraction, such as listening to a story, in contrast to distraction through self-controlled fantasy.

With regard to the decline in hypnotic responsiveness in adolescence, J.R. and E.R. Hilgard (E.R. Hilgard, 1971; J.R. Hilgard, 1970) suggest that the increasing need for reality-based competencies and achievements diminishes the imaginative involvement thought to be an important factor in hypnotizability.

Genetics and Parent–Child Interactions

According to a study by Morgan and associates (Morgan and E.R. Hilgard, 1973; Morgan, E.R. Hilgard, and Davert, 1970) there appears to be a genetic contribution to hypnotizability. In a study of 140 pairs of twins, ages 5 to 22, hypnotizability in monzygotic twins was found to be significantly related both for males and for females. In contrast, no significant relationship was found for dizygotic twins or for nontwin sibling pairs. There was, however, a low but significant relationship between mean parent and mean child susceptibility. In addition, a positive correlation was found between personality resemblance and hypnotizability for either sex child and the like sex parent. No such interaction existed for either sex and the opposite sex parent. These results were interpreted as suggesting an environmental contribution to hypnotizability, based mainly on identification with the like sex parent and modeling of that parent's behavior.

In contrast, highly hypnotizable subjects were found to identify most strongly with opposite sex parents in two retrospective studies of young adults (J.R. Hilgard, 1970; J.R. Hilgard and E.R. Hilgard, 1962). The families of highly hypnotizable subjects were characterized by a combination of warmth and strict discipline, a setting in which the children knew what was expected. J.R. Hilgard hypothesized that these young adults' readiness to conform to authority, even if it seemed rather illogical, increased their hypnotizability.

In a longitudinal study by Nowlis (1969), a stern, restrictive, and punitive home environment at the time the children were in kindergarten was related to high susceptibility to hypnoticlike experiences when the children reached the 12th grade in high school. Cooper and London (1976) concurrently studied parent–child relationship and childhood hypnotizability. Parents of highly hypnotizable subjects tended to rate themselves as more strict, anxious, and impatient than the parents of low hypnotizable subjects.

The role of parent–child relationships in hypnotic responsiveness in children has also been explored from a theoretical point of view, with emphasis on the regressive aspects of the hypnotic relationship. Call (1976) suggests that what is elicited during hypnotic induction is the child's subjectively experienced relationship with the powerful, internalized, omnipotent parent image. Several of the studies cited above lend credence to this view.

Cognitive Development

Although research has found only a low positive correlation between intelligence and hypnotizability, those using hypnotic induction with the retarded child and adolescent must take into account the mental age of the patient. Gardner and Olness (1981) report successful hypnotherapy with relatively mildly retarded children in the 50-to-70 IQ range. However, in their experience, more severely retarded children usually respond poorly to hypnotic induction and suggestions owing to their inability to relate to the therapist, focus attention selectively, and follow instructions.

Imaginative Involvement

It is generally accepted that the use of imagination is an important factor in hypnotic responsiveness. Research by J.R. Hilgard (1970) has shown a positive relationship between various kinds of imaginative involvement and hypnotizability in adults. Highly hypnotizable adults report engaging in a variety of imaginative involvements since childhood. In the highly hypnotizable subjects, imagination was typically related to stimuli outside the person rather than artistic or inner-stimulated imagination.

Vividness of imagery is also positively related to hypnotizability (E.R. Hilgard, 1977), with the highly hypnotizable showing high imagery and the low hypnotizable little imagery. However, imagery itself is not predictive of hypnotizability because many with high imagery are not hypnotizable. The role of imagination in hypnosis apparently involves some ability to make use of the images that are present in some special manner, if imagery ability is to lead to hypnotizability.

Hypnotic responsiveness in children has often been related to their imaginative skills and involvement (Ambrose, 1961; Erickson, 1958; Gardner, 1974a; Gardner, 1978a; Gardner and Olness, 1981). Changes in hypnotic responsiveness with age are often explained in terms of the development and the decline of imaginative skill (Hilgard, 1970). Nevertheless, there has been little research on the relationship between children's imaginative involvement and hypnotic responsiveness.

In one study by London (1966) of a larger number of personality variables thought to be related to childhood hypnotizability, no relationship was found between children's hypnotic susceptibility scores and items concerning use of imagination, including imaginary playmates, extent of dreaming, and imaginative games. A significant correlation was found between age and susceptibility for children low in imagination, but there was no age–susceptibility relationship for children who were high in imagination.

In summary, empirical studies have resulted in few definitive findings about correlates of childhood hypnotic responsiveness. Studies conducted thus far have identified few highly significant variables, with the exception of age. If as London observes, responsiveness is a stable personality trait that is normally distributed in the population, then the task is to assess for which children hypnotherapy is applicable and under what conditions.

Assessment

Hypnotherapy is currently underutilized in most medical settings although it is associated with few risks and negative side effects, has great appeal to children, and provides effective treatment for a wide range of childhood medical problems.

In considering the use of hypnotherapy to treat an individual child with a specific medical problem, the following questions may aid in assessing factors related to the child, the medical problem, and the treatment milieu. Affirmative answers are more likely to be indicative of successful treatment outcomes.

CHILD VARIABLES

1. Has a positive relationship been established between the therapist and child?
2. Does the child have medium-to-high hypnotic responsiveness as assessed by standardized scales? (Scales are discussed in this section.)
3. Would benefits from relief of the problem outweigh secondary emotional gains (*e.g.*, extra attention) the child may currently be receiving as a result of his or her medical problems?
4. Is the child free of underlying serious emotional problems that might be aggravated by the use of hypnosis?
5. Is the child motivated to solve his or her problem and take responsibility for practicing the self-hypnosis skills?

MEDICAL PROBLEM VARIABLES

1. Have possible organic etiologies of symptoms been evaluated and treated if necessary?
2. Has the efficacy of other treatment modalities for the medical problem been explored?
3. Does the literature or personal experience suggest that hypnotherapy could be used as a primary or adjunctive treatment for the medical problem?

TREATMENT MILIEU VARIABLES

1. Do parents agree to the use of hypnosis with their child?
2. Are parents' attitudes about hypnosis favorable? (Preparing parents for the use of hypnotherapy is discussed in a later section.)
3. Will other members of the treatment team, doctors and nurses, cooperate in the use of hypnotherapy with the patient?

In assessing the appropriateness of using hypnotherapy with an individual child, hypnotic responsiveness can be formally evaluated by means of two specially designed scales: The Children's Hypnotic Susceptibility Scale (London, 1963) and the Stanford Hypnotic CLinical Scale for Children (Morgan and J.R. Hilgard, 1979).

The Children's Hypnotic Susceptibility Scale

Cooper and London (1978) have operationally defined susceptibility as the frequency with which a subject acts as a hypnotized person when the responses are elicited by a standardized procedure. A standardized induction procedure and quantitative system for assessing responses to this induction are provided in the Children's Hypnotic Susceptibility Scale (CHSS). London patterned the CHSS after the Stanford Hypnotic Susceptibility Scales for adults (Weitzenhoffer and E.R. Hilgard, 1959, 1962, 1963), rewriting the items to make them more suitable for use with children. The CHSS consists of 22 items, divided into two parts. The ten items in part two, including suggestions for anesthesia, age regression, and visual and auditory hallucinations, are considered more difficult than those in part one. The scale requires 45 to 60 minutes of administration time for each child. A shorter form of the scale, however, results from using part one only (the first 12 items), with little loss of reliability.

In order to assess children over a wide age range, two forms of the test were developed. The form for children ages 5 to 12 and the one for children ages 13 to 16 contain the same items and differ only in the wording of some of the instructions.

The standardization sample for the CHSS consisted of 240 children, including ten girls and ten boys at each age level from 5 to 16. The scale was found to be highly reliable as measured by both simultaneous observations of independent judges and retest performance of the children. The children's mean score of 8.16 for the first 12 items of the CHSS was significantly greater than adults' mean score of 5.25 on the Stanford Hypnotic Susceptibility Scale, suggesting greater hypnotic susceptibility in children. Subjects between the ages of 8 and 16 obtained the highest scores; those between 5 and 7 years obtained the lowest scores. In follow-up studies, Cooper and London (1971) found that, although susceptibility is a remarkably stable trait, correlations decreased in time, as the time interval between testing increased, perhaps indicating the trend towards decreasing hypnotic responsiveness with approaching adulthood.

With regard to validity, the scale is composed of items of hypnotic phenomenon that are themselves samples of the behavior that the test seeks to measure, and thus it provides face validity. Cooper and London suggested that predictive validity is attested to by the demonstration that some of the higher and lower scoring subjects made relatively better or poorer hypnotic subjects at a later date. However, no references to studies are reported.

Stanford Hypnotic Clinical Scale for Children

Morgan and J.R. Hilgard (1979) developed a short, seven-item hypnotic susceptibility scale that can be administered in 20 minutes. Since the scale was designed for clinical use, attempts were made to select items that would provide every child with some success, in addition to discriminating levels of hypnotic responsiveness. Items to which the child was responsive could later be utilized in hypnotherapy. The Stanford Hypnotic Clinial Scale for Children (SHCS-Child) is available in two forms: the standard form for children ages 6 to 16 and the modified form for children ages 4 to 8 who prefer not to close their eyes.

The initial construction was a five-item scale consisting of hand lowering, visually hallucinated television, a dream, age regression, and posthypnotic suggestion to reenter hypnosis at a hand-clap signal. Information was gathered by testing 98 children, ages 5 to 16, on the five-item scale and the Stanford Hypnotic Susceptibility Scale, Form A (Weitzenhoffer and Hilgard, 1959). The latter scale is designed for use with adults, and appropriate modifications in wording were made for use with children. A moderate correlation was found between the two scales (*i.e., r* = .67).

Consistent with other studies of susceptibility in childhood (*e.g.,* Barber and Calverley, 1963; Morgan and E.R. Hilgard, 1973), there was a peak in susceptibility scores on the SHCS-child between the ages of 8 and 12, with a slight decline thereafter. The five-item scale had little discriminating power for children at the peak susceptibility ages. Two more difficult items were subsequently added: arm rigidity, which is considerably more difficult than hand lowering, and an auditory hallucination of the television suggestion. The revised seven-item scale was administered to 170 children, ages 3 to 14 years, who were randomly assigned to one of two induction conditions. One condition consisted of the conventional relaxation-eye closure induction in which the child was urged to close his eyes. The other condition involved an active imagination induction in which the child was given suggestions to fantasize about engaging in a favorite activity, but it was suggested that "it might be easier with your eyes closed." Differences in responsiveness to items were found to depend on age and type of induction used. It is not until age 11 that 90% of the children prefer to close their eyes, and those who close their eyes do not always keep them closed. Motor involvement was a significant factor for the 3 to 6 year olds, and more children in this age range passed motor items under an active imagination induction than under a relaxed induction.

Based on the findings, Morgan and Hilgard developed a modified form of the SHCS for use with the child who does not like to close his eyes, especially the child under 6 years. This form uses an eyes-open, active imagination induction and eliminates the posthypnotic suggestion. Morgan and Hilgard observe that participation of the adult along with the child is necessary both to begin the fantasy and to sustain it for the 3 to 5 year olds. However, by age 6 years, imagination is developed enough for the child to sustain fantasy, although some stimulation by an adult may still be necessary.

Morgan and J.R. Hilgard addressed the fear that the use of a scale is contraindicated in a clinical setting because of problems of rapport. In their experience, if hypnosis was presented in a permissive style, there appeared to be no discouragement over failures. Children appeared quite comfortable, and the experience was positive. Morgan and J.R. Hilgard suggest countering failure on items with comments such as "We're just as interested in what people don't experience as we are in what people do experience" or "We have to find out those things that are best for you."

No information is provided about the reliability of the scales. There are thus far two published studies that have used the SHCS-Child. Morgan and J.R. Hilgard (1979) found that the relationship between hypnotic responsiveness as assessed by the SHCS-Child and the effectiveness of symptom relief achieved through hypnotherapy was "probabilistic only." Of 10 children with ancillary symptoms (*e.g.,* anxiety reaction, depression, insomnia, nausea, high blood pressure), all those scoring medium or high in hypnotic responsiveness showed substantial or excellent symptom relief. Two children low in hypnotic responsiveness failed to improve, although two other low scorers achieved excellent symptom relief, with one reducing blood pressure and the other learning to relax. Hilgard and Morgan did not consider the possibility that these low-scoring children achieved symptom relief through relaxation methods, rather than formal hypnosis. In a study by Zeltzer and LeBaron (1982), hypnotic responsiveness as measured by the SHCS-Child was not correlated with pain and anxiety reduction achieved through hypnotherapy owing to the restricted range of scores. Eighty-one percent of the 35 pediatric cancer patients scored in the highly susceptible range.

In our experience, the SHCS-Child can easily be incorporated into initial hypnotherapy sessions owing to its brevity and the generally appealing selection of items (Hodel et al., 1982a). However, the predictive validity of hypnotic responsiveness scales for children has yet to be established. Greater refinement of the present scales may be necessary, including the addition of more difficult items of hypnotic phenomenon (*e.g.,* hypnoanalgesia), in order to better assess whether symptom relief achieved during the process of hypnotherapy is actually attributable to hypnotic responsiveness. Having addressed issues related to assessment, we now present a six-phase approach to hypnotherapy that we have found useful in our work with children.

Considerations and Techniques With Children

The use of hypnosis with children can be divided somewhat arbitrarily into six phases: (1) preparation, (2) induction, (3) deepening, (4) suggestions, (5) posthypnotic suggestions, and (6) termination. There are important practical considerations and variations in techniques for children and adolescents, as compared to adults, in each of these six phases.

Preparation

As noted earlier, most children over 7 or 8 years of age are excellent, if not the best, hypnotic responders. Given this situation, the critical problem in this phase is more typically that of securing the parents' cooperation rather than that of the child. Parents are best viewed as potential allies for increasing the probability of their child's successful use of hypnosis.

Gardner (1974b) has provided a useful three-step approach to preparation of parents consisting of (1) education, (2) observation, and (3) experience of hypnosis for themselves. The educational step is directed toward defining hypnosis in familiar terms as well as dispelling the myths of loss of control, revelation of secrets, or fear of not being dehypnotized. The parents' misconception about and fears of hypnosis are actively elicited so that they may be corrected and dispelled. Why and how hypnosis might be useful to their child is discussed. We often find it helpful to describe the actual induction, deepening techniques, and probable suggestions that will be given to their child. Parents, with few exceptions, are accepting of the explanations and highly motivated to have their child try this new technique. As with the children, the degree of success with parents is determined more by the relationship skills of the therapist than by his hypnotic skills. The term hypnosis should not be avoided. The use of hypnosis without discussion of it as hypnosis, for fear of losing cooperation, is usually more risky than the rare loss of cooperation of the few parents who might object to the term. We do find that some parents and health professionals feel more comfortable in thinking of the process as "guided imagery" or special use of imagination, but that is best left to their choice. The clinician's fear of parents not accepting "hypnosis" is usually unfounded.

Allowing and encouraging the parents to observe the process with their child is a helpful second step in preparation. We usually try to work first with the child alone to avoid any inhibition the child may feel in the presence of the parents. In the second training session, the child is asked if it is all right with them for their parent to observe. Most children are eager and proud to demonstrate their newly learned skill. Occasionally, the child may not wish to separate from the parents in the first session. In such cases, the initial induction is done in the parents' presence. The child usually separates easily in the next session.

The third step, suggested by Gardner, of having the parents experience hypnosis for themselves has not been found to be necessary or practical in most cases. However, during the observation, some parents do report achieving a light trance, which they experience as relaxing, and they are often comforted, knowing that their child might feel similar pleasant sensations. In any case, such an experience, although not necessary for the child's success, often enhances the cooperation and support of the parent in later phases, in which encouragement of the child may be helpful.

Preparation of the child varies with age and medical situation. Between the ages of 3 and 6 years, hypnosis is introduced through play. The children are usually told that they will be able to learn a way to help themselves to get away from undesirable fear and discomfort related to procedures, and possibly to become more the "boss of their body."

Because of difficulties with sustaining eye closure in this age-group, the preparation and induction focuses heavily on assessing and using the child's preferred methods of play. The distinction between preparation and induction is usually somewhat unclear, in that preparation is brief and concrete, with induction beginning as the child shares his or her favorite television shows, dolls, heroes, or places. Preparation for children between approximately ages 6 and 10 years usually consists of more emphasis on how hypnosis is a skill that will help them relax. They are often told that we will teach them, if they wish, to use their favorite images or pictures to relax and get away from the fears and discomfort and to feel more in charge of their feelings and sensations.

From approximately age 11 years, most children and adolescents understand concepts of relaxation and imagination. Examples of each are elicited from them. The importance of their own initiative and ability to use their imagination for relaxation, dissociation, and production of desirable sensations and feelings is emphasized. Most are eager to begin learning this new skill. As noted earlier, there are a few exceptions in which motivation is suspect and other issues must be addressed before proceeding. With increased public interest in relaxation, imagery, and self-help skills, we have found more adolescents who are somewhat familiar with meditation, yoga, and other forms of "quieting" and relaxation skills. Some familiarity with such phenomena often enhances cooperation, trust, and sense of participation.

Finally, as with preparation for any unfamiliar procedure, children and adolescents do best when the therapists do what they say they will do, as well as respect and reinforce the child's reasoning ability and need for a sense of initiative, competence, and control.

Induction

The choice of method of induction depends to some extent on age, preference of therapist, and situation. A list of induction techniques for different age-groups can be found in Gardner and Olness (1981). Hilgard and Morgan (1978) have demonstrated that between ages 3 and 6 years induction based on imagination is more effective than relaxation. After 6 years, there appears to be little difference in the effectiveness of either technique. To characterize hypnosis as a deeply relaxed state is to limit it unnecessarily. Active, alert hypnosis can be induced, involving strenuous participative activity. Accordingly, children may be in motion during practice sessions, yet deeply involved in active imagination and successful in achieving desired symptom control (Olness, 1981). Insisting that the 3 to 6 year old close his or her eyes is usually counterproductive. Involving children of any age in imaginative play, helping them pretend that they are going on a trip with a favorite character, or that their doll or toy animal is feeling sleepy, or that they are able to play while a procedure is being done on the "friend," often is sufficient for the child to enter hypnosis.

Deepening and suggestions are then given directly to them or indirectly through their "friends" or characters in the stories that are developed. Since many of these children do not close their eyes and do move frequently, the question of whether they are hypnotized is raised. Morgan and Hilgard (1979) have referred to this situation as "protohypnosis." After approximately age 6 years, techniques such as the coin drop, arm lowering, and eye fixation are frequently used. These techniques can facilitate eye closure, which then allows for the use of relaxing visual images and increased involvement in favorite television shows or favorite places.

Induction with adolescents is often similar to that with adults (*i.e.,* taking a few deep breaths, closing their eyes, and imagining progressive relaxation with gradual involvement in favorite scenes). We have found, however, that ideomotor techniques such as arm drop or the coin technique often produce more dramatic results in the first training sessions, allowing the adolescents to experience the power of their imagination in controlling parts of their bodies. Because the ultimate goal is usually to teach skills of self-hypnosis, the adolescents are told that there are many different ways to enter the hypnotic state and that they will gradually find the best techniques for them.

Deepening

To some degree, deepening is another way of saying "involving." In this phase, children or adolescents are guided toward more and more involvement in their imagination. Whether one thinks of this deepening phase as helping the child to disassociate further, to become more involved in the role of being hypnotized, or to enter a trance depends on the therapist's theoretical preferences. Because children seem able to make the necessary shift to the hypnotic state more quickly than adults, the deepening phase is usually shorter than with adults.

Suggestions

Although it may be obvious to experienced hypnotherapists, the difference between inducing hypnosis and giving effective suggestions needs to be emphasized. Although there are often benefits from the deep relaxation and distraction of attention associated with the induction of effective hypnosis, the development of suggestions for the individual child or adolescent can be a difficult task for the beginning hypnotherapist.

It is not unusual for hypnotherapists in training to find themselves at a "loss for words" once they have induced hypnosis. Many training programs emphasize learning a wealth of induction procedures with little attention being paid to techniques for developing effective wording, as well as timing and connecting of suggestions with stimuli in stressful situations. As Dash (1980) has indicated, a verbalization of but a few minutes can produce a medium-to-deep trance in most children. In our experience, the greatest amount of time is spent in interviewing the children to find the words that are most meaningful for them—the words that will produce the images that help them cope with pain and anxiety, feel more confident in controlling their habits, imagine sensations counter to troublesome physiological states, or see and feel themselves coping with and recovering from surgical procedures.

Using a permissive approach, the therapist emphasizes the participation of the child as much as possible with use of favorite images from past experiences, fantasy, television, or movies, which are determined in an interview with the child during the preparation stage, as well as in subsequent treatment sessions. More extensive descriptions of a permissive approach to developing suggestions for many medical problems are provided by Gardner and Olness (1981). However, a few examples might be helpful to illustrate the techniques.

Case 1

Alan S. is a 19-year-old adolescent with leukemia who was referred to one of the authors after showing much distress prior to, during, and after spinal taps and bone marrow aspirations. He had read about the possible benefits of hypnosis for his situation and requested the referral. He was taught a number of induction techniques until he found that the one or two, eye roll, and arm-lowering, were best for him in inducing self-hypnosis. Favorite places and their most involving details were determined, with his help. Because of the prospect of many future spinal taps and bone marrow aspirations, these favorite scenes were developed: (1) being alone in his bed at home on a sunny summer morning, (2) canoeing in Canada early in the morning, and (3) sailing on his favorite lake. In this case, after induction and later self-induction and deepening, he was helped to visualize three doorways and asked to choose one. Talking with the hypnotized patient to monitor depth or involvement was always important in the early sessions. During one particularly difficult spinal tap, necessitating numerous puncturers, the hypnotherapist actually used two of three favorite scenes, shifting from one "doorway" to another. It also became apparent that, at times, suggestions of more active images, such as "you are pulling strongly on the paddle, feeling the strain in your arms," were more effective in reducing distress and pain than were suggestions of peaceful and relaxing images. At other times, combining suggestions of dissociation of the lower half of his body and direct suggestion of anesthesia seemed most effective. The development of the most effective suggestions took place over three or four sessions, with much emphasis on debriefing or carefully checking with the patient after each treatment session.

Case 2

Ann L. is a 5-year-old girl with second and third degree burns on her face and neck received from scalding water that fell off the stove. The primary goal of hypnotherapy in her case was to help her tolerate the change of dressing and soakings done by her mother at home. Eye closure, as often happens, was difficult to obtain until it was determined that her favorite scene was sitting on a large stuffed chair at home. In the training sessions she was able to imagine herself sitting in the chair listening to music and holding her soft blanket while her mother changed the dressing. She was also taught the "switch technique" whereby she could reduce sensation in her face and neck by imagining that the switch in her head that controlled the "pain messages" was turned off by herself. Even with a 5 year old, careful interviewing before, during, and after hypnosis facilitated the development of effective suggestions. This patient, her mother, and the surgeon were amazed at how well she was able to tolerate the necessary procedures. The surgeon was also astonished at the rate of recovery. Obviously, this example is not meant to rule out other explanations for the increased pain tolerance and apparent acceleration of recovery, but rather to emphasize the importance of an individualized approach maximizing the patient's own skills.

Case 3

One final case illustrates the difficulties sometimes encountered when a patient is not well motivated to change his behavior even though he is responsive to hypnosis. Alice S. is an 11-year-old girl with multiple tics, including eyeblinking, shoulder shrugging, and head turning. She was referred by neurology for possible relaxation training, since the tics were viewed by the neurologist as psychogenic. The girl and her parents seem interested in trying hypnosis. Induction using an arm drop was very easy, but Alice S. seemed unable to learn self-hypnosis and usually resisted suggestions that she could control the tics. In fact, it was difficult to develop suggestions with her because she had difficulty thinking of why she would like to be rid of the tics. The tics apparently were a source of much secondary gain, since her parents and grandmother spent much time attending to them. The parents also were not convinced that medication was not the answer and eventually returned to the neurologist for medication, which was somewhat helpful. Ideally, the hypnotherapist will be able to identify the unmotivated child and unconvinced parents before undertaking hypnosis. It may happen, however, that one has proceeded only to find oneself with a hypnotically responsive child with whom effective suggestions are not being developed because the child does not want to change for various reasons.

In summary, the development of effective suggestions is the most important aspect of hypnotherapy. Evoking rather than imposing pleasurable past images and positive coping images is generally more effective. The more skilled the hypnotherapist becomes at involving the child and adolescent in all phases of hypnosis the more likely the suggestion will have the desirable effect.

Posthypnotic Termination and Suggestions

Posthypnotic suggestions are given to the child during hypnosis to increase the likelihood of desirable behavior after hypnosis is terminated. Usually, suggestions are made about practice of self-hypnosis and the ease of subsequent inductions. These suggestions may be strictly verbal or may evoke images of practicing readily and enthusiastically in the future. Since our ultimate goal is usually to teach self-hypnosis, these posthypnotic suggestions for practicing the procedure are very important. Again, a permissive approach is used to encourage the child or adolescent to find his own best ways of induction or entering, deepening, and terminating hypnosis.

Termination is sometimes spontaneous, but usually the therapist guides the child or suggests techniques to the child to help him or her learn to return to an alert, aware, and refreshed state. We often count 1, 2, and 3 to signal the return to a more usual mode of consciousness. Once in a while a child may enjoy the imagery so much or feel rushed, in which case he may not open his eyes on the count of 3. For the beginning hypnotherapist this experience can be disconcerting.

In all such cases, a somewhat more demanding statement for termination is effective. After hypnosis, further discussion with the child about the need for termination may be helpful in reducing such resistance.

After termination, images and suggestions are reviewed with the child, not only to select the more effective ones for subsequent use, but also to give the child the idea that active participation on his part is highly desirable.

Future Trends

There is little doubt that hypnosis is being used increasingly with children in general and particularly with children having medical problems. As more emphasis is placed on treatment of the "whole" child, any technique that offers the child the possibility of symptom relief as well as a greater sense of self-control over responses to medical diagnostic and treatment procedures is likely to gain increased acceptance. The demand, however, for more rigorous scientific examination of hypnosis and hypnotherapy is also likely to increase. Research designs that do not control for threats to internal validity or alternative explanation besides hypnosis, as well as external validity or generalizability to a wide variety of conditions, are likely to have less impact on practice. Fortunately, recent studies of hypnosis in pediatric populations are using larger samples, controlling for alternative explanations with random assignment and appropriate comparison groups, and attempting to measure both independent and dependent variables (Wakeman and Kaplan, 1978).

A number of trends that are likely to continue are evident in hypnosis research and practice with children. First, clinical applications with children in medical settings are increasing both in terms of the range of problems being treated and size of samples. Second, increased recognition of enduring individual differences in children's hypnotic responsiveness has led to a greater demand for routine measurement of hypnotic responsiveness. The development of the shorter SHCS-Child has facilitated this trend, and further refinement of this scale is likely to continue. Third, the finding of greater effectiveness of evoked versus imposed suggestions, both in terms of the quantity and richness of images, is likely to lead to further study of variables associated with the learning of self-hypnosis. Finally, the advances in the psychophysiology of pain (Varni et al, 1982), although not yet clearly linked to hypnosis, should provide exciting possibilities for the future relief, comfort, and recovery of children with medical problems.

References

Ambrose G: Hypnotherapy With Children, 2nd ed. London, Staples, 1961
Azrin NH, Foxx RM: Toilet Training in Less Than a Day. New York, Simon and Schuster, 1974

Azrin NH, Nunn RG: Habit reversal: A method of eliminating nervous habits and tics. Behav Res Ther 11:619, 1973

Azrin NH, Nunn RG: A rapid method of eliminating stuttering by a regulated breathing approach. Behav Res Ther 12:279, 1974

Azrin NH, Sneed TJ, Foxx RM: Dry bed: A rapid method of eliminating bedwetting (enuresis) of the retarded. Behav Res Ther 11:427, 1973

Barber TY, Calverley DW: "Hypnotic-like" suggestibility in children. J Abnorm Soc Psychol 66:589, 1963

Baumann F: Hypnosis and the adolescent drug abuser. Am J Clin Hypn 13:17, 1970

Bensen VB: One hundred cases of post-anesthetic suggestion in the room. Am J Clin Hypn 514:9, 1971

Bernstein HR: Observations on the use of hypnosis with burned children on a pediatric ward. Int J Clin Exp Hypn 13:1, 1965

Call JD: Children, parents, and hypnosis: A discussion. Int J Clin Exp Hypn 24:149, 1976

Cioppa FJ, Thal AD: Hypnotherapy in a case of juvenile rheumatoid arthritis. Am J Clin Hypn 18:105, 1975

Collison DR: Which asthmatic patients should be treated by hypnotherapy? Med J Austr 1:776, 1975

Cooper LM, London P: The development of hypnotic susceptibility: A longitudinal (convergence) study. Child Develop 42:487, 1971

Cooper LM, London P: Children's hypnotic susceptibility, personality, and EEG patterns. Int J Clin Exp Hypn 24:140, 1976

Cooper LM, London P: The Children's Hypnotic Susceptibility Scale. Am J Clin Hypn 21:170, 1978

Crasilneck HB, Hall JA: The use of hypnosis in the rehabilitation of complicated vascular and post-traumatic neurological patients. Int J Clin Exp Hypn 145, 1970

Crasilneck HB, Hall JA: Clinical hypnosis in problems of pain. Am J Clin Hypn 15:153, 1973

Cullen SC: Current comment and case reports: Hypno-induction techniques in pediatric anesthesia. Anesthesiology 19:279, 1958

Dash J: Hypnosis with pediatric cancer patients. In Kellerman J (ed): Psychological Aspects of Childhood Cancer. Springfield, Charles C Thomas, 1980

Diamond HH: Hypnosis in children: The complete cure of forty cases of asthma. Am J Clin Hypn 1:124, 1959

Ellenberg L, Kellerman J, Dash J, Huggins C, Zeltzer L: Use of hypnosis for multiple systems in an adolescent girl with leukemia. J Adoles Health Care 1:132, 1980

Erickson MH: Pediatric hypnotherapy. Am J Clin Hypn 1:25, 1958

Fromm E, Brown D, Hurt S, Oberlander J, Boxer A, Pfeifer, G: The phenomena and characteristics of self-hypnosis. Int J Clin Exp Hypn 29:189, 1981

Gaal JM, Goldsmith L, Needs RE: The use of hypnosis, as an adjunct to anesthesia, to reduce pre- and post-operative anxiety in children. Presented at the annual meeting of The American Society of Clinical Hypnosis, Minneapolis, November 1980

Gardner GG: Hypnosis with children. Int J Clin Exp Hypn 22:20, 1974(a)

Gardner GG: Parents: Obstacles or allies in child hypnotherapy? Am J Clin Hypn 17:44, 1974(b)

Gardner GG: Attitudes of child health professionals toward hypnosis: Implications for training. Int J Clin Exp Hypn 24:63, 1976

Gardner GG: Childhood, death, and human dignity: Hypnotherapy for David. Int J Clin Exp Hypn 24:122, 1976

Gardner GG: Hypnosis with infants and preschool children. Am J Clin Hypn 19:158, 1977

Gardner GG: The use of hypnotherapy in a pediatric setting. In Gellert R (ed): Psychosocial Aspects of Pediatric Care. New York, Grune & Stratton, 1978(a)

Gardner GG: Hypnotherapy in the management of childhood habit disorders. J Pediatr 82:838, 1978(b)

Gardner GG: Hypnosis with children: Selected readings. Int J Clin Exp Hypn 28:289, 1980

Gardner GG: Teaching self-hypnosis to children. Int J Clin Exp Hypn 28:300, 1981

Gardner GG, Hinton RM: Hypnosis with children. In Burrows GD, Dennerstein L (eds): Handbook of Hypnosis and Psychosomatic Medicine. New York, Elsevier, North-Holland Biomedical Press, 1980

Gardner G, Olness K: Hypnosis and Hypnotherapy with Children. New York, Grune & Stratton, 1981

Goldstein A, Hilgard ER: Lack of influence of the morphine antagonist naloxone on hypnotic analgesia. Proc Nat Acad Sci 72:2041, 1975

Hilgard ER: Hypnosis and childlikeness. In Hill JP (ed): Minnesota Symposia on Child Psychology, vol 5. Minneapolis, Lund Press, 1971

Hilgard ER: Divided Consciousness: Multiple Controls in Human Thought and Action. New York, John Wiley & Sons, 1977

Hilgard ER, Hilgard JR: Hypnosis in the Relief of Pain. Los Altos, CA, William Kaufman, 1975

Hilgard JR: Personality and Hypnosis: A Study of Imaginative Involvement. Chicago, University of Chicago Press, 1970

Hilgard JR, Hilgard ER: Developmental-interactive aspects of hypnosis: Some illustrative cases. Genet Psychol Mon 66:143, 1962

Hilgard JR, Morgan AH: Treatment of anxiety and pain in childhood cancer through hypnosis. In Frankel FH, Zamansky HS (eds): Hypnosis at its Bicentennial: Selected Papers. New York, Plenum Press, 1978

Hodel TV, Hoffmann C, O'Grady DJ, Steffen JS: Hypnosis for leukemic children for coping with medical procedural distress. Presented at the American Psychological Association Annual Meeting, Washington, D.C., August 22–26, 1982a

Hodel TV, O'Grady DJ, Steffen J: Hypnosis for leukemic children for alleviation of anxiety and pain. Presented at the American Psychological Association Annual Meeting, Washington, D.C., August 22–26, 1982b

Hoffman E: Hypnosis in general surgery. Am Surg 5:163, 1959

Jones CW: Hypnosis and spinal fusion by Harrington instrumentation. Am J Clin Hypn 19:155, 1977

Kellerman J: Psychological Aspects of Childhood Cancer. Springfield, Charles C Thomas, 1980

LaBaw WL: Adjunctive trance therapy with severely burned children. Int J Child Psychother 2:80, 1973

LaBaw WL: Auto-hypnosis in haemophilia. Haematologia 9:103, 1975

LaBaw W, Holton C, Tewell K, Eccles D: The use of self-hypnosis by children with cancer. Am J Clin Hypn 17:233, 1975

Lazar BS: Hypnotic imagery as a tool in working with a cerebral palsied child. Int J Clin Exp Hypn 25:78, 1977

LeBaron S: Hypnotic treatment of chronic pain and bleeding in hemophilia: Preliminary successes, failures, and problems. Presented at the 31st Annual Scientific Meeting of the Society for Clinical and Experimental Hypnosis, Denver, November 1979

Lewis S: Considerations in setting up psychological consultation to a pediatric hematology–oncology team. J Clin Child Psychol 7:21, 1978

London P: Hypnosis in children: An experimental approach. Int J Clin Exp Hypn 10:79, 1962

London P: Children's Hypnotic Susceptibility Scale. Palo Alto, CA, Consulting Psychologists Press, 1963

London P: Developmental experiments in hypnosis. J Project Tech Person Assess 29:189, 1965

London P: Child hypnosis and personality. Am J Clin Hypn 8:161, 1966

Miller JA: Hypnosis in a boy with leukemia. Am J Clin Hypn 22:231, 1980

Mohlman HJ: Thumbsucking. In A Syllabus on Hypnosis and a Handbook of Therapeutic Suggestions. DesPlaines, IL, The American Society of Clinical Hypnosis Education and Research Foundation, 1973

Morgan AH, Hilgard ER: Age differences in susceptibility to hypnosis. Int J Clin Exp Hypn 21:78, 1973

Morgan AH, Hilgard ER, Davert EC: The heritability of hypnotic susceptibility of twins: A preliminary report. Behav Genetics 1:213, 1970

Morgan AH, Hilgard JR: The Stanford Hypnotic Clinical Scale for Children. Am J Clin Hypn 21:148, 1979

Nowlis DP: The child-rearing antecedents of hypnotic susceptibility and of naturally occurring hypnotic-like experience. Int J Clin Exp Hypn 17:109, 1969

Olness K: The use of self-hypnosis in the treatment of childhood nocturnal enuresis: A report on forty patients. Clin Pediatr 14:273, 1975

Olness K: Autohypnosis in functional megacolon in children. Am J Clin Hypn 19:28, 1976

Olness K: In-service hypnosis education in a children's hospital. Am J Clin Hypn 20:80, 1977

Olness K: Imagery (self-hypnosis) as adjunct therapy in childhood cancer: Clinical experience with 25 patients. Am J Pediatr Hematol Oncol 313, 1981

Olness K, Wain HJ, Ng L: A pilot study of blood endorphin levels in children using self-hypnosis to control pain. Develop Behav Pediatr 1:187, 1980

Peebles MJ, O'Malley F: Problems in mental health consultation facing the professional in training. J Clin Child Psychol 7:68, 1978

Perloff NM, Spiegelman J: Hypnosis in the treatment of a child's allergy to dogs. Am J Clin Hypn 15:269, 1973

Ruch JC: Self-hypnosis: The result of hetero-hypnosis or vice versa. Int J Clin Exp Hypn 23:282, 1975

Sacerdote P: Theory and practice of pain control in malignancy and other protracted or recurring painful illnesses. Int J Clin Exp Hypn 18:160, 1970

Shacham S, Daut R: Anxiety or pain: what does the scale measure? J Consult Clin Psychol 49:468, 1981

Stanton HE: Short-term treatment of enuresis. Am J Clin Hypn 22:103, 1979

Staples LM: Thumbsucking. In A Syllabus on Hypnosis and a Handbook of Therapeutic Suggestions. DesPlaines, IL, The American Society of Clinical Hypnosis Education and Research Foundation, 1973

Varni JW, Katz ER, Dash J: Behavioral and neurochemical aspects of pediatric pain. In Russo DD, Varni JW (eds): Behavioral Pediatrics: Research and Practice. New York, Plenum Press, 1982

Wakeman RJ, Kaplan JZ: An experimental study of hypnosis in painful burns. Am J Clin Hypn 21:3, 1978

Weitzenhoffer AM: A bibliography of hypnotism in pediatrics. Am J Clin Hypn 2:92, 1959

Weitzenhoffer AM, Hilgard ER: Forms A and B. Stanford Hypnotic Susceptibility Scale. Palo Alto, CA, Consulting Psychologist Press, 1959

Weitzenhoffer AM, Hilgard ER: Stanford Hypnotic Susceptibility Scale, Form C. Palo Alto, CA, Consulting Psychologist Press, 1962

Weitzenhoffer AM, Hilgard ER: Stanford Profile Scales of Hypnotic Susceptibility, Forms I and II. Palo Alto, CA, Consulting Psychologist Press, 1963

Williams DT, Singh M: Hypnosis as a facilitating therapeutic adjunct in child psychiatry. J Am Acad Child Psychol 15:326, 1976

Williams DT, Spiegel H, Mostofsky DI: Neurogenic and hysterical seizures in children and adolescents. Am J Psychol 135:82, 1978

Zeltzer L: The adolescent with cancer. In Kellerman J (ed): Psychological Aspects of Childhood Cancer. Springfield, Charles C Thomas, 1980

Zeltzer L, Dash J, Holland JD: Hypnotically induced pain control in Sickle Cell Anemia. Pediatrics 64:533, 1979

Zeltzer L, LeBaron S: Comparison of hypnosis and nonhypnotic techniques for reduction of pain and anxiety during bone marrow aspirations and lumbar punctures in children with cancer. (Abstract) Society for Clinical and Experimental Hypnosis for October 1982 meeting

13 Hypnosis in Surgery and Anesthesia

DABNEY M. EWIN

The intent of the surgeon is to take the patient safely through surgery and on to a rapid return to normal health. This requires the patient's cooperation during diagnostic studies, removal of doubts and fears that cause stressful anesthetic responses, minimizing drug toxicity from chemoanesthesia, early ambulation, and freedom from postoperative complications. Much of this can be accomplished without hypnosis (Egbert, Battit, Welch, and Bartlett, 1964), but adding trance and suggestion achieves these results more efficiently and more consistently. The science of suggestion is taking its place among the other biological sciences that pertain to patient care. It need not be time-consuming once it is learned.

The best time to deal with physical and mental postoperative complications is preoperatively. Good mental preparation should clarify misunderstandings, explain what is to come, protect the patient from harmful conversation in the operating room, and promote the expectation of a rapid and comfortable recovery. Hypnosis helps prevent violent arousal (Werbel, 1965), urinary retention (Doberneck, McFee, Bonello, Papermaster, and Wangensteen, 1961), pain (Kolough, 1964; Papermaster et al, 1960) and hiccups (Kroger, 1969), shortens convalescence (Kolough, 1962), and even promotes healing (Bowers, 1979), perhaps by limiting inflammation (Chapman, Goodell, and Wolff, 1959).

Preparation starts with the referral, and the best referral I have ever received was from a mother who told her child, "I'm going to take you to a doctor who is going to get you well by just talking to you." He *is* well (of long-term asthma). The worst was from a surgical associate who said to his patient, "It probably won't work, but we might as well try hypnosis." It didn't work. The prehypnotic suggestion (Alexander, 1971) given by a trusted person in the waking state sets the stage.

Crile (Crile and Lower, 1914) observed that people fearing death from surgery sometimes die. St. Amant in the Anesthesia Department of the Lahey Clinic has reviewed six such deaths* known in Boston as "Voodoo Syndrome" (Cannon, 1957). Finney (Finney, 1934) refused to operate on patients who expressed such fears, and quoted Halstead as doing the same.

When a patient expresses fears, a good screening technique is to use ideo-motor responses to have the patient visualize himself doing well several weeks after surgery. If he is unable to do this, then some analytic questioning should be done to determine the reason. Several of my patients have had terrifying previous experiences with the curariform drugs wherein they were paralyzed, able to hear, and fearful that surgery would start while they were "awake," not knowing that pain sensation is lost before hearing (Thornton and Levy, 1974).

Until that unlikely day when all surgeons, anesthetists, and staff become aware that surgical patients tend to behave as though hypnotized (Cheek, 1962), one of the most protective preoperative suggestions is to "ignore anything that is said or done in the operating room unless you are spoken to directly by name" (Cheek, 1960). This is valuable prophylaxis against much loose talk during surgery, often about some other seriously ill patient, but which may be heard by the patient (*vide infra*) and interpreted as relating to himself.

Taped preoperative suggestions lower anxiety and transfusion requirements as compared to controls (Hart, 1980), but do not allow the patient to ask questions or interact with the physician (Field, 1974). There is a very high correlation between the answer the surgeon gives to the patient's questions about the number of postoperative days in the hospital and when he will be able to return to work and the actual timing of these events (Dohan, Taylor, and Moss, 1960). This literal carrying out of the surgeon's statement is evidence of the hypnoidal state (concentrated attention) that is available for accepting helpful suggestions (Chaves and Barber, 1976; Rodger, 1964). Follow-up reports (Sheffer and Greifenstein, 1960) indicate that 92% of patients experience fear of and apprehension about surgery and anesthesia.

Disturbing reactions to chemical anesthesia in childhood leave lasting effects. Hilgard (Hilgard, Hilgard, and Newman, 1961) reports that 7.7% of unselected volunteers for hypnotic experiments have headaches or anxiety attributable to some difficulty with a previous chemical anesthesia in childhood. Another series (Cheek, 1960) revealed that 43 of 58 patients resistant to hypnosis had had bad experiences with childhood anesthesia, and this was a factor in a most dramatic case (Yanovski and Bricklin, 1967). Surgery need not be frightening to children, and more attention is being given to the beneficial effects of hypnosis (Daniels, 1962; Scott, 1974).

* Personal communication

Informed Consent

Informed consent is a powerful form of suggestion, and can seriously detract from rapport unless it is handled with aplomb. The surgical consent form at this author's hospital includes the following statement:

> I understand and acknowledge that the following known risks are sometimes associated with this procedure and/or anesthesia: death; brain damage; disfiguring scars; paralysis; the loss of or loss of function of body organs; and the loss of or loss of function of any arm or leg.

The object is to impart the truth to his intellect without letting his subconscious drift off into fantasies of disaster (*i.e.,* keep him *out* of trance). One should avoid anything as direct as "*you* could die, be paralyzed, etc." A possible approach would be, "You know that all major surgery carries risks and complications. No one can guarantee that you won't walk across the street and be hit by a car, but by being careful you expect to cross safely. I can't guarantee the outcome of anyone's surgery, but I intend to protect you in every possible way from complications. You should know that with surgery and anesthesia, there have been reports of almost every problem you can name, including death, brain damage, disfiguring scars, paralysis, the loss of or loss of function of body organs, and the loss of or loss of function of any arm or leg. [pause] Before you sign this consent form, do you have any question you would like answered?" If possible, it helps to have a responsible member of the family present to sign as a witness. Properly handled, the consent form can be a means to increase trust without causing apprehension.

Preoperative Visit

Cheek (Cheek, 1962) has an especially lucid description of the characteristics of subconscious mentation in relation to surgery that is recommended reading for all surgeons and anesthetists. He has had many patients review their surgical experiences in trance, and the knowledge of their fears and reactions to sounds heard under anesthesia and in the recovery room (*vide infra*) leads to the development of a series of highly protective and helpful suggestions to be given preoperatively. The preoperative preparation on the evening before surgery can be given by the anesthesiologist, the family physician, or the surgeon. My approach is roughly as follows:

Touch the patient (take his pulse) (Rodger, 1961).

"What do your friends call you? May I call you that?" This implies a more informal relationship in which the patient can safely confide his feelings without fear or ridicule.

"How do you feel about all of this?" This is really a lead in for the next question. The patient, with a certain air of bravado, may say "Okay, I guess." The "I guess" negates the "okay" and indicates that on a subconscious level he is not fully confident.

"Has there been anything on your mind that you haven't mentioned, even if it seems silly?" Any answer should be taken seriously and dealt with fully. Most often it is a thought about something that happened to another person in surgery, and it should be emphasized that each person is different, and everything possible will be done to prevent any such complication in this case, which is special.

"Would you like for me to help you get relaxed to get a good night's sleep and to go easily through surgery tomorrow?" This idea is universally welcomed.

"If you could do anything else you wanted to tomorrow, where would you go for a laughing place?" He has not thought of this as a laughing matter, but with his worries cleared, an escape into fantasy relieves the remaining tension, and laughing in itself is therapeutic (Cousins, 1976). Even if he is not familiar with Disney's movie, *Song of the South,* which popularized Brer Rabbit's song, "Everybody's Got A Laughing Place," the patient will divine the nature of the question and tell what he does for relaxation—fishing, watching television, going to the beach, or other diversion. This can be used for a later visualization.

"Just close your eyelids, roll your eyeballs up towards the top of your forehead, take a deep breath, and as you let it all out let your eyes relax and let every nerve and fiber in your body go (cadenced) loose and limp and lazy-like, your limbs like lumps of lead (pause). You will have an easy day tomorrow if you do what I say. Tonight you should let yourself feel safe and comfortable, sleeping soundly, accepting the fact that you are turning this over to us now. You can help your body heal best by having an attitude that nothing will upset you. [Repeat] Nothing will upset you. In the morning you won't want to eat or drink anything, so that all of your body functions will be at rest. When you receive your pre-op injection here in your room, you should empty your bladder and let the sedative take effect while you relax and go to your laughing place. From the time you leave your room until you return from the recovery room you should simply enjoy your laughing place and completely ignore anything that people say unless you are spoken to directly by name. [Repeat] Completely ignore anything that people say unless you are spoken to directly by name. When your anesthesia is started, all pain sensation is blocked. Some people hear sounds during their operation, and if you do, you will ignore it because you will be feeling no pain and enjoying your laughing place. You will get a constant supply of oxygen through a small tube in the back of your throat. When the surgery is completed, you will be moved to a stretcher and taken to the recovery room. You will gradually awaken just as you do from natural sleep, relaxed and refreshed. You will keep the arm that is getting IV fluids relaxed and still, and if there is an airway in your mouth when you awaken, simply push it out with your tongue or remove it with your free hand since you don't need it when you are alert. You will wake up remarkably comfortable, with a good appetite, and your normal bladder and bowel functions will resume quickly. You will be up walking later in the day. Whatever you need for comfort will be supplied, and your tissues will heal rapidly.

"Now I want you in your imagination just to picture all that I have just told you taking place, and then project ahead in time to when you feel healed and well and ready to leave the hospital, and when you do that, this finger will rise [touch index finger] and a date or the number of days will come into your mind so you can tell me when it is."

If the date is farther in the future than expected, I enquire what seems to take so long if it could be sooner than that.

"Now is the time for you to practice going to your laughing place, enjoying yourself, totally free of responsibility, just goofing off. Go to . . . [visual imagery of patient's own laughing place] . . . and I'll see you tomorrow."

Less than 10 minutes are required if the opening questions do not elicit unusual fears.

Hearing of Meaningful Sounds Under General Anesthesia

When a patient consciously and accurately reports having heard a statement made while under general anesthesia, it is easy to assume that this is only the result of insufficient anesthetic (Scott, 1974). Crile (Crile, 1947) reported in his autobiography the case of a patient and also his own experience under nitrous oxide. Conscious questioning of 150 patients after cesarean section revealed that three accurately recalled factual events, 46 recalled vague dreamlike experiences, and one recalled hearing her obstetrician telling someone else how to perform the surgery (he had supervised a junior colleague) (Wilson and Turner, 1969). However, only five of 1,328 recently anesthetized patients in another series volunteered recollections (Faithfull, 1969). Brunn (1963) reports hearing from the point of view of the patient. These reports alone should alert the thoughtful surgeon to the fact that he does not know which patient is hearing what is said, or how it will be interpreted. Much more significant, however, is the emerging evidence that patients who are known to be under deep surgical anesthesia hear and record meaningful sounds at an *unconscious* level, and these can be recalled later with the use of hypnosis and ideomotor techniques. Cheek (1959) made the first report of a successful planned attempt to recall this information in 1959, has made numerous supplemental reports (Cheek, 1960, 1962, 1962, 1964), and reviewed the literature on the subject in 1979 (Cheek, 1981). His own studies of over 3000 surgical patients and 15 people who had been unconscious owing to head injuries have led to the development of a reliable technique for bringing to conscious levels what was assimilated at an unconscious level during anesthesia or concussion. In trance, signals are established so that one finger will rise to show the beginning of an episode, another will rise each time something upsetting occurs, and another to indicate the end of the review. The patient is told to let his deeper mind review the episode without trying to have any conscious thoughts, and in less than a minute the beginning finger will rise. If there is no movement of the "upset" finger before the "end" signal is given, all is well and very little will be reported because what was heard was not meaningful enough to the patient to merit his attention in a state in which his survival mechanisms were alert only to danger. What usually happens is that the patient first begins to show signs of distress (frowning, defensive posturing, rapid breathing), then the finger signal for the beginning of the experience with one or more "upset" signals, and through to its finish. At this point, the patient may be able to say what he is reacting to, but often cannot. If he cannot do so, he is asked to repeat the review at a subconscious level and he is reassured that he got through it all safely before and it is all right to simply review the memory as many times as necessary and not repress it any longer. In my experience, two or three such subconscious reviews suffice to bring the experience to a verbal level. This technique was used in cases 1 and 4 of my report on constant pain (Ewin, 1980). When signs of distress occur, scanning should be repeated persistently, since it took 13 reviews of the entire operation for Cheek to get his first success in retrieving the memory (Cheek, 1959).

Prospective studies of unconscious levels of hearing show clearly that patients do hear *meaningful* sounds when given by the *person* to whom they are atuned (surgeon, anesthetist) at an *appropriate time* in the procedure. Studies that neglect these three criteria are flawed, and inhibit progress in understanding this problem because the negative result coincides with comfortable, preconceived ideas that no hearing occurs under anesthesia. Common sense and experience with other life situations are illustrative. Surely the surgical patient has his attention fixed on possible danger, and is alert to anything threatening. Any statement about his health or prognosis is *meaningful* and will be noted, just as a mother whose baby is ill can sleep through a thunderstorm but will react if the baby barely coughs. Meaningless sounds are ignored. The *person* who is speaking is significant. A secretary may ignore a co-worker in the secretarial pool telling her to get to work, but react immediately to the voice of the vice-president calling on the intercom. What the surgeon and anesthetist say is accepted, but tape recordings of an unknown voice are not heeded. The patient is able to accept a suggestion at an *appropriate* time. The order to fire the guns of a battleship upon sighting the enemy is good timing, but the same order given while in home port would be questioned as an error. While the patient is under general anesthesia, the appropriate time to give good suggestions for postoperative comfort is after the main procedure is completed and while the skin is being closed. Two prospective studies have been reported in which the surgeon or anesthetist gave these meaningful suggestions at the right time. In one, 50% of 1500 patients required no postoperative pain medication (Wolfe and Millet, 1960), and in another 70% of 200 patients required none (Hutchings, 1961).

Using these criteria, Levinson (Levinson, 1967) studied ten patients who were in a surgical plane of anesthesia (clinically and by EEG). On a signal, the anesthetist pretended alarm about the patient's condition and need for more oxygen, temporarily halting the operation for rebreathing. Several weeks later, an ideomotor review of the surgery was done under hypnosis, and four of the ten were able to report the experience almost verbatim. Four more showed signs of distress and refused to continue with the investigation. The words were meaningful, the right person said them at a critical time, and only two of ten showed no sign of being affected. In contrast, a widely quoted negative study (Abramson, Greenfield, and Heron, 1966) used tape recordings of an unknown voice at an inappropriate time, and the conclusions were based on EEG tracings rather than hypnotic review (which probably would have been negative, too, under this test condition). Pearson's (Pearson, 1961) suggestions were meaningful, even though taped by an unknown voice, and some response occurred in that matched controls stayed an average of 2.42 days longer in the hospital, even though the treating surgeons did not know whether their patients had been given suggestions or a blank tape.

A review (Trustman, Dubovsky, and Titley, 1977) by scholars not actively using hypnotic investigation gives equal weight to negative studies that ignore these three criteria and concludes (erroneously) that the phenomenon of hearing in fully anesthetized patients remains an open question.

Hypnosis as an Adjunct to Chemoanesthesia

The most reliable and effective use of hypnosis in anesthesia is to augment chemical anesthesia. This produces a calm, cooperative patient under local anesthesia (Crasilneck and Hall, 1975) and decreases the amount of anesthetic required under general anesthesia (Bartlett, 1966; Crasilneck, McCranie, and Jenkins, 1956; Fredericks, 1980; Magaw, 1906; Rodger, 1962; Van Dyke, 1970; Wollmann, 1965).

In 1906, Magaw reported 14,380 anesthetics at the Mayo Clinic without an anesthetic death. She stated: "Suggestion is a great aid in producing a comfortable narcosis . . . during the administration, the anesthetist should make those suggestions that will be most pleasing to this particular subject . . . talk him to sleep, with the addition of as little ether as possible." In stomach cases, "as soon as the stomach is explored and the method of operation decided upon, the ether is withdrawn, the surgeon being able to continue operation, no more being given until time to close the incision . . . thus we are able to complete the operation and avoid vomiting with an exceedingly small amount of anesthetic." Since 1900, anesthesia and surgery have changed much, but humans have not, and they still respond to suggestions, both good and bad.

Special conditions make hypnosis combined with local or regional block ideal. Obstetricians and dentists find it particularly useful, as noted in other chapters. Eye surgery is often done under local anesthesia because postoperative vomiting causes increased intraocular pressure, with possible iris prolapse, hyphema, or disruption of the repair. Many of these surgeries involve elderly, high-risk patients, and particularly in emergent situations, local anesthesia alone may be inadequate. Local anesthesia combined with hypnosis works well (Golan, 1975; Lewenstein, Iwamoto, and Schwartz, 1981).

Crasilneck (Crasilneck and Hall, 1975) has reported several cases in which hypnosis supplementing local anesthesia was the key to success. These include preventing unexpected movements while dissecting the facial nerve under local, EEG monitoring to locate a focus of temporal lobe epilepsy in which the waking EEG was necessary, and a chemopallidectomy for Parkinson's disease in which the patient's tremor had to be observed during the procedure.

Knowing that patients hear under general as well as local anesthesia makes suggestion an important part of every procedure.

Hypnosis as the Sole Anesthetic

Hypnosis as the sole anesthetic for a major surgical procedure is valuable in special circumstances. Its occurrence is well-documented (August, 1961; Esdaile, 1957; Kroger, 1963; Marmer, 1959; Steinberg, 1965; Werbel, 1967), and it can no longer be regarded as a curiosity. It is believed that only highly hypnotizable people (about 10%) (Kroger, 1977) can attain this state, even though Esdaile (Esdaile, 1957) did no tests for hypnotizability on his 3000 surgical patients. *Necessity* (*i.e.,* allergy or unavailability of other anesthetics), *motivation* (will to live, intolerable conditions, concern for others), and *belief* (previously accepted or instilled by the hypnotist), when combined, seem to suffice to produce a trance adequate for anesthesia.

On Christmas Day, 1809, Dr. Ephraim McDowell (Schachner, 1921; Sparkman, 1979) performed the first successful abdominal operation in Danville, Kentucky. His patient was a young woman with an enormous ovarian cyst who implored him to operate because she was unable to function and said she would rather die than continue in the state she was in. She managed herself to do what we would call a distraction technique. She told Dr. McDowell that she would let him know when she was ready. She opened her Book of Psalms and started reading out loud, and when she was sufficiently concentrated on this she signaled him to go ahead. She continued to read out loud through the operation, tolerated it well, healed rapidly without infection, and lived for 32 years in good health after the operation (McCormack, 1932). Mrs. Jane Todd Crawford had *necessity, motivation,* and *belief.* In his report of the operation, Dr. McDowell (Schachner, 1921) made no mention of his patient crying, flinching, going into shock, or having muscle spasm, even when she was turned on her side to empty the blood.

I am personally acquainted with a survivor of the Bataan Death March in World War II who developed acute appendicitis in the prison camp in which no surgical facilities were available. Two fellow prisoners, a caring priest and a surgeon, carried him through. He was not even religious, or of the same faith, but he had *necessity* and *motivation,* and the priest imparted *belief* with the quotation, "with God, all things are possible." The patient turned the matter over to God, concentrated on prayers with the priest while the appendectomy was done under unsterile conditions, and healed without complication. He did not "tough it out" with will power. He was simply unaware of any painful sensations. Similar instances were reported in prison camps in Singapore (Sampimon and Woodruff, 1946), where it was noted that only lack of comprehension (mental deficiency and deafness) distinguished the failures from successes.

There are circumstances in which hypnotic anesthesia is particularly valuable. Lewenstein (1978) uses it to take the guess-work out of suture adjustment in strabismus operations. In poor risk patients, Marmer (1959) reported doing mitral commissurotomy, pneumonectomy, coarctation of the aorta, hysterectomy, thyroidectomy, and hemorrhoidectomy under hypnoanesthesia. Transurethral resection (Lait, 1961), ventral hernia (Steinberg and Pennell, 1965), tonsillectomy (Mihalyka and Whanger, 1959), and ceserean section (August, 1960, 1961; Kroger, 1977) have been done under hypnoanesthesia. Werbel (1965, 1967) and Finer (Finer and Nylén, 1961) did skin grafting after patients had been resuscitated from cardiac arrest. Using only self-hypnosis, physicians have undergone cholecystectomy (Rausch, 1980), transurethral resection (Bowen, 1973), ganglionectomy (Maresca and Boyden, 1960), and excision of nodules in the breast and thyroid (Reis, 1966).

Although they regularly deny discomfort, some of these patients show physiologic signs of distress (Johnson and Barber, 1978) (change in vital signs, sweating, facial expressions), but many do not. Finer's case (Finer, et al, 1973) showed no change in blood pressure, pulse, or catecholamine excretions during vein stripping. Stable vital signs were emphasized in Crasilneck's (Crasilneck, Mc-Cranie, and Jenkins, 1956) case 5 and in Rausch's (Rausch, 1980) cholecystectomy under self-hypnosis.

The major disadvantage to hypnosis as the sole anesthetic is that it is not always successful, and in elective cases it is also time-consuming, since the patient must be rehearsed. Kroger (1977) maintains that only 10% of patients are suitable for planned hypnoanesthesia when other anesthesia is available (*i.e.,* necessity is lacking), whereas August (1960) points out that if a patient is already in labor, no prior conditioning is necessary. Barber (1977) used only an average of 11 minutes each to get adequate analgesia in 99 of 100 dental patients. Uncertainty on the part of the hypnotist invites failure by the patient (Pearson, 1973). Any skilled and confident hypnotist who is interested in administering hypnoanesthesia for a major surgical procedure should be conversant with the detailed preparation and techniques already alluded to (August, 1960, 1961; Cheek and LeCron, 1968; Kroger, 1963, 1977).

Clinical Implications of Hearing Under Anesthesia

Just as good suggestions given under anesthesia can improve convalescence (Bensen, 1971; Daniels, 1962; Hutchings, 1961; Kolough, 1964) and control bleeding during surgery (Cheek, 1964; Clawson and Swade, 1975), complications can result from alarming remarks made at critical times. The patient's mind is alert to danger, and he is likely to make the worst possible interpretation of an unclear statement. When President Reagan was shot, a news item reported that a member of the surgical team said "This is it," and the President blanched, took a notepad, and wrote for a nurse, "What does he mean, this is it?"

Cardiac arrest is a serious complication, and one case is reported in which the procedure was going well until the surgeon remarked that the patient was a "horrible risk," and arrest occurred (Wolfe and Millet, 1960). In another case, I was assisting a resident who made a high abdominal incision beside the xyphoid and inadvertently entered the pericardium. He said, "Look at her heart out here flapping in the breeze," and the patient's blood pressure immediately dropped to 70, with a slow pulse. Two doses of vasopressor got no response, so finally at my insistence the resident reluctantly said to her, "Mrs. E., this is Dr. J., everything's all right; get your blood pressure up." Her pressure returned to 120 in less than a minute, and the procedure was completed without further difficulty. Wolfe (Wolfe and Millet, 1960) reports a patient being explored for cancer whose blood pressure progressively rose to 220 and pulse to 120. When the lesion was found to be benign, the knowledgeable anesthetist said, "Dr. X., isn't it wonderful that this man has no cancer," and the pressure rapidly dropped to 120 and the pulse to 70.

The phenomenon of being "frightened to death" is known in primitive societies (Cannon, 1957) and experimental animals (Richter, 1957). In civilized societies after earthquakes, men and women are found dead who show no signs of injury (Haggard, 1929), and during World War II, 200 of 600 people in a London bomb shelter showed no evident cause of death at autopsy. Survivors reported a wave of silent panic after a bomb exploded nearby (Meerloo, 1969). It is interesting that Richter's wild rats (1957) died only when they were conditioned to perceive the situation as "hopeless." In humans, cardiac arrest has been produced hypnotically (Raginsky, 1959) and by self-suggestion (McClure, 1959).

Older surgeons say that there was a general quiet in the operating room before World War II, and complain of lack of decorum since then. It was at that time that residency programs flourished, with verbal teaching during surgical procedures, discussions of other patients who did poorly, and much casual conversation that would have been unthinkable in the presence of an old time "Chief." It is interesting that an extensive review of the world literature from 1924 to 1945 found only 143 reports of cardiac arrest in 21 years (Barber and Madden, 1945), whereas two reviews at university (teaching) hospitals since World War II reveal over 500 each year (rates of 1:1560 and 1:1669 anesthetics) (Beecher and Todd, 1966; Stephenson, 1969). This is in striking contrast to McGaw's 14,380 anesthetics (1906) in which light anesthesia was supplemented with good suggestions throughout the procedure, without a single death reported in 1906. Granted that much higher risks are taken now and more complicated surgery is done at these hospitals, much routine surgery is also done, and many of these patients have complications. The popular television program M.A.S.H. may be unwittingly setting a harmful example for future surgeons with all the levity, sarcasm, and prognostic remarks that are made in the operating suite.

Other complications have been traced to hearing under anesthesia. Levinson's (1967) patient had a severe postoperative depression after surgery for a benign lesion. In hypnotic review, she remembered having heard the surgeon say that it might be cancer, and subsequently got well when disabused of this idea. Bevivino (1981) reported a remarkable case of a woman who had temporary left arm paralysis from a cerebral aneurysm. When full use returned, the aneurysm was ligated without difficulty, but after surgery, she was again paralyzed in the left arm for no known reason. Nineteen years later the procedure was reviewed hypnotically, and she heard the surgeon say "she'll never be the same after this," which she interpreted to mean that her paralysis would return and be permanent. This idea was removed and she began to exercise. Within 3 months, she was using her hand again to comb her hair and for most ordinary activity.

Burns

Aside from the injury itself, seriously burned patients experience nearly every negative emotion that can add to suffering (Ewin, 1978). Both the burn and its treatments are excruciatingly painful, and fear of the next treatment sets in early. The accident is usually caused by someone's carelessness, so either guilt or anger intervenes. A sense of helplessness and hopelessness resulting in depression is common. Nausea and anorexia hinder the increased food intake necessary to meet metabolic demands. It is easy for these patients to become sullen, obstinate, and uncooperative. Artz (Dahinterova, 1967), one of the early advocates of separate burn centers, is quoted as follows:

> The well-motived, secure, individual did extremely well after even the most severe burn injury, whereas individuals without these resources had considerable difficulty adjusting to the result of a massive injury.

Hypnosis can provide this sense of security and motivation, and a number of clinical reports describe burned patients on critical, down-hill courses who reversed direction and healed promptly following hypnosis (Cheek, 1962; Crasilneck, et al., 1955; LaBaw, 1973; Pellicane, 1960).

Early hypnosis (within the first 2 hours after burning) is particularly valuable in limiting the amount of inflammatory reaction to the thermal injury. Brauer and Spira (1966) showed that up to 4 hours postburn a standard "full thickness" experimental burn could be excised and used as a skin graft, demonstrating that deeper dermal layers are not killed by the heat, but by inflammation (Hinshaw, 1963). Chapman (Chapman, Goodell, and Wolff, 1959) showed that the signs of inflammation (heat, pain, redness, swelling) are a *response* to the thermal injury. Since *stimulus* and *response* are separate, a hypnotically imagined burn *stimulus* can evoke an actual burn (painful blister) (Bellis, 1966; Chapman, Goodell and Wolff, 1959; Johnson and Barber, 1978; Ullman, 1947). Likewise, after a true burn stimulus (but before the natural response has occurred), hypnotic anesthesia inhibits or prevents the inflammation. A burned patient who has accepted the suggestion that his wounded area is "cool and comfortable" is easy to treat, optimistic, and heals rapidly (Ewin, 1978, 1979). This is particularly evident in burns of less than 20% of the body surface. In larger burns, inflammatory response occurs as though the mind had been overwhelmed, but the edema is apparently limited, as shown by the fact that with early hypnosis, these patients may require as little as 50% of the fluid calculated by formula for resuscitation (Margolis, 1981). During the first 2 days following a sizable burn, large amounts of fluid shift from the bloodstream into the injured, swollen tissues. When a patient requires a large volume of fluid to maintain blood pressure and urine output during these first 2 days, he must later mobilize most of this back into the circulation. In older patients with weak hearts, this can result in fluid overload, pulmonary edema, and heart failure. To safely cut in half the amount of fluid given during shock resuscitation could be life-saving.

When a newly burned patient arrives in the Emergency Room, his mind is concentrated and hypnosis is usually easy to induce. Since he may be a stranger to the physician, the first communication is an introduction and suggestion:

VERBALIZATION	COMMENT
Doctor: "I'm Dr. ____ and I'll be taking care of you [pause]. Do you know how to treat this kind of burn?"	This question is to bring to his immediate attention that he does not know and that he must put his faith in the medical team. Precise wording is important because if you ask "Do you know anything about treating burns?" he may know *something* and tell you about butter, Solarcaine, or kiss-it-and-make-it-well, which is a complete avoidance of recognizing the dependence.
Patient: "No."	The standard reply. In the rare instance of a physician or nurse who actually does know about burns, you simply use that knowledge to say, "Then you already know that you need to turn your care over to us and that we will do our best."
Doctor: "That's all right, because we know how to take care of this, and you've already done the most important thing, which was to get to the hospital quickly. You are safe now, and if you will do what I say, you can have a comfortable rest in the hospital while your body is healing. Will you do what I say?"	This exchange lets the patient know that he is on the team and has already done his biggest job, so he can safely lay aside his fight or flight response (he's already fled to the hospital, which mobilizes hormones that interfere with normal immunity and metabolism. It includes a prehypnotic suggestion (Alexander, 1971) that he is safe and can be comfortable if he makes a commitment.
Patient: "Yes," or "I'll try."	With his affirmative answer he has made a hypnotic contract that is as good as any trance.
Doctor: "The first thing I want you to do is turn the care of this burn completely over to *us,* so you don't	Frightened patients tend to constantly analyze each sensation and new symptom to report to the doc-

VERBALIZATION

have to worry about it at all. The second thing is for you to realize that *what you think* will make a great deal of difference in your healing. Have you ever seen a person blush, or blanch white with fear?"
Patient: "Yes."

Doctor: "Well, you know that nothing has happened except a thought, an idea, and all of the little blood vessels in the face have opened up and turned red, or clamped down and blanched. *What you think* is going to affect the blood supply to your skin, and that affects healing, and you can start right now. You have had happy, relaxing, enjoyable thoughts to free up all of your healing energy. Brer Rabbit said 'everybody's got a laughing place,' and when I tell you to go to your laughing place, I mean for you to imagine that you are in a safe, peaceful place, enjoying yourself, totally free of responsibility, just goofing off. What would you do for a laughing place?"
Patient: "Go to the beach . . . or . . ."

Doctor: "Let's get you relaxed and go to your laughing place right now, while we take care of the burn. Get comfortable and roll your eyeballs up as though you are looking at the top of your forehead and take a deep, deep, deep breath and as you take it in, gradually close your eyelids and as you let the breath out, let your eyes relax and let every nerve and fiber in your body go

COMMENT

tor. By turning his care over to *us* (the whole team), he is freed of this responsibility and worry. Next, his attention is diverted to something he had not thought of before.

Even dark-skinned patients are aware of this phenomenon in light-skinned people.
The patient needs something he perceives as useful to occupy his time. The laughing place may be the beach, television, fishing, golfing, needlepoint, playing dolls, etc. It becomes the key word for subsequent rapid inductions for dressing changes, etc.—to simply "go to your laughing place."

It helps the doctor to know what the laughing place is and to record it, because he may enhance it later with some visual imagery.
This simple, rapid induction usually produces a profound trace almost immediately.

VERBALIZATION   COMMENT

[slow and cadenced] loose and limp
and lazylike, your limbs like lumps
of lead. Then just let your mind go
off to your laughing place and . . .
[visual imagery of laughing place.]"

This short bit of conversation does not ordinarily delay the usual emergency
hospital care. Most often, when the patient arrives in the Emergency Room
an analgesic is given, blood is drawn, IV drips are started, and cold water
applications are put in place by the time the doctor arrives. If not, these
can proceed while the conversation takes place. A towel dipped in ice water
produces immediate relief of the burning pain that occurs right after a fresh
burn. Since frost bite is as bad an injury as a burn, the patient should not
be packed in ice, but ice water towels are very helpful. In fact, Chapman
(Chapman, Goodell, and Wolff, 1959) showed that applying ice water to a
burn holds the inflammatory response in check for several hours, so there
is ample time to call for the assistance of a qualified hypnotist if the primary
physician is not skilled in the technique of hypnosis.

VERBALIZATION

Doctor: "Now while you are off at
your laughing place, I want you to
also notice that all of the injured
areas are cool and comfortable. Notice how cool and comfortable they
actually are, and when you can really
feel this, you'll let me know because
this finger (touch an index finger)
will slowly rise to signal that *all* of
the *injured* areas are cool and comfortable."

COMMENT

By this time, the patient has iced
towels on and the analgesic is taking
effect so that he actually *is* cool and
comfortable. It is much easier hypnotically to continue a sensation
that is already present than it is to
imagine its opposite. The suggestion, "cool and comfortable," is anti-
inflammatory, and if he accepts it,
he cannot be hot and painful. From
now on, the word *injured* is substituted whenever possible for the
word burn, because patients use the
word burning to describe their pain.
(Do not specify a particular area,
hand, neck, etc., because while these
areas will do well, some spot you
forgot may do poorly.)

Doctor [after obtaining ideomotor
signal]: "Now let your inner mind
lock in on that sensation of being
cool and comfortable and you can
keep it that way during your entire

I just leave the patient in trance, go
ahead with his initial care, and get
him moved to the Burn Unit. Often,
he will drop off to sleep.

VERBALIZATION

stay in the hospital. You can enjoy going to your laughing place as often as you like, and you'll be able to ignore all of the bothersome things we may have to do and anything negative that is said."
Doctor: "Go to your laughing place."

COMMENT

On subsequent days this is all the signal the patient usually needs to drop into a hypnoidal state and tolerate bed-side procedures, physical therapy, etc.

In burns under 20% of the body surface, the single initial trance generally suffices, while in larger burns, repeated suggestion helps control pain, anorexia, and uncooperativeness (Crasilneck et al, 1955; Ewin, 1973; Knudson-Cooper, 1981; Schafer, 1975; Wakeman and Kaplan, 1978).

Since a thought can produce a burn (*vide supra*), continued feelings of guilt or anger can prevent healing, and should be dealt with during emotional countershock (Mattsson, 1975) a day or two after admission. If the patient is feeling guilty, I stress the fact that the injury was unintentional, he has been severely punished, and he has learned a lesson he will never forget or repeat. If he is angry, I point out that the goal is healing and that it does not interfere with his legal rights to get the best healing possible or to forgive the other person of evil intent. There is no place for anger at his laughing place, and he is instructed to postpone that feeling until healing has occurred.

Infection

Before McDowell's success, abdominal operations were so routinely complicated by infection and death that the oath of Hippocrates included "I will not cut for the stone." Patients with kidney stones would often be in such excruciating pain that they would beg for surgical relief even at the risk of their lives, and compassion might lead a surgeon to over-look experience. Even under modern, sterile conditions, infection is one of the worst postoperative complications.

Does hypnosis reduce infection, and if so, how? Esdaile's (1947) death rate from infection dropped from 45% to 5% when he started using hypnoanesthesia in India. Schafer (1975) noted that the patients he hypnotized on the Burn Unit healed without infection. He graciously credited this to good surgical care, but surgeons know that the major cause of death among today's burn patients is infection. Mun (1974) describes the Monkey God rituals in which participants put skewers through their cheeks and flesh without sterilization, and he comments that "no case of sepsis or tetanus has ever been reported." It has been my experience with the viral infections of warts (1974) and herpes (Ewin and Hill, 1981) that hypnotic intervention is effective. Feller (Feller, Flora, and Bawol, 1976) showed in a cooperative study of 21,000 burned patients that survival was not statistically influenced by the type of topical antibiotic used, or if none was used.

How might hypnosis influence infection? Virulence of the organism and resistance of the patient are the protagonists, and presumably all we can influence with words is the patient's resistance. A reasonable theory derives from comparative physiology: many life-forms have a special inactive state in which survival is enhanced. The tetanus organism in its spore state can survive drying, boiling for 5 minutes, and introduction of antibiotics; in its vegetative state, it is susceptible to antibiotics and even oxygen. The amoebic cyst has been revived after drying for 40 years and is not harmed by ordinary chlorination of drinking water or application of any known medications; in its active trophozooite form, it is destroyed by numerous amoebaecidal drugs. Plants and trees become dormant in wintertime and can be pruned, grafted, or transplanted safely; they are unlikely to survive the same treatment during the active growing period of springtime. The African lung fish (Protopterus) can survive for several years out of water in a state of suspended animation called estivation or summer torpidity. The ground squirrel hibernates to survive winter freezing and food shortage, decreasing heart rate from 300 to 10 per minute and reducing metabolism 30 to 100 times. A deep somnambulistic trance apparently gives humans similar protection against potentially lethal external onslaughts.

Thrombosis and Hemorrhage

It is known that surgical trauma and strong emotions affect bleeding and clotting mechanisms, but authors tend to note this without speculating on the possibility that something can be done to use this effect to benefit the patient. Cannon (Cannon and Gray, 1914) noted that a small dose of adrenalin, as well as pain and excitement (Cannon and Mendenhall, 1914), shortened the clotting time, whereas a large dose lengthened it (Cannon and Gray, 1914). He perceived this as a normal protective mechanism to stop hemorrhage from wounds during the fight or flight response (Cannon, 1939), producing many tiny clots in small vessels. Ideally, the increased blood flow during actual fighting or fleeing would keep large veins open, and the clots in tiny vessels would be dissolved by the rebound release of moderate amounts of fibrinolysin. We now know that when this mechanism is overactivated, clots form in the large veins and diffuse intravascular clotting

(McKay, 1965) occurs in the small veins of all organs, impairing perfusion. The end stage of all this clotting is a bleeding condition appropriately called consumption coagulopathy (Rodriguez-Erdmann, 1965) because so many plasma clotting factors have been consumed that the remaining blood cannot clot. This is the only hemorrhagic diathesis treatable with an anticoagulant (Heparin). In addition, dangerous bleeding occurs when the fibrinolysin system is overactivated, dissolving all of the little clots so that hemorrhage even occurs through the holes of skin sutures. Thus, a normal protective mechanism becomes a dangerous threat when overstimulated.

Under surgical anesthesia, the legs are inactive, whereas the neuroendocrine system may be highly activated. [125]I studies show that clotting in the larger veins occurs after 5% to 16% of major abdominal operations, and 26% to 65% of major thoracic operations (Hirsch and Gallus, 1975). Significantly, Ochsner and De-Bakey (1974) state that "a sense of impending disaster, which seems a nebulous manifestation, is of extreme importance in making a diagnosis of phlebothrombosis. The reason is difficult to explain, but must not be disregarded." Perhaps patients with this much anxiety are simply the ones most likely to clot. President Nixon developed spontaneous thrombophlebitis during the stress of the Watergate hearings. deTakats (1944) reported shortening of the clotting time resulting from fear and anxiety before surgery, and Schneider (1951) studied six patients with recurrent phlebitis, all of whom had a striking shortening of clotting time under stress. Critically ill patients are especially vulnerable (Cheek, 1969). No good prospective study using preoperative hypnosis and monitoring intraoperative and recovery room talk has been done, but it should be investigated. Kolough's (1964) 200 patients included only one with a postoperative clot. Wolfe's (Wolfe and Millet, 1960) 1500 patients and Hutchings' (1961) 200 patients had much shorter hospital stays than controls, but neither report mentions a phlebitis rate after hypnosis.

In his review of surgical uses of hypnosis, Zimmerman (1980) comments that hypnotic control of bleeding is badly neglected except by the dentists. McKay (1965) discusses the role of great stress in disseminated intravascular clotting. In a classic show of serendipity, Yudine (1937) observed that cadaver blood from people who died in great fear (trauma, hanging, etc.) was liquefied (fibrinolysed), and he used it for over 1000 blood transfusions before blood banking was developed. In contrast, he noted that the blood of persons dying slowly of cancer, tuberculosis, and so on formed a coagulum that could not be dissolved. Agle (1962) reported nine patients with autoerythrocyte sensitization who cited emotional stress immediately preceding the eruptions of purpura, and a JAMA editorial (1962) suggests the need for psychiatric investigation of the role of emotional factors in other hemorrhagic states. Even dreams (Cheek, 1963) can stimulate hemorrhage.

Hypnotic control of bleeding in hemophiliacs is well-known among hypnotists, particularly dentists. Lucas (1965) reported 114 dental extractions using hypnoanesthesia without any transfusions, and Dubin's (Dubin and Shapiro, 1974) patient had a high antibody titer against Factor VIII, contraindicating transfusion. Stress reduction seems to play a major part in this, since nearly 80% of their bleeding episodes are spontaneous versus 20% traumatic (Browne, Malley, and Kane, 1960). Fredericks' (1967) patient had already received over 200 transfusions for gastrointestinal bleeding before hypnosis was requested and used successfully. Hemophiliacs tend to bleed when they most desperately wish not to, being victims of the Law of Reversed Effect. Just as surgeons used to "steal" the toxic thyroid, the Massies (1975) describe learning to pack for vacation during the night and drive away in the morning without comment to their hemophiliac son, because his anticipatory excitement would predictably cause him to bleed. LaBaw teaches his hemophiliac patients to control their bleeding with self-hypnosis and has a special summer camp for this. Abramson (1970) taught two teenage boys self-hypnosis, and their needs for cryoglobulin transfusions in a year dropped from 468 to 91 and 365 to 52, respectively. They were not cured, but their conditions were much more manageable.

Cardiopulmonary by-pass surgery is becoming increasingly common and is done under very light anesthesia, increasing the likelihood of conscious as well as unconscious hearing during surgery. One report (Marengo-Rowe, Lambert, and Leveson, 1979) notes that 21% of these patients have excessive postoperative hemorrhage (defined as more than 600 ml chest tube drainage in the first 8 hours) and that no preoperative laboratory tests of hemostatic functioning were useful in predicting these coagulopathies.

Some bleeding can be controlled by simple suggestions of coldness, causing arteriolar constriction. Cheek's (1964) patient got "goose flesh" under anesthesia and stopped bleeding when this suggestion was given.

Emergency and Miscellaneous Uses

Accident victims are easy to hypnotize, and many lesser procedures are simplified by adding it to Emergency Room care. Jameson (1963) reported on 40 emergent patients who had recently eaten or were otherwise unfit for anesthesia, and 38 attained adequate analgesia. He reduced 19 fractures and nine shoulder dislocations, sutured a massive abdominal wound dehiscence, drained abscesses, and performed minor procedures. Goldie (1956) had a similar experience, reducing 26 of 28 fractures and dislocations easily. He concluded that his best success was with patients who came with injuries for which they felt immediate treatment was imperative, while abscesses and foreign bodies that could be left untreated awhile were more resistant to hypnoanalgesia. McCord (1968) controlled nose bleed.

Disorders of the autonomic nervous system often respond to hypnotherapy. Earlier reference has been made to prevention of postoperative ileus urinary retention, and vomiting by preoperative suggestion. Wangensteen's group (1959) Doberneck and co-workers (1960) reported control of symptoms and weight gain in 56% of patients hypnotized for treatment of dumping syndrome when orthodox care had failed. Reflex sympathetic dystrophy (Ewin, 1974; Lewenstein, 1981) is very responsive to hypnosis, and one of my cases recovered after sympathectomy had failed. Relief of Raynaud's syndrome (Braun, 1979; Jacobson, et al, 1973) has been reported in some instances, but failure rate is high and smoking must be stopped concurrently (Ewin, 1977).

Hypnosis has been very helpful on plastic surgery services at which large pedicle flaps are performed. Patients can maintain awkward positions comfortably for 2 to 3 weeks using catalepsy, time distortion, and suggestions of comfort (Kelsey and Barrow, 1958; Scott, 1974; Wiggins and Brown, 1968).

Hypnosis enhances relaxation during office procedures such as pelvic examination and proctoscopy, and also for removing drains, T-tubes, and sutures in apprehensive patients. Werbel (1965) had two patients whose incarcerated hernias reduced spontaneously during preoperative hypnosis, changing an emergent into an elective procedure.

Needle phobia is fairly common and easily treated. I saw one 34-year-old mother of two who had a metastatic lesion in her lung and clearly stated that she would rather die of her melanoma than take chemotherapy by needle. After two sessions, she took her chemotherapy, and at 3 years, her metastasis has disappeared and she is clinically well. Another unusual case was a woman who could not swallow barium for a gastrointestinal series. Since being forced to take Castoria as a child, she had never been able to swallow any liquid "medicine," although she had no trouble taking milk or other beverages. One 10-minute session solved her problem.

Physical therapy and rehabilitation after injury can be facilitated (Crasilneck and Hall, 1975; Shires, Peters, and Krout, 1954) by hypnosis.

In phantom limb pain, Papermaster (Papermaster, et al., 1960) cured seven of seven cases by regressing them back before injury, through hospitalization and surgery with suggestions that on recovery they would awaken free of discomfort, whereas Siegel (1979) used glove anesthesia successfully. For his five causalgia patients, Finer (Finer and Graf, 1968) manipulated blood flow to the extremities, with control of the pain by both increasing and decreasing blood flow.

Venereal warts that keep recurring after removal present a vexing problem. They can become malignant and need to be cured. Suggestion can produce warts (Gravitz, 1981), cure them (Allington, 1952; Cohen, 1978; Sheehan, 1978), and cure them in only the suggested area while leaving others intact (Sinclair-Gieben and Chalmers, 1959). Venereal warts are caused by the same virus that causes the common verruca vulgaris, and they respond to analytical hypnotherapy (Ewin, 1974). My experience with recurrent perianal warts is that even after getting a good ideomotor signal that the patient can let them go, the warts often fail to heal spontaneously as warts do in other areas. In this case, one more surgical or chemical removal suffices, and they do not recur.

The Family and Malpractice Suits

In a malpractice symposium, a successful attorney (Martzell, 1975) said in his lecture, "I don't know what you surgeons do when you come out of the operating room, but the first words you say to the family are written in blood across their foreheads." He was clearly describing a hypnoidal state of emotional focus of attention in which a statement is taken literally as though it were a posthypnotic suggestion. His clients all had a bad result, but even when his investigations revealed no negligence, he was unable to assuage them by reasoning. Because of this, the first words should be the most optimistic consistent with the truth, such as "He's in recovery now, and his blood pressure is stable." After a few moments to let this sink in, emotions are calmed and thinking processes return. Then a statement that he is "still in critical condition" will be dealt with on a more rational basis. A prognosis is usually requested, and it is a poor time to discuss a bad prognosis. It is better to say "It's too early to tell. Let's wait until we get him through this critical period, and then we'll know more."

Family attitudes and pressure may coerce the patient to sue when he has a less than perfect surgical result. There is an unreasoning faith today that science can do anything if handled properly; therefore, a bad result equals improper care. When a member of the family asks me if there is anything he can do, I counter with "Do you believe in God?" To a positive reply, I say, "Then please say a prayer for me, and for the best result possible." This is a reminder that science is still imperfect, and puts the family on the team, with some sense of responsibility for the outcome. The final result is likely to be accepted as the best result possible. When this approach is used, it should not be insincere. A stop by the hospital chapel on the way to surgery can't hurt, and helps keep clear the distinction between a surgeon and God.

References

Abramson M: Self-hypnosis for hemophiliacs. Present at the American Society of Clinical Hypnosis Workshop, University of Minnesota, October 17, 1970

Abramson M, Greenfield I, Heron WT: Response to or perception of auditory stimuli under deep surgical anesthesia. Am J Obstet Gynecol 96:584, 1966

Agle DP, Ratnoff OD: Purpura as psychosomatic entity. Arch Intern Med 109:685, 1962

Alexander L: The prehypnotic suggestion. Comprehen Psychol 12:414, 1971

Allington HV: Review of the psychotherapy of warts. Arch Dermatol Syph 66:316, 1952

August RV: Hallucinatory experiences utilized for obstetric hypnoanesthesia. Am J Clin Hypn 3:90, 1960

August RV: Hypnosis in Obstetrics. New York, The Blakiston Division, McGraw-Hill, 1961

Barber J: Rapid induction analgesia. Am J Clin Hypn 19:138, 1977

Barber RF, Madden JL: Historical aspects of cardiac resusitation. Am J Surg 70:135, 1945

Bartlett EE: Polypharmacy versus hypnosis in surgical patients. Pacific Med Surg 74:109, 1966

Bellis JM: Hypnotic pseudo-sunburn. Am J Clin Hypn 8:310, 1966

Bensen VB: One hundred cases of post-anesthetic suggestion in the recovery room. Am J Clin Hypn 13:273, 1971

Bevivino BJ: Hemiplegia following brain surgery relieved by hypnosis. Presented at the 24th Annual Meeting of the American Society of Clinical Hypnosis, Boston, November 12, 1981

Bonello FJ, Doberneck RC, Papermaster AA, Griffen WO Jr, Wagensteen OH: Hypnosis in surgery. I The post-gastrectomy dumping syndrome. Am J Clin Hypn 2:215, 1960

Bowen D: Transurethral resection under self-hypnosis. Am J Clin Hypn 16:132, 1973

Bowers KS: Hypnosis and healing. Austr J Clin Exp Hypn 7:261, 1979

Brauer RO, Spira M: Full thickness burns as source for donor graft in the pig. Plast Recons Surgery 37:21, 1966

Braun BG: Hypnotherapy for Raynaud's disease. In Burrows GD, Collison DR, Dennerstein L (eds): Hypnosis, 1979. Elsevier/North Holland Biomedical Press, 1979

Browne WJ, Mally MA, Kane RP: Psychosocial aspects of hemophilia: A study of twenty-eight hemophiliac children and their families. Am J Orthopsychiatry 30:730, 1960

Brunn JT: The capacity to hear, understand, and to remember experiences during chemo-anesthesia: A personal experience. Am J Clin Hypn 6:27, 1963

Cannon WB: The Wisdom of the Body. New York, WW Norton, 1939

Cannon WB: Voodoo death. Psychosom Med 19:182, 1957

Cannon WB, Gray H: Factors affecting the coagulation of blood. II The hastening or retarding of coagulation by adrenalin injections. Am J Physiol 34:232, 1914

Cannon WB, Mendenhall WL: Factors affecting the coagulation time of blood. IV The hastening of coagulation in pain and emotional excitement. Am J Physiol 34:251, 1914

Chapman LF, Goodell H, Wolff HG: Augmentation of the inflammatory reaction by activity of the central nervous system. AMA Arch Neurol 1:557, 1959

Chapman LF, Goodell H, Wolff HG: Changes in tissue vulnerability induced during hypnotic suggestion. J Psychosom Res 4:99, 1959

Chaves JF, Barber TX: Hypnotic procedures and surgery: A critical analysis with applications to "acupuncture analgesia." Am J Clin Hypn 18:217, 1976

Cheek DB: Unconscious perception of meaningful sounds during surgical anesthesia as revealed under hypnosis. Am J Clin Hypn 1:101, 1959

Cheek DB: Use of preoperative hypnosis to protect patients from careless conversation. Am J Clin Hypn 3:101, 1960

Cheek DB: Removal of subconscious resistance to hypnosis using ideomotor questioning techniques. Am J Clin Hypn 3:103, 1960

Cheek DB: Areas of research into psychosomatic aspects of surgical tragedies now open through use of hypnosis and ideomotor questioning. West J Surg Ob Gyn 70:137, 1962

Cheek DB: Importance of recognizing that surgical patients behave as though hypnotized. Am J Clin Hypn 4:227, 1962

Cheek DB: Ideomotor questioning for investigation of subconscious "pain" and target organ vulnerability. Am J Clin Hypn 5:30, 1962

Cheek DB: Physiological impact of fear in dreams; postoperative hemorrhage. Am J Clin Hypn 5:206, 1963

Cheek DB: Surgical memory and reaction to careless conversation. Am J Clin Hypn 6:237, 1964

Cheek DB: Further evidence of persistence of hearing under chemoanesthesia: Detailed case report. Am J Clin Hypn 7:55, 1964

Cheek DB: Communication with the critically ill. Am J Clin Hypn 12:75, 1969

Cheek DB: Awareness of meaningful sounds under general anesthesia: Considerations and a review of the literature 1959–1979. In Wain HJ (ed): Theoretical and Clinical Aspects of Hypnosis, p 87. Miami, Symposia Specialists, 1981

Cheek DB, LeCron LM: Clinical Hypnotherapy. New York, Grune & Stratton, 1968

Clawson TA Jr, Swade RH: The hypnotic control of blood flow and pain: The cure of warts and the potential for the use of hypnosis in the treatment of cancer. Am J Clin Hypn 3:160, 1975

Cohen SB: Editorial-warts. Am J Clin Hypn 20:157, 1978

Cousins N: Anatomy of an illness (as perceived by the patient). N Engl J Med 295:1458, 1976

Crasilneck HB, Hall JA: Clinical hypnosis: Principles and applications. New York, Grune & Stratton, 1975

Crasilneck HB, McCranie EJ, Jenkins MT: Special indications for hypnosis as a method of anesthesia. JAMA 162:1606, 1956

Crasilneck HB, Stirman JA, Wilson BJ, McCranie EJ, Fogelman MJ: Use of hypnosis in the management of burns. JAMA 158:103, 1955

Crile G, Lower WE: Anoci-association, p 98. Philadelphia, WB Saunders, 1914

Crile GW: Autobiography, p 197. Philadelphia, JB Lippincott, 1947

Dahinterova J: Some experiences with the use of hypnosis in the treatment of burns. Int J Clin Exp Hypn 15:49, 1967

Daniels E: The hypnotic approach in anesthesia for children. Am J Clin Hypn 4:244, 1962

deTakats G: Nervous regulation of clotting mechanism. Arch Surg 48:105, 1944

Doberneck RC, Griffen WO Jr, Papermaster AA, Bonnello F, Wangensteen OH: Hypnosis as an adjunct to surgical therapy. Surgery 46:299, 1959

Doberneck RC, McFee AS, Bonello FJ, Papermaster AA, Wangensteen OH: The prevention of postoperative urinary retention by hypnosis. Am J Clin Hypn 3:235, 1961

Dohan FC, Taylor EW, Moss NH: The role of the surgeon in prolongation of uncomplicated surgical convalescence. J Surg Gyn 111:49, 1960

Dubin LL, Shapiro SS: Use of hypnosis to facilitate dental extraction and hemostasis in a classic hemophiliac with a high antibody titer to factor VIII. Am J Clin Hypn 17:79, 1974

Egbert LD, Battit GE, Welch CE, Bartlett MK: Reduction of postoperative pain by encouragement and instruction of patients. N Engl J Med 270:825, 1964

Emotions and purpura. Editorial in JAMA, 181:720, 1962

Esdaile J: Hypnosis in Medicine and Surgery. New York, Julian Press, 1957

Ewin DM: Hypnosis in industrial practice. J Occup Med 15:586, 1973

Ewin DM: A case of reflex sympathetic dystrophy of the left hand cured by hypnosis. Presented at the 17th Annual Meeting of the American Society of Clinical Hypnosis, New Orleans, 1974

Ewin DM: Condyloma acuminatum: Successful treatment of four cases by hypnosis. Am J Clin Hypn 17:73, 1974

Ewin DM: Hypnosis to control the smoking habit. J Occup Med 19:696, 1977

Ewin DM: Relieving suffering and pain with hypnosis. Geriatrics 33:87, 1978

Ewin DM: Clinical use of hypnosis for attenuation of burn depth. In Frankel FH, Zamansky HS: Hypnosis at its Bicentennial—Selected Papers from the Seventh International Congress of Hypnosis and Psychosomatic Medicine. New York, Plenum Press, 1978

Ewin DM: Hypnosis in burn therapy. In Burrows GD, Collison DR, Dennerstein L (eds): Hypnosis 1979. Elsevier/North-Holland Press, 1979

Ewin DM: Constant pain syndrome: Its psychological meaning and care using hypnoanalysis. In Wain HJ (ed): Clinical Hypnosis in Medicine. Chicago, Year Book Medical Publishers, 1980

Ewin DM, Hill FE: Analytical hypnotherapy of recurrent herpes genitalis: Report of four cases. Presented at the 24th annual meeting of the American Society of Clinical Hypnosis, Boston, November 14, 1981

Faithfull NS: Awareness during anaesthesia. Br Med J 2:117 (Correspondence), 1969

Feller I, Flora JD Jr, Bawol R: Baseline results of therapy for burned patients. JAMA 236:1943–1947, 1976

Field PB: Effects of tape-recorded hypnotic preparation for surgery. Int J Clin Exp Hypn 22:54, 1974

Finer B, Graf K: Circulatory changes accompanying hypnotic imagination of hyperalgesia and hypoalgesia in causalgic limbs. Zeitschrift für die gesamte experimentelle medizin. 146:97, 1968

Finer B, Jonzon A, Sedin G, Sjöstrand U: Some physiological changes during minor surgery under hypnotic analgesia. Acta Anaesth Scand (suppl) 53:94, 1973

Finer BL, Nylén BO: Cardiac arrest in the treatment of burns, and report on hypnosis as a substitute for anesthesia. Plast Reconstr Surg 27:49, 1961

Finney JMT: Discussion of papers on shock. Ann Surg 100:746, 1934

Fredericks LE: The use of hypnosis in hemophilia. Am J Clin Hypn 10:52, 1967

Fredericks LE: The value of teaching hypnosis in the practice of anesthesiology. Int J Clin Exp Hypn 28:6, 1980

Golan HP: Hypnosis: Further case reports from the Boston City Hospital. Am J Clin Hypn 18:55, 1975

Goldie L: Hypnosis in the casualty department. Br Med J 2:1340, 1956

Gravitz MA: The production of warts by suggestion as a cultural phenomenon. Am J Clin Hypn 23:281, 1981

Haggard H: Devils, Drugs and Doctors, p 298. New York, Harpers & Row, 1929

Hart RR: The influence of a taped hypnotic induction treatment procedure on the recovery of surgery patients. Int J Clin Exp Hypn 28:324, 1980

Hilgard J, Hilgard R, Newman M: Sequelae to hypnotic induction with special reference to earlier chemical anesthesia. J Nerv Ment Dis 133:461, 1961

Hinshaw JR: Progressive changes in the depth of burns. Arch Surg 87:993, 1963

Hirsch J, Gallus AS: 125 I-labeled fibrinogen scanning: Use in the diagnosis of venous thrombosis. JAMA 233:970, 1975

Hutchings DD: The value of suggestion given under anesthesia: A report and evaluation of 200 consecutive cases. Am J Clin Hypn 4:26, 1961

Jacobson AM, Hackett TP, Surman OS, Silverberg EL: Raynaud's phenomenon: Treatment with hypnotic and operant techniques. JAMA 225:739, 1973

Jameson RM: Hypnosis for minor surgical procedures. Br J Anaesth 35:269, 1963

Johnson RFQ, Barber TX: Hypnosis, suggestions, and warts: An experimental investigation implicating the importance of "believed-in efficacy." Am J Clin Hypn 20:165, 1978

Kelsey D, Barrow JN: Maintenance of posture by hypnotic suggestion in patient undergoing plastic surgery. Br Med J 1:756, 1958

Kolough FT: Hypnosis and surgical convalescence: A study of subjective factors in postoperative recovery. Am J Clin Hypn 7:120, 1964

Knudson-Cooper MS: Relaxation and biofeedback training in the treatment of severely burned children. J Burn Care Rehab 2:102, 1981

Kroger WS: Clinical and Experimental Hypnosis. Philadelphia, JB Lippincott, 1963

Kroger WS: Hypnotherapy for intractable post-surgical hiccups. Am J Clin Hypn 12:1, 1969

Kroger WS: Clinical and Experimental Hypnosis (ed. 2). Philadelphia, JB Lippincott, 1977

LaBaw WL: Adjunctive trance therapy with severely burned children. Int J Child Psychother 2:80, 1973

Lait VS: Transurethral resection of carcinoma of bladder under hypnosis: A case report. Am J Clin Hypn 3:200, 1961

Leonard AS, Papermaster AA, Wangensteen OH: Treatment of postgastrectomy dumping syndrome by hypnotic suggestion. JAMA 165:1957–1959, 1957

Levinson BW: States of awareness during general anesthesia. In Lassner J (ed): Hypnosis and Psychosomatic Medicine. New York, Springer Verlag, 1967

Lewenstein LN: Hypnosis as an anesthetic in pediatric ophthalmology. Anes 49:144, 1978

Lewenstein LN: The treatment of reflex sympathetic dystrophy. Presented at the 24th Annual Meeting of the American Society of Clinical Hypnosis, Boston, 1981

Lewenstein LN, Iwamoto K, Schwartz H: Hypnosis in high risk surgery. Ophth Surg 12:39, 1981

Magaw A: A review of over fourteen thousand surgical anesthesias. Surg Gyn Obst 3:795, 1906

Marengo-Row AJ, Lambert CJ, Leveson JE, et al: The evaluation of hemorrhage in cardiac patients who have undergone extracorporeal circulation. Transfusion 19:426, 1979

Maresca RL, Boyden LC: An early experience in hypnoanesthesia. Am J Clin Hypn 2:143, 1960

Margolis CG: Hypnosis in the early treatment of burns: A pilot study. Presented at Burn Workshop 24th Annual Meeting of the American Society of Clinical Hypnosis, Boston, November 10, 1981 (in press)

Marmer MJ: Hypnosis in Anesthesiology. Springfield. Charles C Thomas, 1959

Martzell JR: Presented at Medical Malpractice Seminar, LSU Medical School, 1975

Massie R, Massie S: Journey, p 112. New York, Knopf, 1975

Mattsson EI: Psychological aspects of severe physical injury and its treatment. J Trauma 15:217, 1975

McClure CM: Cardiac arrest through volition. Calif Med 90:440, 1959

McCord H: Hypnotic control of nosebleed. Am J Clin Hypn 10:291, 1968

McCormack AT: Our pioneer heroine of surgery—Mrs. Jane Todd Crawford. The Filson Club Historical Quarterly, 6(2):118, 1932

McKay DG: Disseminated Intravascular Coagulation. New York, Hoeber, 1965

Meerloo JAM: Patterns of Panic. New York, International Universities Press, 1950. Quoted in Cheek DB: Communication with the critically ill. Am J Clin Hypn 12:75, 1969

Mihalyka EE, Whanger AD: Tonsillectomies under hypnosis: Report of cases. Am J Clin Hypn 2:87, 1959

Moore LE, Kaplan JZ: Hypnotically accelerated burn wound healing. Presented at Burn Workshop 24th Annual Meeting of the American Society of Clinical Hypnosis, Boston, November 10, 1981

Mun CT: Trance states in Singapore. Br J Clin Hypn 5:102, 1975

Ochsner EWA, DeBakey M: Thrombophlebitis, phlebothrombosis, and pulmonary embolism. In Lewis D (ed): Chapt. 8N Practice of Surgery: Cardiovascular Surgery. Hagerstown, Harper & Row, 1974

Papermaster AA, Doberneck RC, Bonello FJ, Griffen WO Jr, Wangensteen OH: Hypnosis in surgery: II Pain. Am J Clin Hypn 2:220, 1960

Pearson RE: Response to suggestions given under general anesthesia. Am J Clin Hypn 4:106, 1961

Pearson R: Why doesn't it work for me? Presented at 16th Annual Meeting, American Society of Clinical Hypnosis, 1973, Toronto

Pellicane AJ: Hypnosis as adjunct to treatment of burns. Am J Clin Hypn 2:153, 1960

Raginsky BB: Temporary cardiac arrest induced under hypnosis. Int J Clin Exp Hypn 7:53, 1959

Rausch V: Cholecystectomy with self-hypnosis. Am J Clin Hypn 22:124, 1980

Reis M: Subjective reactions of a patient having surgery without chemical anesthesia. Am J Clin Hypn 9:122, 1966

Richter CP: On the phenomenon of sudden death in animals and man. Psychosom Med 19:191, 1957

Rodger BP: The art of preparing the patient for anesthesia. Anesthesiology 22:548, 1961

Rodger BP: Hypnosis in anesthesia: Some psychological considerations. Am J Clin Hypn 4:237, 1962

Rodger BP: Recognition and use of hypnoidal behavior in the surgical patient. Am J Clin Hypn 6:355, 1964

Rodriguez-Erdmann F: Bleeding due to increased intravascular blood coagulation. Hemorrhagic syndromes caused by consumption of bloodclotting factors (consumption coagulopathies). N Engl J Med 273:1370, 1965

Sampimon RLH, Woodruff MFA: Some observations concerning the use of hypnosis as a substitute for anesthesia. Med J Aust 1:393, 1946

Schachner A: Ephraim McDowell, "Father of Ovariotomy" and Founder of Abdominal Surgery. Philadelphia, JB Lippincott, 1921

Schafer DW: Hypnosis use on a burn unit. Int J Clin Exp Hypn 23:1, 1975

Schneider RA: Recurrent thrombophlebitis, an experimental study of life situations and emotions and clotting time and relative viscosity of the blood. Am J Med Sci 222:562, 1951

Scott DL: Modern Hospital Hypnosis. London, Lloyd-Luke, 1974

Siegel EF: Control of phantom limb pain by hypnosis. Am J Clin Hypn 21:285, 1979

Sheehan DV: Influence of psychosocial factors on wart remission. Am J Clin Hypn 20:160, 1978

Sheffer MB, Greifenstein FE: Emotional responses of patients to surgery and anesthesia. Anesthesiology, 21:502, 1960

Shires EB, Peters JJ, Krout RM: Hypnosis in neuromuscular re-education. US Armed Forces Med J 5:1519, 1954

Sinclair-Gieben AHC, Chalmers D: Evaluation of treatment of warts by suggestion. Lancet, 2:480, 1959

Sparkman RS: Presidential address: The woman in the case. Ann Surg 189:529, 1979

Steinberg S, Pennell EL Jr: Hypnoanesthesia—A case report on a 90 year old patient. Am J Clin Hypn 7:355, 1965

Stephenson HE Jr: Cardiac Arrest and Resuscitation (ed 3). St Louis, CV Mosby, 1969

Thornton JA, Levy CJ: Techniques of Anaesthesia: With Management of the Patient and Intensive Care. London, Chapman and Hall, 1974

Trustman R, Dubovsky S, Titley R: Auditory perception during general anesthesia—Myth or fact? Int J Clin Exp Hypn 25:88, 1977.

Ullman M: Herpes simplex and second degree burn induced under hypnosis. Am J Psychiatry 103:828, 1947

Van Dyke PB: Some uses of hypnosis in the management of the surgical patient. Am J Clin Hypn 12:227, 1970

Wakeman RJ, Kaplan JZ: An experimental study of hypnosis in painful burns. Am J Clin Hypn 21:3, 1978

Werbel EW: One Surgeon's Experience With Hypnosis. New York, Pageant Press, 1965

Werbel EW: Use of hypnosis in certain surgical problems. Am J Clin Hypn 7:81, 1965

Werbel EW: Hypnosis in serious surgical problems. Am J Clin Hypn 10:44, 1967

Wiggins SL, Brown CW: Hypnosis with two pedicle graft cases. Int J Clin Exp Hypn 16:215, 1968

Wilson J, Turner DJ: Awareness during caesarean section under general anaesthesia. Br Med J 1:280, 1969

Wolfe LS, Millet JB: Control of postoperative pain by suggestion under general anesthesia. Am J Clin Hypn 3:109, 1960

Wollman L: Hypnosis for the surgical patient. Am J Clin Hypn 7:83, 1965

Yanovski A, Bricklin B: Spontaneous abreaction during major surgery under hypnosis. Psychiatr Q 41:496, 1967

Yudine SS: Transfusion of stored cadaver blood. Lancet 2:360, 1937

Zimmerman D: Hypnotherapy in surgical management: A review. J Roy Soc Med 73:579, 1980

14 Hypnosis and Pain Control

STUART W. BASSMAN
WILLIAM C. WESTER, II

Throughout the history of mankind, pain has been a perplexing phenomenon. The presence or absence of pain has been the motivation for the development of some systems of philosophy, for the existence of aberrations of human behavior, and for the creation of a large portion of the world's literature (Diamond and Dalessio, 1973).

It was at one time believed that pain was caused by demons or hostile spirits that could only be exorcised by witch doctors or priests. In the Book of Genesis, Eve was condemned to bear children in pain because of her sin of disobedience. In ancient Greek writings, pain is spoken of as a punishment or penalty. Aristotle spoke of pain as the passion of the soul.

Although the scientific world has accumulated considerable information about pain over the past several thousand years, the nature of pain is still a subject of continuous controversy (Bresler, 1979).

The many definitions of pain have ranged from descriptions in which it was seen as a warning signal of threatened tissue damage, an integrated defensive reaction, and a private experience of hurt (Sternbach, 1968). To the average individual, the last description offered seems to be the most relevant. Pain is foremost an immediate subjective experience encompassing all of a person's attention. Pain is more than just a stimulus; its significance comes from its gestalt of having temporal, emotional, psychological, and bodily meanings. It is a distressing experience, and for millions of sufferers, the human costs of pain are incalculable. In terms of medical bills, lost wages, and workman's compensation, the price tag is an estimated $50 billion a year (Bresler, 1979). Pain is one of the most misunderstood and neglected phenomena in modern medicine. It is a drain on the physical and emotional well-being of millions of people, making it difficult, if not impossible, for them to lead happy and fulfilling lives.

Pain as a subjective experience is perhaps the most significant factor in causing people to seek medical aid (Erickson, 1968). Hilgard (1975) has noted that pain is so widespread a phenomenon that pain reduction has become the primary task of the physician, second only to the preservation of life.

Sachs (1977) has indicated that comprehensive treatment of pain should be directed toward alleviating each component of the pain process. This study reports that patients desire a more satisfactory life, with reduced suffering, less interference with daily activities, and less dependence on medication. Most patients did not require total withdrawal of the pain to accomplish satisfactory relief and functioning. The emphasis, Sachs maintains, should not be on how much pain-free living the doctor prefers for the patient (with commensurate dependence and side effects from medication), but rather what is tolerable for the person.

An editorial in the January 14, 1982 issue of the New England Journal of Medicine, entitled "The Quality of Mercy," addressed the important issue of prescribing of pain medicine for patients. It emphasized the concerns physicians should have about dispensing pain medicine and urged them to be especially wary of side effects and drug addiction. The message in the editorial's closing paragraph is brief but to the point—"The quality of mercy is essential to the practice of medicine; here, of all places, it should not be strained."

Unfortunately, and all too frequently, unnecessary treatment methods have been prescribed by doctors in their desire to help the patient. Wain (1980) has noted that many patients have become addicted to opiates, have undergone complicated and risky surgery, or have incurred debt in an attempt to find relief. Some have seen their bodies mutilated, whereas others have had psychologically debilitating effects. Therefore, Wain concludes, it is necessary to find a treatment that is expeditious, inexpensive, nonaddicting, and safe.

We believe that hypnosis is such a treatment modality. It is expeditious and responsive to the psychological and physiological components of pain, and carries minimal risk (Haley, 1967). Hypnotic intervention can serve not only as a primary treatment method, but can also be an adjunct to medical treatments.

The literature on the use of hypnosis in the treatment of pain is too vast to be fully explored in this chapter. We have elected to focus our attention on the use of hypnosis in the treatment of headache pain. The approach described and the scripts presented can easily be adapted for the treatment of other types of pain-related conditions.

Review of Literature

Probably the most common complaint of the medical patient is headaches (Ryan, 1978). It has been estimated that, on the average, 42 million Americans have headaches severe enough to seek medical attention (Diamond, 1979). Approximately 80% of headaches are described as muscle-contraction or mixed muscle-contraction and migraine (Friedman, 1964a). These headaches range in severity from mild and occasional up to continuous or incapacitating. Although more migraine headaches are rated as severe, muscle-contraction headache cases suffer a sizable percentage of severe headaches (Phillips, 1977a).

The Ad Hoc Committee definition (1962) of muscle-contraction headache assumes a skeletal muscle basis, and it is associated with a number of conditional elements: four possible sensations (*i.e.,* ache, tightness, pressure, or constriction); three attributes (*i.e.,* frequency, intensity, and duration); and varied locations (*e.g.,* commonly suboccipital). In spite of its clinical significance, there has been surprisingly little experimental evidence pertaining to the physiological basis of muscle-contraction headaches or of the mechanisms affecting the pain complaint (Phillips, 1977b).

Melzack (1971), however, has shown pain to have both psychological and physiological components. He specified that pain perceptions are not simply a function of physical damage alone. The extent of a patient's organic lesion does not necessarily correlate with the amount of pain that is perceived. Patients can be in highly advanced stages of cancer and not experience any pain, whereas a minor injury can be experienced as excruciating (Redden, 1980). Melzack and Perry (1975) note that pain perception can also be determined by expectation, suggestion, level of anxiety, competing sensory stimuli, and other psychological variables.

Treatment approaches for muscle-contraction headaches that have based their design on the premise that the pain is associated predominantly with sustained contraction of skeletal muscles have been generally disputed, primarily through biofeedback techniques. This treatment modality is based on the assumption that elevated EMG activity should occur in headache states and that an association between EMG activity and ratings of pain should be observable. This implication appears to be unsupported. Although initial research (Budzynski, Stoyva, Adler, and Mulleney, 1973) indicated a relationship between EMG activity and pain report, methodological discrepancies invalidated the results (Haynes, Moseley, and McGowan, 1975).

Subsequent studies have failed to find significantly elevated EMG levels during headache states (Phillips, 1977b; Martin and Mathews, 1978; Harrison, 1980). Martin and Mathews show that there was no significant increase in EMG activity in a group of patients reporting moderately severe headache pain compared with patients reporting slight headache. Harrison noted that EMG biofeedback was found to be questionable both as a criterion measure of treatment success and as a treatment for some tension headache sufferers. However, she did speculate that it may have been the relaxation component of the biofeedback treatment which may have helped some of her subjects. Pierce and Morley (1981) note that in reviewing the literature for using biofeedback as a treatment modality, that it should be scrutinized and reappraised. They suggest that the psychological components involved in headache pain should be more closely examined.

Beatty and Haynes (1979) have stated that muscle-contraction headaches may be a function of other factors in addition to muscle tension on the head and in the neck region. Two of the factors that they specifically indicate are pain threshold and pain tolerance. This parallels the speculation of Kroger (1977). He notes that pain is not a primary sensory modality, like seeing or hearing, but rather is, in part, an emotionally charged percept influenced to an astonishing degree by psychological factors. He goes on to state that allowing for variations in responses in humans, the pain threshold is more dependent on physiological factors, whereas pain tolerance is largely influenced by psychological ones.

The presently accepted conceptualization of muscle-contraction headache pain includes three major components: physiological changes (*i.e.,* muscular-contraction, vasoconstriction-dilation); subjective experience of pain (*i.e.,* distress, aching, pulsing, fatigue, etc.); and behavior that the pain motivates (*i.e.,* medication intake, withdrawal from work and social relations, etc.) (Phillips, 1977a). Frequently, treatment procedures may modify one component while leaving the others unaffected. So, for example, Friedman (1964a) reported that medication has no effect on muscle-contraction headaches. However, perhaps the physiological component was affected, but not the subjective or behavioral.

There are presently two treatment modalities that correlate with all three components of pain: hypnosis and relaxation. In addition, hypnosis has the added ability to raise a person's pain tolerance by its use of coping suggestions (Kroger, 1977; Haley, 1967).

Relaxation

Behavior-oriented treatment methods have been used on the assumption that muscle-contraction headaches are psychophysiologic (psychosomatic) disorders. It is assumed that some individuals react to environmental stress with sustained contraction of the muscles of the head and neck, which lead to a muscle-contraction headache. Although social learning approaches have been employed, behavioral interventions have been primarily aimed at decreasing general physiological arousal and muscle tension levels in the head and neck region (Beatty and Haynes, 1979). As noted by Mitchell and White (1977), most of the behavioral interventions have been directed at the last element in the sequence leading to a headache. Rather than removing sources of stress that may precipitate a headache, the vast majority of studies have used methods aimed at decreasing the patient's responses to environmental stressors.

A review of the literature for behavioral treatments for muscle-contraction headaches reveals that the most frequent interventions have been EMG biofeedback and relaxation training. Relaxation exercises, usually modified from those described by Jacobson (1938), have become generally accepted as the most direct means of overcoming the habitual overcontraction of muscles in tension headache.

Jacobson's theory involved teaching awareness and control of voluntary skeletal muscles (Benson, 1975). The technique for general or entire body relaxation involves having participants lie in a comfortable position, close their eyes, and then maintain contraction on a given muscle group for several seconds. This is maintained until tenseness occurs, and then the muscle group is allowed to relax (Jacobson, 1938). Large muscle groups are selected first because the sensations are more conspicuous, and it is important that the participant be instructed to notice the difference between the two sensations of contracting and relaxing (Jacobson, 1938). As the name implies, progressive relaxation is the systematic application of this technique progressing from one muscle group to the next (Schlutter, 1978).

EMG biofeedback was previously discussed as failing to show a significant relationship between headache activity and elevated EMG activity. However, what was also previously alluded to was the implication that the relaxation component of biofeedback may have therapeutic value (Harrison, 1980).

Chesney and Shelton (1977) studied the effects of three treatment groups on the reduction of muscle-contraction headaches. Subjects were trained to use one of the three relaxation procedures: group 1—taped muscle relaxation; group 2—EMG biofeedback training; group 3—a combination of relaxation and EMG biofeedback training; and group 4—control. Only groups 1 and 3 showed a significant reduction in headache frequency as compared to the no-treatment group. Groups 1 and 3 also yielded significantly shorter headache duration than either the control or EMG biofeedback group. Only the combination group produced a significant reduction in severity of headaches compared to the control group. Finally, there was no significant difference between the biofeedback and control group on any measure. Chesney and Shelton concluded that relaxation seemed to be the most significant treatment factor.

Beatty and Haynes (1979), in a review of the behavioral literature implicated home practice as an important determinant of therapeutic success in the previously mentioned study, in addition to a number of other studies. In evaluating the contradictory findings of a similar study that EMG biofeedback training was the significant treatment factor (Hutchings and Reinking, 1976), the reviewers noted that home practice was required in the Chesney and Shelton study and not in the other study.

However, Beatty and Haynes are quick to note that the effects of assigned home practice have not been subjected to controlled empirical investigation. Kondo and Canter (1977) suggest that home practice is not a necessary component of an intervention package, because they have achieved significant reductions in headache activity in its absence. In explaining long-term outcomes of therapeutic success, Reinking and Hutchings (1981) indicate that continual practice seemed to be an important variable. However, this was based on the responses of only 60% of their original sample in a 1-year follow-up interview.

Beatty and Haynes conclude their review of the behavioral literature with the following recommendations:

1. Although the results for relaxation treatment are highly promising (Chesney and Shelton, 1977; Mitchell and White, 1977; Tasto and Hinkle, 1973; Wickramaskera, 1978), an adequate evaluation of relaxation training as a treatment method for muscle-contraction headache must await controlled comparison with other treatments.
2. The contribution of other specific variables such as the reactive effects of self-monitoring and assigned home practice need to be subjected to controlled empirical investigation.

Hypnosis

Erickson (1968) defines hypnosis as essentially a communication of ideas and understandings to a patient in such a fashion that he will be more receptive to the presented ideas (suggestions) and thereby become motivated to explore his own psychosomatic potentials for the control of his psychological and physiological responses and behavior. There are two cogent observations in Erickson's description. First, patients are not treated *by* hypnosis, but *in* hypnosis. Hypnosis is not a sleep nor a state of unconsciousness, but rather a heightened state of receptiveness to ideas or suggestions. Second, hypnosis enables patients to tap forgotten assets and hidden potentials so as to transcend their normal volitional capacities (Kroger, 1977). Because of his own use of hypnosis for polio, Erickson believed that, as a result of experiential events in one's younger days, there is an accumulated but yet unrecognized reservoir of psychological, physiological, and neurological learnings that make it possible to control and abolish pain.

The use of hypnosis for control of pain and as an anesthesia is well documented (Cheek and LeCron, 1968; Crasilneck and Hall, 1975; Haley, 1967). However, these studies are predominantly a reflection of effectiveness in the clinical setting and thus not subject to experimentally controlled methodology. The reduction of experimentally produced pain has been investigated in the laboratory (Hilgard and Hilgard, 1975; Barber and Calverly, 1965). The Hilgards note that laboratory studies have not as yet produced a sufficient theoretical and experimental framework for the very striking pain relief achieved by clinical hypnosis. Their assessment continues as they strongly indicate that unless experimental studies are carried out in the clinical setting, the information gained in the laboratory will tend to be idle and useless.

Most of the clinical studies relating to hypnosis and muscle-contraction headaches are anecdotal and do not present systematic data analysis. The studies usually involve one patient, include a description of the patient's symptoms before and after treatment, and some description of treatment. Although the design of these studies does not allow for an evaluation of treatment effectiveness, they may be helpful in suggesting possible research (Bernal, 1978).

Blumenthal (1963) recommended self-hypnosis for patients with headaches. There was no description of induction techniques or actual suggestions in this study. Kroger (1963) discusses a series of case histories as well as specific techniques (glove anesthesia, symptom substitution) for helping the patient with chronic headaches. However, Kroger does not differentiate type of headache and thus groups all headaches as being homogeneous, which in fact they are not (Friedman, 1962). In addition, evaluation of the study's effectiveness is difficult owing to Kroger's lack of systematic data analysis. Erickson has described a number of case studies using the interspersing of suggestions for headache reduction (Haley, 1967). These are more detailed reports, but because of the small sample and lack of specific control procedures, the results are questionable.

Drummond (1981) reviewed the last 10 years of the treatment of headache by hypnosis alone and in combination with other therapeutic methods. His findings suggested the urgency of what is needed in the literature:

> There were no reported experimental studies done concerning the use of hypnosis in the treatment of muscle-contraction headaches. In fact only three case studies, one subject per study, were reported. . . . Obviously some well-controlled experimental studies are indicated, perhaps comparing the differential effects of relaxation training, biofeedback training, hypnosis, or a combination of two or more of these.

Three dissertations have been completed that compare the effectiveness of biofeedback and hypnosis in the treatment of muscle-contraction headaches (Bernal, 1978; Schlutter, 1978; Harrison, 1980). The research conducted as a basis for this chapter helps to fill the experimental void regarding the effectiveness of hypnosis and relaxation training in the treatment of muscle-contractions headaches. Following the recommendations offered by Beatty and Haynes (1979), we also evaluated the effects of assigned home practice and the reactive effects of self-monitoring.

One example of the use of hypnosis in the relief of pain was a study by Bassman (1982) on the alleviation of muscle-contraction headaches. The scripts illustrated later in this chapter were designed to provide a standardized procedure for developing a hypnotic trance. Originally designed as part of a doctoral dissertation study, these sets of procedures have evolved into both a training module for those professionals seeking an introduction into the indirect mode of hypnosis, as well as a paradigm for using indirect hypnosis in relief of headache pain.

Although the reader may be predominantly interested in the scripts and therapeutic procedures outline, this was only part of the overall treatment armamentarium. Integral parts of the treatment, which is not included here owing to the need for brevity, are an extensive assessment questionnaire (pretreatment instruments) and evaluative questionnaires (posttreatment instruments). It is always imperative that an in-depth assessment of the patient's psychophysiological health be done at the onset of treatment. Although the pretreatment instruments used in our research were directed primarily at the psychological components of the patient's pain, we used a consultative role with each patient's personal physician. Our role was specifically defined as adjunctive to medical treatment and not as a replacement or substitution for it.

The scripts were developed to include a wide array of techniques that have been shown to be effective in helping people in pain. As he experiences the treatment, the patient can then choose whichever technique may be the most effective in helping him with his particular malady. For instance, some individuals may find the symptom substitution effective, whereas others may prefer the glove anesthesia. The availability of various approaches gives the patient the opportunity to feel the satisfaction of taking an active and responsible part in helping himself. This is quite the opposite of the case in which a patient is the passive recipient of a treatment and thus feels vaguely responsible for his remediation. Once again, you are reminded of our description of treatment in which the patient is not treated *by* hypnosis, but *in* hypnosis.

It is important that the patient experience this therapeutic relationship as collaborative. It is not enough for the therapist to verbalize this approach, but he must actively model this belief. After all, the effects of the treatment will need to be maintained after the actual treatment session ends, and this will be accomplished by continued patient activity.

Appendix 14-1

First Session

INDUCTION	COMMENT
"Before we begin, I am going to outline to you what will transpire this session and how well you will do. You may view this as seeing a preview before investing in going to the movies. This preview will include my getting to know more about you. I'll ask you some questions that will help me so that I may help you.	Therapist establishing: Rapport Interest
"Next, we will discuss your presenting problems and how you have dealt with it. Then, we will discuss your ideas and conceptions of hypnosis and	Empathy Positive response set

INDUCTION   **COMMENT**

then discuss what hypnosis is and how
YOUR use of it will help you . . . yes.
A little later, whenever you are ready to
enter a pleasant and deep hypnotic
state, you could let me know—after all,
you will be the one in control, yes. And
you will learn that all hypnosis is actually
self-hypnosis, but we will come back to
that later on."

The therapist then helps the patient to feel more at ease, as the patient is encouraged
to discuss aspects of his life that he feels most comfortable sharing. Subsequently, the
therapist will gradually focus on the patient's malady and how he has dealt with it. It is
essential that the therapist be empathic toward the patient's reaction to his pain. This is
especially crucial to the headache sufferer, since these patients are most sensitive to the
reactions of others to their ailment. The person with chronic headaches is frequently
defending his pain to others, as the significant others in their lives react with disbelief or
irritation to the malady. The professional is, therefore, cautioned to observe acute sensitivity with regard to this issue. A possible way of reconciling oneself to this situation is
to perceive that whatever is painful for an individual is the ultimate criterion for the value
ascribed to it. So for the patient, the pain is real, if they believe it is. In addition, a
possible benefit of reinforcing the priority of his belief in determining his perception of
pain is that the professional is also providing a framework (hypnosis) to change the patient's
experience of pain.

The session proceeds as the therapist discusses with the patient his conceptions and
possible misconceptions of hypnosis. Most patients perceive hypnosis as having a mystique
about which they feel ambivalent. It is essential for the professional to discuss and assure
the patient of what hypnosis is and is not. This also provides the therapist with the added
opportunity of aligning the patient's expectations with his conception of how self-hypnosis
will help him.

You may note that a consistent pattern of the professional emphasizing and modeling to the patient an attitude of empathy, patient responsibility, and control of his
perceptions, and how their utilization of hypnosis will help him when he is ready to be
helped.

INDUCTION   **COMMENT**

"That's right, get as comfortable   Emphasize patient control and relaxing,
as you would like to in the chair. While nonthreatening atmosphere. The man-
you are getting comfortably settled in ner and the mood of the therapist
the chair, I'm going to show you how   should convey a feeling of reassurance
you will go into a very pleasant trance, that the patient will do very well.
O.K.? . . . yes. I want you to enjoy being
very comfortable. Let me do the work,
you can just relax.

"Now, just watch me. In a little   Therapist models behavior of being a
while, whenever you are ready to begin good subject and also prepares the pa-
at your own pace and your own rate,   tient for what to expect. . . . Simply

INDUCTION	COMMENT
just raise one of your arms. Whichever one you would prefer to use, you are the one in control, and so the choice of arms will be up to you. Now, I'm raising my right arm just above my eye level. I am then clenching my fist, and, as you notice, I am staring at my fist.	knowing what to do and how easy it will be may lessen his anxiety.
"Now, let me explain the rationale and importance of what I am doing. There are four reasons associated with this phenomena: *first*, this demonstrates your ability to concentrate your energy and tension into one focal point, your hand. *Second*, the natural consequence of focusing your energy into part of your body will cause that part to tense, begin to strain, and become uncomfortable and painful. This is a very obvious fact!"	Then a rationale is offered, defining this as a collaborative approach.
"However, what is also very obvious, which we frequently overlook, is our natural ability to rectify this situation (unpleasantness) . . . by ALLOWING ourselves to blink our eyes and then close them as they tire from the strain of staring at our fist. And then correspondingly our tight fist begins to loosen effortlessly, and the focused tension begins to decrease as our hand lowers gently into our lap. Of course, this is a very natural and accepted phenomenon. The *third* reason we do this is because you will also learn to associate these very natural occurrences with going into a very deep and pleasant trance state. For you, your hand will symbolize a lever which you can use to control the depth of a very comfortable trance. So, as your hand or lever goes down, your eyes will blink, then close, and then YOU WILL control your descent into a very relaxing and pleasant hypnotic state. All I will be doing is talking, and all you need to do is relax . . . very, very deeply . . . that sounds O.K., doesn't it? . . . yes. The *fourth* reason for using this approach is that you	See if the patient blinks his eyes when you say this. This is an indication of how open he is to this experience.

Therapist's hand begins to descend . . . softer voice

Therapist is modeling how to be very relaxed and at ease. |

INDUCTION

will learn how to control a focal point of tension or energy and transform it into . . . relaxation! . . . or perhaps just a comforting, gentle experience.

"I don't know what the limits are, of what you can make it, mmmm . . . it is entirely up to YOU . . . Just by utilizing SELF-HYPNOSIS.

"So you will be in control! And by using self-hypnosis you WILL be able to control a portion of, or all of you, if that is what YOU DECIDE!

"Any questions before you will go into a trance?" (Be reassuring, if the client has any questions. Always use a positive response set in answering the patient. For example, "That's good that you feel skeptical about going into a trance. It is a sign of intelligence to doubt, and this will only make you a better subject," or "By your affirming that you are ready to begin and don't have any questions, you indicate that you are highly motivated and will really benefit from self-hypnosis and will be an excellent participant—good!")

"Now, if anyone comes to the door, or if the phone rings, just leave it to me. I know that you can hear any sounds that you wish; [slowly mention immediate sounds in environment] . . . but actually the only important thing for you right now is the sound of my voice and the meaning of what I have to say to you, so you really don't need to give any attention to anything else unless you have a particular interest in _____ [refer to sounds already mentioned].

"So now whenever you are ready to enter a pleasant hypnotic state, simply raise your arm, clench your fist tightly, mobilize that tension through your entire body right into your hand." (Wait until the patient begins to move his hand and then say:) "That's right! Feel that tension move from the tip of your

COMMENT

Therapist gazes thoughtfully, thus encouraging patient imagination and also emphasizing patient sovereignty over himself.

Being so calm and unhurried can be reassuring to the patient. By patient indicating that they were ready to begin and yet you continue to diligently prepare them, may increase their willingness to experience a trance state.

Focusing on the immediate experience that we usually ignore can add to your credibility and also be used as a means of developing a trance.

Speak quickly now.

INDUCTION	COMMENT

head, from the bottom of your toes, all that tension, energy, coming to a head in your shoulder, your arm, your hand!" (Gently elevate the patient's fist above eye level, all the while making sure that it is rigid and hard. While doing this, you say:) "Here, let me show you, your shoulder, your arm, your hand are becoming very hard, like a steel beam or iron girder was running through them, SO HARD! Good! Get in touch with that rigidity, steel! That's right . . . begin to stare at it, so you can watch what is happening, as you experience yourself going into a deep hypnotic trance . . . Because your hand will tire of the struggle and loosen its grip, you will feel this weariness spread throughout all of you. What was once tension, straining uncomfortable—will become comfortable . . . pleasant . . . and you will experience yourself MELTING into the chair; perhaps like butter MELTING into the chair. Now, I don't know how much tension is in your body or how long it will take to centralize in your hand, but there is plenty of time, plenty of time . . . like butter, melting into the chair, softly, at your own pace and your own rate . . . after all, you are the one in control. PLENTY OF TIME, plenty of time . . . [Pauses].

Therapist inducing arm catalepsy

Increased credibility of therapist as he predicts what will happen

"Even as you are sitting in that chair, you have probably not realized it yet, but already the rhythm of your breathing has changed. It is slower . . . it is more comfortable . . . and it is a good rhythm! Your whole bodily process is changing to meet your new level of comfort. Your blood pressure is lowering, your heartbeat is at a comfortable range. I want you to enjoy being very comfortable, whenever you are ready . . . whenever you are ready. . . ."

Therapist giving plausible explanation of patient self-control over their autonomic nervous system

The therapist should not be preoccupied with the patient's progress at this point. After all, this situation has been structured so that when the patient lowers his hand to a resting position he will be in a hypnotic trance. This is one of the reasons that it is important for the therapist to ensure arm catalepsy, so that the patient will necessarily have to lower his arm before which a very brief or long period of time may have ensued. It can also be reaffirming to the patient (and perhaps ironic to the reader) that you are indeed keeping your word to "allow" the patient control over himself. The therapist is thereby reinforcing by his behavior the patient's belief in the sovereignty of the person over himself. It is also interesting to note that a patient might be concerned about this issue of responsibility and control of oneself. Perhaps some patients may wish to believe that if the pain is out of their control, they are subsequently not responsible for the pain and the effects it has on their life.

One of the essential elements of this treatment, however, is for the person to re-own responsibility for themselves and thus have the opportunity to regulate his perception of pain. So rather than debating the authenticity of the pain, we affirm perception of the pain, but also emphasize that it is the patient's perception. And his perception can be changed by using self-hypnosis.

INDUCTION	COMMENT
"In a sense, what we are doing here, corresponds to what happens when you go to a doctor and have the doctor listen to the sound of your heart beating. The doctor does not discover your heartbeat but, by the use of a stethescope, is able to become aware of your heartbeat. That is what we will be doing with hypnosis, becoming aware of the vast potential of something quite natural that is always going on inside of you. That YOU ARE capable of doing, that you are vaguely aware of . . . NOW, you will be able to control your ability to experience and utilize the benefits of the relaxing and the deeply pleasant feelings, that are deep . . . deep . . . inside of you. These feelings are always with you—it's just that sometimes we ignore the obvious." [At this point refer to whatever activity the patient is exhibiting and then add how this indicates that he is entering a deep hypnotic state; i.e., "GOOD, you are *swallowing, staring, smiling, etc.* THAT indicates that you are getting more and more deeply, deeply . . . relaxed . . ."]	Give familiar examples to patient to help him feel at ease.

It is also important for the therapist to be very reassuring and not get involved in a struggle if the patient is having difficulty entering the trance state. Just keep using the patient's behavior as a starting point for demonstrating to him that he is doing very well. BE WITH THE PATIENT! Some other ways of doing this are:

"As you [patient behavior], YOU feel yourself becoming more and more relaxed
. . . As you listen to the sound of my voice, YOU feel yourself become more and more
relaxed . . . It is fine to smile [or other behavior]. Smiling [other behavior] is a way of
relaxing, and IT IS A PLEASANT EXPERIENCE! YES! After all, YOU are the one in
control. Plenty of time, plenty of time . . . You are doing very well, good." [It is also
very helpful to synchronize your hypnotic words with the client's exhalation of breath—
watch the client's shoulders, which will lower when he exhales . . . follow his rhythm. So,
when he exhales, you exhale in a breathy voice with such words as "relax, deep, deeper,
restful, comfortable, peaceful."]

INDUCTION	COMMENT
"It's interesting that when I see [or saw, if hand is already down] your hand up, it reminds me of when I was in school as a child. I remember when my teacher explained to our class that in order to be recognized and acknowledged, one needs to raise one's arm and wait until the teacher says one's name. Well, I was a little confused about this procedure, but it seemed to be the right thing to do. After all, I was there to learn, and this was my first lesson. That's right [patient's name], relaxing very, very deeply. Well, the teacher would say my name, and I would lower my hand—kind of silly, but it worked, [patient's name]. Good, just keep on allowing yourself to melt into the chair, just allowing yourself to be very, comfortable and peaceful. I'll just keep talking, and you can become so deeply relaxed . . . so calm . . . so comfortable . . . No need for you to speak now—just enjoy the really comforting feelings that you are experiencing. Just to help you go even deeper, in a little while, I am going to count down from ten to one. As you hear the numbers going down, you feel yourself going deeper and deeper. I know that some people imagine themselves going down in an elevator, or on an escalator, or a flight of stairs. I don't know what you will imagine as I count down from ten to one, but you will feel yourself feeling more and more peaceful, calm, and comfortable. Almost as if, as the numbers go down, you feel your	Age regression to very early learning experience Very open ended and permissive

INDUCTION

relaxation going up, good. [Watch the
rhythm of the patient's breathing by
observing his shoulders rising with inhalation and lowering with exhalation.
Then say each number as he exhales, in
your own breathy voice.] Ten . . . nine,
deeper and deeper, at your own rate
and at your own pace . . . eight, restful,
in control . . . seven, more and more
deeply relaxed . . . six, calm, a full person in every way . . . five, halfway there,
you are doing very well, good . . . four
(soft voice) . . . three, gently, peacefully, comfortable . . . twoooo, deeper
and deeper, and oneee, good! Now, as
you are sitting there in a relaxed state,
feeling very much at ease and at peace
with yourself, I want you to enjoy feeling
very comfortable. For example, if at any
time you need to readjust your posture
to help you to feel more deeply relaxed
and more at ease, please feel free; after
all you are the one in control.

"In fact, perhaps you can allow
yourself to become aware of how relaxed and comfortable you are . . . Of
course, you can allow your conscious
mind to relax . . . and comfortably and
pleasantly think about a very calm and
restful place, your favorite peaceful
place—it's entirely up to you. At your
own rate and at your own pace . . .
good . . . And you can enjoy this so
much that you can let your unconscious
mind listen to me while your conscious
mind can continue to relax deeply,
deeply . . . For after all, your conscious
mind will remember what is important
for you to know. That's right, you are
doing very well, yesss . . .

"Now, many of the things that I
want to assist you in accomplishing are
governed by your unconscious mind,
and now continue as you are, at ease,
in comfort, relaxing very peacefully, and
at the right time YOU will become aware
of how to take care of your concerns,

COMMENT

From this point on, the therapist may
help the patient to a deeper level of relaxation by simply slurring the "s" at the
end of certain words. So, for instance
"yes" becomes "yesss . . ."

INDUCTION

COMMENT

all of those that you need to deal with here.

"Now, I am going to discuss your problem, and I believe you are going to enjoy the way that I present it to you. I will sketch it in general, and I want you to realize that I am going to ask of you only the things that are actually possible for you to do. There are many things that we can do of which we are unaware. And as I told you before, I will ask you to do only those things that you are capable of doing. The question is, how much are you really capable of controlling in your body?

"Now, if I were to ask you how each of your internal organs, such as your heart, your lungs, or even perhaps how your head functions, you might find it quite difficult to explain. But right now as I speak to you, all of the parts of your body are functioning quite well without your understanding exactly how they operate. So it is not really necessary for you to know how your body works, it is an automatic pilot . . . but yes, there must always be a pilot.

"In your lifetime of experience, you have felt some things, and you have not felt other things because you chose not to. You have had much experience in forgetting things that would seem, upon ordinary thinking, to be unforgettable."

"I remember being in school on some [describe present weather outside] days . . . I would frequently daydream when I got tired of the teacher's lecturing. I used to like sitting by the window, so I could always look outside and wonder . . . mmm . . . there would always be something pleasant to dream about, no matter what was going on in the room. And maybe looking forward to a birthday party, or going somewhere . . . going to visit Grandma . . . or going to school . . .

Always use yourself as a model to encourage age regression.

INDUCTION

"I don't know what you're thinking, but I remember . . . playing in the yard . . . in the school yard . . . looking forward to vacation time, and really having a good time . . .

"I remember my teacher telling us stories all the time; I would enjoy that. Once there was a disagreement between the North Wind and the Sun. The North Wind boasted of being the more powerful, and the Sun merely smiled. Just then, a traveler came into sight, and they agreed to test the matter by trying to see which of them could make the traveler remove his coat. The pompous North Wind was the first to try, while the Sun watched from behind a gray cloud. The North Wind blew a furious blast and nearly tore the coat from its fastenings; but the traveler only held the coat closer in desperation. The North Wind was surprised by this resistance, and its fiercesome gales were soon spent. Shocked by the traveler's resiliency, the Wind withdrew in despair. 'I don't believe you can do it either, mighty Sun.' Then out came the kindly Sun in all splendor, dispelling the clouds that had gathered and sending warmest and refreshing rays down upon the traveler's head . . . neck . . . shoulders . . . chest . . . stomach . . . legs . . . feet. The traveler smiled at experiencing such a wondrous spring day, and thought that this was such a day to take off a coat and greet the SPRING . . . that's fine relaxing very deeply.

"Now, you have the wonderful opportunity to associate relaxation of your body and mind with a very comfortable attitude. For already the pattern of your headaches are changing. Now I'm not sure if the change will be gradual or occur rather quickly. You see, we frequently overlook the gradual changes and are all too aware of the rather swift and quick changes. Nevertheless, it is

COMMENT

Slowly enunciate each part of the body.

Development of new association, one of calmness, relaxation

INDUCTION	COMMENT

occurring even now as you sit comfortably in the chair. For after all, that's the reason you are here . . . So that your headaches will become less severe, less frequent, and, of course, won't last as long . . . until they are gone, and they will leave, when YOU decide they WILL! . . .

Emphasizing patient responsibility

"That's right relaxing very deeply. GOOD . . . you're doing well.

"Now, I don't know what changes you will become aware of first, maybe in the severity of the pain, perhaps in the duration of time, I don't know, maybe in frequency. Perhaps, you might not be aware of the changes while they are occurring, sometimes we overlook the minute changes unless someone brings them to our attention. For after all, you are much more than a headache, much more . . . relaxing very deeply and there's so much for you to become aware of . . . I want you to enjoy being very comfortable. From now on, you have the wonderful opportunity to associate relaxation of your body and mind with a very COMFORTABLE attitude . . .

"In a few moments, I will count from one to ten. When I say the number ten, your hand will begin to rise. The same hand you used as a lever to place yourself into a trance. However, this time your hand will rise up, at your own pace and at your own rate, and when it reaches the same level from which it started when you first raised your hand, you will open your eyes and come out of the trance feeling alert, refreshed, and also very relaxed as if you had just experienced a very peaceful and comforting nap . . .

Clearly enunciate number "10."

"And tonight when you go to sleep, you will really be able to enjoy the comfort of your bed, and you will have a very deep and restful sleep, like one you had a long . . . long . . . time

INDUCTION	COMMENT
ago. And you will awaken in the morning feeling calm and secure, rested, comfortable and confident. Yes, confident in your ability to easily go into and come out of a trance, and to comfortably carry out this treatment. Good, easier and easier.	
"Now, one . . . two . . . three . . . four . . . five . . . six, seven, eight, nine, and TEN. Now, it is up to you, at your own pace and at your own rate. Good."	Start counting slowly and softly, then at five increase volume and tempo.

Second Session

In this session, as in those to follow, the patient should be informed about any forthcoming changes in procedures. It is an important consideration that the patient experience this relationship as collaborative. The rationale for this, is to emphasize that the patient is an *active* and responsible partner. After all, the effects of the treatment will need to be maintained after the actual treatment session ends, which will be accomplished by continued patient activity.

    The therapist should inform the patient that today he will first discuss anything significant either directly or indirectly related to the treatment that has transpired since they were last together. This may include any changes in headaches, feeling more relaxed the time after the last session, a deeper sleep than usual, or anything else that may be relevant. The therapist should record any changes reported by the patient and then emphasize to the patient that changes are happening already. Even changes in depth of relaxation during the last session, or being motivated enough to stay in the treatment should be reinforced. This becomes evidence of your posthypnotic suggestion at the end of the first treatment session, "that the patient will experience some changes, perhaps small at first, but that will increase and eventually add up".

    Review of reactions to treatment since last session:

"How   are you today?"
"Have   there been any changes in headaches, sleep patterns, daily activities?" etc.
Reactions   to last induction—reinforce any positive reactions and remember to avoid what the patient dislikes
Practice   at all? (If applicable)
Record   practices? (If applicable)
Still   self monitoring? (If applicable)
Different   induction today—just more choices to choose from
Describe   induction procedure
After going   through the initial phase as described above, use the following procedure.

INDUCTION	COMMENT
"That's right, get as comfortable as you would like to in the chair. I'm	Preinduction

INDUCTION	**COMMENT**
going to demonstrate another induction technique you can use to develop a very deep and pleasant hypnotic trance. Just watch me. That's all, you will be able to do this very well . . . yes. In a little while, whenever you are ready to enter a trance, all you will need to do will be to clasp your hands together tightly in front of you. Once you have them clasped together, begin to exert tension in that area. That's right, just like you did when you raised your arm the last time. However, this time you will feel the force straining from both of your arms. As you can see, my hands are tightly pressed against each other. I am also watching them closely. In a little while, my hands, my arms, my shoulders, my eyes will tire from the strain and want to relax. Now, I don't know how long this will take. It really doesn't matter how long. But it will happen. First, my fingers will stop straining and tensing, and they will begin to loosen, then my hands will loosen. It will be a little difficult for my fingers and hands to come apart. It will feel as if they were stuck together, but they will begin to come apart. That's right. As they do, I will correspondingly feel my eyes blinking and then eventually closing, and then my hands will come to rest in my lap. It is very relaxing, to say the least. This very pleasant feeling will travel all through your body, almost as if your bloodstream were carrying a very soothing refreshing calming effect . . . Of course, I will be talking throughout the whole time you are doing this, and at times you may feel as if my speech pattern matches the rhythm of your relaxation, that's fine. I will then count down from ten to one, just to help you go even deeper and more relaxed and then, I will continue talking until it's time for you to come out of the trance feeling very, very good . . .	Reassuring

Therapist demonstrates.

Therapist uses very soft voice. |

INDUCTION

"Any questions before you go into a trance?"

Once again, it is important to remember to encourage a positive response set for the patient. Use a tone, mood and attitude that conveys a supportive reassuring message that the patient will succeed. Keep on "being with the patient." Remember to characterize his behavior, attitude, feeling, and even skepticism as either a starting point or effect of being a good subject. Also, any feedback from the patient as to what he liked and disliked in the previous induction (*i.e.,* words, scenes, voice quality, etc.) will be useful additions to this induction. Being aware of the present emotional state of the client may also be helpful. By modifying your style to reflect the patient's unique characteristics, you can only add more credibility to your induction.

"Now, if anyone comes to the door, or if the phone rings, just leave it to me. I know that you can hear any sounds that you wish . . . _____ _____ [slowly mention sounds presently in the environment] but, actually the only important thing for you right now is the sound of my voice and the meaning of what I have to say to you, so you really don't need to give any attention to anything else unless you have a particular interest in _____ _____ [refer to sounds already mentioned].

"So whenever you are ready to enter a pleasant hypnotic state, simply clasp your hands tightly together. Mobilize that tension throughout your entire body right into your two hands. [Wait until the patient begins to move his hands and then say:] that's right! Feel that tension, energy, force flow from all of you and come to a head in these two hands. Focus your attention on what is happening . . . that's right . . . watch

COMMENT

Induction

Therapist stares at hands.

INDUCTION

what happens. I know some people imagine that each one of their hands symbolizes an opposing force. Perhaps one hand represents a wish for something and the other hand represents a power denying the wish. It is up to you what you think about, as your hands press hard against each other. After all, you are the one in control!

"One of the reasons we use this approach for going into a hypnotic trance is that you can watch yourself create a strain, a tension, and then be able to transform it into a very pleasant relaxed state. It really isn't necessary for you to speak; just experience whatever is going on inside of you. I will be right here WITH YOU. So experience whatever you need to in order to relax . . . deeply. I don't know how much tension is in your body or how long it will take you to centralize it in your hands, but we have plenty of time.

"Now, whenever you are ready to go deeply into a hypnotic trance and let go of the tension, just simply allow your fingers to come apart, your hands to let go . . . and eventually settle comfortably in your lap . . . and then your eyes will close and then you will be in a comfortable, relaxed state.

Create curiosity, anticipation for what will happen.

"You will feel very relaxed and experience a deep and pleasant trance state.

"Come out feeling really good, relaxed, confident in your ability to do this without me—after all, all hypnosis is self-hypnosis. I am merely showing you how you will help yourself.

"Perhaps at first you might find it a little difficult to separate your fingers from each other. When you are ready to go deeper, they may feel sort of stuck together, but that's O.K., all you will need to do is merely LET GO.

"I was talking to someone the other day about letting go, and he told me an interesting story. It seems that there is a certain kind of monkey that is found only in China. It turns out that these are very rare and valuable animals. They are called "rice monkeys." They are called rice monkeys because they love rice. Well, for a long time no one knew how to catch these lovely creatures. It so happens that recently a group of animal lovers figured out a rather ingenious ploy for catching them. The animal lovers would take coconuts and cut out a small hole in the middle, large enough so the monkey's hand could fit and also large enough to hold rice. Well, they would leave a number of enticing coconuts around the jungle and then wait, hidden from view. The rice monkeys would then come down from their trees, attracted by the aroma and scent of the rice. They knew that they were quicker than anyone, so even if anyone came, the monkeys could still scurry away. Now, the monkeys easily fit their hands into the coconuts to get the rice, but once they had the rice in their grip, their hands were larger than the hole, and thus they were not able to take them out . . . You could just imagine the squealing monkeys, gyrating and jumping up and down, struggling to get these coconuts off . . . Now, the animal lovers just had to come along, merely lift up the coconuts and attached to each one was a yelping monkey . . . mmmm some scene! . . .

"If only the monkeys would have realized that all they needed to do was to let go of the rice, and their hand would come out of the coconut.

"Now, some people would think that it was the rice that was the downfall of these monkeys . . . No. Others would point to the animal lovers . . . No. Some would think that it was the monkeys' greed, or perhaps their desire and wish for the rice which made the monkey a

INDUCTION

prisoner. No! I would think that it was simply the monkeys' action of not LET-TING GO. After all, if they were to open up their hands, they would be FREEEE NOW . . .

"Now, there is plenty of time, whenever you are ready to become more deeply relaxed. All you need to do is merely separate your hands and let them come to rest in your lap, or merely allow yourself to melt deeply in the chair.

"If at any time you need to read-just your posture, to help you go deeper, feel free—after all, you are the one in control!

"You know, it is (was) interesting watching your two hands pressing against each other. If I were to ask you before you went into this trance if you were lefthanded or righthanded, you would have indicated that you were one or the other. But as I am (was) absorbed in your hands, I see (saw) your hands staying pretty much right in the center of your body. Now, one would think that if you were righthanded, your hands would move to the left because of the stronger force. And if you were lefthanded, they would move to the right. But they stay (stayed) right in the middle. I find that interesting . . . mmmm.

"Well, I guess there is always something more to learn about our-selves. Perhaps, rather than believing that one hand is stronger or more dom-inant than the other, one could believe that our hands just complement each other. I wonder that if we have a thought, a feeling, or a belief that we don't also have a thought, a feeling, or a belief that is different and yet equal in force, equal in magnitude. Although it may initially appear to be opposite, it may be there to create a balance. After all, what is the sound of one hand clapping? Now, how do you deal with an equal and different

COMMENT

Whichever is appropriate

INDUCTION

force, feeling, thought? Perhaps you can shake hands with them, that's one way of making a friend . . . I know that when I write with my right hand, I need my left hand to hold down the paper. Plenty of time . . . just keep on relaxing very deeply.

"I remember last time when we got together, and you were able to lower your blood pressure, change your breathing into a comfortable rhythm, create a very slow, peaceful beating of your heart, yes. Now, before you began learning self-hypnosis, if I asked you to accomplish any of these things, you would have given me a confused and perplexed look. But you have already done it. For even now, as you are sitting comfortably in that chair, you may or may not have realized it already, but the rhythm of your breathing has changed. It has become more comfortable . . . slower . . . more at peace . . . and it is a good rhythm. Your whole bodily process is changing to meet your new level of comfort!

"And, yes, you have done all that . . . as I told you before, I will only ask you to do those things that you are capable of doing. The question is, how much are you capable of controlling in your body . . .

"And now each time as you inhale and exhale, you might be surprised to find yourself more and more comfortable . . . more and more relaxed than you have felt in a long, long time. Almost with each breath, you become more at ease, the tension, the tightness, pain, discomfort can drain from your body. That's right! good.

"And as you allow yourself to become more aware of how relaxed and comfortable you are, you might begin to remember another time, another place, when you were so relaxed . . . so comfortable . . . Now only if you

COMMENT

Assume that the patient has learned self-hypnosis.

Therapist asks open-ended and rhetorical question so that the patient may think about answering it.

INDUCTION

want to, you might recall this favorite relaxing place and really feel how good it is to be there, yes . . . only if you want to. Now, it doesn't really matter that I know where it is, and you don't even have to tell me about it later. For what is important to you, you are the one to decide, yes.

"And as you imagine whatever you need to experience in order to relax deeply, I shall count down from ten to one.

"And as you hear the numbers going down you will feel yourself going deeper and deeper and you may also notice that your favorite place will become clearer and more real to you, and when I reach the number one, you will be even more relaxed and pleasantly hypnotized. [Again, synchronize the numbers with the patient's exhalation of breath.]

"Ten, nine . . . deeper and deeper . . . eight, at your own pace and at your own rate, seven, more and more relaxed . . . six, calm, a full person in every way . . . five, halfway THERE, you are doing very well, four [soft voice] gently, peaceful, three . . . deeper and deeper . . . twooo, comfortable and . . . one . . . good. You are doing very well!

"Now, as you are sitting there in a relaxed state, feeling very much at ease and at peace with yourself, I would like to explain something to you. I want you to enjoy feeling very comfortable. In fact, if you want to, you can enjoy yourself so much you can let your unconscious mind listen to me while your conscious mind can continue to relax . . . and comfortably think about that very pleasant place, your FAVORITE peaceful place . . . Because many of the things that I want to assist you in accomplishing are governed by your unconscious mind, and NOW continue as you are, comfortable, calm, and at the right time YOU

COMMENT

Therapist emphasizing patient responsibility; patient begins to associate countdown with going into a deeper trance.

INDUCTION

WILL become aware of how to take care of your concerns, all of those that you need to deal with here.

"Now I am going to discuss your concerns and I believe you are going to enjoy the way I present it to you. I will sketch it in general, and I want you to realize that I am going to ask of you only the things that are actually possible for you to do.

"If I were to ask you what your goals are for coming here, some of them you would know quite well, while I'm sure that there are other goals you have, which are not as clear. For frequently when we set out to accomplish some things, we wind up achieving more than we set out to; interesting isn't it . . . yes, so only if you would like to, why don't you take a few moments to review for yourself what you would like to achieve . . . and will achieve from now on . . . yes . . . [therapist pauses].

"I'm sure that you understand that your unconscious mind has a tremendous capacity for learning, and as you continue to relax more deeply your new learnings automatically become an integral part of your total personality. You will respond to ideas and suggestions that are most helpful in establishing a new point of view, a new orientation, a new way of life. That's something you want, isn't it? Relief and release, yes . . . deeply relaxed.

"Imagine the rest of your life without your usual headache, because from now on you will begin to notice a change in the usual pattern of your headache and you will never have that same headache again. Your headaches will become less frequent and less severe . . . less frequent and less severe . . . until they disappear . . . and they WILL disappear, when YOU decide they will.

INDUCTION

"Your attempts in the past to relieve your headaches developed tension, anxiety, and frustration. NOW, that is all over! Now you have the wonderful opportunity to associate relaxation of body and mind with the relief of headaches. You will find yourself having a more comfortable attitude, more confidence in HANDLING your ability to control sensations in your head.

"After all, I am sure that you have the ability to imagine yourself without your usual headache, how your life would be different, how would it feel to be relieved . . . mmmm. For a long time it may have felt, it may even still feel, that your headache was or is a constant companion. Now, if I were to ask you if your headache is part of yourself like your heart, back, or even your head, you would respond that, of course, you can live without this ache but you need your heart, your back, your head. After all, you are more than just a headache . . . much more . . . So, you could still be yourself without having this pain . . . relaxing very deeply, good . . .

"And as I talk to you, you will absorb what I say deeply into yourself . . . As you are learning how to relax deeply and utilize the resources that are deep within you, you are developing more confidence in yourself . . . realizing that you are capable of so much . . . more than you thought yourself capable of . . . After all, you are sitting in the chair exceedingly comfortable, very much at ease and in comfort . . . And you enjoy your ability to attain this peaceful and calm awareness . . . just by allowing yourself to become aware of the vast reservoir that is deep within you . . . For you have already achieved so much, haven't you . . . And how did you do it? . . . Perhaps by trusting yourself . . . for all I am doing is talking

COMMENT

Ego-strengthening suggestions

INDUCTION

. . . and you have allowed yourself to experience how wonderful you feel when you are relaxed, yes . . .

"And as you continue to feel comfortable and enjoy how wonderful it feels to be here . . . to experience your favorite relaxing place . . . you may tell yourself that you can return anytime you wish . . . that's right, simply by taking a few moments to relax yourself and letting your imagination . . . your memories, carry you here . . . Each time you come to visit, you will find it more peaceful, even more serene than you remember it to be . . . and more comfortable as new horizons are opened for you to experience.

"It is so easy . . . so accessible . . . so available to you even when you are no longer with me . . . for my voice will be with you . . . it will be the voice of a friend . . . it will be the voice of a gentle breeze . . . it will be the voice of the rain . . . the voice of the wind and yes . . . the voice of the sun! . . .

"And just to show you that you can achieve what you set out to do, and that you are able to use hypnosis to help yourself, in a few moments, I will say the word 'now.' When I say this word, you will begin to count to yourself from one to ten. As the numbers increase, you will feel yourself becoming more and more alert. And when you say the number 'ten,' you will open your eyes, and come out of the trance feeling alert, refreshed and also very comfortably relaxed . . . and tonight when you go to sleep, you will really be able to enjoy the comfort of your bed, you will have a very deep and restful sleep, like one you had a long . . . long . . . time ago. And you will awaken in the morning feeling calm and secure, rested, comfortable, and confident. Yes, confident in your ability to easily go into and come out of a trance,

INDUCTION	COMMENT

and to comfortably carry out this treatment, good, easier and easier.

"Now, it is up to you, at your own
pace and at your own rate. Good."

Third Session

The patient should be informed about any forthcoming changes in procedure, and that the following session will be the last treatment session.

As in the last session, the format will be as follows:

Review of reactions to last treatment session (refer to second paragraph of Session Two for more detail of what to explore with patient)

"How are you today?" and "Has there been any changes in headaches, sleep patterns, medication intake, daily activities, etc.?"

Reactions to last induction, reinforce any positive reactions, remember to discard what patient dislikes

Practice at all? etc.

In this session, the therapist should convey a message of reassurance that the patient will do very well. After all, this time, he will be using essentially his own approach to relaxing and hypnotizing himself. The therapist, by his behavior and language, should convey to the patient that hypnosis is now accessible to him.

After patient feedback or questions, use the following procedure.

INDUCTION	COMMENT

"That's right, you can get as comfortable as you wish in that chair. Before
you develop a very pleasant hypnotic
state, I'm going to discuss what will happen today. You have already demonstrated your ability to relax deeply and
to respond to suggestions very well.
Now, we will go one step further by your
going into a trance without my guiding
you. For now, you have a skill that has
become part of you, that you can rely
on, whether it is in relaxing comfortably
and deeply, in graciously handling headaches, alleviating excess tension, pain,
discomfort, or whatever you choose to
apply it to.

"I know someone who learned
hypnosis for controlling his fear of
speaking in front of groups. Well, he did
very well at that, but what is also very

Pre induction

INDUCTION

interesting is that he once got a sharp metal splinter in the palm of his hand. Ouch! Whew, that's a sensitive spot. Well, he went into a deep trance and numbed his whole hand so he wouldn't experience the pain, and then his wife proceeded to remove the splinter. His wife was amazed and couldn't believe it, and he was relieved of the splinter. So who knows the limits of what you learn here. I'm sure that you have heard of people who have lost weight, stopped smoking, alleviated unnecessary anxiety, and relieved pain with hypnosis. The tools are now with you, the house you build is up to you.

"Now, in a little while, whenever you are ready to enter a deep trance, just close your eyes and go into a very comfortable and pleasant hypnotic state. Now, I have shown you a number of ways of doing this. The first time we got together, you utilized the one-arm lever approach, combined with your staring at your arm. The second time, you used both of your hands clasped tightly together, and then you imagined yourself in your favorite relaxing place.

"Another way we have indirectly referred to in terms of going into a trance has been your recognition of your breathing slowing down as you go into a trance. Well, a variation of this approach is to combine the counting down from ten to one with your exhalation of breath. So every time you breathe out, you will count down and on the tenth breath, you will be comfortably and deeply relaxed.

"You may use any of these techniques, or perhaps you have one of your own that you enjoy and that is equally effective in developing a nice trance state. Now, it is entirely up to you what you choose to use. After all, you know what works best for you.

COMMENT

Preparing patient for forthcoming glove anesthesia

INDUCTION
"Any questions before you go into a trance?"

Once again, it is important to remember to encourage a positive response set for the patient. Use a tone, mood, and attitude that conveys a supportive reassuring message that the patient will succeed. Keep on "being with the patient." Remember to use his behavior, attitude, feeling, and even skepticism as either a starting point or effect of being a good subject.

Also, any feedback from the patient as to what he liked and disliked in the previous induction (*i.e.*, words, scenes, voice quality, etc.) will be useful additions to this induction. Being aware of the present emotional state of the patient may also be helpful. By modifying your style to reflect the patient's unique characteristics, you can only add more credibility to your induction.

INDUCTION
"Now, if anyone comes to the door, or if the phone rings, just leave it to me. I know that you can hear any sounds that you wish . . . _____
_____ [slowly mention sounds presently in environment] . . . but actually the only important thing for you right now is the sound of my voice and the meaning of what I have to say to you, so you really don't need to give any attention to anything else unless you have a particular interest in . . . _____
_____ [refer to sounds already mentioned].
"One other thing before you begin. I won't speak until you signal to me that you are in a deep hypnotic trance. Instead of verbally communicating to me that you have achieved this, just move one of your fingers. Which finger would you prefer to use? [Wait until the patient demonstrates and then say:] O.K.; when I see that finger move, I will know that you are comfortably and pleasantly relaxed. At that time, I will begin to speak, and the sound of my voice will help you to feel even more comfortable. O.K.? [wait until the patient acknowledges that he understands, either by a nod of his head or a verbal assurance, and then you say:] Yes. And I will continue to speak to you, and I will help you

COMMENT

INDUCTION   **COMMENT**

by offering suggestions that will be of help to you. All you will need to do is to relax deeply . . .

"Now, there is plenty of time, plenty of time. . . . You will do very well. Whenever you are ready to deeply relax and be pleasantly hypnotized, you may begin, it is now up to you . . . [Therapist stares straight ahead, while the patient initiates his induction. The manner and the mood of the therapist should convey the belief that the patient WILL be able to accomplish it.]

[Long pause—Patient moves his finger]

"O.K. you can relax your finger and enjoy the comfort of relaxing very deeply, and being pleasantly hypnotized.

"First of all, I want you to enjoy feeling very comfortable . . . [At this point refer to whatever activity the patient is exhibiting and then add how this indicates his being deeply relaxed; i.e., Good, as you swallow, smile, breathe easier, etc. [patient behavior] you feel a deep sense of relaxation and comfort flowing through all of you.) That delightful feeling of relaxation is spreading through the muscles of your face, the gentleness of your brow . . . your neck . . . your shoulders . . . and downward flowing through your chest . . . your back . . . melting like butter into the chair, allowing the chair to hold you . . . feelings of peaceful comfort down through your stomach . . . thighs, legs . . . toes . . . You are becoming more and more deeply, yes deeply . . . relaxed. If at any time you need to adjust your posture, feel free, because I would like you to enjoy feeling very comfortable, yes . . . Can you allow yourself to be aware of how deeply relaxed you are? . . . And now you can enjoy the comfort . . . of going even deeper into the trance . . . yes!

INDUCTION

COMMENT

"In a little while, I am going to ask you to imagine a bright intense beam of light is shining directly into your eyes. Perhaps you will tell yourself it is glaring sunlight shining into your eyes, maybe you will imagine someone holding a bright flashlight into your eyes. Whatever you imagine or tell yourself, you will remember what it feels like as glaring, bright lights shine directly in your eyes . . . It is, of course, very difficult to open your eyes as you imagine this.

"Well, I am going to ask you to try to open your eyes as you imagine this. Yes, to try, to try to open your eyes, but you *won't* be able to, because the harder you try the more they will want to stay *closed . . ."*

"So, [patient's name], now, imagine and tell yourself that a bright ray of glaring light is shining directly in your eyes, glaring bright light directly in your eyes . . . and try, yes try to open them, but you won't be able to because the harder you try, the more they want to stay closed . . . Try, try in the glaring light."

[CHOOSE WHICHEVER RESPONSE IS APPLICABLE]

If the patient responds by struggling to open his eyes, but they remain *CLOSED,* use sections 1 and 2.

If the patient responds by *OPENING* his eyes easily, use section 2 only.

1. [After about 10 seconds of having the patient experience eye closure, you say:] "O.K., relax. You did fine. Now, relax deeply. The light is gone, the sun went behind a cloud. Relax . . . You have demonstrated by your ability to do that, that by the power of your mind, you are able to exert control over your body. Good! You have within you the ability to relax . . . to imagine . . . to utilize your own inner resources to control your

INDUCTION   **COMMENT**

bodily processes. Yes . . . Just to
show you that you can open your
eyes and remain in a deep trance
. . . Open your eyes now, the intense light is gone."

2. [When the patient opens his eyes,
you say:]"That's fine. Now just look
about the room and pick some small
spot to look at steadily as you continue to relax deeply with your eyes
open. And look at any spot THERE
. . . And yes, just keep looking at that
spot . . . That's right, good. You
really don't even need to pay attention to me. And you can enjoy this
so much that you can allow your unconscious mind to listen to me while
your conscious mind can continue to
relax deeply, deeply . . . For after all,
your unconscious mind will hear me.
And while you have been sitting
there, you have been letting your
body breathe itself, using its own natural rhythm . . . slowly . . . easily
. . . and deeply . . . this is your own
way of acknowledging the experience of relaxation and comfort . . .
And now you may imagine or project
on that spot, your favorite relaxing
place, as you CLOSE your eyes, NOW!

"And yes, you can now enjoy
the quiet comfort of going ever
deeper into a trance. And I want you
to enjoy being very comfortable
. . . And you can even allow yourself
to become aware of the ease . . . the
comforts . . . the resources . . . and
even the potentials within yourself
. . . and then perhaps you will have
the experience of SENSING as you
relax . . . the experience of healing
. . . restoring . . . nourishing you.

"From now on, you have as
your resource the ability to release
the tension . . . release the tightness
. . . and enjoy this very pleasant state
of relaxation by just opening up your

INDUCTION

hands . . . (or by raising and then lowering your hand . . .)"

COMMENT

The rationale for this particular procedure is to have the patient demonstrate to himself his ability to elicit a self-hypnotic trance. Furthermore, by including a challenge (eye closure) after he had already acknowledged that he was in a deep trance (by ideomotor signaling) provides a basis for the subsequent glove anesthesia. At this point, the patient is being convinced essentially that he can attain self-hypnosis.

The reader will have noticed that there were two options for the therapist to have chosen in response to the patient's reaction to the suggestion of eye closure. This is to provide the patient with the opportunity of experiencing hypnosis in a manner congruent with his particular needs. So, if the patient needed to open his eyes, or keep them closed, the therapist could continue as he has done throughout the entire treatment procedure of reaffirming that the patient is responsible for his own behavior.

At this point in the treatment procedure, a glove anesthesia technique is introduced to the patient while he is in a trance. The patient is told to continue relaxing, but also to attend and follow the therapist's instructions.

There are many ways of using and demonstrating glove anesthesia to the patient. The critical premise for this approach is that the patient experience a numbness in one of his hands and then transfer this feeling to the affected part of his body. In this case, the individual would bring his hand to his head and then either massage or stroke the most painful area. Essentially, what happens in this particular approach is that by having the patient focus his attention on one of his hands and then the therapist suggesting that a certain feeling will be experienced, such as numbness, tingling, or throbbing, will generally result in patient confirmation of this phenomena.

This is really quite simple to achieve. You, for instance, could stop reading and begin focusing your attention on one of your hands, and within a short period of time, you will become aware of sensations in that area. It is basically focusing one's attention and then labeling that experience. The reason that we use this approach in the treatment is that the patient is given the opportunity TO DO something about his pain rather than experiencing helplessness. The patient may use this as a distraction technique or perhaps in some way that he may define so as to alleviate his discomfort. Once again, we are emphasizing patient responsibility for his perception of pain.

INDUCTION

"Now, as you continue to relax deeply and enjoy the comfort of a very pleasant and deep hypnotic state . . . I would like to explain something to you . . . I'm sure that you can remember at the beginning of today's session I mentioned a person who learned hypnosis for controlling his fear of speaking in front of groups . . . And that he did very well at that, and was also able to use hypnosis to help numb his hand when he hurt it so he wouldn't experience the pain as his wife removed the splinter.

COMMENT

Glove anesthesia technique

INDUCTION

"Now, I am going to share with you a way that you can use a similar approach to help you in controlling your pain or discomfort. Now with your eyes remaining closed, good, and while remaining deeply hypnotized and pleasantly relaxed, I would like for you to imagine that a small table is being placed in front of you . . . on which are some items . . . Now, I will describe three possible items on the small table, there may be more or may be less—that depends on you.

"The first object is a beautiful, soft velvet glove with a smooth silk lining . . .

"The second object is a new brightly colored pail, filled with a sparkling, blue liquid . . .

"The third object is a large jar of hand cream, and the jar is open, revealing a most pleasant and aromatic perfume, mmmm . . .

"Now, I don't know what you are able to imagine, or which of these items seem most interesting to you, but if you proceed as if they are real, you may be surprised to discover that the relief you will experience will also be real . . .

"You see that each one of these objects contains an extremely potent anesthesia, that is something that alleviates pain by numbing that area of your body. I'm sure that in your lifetime of experience you have felt a numbness, perhaps a tingling . . . Maybe when you went to the dentist and you were given novacaine so you wouldn't feel the pain . . . A feeling of numbness . . . that's right.

"Now while remaining pleasantly relaxed and deeply hypnotized, I want you to pick up one of these objects off the small table in front of you . . . Now, it doesn't matter which one you choose, that is entirely up to you. However, I would be interested in your choice, so

COMMENT

An object that is essentially focusing on texture

An object that is essentially focusing on visual stimuli

An object that is essentially focusing on olfactory stimuli

The therapist should repeat the name of the object that the patient chooses, so that he is able to align suggestions with the specific choice.

INDUCTION

could you please tell what it is while remaining relaxed and hypnotized.

"Now, that you have chosen the
[object chosen], place your hand inside
of it. Whichever hand that you prefer
[wait until the patient makes hand ges-
ture and then say:] that's right, you are
doing very well . . . As you place your
left (or right) hand in the [object chosen],
(i.e., silk glove, aromatic cream, pail of
sparkling blue liquid) feel your fingertips
tingle as the anesthetic is quickly absorbed . . . slowly place your hand in
more comfortably . . . more securely
. . . allow yourself to experience the
numbness up to your knuckles . . .
across your palm . . . and the back of
your hand . . . that's right . . . really
allow yourself to experience this, for as
you proceed through these actions, you
will become aware that the relief you
will experience will also be real . . .

"Now, I don't know exactly what
you are experiencing in your left (or
right) hand, for you are the one who is
aware that the sensations feel like a
numbness . . . a tingling . . . a gentleness . . . I don't know, that is up to you
. . . However as the potent anesthetic
seeps even deeper, the skin on your
hand will feel even more constricted
. . . much more numb . . . that's right.
Can you sense the movement of the remaining feelings in your hand as they
glide out your fingertips into [object
chosen] . . . Continue to experience
this, and in a little while I will ask you
to gently place your left (or right) hand
on your head . . . This will give you the
opportunity to transfer the feelings of
numbness in your hand directly to your
head, where you usually experience a
headache, and in exchange any tension,
tightness, pain or discomfort will flow
from your head into your hand . . .
good . . .

"You can now begin to gently

COMMENT

The following instructions can be
adapted to any one of the objects or to
whatever the patient may imagine. The
key is focusing the patient's attention on
his ability to control his perception of
the sensations.

massage or stroke your head and allow the sensations to transfer from your hand to your head . . . [When the patient places his hand on his head, you say:] Yes, that's right, allow all the deep feelings of numbness, flow from your hand into your head . . . That's right . . . the same feelings are now gently seeping into your head . . . Can you allow yourself to experience that once painful area feeling better . . . more comfortable. . . . I am wondering if you are aware of the differences in sensations that have occurred already . . . Slowly and effortlessly stroke your hand around your head . . . as you allow the combination of numbness and relaxation to penetrate all over, yes . . . feels good . . . experience it . . .

"Now, you can repeat the transfer process as many times as you want to, need to . . . for as you [describe patient hand motion], you feel an even greater amount of comfort and relief than you did before . . . And each time you repeat it, you will find it easier and easier. [Therapist pauses.]

"Now, whenever you are ready to conclude this particular procedure, remove your hand from your head and simply shake your hand rather briskly for a few seconds, and all the natural feelings will return to YOUR HAND . . . while you continue to remain pleasantly relaxed and deeply hypnotized . . . [When the patient shakes his hand, you say:] Good . . . After doing this, you may be surprised to notice that you continue to not only feel relaxed and comfortable, but confident in your ability to achieve the goals you have set for yourself.

"As you allow yourself to relax, you will absorb what I say deeply into yourself. You will be able to remember what is important for you to remember.

"As you are learning how to relax

Ego-strengthening technique

INDUCTION   **COMMENT**

deeply and utilize the resources that are deep within you, you are developing more confidence in your abilities . . . potentials . . . and realizing that you are capable of so much . . . more than you thought yourself capable of . . . After all, you are sitting in the chair exceedingly comfortably, very much at ease and in comfort . . . and you enjoy your ability to attain this peaceful and calm state of awareness. And as you continue to remember and use what you find helpful here, you will discover that it becomes easier and easier . . . and the relief that you achieve will last longer and longer . . . As you become more confident in yourself you will no longer fear your headache because you will no longer allow it to control your way of life . . . For you have achieved so much already, just by allowing yourself to become aware of the vast resources that are deep within you . . . You have sensed within yourself a wholeness, a feeling of discovering something special . . . meaningful . . . and fulfilling within yourself . . .

"And while you are relaxing and enjoying how wonderful it feels to be comfortable . . . peaceful . . . and at ease . . . tell yourself that you can return any time you wish . . . that's right, simply by taking a few moments to relax yourself and letting your imagination . . . your memories carry you there . . . Each time you come to visit you will find it more peaceful . . . more serene . . . more natural . . . more invigorating than you remembered it to be . . . And more comfortable as new horizons are opened for you to experience . . .

"It is so easy . . . so accessible . . . so available to you . . . even when you are no longer with me, for my voice will be with you . . . it will be the voice of a friend . . . the voice of a gentle breeze . . . it will be the voice of the

INDUCTION	COMMENT

wind . . . the rain . . . and yes . . . the voice of the sun . . .

"And just to show you that you can achieve what you set out to, and that you are able to use hypnosis to help you, in a few moments, I will say the word "now". When I say this word, you will begin to count to yourself from one to ten. As the numbers increase, you will feel yourself becoming more and more alert. And when you say the number "ten," you will open your eyes, and come out of the trance feeling alert, refreshed and also very comfortably relaxed . . . and tonight when you go to sleep, you will really be able to enjoy the comfort of your bed, you will have a very deep and restful sleep, like one you had a long . . . long . . . time ago. And you will awaken in the morning feeling calm and secure . . . rested . . . comfortable and confident . . . Yes, confident in your ability to easily go into and come out of a trance, and to comfortably carry out your treatment. Good. Yes, easier and easier.

"Now! It is up to you, at your own pace and at your own rate. Good."

Fourth Session

As has been previously mentioned at the beginning of each prior session, the patient should be fully informed about any forthcoming changes in procedure. It is also important to notify the patient that this is the last treatment session. This is subject to be changed if there is an evaluative post-treatment session.

As in the last session, the format will be as follows:

Review of reactions to last treatment session (refer to second paragraph of Second Session for more detail of what to explore with patient)

Reactions to last induction, reinforce any positive reactions, and remember to discard what patient dislikes

Practice at all? etc.

In this session, the therapist should convey a message of reassurance that the patient will do very well. Once again, as in the previous session, the patient will be essentially using his own approach to relaxing and hypnotizing himself. By his behavior and language, the therapist should convey to the patient that hypnosis is now accessible to him. After patient feedback or questions, the following procedure is followed.

INDUCTION

"That's right, you can get as comfortable as you wish in that chair. Before you develop a very pleasant hypnotic state, I'm going to discuss what will happen today. You have already demonstrated your ability to deeply relax and to respond to suggestions very well.

"Now, just as you did the other day, you will go into a trance today without my guiding you.

"For now, you have a skill that has become part of you, that you can rely on, whether it is in relaxing comfortably and deeply, in graciously handling headaches, alleviating excess tension, pain, discomfort, or whatever you choose to apply it to.

"Now, in a little while, whenever you are ready to enter a deep trance, just close your eyes and go into a very comfortable and pleasant hypnotic state. Now, I have showed you a number of ways of doing this. The first time we got together, you utilized the one arm lever approach, combined with you staring at your arm. The second time, you used both hands clasped tightly together and then you imagined yourself in your favorite relaxing place.

"Some other ways we have indirectly referred to in terms of going into a trance have been your recognition of your breathing slowing down as you go into a trance. Well, a variation of this approach is to combine the counting down from ten to one with your exhalation of breath. So every time you would breathe out, you would count down and on the tenth breath, you would be comfortably and deeply relaxed.

"You may use any of these techniques or perhaps you have one of your own that you enjoy and that is equally effective in developing a nice trance state. Perhaps, the one you used the last time we were together. Now, it is entirely up to you what you choose to use.

COMMENT

Preinduction

INDUCTION   **COMMENT**

After all, you know what will work best
for you.

"Any questions before you go into
a trance?"

Once again, it is important to remember to encourage a positive response set for
the patient. Use a tone, mood, and attitude that conveys a supportive reassuring message
that the patient will succeed. Keep on "being with the patient". Remember to use his
behavior, attitude, feeling, and even skepticism as either a starting point or effect of being
a good subject.

Also, any feedback from the patient as to what he liked and disliked in the previous
induction (*i.e.,* words, scenes, voice quality, etc.) will be useful additions to this induction.
Being aware of the present emotional state of the patient may also be helpful. By modifying
your style to reflect the patient's unique characteristics can only add more credibility to
your induction.

INDUCTION   **COMMENT**

"Now, if anyone comes to the   Induction
door, or if the phone rings just leave it
to me. I know that you can hear any
sounds that you wish; _____
_____, [slowly mention sounds pres-
ently in environment] . . . but actually
the only important thing for you right
now is the sound of my voice and the
meaning of what I have to say to you,
so you really don't need to give any attention to anything else unless you have
a particular interest in _____
_____, [refer to sounds already men-
tioned].

"One other thing before you begin, I won't speak until you signal to me
that you are in a deep hypnotic trance;
just as we did the last time. Instead of
verbally communicating to me that you
have achieved this, just move one of
your fingers. Which finger would you
prefer to use? [Wait until the patient
demonstrates and then say:] O.K., when
I see that finger move, I will know that
you are comfortably and pleasantly relaxed. At that time, I will begin to speak,
and the sound of my voice will help you
to feel even more comfortable. O.K.?
[Wait until the patient acknowledges
that he understands either by a nod of
his head or a verbal assurance, and then

INDUCTION

you say:] Yes. And I will continue to speak to you, and I will help you by offering suggestions that will be of help to you. All you will need to do, is to relax deeply . . .

"Now, there is plenty of time, plenty of time . . . You will do very well. Whenever you are ready to deeply relax, and be pleasantly hypnotized, you may begin . . . it is now up to you to relax deeply . . . [Therapist stares straight ahead, while the patient initiates his induction. The manner and the mood of the therapist should convey the belief that the patient WILL be able to do it.]

[Long pause—patient moves his finger.]

"O.K. you can relax your finger and enjoy the comfort of relaxing very deeply. And now you can enjoy the comfort of going ever deeper into the trance . . .

"And I want you to enjoy every moment of it. You can have a feeling of satisfaction . . . In becoming aware of the comforts you can have within yourself. As you allow yourself to become aware of how deeply and pleasantly relaxed you are.

"As you continue to relax comfortably, I am going to offer ideas and suggestions that will be most helpful in relaxing deeper and in helping you. It isn't really necessary for you to pay close attention to what I have to say. You may involve yourself in your own very, very comfortable feelings.

"In it's unique way, your unconscious mind listens and responds to new learnings and experiences.

"As I continue to talk, you may experience yourself feeling more and more relaxed . . . peaceful . . . and calm . . .

"A long, long time ago . . . a famous psychiatrist from Germany emigrated to the United States. Well, she was very famous at that time. First, she had the notoriety of being one of a few women in what was primarily a male-dominated profession. And second, she was known as a wonderful healer . . . She was invited to New York City as a guest of the mayor and stayed in one of the most luxurious hotels. When she arrived at the hotel, one of the guests immediately recognized her. He [note: sex of guest will match sex of patient] enthusiastically volunteered his services to carry her luggage perse, but really to seek help with the heavy baggage, he was carrying inside. From the moment that they entered the room and for the next couple of hours, he unrelented in sharing his concerns, special problems, sorrows, and troubles. The doctor listened intently and continually nodded her head in a reassuring and helpful manner. Well, the guest did not know exactly what happened, or how the doctor did it, but he felt so much better, so relieved . . . He couldn't thank the doctor enough, and feeling nourished and refreshed, left the room. Well, the doctor smiled kindly to herself and thought . . . that one of these days, she is just going to have to learn the English language. "Good! As you [smile, laugh, breathe easier—patient behavior], you feel yourself very comfortably relaxed, deeply relaxed . . .

"That's right, good. And you can enjoy this so much that you can allow your unconscious mind to listen to me while your conscious mind can continue to relax deeply, deeply . . . For after all, your unconscious mind will hear me. And while you have been sitting there, letting your body breathe itself, using its own natural rhythm . . . slowly . . . easily . . . and deeply . . . this is your own way of acknowledging the experience of relaxation and comfort . . .

"And as you allow yourself to become more aware of how relaxed and

INDUCTION   **COMMENT**

comfortable you are, you might begin
to remember another time . . . another
place . . . when you were so relaxed
. . . so comfortable . . . Now only if you
want to, you may recall this favorite relaxing place and really feel how good it
is to be there, yes . . . only if you want
to . . .

"I'm sure that you understand that
your unconscious mind has a tremendous capacity for learning, and as you
continue to relax deeply, deeply . . .
your new learnings will become an integral part of yourself . . . You will respond to ideas and suggestions that are
most helpful in achieving your goals and
establishing a new point of view. That's
something you want isn't it? Relief and
release. . . And yes, you can now enjoy
the quiet comfort of going ever deeper
into a trance. And I want you to enjoy
being very comfortable . . . And you
can even allow yourself to become aware
of the ease . . . the comforts . . . the
resources . . . and even the potentials
that are deep within you . . . then perhaps you will have the experience of
SENSING as you relax . . . the experience of healing. . . restoring. . . nourishing yourself . . .

"From now on, you have at your
disposal the ability to release the tension
. . . release the tightness . . . and enjoy
this very pleasant state of relaxation by
just opening up your hands . . . [or by
raising and then lower your hand . . .]

"In the time we have spent together, you have learned many things.
You will be able to remember those
things that are important for you to
know, clearly, easily, effortlessly. From
now on you will remember that YOU
are quite capable of placing yourself in
this deep restful relaxation . . . and
comfortable hypnotic state whenever
you need to . . . whenever you want to
. . . The suggestions that have been offered to you will work just as strongly

INDUCTION

. . . just as surely . . . just as meaningfully when you say them to yourself as when I said them to you in this room. They will remain deeply embedded in your unconscious to help you help yourself.

"You will remember to use what you have learned in these sessions to prevent, alleviate, or terminate a headache. Pain is a warning that the body gives. It is like an alarm clock that awakens you in the morning. You awaken, and you turn off the alarm. Then you proceed with preparing for the day's work. After all, you are more than just a headache . . . much more . . . much more to be aware of . . . . So, you could still be yourself without having this pain . . . relaxing very deeply, good . . .

"From now on, as soon as you begin to experience a headache, you will simultaneously begin to breathe slowly . . . regularly . . . and deeply . . . yes, just as you are doing now. That's right . . . with each slow, regular, deep breath, the feeling that you are getting a headache will begin to subside, and then leave you completely . . . Or if you begin to feel tension, strain or discomfort, instead of the muscles in your neck and shoulders competing and straining against each other, why not experience it between your left and right hand. You know what to do with THAT tension and how to transform it into a deep hypnotic relaxation. And when your hands would separate, the pain will leave as if it was a puff of smoke rising steadily in the air . . .

"You have also learned that by using the power of your mind, you are able to anesthesize parts of your body. You are now capable of imagining a [object used in glove anesthesia by patient] filled with a potent anesthesia that will help you to numb your hand, your head, or wherever you choose to apply it, yes . . .

INDUCTION

"From now on you have the ability to imagine yourself without your usual headache . . . how your life would be different, how it would feel to be relieved . . . mmmm.

"And now you have the wonderful opportunity to associate relaxation of body and mind with the relief of headaches. As you become more confident in yourself . . . yes . . . You will no longer fear your headache because you will no longer allow it to control your life. You will find yourself having a more comfortable attitude, more confidence in your ability to control sensations in your head.

"As you allow yourself to continue to relax . . . you will absorb what I say deeply into yourself. You will be able to remember what is important for you to remember . . .

"While you have learned how to relax deeply and become pleasantly hypnotized, you have also learned how to use the resources that are deep inside of you . . . You have developed much more confidence in your abilities . . . potentials . . . and capabilities . . . and this positive growth will continue as you become increasingly aware of not only the vast resources that lies within you, but of what is also around you . . . the community . . . the people . . . the environment . . . the SHARING . . .

"Just as you have sensed within yourself a wholeness, a feeling of discovering something quite special . . . meaningful and fulfilling within yourself . . . you are also becoming aware of the specialness of what and who is around you . . . the important people in your life . . . the sharing of who you are . . . your appreciation of yourself and others . . . so much to become aware of . . . so much . . .

"And while you are relaxing and enjoying how wonderful it feels to be comfortable . . . peaceful . . . and at

COMMENT

Ego-strengthening technique

INDUCTION

ease . . . tell yourself that you can return any time you wish . . . that's right,
simply by taking a few moments to relax
yourself and letting your imagination
. . . your memories carry you there
. . . Each time you come to visit, you
will find it more peaceful . . . more serene . . . more natural . . . more invigorating then you remember it to
be . . .

"And more comfortable as new
horizons are opened for you to experience . . .

"It is so easy . . . so accessible
. . . so available to you . . . even when
you are no longer with me . . . for my
voice will be with you . . . it will be the
voice of a friend . . . the voice of a gentle breeze . . . it will be the voice of the
wind . . . the rain . . . and yes . . . the
voice of the sun . . .

"And just to show you that you
can achieve what you set out to, and that
you are able to use hypnosis to help you,
in a few moments I will say your name.
When I say your name, you will begin
to count to yourself from one to ten. As
the numbers increase, you will feel
yourself becoming more and more alert.
And when you say the number "ten,"
you will open your eyes, and come out
of the trance feeling alert, refreshed,
and also very comfortably relaxed . . .
and tonight when you go to sleep, you
will really be able to enjoy the comfort
of your bed, you will have a very deep
and restful sleep, like one you had a long
. . . long . . . time ago. And you will
awaken in the morning feeling calm and
secure, rested, comfortable and confident. Yes, confident in your ability to
easily go into and come out of a trance,
and to comfortably carry out this treatment, good, easier and effectively . . .

"Now, [patient's name], it is up to
you, at your own pace and at your own
rate. Good."

References

Ad Hoc Committee on Classification of Headache: J Am Med Assoc 179:717, 1962

Bandler R, Grinder J: Patterns of Hypnotic Techniques of Milton H. Erickson, M.D., vol 1 and 2. California, Meta Publications, 1975, 1977

Barber TX, Calverley DS: Empirical evidence for a theory of "hypnotic" behavior: Effects on suggestibility of five variables typically included in hypnotic induction procedure. J Consult Psychol 29:28, 1965

Bassman SW: The effects of indirect hypnosis, relaxation and homework on the primary and secondary psychological symptoms of women with muscle-contraction headaches. Unpublished doctoral dissertation, University of Cincinnati, 1982

Beatty T, Haynes S: Behavior intervention with muscle-contraction headache: A review. Psychosom Med 41:165, 1979

Beecher H: Measurements of Subjective Responses: Quantitative Effects of Drugs. New York, Oxford University Press, 1959

Beecher H: Generalization from pain of various types of diverse origins. Science 130:267, 1959

Benson H: The Relaxation Response. New York, Avon Books, 1975

Bernal G: The differential effectiveness of biofeedback and hypnosis for the treatment of tension headaches. Unpublished doctoral dissertation, University of South Carolina, 1978

Bernstein D, Borkovec T: Progressive Relaxation Training: A manual for The Helping Professions. Chicago, Research Press, 1973

Blumenthal L: Hypnotherapy of headache. Headache 2:197, 1963

Bresler D: Free Yourself From Pain. New York, Holt, Rinehart & Winston, 1979

Budzynski TH, Stroyva JM, Adler CS, Mulleney DJ: EMG biofeedback and tension headache: A controlled outcome study. Psychosom Med 35:484, 1973

Burrows G, Dennerstein L (eds): Handbook of Hypnosis and Psychosomatic Medicine. New York, Elsevier/North Holland Biomedical Press, 1980

Cheek DB, LeCron LM: Clinical Hypnotherapy. New York, Grune & Stratton, 1968

Chesney MA, Shelton JL: A comparison of muscle relaxation and electromyogram feedback treatments for muscle contraction headache. In Kamiya J, Barber TX, Miller NE, Shapiro D, Stoyva J (eds): Biofeedback and Self-Control: 1976/77. Chicago, Aldine Publishing, 1977

Crasilneck HB, Hall JA: Clinical Hypnosis: Principles and Applications. New York, Grune & Stratton, 1975

Diamond S: Headache: Its diagnosis and management. Headache, 19:113, 1979

Diamond S, Dalessio D: The Practicing Physician's Approach to Headache. New York, Medcom Press, 1973

Drummond F: Hypnosis in the treatment of headache: A review of the last 10 years. J Am Soc Psychosom Dent Med 28:87, 1981

Erickson MH: Hypnosis in painful terminal illnesses. Am J Clin Hypn 1:117, 1959

Erickson MH: An introduction to the study and application of hypnosis for pain control. In Lassner J (ed): Hypnosis and Psychosomatic Medicine. New York, Springer-Verlag, 1968

Erickson M, Rossi E, Rossi S: Hypnotic Realities. New York, Irvington Publishers, 1976

Friedman AP: Reflection on the problems of headache. J Am Med Assoc 190:121, 1964(a)

Friedman AP: Reflection on the problem of headache. J Am Med Assoc 90:445, 1964(b)

Friedman AP, Finlay KH, Graham JR: A classification of headache. Neurology 12:378, 1962

Friedman AP, Merritt HH: Headache: Diagnosis and Treatment. Philadelphia, David, 1959

Friedman AP, Von Storch JC, Houston MH: Migraine and tension headaches: A clinical study of 2,000 cases. Neurology 4:773, 1964

Gannon L, Haynes S, Safranek R, Hamilton J: A psychophysiological investigation of muscle-contraction and migraine headache. J Psychosom Res 25:271, 1981

Greenleaf E: Defining hypnosis during hypnotherapy. Int J Clin Exp Hypn 22:120, 1974

Haley J (ed): Advanced Techniques of Hypnosis and Therapy: Selected Papers of Milton H. Erickson, M.D. New York, Grune & Stratton, 1967

Haley J: Uncommon Therapy: The Psychiatric Techniques of Milton H. Erickson, M.D. New York, W. W. Norton, 1973

Harding CH: Hypnosis in the treatment of migraine. In Lassner J (ed): Hypnosis and Psychosomatic Medicine. New York, Springer-Verlag, 1967

Harrison S: The Use of EMG biofeedback and hypnosis in treatment of tension headache. Unpublished doctoral dissertation, Texas A & M University, 1980

Hartland J: Medical and Dental Hypnosis. London, Balliere, 1966

Haynes SN, Moseley D, McGowan WT: Relaxation training and biofeedback in reduction of muscle tension. Psychophysiology 12:547, 1975

Hilgard ER: Hypnosis. Ann Rev Psychol 16:157, 1965

Hilgard ER: Pain as a puzzle for psychology and physiology. Am Psychol 24:103, 1969

Hilgard ER, Hilgard JR: Hypnosis in the Relief of Pain. Los Altos, CA, William Kaufmann, 1975

Hutchings DF, Reinking RH: Tension headaches: What form of therapy is most effective? In Kamiya J, Barber TX, Miller NE, Shapiro D, and Stoyva J (eds): Biofeedback and Self-Control: 1976/77. Chicago, Aldine Publishing, 1976

Hypnosis without ritual—A medical tool. Med World News 14:58, 1973

Jacobson E: Progressive Relaxation. Chicago, University of Chicago Press, 1938

Kondo C, Canter A: True and false electromyographic feedback: Effect on tension headache. J Abnorm Psychol 86:93, 1977

Kroger WS: Hypnotherapeutic management of headache. Headache 2:51, 1963

Kroger WS: Clinical and Experimental Hypnosis. Philadelphia, JB Lippincott, 1977

Martin PE, Mathews AM: Tension headache: A psychophysiological investigation. J Psychosom Res 22:389, 1978

McGlashan TH, Evans R, Orne MT: The nature of hypnotic analgesia and placebo response to experimental pain. Psychosom Med 31:227, 1969

Melamed B, Siegel L: Behavioral Medicine. New York, Springer Publishing, 1980

Melzack R: The McGill pain questionnaire: Major properties and scoring methods. Pain 1:277, 1975

Melzack R, Wall P: Pain mechanisms: A new theory. Science 150:971, 1965

Melzack R, Torgerson W: On the language of pain. Anesthesiology 34:50, 1971

Melzack R, Perry C: Self-regulation of pain: The use of alphafeedback and hypnotic training for the control of chronic pain. Exp Neurol 46:452, 1975

Mitchell KR, White RG: Behavioral self-management: An application to the problem of migraine headache. Behav Ther 8:213, 1977

Morgan AH, Hilgard JR: The Stanford Hypnotic Clinical Scale for Adults (SCHS: Adult). Am J Clin Hypn 21:134, 1979

Orne MT: On the social psychology of the psychological experiment: With particular reference to demand characteristics and their implications. Am Psychol 17:776, 1962

Pierce S, Morley S: An experimental investigation of pain production in headache patients. Br J Clin Psychol 20:275, 1981

Phillips C: A psychological analysis of tension headache. In Rachman S (ed): Contributions to Medical Psychology, vol 1. Oxford, Pergamon, 1977(a)

Phillips C: Headache in general practice. Headache 16:322, 1977(b)

The Quality of Mercy. N Engl J Med 306:113C, 1982

Redden J: Self-control cognitive modification techniques in the treatment of low back pain. Unpublished doctoral dissertation, University of Cincinnati, 1980

Reinking R, Hutchings D: Follow-up to: "Tension headaches: What form of therapy is most effective?" Biofeedback Self-Regulation 6:57, 1981

Ryan R: Headache and Head Pain. St Louis, CV Mosby, 1978

Sacerdote P: Theory and practice of pain control in malignancy and other protracted recurring painful illnesses. Int J Clin Exp Hypn 18;160, 1970

Sachs LB: Hypnotic self-regulation of chronic pain. Am J Clin Hypn 20:106, 1977

Saper J, Magee K: Freedom from Headaches. New York, Simon and Schuster, 1978

Sargent JD, Green EE, Walters ED: The use of autogenic feedback training in a pilot study of migraine and tension headaches. Headache 12:120, 1970

Sargent JD, Green EE, Walters ED: Preliminary report on the use of autogenic feedback training in the treatment of migraine and tension headaches. Psychosom Med 35:129, 1973

Schlutter L: A comparison of treatments for pre-frontal muscle contraction headache. Unpublished doctoral dissertation, University of South Dakota, 1978

Spiegel H, Spiegel D: Trance and Treatment: Clinical Uses of Hypnosis. New York, Basic Books, 1978

Sternbach R: Pain: A Psychophysical Analysis. New York, Academic Press, 1968

Sternbach R: Pain Patients: Traits and Treatment. New York, Academic Press, 1974

Sternbach R: Clinical aspects of pain. In Sternbach RA (ed): The Psychology of Pain. New York, Raven Press, 1978

Stickney JH: Aesop's Fables. Boston, Ginn and Co, 1915

The American Society of Clinical Hypnosis—Education and Research Foundation. A syllabus on hypnosis and a handbook of therapeutic suggestions. Chicago, 1973

Tasto DL, Hinkle JE: Muscle relaxation treatment for tension headaches. Behav Res Ther 11:347, 1973

Todd FJ, Elly RJ: The use of hypnosis to facilitate conditional relaxation responses: A report of three cases. J Behav Ther Exp Psychol 1:295, 1970

Wain H: Hypnosis in the control of pain. Am J Clin Hypn 23:41, 1980

Waters WE: Community studies of the prevalence of headache. Headache 9:178, 1970

Wickramasekera I (ed): Biofeedback, Behavior Therapy and Hypnosis: Potentiating the Verbal Control for Behavior for Clinicians. Chicago, Nelson-Hall, 1978

Wolberg L: Short-Term Psychotherapy. New York, Grune & Stratton, 1965

Wolff HG: Headache and Other Head Pain. New York, Oxford University Press, 1963

Zeig J: Teach Seminar With Milton Erickson, M.D. New York, Brunner/Mazel, 1980

15 Hypnosis in Other Related Medical Conditions

SIMON W. CHIASSON

We have not even begun to scratch the surface of the many uses of hypnosis in medical conditions. Fortunately, there is a resurgence of interest by the uninitiated. A high degree of respectability is becoming attached to the use, and renewed enthusiasm on the part of many trained in hypnosis, to put this modality to its proper use.

Patients must be made to realize that they are doing the hypnosis, and we are just teaching them how to go into hypnosis. However, they can be the best subjects in the world, but unless they can actually use hypnosis for some useful purpose, it will not do them a bit of good. This is where we, as physicians, dentists, and psychologists, can actually teach them to use the level of hypnosis they have obtained for the desired objective.

I am going to address myself to the use of hypnosis in several medical conditions: neurology, psychosomatic medicine, physical rehabilitation, ophthalmology, orthopedics, genitourinary practice, obstetrics and gynecology, dermatology, and internal medicine. Unfortunately, we are unable to present reliable statistics at this time, and there are no reliable series that are adequately documented. The biggest controversy is between the believers and the nonbelievers, but every day people are beginning to see the power that people have within themselves to achieve objectives and extend the limits of their abilities. What is needed is a central pooling of all data, as it relates to one particular subject. This should not be too difficult in our era of computers. Nevertheless, we should make every effort to contribute cases and series to present and future literature. In this way, we can all start to visualize modalities and verbalizations used in actual clinical practice and learn from one another. There are good books on mechanisms of hypnosis used in actual clinical practice in the conditions that I am going to mention (Kroger, 1977; Hartland, 1971; Erickson, Hershman, and Secter, 1981; Cheek and LeCron, 1968). However, their approach may be different from yours or mine. In this chapter, I show how I use hypnosis in the areas already mentioned. You may be thinking along the same lines, or you may have an approach that works better for you. Nevertheless, something you may see in this chapter may give you an idea on how better to use hypnosis for a particular condition or for one not even mentioned here.

As students and faculty, we bring to workshops our own expertise in our fields—our knowledge of physiology, pathology, anatomy, normal and abnormal psychology, and thought processes. We learn and teach induction techniques, which are formal at first. We should be like a sponge and learn as many techniques as we can because we never know when one of these may save the day when we are teaching a patient how to go into hypnosis. Although most of us avoid formal techniques, as we become more comfortable and experienced, some little bits and pieces creep into our modalities.

When treating various conditions with hypnosis, I use either an informal induction, or when a formal technique is needed, I use the Chiasson technique, for obvious reasons (see Appendix 15-1).

Following this, I use a fractionating technique for deepening verbalization. I count backward from 100 to 0. The first twenty numbers are done in increments of one, and then from 75 to 0, by fives. I pause at appropriate points to give my verbalization for treating the condition in question.

Neurology

In this field, I have used hypnosis for numerous conditions, such as Bell's palsy, multiple sclerosis (MS), alateral sclerosis (ALS), headaches, essential hypertension, and neurologic changes with pernicious anemia.

The verbalization, repeated at least five times is "Let your muscles relax twice as much as they were a moment ago. As all the muscles relax, your circulation improves inside and outside of your body, and you get oxygen and nourishment to muscles and parts of muscles that they weren't getting to before. As the circulation improves, you get oxygen and nourishment to nerve heads, nerve endings and nerve tissue. This prevents any further degeneration and helps regeneration and (in demyelinating conditions) the covering over the nerves where they should be covered. As the circulation improves, you can use your body's immune mechanism with all of the antibodies, enzymes, and chemicals to go to the right places in your body, to get the desired effect. Your subconscious mind knows how to use the antibodies and enzymes and also knows how to put the chemicals in the right combination to achieve a desired effect, much in the same manner as you would use a chemical formula or a recipe to get the right results for some desired outcome. Under this very special state, your subconscious mind can use all the time it really needs, in which one moment of this special time can be equivalent to much longer periods of regular time. Just as in a dream, you can cover situations that may be equivalent to hours, days, weeks, or even months."

This verbalization has been very effective in the conditions I have mentioned.

My results in treating Bell's palsy with hypnosis have been most rewarding and exciting. It has also been a very provocative experience. One of my friends, a neurosurgeon, claims that it is impossible to close the eye affected by Bell's palsy. However, I later had patients checked by an ophthalmologist, who confirmed the diagnosis. Remember that one of the techniques commonly used is an eye closure technique. Tell the subject to close his eyes and relax the muscles so much that even if he tries, he cannot open them. Then by really trying, he can open his eyes, but it takes a definite muscular effort. Therefore, I maintain that in Bell's palsy the eye is kept open by muscle spasm and that when the patient relaxes, these muscle spasms disappear and the eye closes passively. When the hypnosis is discontinued, the muscle spasm returns and the eye remains open. I merely give the explanation that the nerve is swollen and as the circulation improves the swelling will disappear and the nerve revert to normal. I also mention taste because in some it is lost to part of the tongue. Since there is often paresthesia as the nerve is coming back, I use the explanation that the pins and needles that patients feel is an alarm mechanism, and since we both know the problem, it is a good sign. It means that the nerve is coming back to normal. It would be silly to have the patient get rid of the paresthesia by making the area numb, because that is what we are combatting. I simply tell him that since I know that it is coming back to normal, and he knows that it is coming back, he may as well be comfortable while it is coming back.

MS is helped subjectively, but I do not know of any reversal of demyelination. However, anything is possible. I work on the specific complaint by a variation of the verbalization that I use in my general approach to all problems.

I have had experience with two cases of ALS:

One was a 26-year-old female with two children. She had developed weakness and muscle atrophy a few years after her second delivery. Her family practitioner made the diagnosis, and it was confirmed by the Cleveland Clinic. She was depressed and anxious because she was told that she had, at the most, 6 years to live. She asked to see me, and I spoke to both her and her husband. They were told that we did not know what caused the disease, and that since there was no known medical cure, it might be interesting to try hypnosis. At that time, she was in a bowling league and was so tired that she could bowl only one game. Her hands were too weak to buckle her children's snow boots. Through hypnosis, it became apparent that there was some connection, subconsciously, between her condition and cold. The patient was good at visual imagery and had enjoyed teaching kindergarten before her marriage. She was able to go back and picture herself teaching kindergarten and was told to imagine specifically the craft sessions, which gave her isometric hand exercises. She was told also to picture herself swimming one hundred lengths of a warm pool, and the significance of the stroke was explained in restoring learned mental images and reflex arcs. She was told to picture herself squeezing a ball 100 times. Her session ended by imagining that she was getting bowling instructions from one of the best bowlers, and that she would be able to bowl better than ever. She was to bowl three games, and when she was finished, she was to indicate with a finger response. She had no trouble with her children's clothing and boots, and was able to bowl three games in her league. One day after a particularly good session, she was told she might bowl a fourth game as a reward. That week, her team had a playoff with the team that had won the first half of the season. The other team won two games and they won one, but because they had the high score it was necessary to have a playoff. The patient's spare and strike in the fourth game helped her team to win. She moved away after 5 years, and this Christmas I received a card. It is her seventh year since her diagnosis, and she feels fine. She has taken up golf and is back teaching kindergarten, and she is very grateful for her good health.

The other ALS patient was 54 and had trouble speaking and swallowing and had some ataxia. He was first seen 3½ years ago. He improved objectively and subjectively. He could speak much better, could walk better, and had lost his depression. He was seen for his annual visit at one of our leading institutions, and he overheard the neurologist questioning his wife about who was feeding and dressing him. This had a profound adverse effect on him, and it took 2 months to get him back where he had been. On his next annual visit, he was asked if he had any trouble swallowing, and when he said he had some difficulty at times, he was sent to ENT for a very extensive examination. After his return he told me that he did not want to continue his therapy because he felt that he was wasting my time. Despite his wife's pleading, he has not come back and in a very recent communication she tells me that he is failing rapidly now.

When treating headache patients using the fractionation method of deepening, I tell them that as the muscles relax twice as much as they were before, the circulation improves inside and outside of their body, and especially in the brain and the covering over the brain, and even in the scalp. As the circulation improves, it is completely normal, and the vessels will not shrink down or expand. They are told that both are mechanisms to cause headaches and that while they are relaxed and the circulation is normal, they cannot have a headache. By relaxing, they have less chance of the headache recurring. Some patients are told about the endorphins. The technique I use is to compare the endorphins and the receptor sites to a busy phone, so that the painful stimuli cannot get through. In children I often use the switch boxes, the switches and the colored wires going from their thumb to the switches; it can turn off or turn on a headache. All patients are told that they will not mask any symptoms that would be part of their warning or alarm system, which would indicate possible trouble.

I treat patients for essential hypertension, after excluding causes such as arteriosclerotic vessel changes, stenosis of renal vessels, renal diseases, and so on. The biggest effective component here is the autonomic nervous system. Therefore, I use this system while the patient is under hypnosis. I have him visualize himself being given an injection, and I try to explain in lay terms sympathetic and splanchnic blocks or having a surgical procedure which strips some of these nerve fibers, and that this allows the blood vessels to expand and reduces the pressure that has to be overcome. This can be demonstrated with a constricted balloon by showing how much more pressure is necessary to blow up the balloon when it is constricted. By teaching the patient autohypnosis he can be enabled to handle stressful conditions and control the pressure to a great extent.

I am working with a patient with pernicious anemia, who was told that she had irreversible neurologic changes. However, after continued work with hypnosis and autohypnosis, the patient has feeling and lessening paresthesias.

I am sure that there are numerous neurologic conditions that you can think of that may respond well to your own use of hypnosis. I hope that previous suggestions will be of some help to you.

Psychosomatic Conditions

It is difficult to divorce completely functional from organic conditions. It is doubtful that either condition will exist entirely alone. However, there are more functional overlays with organic conditions than vice versa.

How often have you heard these expressions?

"You make me sick to my stomach."
"You give me a pain in the neck."
"You give me a pain in the butt."

How many unnecessary surgeries have been done in the abdomen, or on the back? How many invasive investigative procedures have been performed? How many unnecessary x-rays have been made?

Our biggest fault in medicine and psychology is that we do not really listen to what the patient or the client is telling us although we may hear what he or she says. The most important thing is to really listen. The next essential is to do an extensive physical examination, or at least have one done. Every system in the body is involved in psychosomatic disease—all our senses, the digestive system from the mouth to the very end, the respiratory system, the circulatory system, the autoimmune system, and even the skin itself. We are all familiar with the loss of smell, sight, hearing, and taste. All of these have been successfully treated by hypnosis. Uncovering and treating these complaints requires probing and the use of hypnosis. A patient capable of going deep enough to come up with the answers for the conversion is usually capable of developing amnesia to put the problems back in the subconscious, if the material is too traumatic. The operator has something to work with, and the patient can be desensitized.

When working on aberrations of the senses, it is important to know how these senses work, and one of the best sources is W.F. Ganong's *Review of Medical Physiology* (1979).

I will just give four anecdotes about the treatment of digestive system complaints.

Case 1

A 52-year-old male, who had been a patient in the hospital for 3 months after having come in for the third time with an intestinal obstruction. He had massive adhesions. After prolonged attempts at conservative management, superalimentation, and correct nutrition, he had surgery. X-rays showed that the alimentary tract was intact and functioning. However, after the nasogastric tube was removed, the patient would vomit each time he was given food or drink. It was necessary to reinsert the tube on three occasions. Eventually, the surgeon asked if hypnosis might help, and he was assured that it could be very beneficial. The patient was directed into the hypnotic state and was given the following explanation. For weeks he had had a nasogastric tube down into his stomach because of his previous obstruction. The tube was a foreign object, and his body did everything to try to get rid of the tube by causing the waves that normally went down his esophagus (the tube that goes from the back of the throat to his stomach) to reverse themselves. Now that he no longer needed the tube, he might as well have the tube removed and let those waves go down the way they normally should. In this way, they could carry down the food and liquid, which were so necessary to his health. He was asked to indicate with his index finger if it was O.K. with him, and he responded favorably. The tube was removed; he began to eat and drink; he went home in two days.

Case 2

A 39-year-old male who was an electronics expert had had intestinal surgery and was on continuous suction because of the production of excessive gastric secretions. He was seen on three occasions and given suggestions of normal secretions for the digestion of his food, starting from the mouth and going into the stomach, and the digestion and absorption of the food from the small bowel. The secretions were down to normal after two sessions, and the nasogastric tube was removed. He was seen again for reinforcement and allowed to go home. He had been there so long that the surgical floor had a party for him before he went home. He was seen by his surgeon 2 weeks later, and he was fine.

Case 3

A 36-year-old female had had surgery for a partial obstruction. The surgery was successful, but she continued having colicky pain and needed heavy doses of narcotics. Since she was also a patient of mine, the surgeon asked me to see her for hypnosis, since all her studies were normal. Under hypnosis she was told that for a long time her bowel had been partially blocked, and because of this she had increased the waves that carry food along the intestine to move the food past the partial block. Now there was no longer a block, but there was swelling and the bowel had gotten in the habit of making these waves stronger; therefore, it caused a colicky pain. Now that the intestine was back to normal, the waves should become more normal and comfortable and she would be surprised that she would be comfortable. This would occur soon because as she relaxed and improved the circulation through her whole tummy, the swelling would disappear, the intestine would be completely normal, and the waves could go along normally and comfortably. The patient was taught self-hypnosis and required no more medication. She was discharged 2 days later.

Case 4

A 54-year-old, unmarried female was referred by a surgeon who happened to be a good friend of hers. She had had painful anal spasms and burning for 15 years. She had been seen by her proctologist and had had psychiatric evaluations at Johns Hopkins and the Mayo Clinic. She proved to be a delightful subject, and under hypnosis, she was asked to see her problem, analyze her problem, and solve it. She was asked to dwell on the fact that someone had been giving her a pain in the butt and that now she would figure out how to solve her problem. She was told to indicate when she had the answers and would become completely comfortable. She gave me progress reports and was doing fine. She needed only one reinforcement 6 months later, when she was going to have a long visit with her family at a summer resort. I have had numerous contacts with her since, and she has had no recurrence.

Respiratory System

Asthma can be organic and have functional overlay, or be entirely functional. This can be helped by reassurance, education, and breathing exercises.

Cardiovascular System

Hot flashes and other vasomotor instabilities such as blushing have been treated by reassurance and autohypnosis and by teaching how a cooling effect on the skin causes constriction of the peripheral vessels. Tachycardia and irregularities have been converted by hypnosis, reassurance, and suggestions that the heart rate would become slower and regular. One case in particular was successful after previous efforts by the patient's cardiologist (who was also a very good hypnotist) to produce the same results had failed. In this case, the aura of the operator made the difference. At this time, the patient was in a cardiac intensive care unit, and her prognosis was poor. Three years have passed, and she has done well, and surviving cancer surgery, as well as a stay in the cardiac ICU. At the present time, her daughter says she is doing very well and is fully active with her grandchildren.

Skin

This area includes neurogenic dermatitis and blushing, as well as many other problems. It is my purpose to give examples to whet your appetite and make you think of the many things you have to offer.

Case 1

The first patient was a 26-year-old female, who had just lost a baby. She had a skin condition with papules, ulcers, and irritation of the skin from her umbilicus to her mid thighs. Her dermatologist told her that it was getting better; she felt it was getting worse, and I agreed with her.

She was asked what she thought would help make her more comfortable, and she said that when she took a cold shower it felt much better. Under hypnosis, she was told that she would feel cool and have no desire to scratch, and that the lesions would heal much faster. Even when the hypnosis would terminate, the cool feeling would persist, and the condition would improve and would heal much faster than she would expect. In 2 weeks, when she returned, the skin condition was completely gone. Two years later she had a recurrence of the dermatitis. I had her go into hypnosis and told her that instead of the itching, she would get a numbness in her left little finger, and the condition would improve. She came back 2 weeks later, and there was no improvement. I asked her why she could not accept numbness of her left little finger as a good substitute. She informed me that she played the organ at church, and this was a hindrance. When we recapitulated, she told me about the cool feeling and reinforcement of this produced complete relief.

Case 2

The second patient was a 43-year-old woman referred by a surgical friend of mine, who never refers an easy case to me, either for hypnosis or gynecology. The patient had a neurogenic dermatitis, and she would shed her superficial skin layers completely every night at 3:00 AM. Her face and neck were like real elephant hide. She had been seen by all the local dermatologists, as well as prominent remote clinics. She had had psychiatric evaluations and was felt to have a high suicidal potential. Fortunately, this was during my earlier years of practice, and I was able to give her a lot of time on Saturday mornings. She was able to undergo hypnosis for 2 hours at a time, was perfectly comfortable, and did not shed for 2 days after the sessions. Eventually, she was able to do well, and her skin was relatively normal. The condition recurred 6 months later, when she had broken her leg. However, she again responded to hypnosis. I lost contact with her after 2 years, but until that time she was doing well.

Warts have been treated successfully by hypnosis by suggesting a loss of blood supply or imagining the lesion being touched with a very hot needle or cold needle, which cause the wart to shrivel up and to drop off.

Condylomat accumunata and herpes will be discussed in the obstetrics and gynecology section.

Physical Rehabilitation

Hypnosis can be used very effectively to aid physical rehabilitation in numerous ways. It has facilitated speech recovery and relieved spasms, and can speed up muscle coordination. The best story I can mention relates to Dr. Milton Erickson. After his second attack of polio, he received a telephone call from two neurologists who had conducted an examination. He was told that he would not be able to walk and that he would not be able to use his right arm. He replied, "You darn fool. How do you think I got over to the phone, and what do you think I am holding it with?" Speaking of Dr. Erickson, he was a master at using hypnosis for rehabilitation, especially where speech was concerned. I had a young man with a severe scoliokyphosis and a 110° angulation. He was to have surgery in Delaware, and he was told that he would require 3 weeks of exercises and relaxation of the muscles before surgery. However, with a few sessions of hypnosis with relaxation exercises and use of a tape, he went for his workup. The surgeons were surprised that his muscles relaxed so well, and he was ready for surgery 1 week after he went there. His surgeons were amazed and wanted to hear his tape.

One case of a stroke victim was a 23-year-old woman who made a much faster recovery from her stroke because of her ability to use hypnosis.

It is possible with a good hypnotic subject to have them use their mental imagery and reflexes to aid in their recovery.

Ophthalmology

The most common problem in this field is connected with the use of contact lenses. Some patients cannot tolerate the lenses at all because of irritations, and some cannot tolerate them for a practical period of time. It is important for anyone working in the field of hypnosis to realize that people wearing contacts have to be reassured that they are not really contact lenses but that they float on a fine film of moisture and can be completely comfortable. (You should be very careful if you use an eye roll test such as Drs. Wain and Spiegel do, since the lenses may pop out).

Hypnosis has been used for blepharospasm. Subjects have been taught how to relax the eyelid muscles either by using an eye catalepsy technique already mentioned earlier in the chapter. Dr. Kripa S. Thakur has successfully used hypnosis on a case of exopthalmos. He would be glad to send you a reprint of the case. Hysterical blindness can be successfully treated by hypnosis.

Case 1

A 21-year-old woman was blind, but with no optic atrophy. She was a senior in college and had achieved a 4-point average with the help of a reader. She read Braille and taught Braille. She was seen because of amenorrhea following a carotid arteriogram. She was an excellent subject and went into a deep trance while being interviewed. She regressed to a time four years before when she was admitted to the hospital after hitting her head on the corner of the television set. It was near a holiday, and she wanted to go home. She described the doctor and his daughter, the nurse, and a seriously ill patient that they had put in the bed next to her. She became a little panicky and was asked to relate what was happening. She said, "The doctor is saying that if I leave the hospital, I will go blind." After the situation was reexamined by her, she accepted the fallacy of such a statement, and there was some improvement in her vision. Another session revealed an episode in which she was walking and as she came near a tree, she was surprised to see that it was laden with fruit. She felt that she must have had poor eyesight not to have seen it sooner. This was discussed with her at great length, with further improvement in her sight, so that she could see houses as she rode along. Another session using regression produced another traumatic event. When she was small and had been out on a very bright winter day, she came into the house and she could not see; her cousin laughed at her, and she was very frightened. The event was discussed with her, and she was given the explanation about the rods and cones in the back of the eye. She made steady improvement and called me one day to say that the ophthalmologist had just removed her from the legally blind status and that she was losing an IRS deduction. It is the only time I can remember anyone being happy to pay the IRS more money.

Hypnosis has been used in ophthalmology to facilitate surgery by removing fear and anxiety, minimizing the amount of anesthesia necessary, reducing pain and discomfort, and improving healing.

Orthopedics

Hypnosis can be used in some cases to relax muscle spasm and provide hypnoanesthesia for disimpacting and reducing fractures. Two cases will be cited.

Case 1

One of our bombastic orthopedic surgeons was going through the emergency department one day and heard a patient making quite a bit of commotion. He said to her family doctor, "Why in the h--- don't you put her to sleep and reduce the fracture?" Her family physician asked him if he wanted to see instant results. He then proceeded to have her go into hypnosis (she had used hypnosis for both of her deliveries). She relaxed the arm; he disimpacted the fracture, reduced it and started to put on the cast. The orthopedist was very impressed.

Case 2

The same orthopedist became an instant believer. He stopped me and told me about the case, saying that he had a real problem case and wondered if hypnosis would help. Apparently, he had a young woman who had fractured her patella. He had operated and put her in a cast, but when he took off the cast, she would not bend her knee. He had thought of giving her an anesthetic and bending the knee, but he was afraid there might be scar tissue that might be irritated and cause bleeding and further scarring. He was told to send her to the office. The patient arrived and was an excellent hypnotic subject. Under hypnosis she was instructed about relaxing the muscles and improving the circulation. She was told to bend the good leg and the stiff leg, and within a short period of time she could bend it. When she saw the orthopedist 2 days later, she could go through a full range of motion.

Hypnosis has been a real benefit in chronic back pain, in which litigation was not involved or had been settled. Some cases will automatically clear up when the patient gets the "Greenback Poultice." The method used is a variation of muscle relaxation, improved circulation as stressed in the preliminary section of utilization of hypnosis with muscle relaxation, and decreasing of the nerve swelling, so that the nerves will not be pinched.

Genitourinary

Hypnosis is being used more extensively in genitourinary problems. Sexual disorders are covered in a different area of this book, but it behooves all of us to be familiar with the sexual system. A comprehensive book on this subject has just been released: *Sexual Problems in Medical Practice* (1982).

The use in oncology patients will be addressed in another section.

Eneuresis is a very vexing problem that has been approached in different ways. I have two approaches that I use. If it is close to a child's birthday and he is a good subject, I merely mention that all boys and girls automatically stop wetting the bed at this particular age. This has been fairly successful. I also use the switch box technique and have him visualize the switch box. He is then told that all he has to do is to activate the switch, and it will keep him from wetting the bed. If the urge builds up, it will flip the switch the other way, and he will wake up.

Hypnosis has been very successful in the treatment of postoperative urinary retention. I have had only one failure in 20 cases. Work on this subject has been previously reported.

Obstetrics and Gynecology

Probably one of the best uses of hypnosis is in the field of obstetrics and gynecology. In obstetrics, it is used in some of the complaints patients commonly have. The nausea and vomiting so frequently associated with pregnancy is best dealt with by this modality. The suggestions given are that the patient will cease to have the dirty metallic taste and replace it with a pleasant taste just like that of her favorite toothpaste. The esophagus (the tube from the throat to the stomach) will stop reversing the waves and begin to have nice smooth waves, taking the food down to the stomach where the digestive juices will start to digest it. Then it will go into the small bowel, where the peristaltic waves will propel it along in a normal fashion and allow digestion to be completed and the food to be absorbed.

Ptyalism, the salivating and spitting which occurs on very rare occasions, cannot be stopped in any other way but by using hypnosis. It is serious and incapacitating, since the patient must always carry a container. Occasionally, itching occurs for no apparent reason. When all medical conditions have been ruled out, this can often be treated with hypnosis. Painful hemorrhoids have been markedly ameliorated by using hypnosis. Heartburn which is often very troublesome can be treated by hypnosis when antacids do not work. After delivery, painful episiotomies, which might not respond to heavy narcotics, can be handled by having the patient relax all the muscles in her perineum. I have the patient relax all the muscles in her bottom, and when she feels that she is relaxed and comfortable, I test her in any way she wants. (The patient can signal with an ideomotor response.)

Condylomata accuminata, venereal warts, have become a vexing problem. We know that with the pregnant patient, the baby can develop a serious condition, congenital papillomatosis, when delivered vaginally by a patient with extensive condylomata. In most cases, they are delivered by cesarean section. I had three cases—two were successfully treated with hypnosis, and the third one failed to respond. Dr. Dabney Ewing has used hypnosis successfully in males (Crasilneck and Hall, 1975).

The following is an outline of the management of obstetrical patients using group techniques (can also be used on individual basis):

1. Complete orientation on the subject of hypnosis
2. Corrections of all misconceptions that present themselves
3. In the group, I use a counting technique from 100 to 0, from 100 to 80 in increments of one, and from 80 to 0 in increments of five, with fractionation of each 20 with suggestions that will help the patient to deepen hypnosis.
4. The patient is then asked to dissociate by picturing themselves doing something that they would find particularly enjoyable.
5. The patient is taught a method of self-hypnosis. The method used is to tell the patient to picture herself at home in a comfortable chair: "Close your eyes and visualize some color scheme, or it may even be a changing color scheme. Now put your right arm on your left shoulder and take a deep breath, and as you slowly let your breath out and let your arm come down by your right side, you will become deeply relaxed." (This is a deepening technique as well as an induction technique.)
6. By this time, most of the class has developed a medium or deep state of hypnosis and response to posthypnotic suggestions. They are given the following suggestions:
   a. "The remaining part of your pregnancy will be easier."

b. "Your labor will be shorter, easier, and safer."

c. "Your delivery will be so much easier and pleasant, and your stay in the hospital so much better and more comfortable."

d. "When you are in labor and when you are in the hospital, you can use your contractions to get more and more relaxed and make all the muscles in your pelvis very numb, loose, and relaxed."

e. The patient is told of the breakthrough periods, and when they are described, they are actually helpful.

f. The patient is seen in the hospital when she is completely dilated if she is having her first baby, or 2½ to 3 fingers dilated if she has had children before. In the beginning, I used dissociation during the delivery, but that was only because of my original fascination, now I feel that the patient should know that she is having the baby, but that it can be comfortable and pleasant. If any adjunctive analgesia or anaesthesia is necessary, the patient may have it. I do not use dissociation for repair of the episiotomy.

g. Each one must use his own verbalization and technique, or if he finds someone's technique useful, he should still adapt this so that he is completely comfortable with the entire procedure.

The following suggestions are for using hypnosis for a cesarean section.

1. Time is taken during each visit to help the subject attain deep hypnosis.

2. Suggestions are first given to produce glove anesthesia and transfer it to the jaw back to the hand, from the hand to the abdomen, and in some cases from the hand to the breast, to show the patient that even in this very sensitive area the numbness can last as long as necessary or for a given time.

3. The patient is then taught to roll the level of numbness up to 2 inches above the umbilicus, and if she is familiar with spinal anesthesia, she can be asked to simulate this without any of the side effects or complications of spinal anesthesia. When the patient is tested, I use an Allis clamp, and give her the suggestion that if she feels any discomfort she has merely to raise her right index finger.

4. The suggestions are repeated on each visit, and the patient is tested. All misconceptions are cleared up and explanations are given.

5. The patient is admitted the night before the cesarean section, and I always like to do a rehearsal, simulating the preparatory noises and conditions that will be met within the operating room.

6. The patient requires no premedication. I usually have a local anesthetic available, because on rare occasions the skin is extra sensitive and although the patient did well in rehearsal, she may be a little tight. However, when the skin has been incised in this latter case I have had no trouble completing the rest of the procedure. The patient always has an IV going and an anesthetist in attendance, because our hospital requires this.

7. The patient is told about each step before it happens. She is told that there will be minimal bleeding and that she can clamp off the blood vessels just as she would shut off a faucet. I use the word "pressure" at any point in the procedure that I feel would cause more stress (*i.e.,* going through the peritoneum, opening the uterus, and stretching the incision by blunt finger pressure) and especially if the head is impacted into the pelvis and has to be disimpacted to deliver it. To avoid pushing on the abdomen, I always use forceps. There is usually no trouble in closing the uterus or peritoneum and fascia. On closing the skin, I again refer to pressure because it seems to have the greatest sensitivity.

8. The patient is given suggestions that her postoperative period will be smooth and uneventful. The muscles will stay relaxed, the blood circulation will be improved, and healing will be better and faster. The bladder and bowel will work normally and she will eat properly.

In gynecology, hypnosis has been used in numerous ways, such as in dysmenorrhea, in which medication has not worked and the condition is incapacitating. Hypnosis can be used in several ways after a good history and physical have been taken. Sometimes the patient has had inadequate information and support prior to the first period. This can be restructured with a good hypnotic subject so that she can reexperience the first period in a comfortable manner. Other methods include teaching the patient glove anesthesia with transfer, having her relax and improve the circulation throughout the pelvis, getting rid of the pelvic congestion, and having her concentrate on forming endorphins so that she can minimize the discomfort. Other patients have been told to picture themselves getting a medication that would lower the substance prostaglandin, that causes the discomfort, bloating, and irritability. Still other good subjects have been told to visualize themselves doing something they would find enjoyable. The principle of time distortion and dissociation is explained to the patient. Therefore, she can have an enjoyable out-of-body experience and when she terminates the hypnosis, the remainder of her period is comfortable. Some patients have used hypnosis to start a late period in which pregnancy was not a consideration. Some have used hypnosis to cut down the duration and amount of bleeding. The pain with herpes genitalia has been alleviated by using hypnosis, and the lesions heal faster. I hope more work will be done on this.

In selected cases, hypnosis can be the anesthetic of choice. I have used hypnosis when I performed a vaginal hysterectomy, a myomectomy, and a laparotomy with oophorectomy, and I am sure many others have also. In these cases, it not only makes the case easier, but the comfort level, healing, and recuperation is so much faster. Most of our D&Cs are done in the office without premedication, or a local or general anesthesia. Reassurance and distraction seem to make it very well tolerated.

Dermatology

Some of the conditions, especially dermatitis, have been covered under psychosomatic problems.

Psoriasis lends itself well to hypnotic intervention. There is a high index of anxiety in causation and exacerbation of the condition. Sometimes when the underlying emotional factors are dealt with, the condition will disappear or be markedly curtailed. The use of dissociation, visual imagery, and picturing themselves using the medication that has worked well for them in the past, together with time distortion, have produced remarkable results. Warts and condylomata and herpes genitalia have all been successfully treated with hypnosis and have been previously presented.

Internal Medicine

One of the most fascinating studies would be the use of hypnosis in cardiac patients. It has been used to decrease the anxiety and distress that many of these patients have. Its use in ulcer patients and other gastrointestinal disturbances is a matter of record. My rationale for management of these problems is adequately covered under the psychosomatic disorders.

Essential hypertension was also covered. Hypnosis can be supportive in the management of hyperthyroid and diabetic patients. Hypnosis can also be useful to the gastroenterologist and cardiologist in some of their invasive and noninvasive diagnostic procedures. Its use in smoking and obesity will be covered in another section.

Appendix 15-1

Chiasson's Technique

Put your arm out straight in front of you. Now bend your elbow and bring the back of your hand just above the level of your eyes.

Make sure that your fingers are together.

Now watch your hand, your fingers will begin to spread and as your fingers spread more and more, your hand will gradually float in toward your face, and when your hand touches your face, your eyelids will close and you can get completely relaxed.

Watch your hand and as your fingers spread more and more, your hand will get closer and closer to your face; and as your hand gets closer and closer, your eyelids get heavier and heavier.

Closer and closer—heavier and heavier. That's right—as your fingers spread more and more—your eyes get heavier and heavier, and when your hand touches your face, your eyelids will close (if they are not already closed), and you can get deeply relaxed.

That's right! Your fingers are spreading more and more and your eyes are getting heavier and heavier and your hand is getting closer and closer, and it doesn't matter which part of your hand touches your face—it can be the back of your hand, your thumb or fingers, but when your hand touches your face, your eyelids can stay closed, you can get deeply relaxed.

Variations of these are used until the hand touches the face and then the subject is told:

O.K., as your hand gradually comes down on to the arm of your chair or into your lap, you can go deeper and deeper—

Let—your toes relax
     your ankles relax
     your feet relax
     your legs relax
     your knees relax
     your thighs relax
     your hips relax
     your tummy—from the chest margin to the top of your thighs—inside and out—
       front and back.

Let—all your chest muscles relax, so that your breathing is slow and easy and with each breath you can go deeper and deeper.

     all your back and muscles
     your shoulders and arms
     your elbows and wrists
     your hands and fingers
     all your neck muscles
     every muscle in your face and even the muscles of your scalp and forehead. Nice
       and loose and relaxed.

From here a deepening technique with utilization of hypnosis for therapy is done.

Each person should adapt his own verbalization to this so that he is completely comfortable and natural with it.

References

Cheek DB, LeCron LM: Clinical Hypnotherapy. New York, Grune & Stratton, 1968

Crasilneck H, Hall J: Clinical Hypnosis: Principles and Applications. New York, Grune & Stratton, 1975

Erickson M, Hershman S, Secter I: The Practical Application of Medical and Dental Hypnosis. Chicago, Seminar on Hypnosis Publishing Co, 1981

Ganong WF: Review of Medical Physiology. Los Altos, CA, Lang Medical Publishers, 1979

Hartland J: Medical and Dental Hypnosis and Its Clinical Applications, 2nd ed. London, Bailliere Gindall, 1971

Kroger WS: Clinical and Experimental Hypnosis, 2nd ed. Philadelphia, JB Lippincott, 1977

Sexual Problems in Medical Practice AMA. American Medical Association, Order Department, OP 120, PO Box 821, Monroe, W. 53566, 1982

16 Hypnosis in the Treatment of Habit Disorders

JUDSON B. REANEY

In common usage, "habit" is defined as "a settled disposition or tendency to act in a certain way, especially one acquired by frequent repetition of the same act" (Onions, 1955). It also may refer to bodily attire. Not curiously, then, even an undesired habit may be as difficult to discard as an old and familiar garment. Hypnosis can be useful in assisting children and adults to eliminate undesired habit disorders including thumbsucking, nailbiting, tongue thrusting, bruxism, overeating, smoking, enuresis, encopresis, tics, intractable coughing, neurodermatitis, hairpulling (trichotillomania), stammering and stuttering, chemical substance abuse, and self-stimulatory behaviors such as rocking and head-banging.

Some habits are initiated or perpetuated by underlying emotional issues. Many may never have been associated with serious psychological factors. Still other habits may once have served an important psychological function and since outlived their usefulness. They remain only to "inhabit" the patient.

Before proceeding with the hypnotic treatment of habit disorders, one must consider whether the habit serves an important function. Is there significant secondary gain? If so, other psychotherapies, alone or together with hypnosis may be indicated.

The answers to other questions may also influence the decision on whether to use hypnosis for habit relief or how best to use it. Is the patient personally motivated to change? How do family structure and predictable sequences of events in the family protect the habit? Are there developmental issues, as in thumbsucking or enuresis? Are underlying physical disorders present, as in retentive encopresis? Thoughtful inquiry will result in the most judicious and effective application of hypnosis for habits.

While there are innumerable ways to approach habits in hypnotherapy, three strategies are particularly to be recommended. First, one should become familiar with the multiple ways to use a symptom described by Minuchin (1974). These are (a) focus on the symptom, (2) exaggerate it, (3) deemphasize the symptom, (4) move to another symptom, or (5) relabel the symptom.

Haley (1970) believes that successful change occurs in patients through therapeutic directives. The therapist may tell the patient to stop doing something, which often increases resistance. Conversely, he can tell the patient to do something different. This is less successful when it consists of giving good advice and more successful when it directs change in the usual sequence of events. Finally, one can direct a paradoxical task, that is, telling the patient to do something the therapist does not want him to do because the therapist wants him to change by rebelling.

Cautela (1975) uses an operant framework to systematize conditioning procedures in which imagery is manipulated to modify behaviors. He labels the process "covert conditioning."

Patients are asked to imagine a particular response and imagine receiving various stimuli. Cautela describes four covert conditioning techniques. When the patient is asked to imagine a maladaptive response followed by a noxious stimulus (*e.g.*, eating ice cream, followed by nausea in an obese patient), it is called "covert sensitization." If imagined adaptive responses are rewarded by imagined pleasant thoughts (*e.g.*, resisting the urge to eat ice cream followed by a pleasant thought in an obese patient), the technique is called "covert positive reinforcement."

"Covert negative reinforcement" is used when patients claim nothing is reinforcing to them. An aversive scene is imagined and is relieved by a shift to imagining the desired adaptive behavior (*e.g.*, an agoraphobic patient imagines being confronted by a rat and is only relieved by next imagining the adaptive behavior of walking down the street on a beautiful day). Finally, "covert extinction" can be used for behaviors being reinforced by situations and others outside the therapist's control. The patient imagines performing the undesirable behavior and then imagines no response in the environment (*e.g.*, a child imagines thumbsucking to compete with his baby brother for attention and then imagines getting no response from his parents).

Some final general comments about habits should be made. While symptom substitution is frequently talked about, in clinical practice it is rarely encountered (Conn, 1961; Gardner and Olness, 1981). If the patient accepts hypnotic suggestions for symptom removal, he is usually no longer in need of the habit. Answers with ideomotor signals to questions about desire to give up the habit, the ability to talk about how life would be different without the habit, and the ability to image the desired outcome in hypnosis all are useful but not absolute predictors of the patient's readiness to eliminate a habit.

Oral Habits

Thumbsucking

A common childhood habit, thumbsucking rarely presents a significant threat to dentition before the age of four. In the early years it is a developmentally appropriate behavior which satisfies infantile oral sucking needs and later serves as a transition object more convenient than a teddy bear or a favorite blanket. As the child grows older, the habitual use of thumbsucking for pleasure and relief from anxiety is less well tolerated by parents and peers alike.

Hypnosis can effectively help children to stop thumbsucking if they wish to give it up. Many children, after learning how to mentally image a favorite place, are willing to trade the good feelings found there for the pleasure of thumbsucking. Raising his hand toward his mouth can be a cue for the child to relax and enjoy his favorite place. The thumbsucking itself can even be used to induce trance, and then the child can be taught he can have the feeling without the sucking.

Mohlman (1973) asks the child to trade sucking his thumb for tucking it comfortably inside his fist. It is then suggested that this will be more pleasant and nearer to the thumb than the mouth. Mohlman also prescribes thumbsucking at certain hours of the day or suggests that the child will only be comfortable if he gives his other thumb equal attention. In a similar technique, La Scola (1973) indicates to the child that there is nothing wrong with sucking, but he needs to be fair. "Playing fair" requires that he suck all his fingers an equal amount of time as his thumb.

Erickson (1958) focused on and exaggerated the symptom by directing a thumbsucking, 16-year-old girl to conscientiously irritate her parents with loud sucking for 20 minutes each day. The parents contracted to give no response, and the habit was quickly extinguished.

Appealing to the child's desire to be grown-up, Staples (1973) asked a child to scold her "naughty thumb" with "I am not going to suck you anymore, because I am a big girl now." Sector (1973a) comments to the child that "Most people grow up to the point where they don't need to, or even want to suck their thumbs." He then innocently ponders aloud, "I wonder how soon you'll be grown up enough for that?" This approach is most successful with the younger child. The older thumbsucker would likely become hostile and resistant.

Nailbiting

Nailbiting, like thumbsucking, may be annoying, but is not injurious to health. Its onset is most often in the grade school years, and it is often accentuated by anxiety. By the time that hypnosis is considered, many other treatments may have been tried, including hardeners, false nails, bitter solutions, or in children, parental nagging.

Many of the techniques for thumbsucking and variations of them work well with nailbiting. The relaxation produced by hypnosis alone may be enough to interrupt an anxiety-nailbiting pattern. Children again can learn to switch from nailbiting to the pleasant images of a favorite place cued posthypnotically by the hand raising to the mouth. Pleasing images of long, polished nails help assure the outcome. Overcoming the habit themselves through powers of imagination give children a sense of control and mastery.

Kroger (1977) directs patients to bite one nail on each hand instead of all the nails. Each of these two nails is elaborately bitten tooth by tooth from left to right and then back again. This is repeated three times "for fun," and can also be done upside down. Growth of the other nails is praised. The patient can be weaned from the biting nails as they wish, although some may be satisfied to keep them.

Children can be started on the road to success by indirect suggestions, as follows: "I can tell you really enjoy those nails. They're all chewed so nice and short. But have you ever had a nice, long nail to chew on? They're the best. I wonder which nail will be the first to grow?"

Covert conditioning is also useful for nailbiting. Secter (1961) described successful covert sensitization with imagery of revolting scenes each time the patient bit his nails. He also reinforced appropriate nonbiting behavior with pleasant images. Bitter tastes and nausea can also be suggested as aversive stimuli whenever nails are bitten.

Tongue Thrusting

Tongue thrusting, the pushing of the tongue against the incisors, can result in dental malocclusion. Most common in children, Secter (1973a) recommends teaching the child new activities for the tongue such as counting all the teeth and then counting their cusps. As in thumbsucking, an appeal to fairness can be made. "All your teeth need the attention of your tongue." The child can learn to explore his mouth, to curl the tongue, and to feel the roof of the mouth.

Other investigators (Barrett and vonDedenroth, 1967; Crowder, 1965) have found hypnosis to be effective in eliminating tongue thrust in as few as one to four sessions. Secter's (1973) covert sensitization technique previously described for nailbiting was simultaneously used in a patient to treat tongue thrusting.

Bruxism

Bruxism, forceful grinding of the teeth, can seriously damage dental surfaces. In addition, it may cause dental or temporomandibular joint pains or headache. Many patients are unaware of their habit, and some may primarily brux in their sleep. In children, it is most commonly found in severely retarded individuals.

Suggestions that bring the bruxing into conscious awareness enable it to be paired with relaxation. Just as raising the hand to the mouth is conditioned in thumbsucking or nailbiting to produce relaxation, teeth clenching is coupled with a relaxing scene or relaxed jaw muscles. Specific instructions can be given for opening the mouth and placing the tongue comfortably between the back teeth as well. This is incompatible with clenching but not with relaxation.

Displacing the tension to another part of the body also can be effective. Secter (1973b) suggests clenching the fists instead of the jaws. In an unusual case, he directed an Army signal corpsman to tap with his right index finger instead of his teeth during tension or sleep.

For nocturnal bruxism, Secter (1973a) recommends a hypnotic meditation upon drifting into sleep of "Lips together—teeth apart." He has also suggested that every time grinding appears in sleep, the patient will awaken and be angry that the bruxing has interrupted his sleep. He can then feel very relaxed and happy and return to sleep.

Occasionally bruxism may be a posttraumatic symptom. Golan (1955) reported such a case in which the bruxism was only reversed after hypnotic regression to the bus crash that initiated the habit.

Overeating

Overeating and resultant obesity are major public health problems in the United States and contribute significantly to the development of hypertension, cardiovascular heart disease, compromised vital lung capacity, diabetes mellitus, degenerative arthritis and other musculoskeletal problems. Chronic overeating and obesity form the basis for big business. Weight reduction programs are being spawned as quickly as fast food restaurants, as the obsession to lose weight tries to keep pace with the obsession to overeat. In such an atmosphere, it has become extremely difficult to assess which treatments are effective and which are ineffective—to sort out the competent practitioner from the charlatan. Perhaps only one simple fact remains: certain overweight individuals can be helped to lose weight by the adjunctive use of hypnosis.

In a comprehensive review of the literature on obesity and hypnosis, Mott and Roberts (1979) found much that is not known about hypnosis and overeating and little that is known. Most of the literature consists of anecdotal reports and studies of selected cases. In these reports, there has been little or no standardization of induction techniques and suggestions or of definitions of obesity and ideal body weight. Few objective measures of hypnotizability have been applied. In addition, replication of findings are not reported. Frequently, hypnosis is not an independent variable, since its use is reported combined with many other treatment modalities such as diets, exercise programs, behavior modification techniques, medications, and group therapy. Maintenance of weight loss is another serious consideration that is frequently overlooked. In a major review of mildly to moderately obese individuals who had initially shown a substantial weight loss through behavior modification, Stunkard and Penick (1979) found that the losses were only moderately maintained over 5 years. Similar studies to assess long-term benefits of hypnotherapy for obesity remain to be done.

Perhaps the most intriguing question waiting to be answered is "Which overweight patients are most likely to benefit from hypnosis?" Two assumptions underly this question. First, there may be factors in an individual that can predict responsiveness to hypnotherapy. Second, there may be subgroups of the obese population that are more likely to be benefited by hypnosis. Degree of obesity may be one factor. Are mildly to moderately obese patients benefited by hypnosis the same as those who are morbidly obese? Underlying psychopathology needs consideration. Wick and associates (1971) used hypnoanalysis for severely disturbed patients and autohypnosis for those who are otherwise judged to be well-adjusted. What differences in response to hypnosis exist between childhood and adolescent onset obesity versus adult onset; and what effects are exerted by age, sex, social class or ethnicity? Hypnotizability may be another predictive factor. Deyoub and Wilkie (1980) recently found that objective measurements of suggestibility were positively correlated with weight loss for hypnotic subjects.

Self-esteem and self-concept, including body image, may be important mediators of successful weight loss. In an important unpublished study of obese adolescent girls, Olness and co-workers (1974) found a significant correlation between the ability to visualize oneself thinner in the future and subsequent weight loss with hypnosis. Girls able to visualize averaged a 9.7-pound weight loss compared to 0.6-pounds for the rest of the group. A dieter may be able to lose weight from 200 pounds to 120 pounds, for example; but without a concomitant change in self-concept, he may then feel unconsciously like a 200-pound person trapped inside a 130-pound body. This conflict is usually resolved by regaining the lost weight.

Specific hypnotic techniques can be applied in both individual and group settings. Frequently, self-hypnosis is useful. Ego-strengthening suggestions may be particularly helpful in raising self-esteem. Likewise, it would seem wise to include suggestions for the patient to develop a mental image of the desired outcome—the "new you." For some, this image will be visual, such as seeing a slimmer self participating in a favorite activity, wearing a smaller size, or seeing an appropriate weight-for-height on an anthropomorphic graph (Kohen et al, 1980). Changing the visual body image can be enhanced by asking the patient to see himself at a desired weight in a special mirror. The mirror then disappears and the patient steps into the new body. Lindner (1963) directs patients to conjure a new self-image from recollections of a photograph of themselves younger, and thinner. Other obese patients may imagine hearing the desired results as compliments from people important to them or feeling the new body in a lighter step. Even a gustatory image of the wished-for change can be developed. The patient learns to see himself in the future as a gourmet, savoring food with a heightened awareness of flavors but requiring only modest amounts.

Numerous direct suggestions to correct overeating can be used. They have the greatest impact when paired with the unique characteristics of an individual patient. Many of these suggestions focus on food, directing that patients, for example, eat a minimum of carbohydrates, adhere to prescribed diets, or develop a taste for low-calorie snacks. Suggestions may also be given to alter the amount of food and way it is eaten, such as, enjoying smaller portions, becoming full when half the meal is eaten, fasting periodically, avoiding snacks between meals, or eating slowly. Direct suggestions can also be made to increase exercise, develop a new interest in sports, or simply walk stairs whenever possible.

Groups of overweight patients can be directed to use a self-hypnotic grace before meals, "I will become uncomfortable if I overeat" (Wollman, 1962). Self-hypnosis was taught to patients by Spiegel and Debetz (1978) to restructure eating habits. The patients were asked to use a self-affirming, three-part meditation: (1) For my body, overeating is a poison, (2) I need by body to live, and (3) I owe my body this respect and protection.

Erickson (1960) reported an indirect approach with three overweight patients in which he commented that the patients had many times before "lost and gained." He then told them they would "gain and lose weight" ending with the loss. At a 6- to 9-month follow-up, all had maintained their losses. Obese patients who complain that personal problems result in anxiety and overeating can have that belief redirected by repeated, casual comments such as "How long have these problems been eating (or gnawing) at you?" or "You seem to be consumed by these worries." Hanley (1967) congratulates patients on relapsing quickly and well. He thus redefines the relapse as a transition to long-term change. One can also indirectly liken the continual daily choices about eating to the encountering of stop signs while driving. The "stop" message is only temporary, giving the driver pause to assess potential dangers and then consider whether he will proceed straight ahead or turn to the left or right.

Many therapists use hypnotic covert conditioning to treat obesity. Nausea is often chosen as the stimulus in covert sensitization because it is significantly aversive to many people and because it is difficult to maintain feelings of nausea and hunger at the same time. Patients are conditioned in hypnosis to experience intense nausea when they imagine dietary indiscretion. In 1955, Hershman described a novel method in which he asked obese patients to imagine observing on a stage an actress with a sad face who evoked negative emotions in them. It was then suggested that breaking their diet would reproduce the negative fantasy. Adhering to the diet was reinforced by an image of the actress looking happy with the associated feelings in the patients of happiness, contentment, and peace of mind (Hershman, 1956).

Cook and VanVogt (1956) reinforced the adaptive behavior of eating small quantities of food with the suggestion that it would feel to the patient as though he had eaten a Thanksgiving dinner.

Smoking

Nearly fifty-five million people in the United States currently smoke cigarettes. When polled, three out of four smokers express a desire to quit, and 60% have tried to stop at least once. While reasons for wanting to stop smoking vary, concerns about adverse effects on health, especially lung cancer, are most common. A more sophisticated smoking population is also becoming increasingly aware of the noncancer health risks of smoking such as ulcers, coronary artery disease, and the harmful effects of maternal smoking on the fetus. At the same time, legislation and increased assertiveness among nonsmokers have made cigarette smoking a less comfortable social habit.

Hypnosis has emerged as a significant and effective form of treatment for cigarette smoking. How it may best be used and to what extent it is effective are still subjects for debate. Various authors have reported numerous hypnotic techniques for smoking, with widely varying and often flawed research methodologies. Reported effectiveness ranges from that of Cohen (1969), who was unable to produce permanent cessation of smoking with hypnosis in any patients, to that of vonDedenroth (1968), who claimed a 94% success rate without relapses. Most authors report more moderate long-term abstinence rates falling between these two extremes (Hall and Crasilneck, 1970; Kroger, 1977; Nuland and Field, 1970; Sanders, 1977; Spiegel, 1978; Stanton, 1978).

Sanders (1977) has aptly described smoking behavior as a multidetermined habit consisting of individual characteristics of the smoker himself, his belief system about smoking, and his environment. To be most effective, the therapist must address this triad in hypnotherapy. To accomplish this, she uses mutual group hypnosis in which one hypnotized client gives suggestions to another hypnotized group member. Other creative problem-solving techniques in Sanders' therapy include group brainstorming about reasons for wanting to be a nonsmoker, time progression and imagery to consider the possibility of change in the future, spontaneous dreaming to assess motivation and rehearse imagery associated with self-control, and self-hypnosis to practice nonsmoker imagery independently from the group. At a 10-month follow-up, 68% of the subjects were still nonsmokers.

To elucidate which variables of hypnosis are related to success in a smoking withdrawal program, Pederson and co-workers (1979) randomly assigned 65 habitual smokers to one of four groups: live-hypnosis plus counseling, videotape-hypnosis plus counseling, relaxation-hypnosis plus counseling, and counseling alone. Of the four techniques, only live-hypnosis plus counseling proved significantly effective, with a 53% abstinence rate at 6 months posttreatment, compared to only 18% for the counseling-alone control group. They concluded that the presence of the hypnotherapist as well as the specific content of the hypnosis session with references to quitting smoking are both necessary elements of a successful smoking withdrawal program.

Hypnosis in individual sessions, while more labor-intense, makes tailoring of suggestions to fit the unique characteristics of the smoker easier. In 1956, Hershman described using the smoker's own verbalizations and motivations in heterohypnosis to curb smoking. Nuland and Field (1970) used an "active, personalized approach focused on the commitment to stop." They fed back during hypnosis the patients' own reasons for quitting smoking and also used meditation during hypnosis to uncover individual motivations. In an uncontrolled, retrospective study, they found that this highly personalized technique had a 60% success rate at 6 months compared to 25% for a less individualized program that they had previously used. Powell (1980) conducted careful interviews with patients to determine why the person wished to quit smoking. During hypnosis, both the therapist and the smoker made suggestions about the reasons that he wished to quit followed by the statement, "I am a nonsmoker. Nonsmokers do not smoke." Lait (1973) uses hypnosis to discover the need for smoking and then suggests that the need will be met be adaptive behavior. He cites as an example a patient who began smoking at 10 years of age to "feel like a big shot." It was then suggested to him that in the future when he refused a cigarette or did not smoke when others were smoking, he would feel like a big shot.

Abrupt cessation of smoking and gradual reduction of the habit have both been suggested as effective therapeutic strategies. Some therapists are even content merely to reduce cigarette consumption to a safer level. VonDedenroth (1968) best represents the gradualists with his technique of setting a "quitting day" 21 days after the start of hypnosis. Stein (1964) advocates a reconditioning technique that stresses an improved qualitative reduction in smoking. Most authors use suggestions for abrupt and complete cessation of smoking. This is especially true of those, led by Spiegel, who recommend single-treatment methods. These therapists believe that one session is enough to produce most of the smoking cessations a therapist is likely to achieve. Using one-session hypnotic approaches, Spiegel (1978) reported a 20% smoking cessation rate at 6 months, and Stanton (1978) reported a 45% cessation rate.

Hall and Crasilneck (1970) use simple directives with their smoking patients, such as, "You simply will not crave nor will you smoke cigarettes again." They also direct that there will be no excessive hunger, frustration, or nervousness, minimal feelings of psychological or physical withdrawal, and restful sleep. Pelletier (1981) uses the direct verbalization to the patient that "You will never desire to place a cigarette to your mouth" and "You will eat in moderation so that you need not gain weight." In a unique twist, he goes on to use the name of the patient's own cigarette and other cigarette brand names to demonstrate how the cigarette industry has been subtly "hynotizing" the patient to smoke.

There is no "Merit," "Triumph," or "Vantage" point in smoking—nothing "Kool" about a cigarette. Properly named, cigarettes would be called "Phlegm," "Cancer," "Cough," or "Emphysema."

Covert conditioning techniques are especially useful in smoking control. They often take their lead from behavior modification programs. One of the most successful behavioral methods is rapid smoking in which the patient is instructed to smoke continually and rapidly until he cannot bear to continue (Schmahl et al, 1972). Barkley and associates (1977) found that group rapid smoking was significantly effective for the treatment of habitual smoking and only marginally more effective than group hypnosis. The combined use of the two techniques might be expected to be even more efficacious than either alone. Many authors recommend the use of covert noxious stimuli such as a horrible taste and smell associated with cigarettes, nausea, images of a stinking bronchial tree, the stale smell of ashtrays, or the experience of a beautiful hike ruined by being out of breath (Hershman, 1956; Kroger, 1977; Watkins, 1976).

Additional Habit Disorders

Enuresis

Enuresis, or bedwetting, is a common childhood problem affecting, to some extent, between 15% and 20% of all 5-year-olds. If no treatment at all is undertaken, the percentage of bedwetters decreases to about 5% by age 7 and to 1% by the early teens. Because of this developmental decline, hypnotic intervention before age 5 is rarely indicated. An understanding of the commonness of this problem alone provides relief to children and anxious parents and in many cases hastens the development of dryness.

Before beginning the treatment of enuresis with hypnosis, the therapist should carefully evaluate the patient to rule out underlying physical disorders. This is particularly true in the case of the recent onset of bedwetting in a previously dry child (secondary enuresis) which may be a symptom of a urinary tract infection or diabetes. While emotional issues can accompany developmental enuresis, they may be the prime cause of secondary enuresis. Recent onset of bedwetting may be the presenting symptom of psychological trauma due to incest, for example. It is essential, then, that careful inquiry precede simple symptom removal.

Hypnosis is particularly suited to the treatment of enuresis because it gives children a sense of self-mastery and competence. These are important developmental issues in the elementary-school-age child. For treatment to be effective, it is important that the child be educated about his problem through age-appropriate drawings, models, and discussion. Care should be taken to use words from the child's own vocabulary. Demystifying the child's own anatomy and physiology allows the child to feel in control of his own body. In hypnosis, the child is then able to develop personalized images that help him to stay dry. These may include images of the bladder as a stretched balloon being pinched shut at the opening, the external sphincter as a garden spigot, or the bladder and "brain-computer" communicating during the night. In the latter, children frequently enjoy imagining the bladder signaling by wires (nerves) "Help, help! I'm full." The brain then sends instructions to either hold on until morning or get up and go to the bathroom.

Gardner and Olness (1981) used an image of the bladder as a muscle that could be trained just as other muscles in the body. Olness reported a similar technique successful for giggle micturition in a 14-year-old boy. LaScola (1968) gave the direct suggestion that the child can only urinate when awake. While patients concentrate on another task such as listening to music, Stanton (1979) suggested that the child will lose the power to pee while lying down and gain the ability to wake up at night. This was paired with indirectly talking about learning to walk, speak, read, and ride a bike. Stanton reported a 70% success rate with this technique. Hartland (1971) stroked the stomachs of bedwetters and suggested a hallucinated feeling of warmth that would strengthen the bladder, enabling it to hold urine all night long.

Erickson (1981) has described two indirect methods for treating enuresis. In the case of a couple who both bedwet, he prescribed that they kneel and wet their bed each night before retiring for two weeks. Having succeeded in sleeping "through" the night without wetting for two weeks, they stayed dry the very first "vacation" night they were relieved from the ordeal and every night subsequently. The second instance involved an 8-year-old boy who was openly resentful and hostile about being dragged to the doctor. Erickson (1981) dismissed the parents and joined the child's resistance by saying that he, too, was angry at the parents for thinking that he could make the boy stop wetting. He suggested that it would serve the parents right if the boy waited to become dry until the end of the school year, which is exactly what the child did.

Several final comments about hypnosis and enuresis should be made: (1) Ideomotor signals are very effective in assessing the child's readiness to become dry. (2) Whenever possible, emphasis should be placed on the "dry" rather than the "wet" beds. (3) Self-hypnosis at home is recommended. (4) Parents should be instructed to let the hypnosis be the child's responsibility. (5) The child should be encouraged to imagine the future results of being dry. (6) Hypnosis can be effectively blended with other modalities, such as daytime start-and-stop bladder exercises, behavior modification calendars, and "bell-and-pad" alarm systems.

Encopresis

Encopresis, or fecal incontinence, is unlike enuresis in that it is not related to developmental or neuromaturational factors. The term encopresis is most often used to refer to constipation associated with soiling. The terms "retentive encopresis" or "soiling" are more appropriately descriptive. Only rarely is encopresis nonretentive, and in such cases, hypnosis is only occasionally indicated as a part of intensive psychotherapy.

Hypnosis can be routinely included in an overall management program for retentive encopresis. The other elements should include a careful history and physical evaluation, education for the child and his family about the problem as well as about normal anatomy and physiology, dietary regulation to avoid constipation, behavior modification techniques such as the use of calendars, and counseling to deal with secondary emotional issues. Enemas are often necessary initially to empty a distended colon that has poor tone. After that, it is preferable in most children to keep the colon empty with flavored oral mineral oil suspensions rather than repeated enemas.

The goal for the treatment of soiling is to avoid constipation and promote regular bowel movements in the toilet. Hypnotic suggestions should thus focus on the development of normal elimination habits and not on the soiling. The relaxation produced by self-hypnosis can assist the child to avoid the "holding habit" when he sits on the toilet. Imagery similar to that described earlier for the bladder sphincters in enuresis can also be used to develop control of the anorectal sphincters. Baumann related an amusing anecdote about an encopretic child who was very interested in the space program. The boy was induced to have a bowel movement in the office bathroom with the hypnotic suggestion that he was to be the first human to defecate on the moon.*

Of final interest is the retrospective study by Olness (Gardner and Olness, 1981) comparing the use of anorectal biofeedback with soiling children to self-hypnosis. The most significant finding was a median time for significant improvement in soiling from onset of therapy of 1 week for biofeedback and 4 weeks for self-hypnosis. Future prospective studies may show biofeedback or biofeedback combined with hypnosis to be the treatment of choice for retentive encopresis when biofeedback equipment is available.

Tics

Tics are found in nearly as many varieties as there are muscles in the body. Those of the head, neck, facial musculature, and upper extremities predominate. Patients are frequently referred for hypnotic removal of tics. As with other habits, one

---

* F. Baumann, personal communication.

must consider the possibility of an organic cause. Lipsmacking, for example, could be either a tic or a psychomotor seizure phenomenon. Gardner and Olness (1981) warn that tics are more likely to be symbolic representations of unresolved intrapsychic conflicts than are other habits.

Questioning the patient in trance with ideomotor signaling responses is very useful to determine if the patient is willing to give up a tic. The therapist can then use symptom-exaggerating or symptom-trading techniques. The patient can be asked to tic more often, to change the rhythm of the tic, to perfect the tic in front of a mirror, or to tic on the opposite side of the body. The patient may be willing to trade down from a major tic of the face to a small tic of the index finger. This newly established habit is much more easily relinquished than the older one. In addition, tension associated with the tic can be displaced into a clenched fist and then thrown away or tied to an imaginary balloon and floated away. Hypnosis can also be used effectively to uncover and deal with psychodynamic determinants of the tic. Spithill (1974) reported the use of hypnotic abreaction and self-hypnosis to treat an eyeblinking tic. A complete induction for a unique nasal snorting tic using an indirect hypnotic technique with symptom prescription can be found in Appendix 16-1.

Intractable Cough

Intractable coughing can be a significant warning sign for organic diseases. Once they are ruled out, hypnosis can be beneficial in relieving the habit. Techniques for coughing are also applicable to habitual clearing of the throat.

Hall and Crasilneck (1970) gave the direct suggestion to a 12-year-old boy that "your excessive abnormal cough will stop," along with suggestions for easy breathing, decreased throat itching, and relaxation in the throat muscles. Gardner and Olness (1981) taught self-hypnosis to a 13-year-old, using imagery of the bronchial tree and cough reflex followed by a suggestion that the cough would stop. The patient also focused on future pleasant events free of coughing. Images of soothing coolness or warmth, emphasis on quiet nasal breathing, or glove anesthesia transferred to the outer throat can also be used effectively.

Neurodermatitis

The itching and the pleasurable relief scratching brings makes neurodermatitis an especially challenging habit to control. Underlying psychological problems may also be significant. Hypnosis for symptom relief can be directed to the itching, the scratching, or both.

Kroger (1977) has listed numerous hypnotic techniques for neurodermatitis including direct suggestions that the itching will disappear, imagery of warmth from the sun, glove anesthesia transferred to the affected area, displacement of itching to another area, negative sensory hallucination of normal skin, and symptom substitution or transformation. Erickson (1981) has recommended cooling images. Some patients might resist suggestions for total elimination of itching but are comfortable "dialing down" the itching to tolerable levels.

Related habits such as nose-picking and excoriation of acne are also treatable by hypnosis. Hollander (1958) used covert sensitization for treating excoriated acne by suggesting the thought "scar" would occur each time picking the face began.

Hairpulling

Habitual hairpulling, or trichotillomania, usually involves pulling out the scalp hair, eyebrows, or eyelashes and may include ingestion of the pulled hair. This can result in the only serious complication of hairpulling, gastric outlet obstruction from trichobezoars. Only small areas of the scalp may be involved, or there can be marked thinning. Hairpulling may be an anxiety symptom like nailbiting, a habit that has outlived its original usefulness, or a manifestation of serious emotional conflicts. Psychological problems in particular should be suspected and ruled out before hypnotic symptom removal.

Covert conditioning and suggestions for relaxation, a sense of control, and lessened anxiety are all useful for treating hairpulling. Because hairpullers often report that they do not experience pain with their habit, many interesting hypnosis techniques are directed toward producing a new awareness of discomfort with pulling. Using hypnosis adjunctively with psychotherapy, Galski (1981) suggested that a 26-year-old severe hairpuller develop a very sensitive scalp as though he had been sunburned. The pain of beginning to pull hair would then trigger a relaxation response and release of the hair. Gardner (1978) hypnotically gave control over pulling to the part of an 8-year-old girl who wanted pretty hair with the phrase, "Stop, please do not hurt." Rowen (1981) used age regression in a 21-year-old to age 7 when the symptom started. He then age progressed the patient back to 21, suggesting that with each succeeding year the hairpulling would become more painful.

Stammering and Stuttering

Like the patient with agoraphobia who begins to fear the fear itself, the stammerer or stutterer fearfully anticipates dysfluency, thus making it more likely to occur. Hypnosis and its associated relaxation can be used in conjunction with a comprehensive speech therapy program to break the stuttering-anxiety-more stuttering cycle. Numerous authors have documented the effectiveness of hypnosis in these speech habit disorders (Falck, 1964; Marchesi, 1977; Moore, 1946; Silber, 1973).

Successful suggestions for treating stuttering and stammering include substituting feelings of relaxation found in the trance, taking an exaggerated breath prior to stuttering, developing an auditory hallucination of oneself speaking normally, or displacing the stutter or stammer to a finger. Habitual dysfluencies are frequently not present when patients speak aloud to themselves, whisper, sing, or speak in unison with others. Suggestions to practice these activities can hasten recovery. Kroger asks patients to concentrate on the end of words, whereas Hall and Crasilneck (1970; Kroger, 1977) recommend "sliding" through a word at the first indication of a problem. Both sources suggest recording the patient's fluent speech in trance and then playing it back to him later.

Paradoxical intent can be used as well. The patient is taught to stammer better and to practice in front of a mirror, and is then asked to give up stammering except in private. Cautela (1975) described covert extinction in which a stuttering boy, fearful of rejection, imagines telephoning a girl. He stutters but gets no indication that she noticed at all. Marchesi (1977) uses nondirect techniques, which include rehearsing speaking in trance under emotional conditions that would usually provoke stammering.

Chemical Dependency

Chemical dependency has qualities of both an addiction and a habit. The degree of each depends upon the abuse substance. Hypnosis can be used to minimize addictive withdrawal symptoms or can be directed toward changing the habit pattern. In either case, hypnosis is rarely indicated as the treatment of choice for alcoholism or other drug dependencies. Rather, it should be employed as one therapeutic modality in a comprehensive treatment program.

Hypnosis may be most useful simply by producing relaxation and substituting it for anxiety and withdrawal symptoms. A prime use of chemicals is to relieve tension and anxiety. Hypnosis enables the patient to become comfortable without drugs. Byers (1975) even trained technicians to teach self-hypnosis for relaxation to patients in an alcoholism treatment program. A patient can also learn to alter his mood with hypnosis. Baumann (1970) taught teenagers who used LSD and marijuana to create a "hypnotic high." Many chemically dependent persons have difficulty dealing with strong emotions, especially anger. Hypnosis can help them develop nonchemical ways to cope effectively with these feelings. Occasionally, hypnotic regression can be useful to help fill in gaps in the memory of significant past events. This newly remembered information can be particularly useful in the first step of an Alcoholics Anonymous-based treatment program in which the alcoholic admits he is powerless over alcohol. LaScola

(1968) has patients review in hypnosis their life before and after drug use began. If they indicate disapproval of the effects drugs have had on their life, he tells them that the past can shape the future and gives ego-strengthening suggestions. On the following visit, he asks the patient to give him advice about a fictitious patient with similar symptoms.

Ashem and Donner (1968) reported that covert sensitization was an effective therapy in alcoholism treatment. As early as 1948, Wolberg (1948) used suggestions of alcohol as a poison or imagining nausea whenever one took a drink. Feamster and Brown (1963) produced a hypnotic aversion to alcohol with a vivid recollection of the worst hangover the patient ever had after any subsequent contact with alcohol. One of the diagnostic clues to chemical dependency is the persistent use of the chemical despite significant adverse results such as illness, loss of a job, arrests, or marital problems. Thus, real-life aversive stimuli have usually failed to curb the habit. Covert sensitization is most likely to work if a particularly strong negative personal experience can be anchored to the drug habit.

Little data are available on the effectiveness of hypnosis in chemical dependency; and because there are multiple, complex variables, good information is unlikely to be forthcoming. In the best published information to date, Baumann (1970) concluded that hypnosis can be useful in adolescent drug abuse when the patient is motivated and fears physical harm to himself if the habit does not change.

Self-Stimulation

Self-stimulatory behaviors in children, such as head-banging, body-rocking, and masturbation, are relatively benign but often bothersome to parents. Reassurance that they are not harmful is always indicated. When these habits keep children from other childhood activities or are public or obsessive, hypnosis can be used. Emphasis should be focused on reducing the amount of time spent in self-stimulation and in limiting the habit to private use. When self-stimulatory behavior is found in association with mental retardation or autism, use of hypnosis is not suggested.

Children can learn to experience the feeling of vestibular stimulation hypnotically without body motion. Imagery such as rocking chairs, boats, or roller coasters can be used. They can be taught to substitute the comfort of a favorite place in self-hypnosis for self-stimulation. Gross body movement may be traded down for finger-tapping or the shaking of a foot. Hypnotic suggestions can be given that each time they begin to masturbate, they will be reminded to go to their rooms. There they will find greater satisfaction in their habit and will need less and less time to enjoy it so that they may then return to other activities.

Appendix 16-1

Sample Induction for a Habit Disorder

The following is an example of the use of indirect suggestion, symptom prescription, and storytelling to eliminate an unusual nasal snorting noise in a 6-year-old girl. The tic had been present for several years.

Therapist: *I just don't understand your parents' concern over your sneezing noise. I bet you don't either. Is that right?*

Patient: *Yes.*

Therapist: *I'm really impressed that such a large noise can come from such a small girl. Your sneeze as you came into my office really announced you well. I could tell you were very special. It was almost like a trumpet or horn. Could you do it for me again?* [Patient demonstrates] *That was great! It would really be a shame for your parents to ask you to give up such a special and useful talent. I suspect they don't understand. Do you think they don't understand?*

Patient: *Yeah, they don't.*

Therapist: *Perhaps you sound like a goose to them—a noisy old gander. I prefer to think of you as a beautiful trumpeter swan. That's a graceful bird with a long neck. Its song is like yours, a trumpet noise. Of course, when they're young they must practice their song to get very good. Otherwise they might not be appreciated, understood, or noticed. Someone might even mistake them for a goose. You know, I'm not sure that I can get your parents to appreciate your sound as I do without your help. Would you like to help me to help them?*

Patient: *Sure.*

Therapist: *Good! Now just as the young swans practiced their trumpeting to become very good, I'd like you to practice too. This will help your parents to hear how good you've become. Of course you're already quite good. I should think that twenty sneezes each morning when you get up and twenty each night before bed should be enough. Make each one a little different, a little better. What do you think?*

Patient: *Okay.*

Therapist: *During the day, each time you come into a room in your house, announce yourself with a trumpet sound. Be sure to check to see that your family notices and appreciates your sound. If someone new comes into the room after you, be sure to blow the trumpet for them too. Can you do this?*

Patient: *Sure.*

Therapist: *Wonderful. I'm not sure how long it will take for your parents to learn to notice and appreciate you as you enter the room, but with your helping them it shouldn't be long at all.*

References

Ashem B, Donner L: Covert sensitization with alcoholics: a controlled replication. Behav Res Ther 6:7, 1968

Barkley RA, Hasting JE, Jackson TL Jr: The effects of rapid smoking and hypnosis in the treatment of smoking behavior. Int J Clin Exp Hypn 25:7, 1977

Barrett RH, vonDedenroth TEA: Problems of deglutition. Am J Clin Hypn 9:161, 1967

Baumann F: Hypnosis and adolescent drug abuser. Am J Clin Hypn 13:17, 1970

Byers AP: Training and use of technicians in the treatment of alcoholics with hypnosis. Am J Clin Hypn 2:90, 1975

Cautela, JR: The use of covert conditioning in hypnotherapy. Int J Clin Exp Hypn 23:15, 1975

Cohen SB: Hypnosis and smoking. JAMA 208:335, 1969

Conn JH: Preparing for hypnosis in general practice. Roche Rep 3:3, 1961

Cook CE, Van Vogt AE: The Hypnotism Handbook. Alhambra, CA, Borden Publishing, 1956

Crowder HM: Hypnosis in the control of tongue thrust swallowing habit patterns. Am J Clin Hypn 8:10, 1965

Deyoub PL, Wilkie R: Suggestion with and without hypnotic induction in a weight reduction program. Int J Clin Exp Hypn 28:333, 1980

Erickson MH: Naturalistic techniques of hypnosis. Am J Clin Hypn 1:3, 1958

Erickson MH: The use of patient behavior in the hypnotherapy of obesity: Three case reports. Am J Clin Hypn 3:112, 1960

Erickson MH, Hershman S, Secter II: The Practical Application of Medical and Dental Hypnosis. Chicago, Seminars on Hypnosis Publishing, 1981

Falck FJ: Stuttering and hypnosis. Int J Clin Exp Hypn 12:67, 1964

Feamster JH, Brown JE: Hypnotic aversion therapy to alcohol: 3-year follow-up of one patient. Am J Clin Hypn 6:164, 1963

Galski TJ: The adjunctive use of hypnosis in the treatment of trichotillomania: A case report. Am J Clin Hypn 23:198, 1981

Gardner GG: Hypnotherapy in the management of childhood habit disorders. J Peds 92:838, 1978

Gardner GG, Olness K: Hypnosis and Hypnotherapy With Children. New York, Grune & Stratton, 1981

Golan H: Further case reports from the Boston City Hospital. Am J Clin Hypn 18:55, 1955

Haley J: Problem-Solving Therapy: New Strategies for Effective Family Therapy. San Francisco, Jossey-Bass, 1976

Hall JA, Crasilneck HB: Development of a hypnotic technique for treating chronic cigarette smoking. Int J Clin Exp Hypn 28:283, 1970

Hanley FW: The treatment of obesity by individual and group hypnosis. Can Psychiatr Assoc J 12:549, 1967

Hartland J: Medical and Dental Hypnosis, 2nd ed. London, Balliere Tindall, 1971

Hershman S: Hypnosis in the treatment of obesity. J Clin Exp Hypn 3:136, 1955

Hershman S: Hypnosis and excessive smoking. J Clin Exp Hypn 4:24, 1956

Hollander MB: Excoriated acne controlled by post-hypnotic suggestion. Am J Clin Hypn 1:122, 1958

Kohen D, Olness K, Colwell S, Heimel A: 500 pediatric behavioral problems treated with hypnotherapy. Presented at the annual meeting of the American Society of Clinical Hypnosis, Minneapolis, November 1980.

Kroger WS: Clinical and Experimental Hypnosis in Medicine, Dentistry and Psychology, 2nd ed. Philadelphia, JB Lippincott, 1977

Lait VS: Smoking. In: A Syllabus on Hypnosis and a Handbook of Therapeutic Suggestions. Des Plaines, IL, The American Society of Clinical Hypnosis Education and Research Foundation, 1973

LaScola RL: In Cheek DB, LeCron LM (eds): Clinical Hypnotherapy. New York, Grune & Stratton, 1968

LaScola RL: Thumbsucking. In: A Syllabus on Hypnosis and a Handbook of Therapeutic Suggestions. Des Plaines, IL, The American Society of Clinical Hypnosis Education and Research Foundation, 1973

Lindner PG: Mind Over Platter. North Hollywood, CA, Wilshire Book Co, 1963

Marchesi C: Quoted in Kroger WS: Clinical and Experimental Hypnosis in Medicine, Dentistry, and Psychology, 2nd ed. Philadelphia, JB Lippincott, 1977

Minuchin S: Families and Family Therapy. Cambridge, MA, Harvard University Press, 1974

Mohlman HJ: Thumbsucking. In: A Syllabus on Hypnosis and a Handbook of Therapeutic Suggestions. Des Plaines, IL, The American Society of Clinical Hypnosis Education and Research Foundation, 1973

Moore WE: Hypnosis in a system of therapy for stutterers. J Speech Disorders 11:117, 1946

Mott T, Roberts J: Obesity and hypnosis: A review of the literature. Am J Clin Hypn 22:3, 1979

Nuland W, Field PB: Smoking and hypnosis. A systematic clinical approach. Int J Clin Exp Hypn 18:290, 1970

Olness K, Fallon J, Coit A, Fry G, Bassford M: Group hypnotherapy in management of obesity in teenage girls. Presented at the annual meeting of the American Society of Clinical Hypnosis, New Orleans, 1974

Onions CT (ed): The Oxford Universal Dictionary on Historical Principles, 3rd ed. London, Oxford University Press, 1955

Pederson LL, Scrimgeour WG, Lefcoe NM: Variables of hypnosis which are related to success in a smoking withdrawal program. Int J Clin Exp Hypn 27:14, 1979

Pelletier AM: Hypnosis in the treatment of obesity and tobacco addiction. Delivered at the Annual Scientific Meeting of the American Society of Clinical Hypnosis, Boston, 1981

Powell DH: Helping habitual smokers using flooding and hypnotic desensitization technique: A brief communication. Int J Clin Hypn 28:192, 1980

Rowen R: Hypnotic age regression in the treatment of a self-destructive habit: Trichotillomania. Am J Clin Hypn 23:195, 1981

Sanders S: Mutual group hypnosis and smoking. Am J Clin Hypn 20:131, 1977

Schmahl DP, Lichtenstein E, Harris DE: Successful treatment of habit smokers with warm, smoky air and rapid smoking. J Consult Clin Psychol 38:105, 1972

Secter II: Tongue thrust and nailbiting simultaneously treated during hypnosis: A case report. Am J Clin Hypn 4:51, 1961

Secter II: Thumbsucking. In: A Syllabus on Hypnosis and a Handbook of Therapeutic Suggestions. Des Plaines, IL, The American Society of Clinical Hypnosis Education and Research Foundation, 1973

Secter II: Bruxing. In: A Syllabus on Hypnosis and a Handbook of Therapeutic Suggestions. Des Plaines, IL, The American Society of Clinical Hypnosis Education and Research Foundation, 1973a

Silber S: Fairy tales and symbols in hypnotherapy of children with certain speech disorders. Int J Clin Exp Hypn 21:272, 1973

Spiegel H: A single-treatment method to stop smoking using ancillary self-hypnosis. Int J Clin Exp Hypn 18:235, 1978

Spiegel H, Debetz B: Restructuring eating behavior with self-hypnosis. Int J Obesity 287, 1978

Spithill AC: Treatment of monosynaptic tic by hypnosis: A case study. Am J Clin Hypn 17:88, 1974

Stanton HE: A one-session hypnotic approach to modifying smoking behavior. Int J Clin Exp Hypn 26:22, 1978

Stanton HE: Short-term treatment of enuresis. Am J Clin Hypn 22:103, 1979

Staples LM: Thumbsucking. In: A Syllabus on Hypnosis and a Handbook of Therapeutic Suggestions. Des Plaines, IL, The American Society of Clinical Hypnosis Education and Research Foundation, 1973

Stein C: A displacement and reconditioning technique for compulsive smokers. Int J Clin Exp Hypn 12:230, 1964

Stunkard AJ, Penick SB: Behavior modification in the treatment of obesity. Arch Gen Psychiatr 36:801, 1979

vonDedenroth TEA: The use of hypnosis in 1000 cases of "tobaccomaniacs." Am J Clin Hypn 10:194, 1968

Watkins HH: Hypnosis and smoking: A five session approach. Int J Clin Exp Hypn 24:381, 1976

Wick ER, Kline M: Hypnotherapy and therapeutic education in the treatment of obesity: Differential treatment factors. Psychiatr Q 45:234, 1971

Wolberg LR: Medical Hypnosis, 2 vol. New York, Grune & Stratton, 1948

Wollman L: Hypnosis in weight control. Am J Clin Hypn 4:177, 1962

17 Hypnosis in Family Therapy

BENNETT G. BRAUN

The *family therapy* movement appears to have been started independently by several clinicians in the mid 1950s. Some observers think the family movement began earlier, with Freud's (1909) involving the father in the treatment of little Han's horse phobia, or with the publication of Fluegel's (1921) book, *The Psychoanalytic Study of the Family*. Others credit Adler with founding family therapy; from 1918 to 1934, he founded many child guidance clinics at which parents were present during child therapy. The orientations of Freud, Fluegel, and Adler, however, focused on the family as it affected an individual, not on the family system or family as a whole.

Contemporary family therapists have moved away from the traditional medical model, in which the family is of interest only to the degree that it acts on the "identified patient," to a more holistic approach, which recognizes the interdependence and mutual influence members of the family have upon one another. Bateson (1956) observed that if an identified schizophrenic patient got better, another member of the family would develop problems. Jackson (1957) stressed the importance of interpersonal interaction styles (the "double bind") on the development of schizophrenia. Wynne (1968) added the concept of pseudomutuality, which suggests that the family's boundaries are elastic and shift to include a member's behavior even if it is very deviant. Bowen (1960, 1961) stressed the triangle as the basic family and human interaction building block.

The tendency to begin to view the family as a unit was influenced strongly by systems theory (Bowen, 1971; Hoffman, 1971; Jackson, 1957, 1960; Kramer and Minuchin, 1974; Speer, 1970). According to *systems theory*, a system is a group of parts that react interdependently and that maintain an equilibrium in an error-activated way (*negative feedback*). If one views the family as a system, an intervention at any point will have repercussions throughout the system.

When looking at the family, one needs to be aware of several subsystems:

1. *Intrapersonal system,* which is usually arbitrarily subdivided into an intraphysic and a somatic system. The equilibrium between these two has been **325**

discussed by Grinker (1953), Alexander and co-workers (1968), and Erickson (1977).

2. *Interpersonal systems*
   a. The *couple* brings their past histories, neuroses, and somatic problems to their relationship and behave toward each other in various ways so as to maintain their own equilibrium.
   b. The *children* have their own system, which interacts with both the individual parent and the couple systems.
   Each individual child interacts with each other child and with the above system.
3. *Society* interacts with and puts pressure on all of the above relationships.

Each of these systems interacts at different levels with negative feedback (maintaining a homeostatic equilibrium, like a thermostat) or *positive feedback* (running away, like an out-of-control atomic pile). A positive feedback system will either plateau out, burn out, or self-destruct, unless an external force is properly applied.

Writers agree that there are many positive and negative feedback chains operating on the family in any situation and that the results are not always easy to predict. An aspect of society may force the family to re-equilibrate or it may produce a deviant who will lock the status quo into place. In part, the strength of the homeostatic status of the system will also determine the outcome. There are also different stages or types of mutual causal processes. There is the drift that may go toward or away from random, and there is the more systematic activity such as is evidenced by a runaway. Finally, there is the problem of levels. The same feedback process may have deviation amplifying effect (positive feedback) on a system at one level and the opposite effect (negative feedback) on a system the next level up. Thus, it is difficult to decipher the cybernetic process at work in a given field at the same time (Hoffman, 1971, p. 308).

An example is the teenager who is abusing drugs. He is involved in a positive feedback system in relation to his parents, causing increasing isolation from them, owing to his rebellious drug use and their increased arguing with him. He uses the drugs to stabilize himself intrapsychically (negative feedback system) and to tighten bonds with some peers (positive feedback system—increased drug use). This behavior unites his parents (negative feedback system) and prevents them from looking at their conflict (potential positive feedback system).

Use of hypnosis with the family as a whole can be of help in the previous example by introducing some calm into an escalating system, by reinforcing this new state and showing the members that good feeling *can* be achieved, by exploring the foundation of the systems, by uncovering and working on the parental conflict, and by helping members discover new options for behavior and reinforcing them. From these can come a new equilibrium and modus operandi.

Family Interaction Styles

Several authors (*e.g.,* Bowen, 1971; Jackson, 1957) have identified family or marriage interaction styles, but the terminology that I have found most useful comes from Kramer (1968). He identifies four main marriage styles that may be generalized to family styles:

1. *United front marriage,* in which the family is overtly harmonious and is seen usually because one of the children is symptomatic. School phobia, pregnancy, drug use, or any of a number of other problems may bring the family to therapy. Most often the family wants the "problem" child "fixed" without submitting themselves to examination.
2. *Over-adequate/under-adequate marriage,* a relationship in which members assume one up/one down positions. One spouse has the symptoms, and the other appears symptom free. When the "sick" one starts to get better, there is a new strain on the relationship, and the other partner often develops problems.
3. *Conflictual marriage,* which is characterized by open conflict and fighting. The conflict may serve to maintain a level of closeness and interaction with which the family members are comfortable. The conflict may also be used to avoid a one-up/one-down position, as is evidenced in the second type of marriage.
4. *Mixed type marriage* which is a combination of two or more of the above types.

The basic styles function to promote a familial homeostatic (negative feedback) system, which resists change in its parts. The goal of therapy is to help the family in its parts. The goal of therapy is to help the family achieve a new homeostatic style that meets their life goals and needs. Guidelines for choosing hypnotic techniques for the various family styles will be discussed later in this chapter.

Applications in Family Therapy

Unlike the therapy groups (*i.e.,* group psychotherapy), the members of the family group actually live the other 22½ hours of the day in close contact with each other. It is understandably hard for a family in treatment to pull down the barriers, confront each other and freely loosen up inhibitions and prohibitions and then reestablish the whole conventional framework as soon as they are home again. Often, the only way to deal with the overflow of feelings is to dissociate the situations (life and family therapy).

To these ends, hypnosis can be a valuable tool to facilitate movements in family therapy, to overcome barriers and inhibitions, and to help create a new framework. The use of hypnosis in group psychotherapy has been reviewed and discussed by Braun (1978). Many of these concepts also apply to the family group.

One general use of hypnosis in family therapy is to give the family a shared pleasurable experience (*e.g.,* relaxation). Although the family members live in the same house, they may not have shared many experiences. Sharing hypnotic relaxation can help build trust and give the family members a common foundation.

A hypnotic experience can help family members tune into themselves and each other; it seems to make them more sensitive. Sometimes, when a person is unable to express his or her thoughts, another family member can supply both the words and the feelings. Of course, this phenomenon occurs without formal hypnosis, but I believe that hypnosis facilitates its occurrence.

Indications and Contraindications

Since it is generally safer to know where not to go and where one's limits are before knowing where to go or what to do, I will start with *contraindications* to the use of hypnosis with families. At this point, there are no absolute contraindications; the contraindications are relative ones. They relate mainly to the skill of the hypnotherapist and his knowledge of family therapy. The therapist must be prepared and willing to deal with unexpected material. One needs to be able and willing to deal with strong abreactions; this is more complicated when other family members are upset also. With relaxation comes a decrease in the strength of the repression barriers. By using muscle control one can control the expression of emotion; to keep from crying a person must control the rate and depth of breathing. I believe that much repressed memory is stored in, or stored in relation to, muscles. Through the use of hypnosis and other relaxation techniques, this information is allowed to surface more easily. Spontaneous age regressions while in a hypnotic trance have been observed, especially in teens and older adults when their parents are present. The parents seem to serve as stimuli for the regression.

These phenomena can be handled by remaining calm and using the hypnotic rapport to keep others calm, while working with the patient. Some things that can be done include calming and strengthening suggestions conveying the knowledge that the therapist is not afraid, helping the patient to desensitize the abreacted material using, perhaps, a multiple abreactive technique, or helping the patient create a new option or ending to the issue, thereby helping him to gain mastery. Much therapeutic work can be accomplished at these times if the therapist remains calm and helps the family to do so. Not only will the individual benefit, but so will the family, especially if they are able to interact appropriately with the upset member during the temporary crisis; a new sense of family mastery and cohesion can result.

Another relative contraindication for the use of hypnosis in families is the patient's personality structure. It may be inadvisable to use hypnosis with borderline and hysteric patients. In these cases, the presence of the family accentuates the risk and may precipitate a crisis. I work with these patients using hypnosis, but only after carefully evaluating both them and the risks. In the borderline patients, the most feared risk is precipitating a psychosis as repressed material comes out and defenses break down. This will not occur if the therapist is sensitive and competent. A more common occurrence is losing the patient as the closeness of the hypnotic relationship is misinterpreted. One also needs to be careful using anreactive techniques, since the patient may get locked in an inappropriate rage. With the hysteric, one needs to be aware of the intensity of the transference that might develop. The hysteric tends to give up critical evaluations of situations to the therapist. In addition, the amount of dependence that exists or gets stirred up by the regressive aspects of hypnosis must be carefully regulated. The presence of the family may inhibit or accentuate this process.

The usual *indications* for hypnosis with an individual also apply with families: pain control, age regression, exploration of feelings, rehearsal in fantasy, and so on. Hypnosis can also help the family to become more emphatic, to limit fighting, to increase trust, to change the mood, to find new materials, and to solve problems. More will be said about these benefits in later sections.

Transference and Countertransference

Since hypnosis is a regressive phenomenon in which a great deal of tuning in is employed to increase empathy and rapport, there is an increased potential for transference and countertransference to occur. The latter needs to be kept as conscious as possible; a co-therapist is often helpful in the process. In working with families, the therapist becomes part of the system, optimally a unique part, which facilitates changes in behavior and family homeostasis towards the desired goals. However, this is not always what happens. The family as a group may have a familiar transference onto the therapist which encourages him to take the role of, say, an omnipotent, hated grandfather. At this time a *rotating resistance* to the use of hypnosis with that family may occur. By rotating resistance, I mean resistance from one family member which, when dealt with, appears in another family member.

In the case of positive transference, the family's rules about closeness may be broken or the family boundaries may be disrupted. Too much closeness of one member to the therapist can be intensified with hypnosis and can be disruptive to therapy. One must watch out for triangling (an alliance, usually unconscious, of the therapist and one family member versus another).

Countertransference issues of the hypnotherapist fall into the broader category of *interface issues.* These are problem areas that the therapist has not worked out in his own family of origin and that can become stumbling blocks to the progress of therapy. With the use of hypnosis, therapists often enter a trancelike state of increased sensitivity to the patients. With this increased sensitivity, there is an increased vulnerability, openness, and tendency for regression of the part of the therapist. This increases the risk of expressing the countertransference and must be guarded against.

Prehypnotic Interview

Before any hypnotic work is done, it is essential to conduct a prehypnotic interview. The following are goals I try to attain with this interview:

1. Gaining rapport
2. Allaying fears and misconceptions, especially the fear of loss of control
3. Understanding the interpersonal contracts among the family members and between each family member and the hypnotherapist
4. Giving some concept of how hypnosis works

During the prehypnotic interview I try to focus the family's attention and to create a mental and physical environment that is conducive to hypnosis. In a conflictual family I may ask people to change chairs to separate combatants or to place a very anxious patient nearer a source of comfort. Sometimes I move myself to accomplish this.

Phases of Hypnosis

Hypnotic work can be divided into five phases:

1. *Induction Phase*—During this phase, the patient's attention is honed down and focused; the patient and the therapist get in tune with each other.
2. *Deepening Phase*—Techniques are added to the induction to deepen the trance and to prepare the patient for the work phase. I might start with a muscle relaxation induction technique and link it to a technique using color imagery to prepare for the induced fantasies.
3. *Work Phase*—This phase may include fantasies designed to produce specific information or specific results (*e.g.,* image of self-assertion, family, interaction, suggestions, etc.).
4. *Termination Phase*—This can be simple or complex and may include posthypnotic suggestions.

5. *Processing*—Though not directly a part of hypnosis, this phase is essential. It is here that one learns what was accomplished and what to change for next time. It is the therapist's learning phase and aids the integration of the experience.

Guidelines

While I will suggest specific techniques and present some general guidelines for using hypnosis with families, I would like to emphasize that the major limitations of the use of hypnosis with families is the therapist's imagination. Of course, normal precautions in choice of technique also apply (*i.e.,* do not use a muscle contraction technique with someone who has back trouble or joint problems).

When I do hypnotic work with families and individuals, I work both in and out of trance during any given session. I also allow time to debrief and sum up out of trance. This helps the individuals to own their own progress and avoids attributing the power of change to the hypnotic procedure, or, even worse, to the therapist. Having time out of trance to process material also helps people integrate their experiences into the reality of here and now.

When using hypnosis and while working with it, take small, obtainable steps. Avoid the urge to push on too fast once things start rolling—and they will. Be aware that the deeply relaxed patients are regressed and therefore more concrete in their thinking. This concreteness is an advantage in that it lowers critical thinking, defensiveness, and the repression barrier. However, if the hypnotherapist moves too fast, he can create confusion, lose rapport, and jeopardize progress.

Making Suggestions

Direct suggestions tell the patient that he or she will or will not be able to do a specific thing. "You will find yourself more relaxed, and when you leave my office your headache will vanish." While direct suggestions may obtain quick results, the therapist who uses them runs the risk of losing rapport and power as an authority figure if the patient is not ready to receive the suggestion. I temper my direct suggestions with, "You will find, with practice, . . ." or "Your pain will continue to decrease gradually over time." This allows some leeway if the "magic" is not immediately forthcoming. Remember that the patient maintains control at all times and can defeat himself and the therapist if he chooses.

Techniques

There are several different ways to use hypnosis in family therapy. Individuals may work hypnotically in the family session on their own issues or problem behaviors. One family member could be in trance and interact with another family member at appropriate times.

Working hypnotically with the family as a whole is the most difficult and often the most rewarding way to work. The difficulties include having to be aware of several people's issues and emotional states, as well as their multiple levels of interaction, both intro- and interpersonally. When working with the family as a whole, pick induction or relaxation techniques that tend to keep people together in their progress or ones in which getting out of phase does not matter.

The *progressive relaxation technique* is good because everyone is working with their feet, legs, and so on at the same time. *Color imagery* and *guided fantasy* techniques also keep people together by having them all concentrate on the same thing at the same time.

A technique that does not require people to progress at the same rate but eventually gets everyone to more or less the same place is what I call a *reverse blink technique*. In this technique the patients are asked to start with their eyes closed and to open and shut them quickly (the reverse of a blink) each time I count a number. Suggestions made between counts encourage deeper relaxations and indicate that eventually the eyes will remain closed and that the individual will continue to relax more deeply with each count. Different members will stop opening their eyes at different times, but eventually all will be relaxed with their eyes closed. At this point other fantasy work can be accomplished. Semi-guided fantasies will have everyone getting to the same place hypnotically by way of different personal routes.

Projection techniques are also useful with families. One such technique is cloud imagery, in which patients are asked to visualize a blue sky with puffs of white clouds; the shapes and images of the clouds can be explored. With another technique, patients are asked to imagine that they are watching their favorite television program. This technique is especially useful for working with children.

Techniques such as age regressions can be used to explore and to relive past events. Remembering and examining past events can bring them into proper prospective and avoid their causing patients to behave inappropriately. If a past event was not shared by the whole family, having them in a trance while someone relives and describes the event helps the others experience it more deeply.

Hypnosis or fantasy techniques with the family as a whole can be aimed at gaining a shared experience, thereby increasing trust and closeness. It can also be used to work on one person's issues and to help the others to identify with that person. For example, a phobic patient may receive a lot of anger from the family. If the others can be helped to experience the paralyzing fear (often recalled and hypnotically augmented from other experiences they have had) and attach it to the phobic object, they can become more supportive and even help in the process of desensitizing the phobic person. This shared experience with mutual cooperation helps bind and move the family closer together.

Fantasy techniques can also be used so that different members can work on their own different problems at the same time. It can also serve to stimulate issues and to bring them to the explicit attention of the family. Often one finds that the same issue has been bothering several members of the family, but for some reason they were not bringing it up.

Using Family Style to Choose Techniques

I shall now return to the three main family types previously mentioned and describe useful techniques for each. It is understood that the suggested techniques can be used with any family type, even though they seem especially well suited for a particular type.

For the *united front family,* relaxation techniques are good to help build rapport, to increase trust, and to decrease guardedness. The family may be able indirectly to express, through fantasy, hostility that is kept hidden. For example, after induction, the therapist may ask each member of the family to be an observer or participant on a space flight to the planet Xeron. The crew consists of a woman or man who is captain, a man or woman who is first mate, and a female, male, or mixed crew to reflect the actual family gender distribution. Have each get a mental image of the rocket on the launching pad and the crew doing their last-minute checkouts. Now they are boarded and settled in. With each number mentioned during the countdown, deeper relaxation is encouraged: ". . . 5 minutes . . . 4 minutes . . . 1 minute . . . 15 seconds . . . 14 seconds . . . 13 seconds . . . 3, 2, 1, 0." The therapist puts more description or patter between the numbers as needed. "BLAST OFF . . . Now you can see the earth moving away from you as you go deeper and deeper into space. Things are going well, the ship is functioning smoothly as you progress toward your destination. Suddenly you find yourself in the middle of a meteor shower, and, through an error, the meteor shields are not up. Your guidance computers are both damaged. You are temporarily lost in space . . . ultimately you have to return to Earth without accomplishing your mission. You are called before your commanding officer to tell what happened, whose fault it was, and how you felt during the trip."

In retelling their fantasies, the family members will reveal things about how they and other members of the family handle stress, how they cooperate, and how they cover things up. This can be done in separate phases so that the therapist can get data while the fantasy is in progress before they have to report to the commanding officer. Information that is revealed here may give the therapist data and a direction to proceed or help the family to look at their dynamics. This is obviously just an example; one can create fantasies to fit any given situation.

For the *over-adequate/under-adequate family,* hypnotic techniques can be used to give direct or indirect strengthening suggestions to the under-adequate member and to teach and support vulnerability in the over-adequate member.

Hypnosis is also a good technique to use with assertiveness training, particularly for the under-adequate member. By using fantasy techniques, the roles can be reversed, giving each a sense of the position and feelings of the other, the isolation and loneliness of the over-adequate one and the helplessness and frustration of the under-adequate one.

One can use fantasy to create role reversal to help produce changes and give a sense of what the other is going through. Another useful technique is the use of the ideal self-image. The patient is asked to create a mental image of himself, not as he is today, but as he would like to be. Ask the patient to describe the image and hold it in memory for later. Then ask him to create an image of himself as he perceives himself today. In reality, the patient is usually somewhere between these two descriptions; getting this feedback from family members is therapeutic. The therapist can also ask the patient to merge these two fantasized images by having them face each other, walk toward each other, and merge into one person. The patient often gains a sense of mastery and freedom to act after this.

In a family in which a phobic person is being scapegoated, hypnosis can be used to help the others gain empathy for the phobic person. After inducing trance for the family as a whole, ask everyone to recall and relive the scariest event of their lives. When the affect is high, ask them to transfer this affect to the imagined phobic person. Sometimes a family member experiencing this process comes up with an interpretation or idea that leads to a heretofore unthought of solution to the problem.

Hypnosis and fantasy technique are useful in the *conflictual family* as a way of breaking into the fight cycle and creating some peace in the presence of the others. These techniques give the family a shared positive experience, which helps increase trust and facilitates the family members' tuning into each other during the rest of the session. One can use fantasy to imagine what the family would be like without conflict and to get in touch with how it would feel to exist without conflict. Often, fear, especially of closeness, surfaces then. Other fears that are frequently observed are those of being under-adequate or of being in a one-down position. The therapist can also use hypnosis paradoxically by creating a fantasy of increased conflict of such proportions that the family members become scared and tired of conflict, thereby facilitating therapeutic work.

Using Hypnosis During Family Crises

When a loved one dies, the emotional impact is usually taken in two phases. The acute phase is often marked by some type of denial. At this time, the family needs support to get in touch with their feelings about the loss. The family hypnotic experience can be a unifying factor. To achieve togetherness and support, the mere act of hypnotic induction is often enough. Active hypnotic or fantasy work at this time may be too stressful for the family and must await the proper timing.

Retirement, like other losses, needs to be mourned. At the time of retirement, the family system is thrown into disequilibrium. Couples that functioned well while one or both were working now have to relate to each other more. Hypnosis can be used to help each accept the loss of their life-style and the old interactive style, and to be more open in their communication. It can be used to change the stimulus value of certain phenomena: "You will become aware of your needs earlier and express them before the old anger is activated." "You will find that your wife's requests will not be perceived as demands, and you will see a reward in meeting them when appropriate and when you are able." "You will find great joy in planning your travels together. You have earned the right to give yourself the luxuries you have worked for."

Another aspect of family therapy, not usually thought of as such, is divorce counseling. As Framo (1977) says: "The goal of divorce therapy, in essence, is to help the partners to disengage from their relationship with dignity and the freedom to form new relationships, with a minimum of destructiveness to self, mate, and children." Hypnosis can be used to this end by projecting into the future and working through loss.

Conclusion

There are as many hypnotherapeutic techniques as there is time for the active imagination to create. One is limited only by the patient's and one's own imagination. Hypnotic fantasy technique can be applied in family therapy with some caution as to with whom and how it is used. Because family therapy is more complex than individual therapy, one must pay attention to more things and more levels of interaction both between individuals and within each one's fantasies and experiences. If you are willing to give the extra energy to do this, you will find the use of these techniques quite rewarding.

References

Alexander F, French T, Pollack G: Psychosomatic Specificity. Chicago, University of Chicago Press, 1968

Bateson G, Jackson D, Haley J, et al: Toward a theory of schizophrenia. Behav Sci 1:251, 1956

Bowen M: A family concept of schizophrenia. In Jackson D (ed): The Etiology of Schizophrenics. New York, Basic Books, 1960

Bowen M: Family Psychotherapy. Am J Orthopsychiat 30:40, 1961

Bowen M: Family therapy and family group therapy. In Kaplan HI, Sadock BJ (eds): Comprehensive Group Psychotherapy. Baltimore, Williams & Wilkins, 1971, p 384

Bowen M: Use of family theory in clinical practice. In Haley J (ed): Changing Families. New York, Grune & Stratton, 1971, p 285

Bowen M: The use of family therapy in clinical practice. Comprehensive Psychiatry 345, 1966

Braun BG: Hypnosis and Fantasy Techniques in Family Therapy. Scientific Meeting, American Society of Clinical Hypnosis, Nov. 1978, Atlanta, Georgia.

Erickson MH: Am J Clin Hypn 20:1, 1977

Fluegel J: The Psychoanalytic Study of the Family. London, Hogarth Press, 1921 and 1960

Framo J: Rationale and techniques of intensive family therapy. In Boszoremnyi-Nagy I, Framo JL (eds): Family Therapy: Theoretical and Practical Aspects. New York, Harper & Row, 1965, p 112

Framo J: Divorce therapy. Advances in Family and Marital Therapy. In press.

Freud S: Analysis of a phobia in a five year old boy. In Starchey J (ed): The Standard Edition of the Complete Works of Sigmund Freud. London, Hogarth Press, 1961. Psychoanalysis of a Five Year Old Boy. (1909), vol 10, p 3

Grinker R: Psychosomatic Research. New York, Grove Press, 1953

Hoffman L: Deviation amplification process in natural groups. In Haley J (ed): Changing Families. New York, Grune & Stratton, 1971, p 285

Jackson D: The question of family homeostasis. Psychiatr Q Suppl 31:79, 1957

Jackson D: Etiology of Schizophrenia. Jackson D (ed). New York, Basic Books, 1960

Jackson D, Lederer W: The systems concept. In Mirage of Marriage. New York, Norton Press, 1968, chap 10

Kaplan HI, Sadock BJ (eds): Comprehensive Group Psychotherapy. Baltimore, Williams & Wilkins, 1971

Kramer C: The theoretical position: Diagnostic and therapeutic implications. In Beginning Phase of Family Treatment. Chicago, Kramer Foundation, 1968

Kramer C: Becoming a Family Therapist. New York, Human Science Press, 1982

Minuchin S: Families and Family Therapy. Cambridge, MA, Harvard University Press, 1974

Speer DC: Family systems, morphostasis and morphogenesis or is homeostasis enough. Family Process 9:259, 1970

Wynne L, et al: Pseudo-mutuality in the family relations of schizophrenics. In Bill H, Vogel E (eds): A Modern Introduction to Family Therapy. The Free Press, 1968

18 Hypnosis and Dentistry

SELIG FINKELSTEIN

Hypnodontics was an important art prior to the discovery of chemical means of pain control. Even then, it was not used so widely that freedom from pain was associated with dentistry. It was a newsworthy event when hypnosis was used as an anesthetic for the extraction of teeth, being reported in the press as a singular event, but not one that was commonplace or even thought to be practical for the average dentist (Stein, 1930). The limited use of hypnosis was not able to create the impression that dentistry was pleasant or painless. Part of the fear of discomfort and pain associated with dentistry came from its practice by nondentists. The physician's medical bag usually contained, in addition to medical equipment, several forceps for the extraction or breaking off of exposed parts of teeth, which was usually an horrendous experience for the patient. Others, such as the blacksmith, with less skill and no knowledge, also had a hand in the process of terrifying the dental patient. However, even with the channeling of dentistry into the trained hands of dentists, it was uncommon for the practitioner to have a feeling of compassion for the patient, as far as control and elimination of pain and discomfort.

Discussion with Dr. Irving J. Naidorf, assistant dean of the Columbia University School of Dental and Oral Surgery, in May, 1981, confirmed that prior to World War II, dental schools not only did not encourage the use of local anesthesia for cavity preparation, but they discouraged its use. Patients were expected to bear the pain, as if it were good for the soul. It was considered enough to say, "This won't hurt," or "Be brave." Repressive and overbearing methods were taught for controlling pediatric dental patients. It was not until after World War II that anesthesia for the cavity preparation became the rule, rather than the exception. Its use has increased since then until, today, it is an accepted and expected modality for operative dentistry. While we now find it hard to understand the callous attitude toward pain that existed previously, not all reluctance to use local anesthesia was due to callousness. The initial agent used for local **337** anesthesia was cocaine, which had an occasional lethal side effect (Beeson, McDermott, and Wyngaarden, 1979). This created an understandable reluctance on the part of many dentists of the era to use cocaine, at that time the only available local anesthetic. Even with the introduction of safe synthetic substitutes, the memory of potential lethalness lingered. The feeling of compassion for the patient, however, which might have prodded the search for safe alternatives, and which might have resulted in rediscovering hypnotic techniques, was not really an important factor at that time.

The change in attitude toward the patient, which resulted in the increased use of local anesthesia, sedatives, and tranquilizers, was necessary for the resurgence of the use of hypnosis in dentistry. No one will take the time and expend the effort to learn the techniques and applications of hypnosis unless concern for the comfort and well-being of the patient is of paramount importance.

The use of hypnosis in the dental office is not a matter of induction techniques. Hypnosis requires a rapport between operator and subject (Sechter, 1965). This is affected by the first contact the patient has with the dental office, usualy by phone. The communication that the patient-to-be is an individual and that someone is interested in his or her well-being is an important first step in the building of the rapport necessary for the successful use of the hypnotic modality. The greeting of the patient upon arrival at the dental office and the general feeling of the office are also important. When the right climate exists, it is then equally important that induction techniques that are comfortable for the operator and acceptable to the patient should be used. However, it should be recognized that hypnosis is only one of the modalities available and is most often used in conjunction with other modalities, if the needs of the patient are to be fully met (Moss, 1957; Carnow, 1973; DiBona, 1979).

Hypnosis is presently much more widely accepted, so that lengthy explanations are not always necessary (Wegner, 1979). The patient can be introduced to the concept of hypnosis and hypnosis itself in a number of ways. The dentist can explain what hypnosis is and what it is not, and clarify some of the more common misconceptions (Cheek and LeCron, 1968; Hartland, 1979; Heron, 1958). An important misconception to correct is that the subject in trance is under the control of the hypnotist. Another important misconception is that only weak-minded persons can be hypnotized. Another that comes into play when hypnosis must be proved, is the misconception that the trance subject has to be zonked out, in order to be hypnotized. Each patient brings individual feelings about hypnosis that may need to be corrected. It is important to listen to the patient. Much can be learned and many difficulties avoided. It is possible to illustrate the trance state by doing an induction with one of the staff, while the patient observes. This gives the patient an idea of where they are going so it makes it easier for them to attain trance. It is obviously a pleasurable state, so it is not something to be feared. It enables the patient to ask questions of the one who has been in trance. Another method of introduction is to have a prerecorded tape with an explanation of hypnosis and an induction to which the patient can listen in the waiting room, before coming into the treatment room.

Various induction techniques are explained in other sections of this book, but there is one technique that I feel is so useful for dentistry that I present it here. It is a progressive relaxation induction, and the explanation and induction for the patient are as follows (Finkelstein, Goldstein, and Barnett, 1979).

"Everything is easier when you are relaxed. There are certain situations in dentistry that require the jaw muscles to be relaxed, so we dentists have to know how to teach patients to relax. Let me teach you an easy method. Relaxation, of course, is a mental process, but it helps to have something physical with which to work. Make yourself comfortable in the chair and shrug your shoulders a little. That's very good. That's all the physical motion necessary. Mentally, move that feeling of muscle relaxation into your upper arms, through your elbows into your forearms, wrists, and hands, so you have a comfortable, relaxed feeling from your right hand, up your right arm, across your shoulders, down your left arm, to your left hand. Now bring this comfortable, relaxed feeling from your shoulders into your chest and stomach, then into your hips, upper legs, and through your knees into your lower legs, ankles, and feet. Bring this comfortable, relaxed feeling from your shoulders into your neck and let it spread up into your head, until it fills your entire head with a comfortable, relaxed feeling. Take a deep breath, and as you breathe out [if the patient has not already closed his or her eyes, insert: close your eyes and] relax very deeply." Watch the breathing and repeat until a really deep breath is taken by the patient. Be careful not to overoxygenate your subject. At this point the patient is ready for whatever supportive measures, such as deepening, hypnoanesthesia, local anesthesia, and so on, may be appropriate.

In this induction, the subject controls the experience and is not challenged, so there is no possibility of failure on the part of the dentist. The suggestions are for the subject to do, which gives the subject control of the situation and whatever is experienced is a function of the subject's own processing. Further support for the patient in trance can be given by having the patient listen to a prepared cassette, either after the induction and deepening, or as the induction and deepening. In my office, I use a tape that has a 12-minute segment consisting of an induction, ego-strengthening, and general health suggestions. The 12-minute segment is repeated on a 90-minute tape (45 minutes on a side), so there are three plays of the segment when the tape is run through. It is possible to interact with the patient while the tape is playing, as the patient in trance can handle several simultaneous things without confusion. The following list includes the principal uses of hypnosis in a dental office:

1. Obtaining the relaxation of the patient
2. Increasing the amount of cooperation by the patient

3. Reducing anxiety and fear
4. Preparation of the patient for local or general anesthesia
5. Production of analgesia
6. Control of bleeding, lessening postoperative discomfort, and speeding healing
7. Control of salivation
8. Control of gagging
9. Control of habits, such as bruxism, thumbsucking, and tongue thrusting
10. Control of dental phobias

It also aids the personal well-being of the dentist:

a) Reduction in working time for many procedures
b) Reduction in fatigue from working
c) More harmonious staff relations

Let us examine the uses in a dental office more closely (Hartland, 1979).

Obtaining Relaxation

A relaxation induction will accomplish this even if the patient does not go into an identifiable trance (Cheek and LeCron, 1968). Patients who assert that they cannot relax, will often report surprise at having relaxed in a dental chair for the first time. It is a real source of satisfaction when a patient, after a series of hypnodontic visits, sits in the dental chair and says, "This is the only place I can really relax." Relaxation can also be used as preparation for some other induction technique, particularly when it is necessary to prove to the patient that he or she was actually in trance.

Increasing Patient Cooperation

The hypnotic experience is a joint venture between patient and dentist and enhances the cooperation of the patient for whatever dental procedures are to be undertaken. The results of a good hypnotic relationship make the dental experience easier for all concerned. The patient feels well taken care of, and fearful resistance is diminished or even nonexistent.

Reduction of Anxiety and Fear

These are emotional states. Whenever emotion and reason are in conflict, emotion will win out (Beeson, McDermott and Wyngaarden, 1979). How many times have you heard someone say, "I know I shouldn't feel like this, but I do." Here, in addition to the relaxed state, trance logic is helpful in overcoming emotional blocks to dentistry (Golan, 1971). In trance, the subject is less critical in accepting ideas, perceptions and behavior. The use of appropriate suggestions can bypass the emotional states of anxiety and fear. To accomplish this, suggest to the patient in trance that an enjoyable, safe activity, far removed from the dental office, be experienced. The patient can be told that the sounds and other sensations in the office can be relegated to the background and the dental experience suppressed in relation to the enjoyable experience. This technique was originally developed for preoperative conditioning of surgical patients by Milton Erickson of Phoenix and David Cheek of San Francisco. It was relayed to me by Dr. Cheek in November, 1978, when I consulted him about this problem. There are other methods of doing this (Cassell, 1979). A good course or workshop in hypnosis would be the proper vehicle for an in depth study of those methods.

Preparation for Anesthesia

Even if the patient has achieved only a light trance, it is possible to have accepted a suggestion of numbness at the site of an injection and that the numbness resulting from the injection will be more profound than ever before (Cheek and LeCron, 1968). For some patients, the feeling of numbness is like a security blanket, and they are loathe to let it go. For others, it is annoying once the need for numbness has passed. With the latter patients, when using the hypnotic state, I tell them that the way the local anesthetic wears off is by the bloodstream carrying it away. I remind them that their capillaries are opening and closing in various places in their bodies, for example, opening in the muscles when exercising, or opening in the digestive tract when food has been eaten. I tell them that although they do not know on a conscious level how to open or close capillaries, their bodies do know. If they want the numbness to go quickly, they should just let their bodies open the capillaries in the area where the anaesthetic was injected. I have had patients eliminate the feeling of numbness in four to fifteen minutes (Finkelstein, 1979). As for general anesthesia, it is possible to decrease and sometimes eliminate premedication. It is also possible to use less of the anesthetic agent to achieve the desired depth of anaesthesia (Cheek and LeCron, 1968).

Production of Analgesia

This has been touched on in the numbing of the site for an injection, but has other ramifications as well (Brustein, 1967; Barber and Mayer, 1977). When the patient is using the trance state and it is likely that the scaling of teeth would be painful, I rub the gums with a cotton swab. As I rub the dry, untreated swab over the gums, I tell the patient that a new, powerful surface anaesthetic has been developed and that he can notice the numbness that is being achieved as it is absorbed by the gums. Many patients have said they wished it had been invented sooner. As the analgesia becomes more profound, we can think of it as complete anesthesia. When the motivation is sufficient, surgery is possible, even if the patient does not think that there was a trance (see case discussed at end of chapter). With the accident patient, particularly when the anterior teeth have been broken or displaced and while the surrounding tissues are contused and lacerated, it is often impossible to either inject a local anaesthetic or use a nose piece for inhalation analgesia. We must recognize that the accident patient is almost always in trance, trance being a coping mechanism (Ewin, 1976). Recognizing the existence of the trance state, we can use our skills to help the patient deepen the trance and attain whatever changes in the physiology are possible and necessary for comfort, while we do the appropriate procedures to repair the damage. To illustrate this, let me cite the case of a 9-year-old boy who had been hit in the mouth with a baseball bat. The upper lip was contused, the upper anterior gingivae was lacerated, and the two upper central incisors were broken, with the pulps exposed. He had been a dental patient previously and had done well with local anesthesia. When I determined that the analgesia nosepiece would be painful and that the tissues were sufficiently lacerated so that an injection for local anesthesia would be imprudent, I suggested to the patient that he make his right hand numb, as if it had novocaine, and when he had accomplished this to let me know by raising his forefinger. (Being an accident patient, he was already in trance.) When he signaled this, I suggested that he transfer the numbness to his teeth and lips and when he had accomplished this, he could let me know by returning his hand to his lap. When he signaled this, the dental treatment was accomplished, while the patient sat very relaxed and smiling.

Control of Bleeding and Speeding Healing

There are many applications of the use of hypnosis in the control of bleeding. It has been used to control bleeding in hemophiliacs and with patients on anticoagulant medication (Golan, 1971; Dubin and Shapiro, 1974; Lucas, 1978–79). The most frequent use in a dental office is after surgery with the average patient. When working with the patient in trance, suggest that it would be appropriate for the socket to fill with blood and clot. This is an indirect suggestion, which, in the trance state, can be accepted and acted upon. In addition, mention that the patient will be pleasantly surprised at how little discomfort he will have and how quickly he will heal. I have found that patients report little or no use of pain medication and little or no swelling. These suggestions can be given even when general anesthesia is being used. David Cheek (1959) and Wolfe and Millet (1960) have shown that the patient can hear and respond to suggestion while under general anesthesia.

Control of Salivation

Although our modern methods of aspiration make control of the fluid content of the mouth, both from salivation and water spray, relatively easy, there are times when it is helpful to have a diminution of the output by the patient. The patient, in trance, can be instructed to turn off the flow of saliva, make the mouth feel dry, or hold back the saliva in order to use it during the next meal. If one suggestion does not accomplish the necessary reduction, the patient can be complimented for what she or he has already accomplished and another suggestion given to make it even better. This can be repeated more than once in order to achieve the degree of dryness desired.

Control of Gagging

Most gagging is an increase in intensity of the normal gag reflex. When this has increased beyond the point of control, the patient can then be classified as a gagger, for whom something has to be done, if dental work is to be facilitated (Jacobson, 1968). There are some patients for whom gagging is an unconscious method of preventing dental work (Kramer and Braham, 1977). The patient who sits in the dental chair and gags just upon opening his or her mouth, before any instrument has even approached the lips, is an example of this extreme type. The treatment approaches vary to suit the individual, rather than the type of gagging (Secter, 1960; Strosberg, 1960). The suggestion to the patient in trance that he will be pleased to notice how comfortable everything will be, can be used with the moderate or extreme gagger. The patient can be instructed to go off somewhere on a safe, pleasant vacation, and nothing that happens in the office will bother him. The suggestion can be made that the patient watch himself from across the room and notice how calm and comfortable the patient in the chair appears to be. Anesthesia of the mouth can, also, be produced to prevent gagging. After a few sessions of gagging control, the patient will start to control the gagging on his own, illustrating the amount of self-control made possible by hypnosis.

Control of Oral Habits

Tongue thrusting is a habit pattern that needs corrective exercises. Suggestion during hypnosis helps make the attitude toward the exercises better. It also facilitates the learning process because of the focusing of attention that exists during trance. The rapport developed through hypnosis increases the likelihood that the child would be willing to do the exercises. Thumbsucking may be part of the pattern of an emotionally disturbed child. It is important to know the individual before attempting to remove this symptom. The disturbed child needs psychiatric care before any attempt is made to control thumbsucking. Since most thumb-sucking is an automatic action, the child may be unaware, on a conscious level, of the act. The posthypnotic suggestion that the child will always be aware of the habit should be used with whatever other suggestions are used. Bruxism is often related to patterns of living that are stressful. Because of the occupation or other situations of the patient, it might be difficult or impossible to alter these patterns, but it may be possible to alter their effects in several ways (Goldberg, 1974). The patient can be given a posthypnotic suggestion to awaken if bruxism occurs and a self-hypnotic sleep induction to get back to sleep. It is also possible to teach the patient a relaxing self-hypnotic induction to use before going to sleep in order to relieve the stress. A relaxation and sleep tape can be given the patient to use to counter the stress.

Control of Dental Phobias

The subject of phobias has been treated in other sections of this book. While treatment of phobias properly belongs in those sections, there is something we can and should do in a dental setting. In dealing with dental phobias, we must realize that a phobia cannot exist without anxiety (Beeson, 1979; Graham, 1974). Using the hypnotic modality to teach relaxation and develop the patient's feeling of comfort in your presence creates a nonanxious climate. In addition, by using hypnosis, the phobic situation can be disguised, so that the patient can interpret what might have been a phobic situation as a comfortable one. This latter method of approach does not cure the phobia, but renders it inoperative. There are three ways to alter or conceal the object or situation that would otherwise trigger a phobic reaction. The first way is to have the patient use negative hallucination to conceal the existence of the phobic object or situation. A second way is to have the subject imagine a pleasant vacation or other situation, of his own choosing, away from the phobic situation. A third way is to have the patient reinterpret the phobic situation so that the sensory stimuli indicating its existence can indicate a pleasant, nonthreatening situation, instead.

Benefits for the Dentist and Staff

Reduction in Working Time

The previously mentioned relaxation induction is very rapid. The trance patient can keep his or her head in any desired position, without moving, spitting, talking, or drinking. This eliminates much nonproductive time and permits a smooth, uninterrupted flow of work.

Reduction in Fatigue From Working

Because of the rapport established through hypnosis, the patient feels comfortable and is very cooperative and pleasant. The stress induced by working with unpleasant, uncooperative patients is eliminated, and the dentist and staff are able to be more relaxed while working (Morse, 1977). This makes the day's efforts more rewarding and less tiring, particularly when so many patients say, "I never thought I would enjoy going to the dentist, but I do!" "This is the only place I can relax."

More Harmonious Staff Relations

It is impossible to use hypnosis successfully unless there is a spirit of cooperation among the staff. The patient in trance is quickly aware of disharmony. On the other hand, pleasant patients contribute to a smooth running office. The staff can also be taught self-hypnosis techniques to control minor problems that might otherwise interfere with smooth interpersonal staff functioning (Miller, 1979).

There are, of course, limitations in a practice that employs the hypnotic modality. Not everyone is a suitable candidate for hypnosis. Not everyone needs or wishes to be hypnotized. There is a general concensus that not everyone can achieve trance, as is witnessed by tests dividing people into the highly hypnotizable, the not hypnotizable, and the large gradient in between (Measures of Hypnotizability, 1978–79). Joseph Barber (1980), however, is amassing evidence that all people are capable of benefiting from the hypnotic experience, through indirect induction techniques. We do have the task of assessing our patient's capabilities in order to determine if the hypnotic modality is suitable. Beyond the assessment of capability lies the assessment of motivation. The observation has been made that patients who have adequately handled whatever was necessary through hypnotic means, will, on other occasions, refuse to use the skills that they have previously demonstrated. This is an area that should be studied in order to determine if motivation can be quantified in such a way that prediction of outcome with the hypnotic modality is possible. The solution might well be a combination of the needs of the patient and the skill of the dentist.

Beyond this, lies the ability to determine if, or which, other modalities might necessarily be incorporated to make the dental treatment a pleasant experience for the patient. Dentistry, unlike a surgical experience such as an appendectomy, is an ongoing consideration throughout the life of the individual. At present, there are no guidelines except the experience and art of the dentist. In the clinical setting, there is no way of doing the same thing several ways. This makes assessment difficult, other than on empirical grounds, and with no real means of knowing if another approach might have been better.

While it is generally agreed that the staff should present a pleasant, harmonious, supportive, and compassionate aura to the patient, no one has defined this or the procedures necessary for its achievement.

Much has been said of our (the patient's) successes, but little of the failures of both sides. Until some statistical knowledge of how often and under what conditions hypnosis helps and to what extent, has been amassed we cannot, with certainty, predict the outcome of any use of the hypnotic modality. Experience does enable us to assess, fairly accurately, the outcome in many instances, but the existence of our failures is evidence of the imponderables that face us at present. It is understandable that failures with the hypnotic modality are not written about. It would be helpful if case histories could be well documented so that the goals, methodologies, and results might be properly assessed. The goals could very well turn out to be unrealistic in terms of patient expectancy and operator skills. The methodology might be inappropriate for the particular subject or operant conditions. The results might turn out to be very different from subjective perceptions.

In short, we do not have a yardstick by which we can measure the need for hypnosis for any patient coming to our offices. The obviously anxious patient can be assisted. The patient who conceals his anxiety should have the support of the hypnotic modality, but may not, because it is used, and should be used, on a selective basis. Perhaps we should teach all patients how to use hypnosis in order to give them more control over their own physiology and comfort. The important issue, beyond the question of the degree of hypnotizability, is how to develop for our armamentarium a flexible methodology, so that every patient can benefit from the compassionate, supportive modality called hypnosis.

Appendix 18-1

Case Example of the Use of Hypnosis in Dentistry

CASE EXAMPLE	COMMENTS
The patient was a 57-year-old married white female, for whom it was necessary to extract a tooth. She had had one lung	This patient had no previous experience with hypnosis and knew nothing about it.

CASE EXAMPLE

and a portion of the other removed because of cancer, so that general anesthesia was a life-threatening procedure. She had a history of laryngospasm with local anesthesia, which could make local anesthesia a life-threatening procedure. I explained that it would be possible to remove the tooth comfortably using hypno-anesthesia. She was not enthusiastic, but did make an appointment for the extraction. When she did come in for the extraction, after postponing the appointment twice, she was seated in the treatment room by the dental assistant. I then entered the treatment room and while washing my hands said to the patient, "Mrs. M., before we start, I'm going to teach you how to relax. As you know, everything is easier when you are relaxed. While relaxation is a mental process, it does help to have something physical to work with, so shrug your shoulders a little. That's very good and that is all the actual physical movement you need to make. Mentally, move this feeling of relaxation from your shoulders into your upper arms, through your elbows into your forearms, wrists and hands, so that you have a comfortable relaxed feeling from your right hand up your right arm, across your shoulders, down your left arm to your left hand. It's all right to close your eyes now. Move the feeling of comfortable relaxation from your shoulders into your chest and stomach and hips . . . into your upper legs and through your knees into your lower legs, ankles and feet. Now move the feeling of comfortable relaxation from your shoulders into your neck and let it spread up into your head, until it fills your entire head with a comfortable relaxed feeling. Take a deep breath and as you breathe out, relax very deeply. You have noticed how relaxing it is when you breathe out, so you can become more deeply relaxed and com-

COMMENTS

A relaxation induction was used for this patient because she could understand that relaxation did make things easier. It actively engaged her in the process, since she was the one who was moving the feeling of comfortable relaxation through her body. It was not something that she was told would happen, but something that she made happen.

The suggestion for eye closure was made when she started to blink and seemed to be keeping her eyes open with an effort.

The suggestion of powerful new topical anesthetic was made to give her trance logic a handle for interpreting any sensation as comfortable. The perceptual distortion was reinforced constantly as the elevator was applied to the tooth and finally as the tooth was removed. Until the tooth was removed, all the suggestions were to the effect that the anesthesia was being instituted and intensified. When the patient was told that it was so numb that she would not feel the extraction, the tooth had already been removed, so there was nothing that she could possibly feel.

The posthypnotic suggestion that the socket will fill with blood, and clot and heal normally is readily accepted in the trance state, even though the exact physiological mechanism that makes this happen is unknown at the present time. Giving a subject the feeling of being refreshed and feeling good and being terrific when she opens her eyes gives her an incentive to come out of trance. The trance state is a very comfortable and

CASE EXAMPLE

fortable each time you exhale. We do have a very effective surface anesthetic, which I am now applying to your tooth and gums. I'm squeezing it into the gum tissue and now, to make sure we have complete anesthesia, I'm going to push it under the gum around the tooth. Notice how the numbness increases as I push it firmly down further and further around the tooth. I'm now going to exert even more pressure to push the anesthetic material under the gum and down around the root of the tooth. The anesthesia has now become so profound you will not be able to feel the tooth being removed . . . The tooth is out, and you can let the socket fill with blood and clot normally. You can be pleasantly surprised at how little discomfort and swelling there will be as the tooth socket heals rapidly in a normal manner. When you open your eyes, you will feel refreshed and very good and very pleased with yourself, and when I count to three, you will open your eyes and feel terrific, because you are. One . . . two . . . three. The patient opened her eyes and commented, "I wasn't hypnotized. The only reason I didn't feel anything was because you tricked me into not knowing when you took the tooth out."

COMMENTS

enjoyable state, and it is wise to give the subject an incentive to terminate it.

No effort was made to point out to the patient that she must have been in trance in order for the tooth to have been removed painlessly. The object was a comfortable extraction, which had been accomplished. Convincing the patient that she had been hypnotized was unimportant.

References

Barber J: Hypnosis and the unhypnotizable. Am J Clin Hypn 23:4, 1980

Barber J, Mayer D: Evaluation of the efficacy and neural mechanism of an hypnotic analgesia procedure in experimental and clinical pain. Pain 4:41, 1977

Beeson PB, McDermott W, Wyngaarden JB: Cecil Texbook of Medicine, vol I. Philadelphia, WB Saunders, 1979

Brustein DD: Hypnotic analgesia. Dent Survey 43:57, 1967

Carnow R: A technic for using nitrous oxide and hypnosis together. J Nat Analg Soc 2:5, 1973

Cassell DK: Eliminating fear with hypnosis. Dent Economics 69:75, 1979

Cheek DB, LeCron LM: Clinical Hypnotherapy. New York, Grune & Stratton, 1968

DiBona MC: Nitrous oxide and hypnosis, a combined technique. Anesth Prog 26:17, 1979

Dubin LL, Shapiro SS: Use of hypnosis to facilitate dental extraction and hemostasis in a classic hemophiliac with a high antibody titer to Factor VIII. Am J Clin Hypn 17:79, 1974

Ewin DM: Treatment of emergency patients facilitated by hypnosis. Panel on emergencies, K. Olness, ch. 19th annual ASCH scientific session. Chicago, 1976

Finkelstein S: Rapid elimination of dental anaesthesia by suggestion in a light trance state. Transnat Mental Health Res Newsletter 21:15, 1979

Finkelstein S, Goldstein Y, Barnett EA: Depth, deepening, and trance maintenance. 22nd annual ASCH workshop. San Francisco, 1979

Golan HP: Control of fear reaction in dental patients by hypnosis. Am J Clin Hypn 13:279, 1971

Golan HP. Hypnosis—Further case reports from the Boston City Hospital. Am J Clin Hypn 18:55, 1975

Goldberg G: The psychological, physiological, and hypnotic approach to bruxism in the treatment of periodontal disease. J Am Soc Psychosomatic Dent Med 20:75, 1974

Graham G: Hypnoanalysis in dental practice. Am J Clin Hypn 16:178, 1974

Hartland J: Medical and Dental Hypnosis. London, Bailliere Tindall, 1979, pp 21–25, 360–373

Heron WT: An Old Art Returns to Dentistry. Chicago, Seminars on Hypnosis, 1958

Jacobson BS: Hypnosis in fixed partial prosthodontics. J Prosth Dent 19:406, 1968

Kramer RB, Braham RL: The management of the chronic or hysterical gagger. J Dent Child 44:111, 1977

Lucas ON: The use of hypnosis in hemophiliac dental care. Ann NY Acad Sci 240:263, 1978

Measures of Hypnotizability. Am J Clin Hypn 21:68, 1978–79

Miller S: Hypnosis—Relaxation for you and your patient. NYS Dent J 45:221, 1979

Morse DR: Overcoming 'practice stress' via meditation and hypnosis. Dent Survey 53:32, 1977

Moss AA: Hypnodontics. Brooklyn, Dental Items of Interest Publishing, 1957, p 12

Sechter I I: Applied psychology in dentistry. Am J Clin Hypn 8:122, 1965

Sechter I I: Some notes on controlling the exaggerated gag reflex. Am J Clin Hypn 2:149, 1960

Stein MR: Anesthesia by mental association. Oral Surg Anesth Dec. 1930, p 941

Strosberg IM: Control of gagging by light hypnosis. Am J Clin Hypn 2:118, 1960

Wegner SD: It's coming of age. The use of hypnosis in the dental practice. Chronicle 42:90, 1979

Wolfe LS, Millet JB: Control of post-operative pain by suggestion under general anesthesia. Am J Clin Hypn 3:109, 1960

UNIT FOUR
Use of Hypnosis With Psychopathological States

19 Hypnosis in Psychiatry

THOMAS R. WERNER

Throughout recorded history, hypnosis has been used by healers for the alleviation of pain and dysfunction. Those who employed hypnosis and those who experienced it sought to explain it through spirituality, mysticism, biological deficiencies, physical forces, pure "psychology," and psychobiology. We continue to grope for a comprehensive explanation that will pass the test of time. Barber (1974), Fromm (1972), Gordon (1967), Hilgard (1975), Spiegel (1978), Weizenhoffer (1953), and many others have contributed to this body of knowledge.

Since Antoine Mesmer's introduction of the hypnotic phenomenon into Western medicine in the 18th century, hypnosis has waxed and waned in popularity and acceptability as a treatment modality. The details of this passage from Mesmer to the 20th century is treated in other chapters of this book. In *Foundations of Hypnosis from Mesmer to Freud*, Tinterow offers an in-depth study of this period. In 1955, the British Medical Association formally approved the use of hypnosis in the treatment of psychological disorders as well as for use in anesthesia. In 1958, the American Medical Association recommended that hypnosis be introduced into the curriculum of American Medical Colleges. Research in hypnosis was encouraged as well as its use in the practice of medicine by properly trained practitioners.

The practicing clinician, if he or she is to be responsive to the needs of patients, must have a variety of psychological and somatic tools available. Should the individual clinician not wish to spend the time to develop skills in the use of hypnosis, it is of importance that sufficient knowledge of its application be possessed so that appropriate referrals can be made to competent practitioners when hypnosis is the treatment of choice.

What is hypnosis? In the interest of limited space, I refer you to other contributors and to the previously mentioned sources for an in-depth treatment of the subject.

The general psychiatrist, in daily practice, is faced with a variety of disorders. The literature abounds with reports of successful hypnotic treatment of many of these problems. I shall deal with those that I have found in my daily clinical practice to be the most frequently encountered and that have been demonstrated to be significantly amenable to hypnotherapy.

Among these disorders found to be responsive to hypnotherapy are (1) anxiety disorders, (2) somatoform disorders, (3) psychosexual dysfunctions, (4) psychological factors affecting physical conditions (psychosomatic disorders), and (5) pain.

Selection of Patients for Hypnotherapy

When evaluating a patient for hypnotherapy, the psychiatrist should approach the patient using the traditional medical system of seeking out the most probable cause of the presenting complaint (*i.e.,* arriving at a diagnosis). Only in this way may he arrive at the most appropriate therapeutic modality. To do anything less would be to treat symptoms, which is well understood to be fraught with danger.

Every patient whom I see receives a complete psychiatric evaluation, which may involve up to 3 hours of clinical interviews. Indicated physical evaluation and laboratory studies are performed. Consultative psychological testing for clarification of issues may also be required. The patient who calls asking for hypnotherapy for a complaint is informed that this evaluation will be performed prior to a decision, in order that the most appropriate treatment may be offered. Following completion of the evaluation, treatment options are discussed. Should no contraindications to hypnosis be noted, and its use offer a benefit over other accepted treatments, it is recommended.

The issue of dangers of hypnosis and contraindications to its use is one that is hotly debated. Certainly, a primary contraindication is a deficiency of knowledge and skills on the part of the psychiatrist. Hypnosis in treatment is, as is the scalpel, as safe or as dangerous as the hand in which it rests. Each psychiatrist must make this decision. In my practice, I consider prepsychotic disorders, severe paranoid disorders, and major affective disorders, especially depressive disorders, as contraindications for hypnosis as the primary treatment. More concerning this may be found in the work of Cheek and LeCron (1968), of Brenman and Gill (1960), and of Meares (1961), as well as in other supplied references. An example is a patient with a phobia for bridges with associated fear of jumping from the bridge in the presence of a clinically identifiable depression. This symptom may be interpreted as a defense against suicidal drives. An explanation that a depression is present and should be treated first ordinarily is accepted by the person who recognizes that much time has gone into arriving at this conclusion. Should the phobia persist after the depression clears, the psychiatrist has more time to consider further treatment strategies including, perhaps, hypnosis.

Tests for hypnotizability have been discussed widely as predictors of response to therapy by many experts, including Wolberg (1948) and Spiegel (1978). I have not found such tests of significant clinical value in predicting outcome. In my experience, a healthy motivation and strong positive expectation of benefit from hypnotherapy have been of greater use. Such tests should be known and used as the clinician finds them helpful. A strongly positive response may certainly be used to enhance motivation and expectation of benefit.

Preparation of the Patient

Hypnosis having been agreed upon as the treatment, time should be spent clarifying with the patient the popularly held understanding of the hypnotic phenomenon and dispelling myths that might interfere with the treatment. Emphasis upon the therapeutic relationship as being one of collaboration in arriving at the mutually agreed upon goal of alleviation of the disorder and of psychological growth on the part of the patient will often prevent resistance and overdependence upon the psychiatrist. In addition, encouragement that most people, in the absence of organic brain disease, have the capacity to experience hypnosis and to develop improved skills in its use with practice aids in preventing discouragement if only a light state is initially achieved. The patient should always know when other approaches to treatment exist as a backup lest anxiety over failure of the hypnotherapy interfere with the initial experience.

Treatment Applications

Anxiety Disorders

Among anxiety disorders for which I have found hypnosis to be helpful in selected cases are agoraphobia with panic attacks and panic disorders unresponsive to imipramine or MAO inhibitors, generalized anxiety disorder, social phobias, and many simple phobias.

It is of importance to determine from experience whether the phobic disorder is of a posttraumatic nature, the trauma being available to simple recall, or consequent to trauma and psychological conflicts that are unavailable to the consciousness of the patient.

I have found posttraumatic phobia to be highly responsive to hypnobehavioral therapy fashioned after that described by Kroger (1976). Rarely has a return of symptoms occurred following a successful treatment of this type of phobia. In contrast, the "psychoneurotic" phobia appears to require an approach that involves retrieval of unconscious information and resolution of the conflict if one is to avoid recurrence of the symptom.

In most anxiety disorders, one is confronted with a patient who feels helpless and out of control of incapacitating symptoms. The first step that I undertake is to support the patient's feelings of returning confidence of control.

Following induction of as deep a trance as appears attainable for the patient, a visual image of a private, safe, relaxing experience is suggested. If possible, this is an experience from the patient's past life or from his fantasy of an ideal situation for him. When the patient indicates by an ideomotor signal that relaxation has been achieved, instructions are given to recall and to feel a small amount of the anxiety associated with the disorder. When this is reported as present, the patient is once again asked to return to the "safe place" and to feel the relaxation. This is repeated with increasingly higher levels of evoked anxiety until the patient reports confidence that the anxiety can be suppressed and replaced with relaxation. Following this, the patient is given Hartland's ego-strengthening suggestions (Hartland, 1966). The entire session, lasting 30 to 45 minutes, is tape-recorded and provided to the patient to use at least once per day until the next visit to reinforce the process.

The following case reports are examples of specific approaches:

A 45-year-old married man, an executive of midlevel, presented with the complaint of 6 months of episodes of lightheadedness, feelings of faintness, palpitations, blurred vision, and severe feelings of apprehension lasting from 5 to 30 minutes. They occurred at the office, while he was at lunch, when he was making presentations to higher level executives in conferences, and, more rarely, at home. His history revealed that the symptoms began a short time after he was passed over for a promotion that a friend received. He was clearly angry at his employer and his friend but could not get in touch with his feelings. His personality was clearly compulsive, and he defended against feeling any affect, especially anger, vigorously. A smile was his constant expression. His physical evaluation was normal, except for moderate hypertension. He expressed strong reluctance to enter insight-oriented therapy.

It was felt that his symptoms reflected concern that he was about to lose control of his anger and act in a way damaging to his interests. A course of hypnotherapy was proposed, in part because he felt it would be successful.

The previously described relaxation and ego-strengthening suggestions were provided, and he used the tape regularly. After a week, he reported confidence that the feelings were controllable. He then was given the suggestion that whenever he found himself beginning to experience the symptoms he could count from 3 to 0 and reexperience the relaxation. In addition, suggestions were added to the ego-strengthening technique that he was in control of all of his feelings and would express them only in a constructive fashion, and that one may have anger, love, and other normal feelings without fear of dangerous behavior. He noted a progressive reduction in frequency and severity of episodes over the following 6 weeks. Anticipatory anxiety for situations in which he had experienced the episodes was treated using visual imagery of being in the situations with coupled feelings of calm, relaxed confidence that his ritual (my term) of counting would be adequate to maintain comfort should he need it. He reported himself symptom free after 11 visits. Approximately 16 months later, he called for a follow-up having had one episode during a family crisis. Still smiling, he asked for a "booster session." Following that, he was heard from 1 year later, when he reported continued freedom from the symptoms. His hypertension has also improved.

There are those who would argue that his conflicts remained unresolved. This, indeed, may be so. However, meeting him at the point at which he was ready to work resulted in restoration of function, satisfaction on his part that he had mastered his symptoms, and a relatively modest outlay of health-care dollars.

A second example is a 25-year-old married woman who presented with a phobic disorder involving crossing the Ohio River bridges from Cincinnati to Northern Kentucky alone, either by automobile or on foot. It had begun 6 months prior to the patient's first visit. The phobia was beginning to spread to other highway bridges in the area but was still mild in intensity for them. The patient's history suggested that the phobia had begun at about the time the patient's husband had taken a job in Northern Kentucky and had suggested that they move from Cincinnati to Kentucky for convenience. The patient was totally puzzled by the symptom and was fearful "that she was losing her mind."

Her history revealed that she had been born in Kentucky and had lived there until age 5, when her parents were divorced. She had moved to Cincinnati with her mother and recalled seeing little of her father thereafter. Her mother was alive and living in Cincinnati.

After 3 months of individual weekly psychotherapy with little evidence of progress, it was suggested to the patient that hypnosis be used in her treatment. After a thorough explanation of hypnosis and how it would be used to help her understand her problem better, she readily agreed.

The patient was able to achieve a deep but not somnambulistic level of hypnosis. She was told that we would travel back in time to her childhood when "something important" had occurred, which would help understand her problem. She was instructed to visualize a calendar. The calendar pages would turn back a year at a time until "something told her to stop." She would signal with an automatic movement of a finger when to stop. We performed this, and she stopped when she was 6 years old. She was then asked to see herself at age 6 and to tell me about it. She was unable to do this. A projective technique was then used in which she was asked to visualize a stage in a theater with a 6-year-old girl on it and to add characters and to set the scene of a one act play starring the girl. She saw the girl in a house crying with a man and woman arguing over her. The woman was saying that she was taking the girl with her, and the man would not allow it. The girl was frightened and wanted to go with the woman but also wanted the man "to be nice to her." The patient was instructed that upon coming out of hypnosis she would remember as much as she could comfortably and that it would help her recall events in her life.

The patient spontaneously recalled that around age 6 she had visited her father in Kentucky for the summer, and that he had refused to permit her to return to her mother.

After much turmoil, with threats of legal action, she was returned to her mother. She recalled never being allowed to visit her father without her mother thereafter. In another session using this information, she was able to reexperience her mother telling her that she should never visit her father alone lest she never see her mother again. It was suggested that as we passed through time to the present she see herself growing up and no longer feeling helpless but more in control of her own future. The phobic anxiety began to recede.

Therapy continued for 4 more months, focusing on now more available feelings of dependency upon mother and upon her husband. She was able to associate this with her earlier experiences with her parents. Residual anticipatory anxiety was relieved with two sessions of hypnosis wherein she experienced herself driving on the bridges relaxed, comfortable, and in control.

Somatoform Disorders

Conversion disorders and somatoform pain disorders are commonly seen in the practice of consultative psychiatry.

Hypnosis may be helpful in the diagnosis of these disorders. *Temporary* restoration of function, such as sight, smell, hearing, taste, pain, temperature, and motor functions, previously reported as absent aids the clinician in diagnosis and proper treatment planning. I emphasize "temporary" because one may be opening a Pandora's box should one remove a symptom prior to understanding the psychological necessity of the symptom both for primary and secondary gain. It is often said that a symptom will not respond to suggestions of removal if it is necessary in the patient's current adaption. Should this be the case, a negative response to suggestion certainly would be of no diagnostic value. The literature abounds with challenges to the concept of symptom substitution. It appears prudent to "give permission" to the patient to restore the symptom if it is necessary. This may be for both primary psychological needs or secondary social needs. An example of a secondary social need would be fear of loss of face with family or friends if the symptom proves to be "in their head." I therefore introduce a closing suggestion such as "upon leaving this hypnotic state, your arm will move as much as it can and stay as stiff as it must. You shall remember as much of this as you can and forget as much as you must." The temporary removal of a pain experience, it would appear, indicates no more than that the patient is suggestible.

Spiegel (1978) and others point out that a hysterical symptom may begin as a manifestation of an intrapsychic conflict but persist independently as learned behavior following a resolution of the conflict. Such a residual symptom could be expected to be removable with no risk of symptom substitution or psychological dysequelibria. However, it is of importance to consider the function that the symptom has acquired in the patient's relationship with the external environment, such as the family, in treatment planning.

In the treatment of some conversion disorders, such as hysterical paralysis, one must intervene even though the symptom may be psychologically necessary if one is to prevent permanent physical damage. An accurate psychodynamic understanding of the symptom often allows for direct suggestion for substitution of a less potentially dangerous symptom. Also, the symptom may be allowed to come and go to a degree to prevent damage from occurring while more aggressive insight therapy is taking place. One may offer a specific change, such as moving the paralysis from one entire extremity to a portion of the hand or foot. One may offer the suggestion that the paralysis will disappear during periods of time during the day, allowing active movement of the extremity. Pain may be moved, for example, from the entire hand to several fingers or to the other hand following use of the hand. Such suggestions should always be given with "permission" for it to be accepted to a degree comfortable for the patient. The choice for several options for alteration with suggestion that the patient may pick any one that is best for him offers further safeguards. The choice itself may offer further understanding of the symptom for the therapist.

An example of an approach is the case of a 43-year-old man with a stiff right arm, which developed after a family argument.

He left the home rather than continue the argument and while driving his automobile around town noted the onset of the symptom. He found it very difficult to move and was unable to work. After being seen in consultation and a diagnosis of conversion disorder being made, hypnosis was offered as a means of relaxation. In a moderate trance he was able to move the extremity with ease. Not psychologically minded, he attributed it to the "relaxation." It was felt that this gentleman needed a treatment that would be socially acceptable to him. He was asked under hypnosis whether he felt hot packs and passive exercises, or diathermy, or whirlpool treatments would be the treatment which would best relax his arm and return it to full use. He chose whirlpool treatments. These were initiated with the suggestion that he would attain the same relaxation as when in hypnosis and that use of the arm would gradually last for progressively longer periods of time until total function returned. While these treatments were taking place, intensive family therapy was initiated with the explanation that the "talking sessions" were to help work out problems that made him tense.

With resolution of the family conflicts, the patient showed increasing improvement in the use of his arm. He was able to return to work after 5 weeks of treatment. The family therapy continued with another therapist for some months thereafter.

Another example is that of a 54-year-old married man with severe low back pain following a fall in his home.

He had been diagnosed as having low back strain but had not responded to treatment. He spent much of his time in a wheelchair or in bed. With reluctance, he agreed to see a psychiatrist for "a psychosomatic evaluation." In all such cases, the family was interviewed as well. It became evident that prior to his accident, he had ruled his family with an iron hand. He controlled the family funds and was very restrictive in his discipline of his three children. Following his accident and disability, his wife got a part-time job and, with it, new-found freedom. His children, ranging from late to early teens, had greater freedom, since father no longer could enforce his will, having lost control of the family funds. It was noted while observing the family together that many subtle messages of invalidism were directed to the father, both verbally and nonverbally. The presence of denied dependency needs satisfaction was also noted. The entire family accepted the recommendation of treatment for father with much ambivalence.

In a nonhypnotic interview, the patient denied any knowledge of back problems. However, under hypnosis when again asked what he knew about back injuries, he stated that "they never get better." Using time regression, he recalled a discussion at his job about a man who suffered a back injury on the job. It was the group concensus that no one ever recovered from such an injury. He accepted that he would not take medical advice from anyone in the group individually but had accepted the group opinion. He was able to discard that opinion. Simultaneously, family therapy meetings were held in which the patient was able to accept the greater independence of his wife and children as well as his needs for support from the family. The focus shifted to his recovery, and the family reinforced his exercises, which had previously been discouraged. He made a slow, progressive recovery and was able to return to work.

In some conversion disorders, more intense and lengthy insight therapy is required. Hypnosis may be incorporated into such therapy as described by Wolberg and others.

Certainly, one must anticipate that many patients' needs for the symptom or environmental reinforcement will result in a poor response or nonresponse to treatment.

Psychosexual Dysfunctions

These disorders, such as erectile incompetence, anorgasmia, premature ejaculation and vaginismus are commonly seen on referral from urologists and gynecologists who have evaluated the patient for physical disorders and found none. Should such patients present as self-referrals, a thorough evaluation for contributing physical pathology should be performed.

In classifying these disorders, one must determine whether they are primary or secondary in nature. The primary disorder has been present from the onset of sexual activity, there never having been a time of normal functioning. The secondary disorder follows at least one experience of normal sexual activity. Primary disorders commonly are manifestations of deeply entrenched psychopathology, which requires intensive psychotherapy. Hypnosis may play a role in this therapy. Advocates of various modes of psychotherapy report positive results, with no one approach clearly dominantly superior.

Primary erectile incompetence may follow a confidence-undermining failure in coitus, which introduces anticipatory anxiety into the next attempt, resulting in another misadventure. His confidence undermined, the man may then avoid further attempts lest he experience a recurrence of painful shame.

Often a complete history reveals an explanation for the first event, such as fatigue, alcohol, medication, anxiety over being discovered, and so on. If the avoidance pattern has not been lengthy, informal suggestions are given in the form of presenting the probable cause, with reassurance that such events are not uncommon and that the person surely will perform adequately the next time. Coming from an authority figure at a time of heightened suggestibility, the reassurance is a potent supportive suggestion.

Should avoidance behavior be of lengthy duration, the following hypnotherapy approach is often successful.

Following induction of a trance state, the patient is time regressed to an earlier successful sexual experience and instructed to first observe the scene and to be aware of how competent a lover he is. Following this, if he is able to experience revivification, he is instructed to feel the sexual abandon in contrast to his more recent anxiety. Next, he is to feel the strength and rigidity of his penis. One may have him stroke his penis while doing so and become aware of the erection should it develop. The awareness of an adequate erection is generally most reassuring. He may be instructed to masturbate to ejaculation should you feel that it would be acceptable to the patient. This is done while reliving the coitus experience. Autohypnosis training is provided so that he may "rehearse" successful coitus.

The next phase is to have the patient visualize another woman attractive to him but not known to him. Under hypnosis, he is taken slowly through foreplay to successful coitus, reinforcing the feelings of abandon and pleasure.

He is instructed to pause at any point at which anxiety intrudes, to relax and to reinforce feelings of excitement and abandon. Having had several anxiety-free experiences, he may then "rehearse" using the image of his regular partner, should he have one, using self-hypnosis. A posthypnotic suggestion may be given that when he next attempts coitus he will feel the same confidence and arousal that he has felt under hypnosis and that he may use self-hypnosis during coitus to strengthen the experience should anxiety begin to intrude. Should the man have a wife or regular companion, it is important to interview her and make her aware of what to expect and to attempt to help her avoid the learned apprehension over another failure, which may be communicated to the patient.

In anorgasmia, one must, if possible, identify the event or conflict that has resulted in the dysfunction and attempt to resolve it.

A case example is that of a 47-year-old married woman who had an active orgasmic sex life up to age 46, when she underwent a hysterectomy for fibroid tumors.

Following recovery from surgery, she found herself anorgasmic and, surprising even to her, disinterested in sex. At the urging of her husband, she saw her gynecologist, who sent her for consultation.

The patient had four children and had been raised to view sex as a procreative process and the pleasure as the reward for procreation. She scoffed at the idea intellectually. In addition, she expressed anger over a memory of hearing her mother-in-law express regrets to another woman that her son no longer had a complete woman for a partner. After several months of psychotherapy exploring her feelings and attitudes toward sex, motherhood, and grief over loss of a cherished body part, her uterus, hypnotherapy was suggested, which she accepted. She achieved a good level of trance in which she was able to accept that orgasm could continue as a reward for her four children and for her continued care of them. She was able to reject the comment of her mother-in-law. She was taught self-hypnosis and instructed to spend time each day when she was alone at home in self-hypnosis reexperiencing earlier coitus with her husband. She suggested that perhaps a vibrator would help "get her started again," and this was supported. After several weeks of "practice" she had coitus with orgasm with her husband and subsequently has had a satisfying sex life with her husband.

One is well-advised to use prudence in working with women if one is to have them experience revivification of an orgasm in the office setting, lest the experience be distorted in the hypnotic relationship. It is my practice to refer to a woman therapist if the patient is unable to accomplish revivification through self-hypnosis at home.

Premature ejaculation is a disorder that often responds easily to Masters and Johnson's technique of pressure on the glans penis to inhibit ejaculation. This, of course, requires a regular partner who is prepared to cooperate. Kroger (1976) describes the use of time distortion, in which the perceived length of time preceding ejaculation is suggested as being longer. This is supported and reinforced by the partner. Visual imagery of nonerotic scenes at insertion and for a period of time thereafter may interfere with the erotic component of coitus, suspending ejaculation until attention is restored to the sexual experience.

Vaginismus results from involuntary spasm of the vaginal muscles and of the perineal muscles. This may appear as a secondary response to a painful or traumatic coital experience, fear of additional pregnancies, rejection of lover, and so on. Hypnosis may be used to enhance muscular relaxation and reduction of anxiety. Often, the woman must at first gently introduce her own finger slowly into the vagina over a number of days, allowing the muscles to relax around the finger. Once she is able to accomplish this, her husband or regular partner may over a period of time perform the same function while the woman uses self-hypnosis for relaxation. Visual imagery of a pleasant experience initially progressing over time to images of gentle, pleasurable penile insertion may be helpful. When there is no regular partner, many gynecologists have graduated dilators, which the patient may use on herself with or without visual imagery. Concomitant psychotherapy is commonly necessary.

Psychosomatic Disorders

Beginning with the concept of organ neurosis, a number of physical disorders have been identified as having psychological factors as either the primary etiology or a major contributing factor. Among these disorders are asthma, ulcerative colitis, mucus colitis, rheumatoid arthritis, atopic dermatitis, migraine headaches, muscular contraction headaches, and essential hypertension.

Over the years, theories of conflict specificity, organ vulnerability, autonomic regression, and many others have risen and receded. Current views of all illness as resulting from multiple factors including nonspecific stress appear to offer the most useful model.

If one can identify in one's patient the life experience or experiences that evoke a level of arousal sufficient to trigger to aggravate the disorder, whatever it may be, hypnosis may prove to be a helpful tool.

Insight psychotherapy with deconditioning techniques to identify and diminish responsivity to a stimulus may often prove helpful in reducing the number of episodes or severity of an illness. The regular practice of self-hypnosis with relaxation shows early indications of being helpful in reducing chronic over-arousal. Certainly, in those instances in which muscle contraction or spasm is a major component of the disorder, an adept subject may find relief with auto-hypnosis.

Pain

Suggestion has been used for the alleviation of pain for centuries under many names. John Elliotson in 1834 and James Esdaile in 1846 first reported the effective use of hypnosis in surgery in large numbers of patients. With the advent of chemical anesthesia, hypnosis receded from the surgical amphitheater. It has continued to be used in obstetrics, minor surgery, and dentistry. General physicians often employ it for the treatment of headaches and other short-term pain experiences. Its use in chronic pain, such as musculoskeletal pain and pain resulting from cancer, is often helpful for limited intervals and allows reduction in use of narcotics. It has been reported to be regularly helpful in about 20% of patients with chronic pain. For a comprehensive presentation of this subject, one should refer to Hilgard's *Hypnosis in the Relief of Pain* (1975).

Induction Sequence

Some years ago when I first became interested in the use of hypnosis as a treatment modality in my practice of psychiatry, the writings of Ainslie Meares (1961), describing his "dynamic induction technique," capture my interest. It did so because it appeared to emphasize the dynamic interaction between the hypnotherapist and the person experiencing the hypnotic phenomenon. Although requiring a greater repertoire of deepening strategies to aid one's patient in enhancing his hypnotic experience, it frees both therapist and subject from the restrictions of a predetermined sequence.

My most frequent initial step in an induction involves instructing the patient, prior to his visit, to wear comfortable clothing. In addition, a patient who ordinarily has been seen on at least one previous occasion has been given a thorough explanation of the hypnotic phenomenon and what he or she may expect with the design of removing unwarranted apprehensions and of enhancing positive expectations.

The patient is offered a seat in a high-backed, winged chair with the option of using a footstool. The subject is then instructed to pick out a spot in the room on which to focus his attention and is asked to take two easy, deep breaths, allowing the air to flow out of his lungs and being aware of the muscles of the rib cage and diaphragm, which are automatically relaxing from a state of increased to decrease tension. The subject is then instructed to allow his breathing to continue in an automatic fashion, and the therapist points out that this sequence of tension and relaxation has occurred automatically since birth. At the same time, suggestions of eye fatigue and lid heaviness are provided, with the reassurance that this is a normal, predictable experience. Should resistance be noted through such signs as corrugation of the forehead or actual widening of the palpebral fissure, the subject is reassured that his lengthening the time it takes for his eyes to ultimately close will facilitate his entering into an even deeper state of relaxation once it is achieved. This very commonly interrupts the resistance, and there is rapid eye closure.

The subject is then asked to follow the easy, regular rhythm of his breathing for a few moments, and the therapist once again emphasizes the automatic relaxation, the "letting go of unnecessary tension" of the muscles of the chest and diaphragm.

Following this, a standard progressive relaxation sequence from scalp to toes is performed, in which it is suggested to the subject that he tighten and then relax each muscle group in order to feel the loss of tension until he feels this occurring spontaneously.

Following this, if there is no contraindication to touching the patient and the patient has been forewarned, one arm is lifted, with the observation, "I am now lifting your arm." An observation of how much muscle tension remains in the arm is made. If the arm is quite heavy and relaxed, the standard arm drop deepening technique is used, with the reassurance that the arm will drop "heavy as a sopping wet bath towel safely into my hand below." Should the arm retain significant muscle tension, which would imply a potentially poor arm drop experience, arm rigidity is induced as a deepening strategy. Should the muscle tension fall somewhere in the midrange, the elbow may be placed on the arm of the chair and automatic movement induced.

If arm rigidity has been induced, one may then reverse it, suggesting profound relaxation, which then is often achieved. One may then proceed with the arm drop. Alternately, one may allow the arm to float in the air, while raising the other arm, suggesting that it too will float as does the first. Then suggestions of magnets being in the palms of the hands with automatic movement toward each other with ultimate locking of the palms are provided with a gentle challenge to pull them apart with a suggestion that "the harder you attempt to pull them apart, the tighter they will become locked." The process may then be reversed by suggesting reversal of polarity of the magnets, causing the hands to drift apart, removing the magnets, and suggesting that the arms will become heavy and slowly descend to the lap or the arms of the chair, where they will become totally and completely relaxed.

If it has been established from the initial interview that the subject has the capacity for vivid visual imagery and is not claustrophobic or acrophobic, it is suggested that the patient visualize himself in an elevator and see the floor indicator as an illuminated number. The subject is then instructed to signal by "allowing a finger of a hand to move as a signal that he or she is ready to press the button for the first floor, which, when reached, will open onto a very, very relaxing scene." The subject is asked to visualize each floor as it passes by seeing the number illuminated as the therapist counts down to the first floor. Suggestions of going "deeper" and of "more and more relaxed and at ease" are made periodically during the descent. The door then opens upon a predetermined relaxing scene, which has been derived from information obtained during a previous clinical interview.

Should the patient not be able to achieve good visual imagery, fractionalization is used. The patient is asked to count within himself as the therapist counts from zero to ten, feeling himself becoming more wide awake and alert while retaining his level of peaceful relaxation. Upon reaching ten, the count is immediately reversed down to zero, with suggestions of entering an even "deeper" or "intense" state of relaxation. This may be repeated a number of times at the discretion of the therapist.

As a test for depth and further enhancement of the hypnotic state, a suggestion of tactile and auditory hallucinatory experiences may be made. Ordinarily, I use the image of a housefly buzzing about the patient's ear and cheek. The patient is instructed to "allow" one or the other arm automatically to brush away the fly when it is heard or felt, which may further enhance deepening.

Having achieved maximum depth for that induction, a posthypnotic suggestion is given for a cue to facilitate more rapid reentry into the hypnotic state at another session. I have found that a suggestion that Spiegel's eye roll technique (Spiegel, 1978) of rapid induction will henceforth produce as intense, or perhaps an even more intense, level of hypnosis in the future and will further enhance its effectiveness.

References

Barber T, Spanos N, Chaves J: Hypnosis, Imagination, and Human Potentialities. New York, Pergamon Press, 1974

Bernman M, Gill MM: Hypnotherapy, A Survey of the Literature. New York, International Universities Press, 1960

Cheek DB, LeCron LM: Clinical Hypnotherapy. New York, Grune & Stratton, 1968

Fromm E, Shor R: Hypnosis: Research Developments & Perspectives. Chicago, Aldine Publishing Co, 1972

Gordon JE: Handbook of Clinical and Experimental Hypnosis. New York, Macmillan, 1967

Hilgard ER, Hilgard JR: Hypnosis in the Relief of Pain. Los Altos, CA, William Kaufman, 1975

Hartland J: Medical and Dental Hypnosis and Its Clinical Applications. Baltimore, Williams & Wilkins, 1966

Kroger WS, Fezler WD: Hypnosis and Behavior Modification: Imagery Conditioning. Philadelphia, JB Lippincott, 1976

Meares A: The System of Medical Hypnosis. Philadelphia, WB Saunders, 1961

Spiegel H, Spiegel D: Trance and Treatment. New York, Basic Books, 1978

Tinterow MM: Foundations of Hypnosis From Mesmer to Freud. Springfield, IL, Charles C Thomas, 1970

Weitzenhoffer AM: Hypnotism An Objective Study in Suggestibility. New York, John Wiley and Sons, 1953

Wolberg LR: Medical Hypnosis, Vol. I, The Principles of Hypnotherapy. New York, Grune & Stratton, 1948

Wolberg LR: Medical Hypnosis, Vol. II, The Practice of Hypnotherapy. New York, Grune & Stratton, 1948

20 Hypnosis With Severely Disturbed Patients

JOAN MURRAY-JOBSIS

Foundations

General Literature

The experimental and clinical literature relating to severely disturbed patients is extensive. For the purposes of this chapter, this review will be limited to a summary of the literature regarding the general theories of the etiology and treatment of schizophrenia, and then to a summary of the more recent literature introducing the techniques of hypnosis into psychotherapeutic approaches in the treatment of schizophrenics and other severely disturbed patients.

There have been decades of debate in the experimental and clinical literature over the causal factors associated with schizophrenia and over the appropriate methods of treatment. Historically, the pre-Freudian clinical view held that schizophrenia was a degenerative disease, organic in nature, and therefore incurable (Kraepelin, 1919). Though not currently an accepted point of view, this position still influences an ongoing belief in the incurability of schizophrenia.

In the late 1800s, Freudian psychoanalytic concepts introduced the view that emotional disturbance was due to environmental/psychological factors and was therefore amenable to psychoanalytic intervention. While an exclusive correlation between psychological factors and schizophrenia was not established, the concept that psychological factors and mechanisms constitute at least an important and necessary part of the etiology of schizophrenia became accepted by the early 1900s (Jung, 1960; Arieti, 1974; Reiss, 1974). Since that time, many psychotherapeutic approaches have been employed with varying degrees of success. The earliest applications of psychotherapy to schizophrenia were psychoanalytically oriented. Representative of these were the therapies of Jung, Federn, and Abraham (Arieti, 1974). Later psychoanalytic approaches were prompted by Klein, Rosenfeld, Segal, Bion, and Winnicott (Arieti, 1974).

368

More recent developments in psychotherapeutic approaches include the direct analysis of John Rosen, in which the patient's vision of reality is shared by the therapist and communication is established directly with the unconscious (Arieti, 1974). Other modern therapists who work with the "world of the psychoses" as a technique for communicating with and restoring the integration of the schizophrenic patient include Margeurite Sechehaye and Ronald Laing (Arieti, 1974).

In contrast, other prominent modern clinicians have worked to communicate with schizophrenic patients while stressing the "world of reality." Harry Stack Sullivan and Frieda Fromm Reichmann represent a psychotherapeutic approach that stresses a supportive but reality-based adaptation of psychoanalytically oriented psychotherapy (Arieti, 1974).

Other current psychodynamic views of schizophrenia stress the environmental factors involving the dislocation of interactions and communications in disturbed families and parent figures (Lidz, 1977; Wynne and Singer, 1963; Bateson, Jackson, Haley, and Weakland, 1956; Alanen, 1966; Bowers, 1961). The psychotherapeutic approaches used for treatment based on this theoretical framework stress re-education of communication and interaction skills as well as insight.

Finally, there is the behavioral position of viewing schizophrenia as a learning problem, a set of learned behaviors that are unacceptable and abnormal. The theoretical framework here is still psychological, but the emphasis is shifted almost wholly to re-educating behavior and away from causal issues and insight (Ullmann and Krasner, 1967; Skinner, 1967; Meehl, 1962; Ayllon, 1962).

Paralleling this development in the psychological theories of schizophrenia in the clinical literature, there has been a simultaneous development of several competing physiological theories emanating primarily from the experimental literature. The argument for a genetic factor as the causal agent in schizophrenia was presented as early as 1938 (Kallmann). Ongoing experimental work continues to appear to support the assumption of some genetic influence in the incidence of schizophrenia (Slater, 1951, 1968; Kallmann, 1953; Book, 1960; Gottesman and Shields, 1966; Kringlen, 1967, 1968; Bleuler, 1968; Pollin, 1969; Swanson, Brown, and Beuret, 1969; Arieti, 1974).

In addition to the genetic theories, a second grouping of physiological theories developed from experimental literature emphasizing the various biochemical peculiarities associated with schizophrenia (Kety, 1959, 1966, 1969, 1972; Heath and Krupp, 1967; Woolley and Shaw, 1954; Friedhoff and Van Winkle, 1967). While the specific chemical agents in question have varied, these researchers have proposed that chemical imbalances are the causal factors in schizophrenia. These studies often have encountered difficulties in separating cause from effect where biochemical discrepancies have been found, the experimental results sometimes being confounded by the symptoms of schizophrenia. The literature appears to indicate some biochemical and metabolic changes related to schizophrenia. However, whether these changes are resultant rather than causal appears to be difficult to determine (Arieti, 1974).

The result of this experimental work has been an emphasis on biochemical rather than behavioral or psychologically oriented treatment. In addition, the clinical experience since the introduction of phenothiazines in the 1950s for the regulation of schizophrenic and other severely disturbed behaviors has further advanced the emphasis on biochemical rather than psychological treatment for severely disturbed patients.

Hypnosis Literature—Experimental

In addition to the literature (both experimental and clinical) regarding schizophrenia and the debate over its psychological versus its physiological origins and treatment, there is also an extensive experimental and clinical literature concerning the use of hypnosis with this patient population. The main issues debated in the literature concerning the use of hypnosis with severely disturbed patients involve the following questions:

1. Are psychotic patients capable of being hypnotized?
2. Is it dangerous to use hypnosis with psychotic patients?

Regarding the first question, evidence that psychotic patients can be hypnotized began to emerge from experimental studies as early as the mid-20th century. Wilson, Cormen, and Cole (1949) established that hypnotic states could be induced in a significant number of schizophrenics and psychotics with organic illness. More than 50% of the patients in this study proved susceptible to hypnosis. Gale and Herman (1956) found similar results in their research. They, too, found that psychotics with both functional and organic etiology were susceptible to hypnosis. They reported that 62% of the psychotic patients studied in their sample were able to enter trance. They also reported that susceptibility to hypnosis was considerably greater for psychotic patients who were in good contact with reality as compared to those who were "out of contact." Heath, Hoaken, and Sainz (1960) further corroborated these earlier findings by demonstrating that a considerable proportion of schizophrenics in their study were hypnotizable. However, this study reported a smaller percentage of hypnotizability than the earlier studies, perhaps because the patient population in this study consisted wholly of catatonics.

Abrams (1964), in a very thorough review of the literature, reported that aside from anecdotal accounts relatively little experimentation had been conducted in regard to the hypnotizability of psychotics. In studies of general suggestibility, results had shown that psychotics were suggestible as a group, but less so than normals. In reviewing the research studies dealing specifically with the hypnotizability of psychotics, Abrams cites the three studies mentioned above and concludes that the literature supported the position that a significant number of psychotic patients are susceptible to hypnosis. Abrams also notes that the literature appeared to indicate that psychotics are somewhat less hypnotizable than normals and less subject to deep trance. He then points out that depth of trance does not bear any direct relationship to the usefulness of hypnosis as a therapeutic tool. In subsequent sections of this literature review article, Abrams also concludes that hypnosis is both safe for psychotics and useful as an adjunct to psychotherapeutic intervention.

However, at about the same time that Abrams' review article was being published, a new, contradictory study was also being reported. Barber, Karacan, and Calverley (1964) reported finding little susceptibility to hypnosis in a sample of 253 chronic schizophrenics. Of the original 253 patients in this study, Barber and co-workers actually tested 192 chronic schizophrenic inpatients using the Barber Suggestibility Scale and compared their basal level of performance on this scale to a second performance using an hypnotic induction procedure or an alternate procedure of task-motivating instructions. The authors concluded from these tests that schizophrenics showed no better performance on the Barber Suggestibility Scale with hypnotic induction than without. They concluded that schizophrenics, therefore, evidenced little or no susceptibility to hypnosis. This study, however, must be considered against the background of Barber's general philosophical position on hypnosis. At that time, Barber held the view that hypnosis was not a real phenomenon and that hypnotic behavior could be explained in terms of "task motivation." In addition, an analysis of the Barber Suggestibility Scale indicates several test items and procedures that would be likely to elicit high anxiety in a schizophrenic, which would block performance (*e.g.,* insistence on eye closure, directions for loss of ability for speech and movement of the body, and the hallucination of extreme thirst). Thus, the results reported in this study should be viewed in the context of the anxiety-provoking test measures used and in the context of Barber's general philosophical position.

Ongoing research continued to accumulate more and more scientific evidence supportive of the hypnotizability of psychotics. Researchers using the Stanford Hypnotic Susceptibility Scale (SHSS) developed by Weitzenhoffer and Hilgard (1959) have shown that psychotics could achieve a level of hypnotizability comparable to that of a normal population of subjects. Kramer and Brennan (1964) and Vingoe and Kramer (1966) found that both acute and chronic hospitalized schizophrenics were just as hypnotizable as the normal college students investigated by Hilgard, Weitzenhoffer, Landis, and Moore (1961). Greene (1969) replicated these results with another inpatient population of 26 psychotics. Greene further found a two-session reliability coefficient of .92 that was virtually the same as the .91 coefficient found in the Weitzenhoffer and Hilgard normative population. In other words, the psychotic subjects showed the same reliability of susceptibility to hypnosis over a two-session trial as did the normative population on which the Stanford Scales were based. Greene (1969) concluded that "hypnotic techniques might have considerable application in the treatment of psychotics who agree to the use of hypnosis or show interest in it."

Following the work of Greene, research reported by Lavoie, Sabourin, and Langlois (1973) also indicated that many schizophrenic patients were susceptible to hypnosis. Of a sample of 60 male psychotic inpatients, 56 achieved some level of hypnotizability using standardized scales of hypnotic susceptibility (SHSS). The authors reported that their psychotic inpatients tended to cluster in the middle range of the SHSS as compared to Hilgard's (1965) normal population, which showed a greater distribution. Also, the psychotic population in this study showed a slightly lower mean (4.80) as compared to Hilgard's normals (5.62).

In 1973, Gordon, using a modified SHSS, compared two groups of 32 chronic schizophrenics and 32 nonpsychotic male patients, who were matched for age, for suggestibility. The mean ages for both psychotic and nonpsychotic groups were 44.44 and 44.40, respectively. The conclusion from this study indicated that the chronic schizophrenic subjects were more suggestible than the normal subjects.

In 1976, Lavoie, Sabourin, Ally, and Langlois published a study designed to evaluate the relationship between hypnotic susceptibility and the capacity for adaptive regression in a random sample of 56 chronic psychotic patients, mainly schizophrenics ($N = 48$). This study was designed to test the theory of hypnosis proposed by Gill and Brenman (1959), which postulates that a regressed subsystem is set up within the ego as the result of hypnotic induction. Aside from its stated main purpose, this study also provided further documentation and evidence of the hypnotizability of psychotics. The original sample consisted of 60 male psychotic patients chosen randomly from the chronic wards of Hôpital Saint Jean-De-Dieu. Four subjects were eliminated from the sample: one for refusal to participate and three for unwillingness to complete the hypnotic procedures. (This was not a volunteer group, but a totally random selection.) The remaining subjects ($N = 56$) had a mean age of 46.96 years and a mean length of hospitalization of 14.59 years, and were composed mostly of schizophrenics ($N = 48$). The mean score on the SHSS-A for this group of chronic psychotic patients was 4.80, with a range from 1 to 9. The authors concluded that this group of psychotic patients clearly evidenced susceptibility to hypnosis. The study further indicated a positive correlation between adaptive regression and hypnotic susceptibility.

In the recent research literature, the only work still suggesting that psychotics are not susceptible to hypnosis is Spiegel and Fink's (1979) paper on "Hysterical

Psychosis and Hypnotizability." In this paper, the authors state that schizophrenics show little or no hypnotizability (as opposed to individuals with hysterical psychosis). Spiegel and Fink also state that their clinical experience with schizophrenics and seriously depressed patients using the Hypnotic Induction Profile indicates decrement patterns on that test which, in turn, indicates little or no hypnotizability in these subjects. In support of this position, the authors refer to the writings of Charcot, Janet, and Breuer and the 19th century theory linking hypnosis with hysteria and denying the applicability of hypnosis for normals or psychotics. The lack of validity of this 19th century position has been well established and need not be discussed further. However, the authors also refer to four more recent studies to support their position (Abrams, 1964; Barber, Karacan, and Calverly, 1964; Vingoe and Kramer, 1966; and Lavoie, Sabourin, and Langlois, 1973). As noted in the previous discussion, three of the studies cited by Spiegel and Fink specifically conclude that psychotics are susceptible to hypnosis (Abrams, 1964; Vingoe and Kramer, 1966; Lavoie, Sabourin, and Langlois, 1973). The results of the Barber study have been discussed and explained. Therefore, the assumption by Spiegel and Fink that the prior literature supports their position of little or no hypnotizability with psychotics appears to be unfounded.

In conclusion, it seems that the weight of the evidence of the experimental literature of the past 30 years clearly supports the conclusion that psychotics can be hypnotized. Whether they are more or less susceptible as a group to hypnosis than the normal population appears to vary according to factors of age, volunteerism, ego integrity, trust, and transference. It also seems evident, in answer to the second question posed previously, that hypnosis itself is a safe modality for psychotics. In all of the literature of work using the SHSS with psychotics, no incidence of harm was reported. It seems likely that just as in psychotherapy in general, the therapist's skillful use of the tool of hypnosis is essential as the primary safeguard for the patient's well-being.

Hypnosis Literature—Clinical

The following clinical studies taken from the literature give further evidence of the safety of hypnosis for psychotics and of their susceptibility to hypnosis.

In the early 1960s, the general consensus in the clinical literature appears to have stressed caution in the use of hypnosis with patients who were psychotic or borderline psychotic (Rosen, 1960). One survey, indicative of this mood of caution (Auerback, 1962), reported that although 45% of the psychiatrists questioned acknowledged having had training in hypnosis and having used hypnosis at one time, only 13% of those same psychiatrists reported continued use of hypnosis. Unpredictability and the fear of precipitating a psychotic episode were given as reasons for the disuse of hypnosis. The argument against the use of hypnosis with psychotics stressed the psychotic patient's tenuous relationship with reality and postulated that hypnosis would increase the loss of ego boundaries and of reality. Thus, it was hypothesized that a person who was borderline would decompensate and one who was already psychotic would decompensate even further (West and Deckert, 1965).

However, as early as 1926 (Schilder and Kauders, 1956), sporadic reports of successful use of hypnosis with psychotic patients began to appear in the literature. Gill and Brenman (1959) reported that one of the best hypnotic subjects in their study was a schizophrenic girl. In attempting to explain the fact that hypnosis was sometimes possible despite severe psychiatric illness, Gill and Brenman hypothesized some variations in degree of ego integrity and ego functioning in psychotics capable of hypnosis.

Bowers (1961) reported good results when hypnosis was used with chronic ambulatory schizophrenics in an outpatient setting after other methods of treatment had failed. She recommended that hypnotic procedures could be useful in the development of a positive relationship with the therapist and in the treatment of at least some chronic schizophrenics. Erickson (1964) reported a case of successful use of hypnotic techniques with a psychotic patient. A 24-year-old paranoid schizophrenic woman with complaints of visual and auditory hallucinations was treated by Erickson with hypnosis using an indirect induction technique and using her resistance. Hypnosis was then accepted by the patient as a positive resource for therapeutic progress. In a second case of the use of hypnosis with a psychotic, Erickson (1965) worked with a 25-year-old psychotic male, whose main symptomatology included confusion and word salad. Indirect hypnotic techniques were employed to engage the patient in a relationship and in therapy.

Reardon (1965) described the successful use of hypnosis as a relaxation technique with severely disturbed patients. Biddle (1967) reported that a variety of hypnotic methods for working with psychotics was potentially positive. Rosen, while emphasizing the need for caution in the use of hypnosis with psychotics, did occasionally use hypnotic procedures with this patient population (Biddle, 1967).

In 1972, Yarnell described the successful use of hypnosis and guided imagery in the treatment of a severely disturbed patient diagnosed as a "neurotic introvert" (with an apparent schizoid character constellation). Desensitization techniques were successfully integrated with hypnotic imagery and symbolic metaphor.

By 1972, Conn clearly asserted that there were no dangers associated with hypnosis other than the usual dangers present in every psychotherapy situation. The emphasis began to shift from concern over hypnosis as a danger to consideration of the sensitivity and skills needed for all therapy work with psychotics. It was hypothesized that therapists who were competent in working with a psychotic population could also safely employ the use of hypnosis with that population.

In 1974, several reports of successful clinical work with psychotics were published, signaling the beginning of an upsurge of such work. Eliseo (1974) reported successful hypnotic work with three patients with organic psychoses. Formal induction techniques were used without concern for depth of trance. In all cases, better orientation in time and place, and reduction in confusion and pain were evidenced.

Scagnelli (1974) reported successful clinical work with an acute schizophrenic. Hypnotherapy was used in conjunction with traditional ongoing, insight oriented psychotherapy. Hypnotic relaxation was used for reduction of anxiety, hypnotic dreams were explored for insight work, and hypnotic imagery was used to develop shifts from a negative self-concept into a more positive one (imagery shifts).

Zeig (1974) reported the use of informal hypnotic techniques with paranoid and schizophrenic patients. Zeig stated, "In cases where I have used a more formal introduction to hypnosis and more formal induction with psychotic people, I have met with little success, seemingly due to resistances and fears which I have not easily allayed." Zeig then described indirect techniques of relaxation and the use of metaphor and puns, which were successful in helping paranoid schizophrenics deal with the control or removal of their "voices."

In addition, a dentist, Milton Newman (1974), reported a case in which he employed hypnosis, working in conjunction with a psychiatrist in the emergency treatment of a 24-year-old woman with a diagnosis of undifferentiated schizophrenia with fugue states and suicide potential. Newman concluded that hypnosis could be useful in the termination of fugue states.

Following this upsurge of reports on hypnotic work with psychotics in 1974, there continued a steady flow of ongoing work in this area. In 1975, Joseph Avampato reported the use of hypnosis with a 42-year-old woman suffering from severe torticollis. The diagnosis of this patient was pseudo-neurotic psychosis, with an overlay of conversion-type hysterical symptomatology masking a schizophrenic disorder. The patient was initially treated for her symptomatology, with approximately 80% to 90% improvement in this area. However, when the therapist attempted to deal with the schizophrenia underlying the symptomatology, he met with continued resistance. The patient refused to share her fantasy life or thought processes and terminated therapy prematurely. Nevertheless, she was susceptible to hypnosis and did employ it successfully for symptom alleviation.

In 1976, John Plapp reported the treatment of a 17-year-old adolescent male using hypnosis as a bridge for making contact and forming the basis of a therapeutic relationship with this resistant patient. The parents of this patient, who were diagnosed as psychotic, shared a *folie a deux* and managed to remain out of the hospital, though isolated in their home. They believed that they were being slowly poisoned by neighbors who were Nazis and Jews. The son, who was the primary patient in this case, was fairly intact but was increasingly withdrawing from outside life and developing paranoid ideation of his own. He was diagnosed as an adolescent schizophrenic. The patient resisted all attempts at therapeutic work but continued to come in for treatment. The boy then requested hypnosis. A simple standard induction procedure was used without apparent success. The patient stated that "it had not worked." However, he then asked to "hypnotize the therapist." The therapist agreed and used this procedure as a unique way of establishing trust with the patient and forming the basis for a beginning therapeutic relationship. Therapy then moved into a more traditional psychotherapy framework.

Also in 1976, Scagnelli reported a summary of hypnotherapy work with eight severely disturbed patients; four were schizophrenic and four were borderline psychotic. Scagnelli detailed the specific problems encountered in the use of hypnosis with this patient population: fear of loss of control, fear of closeness, and fear of releasing negative self-concepts. Procedures for dealing with these typical psychotic fears were detailed. In addition, specific hypnotic techniques that could be used successfully with psychotic and borderline patients were outlined. Techniques for anxiety reduction were considered generally applicable to this patient population. Then, with varying degrees of success according to patient variables, other hypnotic techniques were employed. Techniques of ego building, free association for insight, dream production and analysis, and creation of imagery shifts for positive reintegration of feeling were all successfully used.

In 1977, Scagnelli reported a case study of hypnotic dream therapy with a borderline schizophrenic. This patient was a 24-year-old male with a schizoid character structure. The schizoid withdrawal seemed to be the patient's main defense against a florid psychotic outbreak. When he made progress in therapy through dream analysis or free association, overwhelming psychoticlike imagery and ideation would emerge and the patient would retreat into schizoid withdrawal. Similarly, all relationships in or out of therapy appeared to precipitate extreme anxiety and withdrawal. However, when introduced to hypnosis and its potential use for dream production and analysis, the patient was able to work productively through 14 months of hypnotherapy, resolving most of his psychotic anxieties. He dealt with dream material that involved his identity confusion, incorporation fears, oedipal fears, and fears concerning his own death and destruction. It was important for this patient to learn ways of controlling the hypnotic process. The emphasis on autohypnosis and on creator control of the dream-imagery process appeared to be essential factors permitting the patient to deal with the psychoticlike material without being overwhelmed by it. In addition, it seemed that hypnotic dreams, using symbolic imagery and metaphor, allowed the patient sufficient distance and safety to be able to communicate previously overwhelming and threatening feelings.

Also in 1977, Berwick and Douglas reported successful use of hypnosis with two paranoid schizophrenics. Both patients were women in their early 40s. One woman's paranoid delusional system centered around feelings of being possessed by Satan. The second woman felt that "black magic" was being worked against her. In both cases, traditional techniques were used (eye fixation). The therapists then entered the patient's delusional systems and suggested the enhancement of the patient's powers to overcome the external powers. Both cases responded positively. Although insight was not attempted or achieved, the delusional symptoms appear to have gone into remission in both cases.

In 1978, Gruenewald reported a case of successful use of hypnosis with a multiple personality. The author warns of the potential for therapists when working with hypnosis with multiple personalities to call forth other personalities and to create a subtle demand on the patient to produce more and more dramatic splits or symptoms. Nevertheless, Gruenewald states that hypnosis facilitates access to secondary personalities when working with a case of multiple personality and that hypnosis as a therapeutic mode is a viable and useful form of treatment for this type of patient.

In 1979, Sexton and Maddox reported hypnotic work with three women with psychotic depression. The three women (ages 52, 36, and 29) all displayed confused and delusional thought patterns, catatonic behavior, and some suicidal ideation. No formal induction was used. The patients were directed back (age regression) to an incident related to their current problems, or they were directed forward (age progression) into some future resolution of their problems (with God or a loved one in heaven). In these three psychotic patients, the authors reported a restitution of ego functioning and a decrease in psychotic symptomatology.

Also in 1979, Milton Kline, while reporting work relating to forensic hypnosis and the problems surrounding the use of hypnosis for an insanity defense, incidentally documents hypnotic work with severely disturbed and psychotic clients.

In 1980, Gardner and Tarnow reported on the use of hypnotherapy with an autistic 16-year-old male. The patient had been diagnosed as having early infantile autism. He had had numerous evaluations and attempts at psychotherapy, with limited gains in affective developments and behavioral control. The patient had a history of delayed speech, disinterest in people, limited range of affect, excessive need for routines, and extraordinary music memory. By adolescence, anxiety and anger were producing behavioral problems. He was being seen in psychotherapy on a regular basis when he was referred to hypnotherapy for nail biting. Music was used as the induction technique, and the patient responded positively to hypnotic suggestion for behavior and habit control.

Also in 1980, Scagnelli reported on hypnotherapy with psychotic and borderline patients and the use of trance by both patient and therapist. Both formal induction techniques and informal hypnotic techniques were found to be useful. Autohypnosis was considered an important tool for this patient population, enhancing feelings of control and mastery in the patient and reducing concerns regarding trust. Hypnosis was found useful with the psychotic patient over a broad spectrum of possibilities, including anxiety reduction, ego building, catharsis, and insight work. In addition to the use of trance by the patient, Scagnelli stressed the added advantage of the use of trance by the therapist. The author stated that the use of autohypnotic trance by the therapist produces heightened empathy, thereby helping the therapist to use his own body, mind, and feeling state to become more empathically in contact with the patient and to identify and decode patient feelings.

Baker (1981) presented a rationale for the use of hypnosis with psychotic patients based on object relations theory. He noted that intensive psychoanalytic psychotherapy has proved useful with psychotic patients when modifications toward greater nurturing for dependency strivings and greater confrontation of attempts at flight from involvement are employed by the therapist. He then suggested that hypnotherapeutic techniques can be successfully integrated into intensive psychoanalytic psychotherapy. He stressed the self-hypnosis and permissive induction procedures already established as necessary for work with this population (Scagnelli, 1975, 1976). He then outlined an hypnotic procedure for helping the patient identify and developing a self–other differentiation followed by object introjection and integration. Essentially, the patient is instructed in hypnosis to visualize himself and the therapist, both separately and together, with increasing guidance for both individuation and for closeness. A case example was given of work with a 23-year-old male paranoid schizophrenic. A formal progressive relaxation induction was used.

Thus, the evidence of more than two decades of clinical work appears to indicate more and more clearly that safe and profitable use can be made of hypnosis with the severely disturbed patient population. The literature appears to indicate that the same care that applies generally to therapy should be applied to the use of hypnotherapy with a psychotic population. Essentially, the therapeutic skills and care that are required for good therapy with the severely disturbed patient are equally important prerequisites for successful hypnotherapy with this population.

Assessment of Patient for Hypnosis

Given the preceding conclusions from the literature that psychotic conditions are amenable to psychotherapeutic intervention and that hypnosis is, at least sometimes, both a possible and safe adjunct to therapy with this severely disturbed population, how then do we assess when and how to use hypnosis with this group of patients?

The main issue for determining the advisability of hypnosis with severely disturbed patients (as with the less disturbed) is the control issue. The question of control centers around concerns over the loss of control and trust in the therapist's integrity and empathic understanding not to abuse this control. Although it is frequently stated in clinical hypnosis that the patient is always "in control," nevertheless the hypnotic relationship implies and requires a temporary giving-over of leadership, initiative, and some degree of control to the therapist by the patient. It seems that all patients perceive this subtle alteration in the locus of control and wrestle with this question of control at some level. Even nonpsychotic patients will sometimes find hypnosis unacceptable for themselves because of this control issue.

In the case of nonpsychotic patients, the fears surrounding loss of control usually involve fear of some inner "unacceptable self" emerging if the conscious monitoring-self relinquishes any degree of control. Another neurotic-level fear concerning loss of control is fear of "going crazy" if the conscious monitoring-self is diminished or lets down its alert guard. Some psychotic patients may fear the expression of their id impulses in a fashion similar to the neurotic fear of the "bad" or "crazy" self emerging. Paranoid patients especially may be concerned about id impulses and the emergence of a "bad self." Psychotic patients, in general, may experience difficulty with hypnosis if they fear their hostile or sexual impulses.

However, in the case of psychotic patients, concerns about loss of control are more likely to center around fears of incorporation and loss of integrity of the ego and the sense of self. These fears of incorporation and the concurrent confusion over the identity of the self and the boundaries between self and others are an intrinsic part of the pathology of schizophrenia. It seems logical, therefore, that this central symptom of psychosis that causes much of the difficulty in traditional psychotherapy also causes difficulty in hypnotherapy. Just as fears of incorporation make the formation of a therapeutic alliance with schizophrenics difficult, so also do these fears make formation of an hypnotic interaction difficult.

Some techniques that have proved helpful in assisting psychotic patients in dealing with this temporary shift of control from the self to the therapist include the following:

1. Hypnosis is presented to the psychotic patient as autohypnosis. The patient is informed that he will be helped to learn the techniques of hypnosis so that he can use them for himself. Autohypnosis can enhance the patient's degree of control and mastery over his own mind and body. The patient is generally encouraged to use autohypnosis independently of the therapist and the therapy

session. Autohypnosis then can have the added value of allowing the patient to practice the use of the trance state for his own therapeutic development outside of therapy sessions. This simple technique has the potential automatically to extend the impact and effectiveness of the therapy hour. For example, patients can be encouraged to use autohypnosis to work on anxiety reduction, ego building, and any positive form of behavior modification and social–interpersonal skill development.

2. Eye-opening is permitted and encouraged in initial work with psychotic patients. Eye-closure can often be perceived as a defenseless or vulnerable posture by the psychotic patient. Psychotics typically do not like to be looked at. They will frequently look away from an observer's gaze and avoid eye contact. They frequently do not want others to "see into their eyes" or look at their faces. These psychotic behaviors seem to result from feelings that their emotions can be "read" through their faces and eyes. Schizophrenics generally believe that their inner feelings are worthless, dangerous, or unlovable. They therefore go to great effort to disguise any real show of feelings (lack of affect or inappropriate affect) and asume that if their feelings are discovered, they will evoke criticism rather than acceptance in the observer. Therefore, allowing open-eyed trance behavior permits the patient to check out the therapist intermittently. The patient can see that the therapist is not looking critically at him. This checking procedure usually provides enough reassurance that most patients will eventually maintain eye-closure when they are informed that it is easier to relax and maintain the trance with their eyes closed. Eye-opening also permits patients to check on the permanence of therapist. The therapist does not abandon (disappear) or incorporate (merge with) the patient, and visual checking can provide sometimes needed reassurance.

3. The therapist also "goes into trance" along with the patient. The patient is told in advance that the therapist will go into trance along with him. Frequently, the patient will check to see that the therapist is in a "trancelike" state when he opens his eyes. In this way, the therapist models the safety of trance behavior and the safety of being seen by another in trance (of being vulnerable). In addition, the therapist in trance is carefully looking away from the patient. The patient is seen with peripheral vision rather than direct observation. The result for the patient is less fear of "being seen" (vulnerability) and greater acceptability of being observed and of risking the experience of trance owing to the therapist's modeling of these behaviors.

In addition to the value of this use of autohypnosis by the therapist, the trance state frequently assists the therapist in making empathic contact with the patient. This enhanced empathic contact can assist the therapist in decoding and defining feelings that the patient has defended against and has not yet defined or verbalized.

In summary, when assessing a psychotic patient for possible work with hypnotherapy, the areas of control and trust are of primary concern. The patient's ability to handle the shift in control and his trust in the therapist need to be evaluated sensitively and manipulated toward greater therapeutic tolerance whenever possible, using the permissive techniques and modeling techniques discussed above. The assessment of acceptability of hypnosis can be a delicate clinical issue. In the final analysis, patient acceptance is the primary determinant of the appropriateness of the patient for hypnosis.

A final consideration may be an assessment of hostility. A high degree of hostility would generally mediate against the use of hypnosis. However, in my experience, those patients high in hostility also are nonaccepting of hypnosis.

Intervention Process

General Considerations

Once the assessment has been made and it has been determined that a psychotic patient is accepting of working with hypnosis, there are then some general considerations of the particular needs and sensibilities of psychotic patients to be taken into account when working with this population.

The issue of control/trust that is so important in assessing the acceptability of hypnosis for the patient is not finalized during the initial assessment period. This issue will usually remain continually and crucially important to the patient and to the ongoing success of any hypnotherapy. The patient may need continued reassurance of his ability to reclaim control through eye-opening or through permission to choose not to use hypnosis at times. A permissive attitude by the therapist about when and how hypnosis is employed generally enhances the patient's feelings of control. Also, the therapist will be continually monitored by the patient for trustworthiness in not abusing the hypnotic relationship. As in any therapeutic relationship, the therapist must always keep the patient's well-being as the primary concern. If the therapist slips into serving his own ego needs (*i.e.,* interpreting material before the patient can handle it, demanding patient improvement for therapist feelings of success, *etc.*), the psychotic patient will generally perceive this lack of real concern from the therapist, and trust will be diminished. Therefore, the questions of control/trust are ongoing and similar to those same concerns that are important in any psychotherapy with a psychotic population. Emotional honesty by the therapist will generally be extremely important to a psychotic patient, even more important than having his emotional needs met by the therapist.

Another area of general concern for the psychotic patient is the fear of closeness. Again, this same fear exists and presents problems for the formation and functioning of any psychotherapeutic relationship with the severely disturbed patient population. However, hypnosis generally fosters and intensifies feelings of closeness, thereby raising the question of closeness more acutely. When hypnosis is used with a psychotic patient, it tends to build and intensify a positive transference. On the other hand, if a patient has predominently negative transference feelings for the therapist, it is unlikely that hypnosis will be acceptable or useful because of concerns over lack of trust and control needs. Thus, fears of closeness are related to the previously stated concern over control/trust.

Fear of closeness, however, actually encompasses two conflicting polar opposites. At one end of the pole, the fear of closeness involves fear of being "taken over" or incorporated by the therapist. The schizophrenic typically has had a life-long struggle with problems of identity integrity and difficulties in separation between self and significant others. Therefore, concerns over incorporation in hypnosis or in psychotherapy in general would be a natural extension of schizophrenic symptomatology. At the other pole of this fear of closeness is the fear of being abandoned. The schizophrenic patient typically has experienced life-long difficulty with relationships, beginning with the primary mother–child relationship. The severely disturbed patient typically is struggling with a central problem of an extremely negative self-image, feeling that he is worthless, bad, evil, or worse. In trying to escape from the anxiety and depression resulting from his poor self-image and his "unacceptable" feelings, the schizophrenic creates defenses that tend to alienate him further from satisfying human interaction. The psychotic uses defenses such as withdrawal, blocking of feelings (lack of affect), projection of feelings, and psychotic jargon, all of which tend to limit or eliminate human relationships or doom them to failure. Therefore, the fear of abandonment, as the end result of the closeness involved in the hypnotic or psychotherapeutic relationship, is again another extension of the general symptomatology of schizophrenia. The psychotic typically looks back on a history of hurtful relationships and fears the potential closeness of hypnosis because of fears of both incorporation and abandonment.

In dealing with the fear of closeness as it relates to incorporation fear with the psychotic patient using hypnosis, it is important to give the patient permission for moving in and out of closeness. Typically, the psychotic patient will alternate between approach–avoidance pressures until he feels ready to make a relationship. At that point, if the commitment can be made, the schizophrenic patient may move into an intensely close relationship. However, during the ambivalence stage, the patient typically needs the freedom intermittently to distance both emotionally and physically from the therapist. In practice, this may involve allowing the patient to walk around the room, leave the room, change chairs, request a cessation in hypnosis or therapy, open his eyes, state that hypnosis or therapy is not working, or talk in metaphor and symbols.

In dealing with the opposite polar fear of closeness, the fear of abandonment, there are further therapeutic procedures that can be helpful. First, the therapist needs to demonstrate to the patient that he can limit the closeness of the relationship to an acceptably safe level. The therapist demonstrates this, in part, by meeting patient needs with consistence and reliability. However, the therapist also demonstrates by word and action that he cannot meet all of the patient's needs and that he will not feel guilty or angry about this inability totally to satisfy the patient's neediness. Therefore, the therapist also conveys the message that he does not demand patient progress to assure himself that he is giving enough, nor will he abandon the patient out of anger if the patient does not get well or still needs more than the therapist can give. In other words, the therapist acknowledges that he is not a savior, and the patient is helped to see that the therapist cannot be his idealized symbiotic parent (and, eventually, that such an idealized parent-figure does not, indeed, exist). With this demonstration of both limitations and dependability, the patient can begin to perceive the therapist's ability to control closeness and therefore provide a staying power lacking in former relationships. This demonstration of ability to limit the relationship also provides reassurance and modeling for the patient for the maintenance of individuation within a close relationship, reducing incorporation fears and teaching the acceptability of separate and sometimes conflicting feelings and needs.

Another nonverbal message that the therapist needs to convey to the psychotic patient to allay fears of abandonment and to allow for the closeness of hypnosis and the psychotherapeutic relationship is the message that the therapist does not fear the patient's psychosis and will not be overwhelmed by it. The therapist can demonstrate his tolerance for psychosis by entering into the patient's metaphor or symbolism for communication and, sometimes, by entering empathically into the psychotic feeling state of the patient. The patient typically responds very positively to a therapist who can communicate with him in his own "language" and who can empathically identify his feeling state. Such empathic communication demonstrates not only the therapist's understanding of the patient, but also his tolerance for psychotic thinking. If the patient sees that the therapist is not overwhelmed, this makes the therapist safer, more stable, and less likely to abandon him. It also gives the patient some greater sense of security that he, too, need not be overwhelmed.

In addition to the issues of control/trust and fears of closeness, another general area of concern for the psychotic patient is the fear of shifting a negative self-image to a positive one. Although it would appear logical to assume that anyone would want to develop a positive self-image, the psychotic patient typically fears and resists such a shift in his self-image. It appears that the psychotic's view of the world, his concept of "reality," is tied into his negative concept of himself. If he were to shift from this view of himself as "bad," then he would also have to change his view of the world and of significant others. In particular, the parent who labeled him as "bad" could no longer be viewed as "good" if his own "badness" were shifted. It has seemed to me that a change in self-image involves a total shake-up, a turning upside down of the psychotic's world. This process must feel "psychotic" or "unreal" to the psychotic patient. The closest analogy to this experience of the psychotic may be the experimental work done with normals, having them wear special eyeglasses that invert all of their visual imagery. The disorientation, confusion, and unreality is overwhelming, and the normal brain re-inverts the upside down images within a few days in an attempt to restore the familiar reality of the past.

In any event, the psychotic patient typically resists progress toward an improved self-image. Direct suggestions seem of least value in this area. Indirect suggestions, metaphors, and permissive suggestions to neutralize negative self-messages rather than shifting totally to positive messages seem most promising of results. For example, in communicating with patients about this issue of self-image, the therapist may refer to the patient in the third person or, even more indirectly, through symbolic language.

In addition, indirect messages of the patient's value can be most significantly demonstrated through the medium of the therapeutic relationship. The therapist, by demonstrating his consistent regard and respect for the patient's separate feelings and needs, begins to model and shape self-acceptance by the patient. This is probably the most arduous and most important task of the therapeutic relationship, requiring patience and perseverance by both therapist and patient. This shift in self-concept is central to the improvement of the psychotic and generally cannot be rushed. However, once the patient has begun to accept a more positive view of the self as "real" and desirable, he can then begin to use autohypnotic techniques to disrupt old negative thoughts and behaviors and to superimpose newer, more positive thoughts and behaviors. The patient, at this later stage in therapy, may work on a self-directed behavior modification program using autohypnosis.

Initial Induction Techniques

The initial induction technique with the severely disturbed population includes traditional formal induction procedures as well as indirect and informal techniques.

Typically, patients who are in a nonacute state of remission or who are coherent enough specifically to seek or to accept hypnosis can be introduced to formal induction techniques. This would include many chronic but coherent psychotics. These patients are usually already involved in an ongoing therapeutic relationship with the therapist. Occasionally, a psychotic patient will come to therapy initially requesting hypnosis. In these cases, hypnosis is sometimes an initial bridge to more traditional therapy. Patients exhibiting an interest in and an acceptance of hypnosis are then introduced to the concept of autohypnosis and the potential for this technique to enhance their own self-mastery, control, and independence. Autohypnosis is taught to the patient through a standard relaxation technique, allowing the patient to operate either with or without eye-closure. Various combinations of breathing, progressive body relaxation, imaging counting down a staircase, imaging a safe and relaxing place, and reverse arm levitation are used according to the needs and abilities of the patient. In a few rare cases, extremely agitated patients may be instructed to tense muscles rather than to relax them. It can then be suggested that they can control and direct that tension into energy.

Ongoing fears of control and closeness are ameliorated by allowing patients to determine their own rate of progress and involvement with both hypnosis and therapy in general. Patients are specifically allowed to move in and out of hypnosis as they need and are permitted freedom to move in and out of closeness with the therapist.

In addition to relaxation techniques, hypnotic trance imagery is also taught and practiced as both a deepening technique and as a therapeutic tool for development of insight, catharsis, and reconditioning. Patients are encouraged both by posthypnotic suggestion and direct suggestion to practice their own trance-relaxation state. It is stressed with patients that their ability to develop trance is not really new, that they have been going into trance all their lives, and that now, with hypnosis, they can learn some ways of controlling when and how they go into a trance and what they want to do with their trance.

Once autohypnosis has been introduced, regardless of whether or not a patient chooses to continue in formal trance work during therapy sessions, the groundwork has been laid for hypnotic trancelike interaction and for suggestions from therapist to patient. Frequently, though no formal hypnotic induction has been employed, the therapist may begin speaking to the patient (concerning ego-building ideas, for example) in a trancelike voice. At these times the patient may automatically assume trancelike responses of immobility, eye-fixation, and intense concentration, sometimes nodding in agreement with the therapist's words and rhythm of speech. At such times, it appears that suggestions may have the increased impact and value of typical hypnotic trance-state suggestions. Thus, a patient, once learning autohypnosis, can use it formally or informally with the therapist and can also use it independently of the therapy session.

Unlike the nonacute patient, the acute disoriented psychotic may be more typically engaged in hypnosis through indirect hypnotic techniques. The use of indirect techniques for this category of psychotic is largely dictated by the need to get their attention quickly and dramatically. I and others have described such indirect work with acutely disoriented psychotics (Scagnelli, 1974, 1975; Zeig, 1974; Berwick and Douglas, 1977).

An example of the use of a nonverbal, indirect hypnotic technique, as employed by me follows.

The patient, a 16-year-old girl inpatient, lapsed from a chronic plateau into an acute psychotic state evidencing nonsense jargon, bizarre movements, and eye rolling. Some of her hand and body movements reminded me of dance movements. I began some finger, hand, and arm movements of my own that simulated dancing while communicating that it was nice to dance, that it feels good to dance sometimes. My behavior succeeded in getting the attention of the patient. This focus of attention initiated an hypnotic interaction between patient and therapist. The patient stopped her own movement and focused direct eye contact on me. I then proceeded to give the indirect hypnotic message: "When a baby is unloved and unwanted, it is the mother who is lacking, not the baby. A baby is lovable and if a mother does not love her baby, it is because the mother is sick and cannot love, but not because the baby is unlovable. The baby who was the patient and the young girl she is now are both truly lovable." The therapist had already understood the patient's need for this message from prior therapy because of the patient's history of being abandoned first by her mother and then by a foster mother. The patient, on hearing this message, wept quietly for a few minutes, went over to a sink and looked at her face in the mirror for a long moment, and then wiped away the tears. She was then no longer acutely psychotic and was able to talk coherently about her hurt at being unloved. Subsequently, she was able to resume traditional psychotherapy positively.

Thus, psychotic patients can respond to both formal and informal, direct and indirect techniques of hypnotic induction. The more disorganized patient will probably require informal, indirect techniques adjusted to his needs and abilities.

Hypnotic Techniques in Psychotherapy

Once a patient is amenable to hypnotic intervention, there is a great range of possible hypnotic techniques that may be employed. Some patients will be able to use only one, or a few, of these techniques, and other patients may be able to use all of them. The therapist generally explores with the patient to determine which techniques are potentially useful for him.

Relaxation and Anxiety Reduction. The most universally acceptable hypnotic technique for the psychotic patient is the use of hypnosis for relaxation and anxiety reduction. Severely disturbed patients typically appear to experience excessive anxiety as a common and debilitating symptom. Therefore, the use of hypnosis for anxiety reduction is generally accepted positively. Relaxation through hypnosis serves the twofold purpose of providing symptom relief and establishing early positive reinforcement for hypnosis and for the therapeutic relationship. Direct messages for relaxation can be given as part of an induction or following an induction. Most psychotic patients can comfortably accept direct relaxation suggestions. Occasionally, patient tension may need to be acknowledged and channeled into controlled energy if relaxation cannot be handled directly.

Ego-Building. A second hypnotic technique is ego-building. As noted earlier, this is a resistance-laden area for psychotic patients. The therapist working with psychotics will need indirect communication (metaphor, symbolic language), patience and perseverance. The therapeutic relationship itself will provide the most salient communication of the therapist's value of the patient, and the use of hypnosis can be a major asset in this communication. The therapist in trance can give the patient a nurturance and acceptance that would be difficult for most patients to accept out of trance. Imagery and metaphor can be used more easily in hypnosis and can provide more easily accepted messages of nurturance for the patient. In addition, intonation of the voice of the therapist using hypnosis can convey nurturance. Finally, the intensity of hypnosis seems to heighten the potential of nurturing messages. Also, messages of "strength" and "growing" can be interspersed throughout trance communication. Acknowledgment and acceptance of strengths and limitations can be given by the therapist and gradually assimilated by the patient.

Creative Self-Mothering. In a third hypnotic technique, the patient can be encouraged to employ "creative self-mothering." In this technique, the patient is encouraged to image himself as a baby or young child. Then he is asked to see himself as an adult mothering the baby-self. If a patient can see himself as a child or infant in imagery, usually he can see that infant as lovable and can begin to positively love and re-mother himself. This process not only can provide restitution for the lack of nurturance and mothering, it can also begin a process of self-love that can grow into adult self-acceptance.

Image Shift. Patients are also encouraged to explore "imagery shifts" in hypnosis. In this technique, a patient who recalls a painful memory from the past is encouraged to image this memory. He is then directed to create a happier, alternative image regarding this memory. For example, a patient may recall feelings of rejection by his mother. He forms an image of this feeling, seeing a mother angrily sending the little child away from her. The patient "transforms" this image to one of a mother smiling at her infant son and nursing him as she cradles him in her arms.

The positive imagery shift is generally followed by a flood of positive feelings about the self. It is clear that the patient using this technique knows he has not changed the reality of his childhood. However, some patients are able to discard, through imagery shift, many of the useless negative feelings that are leftover baggage from past realities.

Dream Production and Analysis. Dream analysis has long been employed in psychoanalysis as a major symbolic key to the unconscious. In more recent times, dream analysis has expanded to include "directed daydreams" and hypnotic dreams (Scagnelli, 1977). In the use of the hypnotic dream, the patient is encouraged, in trance, to produce a dream. The dream can be partially structured by the therapist or totally unstructured. The patient is given some silent time for dreaming. Then a report of the dream is requested from the patient in trance and a joint analysis of the dream is conducted both in and out of trance.

A variation of this procedure would be to suggest posthypnotically that the patient dream about a problem at night and report it in the next therapy session, or that a patient have an hypnotic dream at home in his own autohypnotic trance and report it back to the therapist. Most patients seem to prefer the security and structure of the therapist's office for hypnotic dreams, but a few may prefer the greater autonomy and control of the alternative procedures.

With the reduction in anxiety and critical self-monitoring that accompanies hypnosis, a patient generally will have greater access to conflicted material and to unacceptable or unconscious parts of the self. He also will be more open to interpretation of this information by the therapist. It is therefore essential that the therapist working with hypnosis, and especially with the psychotic patient, be sensitive to the needs of the patient and move in uncovering the interpreting only in ways that the patient can handle. The sensitive therapist generally can be the catalyst that helps the patient reinterpret and restructure this information in a way that enhances his potential for positive adult interaction with reality.

Typically the hypnotic dream provides a means of communicating, through symbols and images, material that cannot be transmitted verbally. The hypnotic dream appears to give the patient a vehicle for communicating feelings more fully and safely than words. The dream provides the patient with a tangible way to encounter his feelings and a way to share them with another person (Scagnelli, 1977).

Creator Control of Imagery. As an adjunct to work with the psychotic patient with image shifts, dream work, or any hypnotic work involving imagery, it can be useful to teach and employ the technique of "creator control of images." In this technique, it is explained to the patient that his dream or his imagery is *his* creation. Since he creates these dreams and images, he has the right and the power to change them any time they become too frightening or too overwhelming. Examples of this use of creator control by patients with whom I have worked follow. A patient imaging his mother in an hypnotic dream as a vampire–witch exercized his creator control to shrink the witch down in size until she became less threatening. Another patient, struggling with the image of a witch–mother chasing her, created an alternate image of a witch with her feet stuck in glue so that she could not run. Other patients have simply made frightening images disappear.

Once the patient understands his ability to control images, his sense of power, mastery, and security is greatly enhanced. There is then no limit to the patient's own innovative ways of defusing threatening material.

Free Associations. Patients in hypnosis can typically produce free associations more easily than they would otherwise. The simple suggestion to begin to "share whatever thoughts and images or feelings that come to mind" can usually initiate free association. If the therapist feels it appropriate, he can direct the patient to a particular point in time or a particular problem and then request the patient's associations. While some patients may be reticent in hypnosis and unwilling to share much communication, many others will be able to flow more naturally with free association in hypnosis than otherwise owing to the natural drift of thoughts and images in undirected hypnosis. In addition, the reduction of anxiety and self-monitoring in the trance state tends to promote an uncritical flow of communication.

The therapist can remain totally silent or move in and out of contact with the patient as seems to be required. At times, the therapist might structure the associations or even shift into more direct interviewing. In any event, at some point, usually both in and out of trance, material is jointly interpreted with the patient.

Projective Techniques. Projective techniques can be as useful in hypnosis as in traditional psychotherapy. Again, the lowered anxiety and critical self-monitoring that is typical of hypnosis seems to facilitate the use of these projective techniques. An example of the use of these techniques follows. A patient may be given the suggestion that he descend a staircase. At the bottom of the staircase he will find a room with many doors. The patient may be told that people or memories of past events or answers to problems lay behind each door. The patient is then directed to "see" which door is ready to open and to "explore" what is behind that door. In using this technique, patients may employ all sorts of additional imagery or "helpers." Patients have been known to use allies to aid in opening the doors. Also, magic swords and guides have been used. Some patients may simply choose a door and enter. Once entering through the door, the patient then "looks around" and "discovers" what is to be found.

Another projective technique can be looking at a blank television screen. As the patient watches, images begin to form. Gazing at imaginary clouds and seeing what shapes they begin to take is still another technique. As the reader can see, there is an almost endless variety of projective possibilities in conjunction with imagery and hypnosis. The therapist can provide structure or openended suggestions as the situation suggests.

Again, as with other insight work, after projective techniques are used, interpretation, both in and out of trance, by patient and therapist is in order.

Affect Bridge. The affect bridge is a more specific variation of free association or projective techniques. In this technique, a patient typically reports an intense and distressing feeling state. For example, a patient might report in therapy feeling intensely lonely and abandoned or unloved. Such a feeling state might be reported to the therapist either in or out of trance. The therapist could then direct the patient in trance to intensify that feeling, to stay with it, and to follow it back through time and space to another time when that feeling was very important. This use of current affect to "bridge back" to a prior significant event will usually produce new and valuable material for the patient and therapist to integrate.

When insights and interpretation go well in hypnotherapy, the patient is able to gain greater access to feelings. He is also helped by the therapist to identify and integrate those feelings, either accepting them or growing past them.

Regression. Regression is an hypnotic technique that can be very effective with psychotic patients. Regression can, of course, be used for simple recall of forgotten material and can be a powerful tool for facilitating catharsis. The psychotic patient can sometimes discharge old unvented emotions from the past as the hypnotic experience helps recall and revivification of past events. However, the psychotic, when not acutely overwhelmed by feelings, is understandably cautious about experiencing feelings in hypnosis. In addition to these traditional uses of regression for recall and catharsis, regression with the psychotic also provides a milieu for intensifying re-nurturing by the therapist and for creative self-mothering. Thus, it is in this area of re-nurturing that regression can be more useful for the psychotic patient.

Analysis of the Resistance. In working with imagery and the various hypnotic techniques for insight (dreams, free associations, projective techniques), resistances are likely to occur that will need to be addressed. In the hypnotic mode, resistance will typically occur in the form of imagery and will need to be dealt with through imagery. An example of resistance in hypnosis can be given using the illustration presented previously in which a patient was directed to visualize a room with many doors. A resisting patient might see the room and the doors but then report that "the door won't open." In that case, the therapist might begin to work with and analyze the resistance by asking, "I wonder why the door won't open," or "I wonder what would be behind that door if it could open." The patient might then begin to explore why the door won't open and if there are ways he can get around his problem door, or he might begin to speculate on the contents beyond the door with the distance and safety that such "as if" speculation permits.

Occasionally, a patient might report that he simply cannot image a room with doors at all. In such a case, the patient may truly have poor imagery ability, and a shift into wording that uses thoughts and feelings rather than images may help. If a patient has displayed previous ability in imagery, a current refusal to image is probably resistance and can be dealt with as such. The real key to working with resistance in hypnosis is to remain within the patient's image or metaphor in handling the resistance.

Shaping the Formation of Transference in Positive Directions. An additional technique developed by Baker (1981) specifically for hypnotherapy with psychotic patients defines an early use of hypnosis and imagery to mold a positive transference relationship and a positive introject of the therapist free from past negative contamination. In this technique, the therapist directs the patient to visualize himself and then the therapist, first separately and then together, in gradually increasing degrees of closeness. This process helps the patient early in therapy establish a visual basis of separation of self and other (therapist). It also provides a visual tool for allowing gradual closeness without overwhelming incorporation.

Behavior Modification Techniques. In addition to all of the above techniques, behavior modification techniques can be used with the psychotic patient whenever applicable and acceptable to him. For example, behavior modification techniques can be useful in helping psychotic patients manage or eliminate "voices." Zeig (1974) reported successful results with paranoid schizophrenics and behavior modification techniques to control the locus and intensity of "voices." Patients were encouraged to increase the loudness of the voices and relocate them within their bodies, with the final goal of controlling them in a positive direction. Also, some psychotics may use imagery for behavior rehearsal, desensitization, assertiveness training, anxiety reduction, or any useful goal appropriate to the patient.

In conclusion, working with the severely disturbed patient is enormously complex, requiring building a relationship with the therapist, trust in that relationship, understanding and insight into the negative self-concept and its unreal origins from parents and parental pathology, an appreciation of the lack of correlation between the negative self-concept and current reality, a willingness to separate from old parent attachments and to experience the confusion of having many long-accepted realities and beliefs turned upside down, and, finally, the determination and endurance to persevere in the long, slow counterconditioning process necessary to shift a deeply ingrained negative self-concept to a positive one.

In all of these therapeutic tasks, the use of hypnosis is an invaluable adjunct. In building a relationship, and trust in that relationship, hypnosis is an asset. It is a modality that intensifies and speeds up the normal therapy relationship. It allows for suspension of the critical, judgmental attitudes that frequently is essential for exploration of negative self-concept and for a shift into a more positive attitude. Hypnosis provides a vehicle of communication not accessible to the logical, verbal mind. It provides us and our patients with the communication of imagery, symbols, and metaphor, and allows access to feeling-information that logic and verbalism cannot reach. It is the natural form of dream communication and one frequently used and felt to be safe by psychotics. It provides the patient with a more structured access to his fantasy/trance world and thereby provides a means of controlling that world of fantasy and trance.

Thus, at all stages of therapy—the creative search for understanding, the achievement of insight, the experience of catharsis and emotional release, the creative reorganization of meaning and emotions from the past, and the unlearning of old patterns and relearning and practicing of new interpersonal patterns and habits—at all of these stages hypnosis can prove to be a major facilitator of therapeutic growth.

Assessment of Effectiveness

The means for determining the effectiveness of hypnotic intervention with the severely disturbed patient are, of necessity, largely clinical and subjective. Nevertheless, some of these indicators of effectiveness appear valid and significant.

One of the major ways a therapist can assess the effectiveness of hypnosis with a severely disturbed patient is the patient's acceptance of the hypnosis. For those patients who do not accept hypnosis as a viable technique for all the many reasons of control/trust stated earlier, then clearly hypnotic intervention is not useful. In some cases, initial fears of control/trust can be worked through to a successful utilization of hypnosis. Thus, simply the acceptance of hypnosis by a psychotic patient is one indicator of success and effectiveness.

Secondly, the patient's phenomenological report of his hypnotic experience is a good indicator of effectiveness. If the patient feels that he is working well with hypnosis and with therapy, and if the patient feels good about hypnosis, this is indicative of a positive therapeutic relationship and, most likely, positive therapeutic growth.

If the patient is able to form a working relationship (positive transference) with the therapist, this is an indication of effectiveness of both the hypnotic intervention and therapy in general. The formation and maintenance of a relationship is one of the more difficult aspects of work with the psychotic population. It is also crucial to the therapeutic treatment of this population. Therefore, success in this area is a strong indicator of effectiveness of treatment. Since the use of hypnosis requires some level of relatedness, patients who can work successfully with hypnosis typically have managed to form some level of trust and relationship with the therapist.

Another indicator of effectiveness of hypnosis in therapy with severely disturbed patients is the reduction or elimination of psychotic behavior. Frequently, patients become less psychotic, less disoriented, abandon psychotic jargon, and eliminate or control "voices." Many patients are able to work more constructively in traditional psychotherapy after a period of hypnotic intervention has created an alliance with the therapist and eliminated the need for psychotic jargon.

In summary, assessment of the effectiveness of hypnosis in the psychotherapy of the severely disturbed is largely determined by the progress of the patient, just as therapy effectiveness in general is determined by patient progress. Therefore, positive changes in behavior and subjective feelings of patients are the key indicators. For the severely disturbed patient, because of the severity of his behavioral disturbance, some of his positive behavior changes are more obvious and clear cut than the less disturbed patient. Therefore, in some ways the observations of effectiveness may be more objective.

It is frequently difficult to assess the effectiveness of hypnosis independently of the other psychotherapy techniques since hypnotic techniques may be intimately intertwined with psychotherapy when they are most skillfully employed.

Future Trends

The literature of several decades has established the fact that psychotic patients are susceptible to hypnosis. There still appears to be a lack of concensus as to whether this susceptibility is the same as, less than, or greater than the normal population. Nevertheless, there is clear agreement on the general principle of the susceptibility of psychotics to hypnosis.

In addition, several decades of literature have established a clinical and experimental record of the ability of many psychotic patients to work productively with hypnosis in psychotherapy. In the future, this history of work with hypnosis should, hopefully, become better known and accepted. The old myths of inability of psychotics to be hypnotized or to use hypnosis in psychotherapy may then be put finally to rest.

It also should become more accepted and understood in the future that hypnosis is a safe modality for the severely disturbed patient. Again, the clinical work of the past appears to show us that hypnosis is both useful and safe for psychotics as long as the therapist using the hypnosis has the psychotherapeutic skill, ability, and sensitivity to work safely with psychotic patients in general. A therapist who can work productively and safely with psychotic patients in traditional psychotherapy can typically learn to work equally well with these patients with hypnotherapy. A therapist who is not comfortable with or sensitive to psychotics in traditional therapy clearly would not do well to work with this population with any modality, including hypnosis.

With the growth of acceptance of hypnosis for psychotic patients, the future should show an increase in the use of hypnosis with this severely disturbed population. There should be an expansion of development of new techniques for dealing specifically with psychotic concerns of control, closeness, and shifting of self-concept in the use of hypnosis. Also, there should be continued exploration of both formal and informal techniques of induction and use of trance.

Another area for significant future development in hypnosis is the area of the use of trance by the therapist to facilitate therapeutic work. The use of the autohypnotic trance by the therapist can produce heightened empathy, thereby helping the therapist use his own body, mind, and feeling state as a barometer for patient feelings. The therapist can, through this process, provide feedback to patients, helping them identify and decode confused and unlabeled feeling states. This process of therapist empathic contact with patient feelings, the identification of these feelings, and then the feedback of this identified and decoded information to the patient can be especially helpful in working with psychotics. Since psychotic disturbances center around confused and mislabeled feelings and confused identity, the therapist's assistance in identifying feelings empathically can be most valuable (Scagnelli, 1980).

Frequently, the therapist's empathic abilities are the key to his ability to communicate with psychotic patients. If the therapist can "read" the feeling state of a psychotic patient, he can frequently understand the psychotic jargon, metaphor, symbolism, or other psychotically confused communications. Since the hypnotic trance enhances this empathic capacity, it also enhances understanding and communication in therapy. Therefore, this area of enhanced empathic communication is of tremendous potential for future work in hypnosis with psychotics.

In addition to the specific future developments expected in hypnosis with severely disturbed patients stated previously, there will also likely be major progress toward the development of a theory of hypnosis in psychotherapy in general. It is hoped that this will include a better theoretical understanding of how hypnosis works with the psychotic patient. A theoretical trend that looks promising to this author for future development appears to be emerging in the area of ego psychology and the concept of hypnosis as adaptive regression.

The theory of hypnosis as a form of adaptive regression has been evolving since the early phases of psychoanalytic ego psychology. Those who view hypnosis as an adaptive regression generally hypothesize that a regressed subsystem of the ego is placed in the service of the overall ego during hypnosis. Adaptive regression is considered to be "regression in the service of the ego." Such regression is considered to be subject to voluntary control. It consists of ego-regulated relaxation of defensive barriers, so that earlier modes of perception and cognition can be reactivated and so that normally regressed affects, memories, and primitive experiences can be accessed (Fromm and Shor, 1979; Kris, 1934). Criteria for identifying adaptive regression as opposed to regression proper includes the ability to self-initiate and terminate regressive experiences, the ability to judge appropriate and safe circumstances for regression, and the ability to reinstate normal psychic functioning (Gill and Brenman, 1959).

Against the background of this theoretical concept of adaptive regression, there has been a growing line of thought tending to view hypnosis as regression in the service of the ego. In 1926, Schilder and Kauders formulated the beginnings of the "hypnosis as adaptive regression" theory. They stated the view that only a part of the ego becomes involved in hypnosis and that a considerable portion of the personality maintains its normal relations with the outside world. Shilder and Kauders further proposed that "psychic depth" increases as the ego increasingly permits its reality orientation to be mediated through the person of the hypnotist, and that when the ego retains more of the function of observer, hypnotic behavior may be elicited but may be relatively more mechanical. Shilder and Kauders' concepts imply a central ego controlling regression and form a background for the theory of hypnosis as an adaptive regression put forth later by Gill and Brenman (1959).

Gill and Brenman (1959) developed the concept of an "overall ego" relatively autonomous in relation to id and environment. They theorized that hypnosis induction promotes sensorimotor disorientation and offers a regressive transference relationship as substitution. Unlike regression proper (or pathological regression), hypnotic regression occurs in a subsystem of the ego rather than in the overall ego. That is to say, a part rather than the whole ego is regressed, and the overall ego never totally loses contact with reality. Gill and Brenman built their theoretical model from an observational basis and concluded that hypnotic regression was regression in the service of the ego (Gill and Brenman, 1959; Fromm and Shor, 1979).

Noting that Gill and Brenman acknowledge clinical exceptions which could not be explained by their theories, Gruenewal, Fromm, and Oberlander (Fromm and Shor, 1979) formulated research testing Gill and Brenman's theory that hypnosis involves a process of adaptive regression. While the results of these researchers failed to establish a clear correlation between adaptive regression and hypnosis, the results did support the conclusion that regressive influences are greater in hypnosis than in the normal waking state. The authors note, in summary, that they found cogency in Gill and Brenman's view of the ego in hypnosis. They note that Sterba (1934), following Freud's postulate of an observing ego, suggested a separation of observing and experiencing parts of the ego in psycho-analysis. They consider this concept equally applicable to hypnosis (Fromm, 1965). The authors further note that the concepts of an observing and experiencing ego and of the adaptive regression by a subsystem of the ego have not been thoroughly explored in the literature and deserve further consideration (Fromm and Shor, 1979).

Let us, then, review the Gill and Brenman theory with a view to exploring and explaining some of the clinical exceptions originally noted by them. The authors state that their theory of regression in the service of the ego implies a "strong" rather than a "weak" ego; that is to say, an ego that has the capacity to regress in part while the depth and direction of regression are controlled by the ego as a whole (Gill and Brenman, 1959, p 198). Therefore, they conclude that normal subjects should evidence higher incidence of hypnotizability than neurotic subjects and that hypnosis should be impossible or nearly so with severe psychotics. However, Gill and Brenman note that exceptions to their theory exist with the hysterical neurotics who are highly hypnotizable and that "there are instances in which hypnosis is possible despite severe psychosis" (p 217). Gill and Brenman assume that these cases are exceptions to their theory because they assume that a "strong ego" is essential for hypnotic regression in the service of the ego.

However, it is possible to explain severely neurotic and psychotic patients' ability to use hypnosis and to allow hypnotic regression in the service of the ego if we assume that the patient in the hypnotic transference relationship is giving over the role (or part of the role) of overall ego to the therapist. This, in turn, would clarify why the issue of control/trust is so important to psychotics using hypnosis. In essence, in hypnotherapy with a psychotic patient, the therapist is assuming the role (at least in part) of the overall ego (*i.e.,* the adult, integrative ego) and serving as an anchor that allows the patient to regress under the controlled, safe structure of hypnosis (differing from psychotic regression or pathologically uncontrolled regression). The patient then can gain access to feelings and conflicts, reinterpret this material, and bring it back to the present to be integrated at a more reality-based, adult, and less frightening level. If a psychotic patient does not trust the therapist to take on this role of the adult ego (involving a temporary shift of control to the therapist), then probably he will not be willing to work with hypnosis at all, or may work with hypnosis only at a superficial level. In essence, the therapist may provide some or all of the ego strength in the hypnotic regression with the more severely disturbed patient.

It is probable that less severely disturbed patients also deal with this issue of temporarily giving over the role of adult ego, at least partially, to the therapist and that this is why the control/trust issue is generally important in hypnosis. When patients are more mechanically or superficially in trance, they are probably holding more of their adult ego role to themselves. At such times, their self-monitoring ego would most likely be more prominent. When patients are more deeply in trance with a less active monitoring ego, it is probable that they have placed greater trust and transference in the therapist and have temporarily given over more of the adult ego role to the therapist.

A third alternative pattern can be found in some patients with a high capacity for autohypnosis who may retain most of their own adult monitoring ego but are still able to allow themselves regression in the service of the ego for hypnosis or other creative uses. These patients would likely be individuals with "strong egos" in Gill and Brenman's sense of that phrase. They also would have the ability to allow the reduction of defenses against the id and environment even if a strong trust or transference or support ego were not present.

This re-analysis of Gill and Brenman's exceptions, then, allows us to create a theoretical framework for hypnosis as adaptive regression that allows for and includes hypnosis with severely disturbed and even psychotic patients. This theoretical integration also compliments some of the more recent constructs such as Hilgard's "hidden observer" (Fromm and Shor, 1979). In adaptive regression theory, this hidden observer would be the overall ego that retains its relation to reality. Similarly, this adaptive regression theory complements Fromm's theoretical conclusions that ego receptivity (as opposed to ego activity or passivity) is the primary factor associated with depth in altered state of consciousness (Fromm and Shor, 1979). In adaptive regression theory, this ego receptivity would be associated with the creation of the regressed subsystem within the ego. Ego receptivity (*i.e.,* depth of altered states of consciousness) would be greatest when the subject trusts either the strength of his own overall ego, or the therapist's, or both combined, to allow lowering of defenses, adaptive regression, and receptive access to previously defended material.

Appendix 20-1

Work Sample With Composite Patient—Lisa

This example is a composite taken from work with several severely disturbed patients. The session would begin with an induction process that is meant to be nurturing. It is therefore a fairly slow and lengthy induction process, and it is generally part of the therapeutic process for the patient. This induction process would include a breathing relaxation technique, in which the patient would pay attention to his breathing and follow it into deeper relaxation. Then the patient would be directed to begin a series of progressive relaxation exercises, working with the different parts of the body, relaxing each part of the body. The induction would proceed, possibly, to an arm levitation. The use of this technique would depend on patient variables. Some patients have a strong aversion to physical contact. If a patient seems to have problems with physical contact, the arm levitation would usually be avoided. A levitation can be produced by simply taking the patient's arm at the wrist and the elbow and finding a place where it feels comfortable and then leaving it there, letting the patient experience the dissociation involved in a levitation. When a patient can work comfortably with an arm levitation, it can be useful in giving him convincing evidence of trance and experience with dissociation so that he can recognize the process of dissociation and use it in constructive ways later on in therapy.

Frequently, the induction procedure will continue with some deepening techniques. Again, this may vary according to patient needs. A patient may be asked to visualize a staircase and simply deepen to whatever level of relaxation can be most comfortable for them. A suggestion for imagery may be used both as a deepening technique and also as a technique for exploration and insight in therapy. The patient may be asked to image some very safe, comfortable, relaxing place. Some suggestions of places that can seem relaxing may be presented to the patient, such as beaches, firesides, or simply a very comfortable chair at home. Frequently, the "discovery" of this relaxing place may be tied to counting down a staircase. As the patient descends the staircase, he "discovers" or visualizes his special place of relaxation. This special place is useful for providing the patient with an anchor, a safe place to which he can return whenever therapy becomes stressful.

At this point, the fairly lengthy induction is essentially concluded and we move on into the therapeutic work of the session. The patient then, in hypnosis, may be encouraged to go back in time and, essentially, a regression may be introduced. (Again, this is one example of one type of work that can be done with the severely disturbed patient.) Regression can typically be induced as follows:

VERBALIZATION	**COMMENT**
Therapist: I would like you now to begin to travel back to the near and distant past, to travel back in time, back to some period of earlier existence, perhaps going back to the early years of college, or high school, remembering some of those teachers. Back through the early years of grade school. Perhaps seeing some of the teachers and children, remembering what the rooms and halls look like. Going back, perhaps remember the feelings, some of the very early, early feelings of crawling across the floor, with fingers and hands making a pattern against the floor. Then remembering that very first time of reaching up, reaching up and grabbing some-	Therapist induces regression here and talks to unconscious more and more in feeling rather than logical messages.
	Therapist suggests regression to time prior to time to be explored and then works up to the exploration point in trance.
	Therapist is communicating the capacity of the patient for growth and accomplishment.

VERBALIZATION	COMMENT
thing—a chair, a table— and standing for the very first time upright, alone, on two feet. For the first time seeing that upright view of the world and feeling that sense of power and accomplishment, perhaps taking that very first step and struggling and falling. Feeling the sense of pain and accomplishment and exhilaration and all of the excitement of those first steps, walking and struggling and falling and walking again, and all of the delight and freedom. Now the hands are free to grasp and pick up things. Pretty soon it's running, skipping, hopping . . . then sitting that day in class, seeing those strange shapes on the blackboard and beginning to discover that all those shapes have names, all of those shapes have names—A, B, C—and on and on, so many names. How will we ever get to know all those names? Isn't it interesting that something that seems so impossible to learn, like walking and letters and reading, eventually becomes so easy that we hardly even think about it anymore. All of those names coming together and making sounds, and the sounds making words, and the words making stories. The stories about dog and ball and baby and mother and daddy. It's beginning to be easier and even a little exciting and I wonder how it feels for you in your classroom. I wonder if you would begin to share with me how your classroom looks.	
Patient: I don't see all of my classroom, but I see the blackboard and I see the teacher, that Ms. Dougherty, and I see the words up there and I'm just beginning to know that those are words and they seem hard right now. I see other kids, but they don't seem very important right now.	The patient's response indicates ability to work with imagery and regression.
Therapist: How does it feel sitting there and seeing that blackboard and teacher, Ms. Dougherty, and those words and the other kids?	

VERBALIZATION

COMMENT

Patient: It seems scary, so scary. Those words seem hard and I don't know, I'm afraid I won't know them. I know one word up there, that's "baby." I know that word. I'm scared. What if she calls on me and I don't know the word.

Therapist: Can you take that image and begin to see a happy, smiling self in that classroom, really happy that you know that word "baby," really proud that you know that word "baby." The teacher, Ms. Dougherty, is smiling at you and is very, very happy with you about how well you know that word "baby." She's letting you know that she will help you learn all the other words easily and comfortably, and she's letting you know that you *can learn,* that you really can, and that she'll help you. Can you see that image, feeling good about what you know and feeling that you will really get the help you want and need from that teacher?

Imagery shift is being suggested here by therapist.

Again, message of patient capacity for growth and accomplishment

Metaphoric message that therapist is accepting of patient and will help patient.

Patient: Yes, I can see that. I think I can see that. I see myself knowing "baby" and feeling good. I do know that word. The teacher feels good about me. She'll help me. I can see that, and that feels good.

Patient has made imagery shift here.

Therapist: That's good. It feels much better to remember how good it feels to appreciate what we really do know and to give ourselves the time to learn all the rest, and the teacher will help. The teacher really likes what you already know and how well you work . . . I'd like you now to go back to the earliest, earliest memory in time, in existence, the earliest memory of the little girl, the little Lisa, and even back further to the infant Lisa. Perhaps back to that crawling baby, or back even further. When you find that image of the infant, of the baby, of the little girl Lisa, then I would like you to signal me by moving your right index finger. [At this point, the therapist waits a period of time, and there is no

Metaphor restated of therapist's acceptance and help.

Therapist suggests further regression.

Patient resistance as no ideomotor signal is forthcoming.

VERBALIZATION

finger signal.] I wonder, Lisa, if you would share with me what it is that is happening in your thoughts or images and share with me whether you're having difficulty in finding that image of the infant, the baby, the little girl.

Patient: I can't picture her. I can't picture the baby.

Therapist: Then let's move on up in years and find the earliest picture of the little girl Lisa. Finding some time, some picture, some image of the little girl Lisa, that you can see and feel comfortable with.

Patient: I see the little girl. I see myself as a little girl.

Therapist: How old is the little girl?

Patient: Maybe 5 or 4. I know a picture and I know that's me. I've seen me in the picture.

Therapist: That's good. What is the little girl doing? How is she looking?

Patient: She's standing there. She has short, blond hair, and she's just standing there. She looks okay.

Therapist: I would like you, Lisa, to imagine, to image yourself, the adult Lisa, back there with that little girl Lisa. If you could have been the mother of that little girl, you would have loved her as she should have been loved, could have been loved. When you look at that little girl Lisa, you know very well that she really was lovable and that she deserved all the love that every little girl has always deserved. If you had been there to be her mother, you would have done all of the things that a mother should do. You would have held her and cradled her and rocked her and sung songs to her and maybe talked to her of all of the love of poetry, of words, and music. You would have shared with her all of the happiness of running and playing, swinging and moving, all of the fun of living and learning and growing, and all of the fun of growing up strong and

COMMENT

Therapist accepts resistance and moves around it.

Patient is able to get past resistance.

Creative self-mothering being suggested here by therapist

Message of nurturance from therapist and message for self-nurturance

VERBALIZATION	COMMENT

healthy and well loved. And little Lisa can *still* get some of those feelings of love from you, all of the feelings that *you* can give her, the mothering and the loving that she *always* deserved. The little girl Lisa was truly lovable, just as the grownup Lisa is now lovable.

References

Abrams S: The use of hypnotic techniques with psychotics: A critical review. Am J Psychother 18:79, 1964

Alanen YO: The family in the pathogenesis of schizophrenic and neurotic disorders. Acta Psychiatr Scand 42:189, 1966

Arieti S: Interpretation of Schizophrenia, 2nd ed. New York, Basic Books, 1974

Auerback A: Attitudes of psychiatrists to the use of hypnosis. JAMA 180:917, 1962

Avampato JJ: Hypnosis: A cure for torticollis. Am J Clin Hypn 18:60, 1975

Ayllon T, Haughton E: Control of the behavior of schizophrenic patients by food. J Exp Anal Behav 5:343, 1962

Baker EL: An hypnotherapeutic approach to enhance object relatedness in psychotic patients. Int J Clin Exp Hypn 29:136, 1981

Barber TX, Karacan I, Calverley DS: "Hypnotizability" and suggestibility in chronic schizophrenics. Arch Gen Psychiat 11:439, 1964

Bateson G, Jackson D, Haley J et al: Toward a theory of schizophrenia. Behav Sci 1:251, 1956

Berwick P, Douglas D: Hypnosis, exorcism and healing: a case report. Am J Clin Hypn 20:146, 1977

Biddle WE: Hypnosis in the Psychoses. Springfield, Charles C Thomas, 1967

Bleuler M: A twenty-three year longitudinal study of 208 schizophrenics and impression in regard to the nature of schizophrenia. In Rosenthal D, Kety SS (eds): The Transmission of Schizophrenia. London, Pergamon Press, 1968

Book JA: General aspects of schizophrenic psychoses. In Jackson DD (ed): The Etiology of Schizophrenia. New York, Basic Books, 1960

Bowers MK: Theoretical considerations in the use of hypnosis in the treatment of schizophrenia. Int J Clin Exp Hypn 9:39, 1961

Conn JH: Is hypnosis really dangerous? Int J Clin Exp Hypn 20:61, 1972

Eliseo TS: Three examples of hypnosis in the treatment of organic brain syndrome with psychosis. Int J Clin Exp Hypn 22:9, 1974

Erickson MH: An hypnotic technique for resistant patients: The patient, the technique and its rationale and field experiments. Amer J Clin Exp Hypn 7:8, 1964

Erickson MH: The use of symptoms as an integral part of hypnotherapy. Am J Clin Exp Hypn 8:57, 1965

Friedhoff AJ, Van Winkle E: New developments in the investigation of the relatedness of 3, 4-dimethoxyphenylethylamine to schizophrenia. In Hirnwich HE, Kety SS, Smythies JR (eds): Amines and Schizophrenia. Oxford, Pergamon Press, 1967

Fromm E: Hypnoanalysis: Theory and two case excerpts. Psychotherapy: Theory, Research and Practice 2:127, 1965

Fromm E, Shor R (eds): Hypnosis: Developments in Research and New Perspectives. New York, Aldine Publishing, 1979

Gale C, Herman MA: Hypnosis and the psychotic patient. Psychiatr 31:417, 1956

Gardner GG, Tarnow JD: Adjunctive hypnotherapy with an autistic boy. Am J Clin Hypn 22:173, 1980

Gill MM, Brenman M: Hypnosis and Related States: Psychoanalytic Studies in Regression. New York, International University Press, 1959

Gottesman II, Shields J: Contributions of twin studies to perspectives on schizophrenia. In Maher BA (ed): Progress in Experimental Personality Research 3. New York, Academy Press, 1966

Greene JT: Hypnotizability of hospitalized psychotics. Int J Clin Exp Hypn 17:103, 1969

Gruenewald D: Agoraphobia: A case study in hypnotherapy. Int J Clin Exp Hypn 19:10, 1971

Gruenewald D: Analogies of multiple personality in psychosis. Int J Clin Exp Hypn 26:1, 1978

Heath ES, Hoakin PCS, Sainz AA: Hypnotizability in state hospitalized schizophrenics. Psychiatr 34:65, 1960

Heath RG, Krupp IM: Schizophrenia as an immunological disorder. Arch Gen Psych 114:14, 1967

Hilgard ER: Hypnosis. Annu Rev Psychol 16:157, 1965

Hilgard ER, Weitzenhoffer AM, Landes J et al: The distribution of susceptibility to hypnosis in a student population: A study using the Stanford Hypnotic Susceptibility Scale. Psychology Monograph 75, 1961

Jung CG: Psychogenesis of Mental Disease. London, Routledge, 1960

Kallmann FJ: The Genetics of Schizophrenia. Locust Valley, NY, August Press, 1938

Kallmann FJ: Heredity in Health and Mental Disorder. New York, Norton, 1953

Kety SS: Biochemical theories of schizophrenia: A two-part critical review of current theories and of the evidence used to support them. Science 129:1528, 1959

Kety SS: Current biochemical research in schizophrenia. In Hock PH, Zubin J (eds): Psychopathology of Schizophrenia. New York, Grune & Stratton, 1966

Kety SS: Biochemical hypotheses and studies. In Bellack L, Loeb L (eds): The Schizophrenic Syndrome. New York, Grune & Stratton, 1969

Kety SS: Progress in psychobiology of schizophrenia: implications for treatment. Paper presented at "Treatment of Schizophrenia: Progress and Prospects" Symposium. UCLA, Neuropsychiatric Institute, 1972

Kline MV: Defending the mentally ill. The insanity defense and the role of forensic hypnosis. Int J Clin Exp Hypn 27:372, 1979

Kraepelin E: Dementia Praecox and Paraphrenia 8th ed. Edinburgh, E & S Livingston, 1919

Kramer E, Brennan E: Hypnotic susceptibility of schizophrenic patients. J Abnormal Social and Psychology 69:657, 1964

Kringlen E: Heredity and Environment in the Funcational Psychoses: An Epidemiological-Clinical Twin Study. London, Heinermann, 1967

Kringlen E: An epidemiological-clinical twin study on schizophrenia. In Rosenthal D, Kety SS (eds): The Transmission of Schizophrenia. New York, Pergamon Press, 1968

Kris E: Psychoanalytic Explorations in Art. New York, International Universities Press, 1952 (1934)

Lavoie G, Sabourin M, Ally G et al: Hypnotizability as a function of adaptive regression among chronic psychotic patients. Int J Clin Exp Hypn 24:238, 1976

Lavoie G, Sabourin M, Langlois J: Hypnotic susceptibility, amnesia and IQ in chronic schizophrenia. Int J Clin Exp Hypn 21:157, 1973

Lidz T: The Origin and Treatment of Schizophrenic Disorders. New York, Basic Books, 1977

Lieberman J: Suggested posthypnotic amnesia under active and passive learning conditions in chronic schizophrenia: A quantitative and qualitative analysis. Unpublished master's thesis, University of Montreal, 1975

Meehl PE: Schizotaxia, schizotypy, schizophrenia. Am J Psychol 17:827, 1962

Newman M: Hypnotic handling of a suicidal patient in the fugue state: A case report. Am J Clin Hypn 17:131, 1974

Plapp JM: Experimental hypnosis in a clinical setting: A report of the atypical use of hypnosis in the treatment of a disturbed adolescent. Am J Clin Hypn 18:145, 1976

Pollin W, Allen MG, Hoffer A et al: Psychopathology in 15,909 pairs of veteran twins: Evidence for a genetic factor in the pathogenesis of schizophrenia and its relative absence in psychoneurosis. Am J Psychol 126:597, 1969

Reardon WT: Modern Medical Hypnosis, 4th ed. Wilmington, The Group Hypnotherapy Research Center, 1965

Reiss D: Competing hypnothesis and warning factors: Applying knowledge of schizophrenia. Schizophr Bull 8:7, 1974

Rosen H: Hypnosis: Application and misapplications. JAMA 172:683, 1960

Scagnelli J: A case of hypnotherapy with an acute schizophrenic. Am J Clin Hypn 17:60, 1974

Scagnelli J: Therapy with eight schizophrenic and borderline patients: Summary of a therapy approach that employs a semi-symbiotic bond between patient and therapist. J Clin Psychol 31:519, 1975

Scagnelli J: Hypnotherapy with schizophrenic and borderline patients: Summary of therapy with eight patients. Am J Clin Hypn 18:33, 1976

Scagnelli J: Hypnotic dream therapy with a borderline schizophrenic. Am J Clin Hypn 20:136, 1977

Scagnelli J: Hypnotherapy with psychotic and borderline patients: The use of trance by patient and therapist. Am J Clin Hypn 22:164, 1980

Schilder P, Kauders O: Lehrbuchder Hypnose. (A Textbook of Hypnosis). Corvin G (trans): The Nature of Hypnosis. New York, International University Press, 1956

Sexton R, Meddock R: Age regression and age progression in psychotic and neurotic depression. Am J Clin Hypn 22:37, 1979

Skinner BF: What is psychotic behavior? In Millon T (ed): Theories of Psychopathology. Philadelphia, WB Saunders, 1967

Slater E: An Investigation into Psychotic and Neurotic Twins. London, University of London Press, 1951

Slater E: A review of earlier evidence on genetic factors in schizophrenia. In Rosenthal D, Kety SS (eds): The Transmission of Schizophrenia. London, Pergamon Press, 1968

Spiegel D, Fink R: Hysterical Psychosis and Hypnotizability. Am J Psychiatr 136:777, 1979

Sterba R: The fate of the ego in analytic therapy. Int J Psychoanalysis 15:117, 1934

Swanson DW, Brown EM, Beuret LJ: A family with five schizophrenic children. Diseases of the Nervous System, 30:189, 1969

Ullmann LP, Krasner L: The psychological model. In Millon T (ed): Theories of Psychopathology. Philadelphia, WB Saunders, 1967

Vingoe FJ, Kramer EF: Hypnotic susceptibility of hospitalized psychotic patients: A pilot study. Int J Clin Exp Hypn 14:47, 1966

Webb RA, Nesmith CC: A normative study of suggestability in a mental patient population. Int J Clin Exp Hypn 12:181, 1964

Weitzenhoffer AM, Hilgard ER: Stanford Hypnotic Susceptibility Scale, Forms A and B. Palo Alto, CA, Consulting Psychologists Press, 1959

West LH, Deckert GHD: Dangers of hypnosis. JAMA 192:9, 1965

Wilson CP, Cormen HH, Cole AA: A preliminary study of the hypnotizability of psychotic patients. Psychiatr Q 23:657, 1949

Woolley DW, Shaw E: A biochemical and pharmacological suggestion about certain mental disorders. Science 119:587, 1954

Wynne L, Singer M: Thought disorder and family relations of schizophrenics: II. A classification of forms of thinking. Arch Gen Psychiatr 9:199, 1963

Yarnell T: Symbolic assertive training through guided affective imagery in hypnosis. Am J Clin Hypn 14:194, 1972

Zeig MS: Hypnotherapy techniques with psychotic in-patients. Am J Clin Hyp 17:56, 1974

21 Hypnosis in the Treatment of Sexual Dysfunctions

DANIEL L. ARAOZ

Regression in the service of pleasure.

(KAPLAN, 1979, P 91)

Ellis (1976) made a meaningful distinction between sexual *dysfunctions* and sexual *disturbance.* Only the dysfunctions that upset the individual or the couple become psychological problems or sexual disturbances. On the other hand, any sexual dysfunction, no matter how slight and transitory, becomes problematic when evaluated as such. This "evaluation" is composed of *self-affirmations* and *mental imagery,* both of which we group under the term *cognitions.*

Because "thinking" affects our sexual behavior so deeply, it is not hyperbolic to state that the most important sexual organ in the human body is the brain, not the genitalia. There is mounting evidence (reviewed elsewhere, Araoz, 1981, 1982) of the effects of cognitions on human behavior in general and, especially, on sexual functioning.

This chapter will center on the therapeutic advantages of using hypnosis in sex therapy. It must be emphasized from the start that hypnosis is not proposed as a substitute for traditional sex therapy (Masters and Johnson, 1966, 1970; Kaplan, 1974), but as an adjunct that will greatly enrich sex therapy and often salvage the sexual problem from becoming iatrogenic (Araoz, 1980).

Hypnosis in Sex Therapy

Masters and Johnson's (1966) concept of "spectatoring" and Kaplan's (1979) "turn-off mechanism" refer to the cognitive processes, hypnotic in nature, affecting enjoyable sexual behavior. Neither has been fully developed in the sex therapy literature, considering the self-hypnotic implications they encapsulate. *405*

What the person "says" to himself about sex, the body, pleasure, and even the sexual difficulty he experiences is, more often than not, subconscious and bypasses logic and reason. This hidden or secondary symptom is the main rationale for using hypnosis, since the hypnotic negative effect of the hidden symptom can only be reached at its own level of operation (*i.e.,* subconsciously). Negative self-talk elicits defeatist mental images; hypnosis counteracts both mental activities (self-talk and imagery) positively.

Our claim that these covert processes are self-hypnotic (Araoz, 1982) is based on our understanding of hypnosis as a cognitive *skill* (see Chap. 26). This follows the research findings of careful studies, cited in that chapter, proving that hypnosis is *an alternate state of mind (or mental activity) in which logic and critical processes diminish, while imagination and suggestibility increase, making one more receptive to constructive change.*

With this in mind, it is not difficult to accept hypnosis as a therapeutic method to counteract the hidden symptom. All the "sexpertise" in the world (to use Walen's [1980] neologism) will be an utter waste of time if the negative affirmations and imagery elicited by the overt sexual symptom are not substituted with constructive cognitions. Walen (1980) called our attention to some of the cognitive factors in sexual behavior and advocated a novel diagnostic approach. This new diagnosis for sexual dysfunctions would focus more sharply on the emotional disturbance and inner attitude (the less playful, the more emotionally disturbing) than on mere dysfunctional behaviors.

Sexology has accepted desire as an integral part of the sexual cycle (Lief, 1977; Kaplan, 1979; Araoz, 1980). Another manifestly psychological component of human sexuality is *processing.* Sexual processing is the mental activity by which we monitor our sexual awareness, feelings, and behavior throughout the three phases of the sexual cycle (desire, arousal, and resolution) and beyond.

Regardless of the endocrinological realities affecting both sexual desire and sexual processing (and which are beyond the scope of this chapter), when the latter is positive, there are joy and fulfillment, when negative, there are frustration, guilt, anger, resentment, embarrassment, or any combination of these unpleasant feelings. Hypnosis is effective to change negative into positive sexual processing. This is so because by the time patients arrive for sex therapy, negative processing has become a subconscious habit. Reasoning, logic, and intellectual evaluations are ineffective because they do not reach the level at which the negative processing takes place. Hypnosis does.

Before proceeding any further, we want to underline *self*-hypnosis not het-erohypnosis. There is enough evidence to claim that all hypnosis is basically self-hypnosis (Fromm et al, 1981; Singer and Pope, 1981), but regardless of the theoretical controversy, we have found that sex hypnotherapy is more effective if clients are taught to practice hypnosis on their own from the very beginning. The reader is, therefore, warned that we always have in mind *self-hypnosis* when we refer to hypnosis in the rest of the chapter.

A Brief Look at the Literature

Little has been published on hypnosis in the sex therapy literature despite the fact that the late Hugo Beigel (1897–1978), for example, was a pioneer in sex research and therapy and, at the same time, a world authority on hypnosis. In the hypnosis literature, on the other hand, one finds an abundance of articles and papers, most of them anecdotal. A review by Brown and Chaves (1980) covered over 20 years of publications and suggested the clinical usefulness of hypnosis despite their criticisms. They lamented the lack of scientific research objectively to assess the value of hypnosis in treating sexual dysfunctions. Their advice cannot be dismissed lightly. Nor can one ignore, however, the consistency of about 50 years of clinical reports (Erickson published in 1935 a detailed explanation of his use of hypnosis in a case of premature ejaculation, which I have discussed elsewhere, 1982). Brown and Chaves seemed to look for the objectivity of the experimental laboratory in the clinical reports reviewed, thus weakening the "historical" argument, built on the frequency and consistency of such clinical accounts. Many authors, from different backgrounds, disciplines, and locations, are consistent in pointing to the advantage of hypnosis for treatment of a host of sexual dysfunctions, from premature ejaculation (Erickson, 1935) and erectile problems (Dittborn, 1957) to orgasmic dysfunction (Cheek, 1961) and gynecological disorders (Leckie, 1964), including vaginismus (Schneck, 1965) and several conditions grouped under the label of "frigidity" (Wijesinghe, 1977). This is just a partial list to emphasize the broad scope of sexual dysfunctions for which hypnosis has been employed.

From the early years on to recent developments (Kroger and Fezler, 1976; Kroger and Alle, 1981) the success of hypnosis for sexual problems seems to be in direct proportion to the use of imagery, as opposed to direct suggestions. Very few early authors explained in detail their clinical interventions through hypnosis. Elsewhere, I (1982) examined the methods used by van Pelt (1949) and Beigel (1972), besides those of Erickson, referred to previously. However, more recently, both behaviorally oriented methods (Miller, 1981; Araoz, 1981) and psychodynamic ones (Edelstein, 1981; Barnett, 1981) have been described thoroughly, making it possible for the therapist to apply them to sexual problems.

Applications of Hypnosis in Sex Therapy

The two basic principles for sex hypnotherapy are

1. Imagination and self-suggestion influence (sexual) behavior, or "regression in the service of pleasure" (Kaplan, 1979)
2. From sensuality to sexuality, or the need to proceed progressively and cumulatively

That imagination and self-suggestions influence behavior is sufficiently clear from the work of the cognitive behavior therapists (Meichenbaum, 1978). The second principle comes from the developmental nature of human sexuality and from the need for a comprehensive approach in re-educating adult sexuality.

The applications of hypnosis in sex therapy fall under two broad categories—diagnosis and treatment. Under the latter, several subdivisions are found, as will be indicated later.

Diagnosis

Sex therapy requires a very considerate diagnosis, since, frequently, relational or personality problems on the one hand, or medical conditions, on the other, are masked by sexual dysfunctions. Hypnosis helps in bringing subconscious material to conscious awareness, and thus in establishing a more secure diagnosis. As to the possible medical conditions underlying sexual dysfunctions, the nonmedical sex therapist will be wise in referring the patient for medical clearance before stepping into the case.

Although there are many effective hypnodynamic techniques, I shall present two, one centered on historicopsychodynamic realities, and the other on symptoms and behavior. In hypnodiagnosis, our aim is (1) to define the problem accurately, (2) to discover any subconscious meaning of the problem, and (3a) if there is a subconscious meaning, to decode that message, (3b) if not, to ascertain the client's readiness to give up the symptom (Araoz, 1982). Only after this three-step diagnostic process, meaningful treatment can begin.

Before and after, a symptom-focused technique, encourages the couple to visualize a double screen. On one screen, the current difficulty is represented, as they are involved in a dissatisfying sexual experience. The second screen portrays the near future without the sexual problem. Obviously, the emphasis is on the latter, and the couple is helped to experience fully the perceptions and positive feelings of the future picture and to verbalize them to each other while in hypnosis. *Experiencing* the process of positive change is stressed: How each feels, physically and psychologically, about the change; how their lives are enriched; what emotional asset has been acquired; and so on. (For those who find it difficult to visualize, previous training in visualization will be required. This may start quite simply with a vivid description of a very familiar place, such as one's living room.)

This exercise usually redefines the problem and provides information about its solution. The emphasis should be, as stated, on mentally *experiencing* the change and its effects, based on one's inner resources and wisdom to change, to grow. This elicits new awareness of the symptom: what function, if any, it is fulfilling in the couple's life at present; why the symptom started; why it continued; and so forth.

Subconscious language, on the other hand, can be used as a psychodynamic diagnostic technique. In this case, after the person is in hypnosis, one of the time-honored hypnotic methods of subconscious investigation is used. This method can be either the Chevreul pendulum or (my preference) ideomotor communication. Because authors such as Cheek and LeCron (1968) have explained these methods thoroughly, there is no need to be more explicit here. The only reminder about sexual problems is that all the questions to be answered subconsciously must be posed in very positive terms and that often each member of the couple must be given a chance to answer the questions individually. This does not mean that the couple should not be together during the hypnosis session. On the contrary, I prefer—after an initial individual interview—to see the couple together whenever possible (Araoz, 1978).

The advantage of *subconscious language* is that the clinician obtains useful information that the client may not be ready to handle yet consciously. In this case, the therapist knows either what to avoid or what goal to aim at.

The following clinical vignette may be illustrative.

Roy, a 22-year-old client, had a double symptom of psychogenic erectile difficulties and choking sensations. While investigating the possible connection between the two symptoms through ideomotor questioning, the therapist found that his father had used Roy as an infant several times to perform fellatio on him. On one occasion, when baby Roy did not cooperate, his father beat him, concentrating on Roy's genitals. This memory had been firmly repressed, but the clinician knew what had to be resolved in order to overcome the double symptom.

In clinical practice, diagnosis, as opposed to psychological autopsy, must be an ongoing process. Therefore, the overlap between diagnosis and exploratory interventions in the course of sex therapy is considerable. However, for didactic purposes, we may distinguish between diagnosis proper and exploratory or uncovering techniques.

Treatment

Under this heading, we will consider, first, hypnosis for therapeutic *exploration;* second, hypnosis for *direct* and for *transfer* symptom relief; and, third, for *mental rehearsal.*

Exploratory Techniques. We shall present only one technique, referring the reader to Edelstien (1981) and Barnett (1981), where one finds many important exploratory interventions quite adaptable to sex hypnotherapy.

We chose Watkins' (1978) *ego states* therapy as an effective tool to investigate subconscious or forgotten material. This is an elegant hypnotic method, since clients recognize a dichotomy in themselves, often expressing it as, for example, "one part of me wants to enjoy sex, but another part doesn't let me." On this basis, as seen in Appendix 21-1, the person is led to identify that hidden part (and any other relevant sides of the personality) responsible for the symptoms, affect, mood changes, and so on that the conscious self is unable to control.

The more involved in the hypnotic experience the client is, the less interference appears from rationalizations, intellectualizations, and "facts." Because of this, it is effective to take one's time to help the person really switch to the hypnotic state before starting the sex therapy work. Trance utilization follows trance induction. However, as will be mentioned in Chapter 26, we take induction literally, that is, *to lead* the client *into* an alternate way of using one's mind, and avoid as much as possible the rituals and histrionics of induction.

We look for mental images reflected in the client's speech patterns, for example, "The pressure is so great," "I can't stand it anymore." "I can hear his tone of voice," "If I could only see my way out of this," and so on. We use these to invite the clients to activate their imagination and to enter into the inner experience beyond the conscious, rational, and reality-oriented mental activity. The transition from ordinary thinking and talk to hypnosis (*i.e.,* induction) is, thus, naturalistic, nonartificial, and smooth.

To return to the ego state technique, we use it as a very convenient tool for subconscious exploration, rather than as a comprehensive method, as Watkins (1978) proposes.

Direct Symptom-Relief Techniques. We follow Kaplan's (1979) model of *psychosexual therapy,* integrating *a multiple causal levels concept* for the understanding and treatment of sexual dysfunctions. Thus, we consider symptom relief as a parsimonious *first step* of therapeutic intervention, the next two steps being circumstantial awareness and developmental awareness of conditions affecting sexual functioning.

Therefore, if direct symptom relief is ineffective, we move on to step two (circumstantial awareness), helping clients connect possible conditions, such as excessive alcohol intake or visits from relatives, with the sexual symptom. When this exploration of immediate causes influencing sexual functioning does not produce positive results, we then move to the more complex psychodynamic factors (step three) and explore subconscious dynamics that might interfere with enjoyable sexual behavior.

Thus, when we mention direct symptom-relief techniques, we are not limiting ourselves to this first step. The ego state method, mentioned in the preceding section, may be used effectively in the attempted direct removal or relief of sexual symptoms. In this instance, "the part" responsible for the symptom is asked either to give it up or to substitute it for a less burdensome one. However, in clinical practice it is difficult to separate exploratory interventions of a psychodynamic nature from direct symptom relief through hypnosis, since often the previously mentioned type of request leads to meaningful insights and revelations from the subconscious mind.

A more direct intervention (*the inner computer*) is a technique that uses the hypnotic state for a visualization of a computer room representing one's brain. The dial indicating the functioning of the problematic sexual behavior is clearly seen in one's mind's eye: its size, its colors, its needle, the numbers from 1 to 10, and so on. But the dial is "seen" as set incorrectly. As long as it is set this way, the sexual problem will continue.

Then a knob is also visualized that the clients can use to correct the setting of the dial. The clients are next encouraged to set the dial correctly and to be sure that it stays set this way. It is effective to add at this point the technique of mental rehearsal, so the person becomes familiar with the way his sexual functioning will be, now that this control center in the brain has been reset.

The seeming superficiality of this technique is deceitful. In many cases this is sufficient to produce a remarkable improvement in sexual functioning, since it seems to give the person a new awareness of mastery through his attitudes. The subtle message received is something like this: "Nothing is wrong with you as such; your reactions and responses in the sexual area we are concerned with are wrong. But you have the inner resources and potential to change those reactions."

As stated earlier, if this or the following intervention is not effective, one proceeds to step two, that is, awareness of the person's circumstances surrounding his sexual activity.

Transfer Symptom-Relief Techniques. As the name indicates, these therapeutic maneuvers employ nonsexual or already familiar phenomena or experiences in order to *transfer* them to the sexual symptom, so it can be removed or relieved. This is similar to the well-known approach to the control of pain through hypnosis by which a hand experienced as numb "transfers" its numbness to the painful area and "turns off" the sensation of pain.

Thus, a woman with vaginismus can be taught to relax all over and then concentrate on her pelvic and vaginal areas. In the case of vasocongestive deficiency, the woman can learn to increase normal salivation in hypnosis and then transfer that experience to her vagina when the circumstances are right for sexual activity. Since vaginal lubrication has an important *subjective* aspect, besides the physiological one, it can be connected with another subjective experience, though physiologically different from lubrication.

Men with erectile problems are led hypnotically to experience pleasurable stiffness of one finger in order to transfer it to their penises during a sexual encounter. On the other hand, retarded ejaculation can be corrected by first experiencing in hypnosis an increased sensitivity of one finger, as if it were role playing the patient's penis. The posthypnotic suggestions stress the experience of similar pleasurable stiffness during sex, lasting for as much time as the person decides and no more.

These and similar transfer techniques, either alone or in combination with any other appropriate hypnotic technique, such as the *inner computer,* previously described, and the mental rehearsal method (see next section), reach and alter the mental functioning that is other than external reality oriented. They often produce dramatic improvement of the sexual dysfunction, as data from our Hypnosex program indicate.

Mental Rehearsal. Another technique employed for many physical and psychological conditions, mental rehearsal, works well for sexual dysfunctions because as indicated previously, practically every sex therapy patient practices negative self-hypnosis without realizing it. This is done through negative self-talk and by admitting and often encouraging self-defeating imagery without doing anything against the same.

Mental rehearsal counteracts that cognitive negativism (see also Chap. 26). The client is helped to visualize positive, enjoyable, and playful sexual experiences until they become so attractive in his mind that this is the only type of sex he thinks about and desires. Often patients with many unhappy years in the sexual area, find it difficult to visualize themselves as sexually happy. To overcome this difficulty, it is helpful to ask the patient to see in his mind's eye a fictional movie of one of his sex symbols (actor, athlete, or whoever it might be) several times. When he has succeeded, the therapist helps him slowly change that ideal person into himself. The inability to do this exercise is often an indication of more fundamental psychological problems—other than the sexual one—in need of psychotherapy.

As I indicated before, I seldom use only one technique at a time in clinical practice. Mental rehearsal is usually combined with any other therapeutic intervention used. As a matter of fact, I believe that the earlier clients establish wellness and optimal functioning as their goal, the quicker is the therapeutic process. Current research conducted by Bleck (1981) is accumulating data that seem to confirm our belief and that will be published in the future.

Moreover, not only wellness and optimal functioning are important as goals of sex therapy, but also playfulness and joy in sex. Again, through mental rehearsal one finds, at times, patients who cannot "see themselves" enjoying sex playfully, even though they consciously agree with the concept. This, very often, points to relational difficulties in need of marital therapy.

In summation, mental rehearsal is a flexible therapeutic tool offering diagnostic, treatment, and prognostic advantages in sex therapy. In concluding this section, it should be remembered that we have listed elsewhere specific hypnotic techniques for different sexual dysfunctions (Araoz and Bleck, 1982; Araoz, 1982). Although it is valid and useful to designate specific techniques for specific sexual difficulties, the limitations of this chapter preclude this. However, the current approach to sex hypnotherapy has the advantage of stressing flexibility and creativity on the part of the clinician. Practically any hypnotic technique described previously can be used effectively with any sexual dysfunction. It is up to the clinician who has grasped the principles and theory involved in the use of sex hypnotherapy to accommodate the technique to each individual client and couple.

The Matter of Effectiveness

It must be remembered that the instruments and research designs of experimental hypnosis (or experimental psychology in general, for that matter) are inadequate to assess the results of *sex hypnotherapy*. For instance, the previously mentioned clinical procedure of employing a symptom-centered approach, which, if unsuccessful, can be quickly changed, would not qualify as an experimental way of researching the effectiveness of a particular technique. Here is the crucial difference, then. The clinician's goal is symptom relief, behavioral change, and overall well-being of the individual. The experimentalist's goal is to test the experimental variables. While the person is an end in clinical hypnosis, the subject is often subservient to the experiment in experimental hypnosis.

Keeping this in mind, it is still important to have data to justify one's procedure. If we take hypnosis to mean the mental state in which constructive imagination and self-suggestion prevail, Barber (1979), among others, has shown its benefits to include improved self-esteem and general learning. Since there is no reason to assume that psychogenic sexual problems are unrelated to self-esteem and general learning, his findings can be applied to this area of human behavior as well.

In a limited study conducted by us (Bleck and Araoz, 1981), careful records were kept of 50 couples treated for sexual dysfunctions without hypnosis and of 150 couples who had sex hypnotherapy. Two of the significant results were, first, that therapy length was shortened from a mean of 12 sessions for the first group, to seven for the second. Another interesting difference between the two groups was observed in a follow-up 1 year after termination. Only 10% of those *not* using hypnosis, as opposed to 70% of those couples treated with hypnosis, were still satisfied with the results. Moreover, 72% of the latter group indicated that they had transferred the skill of self-hypnosis to other areas of their lives, such as air travel, visits to the dentist, and domestic upsets.

Steger (1978) reviewed the outcome of cognitive behavioral strategies in the treatment of sexual problems and found it positive. The fact that he does not view hypnosis as one of these strategies is irrelevant to the outcome. Other studies using guided imagery (Wolpin, 1969) also show the effectiveness of this approach. Other methods that we also consider hypnotic, such as implosive therapy (Stampfl and Levis, 1967) and the covert techniques of Cautela (1975), have also been used successfully in sex therapy, as Hogan's (1978) review points out.

It is our hope that more clinicians gather data on the effects of bypassing resistance to change by means of hypnosis. Although clinicians owe much to and have learned much from the experimentalists, we still must be careful not to mimic indiscriminately their methods. They must be concerned with means and standard deviations; we must never lose sight of each individual treated.

Looking Into the Future

The increased effectiveness and popularity of cognitive behavior therapy will probably greatly help unification in the broad field of mental health. On the one hand, it will bring behavior modification practitioners closer to those of a psychodynamic persuasion. On the other, those who use hypnosis under other terms will, it is hoped, become aware of their communality with hypnoclinicians. Kroger stated the need to standardize the labels employed by the different schools*. Since we are all concerned with *cognitions* in the broad sense of the word, we all find it easy to accept the terminology of cognitive behavior therapy and research.

In sex therapy proper, the seeds for attention to cognitive factors were planted very early by Masters and Johnson (1966) themselves, as we indicated initially. Nowadays, sex therapists seem to be quite ready to concern themselves with the negative mental processes that are hidden under the symptoms (Walen, 1980).

Both fields, that of sex therapy and that of clinical hypnosis, will benefit greatly if the former recognizes that hypnosis á la Svengali is passé, and if the latter accepts hypnosis not as an altered state of consciousness belonging to an esoteric elite, but as an *alternate* state that all humans who daydream can enjoy. When hypnosis is considered a natural state, which people can *learn* to enjoy for their benefit, the fears of many professionals in the field of sex therapy—as well as in other related fields—will become senseless and meaningless.

Without hypnosis in sex therapy one would neglect a potentially important facet of human sexuality—what we called sexual processing. Because of the awareness of cognition in human behavior, and especially in sexual functioning, more and more sex therapists are becoming interested in this time-honored though still misnamed therapeutic method called hypnosis, as a perusal of the papers presented at the Fifth World Congress of Sexology (1981) shows.

---

* W. S. Kroger, personal communication, 1981.

Conclusions

I indicated earlier that my therapeutic approach is essentially to teach *self-hypnosis* to patients. I do not hypnotize anybody. I teach them to switch mental channels— if the analogy does not sound too mechanistic—so that they give themselves permission "to stop the world" or "to stop the internal dialogue," as Don Juan teaches Carlos (Castaneda, 1974), so that they can center themselves and become innerly liberated, in the words of Kushel (1979). Any psychogenic behavioral dysfunction, including those sexual, is self-limiting and crippling. Hypnosis frees clients to become what they can be, because it gives them the key to open a door otherwise closed to the conscious mind.

The need for thorough professional training in both fields cannot be too strongly emphasized. Sex therapy and hypnosis combined, more than other areas, lend themselves to quackery and abuse by those who are not serious and ethical professionals. Stories of sexual abuse by so-called experts abound. To establish quality controls in these fields, psychology has organized two national boards, that is, the American Board of Psychological Hypnosis and the American Board of Family Psychology. The former grants diplomas in clinical and experimental hypnosis; the latter concerns itself with sex and marital therapy combined (and also in marital and family therapy). Both boards do this after strict scrutiny of the candidate, who must have several years of experience in each field, and give a comprehensive examination covering theory and application.

Other professions involved in sex therapy and in hypnosis would do well to follow the example of psychology. Minimal competence, ascertained by state license, is not enough to practice in these two delicate fields. Our clients and patients deserve the *advanced* competence and specialization to which the national boards testify. In the absence of national certification, recognized training and supervision should be imperative.

Only with thorough preparation, training, and supervision will we, as professionals, be able to lead people into a "regression in the service of pleasure." Then they will discover in themselves the abundant resources for sexual growth and happiness that are dormant in the inner mind of the average individual.

Appendix 21-1

This is a verbatim transcript of part of a sex hypnotherapy session for psychogenic erectile dysfunction. This is taken from the second session, after ideomotor responses have been taught. Chuck's wife was in the consulting room, at his request.

VERBALIZATION	COMMENT
Therapist: Now that you are feeling so relaxed . . . so good . . . let the part of you . . . responsible for your problem talk to us through your fingers . . . okay?	This section starts after induction. Induction was naturalistic; Chuck was asked to relax and feel comfortable. "The parts" in him is a concept that was smoothly introduced when he was told that "a part" in him wanted to have good sex, while another "part" was blocking him from it.
Client: Yes . . . okay.	
Therapist: So, relax . . . even more if you want. . . . Enjoy . . . the relaxation and when you . . . have become . . . much more relaxed than . . . you . . . are . . . now . . . let your Yes-finger move by itself.	Deepening is suggested, stressing the enjoyable aspects of the experience.
Client: [Right index finger, his Yes-finger, moves very slightly.]	*He* won't move his finger.
Therapist: I noticed a very slight movement. . . . Let your inner mind move your finger again if the slight movement I saw means that you are already much more relaxed than before. . . .	*It* will move, controlled by his inner mind. At this point, it is still not clear whether he is trying to please the therapist, or whether his subconscious mind is responding.
Client: [Finger movement is greater and prolonged.]	A maneuver to ascertain that ideomotor communication *is* taking place
Therapist: Thank you for your response. Chuck, you may want to thank your inner mind for being so cooperative. When you do, your Yes-finger can move again.	This expression of thanks may seem artificial, but it is a way of reminding Chuck of his inner mind, with whom we want to communicate at this point.
Client: [Yes-finger moves.]	The so-called Yes-finger expresses agreement of any kind. So, it is used here for that purpose. Before starting to work on a particular problem, and to avoid future resistance, it is wise to obtain "permission" from the inner mind. Especially in sexual problems, because of their very personal nature, this procedure conveys a respect that facilitates further work.
Therapist: I see we are in agreement, and it makes me feel good. . . . Is your inner mind ready . . . to work . . . on your problem?	
Client: [Nothing happens.]	
Therapist: I'm addressing myself to your inner mind, Chuck. . . . Are you ready . . . to work on Chuck's . . . sexual problem?	
Client: [Yes-finger moves very slightly.]	
Therapist: I'd like to ask you again the same question . . . just so we get a firmer answer. . . . Are you ready and willing to work now on Chuck's problem?	
Client: [Yes-finger moves decisively.]	
Therapist: All right . . . and thank you again. . . . So, let me ask you the first question: Do you believe the two doctors who told you that your problem is *not* physical?	The preliminary work is done. We can now begin sex hypnotherapy. Chuck had consulted an endocrinologist and a neurologist for his erectile problem. It was important to see whether

VERBALIZATION	COMMENT
Client: [Yes-finger moves.]	the subconscious believed their negative findings.
Therapist: Your problem, then, comes from your inner mind. Doesn't it?	A new attempt to focus sharply on the source of his problem
Client: [Left index finger, the No-finger, moves quickly.]	A good example of the subtlty of the subconscious mind in communicating
Therapist: Your problem is *not* physical and is *not* in your inner mind either. . . . Is it then in both your *inner* and in your *conscious* mind?	with the conscious mind. Previously, the therapist had asked about the *source* of the problem. Now he refers to where the problem is (manifests itself?).
Client: [Yes-finger moves quickly.]	
Therapist: All right and thank you again. . . . For a moment I was a little confused. . . . So, now, Chuck, that we know your problem is both in your inner mind and in your conscious mind, may I start with the inner mind?	The subconscious mind is not as literal as some authors seem to believe. What the person knows about his self is his private domain. Therefore, a respectful and nonintrusive attitude on the part of the therapist must be present at all times.
Client: Yes [very softly].	
Therapist: Okay. . . . Is this the answer of the inner mind also?	
Client: Yes. . . . Yes [while the Yes-finger also moves].	The exploration begins with possible events of Chuck's past. In case some inner "part" in Chuck's personality has
Therapist: Thank you. . . . Is there any reason coming from way back in Chuck's past for his present problem?	established a different identity and some distance from his conscious self, this dissociated language is used. This pro-
Client: [No-finger moves.]	cedure also helps the client not to identify his whole self with the problem.
Therapist: Thank you . . . again. Is there anything from before he was married causing his present problem?	
Client: [No-finger moves, and then he says, weakly] No.	
Therapist: Thank you again. . . . All right. . . . I want to ask you another question. . . . It has to do with when he will be able to enjoy sex fully. Chuck, will the whole of you enjoy sex to the full soon?	The incorrect grammar is kept as spoken, to preserve the original dialogue. "The whole Chuck" is referred to in order to integrate the personality "parts" at work which, really, are not in conflict here.
Client: [Nothing happens.]	The silence is an indication that the preceding question was a mistake. A new
Therapist: Let me change that, then. . . . Is there anything that you have to do *before* you can enjoy sex fully?	question is, then, asked, still looking for Chuck's subconscious readiness for change. Another line of exploration is
Client: [Yes-finger moves.]	opened by the client's response.
Therapist: Is what you have to do related to your wife?	
Client: [The No-finger moves.]	
Therapist: Is it related to yourself?	
Client: [The No-finger moves.]	
Therapist: Is it related to your work?	A seemingly unrelated area of his life

VERBALIZATION	COMMENT
Client: [Yes-finger moves.] **Therapist:** Thank you, and . . . stay with this, please . . . and wait a moment there. Perhaps your inner mind wants to let you know very clearly what you must do to end your sexual problem.	may be connected with his sexual problem. Often, the subconscious mind knows what changes must be brought about in one area of one's life in order to change another area.

At this point, the client opens his eyes and tells the therapist that he just realized very clearly that as long as he continues to work for his father (a very meticulous and authoritarian man) he will be unhappy, and he will feel impotent. He also states that he knew this all along, but somehow, now he knows it with more conviction—the type of statement frequently made in these circumstances. In discussing the possibility of changing jobs, Chuck says that there have been plenty of opportunities, but he was always afraid of leaving his father. Now he knows he must do it.

VERBALIZATION	COMMENT
Therapist: Go back into hypnosis now and tell your inner mind that you *will* take steps to leave your present job with your father. **Client:** [Closes his eyes and looks very relaxed.] **Therapist:** When you are ready, let your inner mind move your Yes-finger so we can continue therapy. **Client:** [Yes-finger moves.]	The previous conscious discussion will now be confirmed at the subconscious level.
Therapist: Now, Chuck, tell your inner mind what you told me before . . . that you'll quit your father's employment. **Client:** [Smiles when REM increases noticeably. He is silent.] **Therapist:** Ask your inner mind to allow you to enjoy sex fully while you find another job. . . . Let me know when you have asked your inner mind. **Client:** [Yes-finger moves.]	Whatever the meaning of "talking to one's subconscious mind" is for each person, it conveys a sense of commitment to self. What was agreed upon that had to be changed is processed now at a different level of cognition.
Therapist: This is like bargaining . . . you do what you know you must do to feel potent . . . as a man again . . . and your inner mind . . . takes away your sexual problem . . . you don't need it any more. . . . Sounds fair to me. . . . **Client:** [Yes-finger moves, while saying] Yes.	Going on the assumption that the sexual symptom is a message from the subconscious mind, once the message is heeded, the symptom becomes unnecessary.

A week later, Chuck still had been unable to talk to his father about his decision to change jobs. His sexual problem was still as acute as before. However, he felt optimistic because he knew what to do. Mental rehearsal was used to prepare him for the confrontation with his father. He was asked to practice for 4 days privately before talking to his father. On the fifth day he did, and was surprised at the ease with which he handled the situation.

Sexual mental rehearsal was practiced at the fourth session, again with the injunction of repeating this practice every day. At the fifth session Chuck reported a complete disappearance of his erectile problem and a very good prospect for a new job, which would materialize in about 10 days. One more session was held to solidify the gains. A telephone call 3 months later confirmed the gains made during sex hypnotherapy.

References

Araoz DL: Clinical hypnosis in couple therapy. J Am Soc Psychosom Dent Med 25:58, 1978
Araoz DL: Enriching sex therapy with hypnosis. In Wain H (ed): Clinical Hypnosis in Medicine. Chicago, Yearbook Medical Publishers, 1980
Araoz DL: Negative self-hypnosis. J Cont Psychother 12, 1:45, 1981
Araoz DL: Hypnosis and Sex Therapy. New York, Brunner/Mazel, 1982
Araoz DL, Bleck RT: Hypnosex: Sexual Fulfillment Through Self-Hypnosis. New York, Arbor House, 1982
Barber TX: Training students to use self-suggestions for personal growth. J Suggestive-Accelerative Learning and Teaching 4(2):111, 1979
Barnett EA: Analytical Hypnotherapy: Principles and Practice. Kingston, Ontario, Junica, 1981
Beigel HG: The use of hypnosis in female sexual anesthesia. J Am Soc Psychosom Dent Med 19:4, 1972
Bleck RT, Araoz DL: Sex Therapy and Sex Hypnotherapy. Private report for Dynamic Imagery Associates, Mineola, New York, 1981
Brown JM, Chaves JF: Hypnosis in the treatment of sexual dysfunction. J Sex Marital Ther 6:63, 1980
Castaneda C: Tales of Power. New York, Simon and Schuster, 1974
Cautela JR: Covert conditioning in hypnotherapy. Int J Clin Exp Hypn 23:15, 1975
Cheek D: Gynecological uses of hypnotism. In Le Cron LM (ed): Techniques of Hypnotherapy. New York, Julian Press, 1961
Cheek D, Le Cron L: Clinical Hypnotherapy. New York, Grune & Stratton, 1968
Dittborn J: Hypnotherapy of sexual impotence. Int J Clin Exp Hypn 5:181, 1957
Edelstein MG: Trauma, Trance and Transformation. New York, Brunner/Mazel, 1981
Ellis A: Sex and the Liberated Man. New York, Stuart, 1976
Erickson MH: A study of an experimental neurosis hypnotically induced in a case of ejaculatio precox. Br J Med Psychol 15:34, 1935
Fifth World Congress of Sexology (Abstracts). Tel-Aviv, 1981
Fromm E, Brown DP, Hurt SW, Oberlander JZ, Boxer AM, Pfeiffer G: The phenomena and characteristics of self-hypnosis. Int J Clin Exp Hypn 29:289, 1981
Hogan DR: The effectiveness of sex therapy: A review of the literature. In Lo Piccolo J, Lo Piccolo L (eds): Handbook of Sex Therapy. New York, Plenum Press, 1978
Kaplan HS: The New Sex Therapy. New York, Brunner/Mazel, 1974
Kaplan HS: Disorders of Sexual Desire. New York, Brunner/Mazel, 1979
Kroger WS, Alle JE: Liberating sexually inhibited patients through hypnotic behavioral conditioning. Behav Med 8(9):13, 1981
Kroger WS, Fezler WD: Hypnosis and Behavior Modification: Imagery Conditioning. Philadelphia, JB Lippincott, 1976
Kushel G: Centering: Six Steps Toward Inner Liberation. New York, Times Books, 1979
Leckie FH: Hypnotherapy in gynecological disorders. Int J Clin Exp Hypn 12:121, 1964
Lief HI: Inhibited sexual desire. Medical Aspects of Human Sexuality 11, 7:94, 1977
Masters WH, Johnson VE: Human Sexual Response. Boston, Little, Brown & Co, 1966

Masters WH, Johnson VE: Human Sexual Inadequacy. Boston, Little, Brown & Co, 1970
Meichenbaum D (ed): Cognitive Behavior Therapy. New York, BMA Audio Cassette Publications, 1978
Miller HR: Process Therapy. Paper presented at the Annual Scientific Meeting of the American Society of Clinical Hypnosis, Boston, November, 1981
Schneck JM: Hypnotherapy for vaginismus. Int J Clin Exp Hypn 13:92, 1965
Singer JL, Pope KS: Daydreaming and imagery skills as predisposing capacities for self-hypnosis. Int J Clin Exp Hypn 29:271, 1981
Steger JC: Cognitive behavior strategies in the treatment of sexual problems. In Foreyt JP, Rathjen DP (eds): Cognitive Behavior Therapy. New York, Plenum Press, 1978
Stampfl T, Levis D: Essentials of implosive therapy. J Abnorm Psychol 72:496, 1967
van Pelt SJ: Hypnotism and Its Importance in Medicine. Presented at University College, London, May 1949
Walen SR: Cognitive factors in sexual behavior. J Sex Marital Ther 6:87, 1980
Watkins J: The Therapeutic Self. New York, Human Sciences Press, 1978
Wijesinghe B: A case of frigidity treated by short term hypnotherapy. Int J Clin Exp Hypn 25:63, 1977
Wolpin M: Guided imagining to reduce avoidance behavior. Psychotherapy: Theory, Research and Practice, 6:122, 1969

22 Depression— A Specific Cognitive Pattern

HARRY R. MILLER

SECTION I:

Depression—Research and Clinical Background

Problem

Depression is man's most common serious emotional complaint. Robert Burton's classic book, *The Anatomy of Melancholia* (1642), was three times more popular than Shakespeare's plays (Ford, 1975). In the late 1800s, American physician George M. Beard described melancholia as "the most frequent, most interesting, and most neglected nervous disease of modern times" (Klerman, 1975).

A National Institute of Mental Health report on depressive disorders (Secunda, Katz, Friedman, and Schuyler, 1973) stated that 75% of all psychiatric hospitalizations resulted from depression; in any given year, 15% of all adults have prominent symptoms of depression. Numerous controlled studies indicate that up to 40 percent of depressed people show no improvement following treatment with tricyclic drugs (Beck, 1973); a 50% relapse rate within one year following termination of drug treatment suggests a need for successful psychotherapy (Beck, 1979).

Aaron Beck stated, ". . . there are few psychiatric syndromes whose clinical descriptions are so constant throughout successive eras of history." Classically overt depression is Somatic complaints and signs of all types, Cognitive negativity, Affective dejection, and Behavioral inertia and sensitivity or irritability (SCAB). Depression occurs in all personality types and diagnostic disorder categories.

Current claims are that, ". . . hypnosis is not indicated as a treatment for depression" (*Core Review*, 1981–82). Perhaps an understanding of cognition and hypnosis, as herein presented, will dispel this myth.

Nosology—Classification in DSM-III

Attempts to separate affective illnesses into neurotic and psychotic classifications have been unsuccessful owing to indiscriminant manner of afflication; many inconsistencies exist concerning the concept of neurotic depression (Akiskal, 1978; Klerman, Endicott, and Spitzer, 1979).

The term "depressive neurosis," used in DSM-II, has been dropped in DSM-III. Except to denote associated symptoms of psychosis, higher suicide risk, and greater need for hospitalization and antipsychotic medication, the term "psychotic depression" has no clinical usefulness (Glassman, 1975).

Distinction of endogenous and reactive classifications has become blurred. Endogenous complex symptoms—such as sleep difficulty, anorexia, weight loss, and motor retardation—have been found to have clear causes in many cases (Katz, 1978).

DSM-III divides all affective disorders into two groups: bipolar, consisting of any manic episodes, and unipolar, consisting of only depressive episodes. This broad distinction first described by Leonhard (1962) has been confirmed by the higher frequency of family history of bipolar disorders (Gershon, 1978; Winokur, Behar, Van Valkenburg, Lowry, 1978) with bipolar relatives (Perris, 1966; Angst, 1966; Winokur and Clayton, 1967, 1969). Evidence shows that bipolar disorders are transmitted by X-linked dominant genes (Reich et al, 1969; Winokur and Tanna, 1969), as well as father-to-son transmissions of membrane lithium transport abnormalities in red blood cells (Ostrow et al, 1978).

Unipolar illnesses are three to four times more common than bipolar and more responsive to therapy (Klerman and Barrett, 1975). An absence of genetic marks is found among unipolar depressions.

Animal Research

Experimental Detachment Syndrome of Maternal and
Peer Isolation

Degree of severity of anaclitic depression in infant monkeys, expressed by depressive posturing, self-clasping, rocking, self-chewing, and lack of play reponse, is dependent upon length of separation from mother. Suomi and Harlow (1970,

1971, 1972, 1974) found multiple peer separations resulted in clinging and dependency displays of infantilism, in addition to anaclitic depression.

Movement Restrictions

Suomi and Harlow (1971, 1972) found that normally mothered monkeys also displayed anaclitic depressive phenomena when restricted to vertical cages that isolated them from their peers, even for brief periods. Such social isolation associated with limited movement encouraged rapid onset of permanent and progressive anaclitic depression.

Therapy Implications

Body Contact—Bonding. Suomi and Harlow restored these monkeys to normal behavior by introducing normally reared young females. Less self-directed disturbances resulted; total rehabilitation ensued, demonstrated by increased environmental exploration and peer contact. Although introduction of wire-cloth surrogate mothers resulted in a decreased incidence of self-directed disturbances, the depressed monkeys did not recover completely until full body contact with nonthreatening peers was resumed.

Because of the emergence of infant psychiatry in recent years, DSM-III lists attachment disorders of infancy, ranging from failure to thrive (Bakwin, 1942; Fischoff, 1980; Lozoff, 1962; Call, 1975) to anaclitic depression or withdrawal from mother (Spitz, 1946) into symbiotic dependency upon withdrawal from mother during infancy (Greenacre, 1952; Mahler, 1952). Importance of the physical maternal–infant relationship was termed "bonding" by Klaus and Kennell (1976). Casriel reported phenomenal results of bonding therapy with children and adults (1972, 1973).

Time Does Not Heal. Harlow (1980) found that monkey psychopathologies, like infant detachment syndromes, tend to worsen with time. Realistic estimates reveal that 12% to 60% of disturbances in child psychiatric patients (Petti, 1981; Pearce, 1977) and 62% of behavioral problems in prepubertal children are defined as depressive (Weinberg, 1973). A frequent association between depression and hyperactivity affects 5% to 10% of school-age children (Brumback, 1977). Poznanski (1976) noted a continuing relationship between childhood and adult depression.

Brain Development and Depressive Illlnesses

Freud believed that psychiatric syndromes would yield to knowledge of definite anatomical–physiologic brain patterns. Perhaps depression syndrome will become one of the first clinical states correlated with anatomical psychobiologic functions.

Effects of Body Movement

Harry and Margaret Harlow's experiments with monkey infants and wire-cloth surrogate mothers in 1962 demonstrate the importance of movement in brain development. Monkey infants ignored with wire mesh mothers, clung to the cloth mothers and developed anaclitic depression. However, when cloth mothers were given rocking motions, anaclitic depressive behavior in infants was prevented.

Mason and Berkson (1975) and Eastman and Mason (1975) demonstrated that rocking motion was more important than vision for necessary brain stimulation. Infant monkeys blind at birth and reared with natural mothers did not develop abnormal rocking and isolation practices. Similarly, human infants blind at birth do not develop these abnormal movements.

Dr. Frank Pederson of the National Institute of Child Health and Development observed six variables of development—from social responsiveness to object permanence—and found that holding and moving the infant was the determinant factor in infant mental and social development (Restak, 1976).

Development of Vestibular System and Dendrites

The vestibular system, earliest portion of the brain to mature and responsible for coordination, operates as early as 16 weeks in the fetus. Between the third and fifth months of pregnancy, the fetus forms the majority of brain cells and dendrites. The human brain approaches adult size in number of cells and weight, increases in number of nerve cells, and develops dendritic interconnections until the second year of life.

The vestibular system is important for brain maturation and development. Annelieses F. Korner demonstrated that an oscillated water bed reduced the incidence of sleep apnea (possible crib death) in premature infants to 60%. Continuous irregular movements of the bed stimulated the vestibular centers, thereby stimulating the respiratory centers needed in brain development (Korner, 1975). Stimulation of brain development through the vestibular system during pregnancy is accomplished by continuous movement of the fetus in the amniotic fluid.

Primitive cultures in modern times produce fewer depressive illnesses (Kiev, 1972) and suicides (Benedict and Jacks, 1954), perhaps because infants are carried more by mothers during the early years of brain development than counterparts in industrialized societies (Liedloff, 1977). These infants also learn fewer rationalizations about feelings (Lambo, 1955).

Effects of Environmental Enrichment

Mark Rosenzweig's experiments with rats in 1972 demonstrated that interesting environments produced significant increases in nerve cells, brain enzyme levels, dendritic connections, and brain weight in the area of the cerebral cortex. The brain responds rather than develops according to environmental stimulations. Two hours per day per month of environmental enrichment produces a better developed brain in laboratory animals (Globus and Altman, 1975).

Stimulation of Cerebellum

Dr. James W. Prescott, neuropsychologist of the National Institute of Child Health and Human Development, stated that an organ thought to concern only equilibrium and coordination had a central role in behavior and emotional abnormalities, as seen from the effects of social isolation in animals, infants, and children deprived of movement and environmental stimulation. Dr. Prescott believes that rocking and cuddling stimulate development of the cerebellum, one of the last organs of the brain to crease growth after birth.

Stimulation of Hypothalamus

That stimulation of the posterior hypothalamus produces violence in animals, and stimulation of the anterior hypothalamus caused pleasure in animals, was known as early as 1928 (Restak, 1976). Robert G. Heath, neuropsychiatrist at Tulane, implanted in patients' brains electrodes that stimulated the limbic system (hippocampus and amygdala); these patients avoided self-stimulation, since activity in this area caused experience of fear and rage. Emotion is a unitary process in which either pleasant or unpleasant feelings can be elicited—but not simultaneously (Restak, 1979).

Effects of Maternal–Social Isolation on Emotion Center Development

In 1975, under Dr. Prescott's direction, five isolation-reared monkeys from Harlow's laboratory were sent to Dr. Heath at Tulane. Dr. Heath implanted electrodes into the limbic areas responsible for emotion (hippocampus, amygdala, septal) as well as into the organ responsible for movement (cerebellum). A direct two-way communication between the cerebellum and these emotion centers was discovered, thus establishing the direct causal relationship between maternal–social isolation and a permanent developmental defect in pleasure centers. During brain development in the fetus and first two years of infancy, deprivation of movement and environmental stimulation results in fewer neuronal and dendritic connections in the cerebellum and pleasure centers. The patient later experiences deprivation of pleasure, anaclitic-type symptoms of social isolation, self-directed behavior, and violent behavioral disorders. Deprivation of maternal–environmental stimulation during the first two years of life has a direct bearing upon depressive illnesses.

Therapy Implications

In 1976–77, ten patients–previously violent, self-mutilating, and suicidal—had implantations of cerebellar stimulators. After implantation, their aggressions ceased (Restak, 1976). The commonly prescribed exercise of jogging for depressed patients was done formerly on an empirical basis. Now, the ameliorating effect upon patients is understood because the cerebellum has a direct stimulating effect upon the brain's pleasure system.

Psychosocial Development and Depression

Growth of Myelin Sheaths

Psychosocial development, in relation to depression, closely parallels and derives from stages of brain development. The brain grows fastest at birth, whereas the myelin sheaths are only beginning development. In a 1-month-old infant, the myelin covering has not yet reached spinal cord level.

Growth of myelin sheaths parallels the infant's psychosocial development. Fetal movement in amniotic fluid during the early development of the vestibular apparatus stimulates the areas of cerebral cortex associated with movement; those concerning regulation of speech have not yet developed significantly. Continued movement and sensory environmental stimulation ameliorates further development after birth.

The Four Maturation Stages of Piaget

Earlier maturation of motor and sensory cortexes closely parallels psychosocial behavior in children, as described in four stages by Piaget (1959, 1970): first, sensory-motor movement, birth to age 2; second, preconceptual representation symbolic thinking, ages 2 to 5; third (and somewhat overlapping), operational thinking of relationships between objects, ages 4 to 8; and fourth, formal operations, with development of completely abstract concepts, age 11 onward.

Each developmental stage, as described by Piaget (Rose, 1976), is correlated with the growth of myelin sheaths in the axons. Formal operations handling concepts cannot occur until myelination develops after age 11, particularly in the reticular formation of the brain, which deals with the pain and pleasure centers. The association areas of the cerebral cortex continue myelination into old age.

Whether use of nerve cells in particular areas signals onset of myelination, or whether myelination precedes use of these particular axons, is not yet known.

However, intellectual stages of development are correlated simultaneously with the physical and biochemical development of these associated areas of the brain (Rose, 1976; Marshall, 1968; Altman and Das, 1964).

Therapy Implications

The importance of neurological and psychosocial development can be appreciated when attempting therapy with depressives. The root of a patient's depressive syndrome may be developmental deficiency acquired in infancy, resulting in deficient cerebellar limbic system development or a deficiency in myelination in later childhood, preventing positive pleasure affects or intellectual performance of formal abstract operations.

Psychotherapy to relieve depression accomplishes very little if the patient's neurological center for experiencing positive feelings is deficient, or if the patient cannot handle abstract concepts competently. This explains the large number of depressed patients who respond negatively to tricyclic antidepressants and only slightly to psychotherapy.

Neurophysiology of Depression

Research indicates that a normal person may develop depression by establishing certain neurological pathways owing to conscious mental focus. Understanding psychophysiology provides insight into particular modes of therapy that alleviate depression and explains why some patients require more psychotherapy than others.

Imagery of Body Movements

EEG studies done by Gary Schwartz (1976) indicate that imagining the performance of an act elicits brainwaves identical to those produced by actually performing the act. E. Roy John of the Department of Neurology of Bellevue Hospital in New York used biofeedback techniques in imagery of contractured limb EMG patterns to restore 75% of cases of paralyzed limbs due to upper motor neuron lesions. Two thirds of these recoveries continued outside of the laboratory (Restak, 1976).

Imagery of Emotional Stress

Schwartz demonstrated by group experiments that mental imagery involving different emotional states produced different physical responses while practicing the same physical activity. Groups practicing angry imagery while exercising had very high sustained heart rates and blood pressures, whereas the relaxed imagery group maintained vital signs within normal limits.

Cognitive Habits

In 1976–77, Schwartz demonstrated that emotionally laden thinking results in peripheral organ electrical patterns specific for that emotion. He found this true for happy, sad, or angry imagery, as well as depressive states. Depressives usually generate sad and angry patterns; their happy imagery muscle patterns are markedly decreased.

Schwartz found conscious cognitive habits controlled peripheral nerve-ending patterns in a specific manner, causing symptoms and physiologic findings associated with that cognitive mode, thus explaining motor retardation and other symptomatology of depression. Therapy can evoke changes by encouraging patients to access different cognitive emotions or syntax.

Hemispheric Processing

Conscious emotional focusing is processed primarily in the right hemisphere; factual questions are processed in the left hemisphere (Galin, 1976). Numerous studies have confirmed the emotional and factual logic dichotomy between the hemispheres (Carter, et al, 1982).

When asked factual questions, most peoples' eyes turn to the right, indicating a left hemisphere activation; when asked emotionally loaded questions, most peoples' eyes turn to the left, indicating a right hemisphere activation. Rubin and Racquel Gur (1975) discovered that people who predominantly moved their eyes to the left (right hemisphere-dominant type) had an increased incidence of somatic illnesses. Studies indicate the possibility that the right hemisphere plays a predominant role in unconscious processes (Galin, 1976).

These findings correlate well with the clinical findings of the Spiegels, who stated that the Dionysian hypnotizability type is a person predominantly accessing affect, tending to form depressive illnesses when decompensating. His depressive episodes are characterized by less ability to focus attention consciously; therefore, he is less hypnotizable (Spiegel, 1978). The Spiegels observed that depressed patients cannot consciously focus cognitively; their minds appear to go into more unconscious modes of accessing. They focus on affective modes (right hemisphere) of structuring reality.

Therapy Implications

Psychobiologists concur that all mental activities cause brain changes; that is, imagery and emotions not only affect muscles and organs peripherally, but also the brain. Constant repeated cognitive focus on an emotion (or lack of emotion) could result in brain pattern changes, which may be consistent and automatic, despite any type of psychotherapy. With early establishment of emotional changes in brain and peripheral organ patterns, psychotherapy may be effective. If these are prolonged, definite neurochemical patterns are created within the brain, which can be changed only by the most intense focusing on different thinking patterns or neurochemical changes. This psychophysiology of imagery (hypnosis) has become the hallmark of effective modern psychotherapy.

Imagery and Conditioning. J. B. Watson established tenets of behaviorism by stating that mentalistic concepts have no place in the study of psychology (1919). B. F. Skinner supplied specific means of applying behaviorism by operant conditioning (1953). Wolpe (1958) found that behaviorism could be applied easily to the patient's environment from the physician's office. He introduced the use of imagery (cognitive mediation) to therapy with systematic desensitization, thus rendering behaviorism a practical therapeutic tool.

The introduction of cognitive concepts as mediating factors in behavioral therapy led to the coining of the term "cognitive behavioral therapy." Faulty behavior has been progressively attributed to cognitive factors (Lazarus, 1968; Meichenbaum, 1974; Mahoney, 1974; Goldfried and Davison, 1976).

Overt vs. Covert Conditioning. Cautela (1972, 1977) applied the term "covert conditioning" to imagery procedures manipulating the consequence of behavior, and therefore the physiological and psychological responses. Research demonstrates that no difference exists between overt and covert behaviors; covert (imagined) and overt psychological events obey the same laws (Cautela and McCullough, 1978). The assumption that imagery behavior causes a desired increase or decrease in overt or covert behavior in a predictable manner has been confirmed by 50 years of accumulated data (Cautela and McCullough, 1978).

Research has demonstrated the effectiveness of imaginal (covert) conditioning, as well as proved that it neurologically, peripherally, and sensorily produces the same effects as overt conditioning. The probability of imagined affect or behavior following an incidence of imagined context is great. However, cognitive behavioral therapists emphasize that actual behavioral practice is essential for pairing the imaginal response to the patient's context. Extensive covert conditioning procedures (hypnosis) contributed by Cautela include: covert sensitization (1966, 1967), covert reinforcement (1970a), covert extinction (1971a), covert negative reinforcement (1970b); covert modeling (1971b), and covert response (1976a).

Eight Factors of Successful Hypnosis With Depressives.

1. PARTICIPATION. An increase of patient participation in an imagery scene yields an increase in effect upon behavior (Kozak and Lang, 1976; Lang, 1977).

The scene uses the patient's personal experience and syntax. During imagery, the patient imagines feeling and experiencing the scene as though it is happening.

2. RELAXATION. Imagery is enhanced with any relaxation (Jacobson, 1938; Cautela and Grodin, 1977). A reclining position is more conducive to freedom, spontaneity, free association, and higher vividness of imagery than sitting up (Pope, 1977; Kroth, 1970; Morgan and Bakan, 1965; Berdach and Bakan, 1967; Segal and Glicksman, 1967; Izard, 1971; Tomkins, 1962, 1963; Singer, 1966).

3. CONTROL. The patient must control the imagery scene, outcomes, and behaviors (Richardson, 1969), or therapy will not be effective. Imagery must be vivid, first person, and controlled by the patient, who thus determines the desired behavior and response in the scene. Despite the patient's ability to produce vivid imagery, he must also experience control, or therapy will not be effective because negative or maladaptive thinking will override the scene. Perhaps this is why Kazdin (1977) found that vividness of imagery did not always correlate with behavioral change.

4. MODELING. The patient's actual participation in modeling or mimicking his own ideal is necessary. Bandura (1976) produces a powerful argument that most of human learning is done by observing elders and peers in a modeling role and then mimicking them. His emphasis of the importance of self-efficacy, feeling of accomplishment, and effectiveness in producing permanent behavior changes is accomplished by the patient's establishing his own ideal as his model, then mimicking this ideal in behavior and imagery (Bandura, 1976, 1977a, 1977b.

Beliefs and expectations about reactions and behaviors are paramount in mediating processes of all operant conditioning. Imaginal modeling of self-efficacy ideal is a powerful self-reinforcement, which the therapist can pair in the patient's life processes (Bandura, 1976, 1977a, 1977b). Planned activities and social encounters are mandatory for reinforcement in the depressive's life (Beck, 1979).

Lack of self-efficacy and thinking and affect are strongly related to the helplessness of depression (Beck, 1967; Seligman, 1975; Starker and Singer, 1975; Rizley, 1976). The therapist's ability to structure the patient's imagery exercises to enable him to achieve the desired outcomes by imagery of self-efficacy and everyday experience is of extreme importance.

5. REALITY DIRECTED. The patient chooses and controls the imagery scene, using his model. Directed rather than free imagery gives better results in treating depressives. Schultz (1978) found that free imagery involving a context of the patient's casual choosing gave poor results. Although directed to positive wishes and ideal self-efficacy fantasy, the imagery was repeatedly interrupted by negative broodings and adverse thoughts about present life situations.

Schultz found that task-directed imagery guided the patient away from negative thoughts and syntax. He also found that such directed imagery must include social or interpersonal relationships to produce the lowest level of depression. Schultz developed four types of imagery, in order of descending success. Aggressive imagery gave the highest result; socially gratifying, second; positive, third; and free, the lowest results in lowering levels of depression. Schultz's work is impressive but disheartening, since elevated mood level after directed imagery lasted less than one hour.

6. BEHAVIOR. Imagery involving the patient's control and centered around the patient's ideal modeling role must be mimicked continuously in thinking and behavior in interpersonal relationships. The short duration of imagery practice is effective only on the basis of distractive effect from the depressive's continuous negative syntax (Lazarus, 1968; Feshbach, 1955, 1967; Beck, 1967).

These ideas correlate with the Spiegel's discovery of distractive effects noted in the hypnotic profiles of depressive patients, and the relative difficulty in using hypnosis with depressives (Spiegel, 1978). The short interval of help after time-limited exercises is explained by observations of Meichenbaum and Turk (1976). They found that patients capable of imagining alternative behavior maintain maladaptive syntax, which returns them to former maladaptive behavior or affect. For this reason, Meichenbaum (1974) designed stress inoculation methods to change the patient's syntax, self-statements, and imageries.

7. FOCUS OF SYNTAX ON FACTS, NOT AFFECT. Despite successful effects of imagery in all aspects of psychology, physiology, and behavior in depression, the thinking style of the patient recalls past negative syntax and affects (Araoz, 1981). Imagery covert conditioning (hypnosis) in depression therapy is effective only as associated with changing the patient's cognitive syntactic style.

Feshbach and Beck (1967) theorized circular feedback of negative thoughts and affect into a loop circuit. This theory of mutual reinforcement of syntax and affect in a depressive cycle is supported by studies in college students (Traynor, 1974), high school students (Rychlak, 1973), depressed male psychiatric patients (Schultz, 1976), and general male psychiatric patients (Starker and Singer, 1975).

8. AVOIDING CIRCULAR FEEDBACK MECHANISM. Klinger (1975) believes that contents of fear and guilt prevalent among severely depressed patients caused an acceleration in conscious focusing within the feedback loop of relevant concerns. Klinger theorizes that rehearsing imaginal themes and stories concerning negative affect and cognition in the depressive's attempt toward mastery only tends to make imagery an inner reality within the patient's mind, nervous system, and behavior. This correlates with Meichenbaum's cognitive rehearsal theories (1975, 1977) concerning attempts for mastery in self-control, as well as Schwartz's research (1977) indicating par-

ticipated imagery in the nervous system neurochemically, as if the imagery had actually happened.

Although depressive patients have more undesirable recent events in their lives (Schultz, 1976; Paykel, 1969), Schultz found severity of depression is only slightly correlated with these events. This suggests that a circular feedback process between syntax and affect may be initiated by undesirable environmental cues, while degree of depression may be correlated to previous past cues related to fear or guilt, as suggested by Klinger (1975), and to infant social deprivation and development syndromes, as previously described.

To be most effective in depressed patients, hypnosis must change the patient's cognitive focus. Therefore, a presentation of the psychology and psychiatry of cognition is now necessary.

Depressive Cognition in Psychiatry and Psychology

Freud—A Cognitive Legacy

Early Theory. Early psychiatry followed the stimulant-repression continuum. Medical literature, unifying in the 1800s, was filled with massive confusion of inhibitor-melancholia and the counterpart manias. In 1899, *Epistomology of All Psychopathology,* by Kraeplin, divided all melancholias into two groups. Within this environment, Freudian psychoanalytic theory purported a stimulant (id) repressant (ego) transformation model of mental disease.

Freud originally viewed all emotions as symptoms of lack of ego (repressant) ability against id instinctual drives. His early theory (1895) on the cause of conversion reactions stated that psychic energy was converted into a physical symptom of hysterical nature rather than being discharged. Freud also believed that anxiety was a psychological manifestation of undischarged sexual libido.

In 1923, Freud formulated a theory designating anxiety as the initiator of all defense processes. He continued to maintain his emphasis on ego defense repression of activated id instincts as the central theoretical structure of psychopathology (Mendelson, 1974). Freud believed that depression was an introjection of instinctual hostilities determined by libidinal fixation in the late oral or early anal phases of development.

Depression as Hostility. Research has established complete independence between hostility and depression. Depression as hostility-turned-against itself is not considered necessary or primary in therapy schools today.

Modern studies support the hypothesis that depression is an affective state subserving an ego-adaptive function (Gershon, et al, 1968; Klerman and Gershon,

1970; Weissman et al, 1971). The subconscious mind is thought of as man's best friend rather than a repository of evil and destructive drives of id and superego.

Cognition vs. Affect. Modern cognitive theory is greatly influenced by pervasive Freudian libido theory attributing affect (apprehension, emotion, feelings) as direct expression of instinctual energy alone; and considering cognition only a matter of comprehension and syntactic linear linguistic experience. Although "cognition" is summarized as including *all* processes concerning information processing and problem-solving (Neisser, 1967; Mahoney, 1974; D'Zurilla and Goldreid, 1971), it involves comprehension or syntactic logical linguistic experience and opposes affect.

According to Freud, cognition exists as an either-or relationship to affect (Rappaport, 1951), implying that cognition (syntactical thinking) is an aspect of ego servicing defensive functions repressing the id drives or affect. Emotion is not considered a conscious cognition. When a person focuses attention on emotion, or automatically accesses emotions, he is not "thinking"—he is "feeling." This Freudian influence pervades modern cognitive theories. Unfortunately, Freud's signal theories of primary and secondary process thinking were overshadowed by his emphasis on the libido stimulus-repressant continuum.

Modern Cognition Theory of Depression

A review of research and writings on cognitive assessment and therapy of depression is not necessary. Refer to the fine review works of editors and authors Merluzzi, Glass, and Genest (1981), Shaw and Dobson (1981), Foreyt and Rathjen (1978), Meichenbaum (1977), Rush (1982), Beck (1979), and Clarkin and Glazer (1981).

Literature about depression may be summarized by saying that a depressive has negative affect and negative syntax concerning self. Modern cognitive therapy and research indicates that dealing with depression is dealing with cognition.

A Typology of Thinking Errors. Beck (1979) proposes a typology of thinking errors found in depression, stating that depressives have ideosyncratic ways of rationalizing information. A summary of these follows:

1. Arbitrary inference—drawing conclusions without evidence.
2. Selective abstraction (absolutistic and judgmental)—focusing on a single detail taken out of context and conceptualizing the entire experience, ignoring other details of the situation
3. Over-generalization (invariant and global)—drawing a general conclusion on the basis of a single incident
4. Magnification and minimization (characterizations and discounts)—evaluating a situation or its significance by either means

Information processing is done in syntactic cognition, since "thinking" is held as distinct from emotions. References to the depressive's cognition are referred to in terms of thinking, as the patient forming negative attitudes or concepts about himself (schemas). Beck further states that the patient's beliefs in these negative concepts persist despite factual contradictory evidence.

In literature about cognitions, the patient's thinking is generally referred to in a syntactical sense, with the belief that the emotional tone of the depressed patient follows syntactic conceptions or beliefs made in his mind according to the ABC process of Albert Ellis (1957, 1962, 1977).

ABC Process Sequence. Cognitive therapists concur that symptom manifestation results from perception of the situation, requiring certain emotional or behavioral displays based upon the patient's peculiar beliefs and rationalizations (content). This follows Ellis' ABC process sequence:

A = Activating situations, followed by
B = Beliefs, which automatically trigger emotions as a
C = Consequence.

Inappropriate affect arises because the patient first develops irrational beliefs and self-thinking. Therapy involves changing the patient's syntax or "thinking" in terms of beliefs and self-talk. This usual typology of thinking errors described by Beck as being ideosyncratic of depression is based on Freudian cognitive theory implication that affect is not thinking.

Derivation of this theory of human affect and behavior is based upon observation of admittedly maladaptive symptom manifestations. In other words, by observing a sick process, therapists conclude that this is the way human emotions and behaviors are normally derived; therefore, to establish normality, they must work within the guidelines of this sick ABC process. This is much like the early Freudian preoccupation stating that since all neurotics seem to have sexual problems, the origin of neurosis must be sexual. What is actually seen in patients is a "sick" process affecting all content.

There is little psychological or psychiatric research directed to defining a healthy process. All statements concern only content examinations within this sick ABC process paradigm. Attention must be directed first to the content of the belief systems; then, emotions and subsequent behavior will change, since patients operate in this ABC process.

Neo-Freudian Cognitive Theory of Depression

Neo-Freudian therapists, such as Horney (1950), Sullivan (1953, 1956), and Fromm (1941), placed great emphasis on cognition as it relates to the self-concept of a self-system (Sullivan, 1953). The adaptational psychodynamic school of Columbia headed by Kardiner (1959), the structure of the self by Kohut (1971, 1977), and the object relations theories demonstrate the interest in the cognitions of self-experiences in clinical psychiatry.

In addition to emphasizing self-cognition as the origin of psychopathology, the neo-Freudians contribute implicit understanding of cognition, which modern cognitive therapists have not adopted.

Apart from personality drive theory, neo-Freudian and cognitive schools generally agree with Freudian concepts. However, in contrast to Freudian and modern cognitive therapy, neo-Freudian literature explicitly or implicitly views the self-consciousness as a cognitive experience of *either* emotional affective *or* syntactic linguistic components—not just Freudian or modern cognitive syntactic components. The author adopts the term "bicameral cognition" (two-sided brain) from Julian Jaynes (1976) for this either-or cognition of affect or syntax.

Bicameral Cognition. The goal of well-formed neo-Freudian therapy is achieved in "cognitive repair" (Barnett) of two aspects of cognition—syntax (left hemisphere) and affect (right hemisphere). Joseph Barnett is credited for his work and writings about this either-or aspect of cognition (Barnett, 1966, 1968, 1979). Recognition of bicameral cognition is critical to understanding successful hypnotic treatment of depression and neuroses, as well as to understanding observations of depression and all other neurotic processes.

Understanding bicameral cognition involving *either* syntactical aspects, *or* accessing conscious affect, provides insight into the origin of maladaptive manifestations and also explains the different cognitive styles and personalities. Such understanding implies that when patients are consciously accessing cognitive affect, their behavior arises from cognitive affect rather than being determined by cognitive syntax (*i.e.,* beliefs or self-talk). Further, healthy adaptive processing is a situation-cognitive fact syntax focus-behavior sequence.

Regarding conscious cognitions as *either* syntax *or* affect in this manner indicates that the patient's entire maladaptive processing of all conscious thinking can be pervasively changed in all aspects of conscious focus from cognitive affect to cognitive syntax on facts.

The goal of neo-Freudian therapy is optimal cognitive awareness (affectively and syntactically) with appropriate spontaneity and intimacy in relating to external reality of sensorily perceived facts (Berne, 1976). Normality may be defined as the extent of a person's behavior in relationship to reality, or cognitive syntactic facts. Conversely, maladaption would be those behaviors dictated by cognitive affect or syntax not in relationship to reality.

Normal—Syntactic Thinking on Reality. Humans have the cognitive ability consciously to focus on facts syntactically *or* on affect—but not simultaneously.

Figure 22-1 shows that everyone relates to the facts–affect ratio regarding cognitive focus. The degree of maladaptive behavior is determined by the percentage of time behavior is in relationship to facts (reality), as evaluated sensorily by the general public, as opposed to momentary affect.

People relate to facts cognitively by syntactic thinking; they relate to reality on interpersonal communication only by syntax. Affective thinking (focusing consciously on affect) cannot be communicated linguistically except by syntactic methods.

Maladaptive symptoms and behavior are derived from predominance of the sick ABC process of situation–affect–behavior. The extent of maladaptive behavior and symptoms or personality manifestations is the extent of percentage of daily use of this process in determining opinions, beliefs, and behaviors. Because there may be infinite variety of emotions and feelings from which the patient's behaviors and defensive rationalizations derived, a multiplicity of infinite symptoms and variations in content result. Conversely, normal processing, involving syntactic cognition concerning the facts of any situation referred to the person's ideal preferential judgment, results in the greatest possible agreement and most effective behavior.

Fantasies from yesterday's experiences, feelings have no relationship to present-day factual occurrences, except in the sick ABC process. These feelings explain the patient's sick behavior within this sick process.

A review of imagery in depression illustrating the most durative and effective therapy involves continued and pervasive idealized cognitive syntax on facts, rather than affect. Beck's modern cognitive therapy is effective to the extent that it inadvertently causes syntactical thinking according to facts by peer and therapist coercion and approval. The patient's mind is syntactically directed away from cognitive affect, and guided by ideal self-concepts dealing with facts. The patient cannot think syntactically and affectively simultaneously.

Cognitive Errors Common to Neuroses. Therapists who treat depressives find Beck's enumeration of depressive characteristic syntactic thinking accurate. However, consideration of conscious "cognition" as *either* syntactic *or* affective at any one time reveals that most psychopathologies exhibit the same cognitive processing stated by Beck as ideosyncratic of depressives.

Anxious or phobic patients commit the same cognitive errors in reference to affect. These patients act with arbitrary inference according to affect at the

100%   0

Facts   75%   50%   25%   Affect

$\frac{Fact}{Affect}$ = Behavior ratio

Fig. 22-1. The facts-affect ratio of cognitive focus

time. They focus upon particular affects out of context, conceptualizing their entire experience out of that affect by overgeneralizing according to this single affect. They magnify and minimize according to their particular affective focus. When asked what his problem is, an anxious patient will say that he is just extremely anxious, for some unknown reason. He does not explain syntactically, nor can he justify his symptoms. Therefore, his therapist may say this patient has "free-floating" anxiety.

In the depressive syndrome, patients use syntax to rationalize (admit) or repress affect, readily telling the therapist their thoughts and feelings. The therapist may say, "Well . . . you have some thinking errors." With the depressed patient's focus on syntax, he can explain this to the therapist, but the anxious patient cannot explain his conscious focus on affect. He would have to start thinking syntactically in order to do so.

FACTORS DETERMINED BY PREDOMINANT COGNITIVE TYPE (FOCUS)

1. *Hypnotizability.* The inability of the Spiegels' Dionysian hypnotic types who display emotional decompensation to focus syntactically on suggestions results from cognitive focus on affect. When these same Dionysians become more syntactically oriented, they often become excellent hypnotic subjects because they have increased ability to consciously focus subjectively (affectively). This is hypnosis—subjective thinking *directed* by syntactic orientation in the consciousness of the subject.

When the patient is schizophrenic or has neurotic emotional decompensation because of focusing affectively, he is unable to originate the syntactic direction of his mind to establish desired subjective thinking. These patients are unable to accomplish hypnosis or hypnotic thinking.

The schizophrenic, passive–aggressive, or obsessive–compulsive who is fixed upon syntactic cognition only has difficulty in hypnotic thinking because he cannot allow himself to accomplish subjective or affective cognitions. His defensive syntactic cognition focus will not allow this.

2. *Basic Complaints.* Understanding cognition results in an understanding of symptom manifestations and characteristic patient statements. These patients feel unable to control their lives, their symptoms, or themselves. They do not know how to reverse this feeling. Patients access or focus conscious examination upon internal affect or emotions caused by a given situation; behavior depends upon how they endeavor to change, modify, or enhance internal affect. They have, in essence, relinquished self-control. In this process, the situation always has control, dictating emotions, while the patients passively await evaluation of the given emotion to determine behavior.

3. *Maladaptive Feelings.* Patients understand that their affective or syntactic cognitions are not in relationship to reality; but they relate to reality by affective cognitions, and they sense that affective cognitions are an unrealistic monitor

of reality. Patients say that they think that they may be acceptable as human beings, but that they want to "know" or "feel" acceptable. Syntactic cognitions relating to facts are not as important or compelling to them as their cognitive focus on affect. Or, patients may cognitively focus on defensive syntax, becoming cognitively unaware of the primary negative self-affect of all psychopathology.

4. *Therapy Failure or Recurrence.* After one therapist rids a patient of one symptom, another symptom may arise, or the same symptom may recur. The patient goes from one hapless therapist to another, asking, "Doctor . . . help me change my feelings . . . then I will be able to behave differently." Or, said another way, "Doctor . . . get into my sick process with me . . . and I will make you a failure, too."

Patients who are more well-adapted and self-assured feel that they are in control because they use the process of situation-syntactic cognition of fact analysis-behavior. They sense that they are in control, since their behavior is effective, because of personal judgmental ideal fact analysis.

5. *Lack of Standards.* Most patients have developed a way of processing information that does not allow injection of ideal concepts in relation to reality (facts). Behavior is totally related to passively received affect determined by current situations. Amazingly, patients often do not realize this until confronted.

Therapy by Restoring Syntactic Focus on Facts. Beck, whose *Cognitive Therapy of Depression* (1979) has been the hallmark of modern therapy, insists that patients behaviorally obey the therapist's directions. This action modifies the patient's affect by changing his cognitive focus, as described under the sections involving brain and nervous system development and physiology. Change in affect continues to the extent of conformation by the patient's syntactic thinking, thereby continuing to further and maintain the change.

A sustained change will be accomplished only by altering the patient's persistent, overweening syntactical focus on affect. If left unchanged, this focus on affect results in continuance of symptoms, or relapse. Beck uses disputation about content, which inadvertently directs the patient's behavior according to fact analysis syntax. The number of decisions made according to the new "facts-do" process determines the amount of help the patient receives.

Beck's clinical characterization of depressive illness does not explain the large number of depressives seen in several personality types and pain-prone patients. These patients are diagnosed depressives by psychological testing; however, they neither admit to depression, nor exhibit the characteristic negative affect and self-talk Beck describes. As McLean (1981) states, ". . . thus far, no theory has accounted for the impressive amount of case variation in regard to etiology." How can the therapist recognize these patients without time-consuming testing? Covert depressives are explained according to type of cognitive focus—either syntax or affect. Recognition of these patients is discussed in the next section, Cognitive Types.

1. *Cognitive Focus Need Always Be Considered.* Transferences and resistances to hypnosis (or any therapy) are manifestations of the patient's particular personality derived from and associated with his cognitive focus (Barnett, 1979). Master therapists, such as the late Milton H. Erickson, often base and detail approaches in therapy to particular patients after talking with them for only a few minutes by discerning personality types, cognition styles, and patient reactions. Most therapy is successful only as it is momentarily created according to context and the patient's personality, rather than a demand by the therapist that the patient meet ritualistic requirements.

2. *Personality Types According to Cognitive Predominance.* In Table 22-1, most of the clinical syndromes or personality types are divided according to cognitive focus, with detailed explanations. Clinical syndromes are divided into three large groups, determined by patients who tend to focus consciously on affect and patients who tend to focus consciously on syntax. Since depression occurs among all personality types, an understanding of the cognitions of each personality type is essential to effect proper "cognitive repair."

    a. *Affective Types.* Since syntax or linguistic analogic forms are the means of communication, all psychotherapy (admitted even by Wolpe) is

Table 22-1. Cognitive types of psychopathologies

Personality or Clinical Syndromes	Symptoms Appear As:	Cognitive Type or Focus	Therapy by Restructuring of:
Anxiety Hysteria Phobias Dependency Most sexual Psychosomatics Pain-prone patients Impulse disorders	Nonreality affect	Nonreality *affect* (active, explosive types—defense against negative affect)	*Syntactical* cognition (using patient's focus on affect)
Antisocial personality	Nonreality behavior	Nonreality *behavior* (defense against negative effect and negative syntax)	*Affect* and *syntax* (using patient's focus on behavior)
Obsessive/ compulsive Paranoid Passive/aggressive Depressive syndrome	Nonreality syntax	*Nonreality syntax* (passive, implosive types—defense against negative affect)	*Affective* cognition (using patient's focus on syntax)

necessarily somewhat syntactic by nature. A therapist cannot walk mutely into a room, manipulate a patient into a different feeling or behavior, and mutely walk out of the room without realizing that a syntactic restructuring in the patient's thinking is also being accomplished. This is done either by the patient's syntactic thinking about the environment that the therapist has manipulated, or by direct reassurance from the therapist. In illustration, while a patient afraid of heights is standing upon a balcony, he must tell himself syntactically that this is not so bad . . . that he is feeling better because . . . the affect is not so bad, and so forth. This is self-hypnosis—affect consciously accessed by syntactic direction.

(1) *Syntactic Restructuring.* As this division of all clinical syndromes into cognitive types illustrates, clinical syndromes of anxiety, hysteria, phobias, dependency reactions, sexual, psychosomatic, and pain-prones characterized by display of affective behavior are relieved by restructuring syntactic conditions. This group is helped most effectively by behavioral modification, and all forms of insight therapy. The root cause of affective negative self-cognition or negative self-hypnosis (Araoz, 1981) is corrected by restructuring syntactic thinking, whether by hypnotic age regression, by hypnotic reframing, or by classical insight, cognitive, or behavioral therapies.

Therapy is most effective and durative in depressives when their style is affective cognition. When syntactic restructuring (accepting appropriate present-time reality syntax instead of past affect) is accomplished by hypnosis, its effectiveness will continue as long as the patient continues to think syntactically according to present reality.

Symptoms return because the patient returns to irrational "nonreality" affective focus, demonstrating the need to practice syntactical fact-to-behavior sequencing.

(2) *Pain-Prone Patients.* Therapy becomes difficult if the patient can justify the affect. This is why the pain-prone patient is difficult to treat; he insists upon focusing on affective cognitions, saying, ". . . after all, don't I have a reason to complain with all this pain?" His syntactic cognitions seem justifiable in his syntax of reality; the therapist dares not gainsay because this patient will not understand. The therapist must bargain with him by saying that if the patient cooperates and uses his mind as instructed, he may experience less pain. If he would think syntactically, ". . . the sensation I have is interesting . . . educational . . . comfortable . . . acceptable . . ." he would achieve relief. But this he cannot comprehend affectively.

Projection tests (consisting of sentence completion, thematic apperception, and Rorschach) demonstrate that 83% of pain-prone patients have definite depression (Blumer, 1981). However, the MMPI generally shows that these patients do not have overt depression (Pilling, et al, 1967; Castelnuovo-

Tedesco and Krout, 1970). The patient can successfully rationalize that, "I have pain . . . I have a reason to complain." Appropriately, the pain-prone disorder has been categorized as a "depression spectrum disease" by Winokur (1979). I believe that the depression syndrome is characterized by using syntax to rationalize or obfuscate affect.

(3) *Rationalization of Affect.* The overt depressive cannot successfully rationalize his affect. Unlike the pain patient, the depressive syntactically realizes that his negative affect is not in relationship to reality. Therefore, the therapist has a foothold, because the patient syntactically "knows" that his affect is not appropriate to reality. The pain patient (not conscious of depression) syntactically "knows" that his pain is appropriate to reality, since other people complain of pain.

Cognitive therapists believe that the depressed patient has inappropriate thinking (meaning specifically syntax), and they dare not tell pain patients that they have inappropriate cognitions or thinking. Exclusively fussing about the patient's conscious syntax, cognitive therapists consider affect to be a subsequent secondary phenomenon—not just a second form of or choice of conscious accessing. Thereby, the cognitive therapist finds himself in a double-bind.

(4) *Suicidal Depressives.* Clinical syndromes characterized by cognitive affect, such as anxieties, hysterias, phobias, and dependencies, present the most dramatic forms of depression, with loud crying, extreme withdrawal reactions, and florid expression of all types of affect. Many psychotherapists believe that, because of cultural conditioning, most American men tend to be among the syntactic cognitive types of obsessive–compulsive or passive–aggressive, and that most American women tend to be of the affective types. This explains the female-to-male ratio of two-to-one of the most common clinical expressions of depression, and the three times more common suicidal attempts of women, as compared to men. However, men are three times more successful at suicide than women (for all ages) because they are syntactically (logically–analogically) thinking about carrying out their conscious focus on suicide. Men typically negotiate syntactically about the negative affect, while women typically have no syntactic style of negotiating with the negative affect—they express only their inability to handle the affect by expressing the affect.

b. *Syntactic Types.* Personality types characterized by syntax do poorly with classical insight therapy, whether by hypnotic regression, disputation, free association, or any therapy directed to provide patient insight into the affective root cause. Proponents of classical and later therapies generally believe that negative affect (whether id or self-concept feelings) is the cause.

(1) *Effects of Insight Therapy.* Insight initially directed toward the root cause (feelings) is met with total resistance, failure, and sometimes the disaster

of patient-turning-against-therapist. The patient is unable to think affectively because defensive cognitions are focused on syntactic thinking. Freudian therapists were unsuccessful in attempts to make patients "feel" because their syntactic cognitive focus was to avoid and obfuscate painful affective conditions. Patients were placed in therapeutic binds, being pushed to do what they were incapable of doing. Their personality defense against unpleasant past affect was to use defensive syntax cognitions.

(2) *Effects of Behavior Therapy.* Behavior therapy also works least with syntax cognitive types because, regardless of behavioral circumstance manipulation, the patient relates cognitively according to his defensive nonreality syntax. Passive–aggressives or obsessive–compulsives always have logical (to them) reasons for their behaviors. Continuance of symptoms is a result of continued defensive syntactic thinking.

Therapy with these personality types succeeds only when therapist convinces the patient that his syntactical thinking (which the patient believes is rational) is irrational and inappropriate because

It is guided by affective references that the patient would certainly eschew. The patient is not taking all of the facts into consideration (as he believes).

This approach enlists the patient's cooperation to use much valued syntactical thinking to help himself behave more realistically. Unless a fact focus syntactic process is practiced, no amount of insight will effect change.

3. *Overt Depressive Syndrome.* Since depression is syntax used to rationalize or obfuscate affect, all syntactic types would be expected to be depressed. Barnett noted that these personality types invariably have some degree of covert depression when they present for symptoms other than depression (Barnett, 1979).

The patient with overt depressive syndrome is an interesting exception among those who focus on syntax. The depressive's syntactic negative self-talk openly declares and confesses (rather than obfuscates) negative affect. Unlike other syntactic types, the depressed patient confesses syntactically that affect is not appropriate and is therefore rejectable. Directed cognitive therapy immediately "makes sense" to the syntactic patient with overt depression, because his syntax does not successfully rationalize or obfuscate the affect.

c. *Antisocial Personalities.* The therapy most effective with antisocial personalities does not involve syntactical or affective cognitive orientation, but rather a focus on behavior. Antisocial personalities focus conscious orientation more on behavior than on thinking or affect; this explains why usual syntactic therapy is a devastating failure with most of these patients. Narcissistic personalities most nearly fit into this cognitive orientation in regard to self-considerations.

Antisocials cannot allow conscious relating either to syntactical factual cognition or to affective cognitions. Such a patient focuses upon what *he* is going to do, or what others are going to do (or have done) to *him.* He will usually not focus on concepts syntactically, or on facts affectively. He does little fact analysis in relation to his behavior, and tries not to access affect; he has learned to ease negative self-affect by focusing on behavior. Behavioral outcomes provide the most satisfaction for originally negative self-affect.

Very few overt depressive patients are antisocial personalities. Depression is syntax that rationalizes or obfuscates affect. Teaching the process of situation-fact analysis-do to antisocials will be accepted if orientated around topics of behavior to provide self-help. To disparage the antisocial's syntax or affect yields results as disastrous as talking to a severe obsessive-compulsive about feelings, or to a narcissistic about imperfect motives.

SECTION II:
Hypnotherapy of Depression

Research and Clinical Background

The research and clinical background detailed in Section I provide substantial understanding of aspects of the therapy of depression. These are

1. *Time.* Research illustrates that passage of time worsens rather than alleviates symptoms.
2. *Peer Contact.* Coupled with physical and emotional bonding, peer contact produces total developmental rehabilitation in primates, and is reported to be clinically helpful with maladapted adults, as well as preventative and helpful in children.
3. *Movement.* Physical, maternal, and environmental stimulation develops the brain's pleasure centers, forming neurological capacity for experiencing pleasure and contentment.
4. *Myelination.* Syntactic abilities to direct thoughts in relationship to concepts of reality are dependent upon level of brain maturation and health (myelination).
5. *Mental Focus.* A patient's deliberate conscious mental focus determines both momentary emotional state and physiologic reactions. These are etched in

a neurophysiologic pathway in the patient's nervous system, resulting in future automatic accessing of emotional and physiologic reactions proceeding from conscious cognitive focus. Habitual focus on affect, or on syntax, accesses these pathways automatically, even deepening them. Noting the effect of different cognitive styles and resulting personalities in influencing symptoms presented, therapy, and prognosis provides substantial clinical evidence.

6. *Cognitive Focus.* All psychogenic symptoms and causes are mediated by and may be changed by cognitive focus, which, by definition, includes hypnosis. All effective therapies implicitly or explicitly involve hypnosis.

7. *Imagery.* The most pervasive and effective means of establishing new neurological pathways, behaviors, and emotions is imagery.

8. *Continuous Focus on Fact Required.* Depressed patients, focused on negative affect, continue accessing the same neurophysiologic pathways. Directed hypnosis (imagery) is effective only at that moment, until patients immediately resume refocusing in the old syntax and neurological pathways, when allowed to function again in personal interaction.

9. *Ideal Therapy.* The most effective treatment must be explicitly *directed* by the therapist to focus on facts of reality, but with imagery *content chosen by the patient* with imagination of *ideal self* and with behavior according to *fact analysis only* repeated continuously *in everyday life* by mimicking the *ideal model* maintained in the patient's imagination. This is necessarily a hypnotic technique by definition.

10. *Changing the Sick Process.* An elegant therapy does not deal with the cognitive morass of content rationalizations or schema in the "sick" process, but changes this process to an efficient reality-oriented process. By this means, change is effected in the shortest possible time, in the most durative manner, in the simplest terms for patient understanding, and by the most pervasive application to the patient's particular personality to prevent recurrences. The therapist need not wade *ad nauseum* into content, but continuously ascribes all to the single sick process, and teaches a different single process that may be applied to all future contents or contexts.

11. *Cognitive Process.* A specific cognitive sequence or process unique to the depressive syndrome is described and related to the cognitive pattern of personality syndromes. This sick pattern (process) is more pervasive than just a cognitive distortion by errors, as described by all cognitive therapists to date.

The patient's intensity in practicing his particular cognitive process determines and characterizes the severity of his personality syndrome. By understanding the patient's intensity and type of cognitive process, the therapist can determine the prognosis and the particular cognitive emphasis to achieve patient cooperation in learning the new healthy process.

12. *Physical Stimulation Therapy.* Psychotherapy can do little to affect deficient infant stimulation resulting in poor brain and pleasure system development and in incomplete myelination. In these patients, many approaches may be associated with psychotherapy, such as drug therapy, rolfing, bioenergetics, and the innovative therapy of Don Casriel (involving physical and emotional bonding of patients), which involve physical stimulation. These modalities of therapy are effective through basic emotional and physiological development pathways. The prescribing of physical activity may activate these unpracticed pathways.

Cognitive Process Therapy

Understanding the research and clinical parameters in Section I promotes formulation of a unified hypnosis approach that I term "cognitive process therapy." I have found this process very effective with depressives, as well as with other neurotic manifestations. Based on the bicameral understanding of cognition, cognitive process therapy focuses on process rather than on content.

Definition of Cognitive Process Therapy

Cognitive process therapy uses imagery and hypnotic techniques, giving the patient a normal cognitive process of reference to the facts-do model, as opposed to the previously described abnormal reference to the feelings-do model. The basic defect is the patient's focusing upon feelings, the cause of all maladaptive behavior and symptoms. Patients have problems to the extent that they allow affective cognitions to influence preferential fact-judgment syntactic cognitions.

Cognitive process therapy is based upon the belief that an ideal theory of therapy deals with one simple process for all symptoms or personalities, rather than being concerned with the morass of content differences between patients. An understanding of cognitive style of each personality presenting with depression determines the cognitive emphasis taken with each patient, as well as prognosis.

Procedure of Communication

Approach is determined by an evaluation of the patient's cognitive type (whether affective or syntactic) and intensity of personality type. The patient is then oriented to the new cognitive process of situation-fact-behavior by communicating to him in reference to his particular cognitive type skill, whether syntax or affect.

For example, an obsessive–compulsive or passive–aggressive would not accept a therapist who initially states that the patient's behavior arises from bad feelings. The patient would attack the therapist syntactically. These personality types are best approached by talking about thinking and doing.

Personality types characterized by focus on affect may be persuaded to adopt the new process by demonstrating that thinking according to facts gives better affect. Depressed patients do not resist the syntactical explanations, since they characteristically access syntax. Taibi Kahler (1981) developed effective specific communication approaches within transactional analysis personality types, which he calls "process therapy." Daniel Araoz (1981, 1982) has independently evolved a correction of "negative hypnosis" in sexual function problems by applying a process therapy (Araoz, 1982).

Clinical Application

With understanding and use of the research and clinical background in Section I, cognitive process therapy proceeds in three steps:

First: Evaluation of the patient's cognitive style and personality by *initial interview* with the therapist

Second: Establishment of responsible and reasonable *therapy contract* with patient

Third: *Teaching normal cognitive process,* according to the personality of the patient and evaluation of his understanding of the therapy contract

Initial Consultation Evaluation.   An acronym for the six parameters of situation-fact-behavior is AIM BIG.

A̲BILITY.   The first step in initial consultation involves evaluation of the patient's mental *ability* and social physiological development. Can the patient carry on formal mental operations, such as translating specifics into concepts and concepts into specifics? Can he control the focus of his attention on syntax? If not, the therapist may find the patient nodding in full agreement and giving seemingly congruent answers to questions, when in actuality he does not understand what the therapist is saying.

Some patients cannot relate concepts to specific occurrences in daily life, nor can they relate specific occurrences and derive from them concepts. For instance, the patient may state that a person turns red in the face and screams insulting remarks, but be totally unable to make conceptual inferences about why the person behaves this way, how he feels, or who is the object of the outburst. His cognitive focus may be in the fantasia of affect.

To treat these patients by hypnosis, syntactic verbalizations, disputations, or rationalizations wastes time. Therapies relating to medications or to body stimulation give quicker and more significant relief than psychotherapy. These people (brain-damaged drug abusers and patients with organic brain syndromes, regardless of cause) require direct physical manipulation, coercions, and social manipulation to effect change. I find that about 5% of patients are of this type, implying a psychosocial maturation deficiency, as discussed in Section I.

IMAGINATION. The patient's ability to *imagine* in all representational systems must be questioned specifically. I have found that 10% to 20% of patients have little ability to imagine. Typically, they are able to picture a person, but cannot imagine associated movement, sound, touch, taste, or smell. The image produced is usually statuelike. These patients cannot imagine a telephone ringing, or a person touching them. Their focus on momentary sensory imput and self-talk engenders difficulty with any hypnosis or ideal imagery concepts. These patients must be taught initially to develop and use their dusty imaginations so that subjective thinking by conscious syntactic direction (hypnosis) may be established. This ability enables patients to note significant relief with fewer than three therapy visits.

MISCONCEPTION. The patient's *misconceptions* are noted so that they may be changed, because a continuation of certain misconceptions offers significant roadblocks to following instructions about process practices. These misconceptions may involve "lack of willpower;" actually, such a faculty of mind does not exist. Patients may not understand the concept of mental illness, hypnosis, fees, scheduling requirements, or the nature of their problems.

BIOLOGIC PRIORITIES. The therapist needs to evaluate the presence of *biologic priorities* involved in the patient's symptom complex relating to

1. Life, involving security and existence
2. Death, relating to punishment or prevention
3. Sex, in terms of expression of gender—not sexual dysfunction.

Various symptoms and definitions revolving around these biologic priorities of life, death, and sex are extremely difficult to treat, since the subconscious mind tends to defend tenaciously the only stance learned through the years to help the individual.

INCONGRUENT DEFINITIONS. Patients may have certain *incongruent* definitions of trust, love, gender, guilt, and so on. Incongruent definitions have no relationship to man's imperfect world. For example, if a patient cannot trust someone unless that person is 100% reliable, an imperfect human therapist will not suffice. If a situation must be associated with love (considered a pleasant emotion), human imperfections may hinder therapy. These definitions curb the effectiveness of any therapist and need to be rooted out at the outset of therapy.

GREAT THINKING. Evaluation of the particular patient's personality type is undertaken to discern the type, severity, and prognosis of the personality problem. The author does not rely on psychological or depression assessments. After questioning the patient, an experienced therapist can specifically evaluate general personality and cognitive type, as well as determine whether he is dealing with psychosis or neurosis. Whenever a recognized cognitive type describes symptoms in detail, a therapist recognizes the presence of the depressive syndrome. The therapist avoids taking the patient's "word" about whether he is—or is not—depressed.

Therapy Contract

The therapy contract does not involve a written statement, but consists of guidelines and a mutual understanding between therapist and patient concerning several factors. Without an understanding of these factors, therapy may meet with pitfalls in certain personality types.

I believe that the royal road to successful, fast therapy lies in considering the patient's particular maladaptive personality and environmental context. Upon initial evaluation, I have found that at least 20% of patients will have such severe personality traits (content rationalizations of affect) that only much emphasis of normal process instead of these traits allows for clearing of symptoms. The extent to which these traits are manifested determines the degree of symptom entrenchment (holding defensively to rationalize or obfuscate affect).

The patient needs constantly to be reminded of seven basic factors. An acronym for these seven facts is CHOOSE—OBEDIENT—FRIENDLY—PERSONALITY—APPROACH—to CONTROL—PROCESS. This is also an appropriate admonition for the therapist.

1. CHOOSE. During the initial interview, the experienced therapist makes every observation to determine whether the patient is congruent in his expression of *choosing* to change. The therapist must be aware of the significance of the patient's subconscious use of parenthetic words, phrases, and body language. He should not proceed with therapy unless there is definite establishment of patient congruency in relationship to understanding the factors of therapy.
2. OBEDIENCE. Patients (and attending family member or friend) must be told that continual assistance, coercion, and encouragement must be offered by the family member (friend) living with the patient. Emphasize to the depressed patient that the quickest and most effective therapy involved absolute *obedience* to the therapist's directions in completing daily exercises and assignments. Family members and friends must understand clearly that they are to

participate by encouraging the patient's compliance to instructions in every way.

Evaluation of the family member or friend may indicate a personality problem that contributes to the patient's poor affect and negative syntax. Reinforcement of the patient's negative syntax is to be discouraged; perhaps private sessions with the family member or friend are indicated. In some instances, the therapist may become involved with the patient's entire family. Persistence of depression is a flag that symptoms are serving a homeostatic purpose in the patient's family system.

3. FRIENDLY. A patient's mind is his best *friend*. Symptoms are not occurring because something is wrong with his mind. His "good friend" simply thinks that these symptoms are appropriate because of the information it has received. The mind is a computer, printing out feelings based on its programming. There is nothing wrong with the patient's mind.

4. PERSONALITY. Whenever the severity of the patient's *personality* traits sabotage cognition practice exercises, these traits must be dealt with openly and candidly by explanation and emphasis. Practicing the new process will effectively prevent personality traits from hindering attempts at achieving change. The patient must change himself by doing the cognitive exercises and behavioral assignments.

5. APPROACH. Explain to the patient the specific *approach* therapy will take, and why this approach was selected. Explain the single maladaptive ABC process, illustrating why the normal process of thinking needs to be understood, and assure the patient that exercises will be provided to help him develop a new healthy process of thinking.

The therapist serves as guide, collaborator, and teacher, rather than momentarily doing "something" to make the patient walk out of the office with an entirely different affect. This is contrary to the average patient's understanding of the medical model, since he has experienced other therapies. The patient goes to a doctor, receives a treatment, and walks out of the office, hoping that the therapy that was passively experienced will be effective. Explain that psychotherapy necessarily involves the patient's active participation and practice 24 hours a day *after* he leaves the office. The therapist is teacher and collaborator.

6. CONTROL. The patient must understand that he *alone* can reprogram or change his symptoms. There is no such thing as mind control—this fact must be emphasized to the patient. To proceed with a depressive on the basis of mistaken belief in the "magic" of direct hypnosis will result only in disillusionment and discontinuance of therapy. Efforts at direct hypnosis with depressives are humorous in their ineffectiveness. Indirect and self-hypnosis *controlled* by the patient will develop in him a new process of thinking. The

therapist cannot do it for him. This fact must be sympathetically and sincerely emphasized to the patient.

7. PROCESS. The patient has accidentally developed a personal emotional mental problem because of a thinking *process* acquired in childhood. This is not his fault—but it *is* his problem. Fortunately, *only he* can change his thinking process, since he would not want mind control to be possible.

The patient does not think bad thoughts; the problem is the sequence of his thinking of situation causes emotions causes behavior. He needs to practice (with the therapist's guidance) a healthy process of fact—"real self" analysis—what to do. The patient will *want* to *do* the resulting behavior, since it stems from his own fact analysis of reality (as he wants to behave) according to facts. This is preferable to behaving according to the fantasies of feelings that (as the patient knows) have no relationship to reality. These factors must be repeatedly emphasized, with the patient's agreement. Haggling with the patient about content or thoughts regarding specific events is generally counterproductive or a waste of time.

Teaching Healthy Processing. After the initial consultation, in which the therapy contract and the evaluation of the patient's cognition are established, teaching the new process begins.

After consideration of the six parameters of consultation and constant emphasis on the seven factors of teaching process, actual patient practice becomes ingenuous. However, unless the therapist explains the importance of this exercise, patients will disregard its significance and fail to practice it. Explain to patients repeatedly how the sick process of situation-affect-behavior causes lack of control and abolition of behavior standards, resulting in behavior unrelated to reality. Otherwise, vital imagery and thinking exercises will not be considered worth doing. Patients must understand that the percentage of time that the new process is used equals the percentage of time of subsequent self-improvement.

1. ESTABLISHMENT OF "REAL SELF." Tell patients that there is nothing wrong with their minds, or the way that they want to be. Unknowingly, they have blundered into this unhealthy process in childhood. Patients need to have ideals as individuals—their former standard has been emotion instead of reality. They need to know how they realistically wish to be—physically, socially, emotionally, intellectually, and sexually. I instruct patients to make five columns on paper, specifically detailing these characteristics. This private list (shown to no one, including the therapist) exemplifies the characteristics of the patient's "real self" as he *realistically* wishes to be.

To help patients with the construction of the "real self" image, I ask them to daydream or fantasize while sitting or lying down with eyes closed. These sessions are for 30- to 90-second periods during the day, as often as possible, since frequency is important. Because they wish to have behavior that is more relative to reality, patients imagine being "real selves" in any desired situations—considering *facts only* in the situation, as the real self does—telling themselves what they *want* to do and then *doing* it. They imagine the situation as successful because they went according to facts while ignoring feelings. Before opening their eyes, patients tell themselves, ". . . now . . . these actions and reactions of my 'real self' are going to continue to be mine. . . ."

2. GOING ACCORDING TO FACTS. After opening their eyes, patients practice the second exercise. They continue imagining themselves as "real selves"— going according to *facts only* and ignoring feelings. Maintaining this image in their minds, they progress throughout the day (between imagery exercises) looking and evaluating only in their good "real self" judgment what to do; then telling themselves, "that's what I *want* (or do not want) to do"—and behaving accordingly, ignoring emotions, likes and dislikes, or body sensations.

A helpful illustration demonstrating how to practice the second exercise is as follows: Ask the patient to recall a favorite movie or television star; then ask him if he could pretend to be that person for the rest of the day. He will usually say "yes," thereby providing an assessment of his ability to shift cognitions. Next, tell the patient to practice the second exercise in exactly the same way.

Initially, most patients produce workable images in their minds of the "real self" acting and thinking according to *facts only* in every situation. Patients are to retain this image continually in their imaginations as they go through the day, mimicking the "real self" image as they regard *facts only*, acting as the "real self" would. This thinking exercise thus becomes an automatic type of continual focusing on the "real self" standard of fact-analysis-behavior. If patients follow these steps *exactly*, they progressively experience help—but only to the extent that they practice the second exercise. Peer coercion and social reinforcement helps greatly to enforce acting out according to fact analysis.

Ego-strengthening Techniques

Use of reframing, regression, or direct hypnotic ego strengthening is seldom necessary to handle specific impasses, although these modalities may be effectively applied as needed. Dealing with specific hindrances accompanying depressives will not be effective unless the patient's process is changed.

Necessary ego strengthening is accomplished by convincingly explaining the how's and why's of the sick process to the patient. These patients acquired bad feelings about themselves accidentally during infancy. As adults, they began basing all thinking and behavior upon feelings in futile attempts to "feel" better.

These patients are as acceptable as anyone, living or dead—the only difference is their focus on the false bad feelings. And because of their cognition type, they have been practicing this sick process since infancy. Patients agree and relate easily to this explanation.

Two Sources of Problem Development

First, the patient thinks the process is too simple to work, so he does not follow it, nor carry it out behaviorally.

Second, the patient injects characteristic rationalizations with focus on affect; he does not say, after *fact analysis only,* "That's what I *want*" (or do not want) and act accordingly. Explain to the patient how he prevents himself from following the normal fact-do process; point out to him all other forms of thinking hinder him, since they are part of the sick process. There is no need to dispute his belief systems; instead, contrast outcomes according to affect with outcomes according to normal process. Do not allow him to think or say, "should . . . must . . . ought to . . . got to . . . or, have to"—only *want* to.

When patients understand that they can think only one thought at a time—and when they realize that the choice of thinking according to feelings or facts arises continually before them—they begin to comprehend the issue. Do not allow patients to say, "I can't." Kindly and empathetically stress the factors of teaching this process, and insist on behavior from it.

A Place for Emotions

Women in particular may raise the question, "Where do emotions come in? Aren't people supposed to be emotional?" Explain that emotions are intended as rewards for proper behavior. Only animals and emotionally ill people behave predominantly according to feelings and emotions. Give patients illustrations of a person ignoring emotions and behaving according to the "real self" analysis of *facts only;* and contrast these illustrations with examples of someone behaving according to emotions, likes, and dislikes. Emphasis is made upon explicit practice of this exercise. When the patient returns after the first instruction, the therapist determines how the exercise is being practiced, checking to see if the patient is sabotaging by "thinking" more than the simple exercise requires.

Concluding Remarks

I have used cognitive process therapy with over 300 depressed patients during the past few years, and have found it to be the only psychotherapy providing immediate relief for most patients, and eventually proving helpful in almost all patients. Short-term failures (less than five visits) occur because patients receive abundant environmental reinforcement of the maladaptive process, are borderline or psychotic, or manifest the developmental and neurological deficiencies described.

References

Akiskal NS, Betar AH, Puzantian UR, et al: The nosological status of neurotic depression. Arch Gen Psychol 35:7, 56, 1978

Angst J: Zuratiologie und Noslogy endogener Depressiver. Psychosen Monogr Gesamtgeb Nural Psyc 112:1, 1966

Araoz DL: Negative self-hypnosis. J Contemp Psychotherapy 12:1, 45, 1981a

Araoz DL: Hypnosex: From the job of sex to the joy of sex. Paper presented at 24th Annual Scientific Meeting, ASCH, Boston, 1981b

Araoz DL: Hypnosis and Sex Therapy. New York, Brunner-Mazel, 1982

Bakwin H: Loneliness in infants. Am J Dist Child 63:30, 1942

Bandura A: Effecting change through participant modeling. In Krumboltz JD, Thoresen CE (eds): Counseling Methods. New York, Holt, Rinehart & Winston, 1976

Bandura A: Social Learning Theory. New Jersey, Prentice-Hall, 1977a

Bandura A: Self-efficacy: Toward a unifying theory of behavioral change. Psychol. Rev. 84:191–215, 1977b

Barnett J: Cognitive disorders in the obsessional. Contemp Psychoanal 2:122, 1966a

Barnett J: Cognitive repair in the treatment of the obsessional, procedure IV. World Congress of Psychiatry, Excerpta Medica Congress Series, No. 150, September, 1966b

Barnett J: Cognition, thought, and affect in the organization of experience. In Masserman J (ed): Science and Psychoanalysis, 12:237. New York, Grune & Stratton, 1968

Barnett J: Character, cognition, and therapeutic process. Am J Psychoanal 39:291, 1979

Beck AT: Depression: Causes and Treatment. Philadelphia, University of Pennsylvania Press, 1967

Beck AT: The Diagnosis and Management of Depression. Philadelphia, University of Pennsylvania Press, 1973

Beck AT: Depression. New York, Harper & Row, 1967

Beck AT, Rush J, Shaw BF, Emery G: Cognitive Therapy of Depression. New York, The Guilford Press, 1979

Benedict T, Jacks I: Mental Illness in Primitive Societies. 17:377, 1954

Berdach E, Bakan P: Body position and free recall of early memories. Psychotherapy 4:101, 1967

Berne E: Beyond Games and Scripts. New York, Grove Press, 1976

Blumer D, Heilbronn M: The pain-prone disorder: A clinical and psychological profile. Psychosomatics 22:395, 1981

Brumback RA, Weinberg WA: Relationship of hyperactivity and depression in children. Perceptual Motor Skills 45:247, 1977

Call JD: The adaptive process in early infancy: A research odyssey. In Anthony EF (ed): Explorations in Child Psychiatry. New York, Plenum Publishers, 1975, p 167

Carter BD, Elkins GR, Kraft SP: Hemispheric asymmetry as a model for hypnotic phenomena: A review and analysis. Am J Clin Hypn 24:204, 1982

Casriel D: A Scream Away from Happiness. New York, Grossett & Dunlap, 1972

Casriel D: The acting out-neuroses of our times. In Milman DS, Goldman GD (eds): The Neuroses of Our Time: Acting Out. Springfield, IL, Charles C Thomas, 1973

Castelnuovo-Tedesco P, Krout BM: Psychosomatic aspects of chronic pelvic pain. Int J Psychiatr Med 1:109, 1970

Cautela JR: Treatment of compulsive behavior by covert sensitization. The Psychological Record 16:33, 1966

Cautela JR: Covert sensitization. Psychology Reports 20:459, 1967

Cautela JR: Covert reinforcement. Behav Ther 1:33, 1970a

Cautela JR: Covert negative reinforcement. Behav Ther Exp Psychiatry 1:272, 1970b

Cautela JR: Covert extinction. Behav Ther 2:192, 1971a

Cautela JR: Covert modeling. Presented to the Association for Advancement of Behavior Therapy, Washington, DC, 1971b

Cautela JR: Rationale and procedures for covert conditioning. Advances in Behavioral Therapy. New York, Academic Press, 1972

Cautela JR: Covert response cost. Psychotherapy: Theory Research & Practice 133:97–404, 1976

Cautela JR, Baron MG: Covert conditioning: A theoretical analysis. Behav Mod 1:351, 1977a

Cautela JR, Grodin J: Relaxation: A Comprehensive Manual. Rhode Island, State Department of Education, 1977b

Cautela JR, McCullough L: Covert conditioning: A learning theory perspective on imagery. In Singer JL, Pope KS (eds): The Power of Human Imagination: New Methods in Psychotherapy. New York, Plenum Press, 1978, pp 230, 240, 250

Core Content Review of Family Medicine, 1981–1982 ed. Special section on psychiatry, question discussion 44–B

Diagnostic and Statistical Manual of Mental Disorders, 3rd ed. American Psychiatric Association, 1980

D'Zurilla TB, Goldfried MR: Problem-solving and behavior modification. J Abnorm Psychol 78(1):107, 1971

Eastman RT, Mason WA: Developmental Psychobiology. New York, John Wiley & Sons, 1975

Ellis A: Outcome of employing three techniques of psychotherapy. J Clin Psychol 13:344, 1957

Ellis A: Reason and Emotion in Psychotherapy. New York, Lyle Stuart, 1962

Ellis A: Handbook of Rational Emotive Therapy. New York, Springer Publishing, 1977

Feshbach S: The drive-reducing function of fantasy behavior. J Abnorm Soc Psychol 50:3, 1955

Feshbach S: In Beck AT: Depression. New York, Harper & Row, 1967

Fischoff J: Failure to thrive. In Berlin IN: Stone LA, Noshpitz JD (eds): Basic Handbook of Child Psychiatry. New York, Basic Books, 1980, p 4

Ford H: Involutional melancholia. In Friedman AM, Kaplan HI, Sacock BJ (eds): Comprehensive Textbook of Psychiatry II. Baltimore, Williams & Wilkins, 1975

Foreyt JP, Rathjen DP: Cognitive Behavior Therapy: Research and Application. New York, Plenum Press, 1978

Freud S: Collected Papers. New York, Basic Books, 1917

Fromm E: Escape from Freedom. New York, Rinehart & Wilson, 1941

Galin D: Hemispheric specialization: Implications for psychiatry, In Grenell RB, Gabay S (eds): Biological Foundations of Psychiatry. New York, Raven Press, 1976

Gershon ES: The search for genetic markers in affective disorders. In DiMascio A, Lipton MA, Killam KF (eds): Psychopharmacology: A Generation of Progress. New York, Raven Press, 1978, p 1178

Gershon ES, Cromer M, Klerman GL: Hostility and depression. Psychiatry 31:224, 1968

Glassman AH, Kantor SJ, Shostak M: Depression, delusions and drug response. Am J Psychol 132:716, 1975

Globus A, Altman J: Studies described, in Early Sensory Influences on Regional Activity of Brain ATPases in Developing Rats. In Meisami E: Growth and Development of the Brain: Nutritional, Genetic and Environmental Factors. Brazier, MAB. New York, Raven Press, 1975

Goldfried M, Davison GE: Clinical Behavior Therapy. New York, Holt, Rinehart & Winston, 1976

Greenacre P: Trauma, Growth and Personality. New York, WW Norton, 1952

Gur R, Gur R: Classroom seating and functional brain asymmetry. J Ed Psychol 67:1, 151, 1975

Harlow HF, Harlow MK: Social deprivation in monkeys. Sci Am 207:136, 1962

Horney K: Neurosis and Human Growth. New York, WW Norton & Co, 1950

Izard CE: The Face of Emotion. New York, Appleton, 1971

Jacobson E: Progressive Relaxation. Chicago, University of Chicago Press, 1938

Jaynes J: The Origin of Consciousness in the Breakdown of the Bicameral Mind. Boston, Houghton Mifflin Co., 1976

Kahler T: Managing With The Process Communical Model. San Francisco, Transactional Publishing, 1981

Kardiner A, Karush A, Ovesey L: A methodological study of Freudian theory for the structural hypothesis: The problem of anxiety and post-Freudial ego psychology. J Nerv Ment Dis 129:354, 1959

Katz MM, Hirshfeld RMA: Phenomenology and classification of depression. In Lipton MA, DiMascio A, Killman KF (eds): Psychopharmacology: A Generation of Progress. New York, Raven Press, 1978, p 1185

Kazdin AE: Research issues in covert conditioning. Cogn Ther Res 1:45, 1977

Kiev A: Trans-cultural Psychiatry. New York, The Free Press, 1972

Klaus MH, Kennell JH: Maternal–Infant Bonding. St Louis, CV Mosby, 1976

Klerman GL: Overview of depression. In Friedman AM, Kaplan HI, Saydock BJ (eds): Comprehensive Textbook of Psychiatry II. Baltimore, Williams & Wilkins, 1975

Klerman GL, Barrett H: The affective disorders: Clinical and epidermalogical aspects. In Gershon S, Shopsin B (eds): Lithium: Its Role in Psychiatric Treatment and Research. New York, Plenum Publishers, 1975, p 201

Klerman GL, Gershon ES: Imipramine effects upon hostility in depression. J Nerv Ment Dis 150:127, 1970

Klerman GL, Endicott J, Spitzer R, et al: Neurotic depression: A systematic analysis of multiple criteria and meanings. Am J Psychiatry 136:57, 1979

Klinger E: The nature of fantasy and its clinical use. Imagery Approaches to Psychotherapy. Symposium chaired by J. L. Singer, Chicago, 1975

Kohut H: The Analysis of the Self. New York, International University Press, 1971

Kohut H: The Restoration of Self. New York, International University Press, 1977

Korner AF: Effects of flotation on premature infants: A pilot study. Pediatrics 56:3, 1975

Kozak MJ, Lang PJ: The psychophysiology of emotional imagery: A structural analysis of image processing. Presented as part of an address by the second author to the Netherlands Conference on Biofeedback, Amersfoot, Netherlands, 1976

Kroth JF: The analytic couch and response to free association. Psychotherapy: Theory, Research and Practice, 7:206, 1970

Lambo TA: Journal of Mental Science, 101:239, 1955

Lang PF: Imagery in therapy: An information processing analysis of fear. Behav Ther 8:862, 1977

Lazarus AE: A learning theory in the treatment of depression. Behav Res Ther 6:83, 1968

Leonhard K, Korff I, Schultz H: Temperament in families with monopolar and bipolar phasic psychoses. Psychiatr Neurol 143:416, 1962

Liedloff J: The Continuum Concept. New York, Warner Books, 1977

Lozoff B, Brittenham GM, Trause MA, Kennell JH, Klau MH: The mother–newborn relationship: Limited adaptability. J Pediatr, 91:1, 1977

McLean P: Remediation of skills and performance deficits in depression. In Clarkin JF, Glazer HI (eds): Depression. New York, Garland STPM Press, 1981, p 180

Mahler M: Child psychosis and schizophrenia: Autistic and symbiotic infantile psychosis. Psychoanal Study Child 7:286, 1952

Mahoney MJ: Cognition and Behavior Modification. Boston, Ballinger, 1974

Marshall WA: The Development of the Brain. Oliver & Boyd, 1968

Mason WA, Berkson G: Effects of maternal mobility on the development of rocking and other behaviors in Rhesus monkeys: A study with artificial mothers. Developmental Psychobiology. New York, John Wiley & Sons, 1975, pp 213–221

Meichenbaum D: Cognitive Behavior Modification. New Jersey, General Learning Press, 1974

Meichenbaum D: Toward a cognitive theory of self-control. In Schwartz G, Shapiro D (eds): Consciousness and Self-regulation: Advances in Research. New York, Plenum Press, 1975

Meichenbaum D: Cognitive-behavior Modification: An Integrative Approach. New York, Plenum Press, 1977

Meichenbaum D, Turk D: The cognitive-behavioral management of anxiety, anger and pain. In Davidson PO (ed): The Behavioral Management of Anxiety, Depression, and Pain. New York, Brenner-Mazel, 1976

Mendelson M: Psychoanalytic Concepts of Depression, 2nd ed. New York, Spectrum Publishers, 1974

Merluzzi TV, Glass CR, Genest M (eds): Cognitive Assessment. New York, The Guilford Press, 1981

Miller WR, Seligman MEP: Learned helplessness in depression in man. J Abnorm Psychol 84:228, 1975

Morgan R, Bakan P: Sensory deprivation hallucinations and other sleep behavior as a function of position, method of report, and anxiety. Percept Mot Skills 20:19, 1965

Neisser U: Cognitive Psychology. New York, Appleton-Century-Crofts, 1967

Neisser U: Changing conceptions of imagery. In Sheehan P (ed): The Function and Nature of Imagery. New York, Academic Press, 1972

Ostrow D, Pandey G, Davis J, Hurt S, Tosteson D: A heritable disorder of lithium transport and erythrocytes of a sub-population of manic depressive patients. Am J Psychiatry 135:1070, 1978

Paykel ES, Myers JK, Dinelt MN, Klerman GL, Lindenthal JJ, Pepper MP: Life events and depression: A controlled study. Arch Gen Psychiatry 21:753, 1969

Pearce, J: Depression disorders in childhood. J Child Psychiatry 18:79, 1977

Perris C (ed): A study of bipolar (manic depressive) and unipolar recurrent depressive psychoses. Acta Psychol Scand 42:1, 1966

Petti TA: Active treatment of childhood depression. In Clarkin FJ, Glazer HI (eds): Depression: Behavioral and Directive Intervention Strategies. Garland, 1981, pp 311–343

Piaget J: Language and Thought of the Child. Rautledge & Kegan, 1959

Piaget J: Genetic Epistemology. New York, Columbia University Press, 1970

Pilling LF, Bannier TL, Swenson WM: Psychological characteristics of psychiatric patients having pain as a presenting symptom. Can Med Assoc J 97:387, 1967

Pope KS: The flow of consciousness. Unpublished doctoral dissertation, Yale University, 1977

Pozanski EO, Krahenbuhl V, Zrull JP: Childhood depression: A longitudinal perspective. J Am Acad Child Psychiatry 15:491, 1976

Rappaport D: Organization and Pathology of Thought. New York, Columbia University Press, 1951

Restak E, Sander L, Shapiro T (eds): Infant Psychiatry: A New Synthesis. New Haven, Yale University Press, 1976

Richardson A: Mental Imagery. New York, Springer-Verlag, 1969

Rizley RC: The perception of causality in depression: An attributional analysis of two cognitive theories of depression. Unpublished doctoral dissertation, Yale University, 1976

Rose S: The Conscious Brain. New York, Vintage Books, 1976

Rosenzweig MR, Bennett EL, Diamond MC: Brain changes in response to experience. Sci Am February 1972

Rush AF: Short-Term Psychotherapies for Depression. New York, Guilford Press, 1982

Rychlak J: Time orientation in the positive and negative free fantasies of mildly abnormal vs. normal high school males. J Consult Clin Psychol 41:175, 1973

Schultz DK: Fantasy stimulation in depression: Direct intervention and correlational studies. Unpublished doctoral dissertation, Yale University, 1976

Schultz DK: Imagery and the control of depression. In Singer J, Pope KS (eds): The Power of Human Imagination. New York, Plenum Press, 1978

Schwartz G: Facial muscle patterning in affective imagery in depressed and non-depressed subjects. Science 192:489, 1976

Schwartz G: Psychosomatic disorders in biofeedback: A psychological model of disregulation. In Maser JD, Seligman MEP (eds): Psychopathology: Experimental Models. San Francisco, WH Freeman, 1977, pp 270–307

Secunda SK, Katz MM, Friedman RJ, Schuyler D: Special Report: 1973—The Depressive Disorders. Washington, DC, US Government Printing Office, 1973

Segal SJ, Glickman M: Relaxation and the Perky effect: The influence of body position and judgments of imagery. Am J Psychol 60:257, 1967

Seligman MEP: Helplessness. San Francisco, WH Freeman, 1975

Shader R, Spiegel D (eds): Manual of Psychiatric Therapeutics. Boston, Little, Brown & Co, 1975, pp 275–276

Shaw BF, Dobson KS: Cognitive assessment of depression. In Merluzzi TV, Glass CR, Genest M (eds): Cognitive Assessment. New York, Guilford Press, 1981, pp 361–382

Singer JL: Daydreaming. New York, Random House, 1966

Skinner BF: Science and Human Behavior. New York, MacMillan, 1953

Spiegel H, Spiegel D: Trance and Treatment: Clinical Uses of Hypnosis. New York, Basic Books, 1978

Spitz PA: Anaclitic depression: An inquiry into the genesis of psychiatric conditions in early childhood. Psychoanal Study Child 2:313, 1946

Starker S, Singer JL: Daydream patterns and self-awareness in psychiatric patients. J Nerv Ment Dis 161:313, 1975

Sullivan HS: Clinical Studies in Psychiatry. New York, WW Norton, 1956

Sullivan NW: The Interpersonal Theory of Psychiatry. New York, WW Norton, 1953

Suomi SJ, Harlow HF: Abnormal social behavior in young monkeys. In Hellmuth J (ed): Exceptional Infant: Studies in Abnormalities. New York, Brunner-Mazel, 1971

Suomi SJ, Harlow HF: Depressive behavior in young monkeys. J Comp Psychol 180:11, 1972a

Suomi SJ, Harlow HF: Social rehabilitation of isolate reared monkeys. Dev Psychol 6:487, 1972b

Suomi SJ, Harlow HF, Domek CJ: Affective repetitive mother–infant separation of young monkeys. J Abnorm Psychol 76, 1970

Suomi SJ, Harlow HF, Novak MA: Reversal of social defects produced by isolation rearing in monkeys. J Hum Evol 3:527, 1974

Tomkins S: Affect, Imagery, and Consciousness, vol I and II. New York, Springer-Verlag, 1962–63

Traynor TD: Patterns of daydreaming and their relationships to depressive affect. Unpublished master thesis, Miami University, Ohio, 1974

Watson JB: Psychology from the Standpoint of a Behaviorist. Philadelphia, JB Lippincott, 1919

Weinberg WA, Rutman J, Sullivan L: Depression in children referred to an educational diagnostic center: Diagnosis and treatment. J Pediatr 83:1065, 1973

Weissman MM, Klerman GL, Paykel ES: Clinical evaluation of hostility in depression. Am J Psychiatry 128:261, 1971

Weissman MM, Prusoff BA, Klerman GL: Personality and the prediction of long-term outcome of depression. Am J Psychol 135:7, 797, 1978

Winokur G: Unipolar depression: Is it divisible into autonomous sub-types? Arch Gen Psychiatry 36:47, 1979

Winokur G, Clayton P: Family history studies: Two types of affective disorders separated according to genetic and clinical factors. In Wortis J (ed): Recent Advances in Biological Psychiatry. New York, Plenum Press, 9:35, 1967

Winokur G, Clayton PJ, Reich T: Manic Depressive Illness. St Louis, CV Mosby, 1969

Winokur G, Tanna V: Possible role of X-linked dominant factor in manic depressive disease. Dis Nerv System 30:89, 1969

Winokur G, Behar D, van Valkenburg C, Lowry M: Is a familial definition of depression both feasible and valid? J Nerv Ment Dis 166:764, 1978

Wolpe JB: Psychotherapy by Reciprocal Inhibition. Stanford, Stanford University Press, 1958

23 Hypnosis in the Treatment of Anxiety and Chronic Stress

EDGAR A. BARNETT

Anxiety is a diffuse and often vague feeling of apprehension usually accompanied by uncomfortable body sensations that are peculiar to the individual. Such symptoms as tightness in the chest, pounding of the heart, perspiration, headaches, and urgency of urination are typical manifestations of anxiety.

Anxiety is indistinguishable from fear and in fact derives its name from the German word, *Angst,* meaning fear. In general, Freud ignored any distinction between anxiety and fear, since such distinction, when it is made, usually depends only upon whether the stimulus for the anxiety is obvious or not. If the threatening event creating an anxious response in the individual is a known external event, then the response is usually termed fear. In those cases in which the threat appears to be internal and not conscious, the response is termed anxiety.

Like fear, anxiety warns of impending danger, and must therefore be regarded as a protective emotion essential for survival. However, the source of the danger so perceived is internally repressed and is therefore unconscious. Usually it is either a fear of actual bodily harm or a fear of the loss of a protective love. In any case, the physiological response of fear and anxiety is the same and is due to an increased excretion of adrenaline, which acts upon the body to produce the anxiety/fear response. Anxiety may be simply situational and occur only in certain circumstances (*e.g.,* examination anxiety); nevertheless, such situational-specific anxiety can be so severe as to warrant being termed a phobia. A phobia can be considered to be a special kind of anxiety/fear, related and limited to specific circumstances, which are only apparently directly responsible for the fear response. Since phobias generate an inappropriately great fear response, they should more properly be regarded as particularly intense forms of anxiety in which the aggravating internal factors remain unconscious.

In other cases, the anxiety is not situational but persistent and unremitting. Gellhorn (1965) believed that such chronic anxiety is due to repeated alerting stimuli, which "tune up" the ergotrophic autonomic nervous system to create an excessive discharge in the visceral and motor systems (partly through the medium of the increased adrenaline secretion). It is these alerting stimuli that are referred to as stresses. Selye (1947) noted that, when referring to stress, a distinction should be made between the stimulus and the response to it. In practice, this distinction is difficult to maintain, since an event cannot be regarded as stressful until it produces a stress response. Unlike inanimate objects, a human being cannot be presumed to react in a stressful manner to a particular stimulus prior to its presentation. He must perceive the event to be such that it makes a demand that threatens his ability to cope successfully. Thus, whether an event is to prove stressful depends upon the nature of the event, the resources available to deal with it, and the adequacy of the defenses and coping mechanism. If these are inadequate, an anxiety will result in the individual that induces him to mobilize his resources to the full.

Chronic stress is the result of continued unconscious conflict in which opposing sets of beliefs confront each other. For example, in the case of the examination anxiety, the unconscious belief is in the inevitability of failure and the ostracism to which such failure will lead. This belief is in conflict with the opposite belief that the student has studied as much as possible and has the ability to pass the examination.

It may be that repeated, adverse, and threatening stimuli produce fear or that a single severe stimulus creates the chronic stress/fear response, which is characterized by an intense and long-lasting neuroendocrine reactivity. This response is mediated through the hypothalamus and the pituitary gland to produce the adrenocorticotrophic hormone, which, in turn, stimulates the adrenal glands to secrete adrenaline and cortisone. These latter hormones produce the physical and emotional effects of chronic stress and anxiety.

Apart from the clinically observable effects of anxiety, there is a conscious, subjective awareness created by such physical discomforts as palpitations, sweating, butterflies in the stomach, tightness of the chest, shaking, and so on. These symptoms indicate to the individual that he is afraid, even though he may be unaware of the reason for the fear or may view the apparent reason as inadequate to explain the severity of his symptoms.

Historical Aspects

Freud (1926) initially held the view that anxiety was the result of repression of instinctual impulses and that it correlated with the strength of these repressed impulses. Later (1936), he reversed this relationship between anxiety and repression and suggested that it was the anxiety that caused the repression of unwanted and unacceptable impulses. Horney (1937) believed that anxiety is due to the repression of hostility by the child who cannot afford consciously to experience anger so long as he is isolated and helpless in a hostile world. Feelings of defenselessness are therefore invariably present. Rank (1952) maintained that anxiety originated in the birth trauma, in which the anxiety of separation is first experienced by the newborn. Sullivan (1953) viewed anxiety as being the direct result of fear of mother's disapproval; thus, if mother is uncomfortable so is the child. Rado (1962) pointed out that the psychological state of the mother can influence the behavior of the fetus and that, consequently, guilty fear is the primary cause of most behavioral dysfunction. The alerting signals that evoke unrealistic self-condemnation are guilty fear and guilty anxiety. In the presence of a strong conscience, even normal impulses (*i.e.,* sexual impulses or self-assertion) create a fear of punishment and abandonment. All of the above views assert that anxiety is a normal response to stress.

Chronic Stress

There are three components to the stress reaction: the environment, the appraisal of that environment, and the emotional and physiological response to it. The response of chronic anxiety varies with the age of the individual. In children, it tends to be responsible for such habit disorders as nail biting, thumbsucking, enuresis, and the behavior disorders. In adolescents, anxiety is manifest as lack of self-confidence, feelings of general inadequacy, shyness, and withdrawal, as well as apprehension about sexual adequacy and concern over masturbation. In young adults, anxiety is frequently associated with inappropriately high levels of aspiration and the attempt to achieve impossible goals. Failure is associated with poor self-esteem and withdrawal together with an increased susceptibility to environmental stress that is likely to lead to depression as well as anxiety. In older people, anxiety frequently appears to be the result of repressed anger: a fear of being abandoned and of being lonely prevents expression of that anger toward figures on whom they must depend.

In reality, anxiety is a normal response that signals to the ego the need to erect its psychological defenses. Chronic anxiety appears to be pathological because the threat to the individual is perceived only at an unconscious level. Indeed, the original threat itself may have been removed a long time ago, but the individual at the level of his perception of danger remains unaware of this. As Seligman (1975) pointed out, the individual has not yet received the signal that all is well and that the danger has passed. He therefore feels that he must maintain his unconscious vigilance which, consciously, is experienced as anxiety. Laughlin (1967) maintained that anxiety is probably a component of all psychological problems and is the representation of a persistent conflict between the instinctual drives and the demands of the conscience. It represses the conflict, which, in turn, causes emotional symptoms. Thus, a vicious circle remains in motion.

The Presentations of Anxiety

Anxiety may safely be assumed to be present in every case attending for therapy whether or not typical anxiety symptoms are evident. Only upon closer inquiry might symptoms of chronic anxiety, such as sleeplessness, muscle tension and pains, rapid heart rate, sweating, and so on, be admitted; they may indeed be responsible for the presenting symptom complex. For example, alcoholics have been shown by Brown (1980) to have a much higher level of anxiety than social drinkers, and Eddy (1978) indicated that they use alcohol to reduce this anxiety. Marcheson (1974) agreed and contended that alcoholics cannot be properly treated without attending to the concomitant anxiety. Similarly, McCrae (1978) has pointed out that heavy smokers have a higher level of anxiety than is normal.

It is rare that patients suffering from sleep problems are without anxiety. Celucci (1978) has shown that there is a strong relationship between anxiety and nightmares and other sleep difficulties. In these days of frequent marriage breakdown it is of interest to note Ishizvka's observation (1979) that a common denominator in troubled marriages is the high level of anxiety consistently present; the assumption is that this anxiety is an important factor in the breakdown. In this context, Kupfer (1977) has demonstrated evidence that sexual dysfunction in both men and women is commonly associated with high levels of anxiety. All patients suffering from a physical illness are prone to high levels of anxiety, and this is very likely to be present in those suffering from an intractable disease such as cancer (Labaw, 1977). Thus, it can be seen that the recognition and alleviation of anxiety in these different syndromes will materially affect the outcome of therapy.

An interesting feature of chronic anxiety is its invariable accompaniment with low self-esteem. Conversely, Shahi (1978) found that those subjects who are low in anxiety score high in self-esteem. This tends to support both Sullivan's view (1953) that maternal discomfort produces anxiety in the infant and, more recently, Samuel's (1976) that high maternal anxiety creates children with poor esteem. Interestingly enough, it has been found by Kane (1976) that the anxiety level of convicts is significantly lower than that of a normal population.

Patients who suffer from coronary heart disease have been shown by Pestonjee (1979) to have a higher level of anxiety than normal controls, and subjects who are highly anxious have a marked ability (Cox, 1977) to increase their heart rate. Even the incidence of postoperative complications have a relationship to preoperative anxiety (Lange, 1978).

Therapy

The therapy for all anxieties can be directed to any one of the three areas of the origin of stress. As a first step, attempts may be made to modify the environment in order to prevent the occurrence of events likely to produce stress. Thus, a change of occupation or residence might be advisable. Secondly, an alteration of the individual's interpretation and appraisal of his environment will render him less vulnerable to stress if he can be persuaded that his current tools for assessing his environment are causing him to perceive it as unreasonably dangerous. Finally, a direct assault upon the emotional and physiological response itself can be made to weaken it sufficiently so that perceptions of danger will not produce the previously exaggerated response. In this latter approach, drugs have been found to be of somewhat limited value in modifying the anxiety response. Fortunately, there are other techniques such as progressive relaxation, self-hypnosis, and meditation that can be more effective without creating the side effects of drugs.

Modification of the Environment

All approaches to the therapy for anxiety must first seek to reduce the effect of adverse environmental influences wherever this is possible. A change of job or a reduction in the amount of work is often a necessary first step in modifying the damaging effect of intolerable external pressures. Such an approach allies the therapy to that part of the personality responsible for the anxiety and recognizes the truly protective nature of that anxiety.

Alteration of the Interpretation of the Environment

Desensitization or deconditioning is the behaviorist approach to altering the individual's appraisal of his environment from threatening to harmless. It is based upon the assumption (Wolpe, 1958) that, as in the Pavlovian model, anxiety is due to a conditioning to normally harmless stimuli following a fortuitous association with threatening situations. Therapy is directed at reassociating these stimuli with comforting and comfortable circumstances so that the anxiety is eventually relinquished. In practice, it is accomplished by a systematic decrease of anxiety through the use of muscle relaxation (produced by either drugs or hypnosis) while a hierarchy of anxiety-producing stimuli commencing with the least stressful stimulus is sequentially presented. The addition of biofeedback in this approach does little more than give an external assessment of the relaxation achieved upon suggestion.

In fact, Hurley (1980) has demonstrated that hypnosis is a more effective self-regulatory technique for lowering anxiety than either biofeedback or trophotropic procedures. It is probable that muscle relaxation is the common therapeutic factor of greatest importance in the behaviorist approach to therapy. Daniels (1976) has frequently demonstrated that desensitization in hypnosis is the most successful way of using this technique and has been supported by the observations of many other workers, including Fuchs (1980) and O'Brien (1981). In the latter case described by O'Brien, the desensitization was markedly augmented by post-hypnotic suggestion for pleasant posthypnotic dreams.

Insight and understanding form part of most therapies directed at the alleviation of anxiety. Ellis and Harper (1975) insist that anxiety is based upon the irrational idea that overconcern will ultimately combat what is apparently dangerous and fearsome. Examination of the origin of the cause of such anxiety usually reveals that it does not warrant the fear that is being maintained. Much of the "awfulness" attributed to possible anxiety-producing events does not survive careful examination. By altering his thoughts and self-evaluation, the individual subsequently finds that the fear maintained in stressful situations is erroneous and the chronic feelings of anxiety, frustration and anger that resulted can be modified and even relinquished. The new orientation achieved enables the individual to adapt to his current life situation. Janis and Feshbach (1965) proposed that, when an objective threat of body damage is anticipated, the greater the repressed fear, the lower the probability that sustained emotional relief will result from reasoned communication—even from authoritative persons who are regarded as credible sources of information. Thus it is that, in spite of a reasoned examination of the sources of anxiety by a patient with the aid of a sincere and credible therapist, the anxiety is frequently retained unchanged. In such cases, there appears to be no alternative but to resort to therapies designed to reduce the response to an anxiety-producing stimulus by lessening the body's capacity for arousal. Most drugs that have a depressant action on the central nervous system (*e.g.,* alcohol, morphine, barbiturates, *etc.*) will, in sufficient quantities, have this effect. So will the tranquilizers whose use is exclusively designed for this purpose. Fortunately, there are drugless methods of reducing the anxiety response, chief among which is the use of hypnosis and self-hypnosis. Kazarian (1978) has produced evidence that drugs may, in fact, interfere with hypnosis.

Bartlett (1971) advocated the use of hypnotic techniques involving suggestion without formal hypnotic induction in the treatment of stress. Bowers (1979) believed that hypnotic suggestion may well be a hidden factor in the success of nonhypnotic techniques. London (1970) claimed that the ability to resist stress following hypnotherapy is directly related to hypnotizability.

Hypnotherapy

If hypnosis is understood as the process whereby communication with the unconscious mind is established and maintained (Barnett, 1981), then its advantage in the therapy for anxiety lies in making the resources of the unconscious mind accessible to the patient. Chief among these resources is the ability to produce relaxation and to locate and uncover sources of unconscious conflict.

Hypnotherapy is used in three main ways. The first is the use of direct suggestion in hypnosis to command the unconscious mind to mobilize one of its resources in the amelioration of clinical problems. Once this method has been established by the therapist, the patient can be taught to use the second method— self-hypnosis—in a precisely similar manner to maintain the therapeutic benefits in the absence of the therapist. The third effective use of hypnotherapy in the treatment of anxiety problems is that of analytical hypnotherapy in which the sources of the anxiety are located and reviewed in an ordered manner so that any current irrelevance in the anxiety response is understood at the level from which it originates and the futility of its maintenance appreciated. Analytical hypnotherapy also encourages the individual to discover for himself new ways of dealing with old fears by adequately harnessing innate unconscious resources that had hitherto been overlooked.

Direct Suggestion. Direct suggestion is the method most commonly used in hypnotherapy. When a satisfactory level of unconscious attention is attained following hypnotic induction, appropriate suggestions are directed at the symptoms. For example, a suggestion for greater relaxation than that already produced during hypnotic induction is given. These suggestions are usually enhanced by pleasant imagery so that the patient achieves a pleasant relaxed state during which anxiety symptoms are absent or are minimized. There are many ways in which such relaxation may be used in therapy.

Norton (1978) has demonstrated how effective deep muscle relaxation combined with desensitization can be when treating a severe anxiety in a concert pianist. Lamb (1980) has proven that quite brief periods of relaxation therapy will reduce the state of anxiety in dental patients, although it does not alter the underlying trait anxiety. Stanton (1978) showed that the relaxation from a simple hypnotic induction, followed by a period of a half an hour's silence without any other suggestions being given, is in itself therapeutic in effectively relieving anxiety. Meares (1971), using a predominantly nonverbal group induction followed by a period of quiet, found that in conjunction with autohypnosis this procedure produced a permanent reduction of chronic anxiety. Todd (1970) maintained that this reduction is achieved because hypnosis facilitates the substitution of the tension response by relaxation. Since no physical or emotional problem is without some accompaniment of anxiety, suggestions for greater relaxation are always therapeutically relevant and frequently provide the individual with relief from symptoms whose content of anxiety may be but dimly perceived by either patient or therapist.

Suggestions given in hypnosis to reduce anxiety can be effectively administered in a less direct manner by the use of projective imagery. The patient is encouraged to visualize himself remaining comfortable and relaxed in projected future situations that created anxiety in the past. Frequent repetition of this approach to the relief of anxiety is effective in a proportion of cases and does not demand a great deal of skill from the therapist. Many physicians who have used these simple suggestions for relaxation in hypnosis have found that the demand for tranquilizers drops considerably, especially if self-hypnosis is also employed.

Self-Hypnosis. Nearly all of the suggestions that are effective in heterohypnosis are equally effective in self-hypnosis; therefore, every patient who attends for hypnotherapy should be taught self-hypnosis. Almost all patients who are able to achieve a satisfactory level of hypnosis in the doctor's office can be taught to use self-hypnosis. The instructions for entering hypnosis on one's own are administered during heterohypnosis. Either a posthypnotic cue for entering hypnosis can be learned and self-administered, or a shortened version of the original induction procedure is taught to the patient. The patient should be encouraged to practice the method of self-hypnosis until he or she becomes sufficiently proficient to apply it readily in the anxiety-causing situation. O'Connor (1978) found that the addition of self-hypnosis to therapy with hypnosis and relaxation resulted in a success rate of about 82%. Sodomsky (1974) confirmed this and showed that many patients, when taught self-hypnosis after one to three sessions of hypnosis, can substitute this for their previous medication with tranquilizers. Davidson (1978) discovered that not only the anxiety but also the blood pressure remained low and within normal limits 9 months after the implementation of self-hypnosis. In some cases of extreme stress, Frankenthal (1969) found that survival itself resulted from the use of self-hypnosis.

Analytical Hypnotherapy. Probably the most significant recent advance in the specific therapy of anxiety has been the careful application of analytical techniques in hypnosis. A significant proportion of anxious patients benefit only temporarily or not at all from direct suggestion and self-hypnosis. It must be assumed that for these patients their persistent anxiety serves an important function in the conduct of their lives. There appears to be a significant part of the unconscious mind (an unconscious ego state) that is retaining the anxiety in a purposive manner. The purpose is usually discovered to be a solely protective one and is a defense against an old danger. A limited understanding of this danger has often prevented awareness of its current innocuousness or of the development of other resources within the individual that are adequate to deal with it.

Therapy in these cases is designed first to locate the source of conflict—and the resulting ego state that is perpetuating the anxiety—and then to promote internal communication with those resources within the individual that can resolve the conflict and provide means of dealing with the anxiety.

The analytical approach to hypnotherapy has recently become increasingly popular since techniques have been developed that do not require the depth of hypnosis necessary for some of the older uncovering techniques. This approach renders these methods accessible to all but those subjects highly resistant to hypnosis. Prominent among these methods is the ideomotor questioning technique, which promotes ready access to all of the unconscious resources. It is the ability of the unconscious mind to record every significant happening in an individual's life, and particularly those that have a bearing on his symptomatology, that renders this technique so valuable. Such a technique permits the recovery of significant memories and the location of those resources unconsciously present but dormant in the patient. When these resources are mobilized, the patient is enabled to deal with those problems that have arisen from his experiences.

The most effective method of handling anxiety with the aid of hypnosis incorporates some or all of these approaches in a flexible manner. For example, in every case there is room for some modification in the patient's life-style in order to reduce some of the stress to which he is unnecessarily exposing himself. The induction of hypnosis, using a technique that incorporates suggestions for relaxation, will itself be therapeutic in a significant proportion of cases presented with anxiety. However, the addition of specific suggestions for maintaining mental relaxation posthypnotically, combined with training in self-hypnosis to reinforce these suggestions outside the consulting room, dramatically increases the number of patients who will benefit from hypnotherapy. It must be assumed that those who respond positively do not have a persistent unconscious reason for retaining anxiety or that, during therapy, they have discovered that the unconscious reason for the anxiety is currently unnecessary. For the significant remainder who either do not benefit from suggestions given in hypnosis or relapse after initial improvement, other more specific techniques for dealing with the persistent anxiety must be instituted. While behavioral techniques in hypnosis, such as deconditioning and implosion therapy, will benefit a proportion of these patients, the use of an analytical approach dealing with the persistent unconscious need to retain the anxiety is more likely to be effective and can readily be used in conjunction with any behavioral method.

The following case illustrates my approach to the therapy of anxiety in which all of the previously mentioned techniques are used to some extent.

The patient is a 35-year-old woman who was referred because of her extreme anxiety associated with recurrent headaches, insomnia, attacks of panic, and cold sweats, which tended to come on without any warning. The anxiety was more likely to occur whenever she was with strangers, particularly men. Consequently, she could not enjoy parties and tended to drink and smoke heavily at such gatherings because of her tension. In spite of this anxiety, she managed to be an effective supervisor in her office work, although she lacked the assertiveness necessary to direct an inefficient subordinate. Her inability to express her feelings created difficulty in communicating with her husband; he felt that he never knew what she was really thinking, since she would not discuss anything that appeared to be of concern to her.

Both the patient and her husband agreed that an important area of poor communication was sexual. The patient felt that her husband was sexually cold towards her, while her husband indicated that he had never felt sexually welcome to her and consequently had become averse to having sexual relations with her. The patient admitted an extreme reluctance to express her sexual needs and had felt that her husband would presume their presence without her having to express them.

An explanation of the role of hypnotherapy in the treatment of her anxiety was given to her, and it was emphasized that she would benefit only if she was prepared to cooperate with the therapy since she could not be made to do anything that she did not wish to do. Hypnosis was then induced, using progressive muscular relaxation technique, and she proved to be an excellent subject. Suggestions were given that she would not only be able to cooperate in therapy but would find it easier to relax at future sessions and be much less tense than she had been.

She was seen again one week later and reported that she had felt very relaxed following her first meeting. This relaxation had lasted all day, and, in fact, she had slept very well that night. However, during the interval, her anxiety had returned as strongly as ever. It was therefore decided that an analytical approach was indicated. Hypnosis was once again induced, and she was instructed to orient her mind back to a time before the anxiety began and to indicate when she was there by nodding the head. She did this and soon began to smile, evidently recalling a pleasant early memory. After a short interval, she was directed to come forward in her memory to the first experience which had anything to do with her current anxiety and to indicate when she was there by another nod of the head. She was then encouraged to review this experience in detail and to indicate when this had been completed by a further nod. It is at this point that the following excerpt commences.

VERBALIZATION	COMMENT
Doctor: How old are you there, Sarah?	These questions are designed to reinforce the regression so far achieved.
Patient: I'm 2 years old.	
Doctor: Where are you?	"Where are you?" demands an optimal involvement in the experience located.
Patient: I'm in the kitchen.	
Doctor: In the kitchen?	
Patient: I'm cooking in the oven.	
Doctor: In the oven? Who's doing that?	

VERBALIZATION	COMMENT

Patient: Me.

Doctor: Cooking in the oven? But you are only two. Is the oven hot?

Patient: No.

Doctor: You are just pretending?

Patient: Yes.

Doctor: Okay. That's good. And what's happening?

Patient: The stove falls over.

Doctor: The stove falls over? And what happens?

Patient: A kettle of boiling water falls over.

Doctor: All over you?

Patient: [Tearfully] Over my sister!

Doctor: The kettle does?

Patient: It burns her.

Doctor: Does it burn you?

Patient: No.

Doctor: Does it burn you at all?

Patient: No. I'm stuck in the oven.

Doctor: You're inside are you? And everything falls over?

Patient: Yes.

Doctor: Is there a big bang?

Patient: Yes.

Doctor: Who comes?

Patient: Mum.

Doctor: What does she say?

Patient: "Oh, my God! Thank God you are okay."

Doctor: How is your sister?

Patient: She is riding the kiddie car.

Doctor: Is she okay?

Patient: She looks all right.

Doctor: What happens?

Patient: Mum is changing her diaper on the couch. She's peed herself. She's got all blisters on her leg.

Doctor: How do you feel about that?

Patient: Scared.

Doctor: Scared about what?

At first it seems as if there has been some mistake until it is realized that we are talking directly to the 2-year-old Sarah who is deeply involved in her game of pretense.

Since this experience is the source of the origin of the anxiety, there must be something more that is creating tension. The question, "what's happening?" persuades Sarah to review these events in greater detail. In very few words, this very frightening experience is rapidly and clearly depicted. Sarah, trapped in the fallen oven, is evidently terrified not only by her own desperate situation, but presumably by the screams of her scalded sister.

Mother eventually comes to the rescue, and the end of the calamity for the 2-year-old Sarah appears in sight.

Mother is relieved that she is all right and this is reassuring.

Furthermore, her sister at first appears to be unharmed. However, this is not really so. Her sister is not only very distressed, but she also appears to be injured in an alarming way.

All of Sarah's previous panic returns in full force. Mother blames her for

VERBALIZATION	COMMENT

VERBALIZATION

Patient: Mum says it was my fault.

Doctor: Did you do it?

Patient: No, the kettle of water did it.

Doctor: Yes, the kettle of water did it. You didn't mean to do that did you?

Patient: No.

Doctor: What did you do? Did you climb into the oven?

Patient: Yes. There's a block stuck in the back.

Doctor: A block? One of your playing blocks?

Patient: Yes.

Doctor: How did it get in there?

Patient: I was playing and pushed in the rack.

Doctor: I see—and it got stuck and you had to go in and get it didn't you?

Patient: Yes.

Doctor: You didn't think that the oven would fall over, did you?

Patient: No. I didn't.

Doctor: You wouldn't have gone in there if you had would you?

Patient: No.

Doctor: Okay, 35-year-old Sarah, did you hear that?

Patient: Yes.

Doctor: Two-year-old Sarah has a very frightening experience happening to her, can you help her please? She's scared to death. Give her all the wisdom, all the understanding, and all the comforting that you can and when you have done that nod your head to let me know. She is very scared. You may have to pick her up and love her.

COMMENT

everything. She must be bad for having caused such a terrible thing to happen to her sister, and yet there is a part of her that knows she did not do it. But mother does not agree.

Therapist and patient review the events preceding the accident in some detail, and it is clear that the 2-year-old Sarah's actions appeared very reasonable at the time. She was not clever enough to realize what the consequences of her actions would have been and that going after her playing block would cause such disastrous consequences. It is evident that her mother believes that she should have known. She is extremely distressed, and Sarah is responsible. She decides that she must never be bad again and that the only way she can prevent this is to retain the panic which reminds her not to be adventurous and resourceful and not to follow her instinct. Instead, she must await the instructions of others to avoid the risk of their disapproval. Therapy is directed at locating her current resources of adult wisdom and understanding so that she can understand her mother, as well as 2-year-old Sarah and can discover that she need no longer cling to her old scared feelings, which had unconsciously been retained to protect her from the disapproval of mother figures.

VERBALIZATION

COMMENT

Patient: [Nods after a short interval]

Doctor: Have you done that? Good. Okay, 2-year-old Sarah, now that you have heard that, do you still need to go on being scared?

Patient: [Shaking her head] No.

Doctor: Right. Thirty-five-year-old Sarah, 2-year-old Sarah now feels that she doesn't need to keep the scared feelings that she has had for the past 33 years. Please find a way for her to let all that scared feeling go, and when you have found a way for her to let go of it, please nod your head.

Patient: [Nods]

Doctor: There you are, 2-year-old Sarah, there's a way to let go of that old, out-of-date, unnecessary and uncomfortable scared feeling. It's finished with, over and done with; let it all go. When it has all gone and you are sure it has all gone, just nod your head.

Patient: [Nods and smiles]

Doctor: Has it all gone?

Patient: [Nods vigorously and smiles]

Doctor: That's good. It's about time, eh? Okay. Now let us have a look and see if there is any other Sarah inside who is feeling bad. If there is, nod your head for "yes" and if there isn't, shake your head for "no."

Patient: (Nods)

Doctor: How old are you there?

Patient: Eighteen . . . nineteen.

Doctor: What's happening there?

Patient: I've got a boyfriend.

Doctor: A nice boyfriend?

Patient: He appears nice.

Doctor: That should feel good. What is wrong with that?

Patient: [Grimly] He's mean.

However, she has kept these feelings for a very long time and needs to find a means of relinquishing them. So long as there is no unexpressed need for their retention, a means for yielding can readily be discovered.

Sarah is instructed to let them go and, to her surprise, finds that she does this very easily and feels an extremely comfortable feeling replacing them. She smiles involuntarily. It has been found that, almost invariably, the release of old tensions permits a patient to give a genuine smile, which confirms such a release.

It now becomes important to seek and locate any other experiences that might have contributed to Sarah's general anxiety so that these can similarly be dealt with. Sarah discovers one occurring many years later that bears some of the same characteristics of the first. To all appearances, her boyfriend is nice, but Sarah feels otherwise about him. He frightens her. She does not like him.

VERBALIZATION

COMMENT

Doctor: Is he? What does he do?

Patient: He fights with his father . . . fist fights.

Doctor: That's not nice, is it?

Patient: Selfish.

Doctor: What are your feelings about that?

Patient: I hate him.

Doctor: You hate him. Why do you stay with him?

Patient: His mother won't let me date anyone else.

Doctor: His mother won't let you date anyone else? What has she got to do with it?

Patient: I'm living with his parents.

Doctor: Why are you living there?

Patient: My father accused me of being a slut, and I left home and took a job, and I'm living there. He's my first boyfriend.

Doctor: Do you feel trapped?

Patient: Yes. Larry dates other girls, but I mustn't date any other boys.

Doctor: I bet you are as mad as hell about that, are you?

Patient: Yes.

Doctor: Okay. Thirty-five-year-old Sarah, did you hear that?

Patient: Yes.

Doctor: We have 18/19-year-old Sarah who is really trapped and is feeling terrible. She needs your help. Can you help her? She is feeling angry and helpless and very uncomfortable. I want you to understand how she is feeling, and when you have done that, nod your head.

Patient: [Nods]

Doctor: Now give her all of the wisdom and comforting that you can, and when you have done that, let me know by nodding your head.

In fact, she hates him!

So, why does she stay with him? She must not cause anyone's distress, especially to mother (or to mother figures), so she is powerless, and this increases her anxiety.

Again, Sarah has had further confirmation that she is bad and must not defend herself. She must not respect her own wishes or needs. This does not prevent her from feeling extremely angry, but this anger must be concealed. Its presence only serves to increase her anxiety. Once again, we enlist the aid of her adult wisdom and understanding to see things as they really are rather than as they have been unconsciously interpreted at the time of the original event. And once again Sarah is encouraged to feel that, although all of her uncomfortable feelings were reasonable at the time and really totally acceptable, they are now no longer relevant or necessary for her continued well-being. Not only had she unconsciously retained much hurt and anger, she had also felt guilty about this. This guilt (always present in these cases of anxiety and contributing to it) is also unnecessary. She is encouraged to find a

VERBALIZATION	COMMENT
Patient: [Nods]	means of relinquishing all of these outdated tensions and is able to discover a means of so doing.
Doctor: Okay, 18/19-year-old Sarah, now that you have heard that, do you still need to keep those uncomfortable, scared, hurt, angry, and guilty feelings any longer?	
Patient: [Shaking her head] No.	
Doctor: Okay, 35-year-old Sarah, I want you to find a way for 18-year-old Sarah to let go of those uncomfortable feelings that she now knows that she no longer needs. When a way has been found to do that, your head will once again nod for "yes."	
Patient: [Nods]	
Doctor: There you are, 18-year-old Sarah, there is a way for you to let go of all of those old, out-of-date, and unnecessary tensions. Use that way and, when they have all gone, nod your head.	She releases these irrelevant tensions and feels the comfort of this freedom.
Patient: [Nods and smiles]	She smiles and is now ready to tackle later sources of anxiety and poor self-esteem.
Doctor: All gone? Feels good? It's about time isn't it?	

Therapy continued in this manner until all discoverable experiences responsible for unconscious tension were located and dealt with. Sarah was finally unable to locate any further areas of inner discomfort, and the session concluded with strong suggestions for greater ego strength and increased self-esteem. These latter suggestions were recorded on a cassette to which Sarah was instructed to listen at least once daily.

Her immediate response to this session was a much more positive attitude toward herself. In several instances, she showed satisfactory self-assertion, and her general level of tension was much lower. Further sessions of therapy were devoted to teaching her self-hypnosis for use whenever she became unnecessarily tense. She found that by taking three deep breaths with the eyes closed and repeating to herself the word, "relax" she was able to induce a sufficient level of relaxation at which she could imagine herself in a quiet place by the water where she could give herself any other appropriate positive suggestions.

There were no further attacks of the extreme anxiety with which she had presented, and at the final session, some 6 weeks after therapy had begun, Sarah remarked that not only had she become more relaxed but so too had her husband, who had become very warm and affectionate as well. They were now able to discuss with each other many aspects of their relationship which had hitherto been impossible.

Six months after termination of therapy, a communication with Sarah indicated that, though there were still occasional periods of mild anxiety, she was coping very well and did not feel the need for further therapy.

In the analytical hypnotherapy of anxiety and chronic stress, there is almost always a discoverable experience or series of experiences of a critical nature in which an important and crucial decision has had to be made. This decision is as appropriate as the individual can make it within the limits of his or her resources at that time; inevitably, it has involved the retention of fear as part of the defense mechanism. When these critical experiences have been located and fully determined, an unconscious review of them (using the individual's present resources, made more freely accessible through the medium of hypnosis) makes new decisions possible. It is hoped that these new decisions are ones that indicate that the retention of old fears is no longer necessary. When this fact is fully accepted, it is found that old fears and anxieties are readily relinquished, indicating that anxiety is always purposeful and will not remain when the purpose is no longer seen to exist. This is the rationale of the analytical approach.

Like any other symptom, anxiety may be retained in spite of adequate analytical work because it has come to be a means of obtaining necessary secondary gains. Suggestions for greater ego strength and self-assertion enable the individual to obtain these secondary gains without the need for his symptoms and ensure that they will not remain or return. Such suggestions are given in hypnosis and repeated as often as necessary. They may be reinforced by appropriate instruction in self-hypnosis using these suggestions or by the use of a tape recording of the suggestions.

The persistence of symptoms always indicates that there remains an unconscious belief either that the original cause for fear still exists or that relinquishing of the anxiety will leave the individual inadequately protected.

It must be reemphasized that many patients with anxiety will do well with the training in relaxation that successful hypnotic induction brings and that the addition of specific suggestions for relaxation will enhance this favourable response. Such therapy is well within the scope of almost any hypnotherapist. On the other hand, those sufferers from anxiety who will not respond to this approach require the greater skill of the analytical hypnotherapist who is prepared to deal with long-buried emotional conflicts. It is to be hoped that an increasing proportion of hypnotherapists will recognize the benefits of acquiring these skills that will enable them to aid a higher proportion of those suffering from anxiety and chronic stress.

References

Barnett EA: Analytical Hypnotherapy: Principles and Practice. Kingston, Canada, Junica Publishing, 1981

Bartlett EE: The use of hypnotic techniques without hypnosis per se. Am J Clin Hypn 13:273, 1971

Bowers KT, Kelly P: Stress, disease, psychotherapy and "hypnosis." J Abnorm Psychol 88:490, 1979

Brown RA: Personality measures in Gamma and Delta alcoholics. J Clin Psychol 36:345, 1980

Celucci AJ, Lawrence PS: Individual differences in self reported sleep variable correlations among nightmare sufferers. J Clin Psychol 34:721, 1978

Cox RJ, McGuiness D: The effect of chronic anxiety level upon self-control of heart rate. Biol Psychol 5:7, 1977

Daniels LK: The treatment of acute anxiety and postoperative gingival pain by hypnosis and covert conditioning: A case report. Am J Clin Hypn 19:116, 1976

Davidson GP, Farnbach RW, Richardson BA: Self-hypnosis training in anxiety reduction. Austr Fam Physician 7:905, 1978

Eddy CC: The effects of alcohol on anxiety in problem and non-problem drinking women. Doctoral dissertation, Cornell University, 1978

Ellis A, Harper R: A New Guide to Rational Living. Englewood Cliffs, NJ, Prentice-Hall, 1975

Frankenthal K: Autohypnosis and other aids for survival in situations of extreme stress. Int J Clin Exp Hypn 17:153, 1969

Freud S: Inhibitions, Symptoms and Anxiety. (1926) Standard Edition. London, Hogarth Press, 1960

Freud S: The Problem of Anxiety. New York, WW Norton, 1936

Fuchs K: Therapy of vaginismus by hypnotic desensitization. Am J Obstet Gynecol 137:1, 1980

Gellhorn E: The neurophysiological basis of anxiety: A hypothesis. Perspect Biol Med 8:488, 1965

Horney K: The Neurotic Personality of our Time. New York, WW Norton, 1937

Hurley JD: Differential effects of hypnosis, biofeedback training and trophotropic responses on anxiety, ego strength and locus of control. J Clin Psychol 36:503, 1980

Ishizvka Y: Causes of anxiety and depression in marriage. Psychiatr Ann 9:302, 1979

Janis IL, Feshbach S: Effects of fear-arousing communications. In Proshansky H, Seidenberg B (eds): Basic Studies in Social Psychology. New York, Holt, Rinehart & Winston, 1965

Kane LJ: A comparison of the anxiety levels of felons and noncriminals. Doctoral dissertation, United States International University, 1976

Kazarian SS: Effects of antianxiety agents on relaxation training: A preliminary investigation. Can Psych Assoc J 23:389, 1978

Kupfer DJ, Rosenbaum JP, Detre TP: Personality style and sexual functioning among psychiatric outpatients. J Sex Res 13:257, 1977

Labaw W, Holton C, Tewell K, Eccles D: The use of self-hypnosis by children with cancer. Am J Clin Hypn 17:233, 1975

Lamb DH, Strand KH: The effects of brief relaxation treatment for dental anxiety on measures of state and trait anxiety. J Clin Psychol 36:270, 1980

Lange HV: Anxiety and neuroticism in the development of headache after lumbar puncture operation. (German) Newenartz 49:47, 1978

Laughlin HP: The Neuroses. Washington, Butterworths, 1967

London PT, McDevitt RA: The effects of hypnotic susceptibility and training on responses to stress. J Abnorm Psychol 76:336, 1970

McCrae RR, Costa PT, Bossé R: Anxiety extraversion and smoking. Br J Soc Clin Psychol 17:269, 1978

Marcheson M: Four particularly instructive cases of alcoholism. Rivista Internazionale Di Psicologia E Ipnosi 15:263, 1974

Meares A: Group relaxing hypnosis. Med J Austr 2:675, 1971

Norton GR, MacLean L, Wachman E: The use of cognitive desensitization and self-directed mastery training for treating stage fright. Cogn Ther Res 2:61, 1978

O'Brien RM, Cooley LE, Ciotti J, Henninger KM: Augmentation of systematic desensitization of snake phobia through posthypnotic dream suggestion. Am J Clin Hypn 23:231, 1981

O'Connor LV: Short-term hypnotherapy dealing with the resolution of psychophysiological disorders, symptomatic of anxiety. Dissertation Abstracts International 39, 2B, 991, 1978

Pestonjee DM, Bagchi R: Anxiety and aggression: A study of coronary patients. Ind J Clin Psychol 6:63, 1979

Rado S: Achieving self-reliant treatment behaviour, therapeutic motivations and therapeutic technique. In Psychoanalysis of Behaviour, vol 2. New York, Grune & Stratton, 1962, p 111

Rank O: The Trauma of Birth. New York, Robert Brunner, 1952

Samuels DD: A study of the relationship between maternal anxiety and self-esteem of Head Start children. Doctoral dissertation, Michigan State University, 1976

Seligman MEP: Helplessness. San Francisco, WH Freeman, 1975

Selye H: Textbook of Endocrinology. Montreal, WT Franks, 1947

Shahi SP, Thakur GP: Self-esteem in subjects high, middle and low in anxiety. J Psychol Res 22:111, 1978

Sodomsky ME: Hypnosis in psychiatry. J Kansas Med Soc 6:195, 1974

Stanton HE: A simple hypnotic technique to reduce anxiety. Austr J Clin Exp Hypn 6:35, 1978

Sullivan HS: The Interpersonal Theory of Psychiatry. New York, WW Norton, 1953

Todd FJ, Kelly RJ: The use of hypnosis to facilitate conditional relaxation responses: A report of three cases. J Behav Ther Exp Psychiatry 1:295, 1970

Wolpe J: Psychotherapy By Reciprocal Inhibition. Stanford, CA, Stanford University Press, 1958

24 Hypnotherapy for Anorexia Nervosa and Accompanying Somatic Disorders

KRIPA S. THAKUR

In the last decade, incidences of anorexia nervosa have increased to epidemic proportions. In Western countries, almost one out of every one hundred young women between the ages of 14 and 20 show some signs of anorexia nervosa. Anorexia has a mortality rate of 15% to 20% and causes more morbidity in the family in which it occurs.

A wide variety of therapies, some of them controversial, has been used to treat anorexia, with varying degrees of success. The more common therapies use psychotropic drugs, behavior modifications, family dynamics, and insight development.

The etiology of anorexia remains an enigma. At best it can be regarded as a psychosociobiologic illness. We have not advanced much more in the clinical understanding of anorexia than William Gull, who coined the term *anorexia nervosa* in 1873.

Ten years ago I started using hypnotherapy for the treatment of obesity. At that time it occurred to me to reverse the hypnotic suggestions used for the treatment of obesity in anorexics. The results, especially in weight gain, were encouraging. This chapter reports experience with 90 cases of patients with anorexia nervosa treated with hypnotherapy.

Referrals

Patients and physicians came to know about my interest in anorexia through reports in the local and national press, open-line television programs (sponsored by the various medical associations), and radio talks. Specialists such as psychiatrists, internists, gynecologists, and endocrinologists referred the anorexic patients to me. A few referrals came from the police department when some of the anorexics were caught shoplifting.

Initial Interview

I prefer to interview the patient alone to record the clinical history. The patient is told that her case is mild, moderate, or critically severe, depending on clinical symptoms, and psychological and social complications. I prefer to treat mild to moderately severe cases on an outpatient basis, whereas critically ill patients are advised to be admitted to the hospital. First, an introductory talk is given on misconceptions about hypnosis. The patient is then given a Chevreul's pendulum. She can demonstrate to herself that without conscious efforts, just self-suggestions, she can make the pendulum move. She is then allowed to watch other patients receiving hypnotherapy for various psychosomatic illnesses. Trance induction and deepening, posthypnotic suggestions, and dehypnotizing procedures are demonstrated. She is permitted to ask these patients any questions if she wishes to do so.

At this point I ask if she would be willing to try hypnotherapy for her condition. Usually her answer is no. She may elaborate further that she does not feel ill so she has no need for any therapy, and actually, she should not be in a doctor's office at all.

Breaking the Patient's Resistance and Ego-strengthening

The patient is told: "It is your right to receive therapy from me or not. Your decision is final, but before you decide, I am not sure if you have understood various facts about hypnotherapy. Maybe you would like to see some other patients with anorexia nervosa and how I treat them. Perhaps you would like to speak to them about your fears and about losing control of your eating. I would like you to come to my office and satisfy any questions or doubts. I would like to give you as much time as you want, but I am afraid your time is likely to run out. As you continue to practice anorexia, your body may show signs of decompensation. This is not to frighten you; I am telling you because enough damage has been done already. You may have your own explanations for various symptoms that you have. I sincerely hope that you will listen to the part of your mind that believes that maybe your anorexia nervosa can be treated here after all.

"I cannot tell you what life should mean to you. There must be some purpose and meaning in your life, more than just being reduced to bones, remaining suspicious and withdrawn, and keeping control over your body. I am leaving it up to you to decide to come back to start the therapy. It is only when you have decided this that I will be able to work with you. Our treatment is like a jigsaw puzzle in which you and I set out various pieces. There is no competition between us. Do as much as you can do, and I will try to do my part. You need not become dependent on me; however, in the beginning, I want you to take my advice. While the treatment progresses, you will notice that you have greater control of your body than you ever thought you had achieved by practicing anorexia."

Over the years I have failed to convince about 5% of my patients to lose their resistance.

Cooperation with internists, gynecologists, and dentists is necessary to assess the patient's physical condition. I check urine, electrolyte levels, and electrocardiograms (ECGs). Patients are advised to have initial photographs taken. Photographs are repeated at the end of the therapy and sometimes during the middle of the course (Figs. 24-1 to 24-6). Patients are advised to write in their diaries, check their measurements, calorie intake, and so forth. At some stage of the treatment, I suggest that they see a dietitian as well. Patients are advised particularly to keep some record of their exercise and are definitely counseled against using laxatives and drinking excess amounts of fluids to avoid water intoxication and hypokalemia.

Hypnosis Sessions

Suggest that the patient bring an empty cassette. The sessions are then recorded and the patient is advised to listen to the sessions at home. She usually learns to induce hypnosis, deepen it as required, and dehypnotize herself. During hypnosis

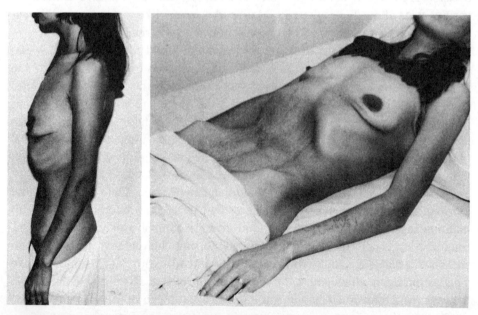

Fig. 24-1. When the patient recovered from anorexia, she requested plastic surgery for removal of the tattoo ("LOVE ME ALWAYS"); "Not necessary," she said.

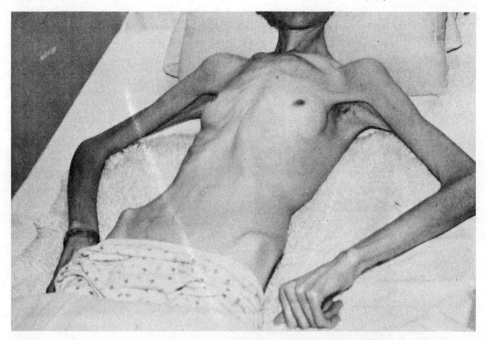

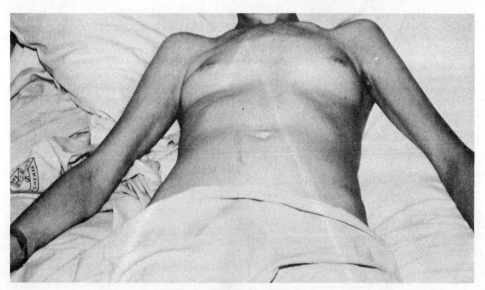

Fig. 24-2. (*Top*) Before hypnotherapy and (*Bottom*) 4 weeks after hypnotherapy (weight gain of 38 lb)

she is taught and demonstrated as many hypnotic phenomena as possible. During that time, reassure her that she is controlling her body even more than she has ever done by any other means.

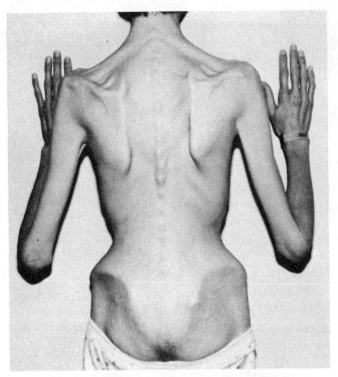

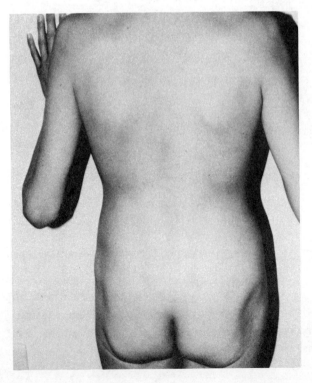

Fig. 24-3. (*Top*) Before hypnotherapy and (*Bottom*) 4
weeks after hypnotherapy
(weight gain of 38 lb)

Other Topics Addressed During Hypnotic Treatment

Weight Gain. The patient is told: "I fully realize that you have no desire to gain any more weight. Actually, you wish to lose more weight, especially on your thighs, hips, and tummy. You don't like them being so round or flabby. I would like you to use your imagination so that as you breathe in, your chest enlarges. Permit your body to increase just the size of the thickness of the thinnest paper you can think of and your size is increasing in the areas that don't really matter much to you. Your weight is increasing, mostly on your breasts, shoulders, arms, legs, and on your back. All the food that you eat has to go to your tummy. For a long time your tummy has not been accustomed to any food so there is some distension and a feeling of fullness. You are quite right when you say that all your weight is going to go to your tummy, but it doesn't stay there. It will be distributed all over the body. I understand your fear. I know you would like to measure your tummy after each meal. Feel free to do so in front of a mirror and keep your measurements. Some day you will realize how futile this exercise is. You don't have much time left for yourself. These rituals take most of the valuable time of your life. Once again, let me remind you that you take your own time to put on more weight. Time does not wait for anyone and it may run out on you. You must attain a certain weight so that your body can function naturally. As you remain relaxed and gradually keep putting on a little more weight, you will become accustomed to that weight. It will become part of your new body image."

Vomiting Control. "You may have noticed that when you are tense, lonely, bored, slightly depressed, or facing a decision, you get an impulse to eat and eat excessively. You feel guilty and then you vomit. Vomiting brings relief. Then you promise yourself that you will never vomit again or, for that matter, will never binge again. By undoing this whole act, you are ready to, under tension, binge all over again. Now, relax a little more and concentrate. Imagine that from your mouth downwards into your tummy and further down it is just a one-way street. All the time the food proceeds in one direction only, that is, downwards. You can make your imagery even more vivid by imagining a large number of cars going on a one-way street. A series of waves of contraction and relaxation are proceeding down the tube from your mouth towards your stomach, right in the center of your chest and from the stomach to your intestines, in your tummy. Think of moments in one direction only. Next, imagine that when you breathe in, you are breathing in through your nose, but as you breathe out, there is an imaginary hole, the size of a quarter, right in the pit of your stomach and the air is coming out from that hole. All of the muscles of your tummy are very relaxed. There is just not enough pressure in your tummy to push the food up for vomiting. When you find that vomiting is not so easy, the channel for escape becomes doubtful. Say to yourself every time that when you vomit, you had no relief from

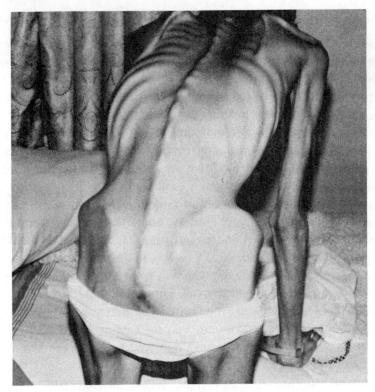

Fig. 24-4. (*Left*) Before hypnotherapy and (*Right*) 7 weeks after hypnotherapy
(weight gain of 35 lb)

the vomiting and, paradoxically, you say to yourself further that you will vomit
again. You are permitted to vomit if required. Now, if vomiting does not give
you relief and you are not undoing any guilt, then your binge-eating becomes
an even more serious problem. You know very well how panicky you get when
you do not vomit immediately after binge-eating. You will be scared to binge-
eat. Binge-eating indeed does give you some relief from tension. Now you are
more likely to face your tensions, your inadequacies, and your fears. You are
more likely to adopt to change, or to become more assertive than to surrender
or try to escape your tensions by binge-eating, guilt, vomiting, and undoing the
whole cycle. Try another exercise. Imagine that you are very tense and are binge-
eating, feeling guilty, and vomiting. Try to use all your senses. Use as vivid
imagination as possible about the circumstances—food, smell, your room, the
toilet—everything as vivid as possible. You vomit and vomit and vomit without
any relief whatsoever, but you keep binge-eating and keep vomiting. You get
absolutely no relief. You simply make a mockery of your symptoms. While you
are so relaxed and calm, you rehearse the whole drama of binge-eating and

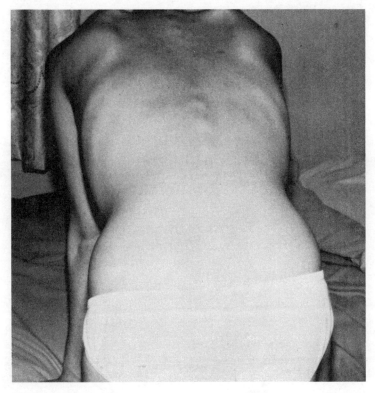

Fig. 24-4. (*Continued*)

vomiting. Because vomiting gives you no relief, the act of vomiting is not rein-forcing binge-eating for the purpose of relieving tensions."

Recommend that the patient listen to her own recorded session of actual vomiting.

Fullness in the Tummy. "There is always a certain amount of gas in your tummy. Remember, for a long time this gas was moving in one direction until the time when you started practicing anorexia. Your alimentary tract is organized in such a way that the digestion proceeds, step by step, from the mouth downwards. If any of the stages are interrupted, then the subsequent steps do not come at the right time. The result is complete chaos in the movements and production of gas in your tummy. I want you to imagine gas movements inside your tummy in one direction. Don't be surprised that you can hear those sounds much louder now that the gas is moving downwards. I can put a stethoscope chest-piece on your tummy and you can hear for yourself that you can make the movement of gas much faster in the downward direction. I appreciate your fears of fullness

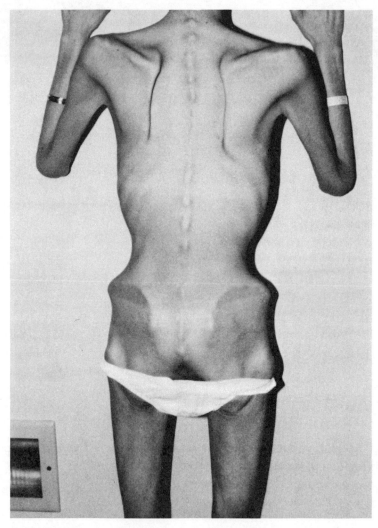

Fig. 24-5. (*Left*) Before hypnotherapy and (*Right*) 7 weeks after hypnotherapy
  (weight gain of 35 lb)

in the tummy. It simply aggravates the feeling that you are going to gain all your
weight in the tummy only."

Constipation. "Now you imagine that there is increased pressure on the left side
of your tummy. Once again, the traffic is going in one direction, downwards, and
is forceful. Allow 10 to 15 minutes every day at the same time in the morning,
before you sit on the toilet seat. You will notice that gradually your bowels start
contracting and pushing the feces downwards. You can imagine, further that a
tight fist is opening and closing on the lower left side of your tummy."

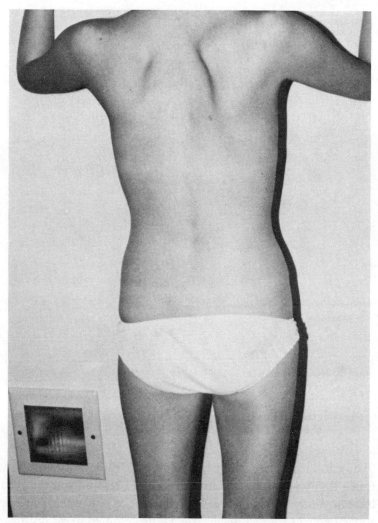

Fig. 24-5. (*Continued*)

Abdominal Cramps. "You have learned how to produce glove anesthesia. Now, anesthetize your left hand and put it at the site of the cramps. All the numbness of the hand is passed on to the tisues of your tummy. Try to breathe out from where the pain is. This will relax the muscles that are in spasms inside your tummy."

Appetite and Hunger. "Now that you can appreciate controlling some functions of your body, let me reassure you that it is quite all right to start being hungry and feeling a desire to eat. You will notice that your sense of smell has increased

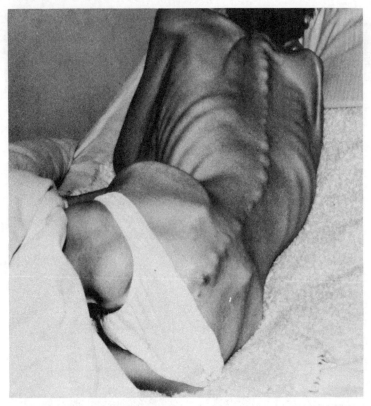

Fig. 24-6. (*Left*) Before hypnotherapy and (*Right*) 7 weeks after hypnotherapy (weight gain of 35 lb)

and that you can taste better. Your saliva is a lot clearer and more tasty. It will never happen that you will lose control of eating. I remind you that you do not eat to please anybody, not even me. You will notice that when you hear noises or have movements in your stomach, you will be tempted to eat healthier food."

Overactivity. "As you relax your body part by part, you have full control of yourself. All muscles are extremely relaxed, just like a Raggedy Ann doll. All muscles are loose and limp. When you are lying in bed, relax and keep relaxing your muscles. There is no need for you to be overactive. Overactivity is a way of keeping yourself excited, to fill the loneliness of your life. It also burns a lot of energy and keeps your weight down. Now, you are deep, calm, and relaxed. I will give you a count of five—at that point, open your eyes and see if you can move your legs or your hands. This is not to challenge you, this is to create confidence in yourself. These suggestions are useful to you and you are quite capable of accepting them. You will find that your limbs are so relaxed that they don't want to move but you know that there is nothing wrong with them. You

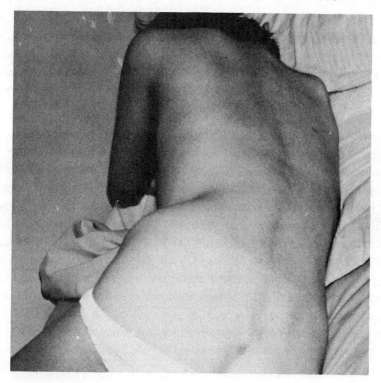

Fig. 24-6. (*Continued*)

can move them if you wanted to, but you don't. I would like to remind you that any form of exercising is dangerous in your present condition."

Migraine Headaches. "I would like you to imagine that your hands are in steaming hot water. They are getting warmer and warmer. Now your fingers are tingling, pulsating, and you can appreciate the warmth. As the warmth increases you feel more relaxed and even sleepy. I would like you to feel cooler and cooler on your forehead and behind your eyes as well as on your temples. As you continue to feel warmer on your hands and cooler behind your eyes, your headache will bother you less and less and in about 10 minutes, it will disappear. The more you practice this exercise, the shorter the time it will take to control your headaches. You will notice that the intensity of the headaches has also become less and their duration is diminished. You are not afraid of headaches."

Breast Augmentation. "As you could increase the temperature of your palm and fingertips, you can also increase the temperature of the skin and the underlying tissues in the center of your chest between the breasts. Imagine that there is a steaming hot towel put there and your skin is getting warmer and warmer. Every time you breathe in, it is as if the air is going into the breasts and they are enlarging. Your breasts are gradually filling into a larger size bra. Practice this exercise about 15 to 30 minutes every day. You will notice that gradually the breasts are enlarging. As your breasts enlarge, then comparatively your tummy looks smaller. You will also become confident that all your weight gain has not gone on your tummy and thighs. Your body looks more proportionate now."

Menstruation. "You are aware of the feelings when you empty your bladder and pass urine. You are also aware of opening your bowels and the feeling you get at your anus. I would like you to become very much aware of the feelings in your vagina. Imagine that something is trickling down the vagina. It's bright, red-colored blood. You have fullness in the lower part of your tummy, a backache, and fullness in your breasts. You gradually become more and more aware of blood coming down the vagina. I would like to remind you again that long before you lost a substantial amount of weight, your mental attitude toward femininity had stopped your period. Excessive exercising has also contributed toward its cessation. It may take a little longer than six months after you have gained sufficient weight for the period to start. If you continue to practice these exercises and you accept yourself psychologically more as a matured woman who is willing to take the responsibilities of a grown-up female, you are likely to start your periods much sooner."

Panic Attacks. "While you gain weight, the total amount of blood in your body increases. You feel that thumping feeling in your head. The body becomes warmer. You are particularly sensitive to this feeling of increased pressure in your head. You are also particularly aware of things happening in your tummy, especially the cramps, and the fullness from gas. You are extremely frightened to note that the clothes you were wearing recently fit so tightly on you. You feel that everything is going to go completely out of control. Let me reassure you. Think of that pendulum. It moved according to your suggestions and when you told it to stop, it stopped. If the movements of the pendulum could be controlled by suggestions only, then the movements of your intestines, increase in body size, your eating habits, and so forth can be controlled by suggestions as well. Gradually, as you are able to tolerate these changes in your body, they will become a part of your new body image. Remember, for a long time your body was simply trying to survive. Your heart was beating slowly. Peripheral circulation in your limbs was poor. You stopped having periods. You grew some fine hair on your body. This was nature's way of conserving energy. Now that you have started eating, the chemical processes of the body called metabolism are enhanced now and many of the things that you feel actually are natural things that of which you deprived yourself while practicing anorexia."

Awareness. "While you were practicing anorexia, you were withdrawn from the world. You concentrated only on controlling your body. You withdrew from all sensations. You avoided stimulation of your nervous system from communications passed on to you from other people and objects alike. You were not interested in music; you didn't pay attention to colors, smell, or taste. You didn't notice the changes in nature, and in seasonal variations. Instead you concentrated more and more on body sensations coming from your tummy. You can reverse the tide now. As you put your two hands together, pay close attention to your fingertips, how cold or warm they are, how all the ridges feel on the skin. Pay attention to the movements of your joints. Listen to every sound that comes to your ears. Pay attention to sense of smell. There is an unlimited amount of stimulus in the environment for your eyes to notice. When you deliberately pay attention, you will find that gradually your sensory awareness increases. You will notice that you are now ready to comprehend communications, especially non-verbal communications, from people. You will be amazed that, instead of thinking back into the past, you enjoy life more in a here-and-now situation. You will not feel as if you are cut off from the stream of life. You are very much a part of it now."

Age Regression. "I would like you to take a journey into your past. Your consciousness works at two levels. You are paying attention to what I am saying and also in your orientation you are going back in time as I direct you. Sometimes you will be more in the past, sometimes you will be more aware of things happening in your present surroundings. Go back as far as possible; you can't fail. You will come across many events of life which may be unpleasant. Let your subconscious mind cope with the unpleasantness. I would like you to deal with the painful experiences in a much more mature manner and, if you can, learn something from those experiences. Don't let them retard your emotional growth any more. I would like you to go back year by year until you are in your preschool years. You can see how small you looked. Perhaps you remember your earlier photographs. You can imagine your voice, your friends, your parents, how your house used to look, and how everybody looked so small. Now, go back farther to that time when you were not speaking. You could hardly walk, and you find that your thinking was quite hazy. You can get images but the words are not there. I would like you to go farther back and now images are really hazy. Now you are actually inside your mother. It is so nice and comfortable and warm and you feel so protected. Now you are going to be born. The birth is going to be a very satisfactory one, without any damage to you in any form. If you remain attached to your mother, your survival is not possible. If you are separated from your mother, then biologically speaking you really do not need your mother.

Look at the symbolism here. This may be the beginning of guilt, that whenever you try to be independent, you will be guilty of not needing your mother. Whenever you surrender to her, then your independence is not there, as if your whole life is going to be a struggle between complete independence or passive surrender. It begins during this early period, when your thinking was just in the form of images. How you were brought up will decide your future. As a baby you have no way of knowing other than looking at your mother's face, how you were developing and progressing or otherwise. You saw your reflection, the way images were reflected back to you from your mother's face. Let your subconscious mind recollect and even pass through some of the experiences. You were passing through a very critical phase in self-development. When something went wrong, the correct images were not reflected back. You were treated continuously more for your bodily than for your mental development. As growth continued, you received impressions that control of your body was much more important. You were not given enough credit for mental development; it was not even acknowledged. You continuously tried to please others. You would do everything to please your mother and other significant people. Now, as age advances, some minor thing happens, maybe a remark from your gym teacher or some friend during exercising, that you had slightly bigger hips or thighs. Even your mother may have remarked that you are going to take shape like her body. You suddenly decompensate. You get obsessed with controlling your body more than ever. Other things gradually start developing, along with the fear of losing control of your body. You remember that thin is beautiful and society is geared towards keeping the body thin. You look at many fashion magazines; you have calorie books and diet books. You started exercising, using laxatives, vomiting, and became more secretive. As you lost weight, you received more and more attention from your family members. It certainly appeared to you that if you controlled your body, you were exempted from controlling your world. You didn't have to take much responsibility as a mature person. You don't have to deal with people. All that was necessary was to control your body to get attention. As your physical condition deteriorated, you lost all perspective. Even your thinking, and your power of concentration, became less efficient. Now that you have reached your present age, I appeal to your subconscious mind that you can rewrite your past. If it is true that you are the result of events that happened in the past, then, by the same logic, what you do now to yourself is going to give you a different future, one much more prosperous, and more healthy. You are going to have a more joyful life. You are going to have a different existence from what you have had so far. You are going to live your life much more fully. You have a lot to contribute to life. During this process of finding purpose and meaning in life, you will enrich this world and yourself."

Age Progression. "I would like you to visualize yourself for the next 24 hours relaxing, keeping calm, eating healthier foods, tolerating the panic feelings and allowing yourself to be healthier and healthier, even though it means increasing your body size proportionately a little larger than what you had yesterday. I would like you to draw how you see yourself. I would like you to draw your body shape depicting your fears, deformities. I would also like you to draw some pictures that look comparatively healthier and of better shape. I would also like you to plan how you are going to spend the next 24 hours. There will not be any vacuum in your time when you know what you were supposed to be doing. Let your life become more organized without anorexic rituals. As much as possible, I would like you to see what things you can do in the next 24 hours that are not part of your anorexia."

Course

The patients who were treated in the hospital showed better progress than the outpatients. The environment in the hospital is much more controlled than the external environment for the outpatients. Family members were not permitted to visit or communicate in any way with hospitalized patients. Outpatients continued to struggle with their changing and preformed images of anorexia. The family members, however, changed their attitudes when they found that the anorectic was really changing her habits and was not manipulating them. Many patients got panic spells and they temporarily discontinued the therapy. They were not punished or reprimanded in any way and were allowed to rejoin the therapy when they were ready to come back. Some disturbed families complicated the matter to such a degree that the therapy had to be discontinued.

Results

On the whole, the weight gains were much higher among the hospitalized patients than among the outpatients. There was a wide range in the weight gains; as much as 8 to 10 lbs weight gain was achieved every week for a period of 4 to 5 weeks in the hospital. The outpatients gained 2 to 3 lbs per week. The weight gain essentially depended on the limit the patient had set for herself. It took much longer to break that barrier established by the patient herself. For example, if the patient had decided to weigh only 99 pounds, then even if she gained a few more pounds, she would lose them and return to 99 pounds. In general, patients were pleased that they could control most of the physical symptoms of anorexia. Psychological development was much more difficult to accomplish. Those anorectics who were supported by their family members were able to adjust to their new image. Social adjustments also improved when the anorectic was able to accept her new body image, became more assertive, and at least tried not to do things just to please people.

Follow-up

Most of my patients kept in contact with me either by writing, telephone calls, or by letting me know, about their progress through friends or relatives. Those who became well-adjusted in their social and family environment did not think it necessary to talk about anorexia nervosa and were reluctant to come to see me as a doctor. When I tried to contact them, they did not avoid me and let me know how they were doing. On the whole, those patients who kept some contact with me maintained their remission. Approximately 10% of the patients did not make satisfactory adjustment to their psychosocial life. Those patients whom I treated in the earlier stage of illness made much more satisfactory progress. Those patients who had anorexia nervosa for longer than three years made comparatively poor adjustment to nonanorexic life. Approximately 25% of my cases were bulimic. These patients made a poorer adjustment to nonbulimic life. Even when they stopped compulsive vomiting, they continued to feel an emptiness in life and required more frequent visits and more contact for supportive therapy.

Summary

An eclectic approach was used to treat anorexia nervosa patients through the medium of hypnotherapeutic techniques. The anorectics received the impression that someone did care for them. Hypnotherapeutic techniques also helped to modify various body functions, thus helping the patient to gain more control over her body. As the patient became less anxious and was able to alter her pathological way of living, her world and her family members started reflecting a different image of her, thereby supporting the patient and encouraging her to adopt to a more mature way of living. The patients became more assertive and were less fearful of leaving their anorexia nervosa behind to go into this world looking for greater purpose and meaning in their lives.

Acknowledgments

I am grateful to Dr. Aruna Thakur, FRCP(C), Consultant Psychiatrist, Saskatoon, who gave autogenic training and biofeedback to the patients.

All photographs were taken by Clasina H. A. M. Stokvis, SRN, SCM, MTD, Director of Staff Development, Saskatoon City Hospital. Her help is greatly appreciated.

Suggested Reading

Bruch E: Eating Disorders, Obesity, Anorexia Nervosa, and the Person Within. New York, Basic Books, 1973

Cheek DB, LeCron LM: Clinical Hypnotherapy. New York, Grune & Stratton, 1968

Crasilneck HB, Hall JA: Clinical Hypnosis. New York, Grune & Stratton, 1975

Crisp AH: Anorexia Nervosa: Let Me Be. New York, Grune & Stratton, 1980

Dally P, Gomez J: Anorexia Nervosa. London, Heinemann, 1979

Frankl VE: The Unheard Cry for Meaning. New York, A Touchstone Book, 1978

Jencks B: Your Body, Biofeedback At Its Best. Chicago, Nelson–Hall Paperback, 1977

Kroger WS, Fezler WD: Hypnosis and Behavior Modification. Philadelphia, JB Lippincott, 1976

Polhemus T (ed): The Body Reader: Social Aspects of the Human Body. New York, Pantheon Books, 1978

Rizzuto AM, Peterson RK, Reed M: The Pathological Sense of Self in Anorexia Nervosa, Vol 4, No 3. Philadelphia, WB Saunders, 1981

Thakur KS: Treatment of anorexia nervosa with hypnotherapy. In Wain HJ (ed): Clinical Hypnosis in Medicine, p 147. Miami, Symposia Specialists, 1980

UNIT FIVE
Distinctive Innovations for the Practitioner

25 Forensic Hypnosis

MARTIN T. ORNE: PART I
NEIL S. HIBLER: PART II

Introduction

This chapter consists of two independent parts. Part I reprints Dr. Orne's already classic paper explaining aspects of the hypnotic process that affect the use of hypnosis for forensic purposes. He discusses the theoretical basis for understanding the many forensic issues that arise from the very nature of hypnosis itself. In Part II Dr. Hibler addresses the logic and discusses the procedures employed by agencies within the federal government in using hypnosis as an investigative technique. He provides the reader with an understanding of how the process is carried out and the kinds of safeguards that are employed.

Permission

"The Use and Misuse of Hypnosis in Court" was reprinted by permission of the author, Martin Orne, M.D., Ph.D. and by the International Journal of Clinical and Experimental Hypnosis from the October 1979; *International Journal of Clinical and Experimental Hypnosis,* Copyrighted by The Society for Clinical and Experimental Hypnosis, October, 1979.

PART I

The Use and Misuse of Hypnosis in Court[1]

Martin T. Orne[2,3]
*The Institute of Pennsylvania Hospital
and University of Pennsylvania*

ABSTRACT: The various forensic contexts in which hypnosis has been used are reviewed, emphasizing its advantages and pitfalls. The technique

Manuscript submitted June 28, 1979; final revision received August 14, 1979.
[1] The substantive work carried out in our laboratory relevant to this paper and its preparation was

may be helpful in the context of criminal investigation and under circumstances involving functional memory loss. Hypnosis has no utility to assure the truthfulness of statements since, particularly in a forensic context, subjects may simulate hypnosis and are able to willfully lie even in deep hypnosis; most troublesome, actual memories cannot be distinguished from confabulations either by the subject or by the hypnotist without full and independent corroboration. While potentially useful to refresh witnesses' and victims' memories to facilitate eyewitness identification, the procedure is relatively safe and appropriate only when neither the subject, nor the authorities, nor the hypnotist have any preconceptions about who the criminal might be. If such preconceptions do exist—either based on information acquired before the hypnotic procedure or on information subtly communicated during the hypnotic procedure—hypnosis may readily cause the subject to confabulate the person who is suspected into his "hypnotically enhanced memories." These pseudomemories, originally developed in hypnosis, may come to be accepted by the subject as his actual recall of the original events; they are then remembered with great subjective certainty and reported with conviction. Such circumstances can *create* convincing, apparently objective "eyewitnesses" rather than facilitating actual recall. A number of minimal safeguards are proposed to reduce the likelihood of such an eventuality and other serious potential abuses of hypnosis.

Over the years, much of the forensic interest in hypnosis has dealt with the question of whether an individual can be compelled to carry out antisocial behaviors[4] and the implications that such a possibility would have for the concept of legal responsibility. More recently, however, there has been a sudden upsurge of legal cases throughout the country which have involved the use of hypnosis in an entirely different context. These cases employ hypnosis (a) to enhance a

supported in part by grant MH 19156 from the National Institute of Mental Health and by a grant from the Institute for Experimental Psychiatry.

[2] For their help in clarifying the issues involved, I wish to especially thank my colleagues at the Unit for Experimental Psychiatry: Emily Carota Orne, David F. Dinges, William M. Waid, Alan S. Lert, William H. Putnam. Special appreciation is due to John F. Kihlstrom and Robert A. Karlin for their substantive suggestions. I am particularly grateful to Nancy K. Bauer, Lani Pyles MacAniff, Joanne Rosellini, and Mae C. Weglarski for their assistance in editing, formatting, and referencing during the preparation of this manuscript.

[3] Reprint requests should be addressed to Martin T. Orne, M.D., Ph.D., Unit for Experimental Psychiatry, The Institute of Pennsylvania Hospital, 111 North 49th Street, Philadelphia, Pennsylvania 19139.

[4] For a detailed discussion of these issues, see Barber (1961), Orne (1960, 1962), Orne and Evans (1965), and volume 20, issue number 2, April 1972 of the *International Journal of Clinical and Experimental Hypnosis,* a special issue of the journal which includes relevant papers by Coe, Kobayashi, and Howard (1972), Conn (1972), Kline (1972), Orne (1972a), and Watkins (1972).

defendant's memory in order to bring out new information which might clear him of the accusation against him, or (b) to increase the recall of witnesses or victims who had observed a crime, either to facilitate the pre-trial investigation or to enhance memory sufficiently so that following hypnosis the individuals could serve as eyewitnesses in court. Finally, hypnosis has been used to help in the psychological and psychiatric evaluation of defendants, especially to determine their state of mind (Kline, 1979).

Because of our laboratory's work on the nature of hypnosis, I have become involved in a number of cases where our work was directly relevant to the proposed forensic use of hypnosis. Of particular relevance were our empirical studies dealing with: the nature of hypnotic age regression (O'Connell, Shor, and Orne, 1970; Orne, 1951); the potential use of hypnosis in interrogation (Orne, 1961); the question of whether antisocial behavior can be elicited by the use of hypnosis (Orne, 1962, 1972a; Orne and Evans, 1965); the nature of posthypnotic behavior (Orne, 1969; Orne, Sheehan, and Evans, 1968; Sheehan and Orne, 1968); the simulation of hypnosis (Orne, 1971, 1972b, 1977); and posthypnotically disrupted recall (Evans and Kihlstrom, 1973; Kihlstrom and Evans, 1976, 1977; Nace, Orne, and Hammer, 1974; Orne, 1966).

The purpose of the present paper is to review the major issues concerning some of the forensic uses of hypnosis, to illustrate the difficulties which may be encountered by examining the relevant scientific evidence as well as some of the relevant legal cases, and finally to propose some general guidelines about the use of hypnosis in a way which should minimize the likelihood of a serious miscarriage of justice—instances of which would otherwise be likely to proliferate.

The Use of Hypnosis to Legitimize New Information and Increase Credibility

In the past few years there has been a sharp increase in the use of hypnosis—by prosecutors and defendants, plaintiffs and respondents alike—to enhance memory for events associated with a crime or civil suit. In most cases, the court has ultimately refused to admit hypnotically elicited material as evidence. An examination of some of these cases illustrates most of the problems that can occur in the forensic use of hypnosis if appropriate safeguards are not employed.

To Exonerate a Defendant

At one time, both hypnosis and "truth serum" (sodium amytal and pentothal administered intravenously) were thought of as techniques which could elicit truthful information. Since it is widely believed by laymen that there is a virtual certainty of obtaining truthful information when a subject's critical judgment is diminished by either hypnosis or a drug, it is hardly surprising that efforts have been made to introduce hypnotic testimony in court as a way for the defendant to demonstrate his innocence to a jury. The courts, however, have recognized that hypnotic testimony is not reliable as a means of ascertaining truth and appropriately rejected both of these techniques as means of determining factual information.[5]

Although these early decisions were usually accompanied by gratuitous deprecatory remarks about hypnosis, the wisdom of the decision itself is supported by scientific data. Thus, experience with the real-simulator design (Orne, 1959, 1971, 1972b) shows that it is possible for an individual to feign hypnosis and deceive even highly experienced hypnotists (see Hilgard, 1977; Orne, 1977; Sheehan, 1972). Further, it is possible for even deeply hypnotized subjects to willfully lie (Orne, 1961).

While the courts rejected the use of hypnosis as a truth telling device, recognition of hypnosis as a valid therapeutic modality by the American Medical Association and the American Psychological Association has contributed to a new trend in the use of hypnosis in legal cases. Because hypnosis has been widely used in a therapeutic context to help individuals remember material for which they had amnesia and since many defendants claim to be unable to remember the events for which they are being tried, it seemed reasonable to consider that hypnosis might help refresh their memory so that they might better assist in their own defense. In other cases it has been proposed that hypnosis could be useful in ascertaining the defendant's state of mind at the time of the crime. By this back door, then, hypnosis was reintroduced into the courtroom, and efforts were made to introduce hypnotically elicited testimony to juries.

An excellent example of this strategy occurred during the retrial of a convicted murderer in Ohio (*State v. Papp,* 1978). The defendant claimed to be unable to remember some of the events that transpired at the time of the crime, and the court authorized that the defendant be hypnotized to assist in his defense. While apparently age regressed to the time of the crime, the defendant exonerated himself, leading the press throughout the state to proclaim his innocence. After viewing the videotape-recordings of the hypnotic sessions which, according to the prosecution expert, revealed some anomalies in Papp's response to hypnosis, the hypnotist hired by the defense was persuaded to administer specific tests to assess possible simulation. The defendant behaved in a manner which was typical of simulating subjects, and the videotape-recorded result was sufficiently clear that it was not effectively disputed by the defense. Consequently, no attempt was made to introduce

---

[5] Cf. *People v. McNichol* (1950), in which the court rejected as hearsay and self-serving declarations which defendant made under the effect of truth drugs and which defendant sought to have admitted as evidence. See generally Wigmore (1974).

the videotape-recording purportedly demonstrating the defendant's innocence in court.

Because the defendant in a legal case is highly motivated to utilize the hypnotic situation to aid his cause, great care must be taken in the interpretation of hypnotic material. It must also be kept in mind that the hypnotic session, which may involve displays of considerable affect, is extremely arousing and compelling to the naive observer. A classic example of this kind occurred 2 years ago in California (*People v. Ritchie,* 1977), where an individual was accused of killing a 2½-year-old child. When confronted with an overwhelming amount of circumstantial evidence, the defendant requested that he be hypnotized to enable him to remember details which he could not recall. Under hypnosis he relived the experience in an exceedingly dramatic fashion, remembering material indicating that his wife committed the murder and clearing himself. Through an analysis of the videotape-recording of the hypnosis session, it was possible to document how the defendant had inadvertently been led by the hypnotist and also to demonstrate a number of intrinsic inconsistencies which clearly indicated that the version the defendant relived under hypnosis was, consciously or unconsciously, confabulated to serve the needs of his case. After extensive testimony, the court excluded the hypnotic evidence because of its unreliability.

To Recall Relevant Details in Civil Suits

Similarly, hypnosis has been used to help plaintiffs in accident cases remember details of the incidents. For example, in a Canadian case (*Crockett et al. v. Haithwaite et al.,* 1978), a woman and a male passenger were found in a car which had run off the road and hit a tree; the passenger was dead and the driver seriously injured. British Columbia law is such that if the driver had been careless or distracted, her insurance would be liable to the estate of her dead passenger and she herself would have no substantial claim; however, if another car caused her to run off the road, her insurance company would not be liable and she herself would be able to recover very substantial damages from a special fund created for the purpose. At the time of the accident, however, the woman reported no recollection of such a car. Some time later her attorney referred her to a psychiatrist for help with emotional difficulties stemming from the accident and also requested that he might seek to facilitate her memory for the accident. There is little doubt that the driver and her lawyer were clearly aware of the substantial difference it would make whether or not another vehicle had been involved in the accident; thus it is hardly surprising that under hypnosis she remembered a van coming toward her and forcing her off the road. If the driver had simply stated that one day she suddenly remembered that a van had forced her off the road, a jury would be likely to reject such "spontaneous" memories as self-serving and not trustworthy. Memories which are recalled via the use of hypnosis, however, are more apt to be taken at face value. This case was ultimately settled on the courthouse steps. Even so, it represents a use of hypnosis closely analogous to hypnotizing a defendant and open to all the caveats involved in such a use.

The Nature of Hypnotic Recall

When hypnosis is used with a defendant or plaintiff who has much to gain by recalling one set of memories rather than another, motivational factors are superimposed upon the basic mechanisms involved in hypnotically aided recall. While these motivational factors complicate the picture, the basic facts about the phenomenon of hypnosis and its effects on recall apply to all circumstances where hypnosis is employed. The unreliability of hypnotic recall is due both to factors inherent in the nature of hypnosis and properties of the human memory system.

Age Regression

While direct suggestion is sometimes used to facilitate recall in hypnosis, the procedures most widely employed involve some form of hypnotic age regression. This dramatic phenomenon appears to enable individuals to relive some past event which might have occurred many years ago. However, it is a method that can be equally effective in helping an individual to relive recent events, particularly if they involve some trauma leading to motivated forgetting manifested by the inability to recall significant events. Not only are extensive clinical observations available concerning hypnotic age regression, but it has also been studied systematically in the laboratory, providing data which shed much light on the nature of the process, and on the critical issue of the historical accuracy of hypnotically elicited recall.

When a hypnotized individual is told that he is 6 years old and at his birthday party, for example, he will begin to act, talk, and to some degree think like a child. He may play as a child would; address the friends who apparently were at his birthday party; and describe in detail the room where the party is occurring, the people who are in attendance, the presents he is receiving, and so on. The naturalness with which these descriptions are given and the conviction that is communicated by the individual are compelling even to trained observers. The feelings which are expressed appear appropriate to a child more than to an adult, and the entire phenomenon is such that it is generally described as beyond the skills of even a professional actor. In a therapeutic setting, the material that is recovered during hypnotic age regression is often of great importance to a patient's treatment. As

Breuer and Freud (1895/1955) discovered at the end of the 19th century, the reliving of traumatic events may result in the cure of troublesome pathological symptoms, lending credence to the historical accuracy of these events. For these reasons, there is a widely held belief among both laymen and practicing clinicians that the events relived during hypnotic age regression are historically accurate.

Typically, age regressed individuals will spontaneously elaborate a myriad of details which apparently could only be brought forth by someone actually observing the events as they transpired. It is these details which sophisticated clinicians find most compelling and occasionally cause them to testify that they know with certainty that the individual was truly regressed. It is rare indeed, however, for the clinician to have the time, energy, or need to be certain that would cause him to verify the accuracy of an individual's description of events that transpired many years ago in childhood. Unfortunately, without objective detailed verification, the clinician's belief in the historical accuracy of the memories brought forth under hypnosis is likely to be erroneous. Freud's early "infantile seduction" theory of hysteria gives dramatic evidence of this.

Freud originally believed that seduction in childhood by an adult, usually the father, was the etiological factor in hysteria (see Ellenberger, 1970) because in hyponosis his patients dramatically relived such an event and typically showed considerable subsequent improvement. It was some years later that Freud realized the seduction scene that the patients relived in treatment accurately reflected the fantasies of the patient but did not accurately portray historical events. Often the relived episodes combined several actual events and many fantasies. This in no way detracted from the usefulness of reliving these events in treatment where the purpose is to help the patient gain relief from his symptoms. Consider, however, the catastrophe which would have resulted if Freud had acted upon his patient's recollections and had urged the authorities to imprison the fathers for incest!

Experimental work with hypnotic age regression is possible because hypnosis is a phenomenon that can readily be induced in normal individuals. It is sometimes possible to obtain materials that an individual has not seen since he was 6 years old, then to age regress him back to that time, and while he is talking, acting, and writing like a child, to have him produce these same materials—for example, childhood drawings. Characteristically, the productions superficially resemble those of a child. One tends to accept them as "typical" of what a 6-year-old would have done, *unless* they are compared to what the individual had actually drawn as a child. In an early study (Orne, 1951), however, an expert in children's drawings examining a series of age regressed productions indicated that these were not done by children but showed "sophisticated oversimplification."

Since that time, other experimental studies have sought to document the historical accuracy of material produced during hypnotic age regression. The best known is an interesting monograph by Reiff and Scheerer (1959) who compared five highly responsive subjects age regressed to ages 10, 7, and 4 with three groups of role playing subjects instructed to act as if they were 10, 7, and 4 respectively. The results seemed to document cognitive processes characteristic of children of the appropriate age in the age regressed subjects, but not in the controls. In our laboratory, this study was extended and replicated with necessary additional controls (O'Connell et al., 1970). With larger samples and controlling for subtle experimenter bias, it became clear that both modest increase in recall as well as increased confabulation occurred within the same subject in the same age regression session. There were many times that subjects provided us with what appeared to be factual material relating to events that occurred many years ago (*i.e.,* their school's name, their teachers' names, school mates who sat next to them in the fifth and second grades). The subjects would describe their classmates so vividly and with such conviction that we were surprised indeed to find, when we went to the trouble of checking the actual school records, that some of these individuals had not been members of the subject's class; nor was the factual recall better than that of unhypnotized controls.

The hypnotic suggestion to relive a past event, particularly when accompanied by questions about specific details, puts pressure on the subject to provide information for which few, if any, actual memories are available. This situation may jog the subject's memory and produce some increased recall, but it will also cause him to fill in details that are plausible but consist of memories or fantasies from other times. It is extremely difficult to know which aspects of hypnotically aided recall are historically accurate and which aspects have been confabulated. The details of material that is confabulated depend upon the subject's total past experience and all available cues relevant to the hypnotic task. Subjects will use prior information and cues in an inconsistent and unpredictable fashion; in some instances such information is incorporated in what is confabulated, while in others the hypnotic recall may be virtually unaffected.

As a consequence of these limitations, hypnosis may be useful in some instances to help bring back forgotten memories following an accident or a crime while in others a witness might, with the same conviction, produce information that is totally inaccurate. This means that material produced during hypnosis or immediately after hypnosis, inspired by hypnotic revivification, may or may not be historically accurate. As long as this material is subject to independent verification, its utility is considerable and the risk attached to the procedure minimal. There is no way, however, by which anyone—even a psychologist or psychiatrist with extensive training in the field of hypnosis—can for any particular piece of information determine whether it is an actual memory versus a confabulation *unless* there is independent verification. Thus, there are instances when subsequently verified accurate license plate numbers were recalled in hypnosis by individuals who previously could not remember them. In the Chowchilla kidnapping case (Kroger and Doucé, 1979), the license plate number was helpful in the initial investigation of the case (although ultimately not required in the courtroom because of the abundance of other evidence available). On the other hand, a good many license plate numbers that have been recalled under hypnosis by witnesses in other cases in fact belonged to individuals where it turned out, after investigation, that neither they nor their cars could have been involved.

Hypermnesia by Direct Suggestion

Another approach which has been used to increase memory is direct suggestion. While generally used to enhance recall for recent events, it can also be employed to induce hypermnesia for the distant past.

Stalnaker and Riddle (1932) used direct suggestion to facilitate recall of long forgotten memories, shedding light on the mechanism of hypermnesia. It was suggested to deeply hypnotized subjects that they would recall prose and verse that they had committed to memory in grade school. In hypnosis, these subjects appeared to remember the material far more easily, with far better recall, than in the wake state. Careful analysis, however, showed that, while some additional material was recalled in hypnosis, the amount was far less than it first seemed; in fact, subjects showed a pronounced tendency to confabulate so that many of the new phrases "recalled" had simply been improvised in a style that superficially resembled the author's. Often these confabulations were sufficiently good so as not to be easily recognized as such on casual examination. This study clearly established two tendencies in hypnotic hypermnesia: (a) a modest increase in the amount of material available to memory, and (b) a tendency to confabulate—to fill in those aspects which the individual cannot remember, in an effort to comply with the suggestions of the hypnotist. More recent studies, such as those of White, Fox, and Harris (1940), Sears (1954), and Dhanens and Lundy (1975), appear to show increased recall of meaningful, though nontraumatic, material in hypnosis. (No such effect has been demonstrated with nonsense syllables.) However, when the effects of hypnosis on increased memory are compared with those of increased motivation (Cooper and London, 1973), and procedures analogous to hypnosis with unhypnotizable subjects (Dhanens and Lundy, 1975), there is no significantly greater increase in recall with hypnosis. Thus, the widely held belief that hypnotic suggestion can not only increase the amount but also the reliability of the material recalled ignores the motivational factors on the one hand, and the concurrent dramatic increase in the "recall" of inaccurate information on the other. This is illustrated in the Stalnaker and Riddle study (1932). Depending upon how they scored their material, these investigators could observe a 65% increase in memory for material learned many years earlier when recalled during hypnosis rather than in the wake state. Such a figure is obtained if one simply looks at the amount of more accurate memories that are brought forth. At the same time, however, subjects in the hypnotic condition vastly increased the amount of inaccurate details that were "remembered."

The apparently increased recall in hypnosis can in large part be understood if one takes into account the deeply hypnotized individual's tendency to manifest a decrease in critical judgment. The same process which increases suggestibility by permitting the subject to accept counterfactual suggestions as real also makes it possible for the subject to accept approximations of memory as accurate. In the wake state he is unwilling to consider approximate or fragmentary memories as acceptable recall; however, in hypnosis he alters his criterion of what is acceptable and brings forth accurately recalled fragments mixed with confabulated material.[6] When hypnosis is used in the context of gathering investigative leads, such a change in criterion is desirable since it will cause a witness to bring forth bits of information which he would not otherwise have felt confident enough to report—provided, of course, one recognizes that these fragments are made available at the cost of adding other details which are likely to be inaccurate. Further, neither the subject nor the expert observer can distinguish between confabulation and accurate recall in any particular instance. The only way this can be accomplished is on the basis of external corroborative data.

The Confusion of Memories During Hypnosis With
Waking Recall and Its Effect on Subjective Conviction

When a subject is hypnotized and told to remember the events of a particular day (and awakened without amnesia suggestions), he may be able subsequently, in the wake state, to describe his recollections in hypnosis and clearly differentiate them from his earlier recollections before being hypnotized. It is another matter, however, if the subject is convinced before being hypnotized that he will have the "true facts" that he is now unable to remember, or if prior to awakening, the subject is given the suggestion that he will wake up and remember everything, including the details of what actually occurred on that particular day, and that he will be able to recall all details as vividly and clearly in the wake state as in hypnosis. Under these circumstances, he will typically awaken and confound the hypnotic memories with his waking memories. Such suggestions, which are now widely used for forensic purposes, result in the individual's tending to accept the events he relived in hypnosis as if they were what actually happened. The previous gaps or uncertainties

---

[6] This process may well be analogous to a change in subjective criterion of sensory thresholds of the kind which led to the application of signal detection theory to problems of psychophysics.

in his memory are now filled in, and the events as they were relived in hypnosis become his recollection of what actually occurred on the day in question.

The witness who testifies following such a procedure may even fail to be able to distinguish which of his memories occurred in hypnosis and which came about as part of his normal waking recollection. Instead of differentiating between his earlier fragmentary recall and the gaps that have been filled in—perhaps by pseudomemories created during hypnosis—he experiences the totality as his recollection of what had originally transpired. It is this new recollection that is convincingly reported when the individual is asked what happened. Even though prior to hypnosis he had been very uncertain about his memory, had changed his story many times, and had not reported many of the details that emerged only during hypnosis, he will now report his "memories" consistently and with conviction. As a consequence, memories which occurred only during hypnosis may be incorrectly presented in court as though they represented recollections based on original memory traces of the events that actually occurred on the day in question.

Hypnotic Recall As Part of Basic Memory Processes

The idea that one can in hypnosis somehow reactivate original memory traces stems from a widely held view (especially among lay hypnotists) that memory involves a process analogous to a multi-channel videotape-recorder inside the head which records all sensory impressions and stores them in their pristine form. Further, there is a belief that while this material cannot ordinarily be brought to consciousness, it can be accessed through hypnosis; this mechanism is presumed to make possible the phenomenon of age regression or revivification. Suffice it to say that such a view is counter to any currently accepted theory of memory and is not supported by scientific data (for reviews, see for example, Hilgard and Loftus, 1979; Jenkins, 1974; Putnam, 1979; Roediger, 1979). As Bartlett (1932) pointed out many years ago, memory is continuously changing and is *reconstructive* as well as reproductive. It is possible that highly traumatic, emotional material that is repressed could be less subject to the kind of continuing changes seen with relatively neutral material, but even this is doubtful since, as has been pointed out earlier, many of the memories recovered in psychotherapy include material which is not historically accurate.

Particularly relevant to our consideration here, however, are the observations discussed by Hilgard and Loftus (1979) indicating that free narrative recall will produce the highest percentage of accurate information but also the lowest amount of detail. Conversely, the more an eyewitness is questioned about details, the more details will be obtained—but with a marked decrease in accuracy. This observation, based on research with unhypnotized individuals, is virtually certain to apply to hypnotized subjects as well.

From Hypnotic Enhancement of Recall to the Creation of Memory

While the laws which govern memory inevitably apply to hypnotic recall, it is difficult to disentangle which aspects of hypnotically enhanced memories represent accurate recall and which represent fantasies that are confabulated to approximate what might have occurred. The extent to which the process of confabulation may be stimulated by hypnosis becomes obvious when, instead of being asked to relive a prior event, the subject is given suggestions to experience a future event—about which no memories could possibly exist. For instance, in age progression (Kline and Guze, 1951), a subject is given the suggestion that it is the year 2000 and asked to describe the world around him. Such a suggestion, given to the deeply hypnotized individual, will lead to a vivid and compelling description of all kinds of new, as yet unseen, scientific marvels. Obviously, the plausibility and the precise nature of the subject's description will depend upon his scientific knowledge, his reading, and his intelligence.

The same process that allows a hypnotized individual to hallucinate the environment of the year 2000 can also be involved when he is urged to recall what happened 6 months ago, especially if he lacks the clear, waking memory to permit him to recall details accurately. Unfortunately, such pseudomemories can and often do become incorporated into the individual's memory store as though they had actually happened. It is worth noting that this can occur even with bizarre memories such as when people "recall" their past lives and become convinced that these events really took place or, in other instances, when individuals under hypnosis remember encounters with flying saucers and become convinced they have actually communicated with beings from another galaxy. In such instances, the sophisticated listener smiles about the individual's assertions since it is obvious that they represent pseudomemories. Unfortunately, if such pseudomemories relate to events which occurred 6 months ago and are eminently plausible, there is no way for either the hypnotist or the subject or a jury to distinguish between them and actual recall of what occurred.

The content of pseudomemories when they are wittingly or unwittingly induced during hypnosis is, of course, not random. If someone has just seen a science fiction film one can usually recognize elements of that film in his description of what is going on about him in the year 2000; similarly, if a witness is hypnotized and has factual information casually gleaned from newspapers or inadvertent comments made during prior interrogation or in discussion with others who might have knowledge about the facts, many of these bits of knowledge will become incorporated and form the basis of any pseudomemories that develop. Furthermore, if the hypnotist has beliefs about what actually occurred, it is exceedingly difficult for him to prevent himself from inadvertently guiding the subject's recall so that he will eventually "remember" what he, the hypnotist, believes actually happened.

A simple experimental demonstration which I have often carried out is directly relevant to the circumstances of attempts to hypnotically enhance recall. First, I carefully establish and verify that a particular subject had in fact gone to bed at midnight on, say February 17, and had arisen at 8 a.m. the following morning. After inducing deep hypnosis, it is suggested that the subject relive the night of February 17—getting ready for bed, turning out the light, and going to sleep at midnight. As the subject relives being asleep, he is told that it is now 4 a.m. and then is asked whether he has heard the two loud noises. Following this question (which is in fact a suggestion), a good subject typically responds that the noises had awakened him. Now instructed to look around and check the time, he may say it is exactly 4:06 a.m. If then asked what he is doing, he may describe some activity such as going to the window to see what happened or wondering about the noises, forgetting about them, and going back to sleep.

Still hypnotized, he may relive waking up at 8 a.m. and describe his subsequent day. If, prior to being awakened, he is told he will be able to remember the events of February 17 as well as all the other things that happened to him in hypnosis, he readily confounds his hypnotic experience with his actual memory on awakening. If asked about the night of February 17, he will describe going to sleep, and being awakened by two loud noises. If one inquires at what time these occurred, he will say, "Oh, yes, I looked at my watch beside my bed. It has a radium dial. It was exactly 4:06 a.m. . . . ." The subject will be convinced that his description about February 17 is accurately reflecting his original memories.

The subject's altered memory concerning the night of February 17 will tend to persist (unless suggestions are given to the contrary) particularly because the subject was asleep at the time and there are no competing memories. The more frequently the subject reports the event, the more firmly established the pseudomemory will tend to become. In the experimental demonstration, we are dealing with an essentially trivial memory about which the subject has no strong inherent motivations. Nonetheless, the memory is created by a leading question, which, however, on casual observation, seems innocuous.

In a life situation where hypnosis is used to enhance recall, the same mechanisms which we have purposively employed in the laboratory to create plausible pseudomemories which the subject accepts as his own may easily occur inadvertently. It must be emphasized that one is not usually dealing with a conscious effort on the part of the hypnotist to distort a witness's memories; on the contrary, the process by which the hypnotized subject is affected typically occurs outside of the hypnotist's awareness. Thus, if the hypnotist knows that two shots have been fired at approximately 4 a.m. on the night of February 17, what seems more natural than to inquire of a witness whether he had heard any loud noises? Further, since usually the witness also knows something about the case and the kinds of memories which would be relevant and important, it may be sufficient simply to inquire at critical times, "Did you hear anything?" in order to lead the responsive hypnotized subject to create the desired "memories."

Lifting of Amnesia Versus "Refreshing Memory"

Traditionally, hypnosis has been a widely used procedure to treat spontaneous amnesia. Similarly, when hypnosis has been used to treat traumatic neuroses, previously amnesic material would suddenly become accessible to consciousness, usually accompanied by profound affect as the patient relives the experience. As abreaction proceeds, the patient's sudden awareness of a myriad of details becomes clear from the manner in which he reexperiences the events. The therapist, seeking to help the patient become aware of feelings, encourages the process of reexperiencing and allows the expression of affect to run its course. The therapist is careful to avoid interrupting the largely spontaneous experience of the patient; though he may well want to know more about some important details, questions are postponed in order not to interfere with the process.

It is characteristic of repressed memories that they suddenly come to consciousness as an entire experience rather than emerging detail by detail. In short, the procedure leads to a narrative exposition as the patient relives the experience. While there is no certainty about the historical accuracy of these memories, when they emerge largely spontaneously and without undue pressure, they are more likely to contain important and accurate information.

Since these instances involved pathological conditions, the approach—even if legal issues were at stake—was essentially therapeutic, and hypnosis was carried out by psychologists or psychiatrists in the context of a traditional doctor–patient relationship. In contrast, hypnosis has more recently been used in circumstances where there is no evidence of pathological memory loss. Here, based on the assumption that every memory is somehow recorded, hypnosis is purported to be simply a means of "refreshing memory." As such, it is claimed that there is no issue of therapy involved.

As a consequence, hypnotic technique is typically altered to prevent the subject from expressing intense feelings that would raise therapeutic issues and would tend to be frightening to lay observers. Thus, it is suggested to the subject that he can visualize the events that he seeks to recall on a special television screen; this screen can, as in televised sports events, move forward or backward through time, allowing events to be seen in instant reply, slow motion, or frame by frame. Further, it is explained to the subject that he need not experience any discomfort, that he can merely observe the screen and see the events unfold—as if he were a spectator rather than a participant (e.g., Reiser, 1974). Suggestions are given, such as, "It is just like watching a television show except that you not only can see it but you can control and even stop the motion; you can be there, but you need not experience pain or fear." Since hypnotic subjects who have been emotionally affected are wont to take the opportunity to relive the experience, there is often some struggle between the hypnotist attempting to keep the affect bottled up and the subject seeking to express it.

This type of "objective" reliving, rather than the "subjective" reliving generally encouraged by trained therapists, seems to bring forth fragmentary recall based not so much on the subject's reliving the experience as upon the hypnotist's detailed questions about what is occurring. Typically, the subject is repeatedly asked to "stop the film and look at the face carefully," and is then asked further questions about the details of the face. The same is generally done in relation to all potentially important details. Since this type of procedure involves a great many questions about details, it will, of course, elicit many more details than a narrative. By the same token, as the work summarized by Hilgard and Loftus (1979) has indicated, it will result in vastly lowered accuracy of the material that is obtained. Further, such a procedure maximizes the potential input of the hypnotist about what is wanted, making it even more likely that the subject's memories will more closely resemble the hypnotist's prior conceptions than would ordinarily be the case.[7]

Unfortunately, no meaningful research is available to document the relative merit of facilitating the reliving of a traumatic event versus the attempt to prevent the affect from being relived by using specific suggestions and questions to increase the amount of memory-like material being brought forth. Considerable experience in the clinical and forensic use of age regression and related techniques suggests that the patient has a higher likelihood of producing uncontaminated memories if allowed to initially relive the events without much questioning by the hypnotist. Further details can then be elicited by questioning the second or third time the material is brought forth. It is interesting that the interrogation technique advocated by Loftus (1979), based on an entirely different body of data with waking eyewitnesses, is remarkably similar to that which evolved with hypnotic subjects.

---

[7] It is, of course, quite useful at times to use metaphors such as "stopping a videotape" and "instant replay" when working with hypnosis. However, no competent hypnotherapist would, in using such a metaphor confuse it with the manner in which memory is organized. He would also recognize that he is putting great pressure on the subject to produce something, and the greater the pressure, the more likely the development of guided confabulations.

The Effect of the Hypnotic Context on Refreshing of Memory

While the effect of hypnosis is most clear-cut in the realm of memory when one is dealing with circumscribed areas of pathological amnesia, the dramatic lifting of amnesia (with which most laymen are familiar from its portrayal in films, novels, and the media), is the exception rather than the rule. With the increasing use of hypnosis, particularly with individuals *without* any obvious memory disturbance and *without* the ability to enter profound hypnosis, the clear demarcation between effects specific to hypnosis and what may occur in everyday interrogation with unhypnotized individuals becomes blurred. While there is no doubt that the kind of processes involved in hypnosis can also be shown to occur under many other cicumstances and that the basic laws governing human memory are not negated because the individual is hypnotized, it would be quite wrong, however, to assume that the hypnotic *procedure* brings about no important changes.

Some advocates of the wide use of "forensic hypnosis" have argued that we need not be concerned about the kinds of issues that have been described earlier, because these problems occur even in the wake state and are certainly negligible if the subject is only relaxed and not deeply hypnotized. It is ironic that this kind of disclaimer is made by the very individuals who tout the unique effectiveness of hypnosis as an aid to criminal investigation. One cannot have it both ways! The reason why hypnosis is used as a forensic tool is that it is effective in eliciting more details. This is so even with individuals who are not particularly hypnotizable, but who cooperate in the hypnotic situation. It is being in the hypnotic situation itself that may profoundly alter some aspects of the subjects' behavior and experience (London and Fuhrer, 1961). Thus, there is a strong expectancy that hypnosis will facilitate recall. The subject in the hypnotic situation feels relaxed and less responsible for what he says since he believes that the hypnotist is both an expert and somehow in control. The hypnotist in turn makes certain that the subject cannot "fail." Hypnotic technique involves the extensive use of reinforcers through frequent verbalizations, such as "Good," "Fine," "You are doing well," and so on, which are novel, satisfying, and reassuring, particularly in a police interrogation situation. Not surprisingly, the subject wants to maintain the level of approbation; consequently, when the hypnotist stops his expression of approval (simply by omitting to say "Good"), he clearly communicates that something else or something more is wanted. It requires only a modest decrease in the level of support to alter the subject's behavior after which there is a return to the previous frequent level of reassurance. Similarly, in the relaxed and apparently benign context of hypnosis, an individual may be generally less anxious and less critical—allowing himself to bring forth bits of information about which he is uncertain but that may in fact be accurate and important—information that would not be brought forth in a context where the individual is made to feel responsible for his memories and challenged about their consistency. Thus, one might say that the hypnotic situation itself serves to change the subject's "guessing strategy."

To date, little systematic research has sought to distinguish between different kinds of effects that the hypnotic situation may exert on recall. Some mechanisms may require a profound level of hypnosis and relate primarily to the recall of material which is actively kept out of awareness; other mechanisms may be involved in the recall of meaningful details in emotionally neutral contexts.

Finally, there are aspects of the hypnotic situation that are not related to hypnotic depth, but nonetheless facilitate the increased reporting and acceptance of detailed information. For example, once a series of details are reported and accepted as valid by the hypnotist, that very fact serves to help convince the subject about the veridicality of these memories—memories that might previously have been extremely tentative and about which the individual had little or no subjective conviction. While there has been little systematic exploration of the means by which the hypnotic context itself may alter the experience of individuals who are only lightly hypnotized from a pragmatic point of view, it is necessary to recognize that these effects exist and may be profound. While careful research will be needed to clarify precisely which kinds of individuals—under what circumstances, relating to what kinds of memories, and in response to which specific techniques—will be more or less likely to yield reliable information, in the absence of such data, it seems best to illustrate these issues in a life context by a selective review of relevant legal cases.

The Use of Hypnosis With Witnesses or Victims to Enhance Memory

Given the limitations of the hypnotic technique to facilitate recall, it becomes crucial to distinguish between apparently similar applications which in fact are very different and which consequently range from entirely appropriate to completely misleading. The key issue is not only the possible benefits that material obtained under hypnosis might accrue but also the need to assess the potential harm that would be caused by erroneous information. The use of hypnosis in an investigative context, with the sole purpose being to obtain leads, is clearly the area where hypnotic techniques are most appropriately employed. Thus, we will examine separately the situation where hypnosis is used exclusively to provide leads in a context where the facts are *not* known and contrast it with the use of hypnosis where a suspect has been identified and an effort is made to help a witness recall sufficient details to permit them to testify in court; there is less emphasis here on the uncovering of details unknown to the investigating officers but rather to help the witness remember them. We will then consider yet a third situation where a witness may have given a number of conflicting statements and hypnosis is utilized in an effort to "help the witness remember what really happened;" here the search is not for new facts at all nor is the emphasis on independent verification. Rather there is an effort to use the hypnotic session itself as a means of verifying the witness's statement. The overall effect is to help the witness become reliable in his statements while reassuring both the authorities and the witness himself about the validity of these statements.

When Facts Are Not Known or Presumed

There are many cases involving a victim or a witness to a crime who cannot recall potentially important details and where the enforcement authorities are equally in the dark. In cases of assault, for example, hypnosis has made it possible for the victim to recall the assailant's appearance, enabling police artists to draw a reasonable likeness. To the extent that the victim or witness, police, artist, and hypnotist alike share no preconceived bias about what might have occurred, the situation approaches the ideal case for hypnosis to be most appropriately employed: to develop investigative leads.

Hypnotic suggestions may directly or indirectly enhance memory by providing contextual cues, and the relaxed environment of a sensitively conducted session may help diminish the anxiety which otherwise interferes with attempts to recall. Several cases of this type are described by Kroger and Doucé (1979). Many of the limitations of the technique—even under such circumstances—have been emphasized earlier, while other pitfalls are described by Kroger and Doucé. Given appropriate care, however, hypnosis has provided important new information to the authorities in many instances. If the sole purpose of the hypnotic session is to provide clues which ultimately lead to incriminating evidence, the fact that hypnosis was originally employed becomes irrelevant. However, if there is even the vaguest possibility that hypnotically enhanced recall is to be used in court, it is essential that the entire contact of the hypnotist with the subject be videotape-recorded in order to allow an independent assessment of the events preceding, during, and following the hypnotic session to determine whether or not the memories might have inadvertently been guided by cues in the situation.

When Significant Facts Are Known or Presumed

An increasing number of instances are finding their way into law courts where hypnosis is used to help "refresh" the memory of a witness or victim about aspects of a crime which are known to the authorities, the media, or the hypnotist and may involve presumed facts that in one way or another have been made available to the subject. Of course, the witness or victim cannot testify on this matter unless he is able to remember it personally. Particularly when the interrogation focuses on some relevant detail and involves leading questions, there is the greatest likelihood of mischief. A "memory" can be created in hypnosis where none existed before. While cases of this type were once rare, there has been a dramatic increase in the number in recent years. Although the source of the factual information may vary widely, all of these cases have the quality that information is somehow introduced into the subject's memory which causes him to testify to the facts as if they were based on prior memories.

A Pennsylvania case (*United States v. Andrews,* 1975) illustrates the kind of problem that may occur. Two seamen recuperating from illness were working in an office when a sailor appeared in the doorway, aimed a pistol at one of the sailors, shot at his head, and fled the scene. Fortunately, the intended victim moved quickly and suffered only a grazing wound to the ear. When the seamen were shown pictures of individuals who might fit the description and could have been in the area, the victim was unable to identify anyone. The witness, however, identified one of the pictures as the assailant. Subsequently, at a preliminary hearing, the victim was present when the witness identified the defendant as the assailant. The victim, however, indicated that the accused looked like but was not the assailant. The victim was then hypnotized on two occasions by an experienced Navy psychiatrist to facilitate his recall. During the first session, he was still unable to make an identification; however, during the second session he claimed to recognize the defendant who had previously been identified by the witness as the assailant.

At the General Court Martial, the issue of the role of hypnosis was raised by the defense and I was asked to testify as an expert. My testimony pointed out that the victim's reaction to hypnosis would probably have been the same whether or not he could actually remember the assailant. Thus, if he continued to be unable to remember him—which was highly likely considering the difficulties encountered in eliciting the recollection—he would have been prone to confabulate an individual who appeared to be the most likely candidate. He had seen the defendant accused during the preliminary hearing and was aware that the witness had identified him with certainty; further, that it was the general belief of the prosecution that the defendant was guilty. The hypnotic session altered the victim's memory and, while he would now testify to what he erroneously believed his original memory to have been, he was in fact testifying on the basis of what he had been led to recall during hypnosis, which was quite different from his actual earlier memories.

In this instance, the military judge ruled as a matter of law that the victim could testify to those things that he had previously testified to but that since his memory was altered by hypnosis he was not permitted to identify the defendant.

In the weeks following this event, two individuals who had left for overseas the evening of the incident returned from Germany and independently corroborated the defendant's alibi, making it extremely unlikely that he was the actual assailant. In this case, it is interesting that the effect of hypnosis on the victim's memory persisted, and well over a year after the event he still asserted his conviction that the defendant had in fact fired the shot which nearly killed him.

Another example is a recent capital case in Milwaukee, Wisconsin (*State v. White,* 1979). A 20-year-old Indian girl nicknamed "Sweetie Pie" had been found strangled several years before. The case had not been solved but had raised considerable attention and concern and had not been closed. Sometime later, another girl contacted the police because her boyfriend had beaten her several times and she wanted him to seek psychiatric help. When questioned, she admitted that on occasion he had choked her, presumably in an attempt to frighten her. The authorities became more interested at that point, particularly when it turned out that the boyfriend, also an Indian, had known "Sweetie Pie." At that point, the girlfriend became uncooperative because she had wanted only to induce the boyfriend to seek treatment and had no wish to have him become involved with the police. On further investigation, however, it was found that the boyfriend did not have an alibi for the time in question, and the authorities talked at length with his former wife from whom he had been separated about a year, and her sister. Both women had lived with the defendant and had children by him.

The wife, who maintained some relationship with the defendant, was not particularly helpful to the authorities, but the sister, who was felt to be more willing to discuss matters, was interviewed on several occasions by police officers. She was asked whether she had been beaten up and indicated that there were times when this had occurred but claimed that she could not remember much else. When it was suggested that she and the former wife participate in a hypnotic session, they agreed to do so. The hypnotic session was carried out by a well trained psychologist. Prior to hypnosis, he showed a gruesome picture of the dead body to the sister who had also been a close friend of the murdered girl. He then induced hypnosis, and shortly thereafter said,

> For a moment I want you to think about just you and me and Sweetie Pie, who got strangled, thrown out on the road, taken to the morgue, put in a box, and buried in the ground. Now somebody did that. I don't know who, and you may not know who, but you know that Joe White is a suspect in this case, don't you? Do you think that there is any reason why Joe White should or should not be a suspect in this case? [N.T. p. 8]

At the end of the session, which included an age regression-like procedure that did not work very well despite the subject's otherwise good response to hypnosis, there was a posthypnotic suggestion given that she would be thinking about telling the truth, how good it would feel to tell the truth, and that she was going to tell the truth. Within a week after the session, the sister called the police and told them how the defendant had often choked her, that he seemed to enjoy it, and that one time shortly after the murder he was choking her and said something to the effect, "If you don't behave, the same thing can happen to you that happened to Sweetie Pie." When she asked whether he had killed "Sweetie Pie," he allegedly broke down crying and said that he had not intended to but admitted that he did.

The case against the defendant was primarily based upon the sister's hearsay testimony which became available shortly after the hypnotic session. After a lengthy hearing, the court ruled that as a matter of law she could not testify before a jury because, thanks to the hypnotic session, the presumed memory was likely to have been created rather than remembered. It is unlikely that anyone will ever know for certain whether the defendant was or was not responsible for the murder. There was no doubt in the sister's mind, however, as to the kind of memory which was wanted, and the sister was amply motivated to testify against the defendant. She had continued to live with the defendant, supposedly knowing that he was a murderer, for many months until he rejected her. Consequently, her testimony would have been totally discounted if it had not come after the hypnotic session. The court recognized the danger of permitting hypnosis to be used in a context where it is more likely to create a memory than to refresh it.

Whereas in the first case the identity of the defendant became known to the victim during a pretrial hearing, and in the second case the nature of the memory was shaped by conversations with the police officers, with the sister, and particularly by the way the hypnotic session was conducted, it is equally possible for the suggestion about what to recall to come from entirely different sources unrelated to and long before hypnosis. For example, in the Minnesota case of *State v. Mack* (1979), a physician insisting that a laceration must have been made by a knife led to a total reorganization of an apparent victim's memory about how she had acquired an internal wound. In other cases, the media have provided the critical information, while in still others, the manner in which a lineup was conducted facilitated the creation of "memories" at hypnotic sessions conducted at a later date (e.g., *State v. Peterson,* 1979).

In addition to criminal cases, it is not uncommon to find something of this kind in civil cases where an individual is helped by hypnosis to remember details of an accident he had been unable to recall previously. By the time hypnosis is carried out, it is generally clear to the subject which of the possible events that could have occurred would be most helpful to his case. Though it is possible that accurate information is recovered, the important effects that motivation can exert on memory—hypnotically enhanced or otherwise—must be taken into account in assessing the "memories" that are obtained.

To Affirm the Reliability of the Witness's Statement or to Create an Apparently Reliable Witness

Many witnesses are unreliable in the sense that they tell somewhat different stories each time they are asked to tell what had occurred. These differences may relate to important details of the crime. The adversary system upon which Anglo-Saxon justice is based is particularly effective in unmasking the unreliability of witnesses by means of cross-examination before a jury.

The effect of hypnotizing witnesses of this kind, presumably to help refresh their memories, is generally dramatic. Even if the subject is not particularly responsive to hypnosis, reviewing the events in the hypnotic context and having the memories legitimized by the hypnotist generally fixes one particular version of the testimony in the witness's mind which is then faithfully and reliably reproduced every time. In these cases, hypnosis does not serve to produce any new information, but the procedure can bolster a witness whose credibility would easily have been destroyed by cross-examination but who now becomes quite impervious to such efforts, repeating one particular version of his story with great conviction.

To appreciate the effect of hypnosis in these kinds of cases, it is important to view the use of the technique in its broader perspectives. Often it will involve a witness about whom the prosecution has considerable doubts. In one California case (*In re Milligan,* 1978) for example, the prosecution's star witness was a 14-year-old girl who had told many different stories to the police at different times and readily changed her story during early depositions. Indeed, she repeatedly stated that it was impossible for her to say whether her recollections were a dream or represented actual events. The case involved the murder of the witness's aunt, sister, grandmother, and cousin, and there was some serious question as to the degree of possible criminal involvement of the witness herself.

The witness was hypnotized and again told her story to the district attorney and the police. However, now it was during hypnosis which everyone agreed would reliably help her recall and she would know whether her memories related to real events or to her dreams. Simply carrying out the hypnotic session committed the prosecution to view that the witness was not criminally involved since it would not be permissible for the state to hypnotize a defendant—especially a minor. Somehow the witness became reassured that she would be safe and her story became remarkably stable, virtually unshakable on cross-examination.

In a real sense, the hypnotic procedure also helped change the prosecution's attitude toward the witness. She was accepted as having no part in the crime, and instead of being considered as an unreliable juvenile, became an exceedingly effective witness whose testimony led to the conviction of the other individuals involved. This was so despite the fact that the story she brought forth under hypnosis and on subsequent occasions contained a number of incorrect statements recognized as such by the hypnotist but ignored. Hypnosis had not resulted in accurate memories, but rather had served to produce consistent memories. Further, the technique served to reassure the law enforcement officials that the witness was in fact telling the truth, an aspect which was perhaps as important as the effect the hypnotic session had in stabilizing the witness's recollections.

In the case of *State v. White* (1979), a senior law enforcement official was asked under oath about his views of hypnotically aided testimony and he succinctly expressed widely held beliefs when he testified that hypnosis lends "credibility and strength to your investigation." [N.T. p. 13] Perhaps the most interesting, as well as the most frightening, consequence of this belief is illustrated by a New Jersey case (*State v. Douglas,* 1978). A woman was stopped at a light and two black men entered the car and forced her at gunpoint to drive to a deserted place on the outskirts of town. When they arrived there, the man in the front seat attempted to rape the woman. When she protested that she was pregnant, the man on the back seat with the gun told the attacker to stop. They took the woman's purse, made her leave the car, and threatened her that if she contacted the police, terrible things would happen to her family. On getting back to her home, the woman immediately reported the attempted rape, as well as the theft of her car and valuables. At the police station, she was shown mug shots and identified one man and picked out another as a look-alike. Subsequently, she received several threatening notes which were turned over to the police. She continued to be unable to identify the second individual involved in the crime, and finally the police persuaded her to undergo hypnosis. Although the police had videotape- as well as audiotape-recording equipment available, it was claimed that the equipment would not work, and hypnosis was carried out without any objective record of what occurred. During the hypnotic session, however, the victim identified the look-alike as the individual who was involved in the crime.

It turned out that the district attorney had been quite skeptical about the case but was finally convinced to prosecute by the hypnotic session. However, when it was learned that the use of hypnosis would be vigorously challenged and that the public defender's office was prepared to use this case as a vehicle to prevent the abuse of hypnosis by the police, the district attorney decided to have another look at the facts of the case. She was struck by the peculiarity of the handwriting in the threatening notes, and for the first time submitted these to a handwriting expert who identified the writing as that of the woman who had filed the charges. When the alleged victim was confronted with this fact, she confessed that there had never been an attempted assault, that she had never met the two men whom she had accused, and that she had generated the complaint and the threatening notes in an effort to reawaken the interest of her husband who was in the process of filing divorce proceedings against her.

The appalling aspect of this case is that it was the hypnotic session which initially prompted the district attorney to cast doubt aside and proceed with the prosecution. The hypnotically enhanced memories would have been the basis for the victim's testimony and might well have led to the conviction of two innocent individuals who happened to have been in the collection of photographs available to the police and did not happen to have excellent alibis. It was only when the district attorney became aware that the defense would have appropriate expert help to challenge the totally inappropriate way in which hypnosis was employed in this case that a more careful review of the evidence uncovered the true state of affairs. Far from being helpful to the prosecution, the manner in which hypnosis was employed actually served to confuse the authorities.

The Role of the Expert in Forensic Hypnosis

It is not possible in the context of a single article to more than touch upon the complex issues involved in the forensic use of hypnosis. However, it behooves those of us experienced in the clinical use of hypnosis to use extreme care when we use our skills in a forensic context. We should keep in mind that psychologists and psychiatrists are not particularly adept at recognizing deception. We generally arrange the social context of treatment so that it is not in the patient's interest to lie to us, and we appropriately do not concern ourselves with this issue since in most therapeutic contexts it is helpful for the therapist to see the world through the patient's eyes in order to ultimately help him to view it more realistically.[8]

As a rule, the average hotel credit manager is considerably more adept at recognizing deception than we are. Not only does his livelihood depend upon limiting errors of judgment, but he is in a position to obtain feedback concerning those errors of judgment, whereas in most treatment contexts the therapist is neither affected by being deceived nor even likely to learn about the fact that he had been deceived at a later date. While military psychiatrists and other health professionals who are required to make dispositional judgments on a daily basis do become adept at recognizing manipulation and deception, only a few colleagues who are experienced in the use of hypnosis have had this type of background. Consequently, they have little experience or concern about being deceived or used. On the other hand, a defendant in a murder trial or, for that matter, a witness or a victim in a crime of violence may well have an axe to grind, and it is essential that we recognize that in a forensic context the unwary expert witness may become a pawn either for the prosecution or for the defense. With

[8] See Lindner (1955) for a superb description of the kind of countertransference which leads to the uncritical acceptance of the patient's views that, on the one hand, makes treatment possible, but on the other can be a source of serious difficulties.

the increasing popularity of hypnosis in the courts, it is essential that those of us who have an interest in these matters develop the necessary sophistication and judgment in the forensic context, much as we have had to acquire it in the therapeutic context. It would be foolhardy indeed to assume that familiarity with one context is sufficient to allow us to function effectively in the other. On the contrary, the ground rules governing the two situations are vastly different, and we must guard against being coöpted—wittingly or unwittingly—by prosecution or defense. In the long run, the only expert who can help the administration of justice is one who is able to maintain an independent perspective rather than see himself as working for either the defense or the prosecution.

Safeguards for the Forensic Use of Hypnosis

The use of hypnosis and related techniques to facilitate memory raises profound, complex questions, and it is likely that the individual will be protected only if these issues are dealt with at the highest level of our court system. There are instances when hypnosis can be used appropriately provided that the nature of the phenomenon is understood by all parties concerned. It must be recognized, however, that the use of hypnosis by either the prosecution or the defense can profoundly affect the individual's subsequent testimony. Since these changes are not reversible, if individuals are to be allowed to testify after having undergone hypnosis to aid their memory, a minimum number of safeguards are absolutely essential. Based upon extensive review of the field and my own experiences in a considerable number of circumstances, I have proposed the following minimal safeguards in an affidavit (Orne, 1978) in the case of *Quaglino v. California* (1978) which was filed with the Supreme Court of the United States.[9]

1. Hypnosis should be carried out by a psychiatrist or psychologist with special training in its use. He should not be informed about the facts of the case verbally; rather, he should receive a written memorandum outlining whatever facts he is to know, carefully avoiding any other communication which might affect his opinion. Thus, his beliefs and possible bias can be evaluated. It is extremely undesirable to have the individual conducting the hypnotic sessions to have any involvement in the investigation of the case. Further, he should be an independent professional not responsible to the prosecution or the investigators.

2. All contact of the psychiatrist or psychologist with the individual to be hypnotized should be videotaped from the moment they meet until the entire interaction is completed. The casual comments which are passed before or

---

[9] A recent Wisconsin Circuit Court opinion by Judge Wedemeyer in the case of *State v. White* (1979) explicates and expands upon these safeguards (Slip opinion, Pp. 11–13).

after hypnosis are every bit as important to get on tape as the hypnotic session itself. (It is possible to give suggestions prior to the induction of hypnosis which will act as posthypnotic suggestions.)

Prior to the induction of hypnosis, a brief evaluation of the patient should be carried out and the psychiatrist or psychologist should then elicit a detailed description of the facts as the witness or victim remembers them. This is important because individuals often are able to recall a good deal more while talking to a psychiatrist or psychologist than when they are with an investigator, and it is important to have a record of what the witness's beliefs are before hypnosis. Only after this has been completed should the hypnotic session be initiated. The psychiatrist or psychologist should strive to avoid adding any new elements to the witness's description of his experience, including those which he had discussed in his wake state, lest he inadvertently alter the nature of the witness's memories—or constrain them by reminding him of his waking memories.

3. No one other than the psychiatrist or psychologist and the individual to be hypnotized should be present in the room before and during the hypnotic session. This is important because it is all too easy for observers to inadvertently communicate to the subject what they expect, what they are startled by, or what they are disappointed by. If either the prosecution or the defense wish to observe the hypnotic session, they may do so without jeopardizing the integrity of the session through a one-way screen or on a television monitor.

4. Because the interactions which have preceded the hypnotic session may well have a profound effect on the sessions themselves, tape recordings of prior interrogations are important to document that a witness had not been implicitly or explicitly cued pertaining to certain information which might then be reported for apparently the first time by the witness during hypnosis. [Orne, 1978, pp 853–855]

In sum, an effort has been made to outline some of the major issues that must be considered for the forensic use of hypnosis, and particularly if hypnotically enhanced recall is to be used in court. It is possible to document, as has been done here, some of the circumstances where hypnosis has worked against the judicial process. Much of what has been said about memory and hypnosis in this paper has already been documented empirically; however, further rigorous research is needed. Future work will need to direct itself to the task of spelling out the circumstances under which the likelihood of confabulation is maximized, the specific effects which result from the hypnotist's preconceptions, the consequences of allowing the reexperiencing of relevant affect as opposed to suppressing it during the process of recall, the different effects which hypnosis may have on the recall of different kinds of material on the one hand and on the other to assess whether hypnosis has different effects in facilitating recall of material that was purposively learned as that incidentally noted. At the present state of knowledge, it is relatively easy to point to some clear-cut abuses and try to identify some relatively safe and appropriate applications of hypnosis. As serious research addresses the question of the effect of hypnosis and the hypnotic context on memory, it will become possible to be increasingly specific about other circumstances where hypnosis may play a legitimate role as opposed to those where its use will serve only to further confuse an already blind justice.

References

Barber TX: Antisocial and criminal acts induced by "hypnosis": A review of experimental and clinical findings. Arch Gen Psychiatry 5:301–312, 1961

Barber TX, Calverley DS: Empirical evidence for a theory of hypnotic behavior: Effects on suggestibility of five variables typically induced in hypnotic induction procedures. J Consult Psychol 29:98–107, 1965

Bartlett FC: Remembering. Cambridge, Cambridge University Press, 1932

Breuer J, Freud S: Studies on hysteria, vol II. Strachey J (ed and trans): The Standard Edition of the Complete Psychological Works of Sigmund Freud. London, Hogarth, 1955 (originally published 1895)

Coe WC, Kobayashi K, Howard ML: An approach toward isolating factors that influence antisocial conduct in hypnosis. Int J Clin Exp Hypn 20:118–131, 1972

Conn JH: Is hypnosis really dangerous? Int J Clin Exp Hypn 20:61–79, 1972

Cooper LM, London P: Reactivation of memory by hypnosis and suggestion. Int J Clin Exp Hypn 21:312–323, 1973

Crockett et al. v. Haithwaite et al., No. 297/73, (Sup. Ct., B.C. Can. February 10, 1978; unrep.)

Dhanens TP, Lundy RM: Hypnotic and waking suggestions and recall. Int J Clin Exp Hypn 23:68–79, 1975

Ellenberger HF: The Discovery of the Unconscious. New York, Basic Books, 1970

Evans FJ, Kihlstrom JF: Posthypnotic amnesia as disrupted retrieval. J Abnorm Psychol 82:317–323, 1973

Hilgard ER: Divided consciousness: Multiple controls in human thought and action. New York, J Wiley & Sons, 1977

Hilgard ER, Loftus EF: Effective interrogation of the eyewitness. Int J Clin Exp Hypn 27:342–357, 1979

Jenkins JJ: Remember that old theory of memory? Well, forget it! Am Psychologist 29:785–795, 1974

Kihlstrom JF, Evans FJ: Recovery of memory after posthypnotic amnesia. J Abnorm Psychol 85:564–569, 1976

Kihlstrom JF, Evans FJ: Residual effects of suggestions for posthypnotic amnesia: A reexamination. J Abnorm Psychol 86:327–333, 1977

Kline MV: The production of antisocial behavior through hypnosis: New clinical data. Int J Clin Exp Hypn 20:80–94, 1972

Kline MV: Defending the mentally ill: The insanity defense and the role of forensic hypnosis. Int J Clin Exp Hypn 27:375–401, 1979

Kline MV, Guze H: The use of a drawing technique in the investigation of hypnotic age regression and progression. Br J Med Hypn Winter:1–12, 1951

Kroger WS, Doucé RG: Hypnosis in criminal investigation. Int J Clin Exp Hypn 27:358–374, 1979

Lindner R: The Fifty-Minute Hour. New York, Rinehart & Farrar, 1955

Loftus EF: Eyewitness Testimony. Cambridge, MA, Harvard University Press, 1979

London P, Fuhrer M: Hypnosis, motivation and performance. J Pers 29:321–333, 1961

Milligan, In re, No. J-17617 Super Ct. Cal., Monterey Co. (jdmt. June 29, 1978; unrep.); Appeal pendg., Ct. of Appeal, 1st Appl. Dist., San Francisco, Cal.

Nace EP, Orne MT, Hammer AG: Posthypnotic amnesia as an active psychic process. Arch Gen Psychiatry 31:257–260, 1974

O'Connell DN, Shor RE, Orne MT: Hypnotic age regression: An empirical and methodological analysis. J Abnorm Psychol 76(monograph suppl no. 3):1–32, 1970

Orne MT: The mechanisms of hypnotic age regression: An experimental study. J Abnorm Psychol 46:213–225, 1951

Orne MT: The nature of hypnosis: Artifact and essence. J Abnorm Soc Psychol 58:277–299, 1959

Orne MT: Antisocial behavior and hypnosis: Problems of controls and validation in empirical studies. Presented at Colgate University Hypnosis Symposium, Hamilton, NY, April 1960

Orne MT: The potential uses of hypnosis in interrogation. In Biderman AD, Zimmer H (eds): The Manipulation of Human Behavior. New York, J Wiley & Sons, 1961, pp 169–215

Orne MT: Antisocial behavior and hypnosis: Problems of control and validation in empirical studies. In Estabrooks GH (ed): Hypnosis: Current Problems. New York, Harper & Row, 1962, pp 137–192

Orne MT: On the mechanisms of posthypnotic amnesia. Int J Clin Exp Hypn 14:121–134, 1966

Orne MT: On the nature of the posthypnotic suggestion. In Chertok L (ed): Psychophysiological Mechanisms of Hypnosis. Berlin, Springer–Verlag, 1969, pp 173–192

Orne MT: The simulation of hypnosis: Why, how and what it means. Int J Clin Exp Hypn 19:277–296, 1971

Orne MT: Can a hypnotized subject be compelled to carry out otherwise unacceptable behavior? A discussion. Int J Clin Exp Hypn 20:101–117, 1972a

Orne MT: On the simulating subject as a quasi-control group in hypnosis research: What, why and how. In Fromm E, Shor RE (eds): Hypnosis: Research Developments and Perspectives. Chicago, Aldine-Atherton, 1972b, pp 399–443

Orne MT: The construct of hypnosis: Implications of the definition for research and practice. Ann NY Acad Sci 296:14–33, 1977

Orne MT: Affidavit of Amicus Curiae, *Quaglino v. California,* U.S. Sup. Ct. No. 77-1288, *cert. den.* 11/27/78. In Margolin E (Chm): 16th Annual Defending Criminal Cases: The Rapidly Changing Practice of Criminal Law, vol 2. New York, Practising Law Institute, 1978, pp 831–857

*Orne MT: The use and misuse of hypnosis in court. Int J Clin Exp Hypnosis 27:311–341, 1979

Orne MT, Evans FJ: Social control in the psychological experiment: Antisocial behavior and hypnosis. J Pers Soc Psychol 1:189–200, 1965

Orne MT, Sheehan PW, Evans FJ: Occurrence of posthypnotic behavior outside the experimental setting. J Pers Soc Psychol 9:189–196, 1968

People v. McNichol, 100 Cal. App. 2d 544, 224 P.2d 21 (1950)

People v. Ritchie, No. C-36932 (Super. Ct., Orange Co., Cal. April 7, 1977; unrep.)

Putnam WH: Hypnosis and distortions in eyewitness memory. Int J Clin Exp Hypn 27:437–448, 1979

Quaglino v. California, cert. den. 11/27/78,—U.S.—, 99 S. Ct. 212, *pet. rehearing den.,*—U.S.—, 99 S. Ct. 599 (1978)

Reiff R, Scheerer M: Memory and Hypnotic Age Regression: Developmental Aspects of Cognitive Function Explored Through Hypnosis. New York, International University Press, 1959

Reiser M: Hypnosis as an aid in a homicide investigation. Am J Clin Hypn 17:84–87, 1974

Roediger HL: Implicit and explicit memory models. Bull Psychonom Soc 13:339–342, 1979

Sears AB: A comparison of hypnotic and waking recall. Int J Clin Exp Hypn 2:296–304, 1954

Sheehan PW: The Function and Nature of Imagery. New York, Academic Press, 1972

Sheehan, PW, Orne MT: Some comments on the nature of posthypnotic behavior. J Nerv Ment Dis 146:209–220, 1968

* Article from which Part I of this chapter was reprinted.

Stalnaker JM, Riddle EE: The effect of hypnosis on long-delayed recall. J Gen Psychol 6:429–440, 1932

State v. Douglas, Ind. No. 692-77 (Union Co., N.J., vac. 5/23/78)

State v. Mack, Minn. Sup. Ct. #50036 (Pretrial probable cause hearing cert. as important and doubtful question January 30, 1979, by Dist. Ct., Co. of Hennepin, 4th Judicial Dist., under Minn. Rules of Crim. Proc. #29.02, subd. 4) 292 N. W. 2d 764 (Minn.), 1980

State v. Papp, No. 78-02-00229 (C. P. Summit Co., Ohio, Lorain Co. No. 16862, March 23, 1978; unrep.). Appeal, U.S. Sup Ct. No. 79-5091, *cert. den.* 10/1/79

State v. Peterson, No. CCR79-003 (Cir. Ct., Hamilton Co., Ind. July 12, 1979; uprep.)

State v. White, No. J-3665, (Cir. Ct., Branch 10, Milwaukee Co., Wisc., March 27, 1979; unrep.)

United States v. Andrews, General Court-Martial No. 75-14 (N.E. Jud. Cir., Navy-Marine Corps Judiciary, Phila., Pa. Oct. 6, 1975)

Watkins JG: Antisocial behavior under hypnosis: Possible or impossible? Int J Clin Exp Hypn 20:95–100, 1972

White RW, Fox GF, Harris WW: Hypnotic hypermnesia for recently learned material. J Abnorm Soc Psychol 35:88–103, 1940

Wigmore JH: Evidence (Chadburn rev), vol 5, sec 1360. Boston, Little, Brown & Co, 1974

PART II

Investigative Aspects of Forensic Hypnosis*

Neil S. Hibler

It appears that each time a new and innovative technique is introduced to do a job more easily or quickly, it becomes somewhat of a fad. So it seems with hypnosis in law enforcement. The infectious appeal this technique has achieved seems reminiscent of many other promising "panaceas" in the investigative field. Unfortunately, all too often the anticipation with which new techniques are popularized exceeds their actual realization—and, as a result, the technique raises question as to its own reliability and validity.

As described earlier in this chapter, hypnosis is fraught with potential forensic difficulties arising from its very nature. In hypnosis, suggestion can easily taint the perceptions of an interviewee, and the filling in of memories, or confabulations, can easily occur where an interviewee's need for closure or an eagerness to please inquirers overcomes actual memory. Worse yet, because of the compelling genuineness with which hypnotic statements are offered, those naive to these serious limitations would be confident that information derived from trance was accurate (Margolin, 1981). Other discussion has focused on interviewees' confusion over what is recalled and that which is imagined; suggesting that persons who have been hypnotically interviewed may not be suitable wit-

* This is a work of the United States Government within the meaning of Title 17, United States Code.

nesses at all (Diamond, 1980). Despite these issues, employment of hypnosis as an enhancement to memory has certainly been well intended. While hypnosis has been used as an investigative aid for at least a quarter century (Arons, 1967; Block, 1976), the proliferation of its use has occurred owing largely to a reawakening of the technique in law enforcement by Dr. Martin Reiser of the Los Angeles Police Department (Reiser, 1980). In establishing hypnosis as an available technique for law-enforcement personnel, Reiser trained a select group of police lieutenants. These officers, in turn, were dispatched to use hypnosis in the course of investigations. Owing to the influence of the hundreds of officers around the country who have since been trained and who strongly advocate hypnosis as an investigative tool, the concept has become well-known in the police community.

It is important to realize that police face a formidable task in conducting investigations. Officers deal with physical evidence that is frequently minute, fragile, or perishable, and must develop other details from the observations of persons who were unexpectedly confronted with often dramatically traumatic experiences. In these memories may lie the most critical information, and hypnosis often holds promise in enhancing descriptions that might not otherwise be available. Yet, there is a clear need for investigators to be certain that hypnotically obtained information is correct. Herein lies the controversy of forensic hypnosis and the caution to all who would use hypnosis for investigative purposes. In fact, concern regarding the accuracy of hypnotic recall prompted a unified effort within the Federal investigative community.

In early 1978, an *ad hoc* forum was convened to assure the development of uniform guidance within the Federal community. The record in the civil arena was clear; the many and varied private and departmental uses of hypnosis often led to applications that could not meet their test in court. The result has been a myriad of court decisions that sporadically endorse or reject hypnosis because of often ill-conceived applications. Therefore, Federal investigative agencies coordinated to devise a uniform model that addressed the issues.

The Federal use of forensic hypnosis is based on the premise that hypnosis is a technique for memory refreshment, not memory verification. The basis of this position is that if hypnotically derived information is to be of investigative value, it must be independently corroborated. Therefore, the purpose of hypnosis is to derive investigative leads, and not to evoke testimony. Simply, the potential difficulties inherent in the use of forensic hypnosis are nullified when independent corroboration becomes the criteria for evaluating hypnotically obtained information (Hibler, 1979, 1980; Teten, 1979).

Within the "Federal Model," a "team approach" was developed to use the best qualified personnel to conduct interviews. This pragmatic compromise uses the expertise of mental-health professionals as hypnotists and trainers of investigators as interviewers. Doctors simply are not familiar with investigative procedures, nor are they prepared to handle many forensic requirements, such as making an advisement of rights or securing materials as evidence. Likewise, investigators are not suitable hypnotists. They lack the professional experience and skill required fully to employ hypnosis and tend to the needs of victims of often traumatic crimes, and they are less credible expert witnesses than doctors in attesting to the use of hypnosis. The result is that the Federal Government's "team approach" to forensic hypnosis provides a comprehensive capacity for dealing with the needs of both the investigation and the interviewee (Ault, 1979, 1980; Hibler, 1980).

As this chapter continues, the Federal Model is further explained in three major areas of discussion: procedures for case review, interview preparation and conduct, and investigative continuation.

Procedures for Case Review: When to Use Hypnosis

Forensic hypnosis is not a panacea. The instances in which hypnosis is suited for application tend to be well defined, and occur with only modest frequency. To assure that hypnosis is employed in appropriate situations, requests for forensic hypnosis in Federal investigations receive multiple levels of review to determine if hypnosis is the only, or even the best procedure for the investigation.

Although each government agency is autonomous and functions independently, each employs similar safeguards in their screening procedures. For example, in the Air Force Office of Special Investigations, field requests for hypnotic interview are forwarded to Headquarters, where supervisory personnel review the status of the case and when indicated, offer suggestions for alternatives to hypnosis. Sometimes, this results in simple advice that was not previously considered. One such example was an instance in which an investigator, eager to request hypnosis, had not fully interviewed witnesses of a crime. His impatience was reflected in his initial contact with the neighbor of the suspect (who was thought to have murdered her husband). The investigator needed to ascertain the time at which the suspect arrived home after shopping, reportedly to find that her husband had been shot to death. Questions had to be raised, however, because of well-known tensions between the suspect and her husband and because of various inconsistencies in her prior statements. Unfortunately, the neighbor said that she was unable to help—after she was told by an investigator that she needed to be absolutely certain as to the time she witnessed the suspect driving into her garage. In fact, he added: "Would you be willing to testify to this in court?" Case reviewers of the investigation suggested that the potential witness be reinterviewed by an agent not familiar with the case. This second investigator apologized to the witness for her having to repeat her recollections, and simply asked her if she could indicate what time the suspect arrived home. Much to his surprise, the neighbor now provided a precise time, adding that she noticed the suspect arrived home while she had gotten up from her chair during a television commercial. The precise time was further confirmed by the witness' husband, who was quite able to recall his wife getting him something from the kitchen during a break in one of their favorite television programs.

In another example, a telephone call was received from a field office requesting a hypnotic interview of a service station attendant who was the victim of an armed robbery. The purpose of the hypnotic interview was to ascertain whether a tatto on the gunman's right forearm was a rearing stallion or a unicorn. Other details developed in the case included an excellent description of the gunman, a "get away" driver, and the vehicle used in the crime. When the special agent requesting the interview was told that he would need to use formal channels for the request, and that he would need to respond to a number of administrative requirements, he exclaimed, "Hell, it will take a month to do that—we'll have it solved by then!" It took only 3 weeks.

Requests for consultation by the forensic science staff may also be indicated. These forensic specialists have graduate degrees in forensic pathology, physical science, and laboratory techniques; they consider the special processing of physical evidence that might preclude the need for the use of hypnosis. Whenever possible, consideration of forensic hypnosis is withheld until laboratory procedures are completed and the importance of that data is known. Because of the many issues that make application of hypnosis in an investigation a complex task, only major felony offenses are considered suitable for the expenditure of the time and effort that this technique requires. Hypnosis is typically employed only as a last resort in the hope that other investigative procedures will be successful and then alleviate the need for hypnotic intervention. Even then, some serious crimes that have been considered with the utmost care and have been afforded extensive investigative effort may still not be suitable. In the Air Force's experience, about one third of the cases in which hypnosis is requested are solved without hypnosis. About one third more of these requests are considered ill suited for the procedure at all; the majority of instances do not need nor benefit from the technique.

Indiscretions or errors in investigative procedure—although not violations of the law—may nonetheless severely restrict or even prohibit the use of hypnosis. For example, presentation of a suspect for identification to a witness, in other than a well-considered actual or photographic lineup, may lead a witness or victim to believe that the suspect is involved regardless of his initial opinion. For this reason, cases in which no suspect has been developed are better for hypnosis; there is a clear preference for investigations in which the subject or subjects are unknown. Simply, if there are no indications as to who might be responsible for the crime, there is significantly less likelihood that inadvertent suggestions will play a role in implanting ideas in the mind of an interviewee.

If a suspect has been developed, hypnosis might be used carefully to develop information that can probably be corroborated, but is not tainted by the prior identification of a suspect. For example, in cases in which subjects are identified, the use of a police artist or other composite technique would be in question if the suspect was known to the hypnotic interviewee. However, under some circumstances it may be worthwhile to consider a hypnotic interview to develop the details that are identifiable for the suspect (for example, description of an automobile, weapon, etc.), but which are known to the interviewee only through the criminal act in which he or she was a witness or victim. One case that illustrates this logic involved the brutal rape of an office clerk. Days after reporting the incident she happened to notice someone who "looked like" the rapist. It is, of course, quite common in the aftermath of rape for victims to believe they have again encountered their attackers. This is a natural form of vigilence that occurs as the victim adjusts to her intense sense of vulnerability. Yet to be sure that the features of an innocent individual were superimposed in her hypnotic memory, only the automobile used in her abduction was pursued hypnotically.

A similar issue deals with the potential interviewee's sense of pressure either to increase the credibility of his earlier statements, or to please authorities. Therefore, information about the case that has been shared with the victim or witness becomes quite important, as it could possibly be confused with his own memories of the incident. Further, if some logical conclusion has been inadvertently suggested, there may well be tainting of the interviewee's recollection, particularly if there has been pressure to produce results.

Another consideration in case review is to estimate the likelihood that recall may be enhanced by hypnosis. The intent here is to consider the extent to which an individual may actually have additional memories for enhancement. Failure specifically to consider aspects of the incident that are critical to the case, and their likelihood for enhanced recall, only tends to increase the interviewee's pressure to perform. To assure that goals are clearly evident, hypnosis is not used as a "fishing expedition." Rather, in each case, there is a careful examination of the details of a potential interviewee's nonhypnotic statement that might be developed. Then an assessment is made of the relative investigative value of information that might be expected from a hypnotic interview. To accomplish this, it is sometimes necessary to reenact the event.

In the careful retracing of the incident, it may be possible to clarify what the witness or victim might have seen or heard. This is the best way to explore the potential acuity of these perceptions. For instance, the effects of lighting, distances between witnesses and subject, and other factors can be more clearly understood. Hypnosis can allow only for a detailed review of an experience. Hypnosis does not provide telescopic vision, the ability to hear whispers at great distances or any other magical effects. Sometimes, scrutiny of existing statements or reenactments also reveals inconsistencies that question an individual's credibility.

There is no issue more central to the investigative use of hypnosis than the validity of information derived through the process. As all of the controversies surrounding hypnosis appear to stem from whether or not hypnotic recall is accurate, it has been the position of the Federal investigative community that hypnotically derived information is considered to be of prosecutive value only if it is independently corroborated. This precaution has served well to avoid controversies in which hypnosis would otherwise be relied on as the trier of fact. Further, much investigative effort can be wasted in attempts to confirm intentionally misleading hypnotic statements. To further assure the appropriate use of hypnosis, a polygraph examination is requested whenever an investigation raises concerns about the credibility of statements from a potential hypnotic interviewee. While the polygraph itself is not a conclusive procedure, nor is it without its own controversies, the motivation of personnel to undergo the polygraph and its generally acceptable results have been an important means with which to further define the intent and cooperation of potential interviewees. In fact, when a polygraph examination is considered necessary, it must be successfully passed prior to further consideration of hypnosis.

Who ought to be hypnotized? Certainly victims of and witnesses to crimes are the likely candidates for memory enhancement. Yet the use of forensic hypnosis with suspects presents a particularly strong debate. This is because of the potential for hypnosis to confuse a suspect's memory and therefore possibly alter his capacity to stand in his own defense. For this reason, the Federal investigative community, with the exception of the Air Force, does not allow the hypnotic interview of suspects. The Air Force, however, has adopted the position that if the defense is intent upon using hypnosis, they may well do so on their own. Therefore, as the government has the capacity to provide trained doctors, investigators, and recording equipment, it is only fair that this investigative procedure be available to the prosecution and the defense as well. Interview requests by a defense counsel receive the same careful, critical case review and evaluative considerations as would any other case. Yet the type of situation in which a suspect interview would be appropriate would seem limited. For instance, one possible suspect interview scenario could include a situation in which the accused professes innocence of an act, but has had difficulty in accounting for his whereabouts at the time of the crime. Here hypnosis might be helpful in developing a defense by producing leads which, upon confirmation, would establish a creditable alibi.

There is one other group that may benefit from the enhanced recall afforded by hypnosis. Operational personnel (undercover agents and informants) are sometimes exposed to critical events that cannot be reported in sufficient detail because of the quantity of things happening, their intensity, or the delay in time between the event and subsequent debriefing. As with all other applications of this technique, case review needs to address the possibility of prehypnotic suggestion, credibility, and interviewee motivation.

Preparation to Request Forensic Hypnosis

In preparation for using forensic hypnosis, it must be confirmed that the hypnotic interviewee is clearly a volunteer for the procedure. This is not only an ethical prerequisite, but an important safeguard to prevent actual or implied coercion, which would further complicate the course and results of the interview. Also, the prosecuting attorney needs to be aware of the intended interview. Coordination with prosecutors should underscore the concerns hypnosis may raise, which could have a strong effect on the preparation of the case for trial. Further, there is a strong ethical concern for the well-being of the interviewee, and his capacity to undergo the recall of events that may have been intensely traumatic. For this reason, a potential interviewee's medical records are reviewed with particular attention to psychiatric history. Where current mental health issues are revealed, the attending practitioner is approached to ascertain his opinion as to the appropriateness of such an interview. When records are not available, interviewees are asked whether they have received psychological assistance, and further, these points are explored and clarified by the hypnotherapist at the time of the interview.

Interview Approval, Preparation, and Procedure

Cases that meet all of the forensic, investigative, and hypnotic prerequisites are presented for approval consideration to a senior official within the headquarters of the investigative agency. This requirement sets forth yet another level of review, which is, importantly, separate from the intensity of the case at the level at which it is being investigated, and the possible pressures that might otherwise force a less well-considered judgment. If the request for hypnotic interview is approved, the case is then referred to a hypnosis coordinator who arranges for the actual session.

Hypnosis coordinators are well-experienced special agents who have been trained to assist hypnotherapists by conducting numerous forensic and administrative details before, during, and after the interview. The annual training these investigators receive maintains their proficiency, updates their knowledge, and allows for critical review of their work.

Preparing for the Interview

The hypnosis coordinator contacts the case investigator and the hypnotherapist, and initiates planning for an interview location and date. Preferable locations would include space in a hospital or doctor's office. The room to be used needs to be private and to assure that there will be no interruptions, and, further, this space needs to be well illuminated as well as quiet, so that there will be no interference with the recording of the session. Also, the space needs to be large enough so that television equipment and participants may be positioned and a reclining chair may be used for the interviewee. Figure 25-1 depicts the layout of an interview setting.

On the actual date of the interview, the session needs to be carefully scheduled so that all parties are free of other obligations that might distract them from the task at hand. The session ought to begin early enough in the day so that the need for meals or the end of day does not interfere; sessions typically take 2 to

Fig. 25-1. Positions of personnel and equipment

3 hours, or longer. Further, the hypnotic coordinator must have copies of appropriate consent forms on hand, a clipboard (for automatic writing), and incidental items, such as a box of facial tissues. He makes sure that the television equipment is functioning, that there is a sufficient supply of recording tape and, if a female is to be interviewed, that a chaperone is present. Additionally, if facial composites are expected to be used, either a police artist should be made available or a Smith and Wesson Identi-kit needs to be obtained.

The television equipment that is utilized should incorporate separate microphones for the hypnotherapist, interviewee, and hypnotic coordinator. As may be seen in Figure 25-2, the hypnotherapist, interviewee, and hypnotic coordinator sit together so that they may be on camera. Preferably, voice recordings are controlled by use of a sound mixer, rather than by using dynamic or self-regulating microphones, which tend to record distracting extraneous noise. A date–time generator should also be provided to imprint the date, hour, and elapsed minutes and seconds on the video image, so that each moment of the interview may be followed. The camera operator adjusts all equipment during the interview, and as depicted in Figure 25-3, is positioned to videotape the session.

In addition, the camera operator is instructed to give a nonverbal signal to the hypnotherapist 10 minutes before he must put a fresh cassette into the recorder. The camera operator also needs to ensure that the recording equipment

Fig. 25-2. Mental health professional, interviewee, and hypnosis coordinator

Fig. 25-3. Audiovisual recording apparatus

functions appropriately, and should focus the camera on any activity during the session that may be of particular importance. For example, ideomotor signaling and automatic writing may require close-up shots. The case investigator is also present, sitting near the hypnotic coordinator (but is not on camera). The case investigator's role is to notify the hypnotic coordinator of information that is developed during the course of the interview that is of particular importance, either because it is new information or contrary to that which was previously stated. This is done by having the case investigator write down comments such as "Develop more detail about the automobile." Then he passes this note to the hypnotic coordinator. Upon receipt of such a note, the hypnotic coordinator initials the note and writes the time at which it was transmitted. As appropriate to the course of the session, the hypnotic coordinator will ask nonleading questions that address the concern raised by the case agent. This precaution is taken to assure that suggestive or leading questions do not occur, while at the same time being sure that details of investigative importance are pursued. By design, the hypnotherapist and hypnosis coordinator know very little about the case. This is to preclude any *a priori* conclusions that might otherwise be reached, as well as to further minimize the potential for cueing, which would suggest information known to investigators. Prior to the interview, the coordinator also provides the hypnotherapist with a detailed overview of the procedures to be followed, emphasizes precautions regarding leading questions, and clearly establishes that the interview is considered a forensic-medicine procedure, which is under the practitioner's charge. This is an important safeguard for the well-being of the interviewee, as the hypnotherapist may terminate the interview at any time if it is necessary in the best interests of the interviewee.

To assure that an interviewee is participating with fully informed consent and voluntariness, a standardized informed consent form is used. The format for this form is depicted in Appendix 25-1, and in Appendix 25-2 there is a modified form to be used if the interview is being monitored by others. Additionally, a prepared statement is used to obtain permission to use the recordings for training purposes, should the session seem to have value as an educational aid (Permission to Release form, Appendix 25-3). This form, however, is not presented until after the interview has been concluded.

The doctor needs to be allowed the opportunity to be certain that the interviewee is well suited to experience hypnosis and the recall of potentially traumatic events. To accomplish this, the doctor may have a private clinical interview with the interviewee if it is felt to be necessary. This interview addresses the mental status of the interviewee and does not include any discussion of the case. Other than this possible interaction, however, all proceedings are tape-recorded.

On occasion, interviewees state that they would feel more comfortable having a friend present during the interview. Any such additional persons, to include a chaperone if one is used, should sit far in the rear of the room, and while present, they usually cannot hear any of the dialogue. Consequently, these persons do not respond to the contents of the interview, and as a final precaution, all persons who are to witness the interview are cautioned not to make any responses which would influence the proceedings. An alternate and superior way of ensuring that the interview is free of interference is to have interested parties monitor the session by means of a remote television monitor which is located in another room.

The form and flow of the interview follows a predetermined script. The script structures the interview so that it includes all necessary precautionary considerations while providing a structure with which to enhance the familiarity of roles and development of information. A copy of the script that is employed throughout the interview is appended to this chapter as Appendix 25-4. Its use is demonstrated in a transcript for a forensic hypnosis session, which is included in the following case discussion.

Case Example and Transcript of Interview*

Miss L. reported to authorities that she had been raped by a motorist who offered her a ride to work. She stated that she would not have ordinarily

---

* Names of persons and places in this investigation have been changed to protect identities, and this transcript has been edited and condensed from the original 4-hour session.

accepted a ride, but she had recently fractured her ankle, and was wearing a partial cast, which made a brief walk to work quite cumbersome. Miss L. told investigators that at approximately 6:30 in the morning she was hailed by a motorist whom she recognized as a person she had met while at a nightclub some 2 weeks earlier. She reluctantly entered the car, and the two engaged in small talk until the driver turned in the wrong direction. She protested, but was told that he "wanted to show her something." The auto was driven to a deserted area, where the driver produced a gun and demanded that she undress. She hesitated, and a pistol was put to her head with the threat that he would have his way whether she was dead or alive. She then followed his instructions, and was subjected to sexual intercourse. She was allowed to dress and eventually was driven to her residence, where, she reported, he threatened to kill her if she went to the police. She went directly to her room, bathed, and then reported the assault to authorities.

The investigation included a thorough, medical rape protocol examination. Further, locations at which she was picked up and dropped off were canvassed in the hope of identifying witnesses. Also, interviews were conducted of personnel at the nightclub where she had met the suspect on an earlier occasion. Miss L. attempted to generate a facial composite of her suspect, but was unable to do so. In the following 2 months, she encountered one brief, chance contact with her alleged assailant, at which time he again threatened her life. Following that, she relocated to another geographic area, out of concern for her safety.

A review of other sexual assault cases within the military community and neighboring towns, failed to reveal any similar crimes. One local police department did report apprehending a speeder following a high-speed chase. While these two incidents had no obvious relationship, the color of the speeding automobile and the general physical description (age, height, and weight) of the driver were in keeping with those of the rape subject. A photographic lineup, which included a photo of the speeder, was constructed and presented to the rape victim. She reported, however, that she had never seen any of those individuals before. Finally, after some 2 months without any investigative developments, the case was considered for final review prior to closure. As a result of this review, a request was made for a hypnotic interview as a possible means with which to enhance the victim's recall of the subject, the handgun used in the assault, and the subject's vehicle. Headquarters' review of this investigation generated a request that the victim be reinterviewed to clarify numerous details of her earlier transcripts. Upon reinterview she repeated what she had stated previously, with the exception that in this subsequent contact, she was emphatic that the suspect held the gun to her head during intercourse. Due to a variety of subtle concerns about her motivation to assist investigators, it was then recommended that the victim be given a polygraph test regarding the major elements of her statements. She consented to polygraph, and, after some initial uneasiness, she was cooperative, advising that she had altered several aspects of her statements so that she would appear to be more clearly the victim of a violent act, and in so doing protect her own pride and dignity. Coordination for the request to use hypnosis then commenced.

The victim willingly volunteered for a hypnotic interview, and added that she had never received treatment from a mental-health professional. Next, the prosecutor for the case was contacted for coordination. Approval for the use of forensic hypnosis was granted by the headquarters of the Federal investigative agency, with the understanding that details of the suspect's vehicle would be particularly important. Also important would be details of the meetings in which the victim and the subject talked prior to the rape and of the chance encounter some days after the rape, which might identify other witnesses. The following is a summarized transcript of Miss L.'s forensic hypnosis interview.

Hypnosis Coordinator: *This interview is being conducted at Miller Air Force Base, New York. It is the 2nd of March, 1981. The time is now 8:30 in the morning. Persons present are myself, Special Agent John Smith, Air Force Office of Special Investigations. To my right is Miss L., and to her right is Dr. Neil S. Hibler; off-camera are Special Agent William Jones and Special Agent Richard Scott, Air Force Office of Special Investigations, and Mrs. Wendy Appleton. Miss L., it is clear that we're using television equipment to videotape what occurs this morning. Is that all right with you?*

Interviewee: *Yes.*

Hypnosis Coordinator: *The purpose of this interview is to discuss the circumstances of a sexual assault that Miss L. has reported to have occurred on December 14th, 1981, at Miller AFB. I would like to now turn your attention, Miss L., to Dr. Hibler who is going to speak with you about hypnosis and the procedures which are used in hypnotic interviews.*

Mental-Health Professional: *Miss L., may I call you by your first name?*

Interviewee: *[Nods yes.] My name is Elizabeth, but I like to be called "Betty."*

Mental-Health Professional: *Okay, Betty, I'd like to explain some things to you about hypnosis and how we would like to use it as an aid in working in this investigation. First, perhaps you could let me know if you've encountered hypnosis before?*

Interviewee: *No, I've never been hypnotized. I only know what they say on TV and the movies.*

Mental-Health Professional: *Okay, perhaps then I might explain some of* *what I feel is important to know about hypnosis. I define hypnosis as an altered state of consciousness. Let me say that another way; it's a very natural way of being relaxed. There are a number of qualities that also might be used to explain this "altered state." One I have already alluded to, for in its natural form it's quite relaxing. About the other qualities, hypnosis is a state in which each of us has the potential to alter our perceptions. Altering perceptions can be useful in medical and dental applications of hypnosis to relieve pain, and sometimes control bleeding. It's also a potent way to control anxiety, and therefore has many applications for emotional adjustment, such as in psychotherapy. One psychotherapeutic application is something that doctors call an age or time regression, which allows individuals to reexperience critical events in their lives. This is the application which is used to aid investigations. What may be helpful here is for you to reexperience that morning on that day in December, and in so doing, provide myself and Mr. Smith an understanding of what happened to you.*

Let me talk a little bit more about trance itself. If you would like to proceed with the interview today, I will help you to experience hypnosis, and we'll talk about that—what that feels like. Then, when I feel you're ready, and you feel it's okay, we'll use time regression to go back to the day in which the incident occurred. I've mentioned that, in its natural state, hypnosis is most comfortable, and explained this is why hypnosis is so helpful in dealing with anxiety. Unfortunately, there are often misconceptions about hypnosis; perhaps I might address a few of these.

In hypnosis, you will be in control of your thoughts and actions, just as you always are. For example, if a fire alarm were to sound, even while you were deep in trance, you would be able to get out of the chair and exit the building just the same as you always would. Further, you won't do anything in hypnosis that you don't want to do. For example, if there is some area that a question asks about that you're uncomfortable with, you need not answer, just please let me know. I'd like to know if you are uncomfortable because a question deals with something that's private, or if it's something else that you're anxious about. For, if it's okay with you, I believe I will be able to help you deal with something, for example that you're anxious about. We will not pursue any area that you do not want us to. Also, I'd like to add that most people can be hypnotized, if they want to be. Incidentally, there are different capacities to experience hypnosis among people, and trance itself has varying depths or degrees. While you're experiencing hypnosis, we can talk about how trance feels, and its depth, and so on. Please feel free at any time to ask any question that you may have.

Now let me tell you how we conduct an interview. In using hypnosis in forensic applications, we use a standardized format. One of the details is my talking to you and explaining hypnosis, and answering any questions that you may have, just as we're doing now. After we're through with our conversation, Mr. Smith will go over an informed-consent certificate with you, which he'll ask you to read and, if you concur, to sign. After that, we'll be talking about the incident in question—without any hypnosis at all. You see, Mr. Smith and I know almost nothing about your investigation; we would rather hear about it from you. After we've discussed what you recall of the event now, in detail, I'll let you experience trance so that you can become familiar with that. Trance induction, or the way in which you enter trance, can be very varied, and I'll use several ways today so that you can tell me which ones you prefer. I'll also be doing some deepening with you, so that you can access different levels of trance. Earlier, I mentioned age or time regression; this is a form of time distortion, which will enable you to reexperience that incident of weeks ago. As you reexperience that incident, you may well feel the emotions now that you felt then. That's why I'm here; if you were to have difficulty with that, just let me know; I can help you. We'll also be using some inquiry techniques. Sometimes we call these television techniques, because they're like the production effects used in television sports events. For example, if you've watched a professional football game or baseball game, you've seen stop action, instant replay, focusing in, and so on. Mr. Smith will assist in asking questions of you and speaking with you in trance. Finally, I would add that often we use something we call posthypnotic suggestion, which is a way of allowing your recall to continue after trance, because sometimes the memory that you have refreshed with hypnosis comes back with yet additional details after trance. Do you have any questions, any questions at all?

Interviewee: *No, I'll ask if anything comes to mind.*

Mental-Health Professional: *Fine then. Mr. Smith now has the informed-consent form for you to review.*

Hypnosis Coordinator: *Miss L., may I call you "Betty," too?*

Interviewee: *That'll be fine.*

Hypnosis Coordinator: *Please read this informed-consent certificate carefully and feel free to ask any questions that you may have. If you concur, I will ask you to sign the form, and Dr. Hibler to sign* *advising that he has counseled you, and then I'll sign as a witness. Here [gives form to interviewee], take your time; read this carefully.*

Interviewee: *[Reads form, nods in agreement and signs] [Hypnosis Coordinator and Mental-Health Professional also sign]*

Hypnosis Coordinator: *Fine. Now, would you tell Dr. Hibler and me about the incident that occurred on the 14th of December.*

Interviewee: *Like I said, I had seen him before. The weekend before the incident, I was in the club and he came over, introduced himself, and offered me a ride home. I left with him, but decided to walk home, and I didn't see him again until that morning.*

Hypnosis Coordinator: *Okay, tell us about that.*

Interviewee: *Well, I had my leg in a cast, and was hobbling down the street when a car pulled up. At first I kind of hoped it wasn't stopping for me. You see, I didn't really know anybody here, and I wasn't sure why anyone would stop for me. I saw it was him though, and I did get in the car—he offered to drive to work. But he didn't take me to work, he drove me to some secluded place and took advantage of me. Afterwards, he took me back to in front of my place, just dropped me off. That's all.*

Hypnosis Coordinator: *Betty, let me ask if you would tell Dr. Hibler and me more about what has occurred. Would that be all right?*

Interviewee: *[Nods in agreement] When I first saw him, I was at the club. He came over, asked me where I was from. We just talked for a few minutes. It was late, and I told him I had to leave. He walked me out, and said he would give me a ride in his car, but my place was just down the street. I walked the rest of the way by myself.*

Hypnosis Coordinator: *I wonder if you could tell us more about when this occurred, or possibly if you were with others at the time?*

Interviewee: *The club thing was about a week, maybe 2 weeks before that morning. I wish I was with someone then, but I was alone.*

Hypnosis Coordinator: *Betty, you said that he walked you out, and offered you a ride. Did you see what he would have given you a ride in?*

Interviewee: *His car was parked right outside, but I don't know anything about cars; I couldn't tell you anything about it.*

Hypnosis Coordinator: *Perhaps there was something that suggested whether it was new or old?*

Interviewee: *Oh, it was new. It was bright, shiny. He seemed very proud of it.*

Hypnosis Coordinator: *Betty, tell me more about "bright and shiny." What made it look that way?*

Interviewee: *It was very clean. Dark in color, maybe, but I really didn't get a chance, maybe I didn't pay attention until that morning. Now, I'm just not sure.*

Hypnosis Coordinator: *That's all right, Betty. I wonder if there is anything else that comes to mind?*

Interviewee: *That morning, he was all dressed and everything. I wonder what he was doing up at that hour? Anyhow, he was weird. He really got a kick out of scaring me. I just don't understand. He wanted to hurt me, he just didn't care.*

Hypnosis Coordinator: *Betty, what else can you tell us about that morning of the incident?*

Interviewee: *What do you mean? I've told you everything.*

Hypnosis Coordinator: *I appreciate your going over this again, Betty. Perhaps there is something else that comes to mind as you think about his car.*

Interviewee: *No, it was early, I just wasn't thinking about his car, I'm sorry.*

Hypnosis Coordinator: *Not at all, Betty. You're doing just fine. I would like Dr. Hibler to now talk with you some more about hypnosis and how we use hypnosis in this kind of interview.*

Mental-Health Professional: *Betty, I wonder if you have any questions so far?*

Interviewee: *No, not so far.*

Mental-Health Professional: *Okay, then I'd like to allow you to experience hypnosis so we can talk about that. And, when I feel you are ready, and when you say it is okay, we'll use hypnosis in reexperiencing whatever incidents are important. Will that be all right?*

Interviewee: *Okay.*

Mental-Health Professional: *Fine. Betty, if you would, please go ahead and lean back; just allow yourself to get comfortable. You will notice that this is a recliner. Perhaps you would like to slide back a little and see how that feels. That's fine. Now, Betty, just let your eyes close naturally, and let the chair support more and more of your weight.*

A naturalistic induction was accomplished using progressive relaxation and deepening by simple count-down suggestions coupled with imagery of the descent of a spiral staircase. Limb catalepsy was demonstrated, and hypnoanalgesia developed on the back of her right hand. Betty talked about what it felt like to be in trance during this initial hypnotic experience and nonverbal cues were practiced for deepening, by touching her right shoulder, and alerting, by touching her left shoulder. The transcript now continues. Betty is in trance.

Mental-Health Professional: *Betty, you're certainly ready to go back in time now. Will that be all right?*

Interviewee: *Yes.*

Mental-Health Professional: *For Betty, today is the 2nd of March, going all the way back, Betty, all the way back. Now it's the first of March, That's right, and the 28th of February, 27th, 26, 25, and the day before that, and the day before that, and the week before that, all the way back . . . all the way back, all the way back to sometime important to this incident. All the way back, that's right, that's right. As clear as it can be, now, you're there. Tell us, Betty, what is happening now?*

Interviewee: *. . . Now it's the morning of the attack. I've walked out of my building . . . and I'm walking down the sidewalk [pause].*

Mental-Health Professional: *Okay, what is happening now?*

Interviewee: *A car is passing me . . . slowing down. It stopped. It kind of startles me, and I look at the license plate—it's local. As I walk by, I see the driver motioning to me. It's . . . it's the guy I met at the club. He is asking me if I want a ride. I say, "Well, okay." It takes me a minute to get into the car, with my cast and all.*

Mental-Health Professional: *And now, what is happening?*

Interviewee: *We're driving down the street. He's talking, but I'm not listening. What? He's turning . . . the wrong way. "Why are we going this way? This isn't right."*

Mental-Health Professional: *Um-hmm.*

Interviewee: *He's saying he wants to show me something. [Interviewee is becoming visibly anxious. Her body becomes stiff, her voice quivers.] He's telling me that he wants to get it on. I try to get out of the car, but he stops me. Oh, my God—a gun, he's got a gun. He's telling me to take my clothes off. I start, but he pushes, hits me. He says it's not fast enough. [Tears are now rolling down the victim's face. She is trembling.]*

Mental-Health Professional: *I understand, Betty. . . . Go on.*

Interviewee: *I'm trying . . . [crying and shaking as she speaks]. But I can't get my pants over my cast. He's pushing, hitting me, telling me "hurry up." [There is a long pause, silence in which she quietly sobs.] He's looking at me, . . . touching me, he takes advantage of me.*

Mental-Health Professional: *I hear you, Betty. I hear you.*

Interviewee: *He's done. I get dressed; he drives me back to my* apartment. I'm getting out of the car, he says "Tell anyone and I'll kill you." He tells me he knows where I live, and that he'll kill me. I'm stunned . . . out of it.

Mental-Health Professional: *Okay.*

Interviewee: *I go to my room, undress, and shower. I put my robe on, and one of the girls, my girlfriend sees me, she sees something is wrong. I tell her that I have been raped. She hugs me. I call the police. . . . That's all.*

Mental-Health Professional: *Okay, Betty. How do you feel now?*

Interviewee: *Okay. I'm okay.*

Mental-Health Professional: *All right then, Betty, I'd like you then to rewind all of that memory, all the way back, all the way back to the very first time you see this individual . . . all the way back. [Pause] There. How's that?*

Interviewee: *Okay. I'm at the club.*

Mental-Health Professional: *This time, Betty, as you tell us what you're experiencing, Mr. Smith and I may be asking you questions or focusing on something so we understand that better. Would that be okay?*

Interviewee: *[Nods in agreement.]*

Mental-Health Professional: *Okay, Betty, go ahead then, what is happening now?*

Interviewee: *I am at the club. I'm sitting by myself. The music is really fine. [Interviewee is sitting quietly, as if listening—tapping her foot rhythmically.] He's over there, I think he's going to come over and talk to me. He's looked this way a couple of times now.*

Hypnosis Coordinator: *I wonder, Betty, who has been looking your way?*

Interviewee: *He is. The guy who attacked me. He's coming over. He's standing with his hands on the back of the chair next to me. He says his name, then, "What's yours?" I tell him. It's noisy, I could just barely hear him. [There's a long pause where the victim appears to be intently listening, then she breaks out into a big smile.]*

Mental-Health Professional: *Betty, you're smiling?*

Interviewee: *He's talking with some other guys now. I know one of the guys he's talking to.*

Hypnosis Coordinator: *Who's talking to the other guys?*

Interviewee: *Mark, the guy who raped me. Oh . . . that's his name. I remember, he said his name was Mark. Mark is his name. That's all he told me. He said his name was Mark.*

Hypnosis Coordinator: *And, Betty, you say he's now talking to some other guys?*

Interviewee: *Yes, he's talking to Animal and some of the guys Animal hangs around with.*

Hypnosis Coordinator: *Animal? Tell me more.*

Interviewee: *I know him from work. He is called Animal because he opens beer cans with his teeth. He is big. [Pause] Mark is coming back now, He wants to know if I'm going to hang around. I'm telling him, "No, it's late; I have to go home." Now he's walking me to the door. He is asking me if I want a ride—I'm not sure. We walk to his car.*

Hypnosis Coordinator: *Tell us more about the car, Betty.*

Interviewee: *It's new. It's brand new. It's bright red.*

Hypnosis Coordinator: *Go on, Betty, what else might you be able to tell us about that car?*

Interviewee: *He's opening his door now, he's taking out something from under the seat. It's a baggie. It's almost half full with white powder. He says, "You want to snort some coke?" I tell him, "No, and I'd rather walk home." I'm walking home now, it's not far.*

Hypnosis Coordinator: *I wonder, Betty, if you see him again?*

Interviewee: *That morning, the day he raped me.*

Mental-Health Professional: *Okay, Betty, it's now that morning. [Pause] That's right, it's that morning. What is happening now?*

Interviewee: *I see his car pulling up. I recognize him.*

Hypnosis Coordinator: *Stop action here, Betty. What else can you tell us about that car?*

Interviewee: *It's red, it's the same car. I see the side of it now.*

Hypnosis Coordinator: *You may need to move the film, in your mind, backwards or forwards a little bit if you need to see the car even a little better.*

Interviewee: *I see the back now. I don't see the front at all, just the back when he pulled to the curb.*

Hypnosis Coordinator: *Okay, Betty. What about the back? Tell us more about that.*

Interviewee: *It has a license plate; it's red on white.*

Hypnosis Coordinator: *Okay, Betty, go on.*

Interviewee: *I don't see it that well. It's not clear.*

Mental-Health Professional: *Betty, in just a moment, I'd like to place a clipboard in your lap. On the clipboard is a piece of blank paper. Are you right-handed or left-handed?*

Interviewee: *Right-handed.*

Mental-Health Professional: *Okay, I would like to help you with something called automatic writing. I'm going to put a pencil in your right hand, and place your hand on the clipboard. After I do that, your hand will begin to move by itself, like a stylus. The pencil in your hand will move about the paper in a way that has special meaning for you. Later, when you look at what you've drawn or written, it may make a great deal of sense to you. I'm putting the clipboard in your lap now, Betty. And now I'm placing your left hand on one end of it so that you may hold it still. Now I'm putting a pencil in your right hand, Betty. Now I'm putting your hand on the clipboard. Your right hand and arm now begin to move. Let that happen all on its own, that's right. Let me know when you are done.*

Interviewee: *[The interviewee's hand begins to move about the paper. The pencil draws an image which becomes increasingly more clear.] I am done. [The interviewee has drawn a rectangle which has rounded corners and a small rectangle within its bottom border. Within the smaller rectangle are the capital letters: JEFFERSON.]*

Mental-Health Professional: *Okay, Betty. In trance, opening your eyes won't disturb a thing. I want you to open your eyes now, and tell me about what you have drawn—what it means to you.*

Interviewee: *[Opens eyes, looks at what she has drawn] It's a license plate. It's red on white, Jefferson County.*

Mental-Health Professional: *Okay, Betty, let your eyes close, and now let yourself go even deeper. May I help you with that?*

Interviewee: *Yes.*

Mental-Health Professional: *You are on your way to work on that morning, and the car is pulled up to the curb, go on. Let me show you something we call ideomotor signaling. I am going to place your right hand here on the arm of the chair so your fingers are stretched out comfortably. Each of your fingers, not your thumb, will be able to respond by rising, and in so doing, signaling, "yes," "no," "I am not sure," and "I don't care to say." Notice now, that as I gently stroke your index finger, it rises. This is your "yes" finger; each time it rises it says that the part of you which knows you best says "yes." That's right; up, up, up—good. Let your "yes" finger return to the arm of the chair. [This is repeated for the middle, ring, and little finger, to signal "no," "I am not sure," and "I don't care to say."] Now I wonder which finger will raise when I ask, "May Mr. Smith and I ask some questions of your fingers?"*

Interviewee: [*Index finger—the "yes" finger, rises.*]

Mental-Health Professional: *Okay, now let that finger return to the arm of the chair, as Mr. Smith asks your fingers some questions.*

Hypnosis Coordinator: *I wonder what finger will raise when I ask: Did the car have a license plate?*

Interviewee: [*Her "yes" finger rises, then returns to the arm of the chair.*]

Hypnosis Coordinator: *Now go where you see the license plate as best as you can. I wonder what finger will rise as I ask: Can you see it as best as you can?*

Interviewee: [*Her "yes" finger rises and then returns to the arm of the chair.*]

Hypnosis Coordinator: *I wonder what else might be on that license plate?*

Interviewee: [*Her "I am not sure" finger rises and then returns to the arm of the chair. Long pause*] *I just didn't get a good look at the license plate. It isn't clear to me at all.*

Hypnosis Coordinator: *Will it be all right to come back to this later?*

Interviewee: [*Her "yes" finger rises and then returns to the arm of the chair.*]

Hypnosis Coordinator: *Okay, now Dr. Hibler and I will ask any questions that may be helpful as you tell us more about your experience.*

Interviewee: *He's telling me to get in, he'll give me a ride. I really don't want to, but it's hard walking with my cast on. I'm opening the door, swinging around to get in. I'm in the car now.*

Hypnosis Coordinator: *Okay, stop action here, Betty. What else can you tell us about the car now?*

Interviewee: *It has a red interior, same color as outside. It's a Chevrolet.*

Hypnosis Coordinator: *What about it suggests that it is a Chevrolet?*

Interviewee: *It says that on the dashboard. It says, in silver letters: Chevrolet.*

Hypnosis Coordinator: *I wonder what else you might see on the inside of the car.*

Interviewee: *That's all. We're driving now . . . he's turning the wrong way. I don't want to be raped, I don't want this to happen.*

Mental-Health Professional: *Stop the action right here, Betty. I'm going to help you feel more comfortable now. Take a nice deep breath, Betty, and hold it. That's right. Now let it go. And, as I touch your right shoulder, let yourself release that tension—going even deeper, that's better. Let me know if you're ready to go on, Betty. And, as you go on, let me know if at any time you're uncomfortable. I am here to help you.*

Interviewee: *Okay. We're driving along the shore road to the pine woods. He's parking there. I know something is wrong. He's telling me that he wants me. I say: "No. Take me home." He pushes me. He . . . he's pulled out a gun. He's pushing the gun in my face.*

Hypnosis Coordinator: *Stop action right here, Betty. What else might you tell us about the gun.*

Interviewee: *It's a pistol, a six-shooter; it's big, black. He's pushing it in my face. He's saying: "Take your clothes off. Hurry, damn it." He's cursing at me. I'm taking off my blouse. I don't want to do this. He keeps telling me to hurry. He's pushing, . . . hitting . . . That pistol!*

Mental-Health Professional: *I hear you, Betty. I hear you.*

Interviewee: *I can't get my slacks over my cast. He's really angry. He wants me to hurry.*

Mental-Health Professional: *I understand, Betty. I understand.*

Interviewee: [*The victim is tense, trembling, tears rolling down her cheeks, sobbing as she speaks.*] *He's looking at me . . . touching me . . . No . . . No.*

Mental-Health Professional: *Betty, I'm putting a Kleenex in your hand. Stop here for a moment, wipe your tears. Part of you knows . . . that you will survive, part of you knows that you will be safe again. When you're ready, go on.*

Interviewee: *He's getting on top of me. He's having intercourse with me.*

Mental-Health Professional: *I hear you.*

Interviewee: *He's done. He's getting off me. No . . . my God . . . I don't believe it. My God, my God, my God! There is blood everywhere. My God.*

Mental-Health Professional: *Stop action here, Betty. Take a deep breath. Hold it. Let it go. Letting go . . . that's right . . . that's better. Tell me, Betty what's happening now. I don't understand.*

Interviewee: *The pistol, he's using the pistol in me. My God, my God. He's pulling that thing in the back of the pistol, and telling me if I move he'll shoot me that way (shuddering), Oh my God.*

Mental-Health Professional: *Let's pause here for a moment, Betty. Catch your breath. That's better. I don't understand, Betty, you said: "Blood everywhere?"*

Interviewee: *Yes, I'm on my period. He thinks it's funny. He's laughing.*

Hypnosis Coordinator: *Okay, Betty. When you're ready . . . what happens next?*

Interviewee: *He just says: "Get dressed." I put my clothes on and he drives me home. As he drops me off, he tells me that if I say* *anything to anyone, he'll kill me. I am stunned. I walk to my room . . . blood everywhere. I shower . . . I feel dirty, so dirty. I put on a bathrobe. My girlfriend comes in. She sees something is terribly wrong. I tell her. We call the police.*

Hypnosis Coordinator: *Okay, Betty, let's stop here. I wonder if there's any other time that you may have seen this individual?*

Interviewee: *Yes, I was in the cafeteria about a week later, and I saw him in line ahead of me.*

Mental-Health Professional: *You're there now, Betty. [Pause] What is happening now?*

Interviewee: *I see him, but I try to pretend that I don't, only he's seen me. I don't know what to do. He comes over and stands by me. He looks at me. He says: "Remember, you know what not to do to stay alive."*

Hypnosis Coordinator: *You see him now, Betty. Tell me what you see?*

Interviewee: *A blue short-sleeve shirt and open collar . . . he's in uniform.*

Hypnosis Coordinator: *What else might you tell me about his uniform?*

Interviewee: *He has four stripes; he's a Staff Sergeant.*

Hypnosis Coordinator: *What else?*

Interviewee: *[Squinting] I see his name tag. But, I can't read it, it just fades away.*

Mental-Health Professional: *Betty, I'm again going to put the clipboard in your lap, and let you hold the pencil—as you did before. Would that be okay?*

Interviewee: *[She nods her head. Yes.]*

Mental-Health Professional: *I'm putting the clipboard in your lap now, your left hand on the clipboard now, the pencil in your right hand like this, and now your hand on the clipboard, there. Just as before, Betty, let your hand work on its own. Let your hand make whatever mark it needs to to help your understand this better.*

Interviewee: *[The victim's hand begins to move, spelling capital letters across the page.] That's it; I'm done.*

Mental-Health Professional: *Okay, Betty [still deeply in trance], open your eyes and tell me what you see.*

Interviewee: *It says: FULLER. Fuller, that's his name, Mark Fuller.*

Mental-Health Professional: *Okay, Betty, let your eyes close now. That's right—letting you go even deeper than before. You are still in the cafeteria, what is happening now?*

Interviewee: *That's all. I haven't seen him since.*

Mental-Health Professional: *Okay, Betty, we can stop here. [Pause] Mr. Smith, would like to ask some questions of Betty?*

Hypnosis Coordinator: *No, that's all for now.*

Mental-Health Professional: *Anything you'd like to say or ask while you're still in trance?*

Interviewee: *No. I'm okay.*

Mental-Health Professional: *Very well. Betty, as we come back in time you may bring with you a full measure of memory of all that's happened, remembering perhaps even more details later, for sometimes even other things come to mind. Would that be okay?*

Interviewee: *Yes.*

Mental-Health Professional: *All right. Coming forward in time now, all the way to the second of March, 1981. It's mild-morning now. Awakening in a minute or two, but not longer,—alert and feeling refreshed, and rested, and clear-headed, and perfectly fine. [Pause]*

Interviewee: *[Arouses slowly, opens her eyes, looks around the room]*

Hypnosis Coordinator: *There. How do you feel now, Betty?*

Interviewee: *Better. I feel good.*

Hypnosis Coordinator: *Are you out of trance now?*

Interviewee: *Yes.*

Hypnosis Coordinator: *Fine. We're going to take a break now. The time is [states the current time from the elapsed-time generator image on the television monitor], and this will conclude the first tape and this series for this investigation. I must caution all personnel present that during the break, no one is to discuss anything regarding the investigation or what has been discussed this morning.*

After a brief intermission, the session was reconvened with the hypnosis coordinator initiating the new tape by stating aloud the time indicated on the television screen, confirming that no one had discussed the investigation during the break, and stating that all that were present during the first tape were again present. The mental-health professional and hypnosis coordinator talked with Betty concerning her experience of hypnosis, what that felt like, and her memory of what occurred.

While out of trance, Betty was also presented with the current copy of the Auto Mug Book (Fetridge, 1980) and asked whether any of the autos contained within this book were similar to the one used in the assault. She carefully examined the photographs of the automobiles contained in this automobile recognition guide, and picked out a compact model Chevrolet and that of another General Motors manufacture. Betty was also presented with the 1980 Motor Vehicle License Plate Guide, and asked to identify the colors, shapes, or other details of these sample license plates for the 50 United States, to determine which seemed most like the one she remembered on the suspect auto. She identified the New York license plate as being of the right color and form, noting that one other state was also quite similar. Finally, the Hypnosis Coordinator worked with Betty in developing a facial composite by use of a Smith and Wesson Identi-Kit II.

At the conclusion of this discussion, the session was ended by the hypnosis coordinator giving a verbal statement as to the time the interview was ending.

After the interview, the doctor spoke for some minutes with Betty, exploring the potential for rape crisis counseling with an appropriate rape crisis center. The hypnosis coordinator received the two video cassettes of the session as evidence, appropriately tagged these items, and secured them in the local investigative agency's evidence room, so that these recordings would be protected. Further, he advised local investigators that if the tape needed to be reviewed, it should be carefully copied onto other cassettes, so that the original recordings did not experience any unnecessary use. Finally, the Hypnosis Coordinator advised the local investigative office that upon closing the case, either because of a lack of a successful conclusion or, following a trial proceeding and sentencing action, the tapes would be signed out of evidence, attached to the investigative case file as transcripts of the interview, and retained with the case file in headquarters office records (for a minimum of 20 years).

In addition to the various considerations that were a part of the review process in considering hypnosis in this investigation, was a potential for self-incrimination on the part of the interviewee. For example, had she replied that she did in fact use drugs on the evening that she first met the suspect, she would have been required to have been advised of her rights. This would have been accomplished by the doctor terminating trance and the Hypnosis Coordinator administering a rights advisement, to include the right to counsel. Further, the interview would not have been permitted to proceed without coordination with the prosecuting attorney.

Continuing the Investigation

Forensic hypnosis is used to enhance memory so that investigative leads might be generated. Hypnosis is used as a conduit—a means with which to further identify elements of possible investigative importance. Just what value exists in hypnotically recalled information, however, must await confirmation by further investigation.

As in any continuing investigation, confidentiality must be maintained throughout the conduct of the case. This is an important safeguard to avoid contamination of the witness' recall prior to hypnosis; the same safeguard needs to be maintained after the hypnotic interview. For these same reasons, therapeutic applications of hypnosis with crime victims need to be carefully considered. On occasion, for example, a practitioner with good intentions will employ hypnosis and systematic desensitization in dealing with the trauma of a crime. Yet, any use of hypnosis without tape recording would potentially serve only to further question a victim's or witness' capacity to accurately remember. Consequently, it seems best to withhold any solely therapeutic application of hypnosis with crime victims or witnesses until the investigation is closed, or trial proceedings are concluded.

Interviews have the potential to produce a considerable amount of information that is either the same as that given prior to using hypnosis, information that is different (that is, in conflict with that which was said earlier), or information that is entirely new. In continuing the investigation, hypnotically derived details that are of possible significance are pursued. For example, in the interview transcript discussed earlier, the mutual acquaintance of the victim and the suspect was contacted to ascertain the identity of the suspect, military facility parking registration was reviewed for a match to the victim's descriptions of the suspect's automobile, and a review was made of all personnel in the facility who might be identified by the name she recalled in hypnosis. Note that while many details of her statements were unchanged by hypnosis, other details varied considerably. For instance, prior to trance, she had stated that she simply walked home from the club where she had met the suspect, but in trance spoke about his presentation of drugs. This was certainly a difference in her recall. Further, just before hypnosis she did not report any recollection of her final meeting with the suspect. Perhaps she suppressed this memory due to its threatening nature. Yet her recall of meeting her assailant in the cafeteria produced details, developed with hypnosis. The most basic question remains: What, among these details, is accurate? To be certain, the answer must await the outcome of continued investigation.

Conclusions

How effective is investigative hypnosis? And what reaction does forensic hypnosis receive in the courtroom? Certainly, these questions test the merit of this investigative tool; here lies its future as well.

Various agencies report mixed successes with the technique, owing largely to different criteria for success. Early analysis of hypnotic results within the Los Angeles Police Department reflected approximately a 7% case resolution due to hypnosis.* Yet, the criteria for selecting cases in which the technique was employed, and the criterion for success, were largely undefined. The Federal Bureau of Investigation, which employed the Federal Model, has reported that in a sample of 65 hypnosis cases, 12 perpetrators were identified, three of whom were convicted.† The Air Force's use of the Federal Model has resulted in solving, to the case investigator's satisfaction, approximately 12% of the instances in which it was employed. These may seem like small odds, but considering that the cases involved are essentially "dead" investigations, a trail gone cold, these odds are clearly better than no chance at all.

The purpose of this chapter has been to alert those who would consult with law enforcement to responsibilities well beyond simply inducing trance. The actual hypnotic interview is perhaps at best only one third of the critical process. The interview is no more nor no less important than careful case review for suitability, or confirmation of information that is developed. To date, many unfortunate precedents have occurred in the courtroom. Doctors with good intentions have applied their trade without realizing that hypnosis was ill-suited to the situation in the first place. Worse yet, the products of their efforts were considered on their face value and, consequently, unwarranted prosecutive action occurred. As the well-known dictum advises: "Bad cases make bad laws." So it has been with forensic hypnosis (Margolin, 1981).

Until the nature of human memory and hypnosis are better known, all of the controversies will remain. Amidst such turmoil, it would appear that a conservative, criterion relevant plan for using forensic hypnosis is a surer route to justice. The Federal Model was developed because of the many controversies concerning forensic hypnosis, and while this plan does not resolve them, it avoids each by assuring that hypnosis is neither a replacement for traditional means of law enforcement, nor a trier of fact. Instead, it is a cooperative effort, employing professional expertise from mental health and law enforcement to assure both the well-being of the person interviewed and the likelihood of resolving crime. Forensic hypnosis is an important investigative tool, which is used to enhance the memory of a victim or witness to develop investigative leads, but that is not enough. Hypnotically obtained information needs to be independently corroborated. Without this confirmation, it is not any easier to understand what actually happened and, after all, that is why hypnosis was used in the first place.

---

* Reiser M: Personal communication, 1977
† Teten H: Personal communication, 1981

Appendix 25-1

Consent for Hypnosis No. 1

I hereby agree, voluntarily and freely, to undergo hypnosis, and be interviewed under hypnosis in order to assist the [insert name of your investigative agency] with an investigation in progress. I understand that, unless I request otherwise, a special agent of the [name of your investigative agency] may be present during the interview. I also understand that a transcript or other means of preservation may be made of the interview and that the transcript or other method of preservation may be used for any lawful purpose connected with the investigation or action based thereon.

_____, a mental-health professional, has explained the procedure(s) to be used and that, while recalling details of unpleasant events, I may experience some discomfort; but that apart from such discomfort there are no known risks or expected complications from the procedure to be used. The purpose of the interview under hypnosis is to assist my memory in recalling the following: _____

_____

_____

WITNESS   INTERVIEWEE

DATE AND LOCATION
                                           DATE & LOCATION

I have personally counseled the interviewee on the purpose of the interview and on the procedure to be performed.

                            MENTAL-HEALTH PROFESSIONAL

                            DATE AND LOCATION

Appendix 25-2

Consent for Hypnosis No. 2

I hereby agree, voluntarily and freely, to undergo hypnosis, and be interviewed under hypnosis in order to assist the [insert name of your investigative agency] with an investigation in progress. I understand that, unless I request otherwise, a special agent of the [name of investigative agency] may be present during the interview. I also understand that a transcript or other means of preservation may be made of the interview and that the transcript or other method of preservation may be used for any lawful purpose connected with the investigation or action based thereon.

_____, a mental-health professional, has explained the procedure(s) to be used and that, while recalling details of unpleasant events, I may experience some discomfort; but that apart from such discomfort there are no known risks or expected complications from the procedure to be used. The purpose of the interview under hypnosis is to assist my memory in recalling the following: _____

_____

I have also been informed that the interview room is equipped with a one-way mirror and intercom system or remote television monitor, and, unless I desire otherwise, other persons who will be fully identified to me will be watching and listening to the interview.

_____ _____
WITNESS   INTERVIEWEE

_____ _____
DATE AND LOCATION   DATE AND LOCATION

I have personally counseled the interviewee on the purpose of the interview and on the procedure to be performed.

_____
MENTAL-HEALTH PROFESSIONAL

_____
DATE AND LOCATION

Appendix 25-3

Release for Use of Video Transcript

_____
DATE

_____
LOCATION

I, _____ participated in a hypnotic interview at _____
_____, on _____. With my prior consent, the complete hypnotic interview session was recorded on videotape, and I am identified in that tape. I understand

that hypnotic interview was conducted as an aid in an official investigation conducted by [insert the name of your investigative agency]. I have been advised by Special Agent _____, of the [name of your investigative agency], that the video transcript may be beneficial in the training of law enforcement personnel and individuals associated with forensic medicine. In consideration of the fact, I freely give the [name of your investigative agency] my consent to use the video transcript for training purposes, to include making it available to other law-enforcement agencies and forensic-medicine personnel.

_____
SIGNATURE

WITNESS:

_____

_____

Appendix 25-4

Forensic Hypnosis Script—The Interview
(*Everything is recorded on tape.*)

A. *Hypnotic coordinator*
　　Opens the interview
　　　　Place:
　　　　Date:
　　　　Time:
　　Identifies persons present (also identifies persons remotely monitoring the interview, if this is done
　　Requests (and receives) permission from interviewee to record the entire proceedings on videotape
　　States the purpose of the interview
　　Turns attention to the mental-health professional
B. *Mental-health professional*
　　Explains hypnosis (which may include)
　　　　Asking the interviewee if he has been previously hypnotized
　　　　Asking what the interviewee knows or what he has heard about hypnosis
　　　　Defining hypnosis
　　　　Explaining misconceptions
　　　　Describing trance characteristics and experiential qualities

Explains procedures to be used (which may include)

    Trance induction

    Deepening

    Time distortion

    Mentions potential "risks" (*e.g.,* reexperience of emotions connected with the event)

    Inquiry techniques (*e.g.,* television techniques, etc.)

    Mentions that hypnotic coordinator will assist

    Posthypnotic suggestion

C. *Hypnosis coordinator*

    Obtains informed consent.

        Before interviewee signs form, asks "Are you in hypnosis now?" (A negative reply is necessary.)

    Asks interviewee to describe the event in question

        This is a detailed recounting, allowing the interviewee to review the event as he pleases (do not pump).

    Turns attention to mental-health professional.

D. *Mental-health professional*

    [Optional] May wish at this time to

        Conduct hypnotizability tests

        Conduct practice trances

    Conducts induction

    Enacts age (time) regression

        Test trance depth by observing or enacting hypnotic phenomena

    Turns attention to hypnosis coordinator.

E. *Hypnosis coordinator*

    Conducts inquiry (use present tense).

        Lets the interviewee describe the event spontaneously, or with minimal encouragement. After the entire event is mentioned the first time, then follows in a detailed description, assisted with television techniques, etc.

    The mental-health professional also . . .

        May deal with emotionality

        Deepens trance (as needed)

        Near end of interview, uses posthypnotic suggestion for later recall in greater detail, etc.

Note: SELF-INCRIMINATING STATEMENTS: If the interviewee incriminates himself, have the mental-health professional terminate the trance; have the interviewee acknowledge (verbally) that he is out of trance; and the hypnotic coordinator will advise the interviewee of his rights. Finally, the prosecuting attorney will be contacted prior to any reinterview.

    Returns attention to the mental-health professional.

F. *Mental-health professional*

    Terminates trance

G. *Hypnosis coordinator*

    Asks interviewee to discuss what they said in trance; develops details

    Where appropriate, obtains composite sketch, or Identi-kit composite, or conducts photographic lineup.

Last thing to be done before termination of videotaping is to ask the interviewee: "How do you feel?"

Be sure tape includes the interviewee giving a response that he is okay.

End interview—say aloud the time indicated on the date–time generator and announce that the interview is concluded.

Breaks

Breaks will be needed to change tape, use the lavatory, or possibly allow for meals. Trance should be terminated before breaks, and (on tape) a precautionary statement made not to discuss the case.

The mental-health professional will be asked to terminate and reinitiate trance as needed.

References

Arons H: Hypnosis in Criminal Investigation. Springfield, IL, Charles C Thomas, 1967

Ault RL: FBI guidelines for the use of hypnosis. Int J Clin Exp Hypn 27:4, 1979

Ault RL: Hypnosis—The FBI's team approach. FBI Law Enforcement Bull 49:1, 1980

Block EB: Hypnosis: A New Tool in Crime Detection. New York, McKay, 1976

Diamond BL: Inherent problems in the use of pretrial hypnosis on a perspective witness. Calif Law Rev 68:2, 1980

Fetridge JR: Automotive Index (Auto Mug Book). Issaquah, WA, Motor Vehicle Manufacturers Association of the United States, Inc., 1980

Hibler NS: The Use of Hypnosis in the United States Air Force Investigations. Paper presented at the American Psychological Association Eighty-Seventh Convention, New York, 1979

Hibler NS: Administrative Aspects of Forensic Hypnosis. Presented at the Twenty-Third Annual Scientific Meeting of the American Society of Clinical Hypnosis, Minneapolis, 1980

Margolin E: Hypnosis enhanced testimony: Valid evidence or prosecutor's tool? Trial 17:10, 1981

Reiser M: Handbook of Investigative Hypnosis. Los Angeles, LEHI, 1980

Teten HD: Lawscope: Hypnotized witnesses may remember too much. Am Bar Assoc J, February 1978

Teten HD: The FBI's Policy and Concerns in the Use of Hypnosis. Presented at the American Psychological Association Eighty-Second Convention, New York, 1979

US Department of Transportation: 1980 Motor Vehicle License Plate Guide. Washington, DC, 1980

26 Hypnosis in Management Training and Development

DANIEL L. ARAOZ

> *Possunt quia Posse Videntur*
> *They can because they see themselves able.*
>
> VIRGIL

Contrary to the approach taken by most authors, in this chapter I use the term hypnosis in a broad, general way, considering it to be the modality of "thinking" (or using one's mind) that is *experiential* as opposed to sequential, logical, and critical. In this view, and using both old and modern expressions, hypnosis is *primary process* or *right hemispheric* thinking, essentially the same as guided imagery (Mowrer, 1977), directed daydreams (Desoille, 1965), covert techniques (Cautela, 1977), or dynamic imagery (Araoz, 1981a). Moreover, much of what comes under the name of cognitive-behavior modification (Meichenbaum, 1977) is considered here as essentially hypnosis, especially the techniques of mental rehearsal and the use of imagination.

Hypnosis in Management Training

Looked at in this way, Dale Carnegie (1944), Norman Vincent Peale (1974), and Maxwell Maltz (1960), just to mention three of the best-known modern authors dealing with the mind in a popular way, taught a long list of hypnotic techniques, though never mentioning hypnosis. One of their forerunners was James Allen, whose 17th century essay, *As A Man Thinketh,* teaches how to use the inner mind to transform one's life by changing one's view of things.

The use of "hypnosis" by consultants in management training and development is found at the three basic levels of organizational structure. Thus, for first-line managers and supervisors, "hypnosis" serves the purpose of fostering a positive attitude towards themselves, their employment role, and the people under them, more creative use of their imagination, and, finally, greater control over any negative thoughts or attitudes.

Secondly, the goal of hypnosis in professional consulting is also to reach the employees at the lowest level through the first-line managers, so the former learn to enhance their own attitude towards work and life in general.

Thirdly, and by no means lastly, hypnosis helps at the executive level, providing techniques to manage stress, the "burn-out" feeling and frustration, while, at the same time, teaching executives methods to use more fully their inner-mind potential for creative problem solving and decision making.

The justification for using "hypnosis" in professional consulting for management is given in the theory of negative self-hypnosis (Araoz, 1981a). This is composed of (1) noncritical negative thinking, which becomes an activation of *negative subconscious processes,* (2) active *negative imagery,* and (3) powerful (posthypnotic) self-suggestions in the form of *negative affirmations* about one's self. Thus, a negative attitude is the effect of negative self-affirmations and imagery. The "failures" in any field, upon analysis, turn out to be people who indulge in images of failure, reinforcing them with negative self-talk. These two mental processes become a cycle of negative beliefs which, as Ellis (1973) has repeatedly stated, leads to feeling negatively, and to either acting in self-defeating ways or refusing to act positively.

A Look at the Literature

A sample review of books used in business and industry for training and development gives us abundant evidence of the presence of negative self-hypnosis as a self-limiting, self-defeating, impoverishing process with many characteristics of hypnosis, especially the three mentioned above.

Thus, selecting a mere handful, Hill's (1937) 13 steps to riches include *Autosuggestion, Imagination, Brain,* and *The Sixth Sense,* in which many hypnotic techniques to counteract negative self-hypnosis are offered. Carnegie (1944) proposed controlled use of imagination and self-suggestion to stop worrying and start living. Bristol (1948) presented ways of turning desire into reality through *suggestion, mental pictures,* and *belief,* not allowing negativism to interfere with our subconscious "power." Maltz (1960) centered his psychocybernetics around a positive self-image, developed through techniques of self-hypnosis, because a negative self-image is emotionally crippling. Simmons (1965) devised a "plan for living" based on "inner space" and the subconscious mind, as a protection against old attitudes of defeat. Andersen (1966) built on Maltz's teaching. His "imagineering ideas," the "quick shift of adversity into achievement," and "making oneself into an opportunity magnet" are hypnotic methods to bypass the familiar negative frame of reference and activate new inner potentialities. For over 40 years, Peale (1974) has developed techniques of positive thinking, emphasizing the danger of "building a case against oneself" and suggesting how to develop inner motivation by discovering one's (subconscious) *true* self.

Finally, almost four centuries ago, Allen (circa 1600) stated that "mind is the Master-power that moulds and makes," and commented on the effect of thought on achievement: "A man can only rise, conquer, and achieve by lifting up his thoughts . . . he is limited only by the thoughts he chooses" (p 42). Or, to develop Virgil's concise statement quoted at the beginning: If you don't experience yourself internally as succeeding, you'll fail; if you allow yourself to rehearse mentally your achievements, they will be yours.

Unfortunately, this truth has been overshadowed by "the hardware of learning," namely, visual aids, and also by "outward" rehearsal, such as role playing. In the original *Training and Development Handbook* (Craig and Bittel, 1967) of the prestigious American Society for Training and Development, not one word was mentioned about the use of imagination, visualization, or subconscious learning. The one chapter devoted to the learning process followed the S—R model, not even referring to the S—O—R paradigm, in which the focus is on the "organism" connecting the "stimulus" and the "response." The second edition (1978), however, does include topics related to imagination, including also a good discussion of the behavioral sciences in the field. The point is that only recently has the field focused on this aspect of human functioning.

More recent works (Friedrich, 1981) continue to ignore the active use of imagination techniques in management training and consulting, though they give lip service to the importance of imagination without studying it systematically in human functioning (Goleman, 1981). One may conclude that management training and development is still deprived of what "hypnosis" can offer.

Hypnosis or "Hypnosis"?

In professional consulting, the term hypnosis itself is taboo, as well as references to *induction, trance,* or *deepening* techniques. But, as was explained above, *the concept* of hypnosis and its applications are used in a broad, general way. Consequently, people are not assessed for hypnosis—no "hynotizability scales" are administered, and there is no concern about "hypnotic depth." Because of the aversive attitude towards clinical concepts in the field of professional consulting, I developed the term *dynamic imagery.* Consequently, in this chapter, dynamic imagery refers to "hypnosis," namely, *the use of one's mind bypassing critical-analytical thinking,* or the activation of right-hemispheric activity.

In professional consulting, the *operating assumption* is that all managers and executives are able to benefit from dynamic imagery, refusing the experimental findings of hynotizability percentages in the general population. If a person dreams, according to this assumption, he can use "hypnosis." The question becomes, rather, one of *hypnotizing ability.* Can the consultant be creative enough—á la Erickson—to use "hypnosis" with this client? Can he reach the clients to help them learn "hypnosis"?

This touches on the issue of hypnosis as a skill, which is implicit in the operating assumption. The person who finds it difficult to engage in "goal-directed daydreams" or "guided imagery" can and should be trained to acquire this new skill. Studies by Barber, Spanos, and Chaves (1974) indicate the ability to enter hypnosis to depend on a positive mental set of TEAM, that is, *Trust* in the professional worker, positive *Expectations,* cooperative *Attitude,* and right *Motivation.* Research by DeStefano (1977), Katz (1978, 1979; Katz and Crawford, 1978), and Spanos (Spanos and Barber, 1971, 1972) confirmed the cognitive aspects of the ability to benefit from hypnosis, whereas Diamond (1974, 1977a, 1977b, 1978), Kinney and Sachs (1974), and Reilley, Parisher, Carona, and Dobrovolsky (1980), as well as Sachs and Anderson (1967), emphasized the learning of the hypnosis skills, which improved the ability to use hypnosis.

This is the view shared by those who use dynamic imagery in professional consulting, as a survey of 158 management consultants* conducted by Dynamic Imagery Associates (Araoz, 1981b) demonstrated. Of those researched, 92% indicated "frequent use of imagination techniques for planning and decision making." Looking more in detail at the results of this survey, we find that 87% "encouraged methods of self-suggestion" 59% "preferred mental rehearsal to mere logical planning," and 57% used "mental rehearsal to enhance role playing and, eventually, actual performance." To the question of whether they had had formal training in hypnosis, 32% responded affirmatively. However, 92% mentioned at least one of the following five authors as influential in their learning and using these imagination techniques: Maltz, Carnegie, Hill, Peale, and Anderson—in that order. Two of these authors were mentioned by 79%, three by 54%, four by 14%, and all five by 8%.†

---

* A survey on the uses of dynamic imagery—"hypnosis," as understood in this chapter—was mailed to 400 professional consultants to business and industry, working in 20 large cities in the United States. Of the 217 responses returned, 158 were complete, 31 denied using dynamic imagery, and 28 were not filled out properly or completely.

† These authors were selected because they have been known for many years now. Many other writers have come on the scene since "the old-timers," and in no way do I want to imply that they are less effective. They are simply less seasoned.

Regarding the effectiveness of these techniques, two factors were considered, that is, length of use and results. As to time, 32% had been employing them for over 20 years, 11% for 10 to 19 years, and 21% for 5 to 9 years. Thirty-six percent had started to use them in the last four years. None had discontinued their use owing to ineffectiveness.

The results of these techniques were tabulated as follows: 63% used them "most of the time," and 77% were "very pleased with them." None found this approach "counterproductive or unhelpful." Finally, as to who benefits from these techniques, 74% indicated that "*most* of their clients profit from them." Sixteen percent stated that "some people find it hard to use their inner minds," but 12% agreed that "with some training, they learn to use them to their benefit." None denied their effectiveness.

This brief description is enough to give an idea of the use of "hypnosis" by professional management consultants, not necessarily trained in hypnosis (68% of those using it had no formal hypnosis training, as I mentioned).

Application of Hypnosis in Management Consulting

When and in what circumstances are these techniques employed? Besides hypnotic relaxation techniques to cope with executive or managerial stress, there are four instances in which dynamic imagery is used in management training and development. These are as follows:

1. When it is necessary to change negative beliefs, namely, to counteract negative self-hypnosis
2. To mentally rehearse situations, so that failure becomes less threatening, and difficult tasks become more attractive
3. When a person must counteract intellectualizations and resistances encountered along the way to change
4. After change has taken place, to reinforce, generalize, and maintain the gains made

These four situations provide the basis for four different techniques. Each will be discussed at some length after these preliminary generalizations.

First, that which experimental and clinical hypnosis describes as *hypnotic induction* becomes a simple and respectful invitation to use one's imagination. Dynamic imagery is usually presented as an "exercise" or "practice" to activate "the inner mind" or "the supermind." Often the concept of "giving oneself permission" is introduced. "To think in mental pictures," "to be part of a cartoonlike daydream" are common directives. Consequently, the transition from ordinary thinking and communicating to "hypnosis" is smooth, natural, and nonthreatening. One wants to *minimize* the differences, not to maximize them, as the entertainer does, nor even to define and point them out, as is done in the laboratory and by most hypnotherapists.

Second, there is great emphasis on *practice* and repetition. Once the clients have experienced dynamic imagery with the consultant's coaching, usually in a group situation (seminar or workshop), they are encouraged to do it over and over again, during the program and at home, until they master and possess the skill of dynamic imagery. From "hypnosis" as a quasi-magical procedure, one moves to the choice and decision elements in using this technique.

Third, *slogans,* catchwords, and adages are employed as ways of triggering that which clinicians and experimentalists call posthypnotic suggestions. In the tradition of Emile Coué (1922), with his famous maxim, "Everyday in every way, I am getting better and better," the task is to find a phrase with meaning for the person's problem.

Changing Negative Beliefs

By the time a consultant is hired, the executive or manager has already tried several other "solutions" to the problem: informal consultation with peers, application of "new" techniques read in books or magazines, organizational changes, and so on. Usually, not only the person responsible for these "changes" is quite despondent at this time, but also the other people in the organization have surmised that "something is wrong." Discouragement, apprehension, and confusion are prevalent, though dissimulated.

Preliminary to any intervention by the consultant, there must always be a thorough assessment of the situation. Once the consultant has ascertained that there are negative beliefs in need of modification so that productive change can take place in the organization, the dynamic imagery program is presented as comprising eight steps:

1. Write five of your negative statements.
2. Write about five of your corresponding mental pictures.
3. Share one of #1 and #2 with group.
4. Find positive statements to counteract #1.
5. Create positive imagery to counteract #2.
6. Discuss with group.
7. Self-hypnotize with #4 and #5.
8. Practice and keep record of practice for two weeks.

Step One—Negative Affirmations. The clients—executives, managers, or supervisors—are instructed to write down on a piece of paper (not on the blackboard) at least five negative statements of their own about the current problem or situation. These papers are *not* shared with others, and thus the clients can be very truthful and honest.

Step Two—Negative Imagery. The clients are asked to describe briefly next to each statement the type of mental image or visualizations that accompany each statement. At this point, the consultant may need to help them complete this double task by giving examples taken from the initial assessment. Thus, for instance, one statement heard might be something like "This is an impossible task." The consultant then asks, "What comes to mind when you say or hear this?" and reminds the clients that no matter how "crazy" the mental pictures, they must recognize them as their own. Next, the consultant might give the following as an illustration of mental imagery triggered by such a negative statement:

Pandemonium   at the branch store
Showcases and storage shelves   disrupted and overturned
Dust and smoke   all over
Lights   out
People   screaming

These are given as an example of the negative images that negative statements might produce. Then the clients are encouraged to perform their task of writing down their own, peculiar images corresponding to each one of the five negative statements written earlier.

Step Three—Sharing. The sharing of *one* negative statement and imagery with the group is done to provide social support and to make the clients realize that imagery can be ridiculous, bizarre, or "way out." This dramatizes the damaging effect of negative imagery on a person's feelings and actions. The fact that they must select only *one* negative element out of five allows them to protect their privacy.

Step Four—Positive Affirmations. Now it is time to develop acceptable positive statements to counteract the statements of Step One. Clients are asked to write a statement antagonistic to each of these negative ones. Thus, if one of the negative statements was "The competition is impossible to beat," the positive counterpart could be "I must find the secret of beating the competition." As you realize, the difference is tremendous. In the admission of lack of knowledge, there is an implicit message of hope—"I can learn"—and a clear statement of *the possibility* of doing it. Some effort might be necessary to find positive counterparts to the self-defeating statements, but, with the help of the consultant, people do find beautiful butterflies to replace the worms.

Step Five—Positive Imagery. The same process of finding positive substitutes is done with the negative imagery, recorded in Step Two. Here, the consultants must insist that their clients build up a very rich imagery, involving as many senses as is possible. Thus, if one negative statement in Step One was accompanied by a mental picture of a customer ridiculing the salesman, abusing him verbally, and dismissing him in anger, the positive imagery could present a friendly, inquisitive, and polite customer with whom it is a pleasure to deal. Again, in imagination, one must see the picture, hear the voice, experience the sensations, and so on.

Step Six—Group Discussion. The group discussion at this point serves to enrich the positive statements and images. One person helps the other with suggestions, anecdotes, or personal experiences. The consultant must guide the group discussion to avoid waste of time, lengthy and boring accounts, or irrelevant material. The polite but firm intervention of the consultant is of paramount importance here.

Step Seven—Use of #4 and #5. Finally, we are now prepared for the hypnotic use of Steps 4 and 5 (see Appendix 26-1 for a transcript of this step). Each client is encouraged to follow this simple procedure: (a) Use your imagination to experience yourself in a quiet, comfortable, and relaxed place, preferably outdoors. All inner senses that apply should be engaged. (b) In that place, use your positive statements and imagery, as if you were thinking about all this. (c) Linger on the good feelings triggered by b. After trying this sequence in the group, all should share the experience, including the difficulties they encountered. Then, they should try again and again in the group session until all have experienced this new way of using their minds. Note that the participants use their own *individual* positive statements and imagery, without necessarily sharing them with the others in the group. They practice in the presence of the others, not as an interrelating group. The others are there for support, encouragement, and reinforcement.

It should also be noted that the consultant needs to be supportive, encouraging, and willing to work independently with those who may have more difficulties than the others.

Step Eight—Practice to Master Skill. A strong pitch must be made in favor of practicing for the next 2 weeks after the seminar—and of keeping a written record of such practice. The rationale is that this is a new skill that must be mastered through repetition and practice. Beliefs can and do change (we all know of religious conversations), but we can teach our clients *how* to do it. And the method outlined above, using hypnotic principles and techniques, is a system for change.

Mental Rehearsal

When a client finds it difficult to face specific situations, he is invited to build up the difficult or new situation in his imagination and then proceed to "think" about it in great detail. This is also done first in the group and later at home—

until the scene becomes so familiar that it does not produce any anxiety or negative feelings.

It goes without saying that the four applications of hypnosis in management training and development overlap generously. Thus, in this instance, the difficult or new situation may have many elements of negative self-hypnosis and, as such, require the application of the eight steps described previously.

These principles of mental rehearsal are the ones used in sports (Nideffer, 1976) or in some therapeutic situations (Kroger and Fezler, 1976), and apply equally well to the new or difficult situations that an executive or manager might need to face.

Counteracting Resistance to Change

In management consulting, resistance to change frequently comes from anxiety-producing "thoughts" about a particular situation. Resistance to change often yields to mental rehearsal, since mental exposure to situations that used to generate anxiety can reduce that anxiety. But at other times, the resistance takes a more intellectual form and manifests itself in reasons, arguments, and excuses one gives oneself. In this case, the consultant may proceed by asking his client to vividly remember a previous situation when resistance of this type was present, and to relive it very intensely. Once the person has accomplished this "age regression," another set of circumstances is recalled, when the assignment, job, trip or whatever that had given rise to that resistance was thoroughly enjoyed or resourcefully accomplished. The client is encouraged to relive this latter situation very vividly and realistically, focusing on the positive feelings of pride, satisfaction, accomplishment, and even joy, which he experienced then.

These positive feelings are used, then, as a vehicle to connect with the current situation that creates the intellectualizations against the task at hand. The same procedure is repeated several times, stressing the positive feelings, and the client is encouraged to practice this exercise alone, after the seminar, as was mentioned before.

Reinforcing Gains

In this case, gains have been made, the "not-okay boss," has become an "okay boss." In order to reinforce, maintain, and even extend or generalize these gains to other areas of functioning, clients are taught to take mental breaks during the day or at least once in a while during the week. This is similar to the commitment made by those who learn transcendental meditation, to devote two 20-minute daily sessions to its practice.

Once the clients have experienced the benefits of dynamic imagery and once they have mastered its use, it becomes logical that one does not have "to sell" them on the idea of regular practice. They will *want* "to buy" it. It is important, however, to give them suggestions for daily practice and to establish new connections between simple, routine activities and dynamic imagery.

For instance, all humans must relieve themselves daily. These "unmentionable" behaviors can become ready-made opportunities to relieve oneself mentally as well. In the practice sessions, the injunction is given that every time the clients go to the bathroom, they shall recall the positive feelings that they experienced in connection with the gains made. The same anchoring of good experiences and particular behaviors can be established with waiting for a red traffic signal to turn green, riding an elevator, sitting down on a particular chair, entering a particular room, looking through a particular window, and so on.

The connection is initially made as a "posthypnotic suggestion." Thus, when the clients are learning these hypnotic techniques in a seminar with the consultant, they are told to choose one such insignificant occupation and to say to themselves right then and there, "Next time I stand by that window, I'll reexperience all these good thoughts and feelings, and every time I stand by that window, those good feelings will fill me completely" and so on.

In this manner, the practice session becomes the new mental reprogramming, so that subconscious connections are established for the client's benefit. Thus, the clients voluntarily and consciously decide what connections to create. Then, using hypnotic techniques, they generate those mental connections between an indifferent event or action and the feelings they want to reinforce. At that point, they may consciously forget about the connection made, since, subconsciously, the indifferent action or event will trigger the feelings that they have chosen to strengthen.

Thus, these four approaches—hypnotic in essence and technique, though never described as hypnosis—may be employed to great advantage in management consulting and training. Obviously, the fourfold division is more academic than practical, since often two or more of these modalities are combined in the same training session.

How to Assess Effectiveness

The survey mentioned earlier (Araoz, 1981b) indicated that these techniques are extremely effective. The assessment of cognitive behavior therapy—which I consider cognitive–emotive (Maultsby and Ellis, 1974) and, therefore, hypnotic—is well documented as effective (Wilson, 1978; Meichenbaum, 1977). My article on negative self-hypnosis (1981a) explains the intrinsic and essential efficacy of this approach. Once negativistic "thinking" is recognized, the only way to stop it is by "thinking" positively. The techniques with which we are dealing effect this change by their very nature. As two physical bodies cannot occupy the same physical space, so, too, dynamic imagery is antagonistic and contradictory to negative self-hypnosis.

As was mentioned before, the real challenge is to teach these techniques to executives and managers. Thorough training on the part of the consultant seems to be an imperative prerequisite to meeting this challenge. In the survey referred to previously, data were unclear regarding how many of those to whom imagery methods were proposed did not accept them, did not learn them, and did not use them. We have only the general statement that 74% reported the majority of clients benefiting from them.

Lieberman's (1977) exciting paper on the inadequacy of the scientific method for understanding hypnosis should make us stop and re-evaluate our cherished belief in that method as the best (only?) way to attain the truth. In professional consulting, especially, pragmatism is paramount. That which has been accepted for so long—at least since the early 1940s, with the works of Carnegie and Peale translated into 20 other languages—has a *validity* that it would be foolish to dismiss lightly.

To repeat what was stated several times before, once my view is accepted that imagery techniques and cognitive restructuring methods are hypnosis, then we have mountainous evidence of its efficacy. If we insist, however, on experimental data, then we have no evidence at all.

What the Future Will Bring

Barber (1980) has been very involved in the application of self-suggestions for personal growth in educational settings. The basic assumptions underlying his proposal apply equally well to management training and development. These are as follows:

1. Humans are constantly engaged in self-talk.
2. What they say to themselves affects their enjoyment of life and their coping with life's demands.
3. Some self-talk is negative and harmful, enhancing negative feelings.
4. With formal training, humans can learn to reduce negative self-talk and increase positive self-suggestions.

5. Thus, people can increase their life enjoyment, their coping abilities, and the use of their personal resources.

More and more, with the popularity of the cognitive therapies, of which Ellis (1962) has been a leader, we are realizing that "thoughts" (self-talk plus imagery) shape life-styles, either negatively or positively. The resurgence of a keen interest in "suggestology" (Lozanov, 1978) is seen in Europe, as well as in the New World, encouraging serious research on the very nature of hypnosis and suggestion, and leading students of the subject to see *suggestion*—which to be effective must always become self-suggestion (Barber, 1980)—as the big umbrella over hypnosis, guided imagery, self-talk, and much of pathology, both physical and psychic, as well as over much of healing.

In management training and development, as was mentioned in an earlier section in which the literature was reviewed, hypnotic principles and even techniques have been accepted for a long time. The future trend seems to be more integrative, applying much of the research data from "scientific hypnosis"—both experimental and clinical—to other areas, such as education, sports, and, yes, management training and development.

Conclusions

The real abuses of hypnosis in police work have forced professional societies to condemn its use and to separate themselves from all those who, not being clinicians, employ hypnosis in their work. This large group includes the professional consultants. However, the difference between condemning a person for "crimes" confessed during hypnosis and using it for the purposes outlined in this chapter is, obviously, vast. Because of the professional groups' condemnation, however, most clinicians and researchers in the field are not aware of the beneficial effects of hypnosis in other areas—particularly in management consulting.

The paradox is that many consultants, I suspect, would deny using hypnosis, not knowing that all techniques involving mostly imagination are hypnosis. It is like the definition of a follower of Christ found in the Gospel According to St. Matthew: "Whatsoever you did to the least of my brethren, you did it to me; I was hungry and you fed me; . . . I was in prison and you didn't visit me" and so on. Many professional consultants use hypnosis without realizing that what they do *is* hypnosis. Then they ask, "When do we use hypnosis?" And the answer is clear: Whensoever you used these techniques, you used hypnosis.

Professional associations might be imposing unnecessary limits on themselves by dismissing or ignoring those who, without being physicians, psychologists, dentists, or social workers, find in hypnosis an important professional tool. By believing that they are the only experts, and that hypnosis, in someone else's hands will be abused, they may be closing the door to many exciting possibilities of making *their* own use of this powerful tool more effective in their fields of expertise.

On the other hand, an important current ideological trend, as reflected in this chapter, stresses the "naturalistic" aspect of hypnosis (Erickson and Rossi, 1979). One of the practical consequences of this view is the application of hypnosis in many other fields, besides the ones considered traditionally professional. If hypnosis can be applied naturalistically, it may be used effectively by students (Barber, 1980), athletes (Nideffer, 1976), and many others, including business people at all levels.

We, the "traditional professionals," have the training, expertise, and background to teach this skill to the others. But we stand doggedly by the dubious principle of professionalism—others are not professionally equal to us—while the "other group" obtains training anyway and keeps using "hypnosis" anyway. Perhaps our posture and policy would be more effective if changed: we could accept the fact that, if there is naturalistic hypnosis, others will learn it, use and, also, abuse it. Abuse is not the monopoly of hypnosis, since all human things can be abused: conversation, trust, love. Rather than seeing "the others" as enemies, we could establish liaisons, not just acknowledging their existence, but cooperating in order to help them and, yes, learn from them. As in the Christian churches, ecumenism is an important practical concept; so it could be in our hypnotheology, too. Perhaps our stand should become even firmer regarding the application of hypnosis in any area for which one is not specifically competent. No psychologist would attempt to use hypnosis for dental purposes without the cooperation of a dentist. This obvious procedural rule should apply strictly across all borders. However, this is more easily said than done. Is a psychologist trespassing into medicine when he helps someone cope with physical pain? Applied psychology, obviously, is much more difficult to define, since in many cases it involves human interaction. A more flexible understanding among professions will not water down any, but, paradoxically, enrich all by the exchange. I hope that the adolescence of our professions will soon be over, so that all of us who practice hypnosis may communicate with respect and openness in order to learn from each other and grow as people and as professionals.

This is, sadly, not a new difficulty among professionals. But we may still hope, joining Augustine of Hippo's fourth century clamor:

In things that are absolute, let there be unity,
In things that are doubtful, let there be freedom,
In everything, let there be compassion.

Appendix 26-1

The following is a verbatim transcript with commentary of Step Seven (see text). The ellipses (. . .) between sentences indicate a pause.

VERBALIZATION

"As you are sitting there . . . make yourself as comfortable as possible and . . . consider whether you may . . . give yourself permission to take . . . a mini-vacation . . . we all need . . . breaks once in a while . . . You may say to yourself: . . . It's okay, . . . to give myself this brief vacation . . . to relax . . . my mind. . . and switch to another mental channel . . . I want to enjoy this experience of . . . giving myself a short . . . break by switching . . . mental channels . . . I can shift around a bit to make myself even more comfortable . . . I take a deep breath . . . relaxing more . . . and . . . another breath, letting much of my tensions go . . . thinking that each breath I take from now on, will increase my well-being and relaxation . . . Feeling good . . . Untense . . . at ease . . .

"In fact, I start feeling so . . . relaxed . . . that I can remember other times I felt very, very . . . relaxed . . . my best vacation ever . . . Beautiful place . . . outdoors . . . the sun shining . . . yet so pleasant . . . Bright colors . . . the peaceful nature sounds . . . just right . . . so relaxing . . . the scents and perfumes of the place . . . feeling so-o-o good . . . wonderful . . . nothing to distract me from my good feelings . . . Tasting the beauty of the place . . . Experiencing myself right there . . . Relaxing . . . enjoying every second of it . . . and . . . thinking positively about myself . . . It comes so natural . . . to think now positively . . .

COMMENT

Starting from where the client is, the idea of a mental pause is introduced. Emphasis is placed on *the permission he can give himself* to have this break.

To underline one's control and responsibility in self-hypnosis, the first person singular is used from the start.

The enjoyment of the experience is stressed.

Letting go of all tensions may sound impossible to many executives; so, avoiding any possible mental argument, the invitation is made to let *some* tensions go.

As an anchor for relaxation, the memory of a beautiful, relaxing place is used.

The five inner senses are slowly introduced.

The slow tempo increases the relaxation and effects the switch of mental channels to the experiential mode of thinking.

Reference is made to the material the client worked on in Steps 4 and 5 (see text).

VERBALIZATION	COMMENT
But, I'm in no rush . . . Before I use my positive statements and imagery, I can visualize a 12-inch ruler, 12 being the highest degree of mental relaxation I can have . . . I'll let a number pop into my mind . . . any number from 1 to 12 . . . If the number is below 6, I am not ready yet to reprogram my mind with the positive statements and images I chose for myself previously. So . . . I'll linger a bit . . . longer . . . in my beautiful place . . . enjoying . . . everything about it . . . the total beauty of the place . . . filling all my senses . . . When the number that pops into my mind is 6 or higher . . . my subconscious tells me that I am ready for my positive reprogramming . . . very relaxed and at ease . . . in my beautiful place . . . starting to think positively, according to the positive statements and images I chose before . . . I don't have to remember now each word I wrote . . . just the general idea . . . Seeing myself in that positive situation . . . feeling good . . . picking up every detail of my positive situation . . . enjoying it . . . Repeating to myself the positive statements that I associated with my positive situation . . . Allowing these positive messages to sink deeply into my innermost being . . . Lingering on the good feelings that come from my positive images . . . good feelings . . ."	The "induction" itself is used to train the person in self-hypnosis. The "depth" self-report is used to provide structure in the self-hypnosis sequence. The arbitrary choice of 6 is suggestive of the need to be relaxed (in an altered state) before proceeding. Now the client is invited to repeat to himself the positive affirmations and to use the positive imagery they prepared individually in Steps (4) and (5). The good feelings generated by the positive self-suggestions and imagery are emphasized. To do this, the last few sentences are usually repeated several times in slightly different ways.

References

Allen J: As A Man Thinketh. (Originally published in the 1600s). Minneapolis, Personal Dynamics Institute (no date)

Andersen US: Success-Cybernetics. West Nyack, NY, Parker, 1966

Araoz DL: Negative self-hypnosis. J Contemp Psychother 1981

Araoz DL: A Survey of Imagination Use in Professional Consulting. New York, Dynamic Imagery Associates, 1981b

Barber TX: Self-suggestions for personal growth and the future of hypnosis. Paper presented at the American Psychological Association, Annual Convention, Montreal, September 1980

Barber TX, Spanos NP, Chaves JF: Hypnotism: Imagination and Human Potentialities. Elmsford, NY, Pergamon Press, 1974

Bristol CM: The Magic of Believing. Englewood Cliffs, NJ, Prentice-Hall, 1948

Carnegie D: How to Stop Worrying and Start Living. New York, Simon & Schuster, 1944

Cautela JR: Covert conditioning: Assumptions and procedures. J Ment Imag 1:53, 1977

Coué E: Self-Mastery Through Conscious Autosuggestion. London, George Allen and Unwin, 1922

Craig RL (ed): Training and Development Handbook, 2nd ed. New York, McGraw-Hill, 1978

Craig R, Bittel L (eds): Training and Development Handbook. New York, McGraw-Hill, 1967

Desoille R: The Directed Daydream, monograph no. 8. The Psychosynthesis Research Foundation, 1965

DeStefano R: The "Innoculation" Effect in Think-With Instructions for "Hypnotic-like" Experiences. Doctoral dissertation, Temple University, 1977

Diamond MJ: Modification of hypnotizability: A review. Psychol Bull 81:180, 1974

Diamond MJ: Hypnotizability is modifiable: An alternative approach. Int J Clin Exp Hypn 25:147, 1977a

Diamond MJ: Issues and methods for modifying responsivity to hypnosis. Ann NY Acad Sci 269:119, 1977b

Diamond MJ: Clinical hypnosis: Toward a cognitive-based skill approach. Presented at the 86th annual convention of the American Psychological Association. Toronto, Canada, August 1978

Ellis A: Humanistic Psychotherapy: The Rational Emotive Approach. New York, Julian, 1973

Ellis AR: Reason and Emotion in Psychotherapy. New York, Stuart, 1962

Erickson MH, Rossi EL: Experiencing Hypnosis. New York, Irvington, 1981

Friedrich O: The money chase. Time, May 4, 1981

Goleman D: The new competency tests: Matching the right people to the right jobs. Psychology Today, January 1981

Hill N: Think and Grow Rich. New York, Hawthorn Books, 1937

Katz NW: Hypnotic inductions as training in cognitive self-control. Cogn Ther Res 2:365, 1978

Katz NW: Increasing hypnotic responsiveness: Behavioral training vs. trance induction. J Consult Clin Psychol 47:119, 1979

Katz NW, Crawford VL: A little trance and a little skill; Interaction between models of hypnosis and type of hypnotic induction. Presented at the Society for Clinical and Experimental Hypnosis, Ashville, North Carolina, October 1978

Kinney JM, Sachs LB: Increasing hypnotic susceptibility. J Abnorm Psychol 83:145, 1974

Kroger WS, Fezler WD: Hypnosis and Behavior Modification: Imagery Conditioning. Philadelphia, JB Lippincott, 1976

Lieberman LR: Hypnosis research and the limitations of the experimental method. Ann NY Acad Sci 296:60, 1977

Lozanov G: Suggestology and Outlines of Suggestology. New York, Gordon and Breach, 1978

Maltz M: Psychocybernetics. New York, Simon and Schuster, 1960

Maultsby MC, Ellis A: Technique For Using Rational–Emotive Imagery (REI). New York, Institute for Rational Living, 1974

Meichenbaum D: Cognitive-Behavior Modification: An Integrative Approach. New York, Plenum, 1977

Mowrer OH: Mental imagery: An indispensable psychological concept. J Ment Imag 1:303, 1977

Nideffer RM: The Inner Athlete. New York, Crowell, 1976

Peale NV: You Can If You Think You Can. New York, Fawcet Crest, 1974

Reilley RR, Parisher DW, Corona A, Dobrovolsky NW: Modifying hypnotic susceptibility by practice and instruction. Int J Clin Exp Hypn 28:39, 1980

Sachs LB, Anderson WL: Modification of hypnotic susceptibility. Int J Clin Exp Hypn 15:172, 1967

Simmons CM: Your Subconscious Power. North Hollywood, CA, Wilshire Book Company, 1965

Spanos NP, Barber TX: Cognitive activity during "hypnotic" suggestibility: Goal-directed fantasy and the experience of non-volition. J Person 40:510, 1972

Spanos NP, Barber TX: Goal-directed fantasy and the performance of hypnotic test suggestions. Psychiatry 34:86, 1971

Wilson GT: Cognitive behavior therapy: Paradigm shift or passing phase? In Foreyt JP, Rathjen DP (eds): Cognitive Behavior Therapy: Research and Application. New York, Plenum Press, 1978

27 Clinical Application of Hypnosis in Sports

BEATA JENCKS
ERIC KRENZ

In this chapter, the term *sports* includes recreational activities such as jogging, bowling, and golf, as well as collegiate and professional competitive athletics at the highest levels. We have worked with subjects in both categories, and while methods and procedures applied will differ somewhat between instructions for recreational and professional purposes, the basic principles remain the same. For our explanation of the terms *hypnosis* and *altered states of consciousness,* see Chapter 3. This chapter covers only the practical approach to improvement of performance in sports through hypnotic methods.

Foundations

Literature

J.H. Schultz drew attention to the relationship of self-hypnotic methods to physical exercise, especially gymnastics, in his first book on autogenic training in 1932. In this work, he also referred to a 1922 congress for psychophysiological conditioning of performing artists (künstlerische Körperschulung). In relation to this, he discussed the work of Duncan, Dalcroze, Mensendieck, and other early teachers of psychophysiological conditioning. The work of these and other early teachers in the performing arts and gymnastics (Jencks, 1977a) employed hypnotic procedures, although not defined as such, during relaxation and movement. Great improvement of sportsmen's performance was mentioned in the first English edition of Schultz's book (Schultz and Luthe, 1959), with training and performance becoming less strenuous and exhausting after varied periods of autogenic training. Lindemann's (1957, 1958) use of autogenic training in his three solo crossings of the Atlantic Ocean in dugout and fold-boats was an impressive example of the value of hypnosis in sports.

In the English literature, Thomas wrote a not widely available article on "Hypnosis in Athletics" as early as 1955. Kroger (1977) reported having used hypnosis for improving athletic ability in competition baseball, football, and golf with "good to spectacular" results, and "without deleterious effects." His approach seems to have been clinical, with posthypnotic suggestions and sensory-imagery condition. Johnson (1961a, 1961b) used with good results hypnoanalysis of body movements for detecting errors in technique, and for age regression to uncover inhibiting childhood events.

A comprehensive program, based on research, was devised in Japan by Naruse (1963, 1964a, 1964b). Hetero- and self-hypnotic methods were used, including autogenic training, modeling, motivating suggestions, meditation, therapeutic imagery, anxiety-reduction techniques, mental rehearsal, and mental warm-ups. The athletes included 125 Olympic champions, as well as high school students.

Pulos (1969) employed hypnosis for team sports, using stepwise deepening and imagery practice. Mitchell's (1972) book reported case studies of hypnosis research with high school, college, and university athletes. Jencks (1977b) investigated the spontaneous occurrence and use of altered states of consciousness in physical peak performances and designed from the results a multiple-purpose teaching program for athletes.

Books that do not specify "hypnosis," but use oriental methods of meditation and body work (Tohei, 1966; Huang, 1973; Gallway, 1974, 1976; Spino, 1976) should not be overlooked among the foundations of hypnosis in sports or for the design of future programs. However, much of the fashionable and fancy must be disregarded and only the useful retained.

In Sweden, Uneståhl (1979a, 1979b) has used a program called "Inner Mental Training," which was designed to enable the athlete to "consistently achieve optimal performance." The program, prerecorded on cassette tapes for use over a 12-week period, systematically teaches athletes various hypnotic techniques. These include the following:

1. Progressive relaxation to produce muscular and mental relaxation
2. "Triggers" or cued responses to shorten the procedures
3. Mental imagery to produce a mental room (Jencks, 1974), which the athlete decorates to individual taste and which must contain a blackboard to write messages on, a motion picture screen to see himself performing, and an "energy machine." It is suggested to the athlete that this mental room can be used as a place to rest or to do whatever work is needed. The athlete is taught to use this imagery even amid such negative external disturbances as talking, whistling, or loud noises.
4. The athlete's being taught to allow the brain to release proper ideomotor performance responses at appropriate times

This short review of literature is by no means comprehensive but covers examples of the earliest and most useful approaches to use of hypnosis in sports.

Movement Hypnosis

The rhythmic movement of cradling an infant, the random movements of *movements passives,* and the free movements of T'ai Chi all induce hypnotic states (Jencks, 1979a). Foot soldiers have accomplished unbelievable feats owing to the hypnotic state induced by marching, reinforced by rhythmic drums or music.

Runners, joggers, and gymnasts go spontaneously into altered states of consciousness, although this is not commonly recognized. Rhythmic running movements often induce a trance state in which the upper body seems to proceed in a straight line while the legs seem to roll like wheels, and marathon runners devise all sorts of imagery for motivation and diversion. The present popularity of jogging and running may be due as much to the remedial stress-reducing effect of the self-induced hypnotic state as to the general health-promoting aspects. Folk dancing, especially when based on tradition and performed with feeling, induces hypnotic states, and so does disco dancing. Moreover, the smooth interaction of ice skating or tennis partners and the concentration interplay in team sports are states of movement hypnosis. Thus, when wholly participated in, all sports can spontaneously induce hypnotic states.

Training Attitudes and Athletes' Natural Hypnotic Capabilities

It has been the attitude of coaches and athletes that intensive physical training, discipline, and willpower are important factors in athletics; pep talks by coaches usually evoke unrecognized hypnotic states. Lately, group or individual training with such standard relaxation methods as transcendental meditation, Jacobsonian progressive relaxation, and floatation tanks have become popular. Individual athletes have also been referred to clinicians for improvement of performance, with the consequence that the therapist has applied the medical model of hypnosis.

The supposition by Vanek and Cratty (1970) that superior athletes are often difficult or impossible to hypnotize was based on the old-fashioned view of hypnosis as a power tool, on inadequate procedures, and on the medical model. Athlete's reports and our observations indicate that athletes go spontaneously into hypnotic states during training and during the competitive performance. Examples of natural hypnotic states of athletes are Joe Louis' well-known behavior of falling asleep on the training table, so that he had to be awakened for the fight; the athlete's staring, vacant look of readiness at the start of a ski jump; the spontaneous speeding up or slowing down of time perception during self-initiated imagery rehearsal or performance analysis; the self-chosen, purposeful image of an excellent college football lineman of being a "wolf, ready to pounce;"

and the capability to disregard all other stimuli but those pertaining to performance.

While there is no one definitive characteristic of an athlete, world-class athletes seem to have acquired a number of common mental qualities. They tend to have the abilities to evoke imagery through mental control, to set definitive goals, and to concentrate. Many are able mentally to slow down time for analyzing a task while performing it. Unestähl* indicated that world-class skiers also have the ability to estimate the time of their performance to the 100th of a second when asked to imagine themselves performing the task. Many of the world-class athletes report that they remember their best performance rather than the worst, while average athletes and neurotics usually forget positive experiences and images, and remember the negative ones.

When self-induced hypnotic states are recognized and explained to the athletes, and they are offered more training to achieve greater skill in these, they gladly cooperate. Athletes may be justifiably resistant to "treatment by a therapist," but, owing to their intense motivation for improving performance, they easily establish positive rapport with a specialist in sports hypnosis.

However, only a few great athletes can cope with anxiety in the way Joe Louis did. In general, time pressure, the necessity to win at all costs, expectation, physiological inadequacies, and the like are great stressors, and the universal response to these is anxiety. Naruse (1964b) found that of 125 Japanese champions of the 1960 Olympic Games in Rome, only 20% had attempted to develop some means of dealing with the anxiety reactions that had been experienced by almost all of them. Of the 20% who attempted to deal with their anxiety reactions, only a few did so in a systematic fashion with reliable results.

It is our opinion that, first, anxiety evoked by healthy, self-induced tensions should be mastered by self-induced stress amelioration procedures rather than by psychotherapy; second, the special needs or problems of athletes must be filled individually in addition to routine programs; and, third, programs should be constructed combining the most useful aspects from the Swedish and Japanese procedures, with the addition of Jencks' breathing measures and any other useful techniques. Table 27-1 and Table 27-2 combined show the hypnotic methods and procedures that seem most appropriate for achieving diverse purposes in sports.

Assessment of Subjects and Interventive Processes

It is apparent from the comprehensive Japanese and Swedish programs and the entries in Table 27-1 and Table 27-2, that no single approach of hypnosis is

* Unestähl L: Personal communication, 1980

Table 27-1. Hypnotic Procedures for Athletic Purposes—Examples of Hypnotic Standard Procedures

	1	2	3	4	5	6	7	8	9	10	11	12	13	14	15	16
1. Train sensory awareness	✓	✓	✓		✓	✓	✓			✓		✓	✓	✓		✓
2. Train sensory disregard		✓	✓		✓	✓	✓			✓		✓	✓	✓		✓
3. Increase concentration		✓	✓		✓		✓			✓		✓	✓	✓		✓
4. Control anxiety and other emotions	✓	✓			✓	✓	✓			✓	✓	✓	✓	✓		✓
5. Increase relaxation		✓			✓	✓	✓				✓		✓	✓	✓	✓
6. Increase invigoration			✓		✓	✓	✓						✓	✓	✓	✓
7. Control tension level and muscle tonus		✓	✓	✓	✓	✓	✓			✓	✓	✓	✓	✓	✓	✓
8. Increase motivation			✓		✓					✓		✓				
9. Establish the "feeling of readiness"			✓		✓			✓	✓	✓		✓				
10. Rehearse skills	✓							✓	✓	✓						
11. Analyze performance	✓							✓	✓							
12. Analyze problems	✓							✓	✓							
13. Help to solve problems	✓				✓			✓	✓							
14. Teach slowing and speeding of time perception	✓					✓										
15. Increase self-esteem		✓			✓		✓			✓		✓		✓		
16. Reinforce feelings of success	✓	✓	✓		✓		✓	✓	✓	✓		✓				
17. Control appropriate remembrance	✓				✓	✓				✓						
18. Control mental and physical activity level		✓	✓		✓		✓			✓	✓	✓		✓		
19. Aid flexibility, equilibrium, and easy movement				✓	✓		✓					✓		✓		
20. Increase vital capacity and endurance			✓	✓	✓	✓	✓		✓			✓				✓

[578]

Table 27-2. HYPNOTIC METHODS AND PROCEDURES
APPLICABLE TO SPORTS (To be matched by number to
Table 27-1)

1. Age regression and progression (Kroger, 1977)
2. Schultz's standard autogenic training (Schultz and Luthe,
   1969; Jencks, 1973a)
3. Avatara Yoga (Deussen, 1906; Pulos, 1969)
4. Awareness through movement (Feldenkrais, 1949)
5. Breathing measures (Jencks, 1974, 1977a; Pálos, 1974)
6. Direct suggestions for athletes (Jencks, 1979a; Unestáhl,
   1979)
7. Hatha Yoga (Vishnudevananda, 1960)
8. Ideomotor movements (Cheek & LeCron, 1968)
9. Imagery analysis (Jones, 1980)
10. Imagery rehearsal (Pulos, 1969)
11. Imagery relaxation (Jencks, 1979a, 1979b)
12. Kung Fu (Minick, 1974)
13. Progressive relaxation (Jacobson, 1938)
14. Sensory awareness training (Jencks, 1974, 1977b)
15. Shiatsu (Namikoshi, 1972)
16. Yoga breathing (Jencks, 1977)

adequate or sufficient in sports for every subject or purpose. Appropriate methods must be combined (Jencks, 1973a, 1973b, 1978) for specific purposes. However, for the psychologically healthy athlete or sportsman, clinical therapies must be changed into *teaching models* of instructor-directed or self-induced problem-solving hypnotic strategies and exercises (Haley, 1976).

The following was observed in work with those who are psychophysiologically healthy, especially athletes:

1. The subject's innate but usually unrecognized ability for working with and in altered states of consciousness must be the basis for further work.
2. Results are expected immediately by the subject, and therefore long-term strategies must be accompanied by immediate success-producing measures.
3. Responsibility for practice, results, and individual changes in procedures can be assigned to the subject.
4. Training can be relied on, but must continually be adjusted to show progress, lest boredom ensue.

The techniques used are not new. Suggestions like Pulos' (1969) to "play like a tiger" are basically the same as the old yogic practice of Avatara Yoga (Deussen, 1906) in which a person assumes in his imagination some "aspect of Vishnu," be it a lion or a fish or, in modern terms for the athlete, a wolf, a tiger, or an exemplary champion.

Hypnotizability as measured by tests is never ascertained in our procedure. Rather, the subject's natural hypnotic abilities and his spontaneous use of these are assessed. Then a teaching process ensues, which might include group instruction for improving natural hypnotic abilities, for deconditioning inappropriate reactions, and for developing the use of additional hypnotic procedures. Multiple methods are offered to the subjects so that if one method does not produce results for the athlete, another might.

A General Training Program

The basic contents of a general training program are as follows:

1. The subject's working knowledge of Jencks' (1974, 1979b; also see Chap. 3) respiration exercises for special purposes
2. A good self-hypnotic method that is body-related, progresses with its instructions over 4 to 6 weeks, relaxes the body but keeps the mind active, and allows the insertion of special instructions. Schultz's standard autogenic training (Schultz and Luthe, 1969; Jencks, 1973a, 1975), modified for athletes (Krenz, 1982; see Appendix 27-1), is such a method.
3. Additional work according to the subject's needs. This may include the heterohypnotic suggestion sequence (see Appendix 27-2); direct suggestions for motivation; control of physiological reactions and emotions by influence of sympathetic–parasympathetic responses; control over reactions to the environment by use of imagery exercises; self-analysis of behavior, emotions, and inhibitions with the aid of ideomotor finger movements; and the solution of problems by imagery exercises. The duration of the individual programs may be varied according to the progress and needs of the athletes.

Jencks' respiration exercises are immediate success-producing, extremely simple interventions. Exhalations versus inhalations are varied with the following: muscle relaxation versus muscle tension, feelings of drowsiness versus feelings of alertness, warmth versus coolness, moving forward versus moving backward, and the like. Emphasis is given to that part of the breath's cycle that supports the intended action, sensation, or physiological state.

The breathing response for proper arousal was especially invented for athletes, who generally tend to interpret relaxation in terms of lethargy, and invigoration in terms of tension. Such interpretation of the semantics of relaxation and invigoration exercises may hinder instead of help their ability to reach the proper level of arousal necessary for optimal performance of a given task. Krenz (Krenz and Jencks, 1980) invented a term to which athletes respond easily and properly, the "proper level of *non-tightness.*" The level is reached by balancing inhalation and exhalation against each other, and Krenz called this process for use by athletes "Jencks' Breathing Response for moving to the Proper Level of Non-tightness." Thus, if, during the course of a game, a player becomes emotionally upset, he takes a deep breath, exhales until he reaches the proper level of nontightness, and continues to play at his best.

The modified autogenic training program (see Appendix 27-1) can be amplified by the following exercises. First, the subject should analyze the evoked sensations throughout the body prior to and immediately following each exercise series. This greatly increases sensory awareness and demonstrates success. Second, the athlete can be taught to think the formulas of heaviness and warmth in the limbs with open eyes, or to open and close the eyes according to self-command. This increases sensory awareness and self-command for everyday activities. Third, feelings of readiness, confidence, or concentration can be evoked on command by inserting such formulas as "arms and legs alive and ready," "solar plexus warm and confident," or "forehead cool and concentrated" during three consecutive inhalations with eyes open. Fourth, suggestions for appropriate remembrance of success and forgetting of failure may be inserted. Fifth, performance analysis, analysis of problems, and imagery confrontation with problems and their solution can be practiced. Sixth, for mental rehearsal, the athlete can be instructed to perceive himself performing the athletic task perfectly in his mind five to ten times by feeling, seeing, hearing, and otherwise noticing with all senses the aspects of the task. Then the athlete reports and is asked now to "step in and perform" the task approximately 20 times.

Of course, these amplifying hypnotic exercises can also be practiced without the modified autogenic traning program. However, the continuous progression and flow of this "carrying vehicle" of self-hypnosis makes the responses to the additional instructions more facile and natural.

The heterohypnotic suggestion sequence (see Appendix 27-2) includes progressive relaxation, direct suggestions, appropriate breathing instructions, and an introduction to the breathing response for "achieving the proper level of nontightness." It can be shortened or modified to meet the individual athlete's needs and the demands of the situation. This sequence may be used additionally when an athlete has difficulties with the Autogenic Training (Appendix 27-1).

Ideomotor finger responses (Cheek and LeCron, 1968; Jencks, 1977b) are useful for ascertaining the cooperation of athletes in guided imagery exercises, for asking simple questions during hypnotic analysis of problems, and for working out conflict situations. Instructions can be simply: "Just sit there comfortably, feet solidly on the floor, hands on your thighs, close your eyes, exhale, and think of your forefingers. Allow them to decide which is the 'yes' and which the 'no' finger." Such decisions are necessary before each use of the fingers, since they may switch connotation. Simple questions can then keep the operator in touch with the subject's progress without too much intervening talk during imagery exercises. For solving conflict situations instructions can be, "Now put one side of your conflict into one forefinger and the other side into the other. Allow both fingers to move spontaneously while you review with good common sense the aspects of both sides of the conflict and feel which finger wins." For multiple choice situations, instructions are, "Close your eyes and review your choices one after the other three to five times, while you allow one forefinger to move spontaneously. Find out which is most important, according to strength and number of finger movements."

Group Instruction

Group instruction in classes of up to 60 students has been successfully given for Jacobson's progressive relaxation, for Jencks' breathing exercises, and for Schultz's standard autogenic training. Instructions in these long-term conditioning methods usually follow preliminary simple instructions for introducing the students to a light hypnotic state. The wording for such instructions could be approximately, "Allow your bodies to align themselves on your uncomfortable bucket chairs in the field of gravity. This field goes in a straight line between outer space, your body, and the center of the earth. . . . Allow your eyes to close, inhale deeply, and then allow the breath to stream or flow out through your slightly parted lips, while you imagine going down . . . , going down in an elevator, floating down, or going down in any other way, along the guide rope of your exhalation. When you reach the lowest place during this exhalation, check your feelings and compare them to what you felt before the exercise. Then inhale, stretch, open your eyes, and be back in the present." It is important in this short exercise to give matter of fact instructions for hypnosis-inducing physiological means, using the imagination. Also, the hypnotic state is ended by means of physiological reactions due to stimulation of the sympathetic nervous system, instead of by suggestive means like counting. Hypnotic work with groups of healthy participants should adhere to physical and physiological principles and should avoid suggesting reactions that subjects may check out as "not true." Such instructions as "try and feel for yourself" or "experiment with it" are appropriate. After discussing the effects of such a simple exercise, the longer methods can be introduced.

Long-term Versus Immediately Acting Strategies

Long-term methods are (1) those that condition striate muscle relaxation (*e.g.,* Jacobson's progressive relaxation), (2) those that condition automatic nervous system reactions (*e.g.,* Schultz's autogenic training), and (3) those that condition the mind, as do the oriental meditation methods.

Examples of immediately acting strategies are heterohypnotic measures that get results immediately, or the use of respiration (see Chap. 21).

After thorough conditioning, long-term methods also result in immediate reactions. For instance, after conditioning a progressive relaxation, all voluntary muscles may be relaxed simultaneously; similarly, the reactions of the first five exercises of Schultz's standard autogenic training can be evoked during one long exhalation, while the sixth is evoked during the following inhalation.

Assessment of Effectiveness

Studies by Castaneda, McCandless, and Palermo (1956), Sarason (1961), and Martens (1977) demonstrated that excess levels of stress and anxiety can have a detrimental effect on athletic performance. Research (London, Ogle, and Unkel, 1968; Pulos, 1969; DeMers, 1979; Krenz, Gordin, and Edwards, 1982) has indicated that the use of altered states of consciousness can be beneficial for reducing such excess stress and anxiety levels, thereby aiding athletes in performing to their optimal level.

While it is difficult empirically to assess the effectiveness of a hypnotic intervention, self-reports from athletes with whom we have worked have been useful in assessing various techniques employed.

Athletes in various situations and sports have used the techniques discussed previously for counteracting excessive stress and high anxiety levels, and for improvement of specific or general aspects of performance. Although dramatic improvement in performance is not the norm, athletes have reported that they achieve greater control of their reactions to the environment.

We have also supervised the use of altered states of consciousness with high school level athletes. In one local high school, approximately 50 male and female athletes were taught Uneståhl's (1979b) "Inner Mental Training." At the end of the season, the team finished in fourth place in the state instead of its predicted eighth place. A second high school team of over 40 athletes used a hypnosis program that consisted of relaxation training, mental imagery, and confidence building from 1975–1980. The team finished 3 of these years as State Champion and was second in the state for the other 2 years. A third local high school used a program of autogenic training and diverse self-hypnotic approaches with 20 ice hockey players from 1979–1981. The first year after using the techniques, the team finished second in the state, and the next year it was State Champion. All of these teams have reported an improvement in confidence, concentration, and performance.

In a study (Krenz and Henschen, 1980; Krenz and Jencks, 1980) of the 1979–1980 University of Utah men's basketball team, five players were given a suggestion intervention for better performance and control. The intervention varied for the experimental group from 2 to 6 weeks. The control group consisted of the remaining five players, who did not receive an intervention. Team statistics for the season indicated that, while all players improved during the season, the experimental subjects showed greater improvement than the control subjects.

Also, the element of time was important in the effectiveness of the intervention. The subjects who improved most had participated for 5 to 6 weeks, while those who showed improvement to a lesser degree had participated for only 2 to 3 weeks. Of those who had participated in the experimental group of this study, three continued to play on the 1980–1981 University of Utah men's basketball team. The team played in the NCAA semi-finals, and the three athletes continued to use the techniques that they had previously learned. One of these athletes lacked emotional control, which resulted in a flaring temper on the court and loss of control over his playing ability. After learning to use his breathing appropriately and achieving the proper level of nontightness, he reported that he felt more in control of his temper and could move without thinking to the proper level of nontightness for improving his performance. The other two athletes had reported excessive stress and anxiety while performing because of disturbing environmental distractions. After participating in the 1979–1980 research study, both reported improvement in controlling their negative reactions to the environment. All three of these athletes were drafted by professional teams. One was dropped, but the other two signed contracts and have demonstrated excellent performance. Both have reported that they continue to use the techniques learned at the University of Utah.

Another player from the 1980–1981 basketball team asked for help during the NCAA semi-final playoffs, complaining that his free-throw shooting needed improvement. While we prefer to use a systematic program that teaches the athlete a series of exercises for mental control, this athlete received only 4 days of concentrated training with the breathing response learning to move to the proper level of nontightness, and he significantly improved his shooting from the free-throw line.

Members of the University of Utah's 1980–1981 women's gymnastics team and the 1980–1981 men's ski team both participated in research conducted to measure the effects of an altered state on stress and anxiety while performing a complex motor task (Krenz, Gordin, and Edwards, 1982). From this study it was concluded that excess levels of anxiety can be reduced through the use of posthypnotic suggestion. At the conclusion of the season, both teams finished in first place in national competition. Both teams are continuing to employ the techniques learned during the research study.

The authors also are working with the 1980–1981 National Champion Intercollegiate Gymnastics team during the 5 months of precompetition practice. The modified autogenic training program (see Appendix 27-1) with special formulas, as well as the hypnotic techniques and suggestions (see Appendix 27-2), are being used.

It is the authors' opinion that the hypnotic techniques described in this chapter are most effective when taught prior to the competitive situation. At this time, athletes perfect their performance and are relatively free of the stress and anxiety of competition. When hypnotic techniques are implemented during the preseason training schedule, the athletes not only develop their performance skills, but also learn greater control of their bodies, emotions, and minds.

Since athletes are the best judges of the effectiveness of a hypnotic technique for attaining optimal performance, they should be encouraged to experiment with different techniques and, under supervision, use and develop the most appropriate ones. On the basis of the studies reported earlier and of subjective reports, we conclude that the techniques described in this chapter are effective in aiding athletes at all levels of competition to perform closer to their optimal levels.

Complete failures with hypnotic work by athletes have not occurred under our supervision. However, at times the expected results appeared to decrease owing to the following reasons: physical problems that could not be overcome; poor cooperation of a group with a new, unknown instructor; failure of the athletes to use taped instructions or negligence to discuss questions about the taped methods; and lack of knowledge or misunderstandings by instructors and athletes with respect to the special problems of athletes and the availability of appropriate remedial measures.

Future Trends

There is no doubt that, owing to the athletes' eagerness to improve skills and to the availability of a program such as the one described in this chapter, which is presently taught through the Health and Physical Education departments at the University of Utah, a bright future may be forecast for the relatively new field of hypnosis in sports. However, this bright future could be modified by the climate of opinion about hypnosis, by hypnotic methods being taught under other names (Benson, 1975; Frederick, 1981; Setterlind and Uneståhl, 1978), and by experts in medical hypnosis opposing hypnotic work with athletes (AMA Newsletter, 1960).

Athletics and schools are much in the public eye, but the general public still disapproves of hypnosis. This negative attitude is encouraged by the emphasis placed by public media on the "magical" and "power" aspects of hypnosis. Also, the public attitude will remain confused as long as misunderstandings and differences of opinion remain between experts in hypnosis and experts in fields that use the same procedures under different names. The following are some examples of this.

Jacobson, who devised progressive relaxation (Jacobson, 1938) still maintains that it is not hypnosis. As a result, it has been experimented with and taught in public schools (Frederick, 1981) and was reported under the auspices of the

Biofeedback Society of America (BSA). Many aspects of biofeedback incorporate hypnosis, but the BSA seems to disapprove of the word "hypnosis." Schultz's autogenic training is taught under BSA auspices as being something different from hypnosis, although Schultz himself called autogenic training a "self-hypnosis," and in Germany it is recognized as hypnosis. Green's (1981) statement to the BSA that Schultz ". . . gave up the use of hypnosis as an undependable medical tool more than half a century ago" is utterly erroneous. Schultz practiced medical hypnosis, including autogenic training, until his death in 1968.

Further, not only are many experts uncertain as to what hypnosis consists of, but old and new terms are confusing. In Sweden, methods that include progressive relaxation and imagery exercises are called "hypnotic" for athletes (Unestähl, 1979a) and "relaxation" for grade school and high school instruction (Setterlind and Unestähl, 1978). In Southern Europe, the term hypnosis has been replaced by "sophrology" (Chertok, 1981), just as once "hypnosis" replaced "mesmerism." And, yet, this oldest term has prevailed. In a preschool program for asthmatic children (Jencks, 1981) a lay aid remarked when the children were blowing imaginary soap bubbles for extending their lung capacity, "How they blow their bubbles!—All mesmerized!"

We wish to repeat that we use the terms "hypnosis" and "altered states of consciousness" interchangeably, depending on the attitudes of subjects. However, it is explained to subjects who are apprehensive of "hypnosis" that both are basically the same, and that individuals are repeatedly using self-induced hypnotic states without realizing what they are doing.

In view of this, one should look to the future of hypnosis in sports with qualified optimism.

Appendix 27-1

Schultz's Standard Autogenic Training, Modified for Athletes

First Week—Heaviness of Limbs

The subject sits or lies in a comfortable position with eyes closed and repeats the formula "comfortably heavy" during seven consecutive exhalations each for (1) the preferred arm, (2) the nonpreferred arm, (3) both arms, (4) the preferred leg, (5) the nonpreferred leg, (6) both legs, and (7) arms and legs. The entire sequence is repeated three times. This procedure takes about 10 minutes. The 10-minute procedure is repeated three times a day, the last time just before falling asleep. The subject should not feel guilty if the procedure is not completed, but should always analyze how the body feels at the beginning of the session compared to the end, as a proof of the efficacy of the method. Since athletes do not like to spend 10 minutes three times a day on these exercises, they are encouraged to decrease the number of repetitions day by day from seven to one. Thus, by the end of the week, they are capable of achieving heaviness with one repetition for each arm and leg.

Second Week—Warmth of Limbs

First, repeat once the suggestion "arms and legs comfortably heavy." Then follow the previously discussed progression for the formula "comfortably warm," seven times for each limb, repeating the sequence three times. For the remainder of the week, this whole procedure is repeated three times per day, decreasing warmth day by day from seven repetitions to only one at the end of the second week.

Third Week—Heartbeat

First, formulas "arms and legs heavy" and "arms and legs warm" are repeated one time each. Then the formula "heartbeat calm and regular" is repeated seven times. This sequence is repeated three times, and the whole procedure repeated three times per day. During the third week's training, repetitions of the heart formula also are reduced from seven to one. Athletes are well acquainted with the beating heart from a positive attitude, and we never observed difficulties with this exercise.

Fourth Week—Respiration

First heaviness, warmth, and heartbeat are repeated, one repetition each. Then the formula "it breathes me" or "breathing" is added seven times. For achieving this passively, the following is explained: If you hyperventilate, you pass out and breathing returns to normal. If you hold the breath, you pass out and breathing returns to normal. As soon as you relinquish the conscious control, the unconscious takes control. Allow the breathing to happen, and analyze the breathing in your body. This increases sensory awareness, self-control, confidence, and self-esteem. The breathing formula is again reduced from seven repetitions to one during the regular training of the fourth week.

Fifth Week—Solar Plexus or Center of Body

First, the previous four formulas are repeated once, as described earlier. Then, the formula "solar plexus (or center of body) comfortably warm" is repeated seven times. During the fifth week's training, these repetitions are again reduced from seven to one. All suggestive formulas for the first five weeks are taught during consecutive exhalations.

Sixth Week—Cool Forehead

First, the previous five formulas are repeated once, during consecutive exhalations. Then the formula "forehead pleasantly cool" is added during seven consecutive *inhalations.*

During the weekly practice of three sets three times per day, this formula is also reduced from seven repetitions to one.

Seventh Week—Shortening of Exercise

The athletes are now instructed to think the first five formulas "heaviness-warmth-heartbeat-breathing-solar plexus" during one long, relaxing exhalation and "cool forehead" during the following inhalation. This is repeated three times.

Appendix 27-2

Heterohypnotic Suggestion Exercise

The induction recommended for use with athletes is a combination of a standard progressive relaxation, appropriate breathing, and suggestion. The important feature of this suggestion exercise is the use of the term "proper level of nontightness." The term was devised by Krenz (Krenz and Jencks, 1980) because athletes tend generally to interpret relaxation in terms of lethargy and invigoration in terms of tension. It is a level at which inhalations are balanced with exhalations to enable athletes to reach the proper level of arousal necessary for optimal performance. An example of the suggestion for this is as follows:

"It is interesting that now, as in the future, *you will be able to move to the proper level of nontightness at any time* by simply taking a deep breath . . . , holding it with your eyes open: open your eyes! Hold your breath and release it! And you will automatically move to the proper level of nontightness at whatever time and for whatever task lies ahead of you. You can use this in the middle of any task, and you can always move to the proper level of nontightness with greater concentration, with open eyes, and you can do this at any time. . . . And now allow your eyes to close again. And any time you need to, you can move to the proper level for your task by taking a deep breath, and holding it. . . . And when you release it, you will automatically move to the proper level of nontightness with greater concentration. . . . And you can do this at any time, for any task, with open or closed eyes. And you will also feel confident in your ability to do whatever task is ahead of you."

References

AMA Newsletter: M.D.'s frown on hypnosis of athletes. July 11, 1960

Benson H: The Relaxation Response. New York, William Morrow, 1975

Castaneda A, McCandless B, Palermo D: Complex learning and performance as a function of anxiety in children and task difficulty. Child Dev 27:327, 1956

Cheek DB, LeCron LM: Clinical Hypnotherapy. New York, Grune & Stratton, 1968

Chertok L: Sense and Nonsense in Psychotherapy. New York, Pergamon Press, 1981

DeMers GE: Effects of Posthypnotic Suggestion in the Performance of a Fine Motor Skill Under Stress. Unpublished doctoral dissertation, University of Utah, 1979

Deussen P: Vier Philosophische Texte des Mahâbhâratam. Leipzig, Brockhaus, 1906

Feldenkrais M: Body and Mature Behavior. New York, International Universities Press, 1949

Frederick B: Progressive relaxation: A core element in a physical education program. Presented at the meeting of the Biofeedback Society of America, Louisville, Kentucky, March 1981

Gallway WT: The Inner Game of Tennis. New York, Random House, 1974

Gallway WT: Inner Tennis, Playing The Game. New York, Random House, 1976

Green E: Autogenic training vs. hypnosis. Newsletter of the Biofeedback Society of America, May 1981, p 4

Haley J: Problem-Solving Therapy. San Francisco, Jossey-Bass, 1976

Huang AC: Embrace Tiger, Return to Mountain. Moab, Real People Press, 1973

Jacobson E: Progressive Relaxation. Chicago, University of Chicago Press, 1938

Jencks B: Exercise Manual for J.H. Schultz's Standard Autogenic Training and Special Formulas with Appendixes on Procedures with Children and Advanced Autogenic Training. Salt Lake City, Jencks, 1973a

Jencks B: Problem-oriented, psychophysiological combination therapy. Presented at the 53rd meeting of the Western Psychological Association, Anaheim, CA, 1973b

Jencks B: Respiration for Relaxation, Invigoration, and Special Accomplishment. Manual. Salt Lake City, Jencks, 1974

Jencks B: Relaxation and reconditioning of the autonomic nervous system for children: The autogenic rag doll. Presented at the meeting of the American Society of Clinical Hypnosis, Seattle, 1975

Jencks B: Hypnosis and athletes. Presented at the meeting of the American Society of Clinical Hypnosis, Atlanta, 1977a

Jencks B: Your Body: Biofeedback at its Best. Chicago, Nelson-Hall, 1977b

Jencks B: Psychophysiological Combinationtherapy. Presented at the meeting of the First European Congress of Hypnosis in Psychotherapy and Psychosomatic Medicine, Malmö, 1978

Jencks B: Movement Hypnosis: Therapies and Research. Presented at the meeting of the American Society of Clinical Hypnosis, San Francisco, November 1979a (reprinted from Svensk tidskrift for hypnos, 1979, pp 15–23)

Jencks B: Relaxation and invigoration for skiers. J US Ski Coach Assoc 3(2):9, 1979b

Jencks B: Hypnotic Factors in the Design of a Preschool Asthma Family-Education Program. Presented at the meeting of the American Society for Clinical Hypnosis, Boston, November 1981

Johnson WR: Body movement awareness in non-hypnosis and hypnosis. Res Q 32:263, 1961a

Johnson WR: Hypnotic analysis of aggression blockage in baseball pitching. Am J Clin Hypn 4(2):102, 1961b

Jones G: Radio interview. November 27, 1980

Krenz EW: Modified Autogenic Training. In preparation, 1983

Krenz E, Gordin R, Edwards SW: Effects of Hypnosis on State Anxiety and Stress in Male and Female Intercollegiate Athletes. Presented at the Ninth International Congress of Clinical Hypnosis and Psychosomatic Medicine, Glasglow, 1982

Krenz EW, Henschen KP: Relaxation Training and Basketball Performance. Unpublished manuscript, 1980 (available from Keith P. Henschen, College of Health, University of Utah, Salt Lake City, Utah 84112)

Krenz E, Jencks B: Utilization of Hypnosis in Sports. Presented at the meeting of the American Society of Clinical Hypnosis, Minneapolis, November 1980

Kroger WS: Clinical and Experimental Hypnosis. Philadelphia, JB Lippincott, 1977

Lindemann H: Allein über den Ozean. Frankfurt, Heinrich Scheffle Verlag, 1957

Lindemann H: Alone at Sea. New York, Random House, 1958

London P, Ogle M, Unkel I: The effects of hypnosis and motivation in resistance to heat stress. J Abnorm Psychol 73:532, 1968

Martens R: Sport Competition Anxiety Test. Champaign, Human Kinetics Publishers, 1977

Minick M: The Kung Fu Exercise Book. New York, Simon and Schuster, 1974

Mitchell WM: The Use of Hypnosis in Athletics. Stockton, Mitchell, 1972

Namikoshi T: Japanese Finger Pressure Therapy-Shiatsu. San Francisco, Japan Publications, 1972

Naruse G: Hypnotic treatment of stage fright in sport. Proceedings of the annual meeting of the Society of Clinical and Experimental Hypnosis, New York, 1962

Naruse G: "Agari" no taisaku ni tsuite (On a treatment of stage fright). Olympia 6:29, 1964a

Naruse G: Hypnotic treatment of stage fright in champion athletes. Psychologia (Jpn) 7(324):199, 1964b

Pálos S: Atem und Meditation. Munich, OW Barth Verlag, 1974

Pulos L: Hypnosis and Think Training With Athletes. Presented at the meeting of the American Society of Clinical Hypnosis, San Francisco, 1969

Sarason IG: The effects of anxiety and threat on the solution of a difficult task. J Abnorm Soc Psychol 62:165, 1961

Setterlind S, Unestáhl L: Introducing Relaxation Training in Swedish Schools. Unpublished manuscript, 1978 (available from S. Setterlind and L. Unestáhl, Department of Sport Psychology, Örebro University, Sweden)

Schultz JH: Das Autogene Training. Leipzig, G Thieme Verlag, 1932

Schultz JH, Luthe W: Autogenic Training. A Psychophysiologic Approach in Psychotherapy. New York, Grune & Stratton, 1959

Spino M: The Innerspaces of Running—Beyond Jogging. Millbrae, CA, Celestial Acts, 1976

Thomas SE: Hypnosis in athletes. Hypnosis 1:11, 1955

Tohei JK: Aikido in Daily Life. Tokyo, Rikugei, 1966

Unestáhl L: Självkontroll Genom Mental Träning. Örebro, Veje Förlag, 1977

Unestáhl L: Hypnotic Preparation of Athletes. Unpublished manuscript, 1979a (available from L. Unestáhl, Department of Sport Psychology, Örebro University, Sweden)

Unestáhl L: Inner Mental Training. Unpublished manuscript, 1979b (available from L. Unestáhl, Department of Sport Psychology, Örebro University, Sweden)

Vanek M, Cratty BJ: Psychology and the Superior Athlete. London, Macmillan, 1970

Vishnudevananda S: The Complete Illustrated Book of Yoga. New York, Julian Press, 1960

28 Hypnosis in Education and School Psychology

RAYMOND W. KLAUBER

Hypnosis enriches the educational process; rather than being the method of change, it supplements the established practices of instructing and counseling. The inclusion of hypnosis helps some students to overcome the obstacles that impede learning and growth while helping others exceed the normal progress of traditional instruction.

The underlying theoretical view of this chapter is Adlerian. That Adlerian views should be combined with hypnotic suggestions might surprise those familiar with Adler's opposition to hypnosis (Adler, 1954). Fortunately, the practice of hypnosis has changed. The commanding stage hypnotist who held others under the power of his spell is a style generally unacceptable today among professionals incorporating hypnosis into their practice.

The topics of this section of the chapter are limited to those areas in which I, in my practice of psychology, have found hypnosis to be helpful. These areas include instruction (reading), emotional learning blocks, interest and attention, discipline, and study habits. Further help through hypnosis is possible in the expression of learning by overcoming test and performance anxiety. Vocational choice and romantic difficulties, two areas of possible concern to university students can be helped through hypnosis. My years of practice of school psychology at the Forsyth School helped me to realize the potential use of hypnoticlike techniques in education.

Research

Hypnotherapy is an effective procedure for some children and adolescents with educational difficulties. These difficulties include reading, arithmetic, memory blocks, classroom behavior, and school motivation. Help can also be provided for students with test anxiety, performance anxiety, and vocational guidance needs. How much effect does hypnosis have in education? Since hypnosis is seldom used in the classroom, especially below the college level, its effectiveness for students of different ages and settings and its actual educational uses are hard to estimate. Also, even similar experiments have shown differences in results. Only one thing is consistent and that is the fact that hypnosis can and does sometimes help with the educational process. However, dependent on the situation, technique used, and goals, hypnosis has varying degrees of effectiveness. As many researchers have found, some students respond with equal educational improvements from nontrance suggestions. For those who are responsive to the techniques and suggestions through hypnosis, hypnosis can be an effective tool in assisting them to improve their learning skills based on their individual needs. The educational process begins at the same time the child is reaching an age suitable for hypnosis. During much of the elementary and secondary educational years, the young person will be at his peak of hypnotizability.

Emotions and Recall

Initially, in looking at the effects of hypnosis on education and learning, some researchers believed that the emotional mood of the subject might affect learning and recall results. This is a plausible idea, since many of us have experienced the effects our mood has on us when we are trying to concentrate and study. Nearly everyone has experienced a limitation of his ability to concentrate when extreme emotions of happiness or sadness existed. The question looked at by the researchers was whether a person's mood served as an important factor in learning, memory storage, and retrieval.

Rapaport (1942) suggests that emotions retrieve memories that were stored when these same emotions were previously experienced. For example, grief associated with personal loss of a spouse during adulthood may retrieve memories related to a childhood grief for loss of a parent.

In a study by Bower, Monteiro, and Gilligan (1978), hypnotized subjects learned a word list while experiencing happiness and sadness. They were asked to recall the list within 1 day, while in the same or opposite mood. Using a relaxation, eye-closure method of hypnosis, subjects put themselves into a happy or sad mood. Retention was not necessarily dependent on learning and testing moods, except in multi-list situations, which could be affected by confusion and interference of memories otherwise. A compromise conclusion that can be accepted is that an emotional mood is best considered an extra cue in retrieval of memories.

Cooper and London (1973) tested the ability to recall meaningful information related to a rare chemical. The variables studied to determine their effect on recall included hypnotic susceptibility, trance or waking state, and the order of testing (hypnosis first or waking state first). Results showed that memory was increased regardless of whether suggestions were given in a waking or hypnotized state and regardless of the order in which these suggestions were given. Cooper and London's thought-provoking explanation is that hypnosis may be most effective on memory for emotionally charged, relevant, meaningful material. Remembering facts on a rare chemical were not considered emotionally charged.

Expectations of and Motivation for Hypnosis

Before becoming more specific regarding hypnotic effects on individual educational aspects, some consideration must be given to the expectations students have for the effects of hypnosis. This idea of essential importance was not always considered in the experimental results of studies. For example, the subjects' expectations for positive results of hypnotic suggestions may cause more recognition of common words than the actual improvement from hypnotic suggestion (Brightbill and Zamansky, 1968).

Harley and Harley (1968) felt that expectations for hypnosis to help possibly played a role in results. They hypothesized that subjects who knew beforehand that hypnosis would be used did not put as much effort into learning in their waking state. Thus, hypnosis appeared to be unduly effective in evaluation of results of the learning process.

Students being tested for research studies may have increased motivation to please the tester and thus, consciously or unconsciously, restrict their initial performance leaving them room for future improvement. If the subjects believe that the tester is hoping for better results under hypnosis, they may perform better during the experimental than the control conditions. Furthermore, those anxious about impending hypnosis induction may have a disrupted performance. When anxious subjects are more relaxed because hypnosis is not anticipated, they perform closer to their maximum capacity (Brightbill and Zamansky, 1968).

In a study by Holcomb (1970) expectations played a different type of role. He noted in his experiment with hypnosis and reading improvement with seventh grade boys that the excellent cooperation of the school, parents, and the very eager youngsters themselves probably affected the results. Everyone was eagerly anticipating the results from the hypnosis and cooperated enthusiastically.

In an experiment by Spanos, Ansaii, and Stam (1979), looking at age regression and eidetic imagery, it was found that adults, before or after hypnosis, were not able to perform random-dot stereogram tasks. These tasks involved viewing a 100,000-dot stereogram and then, from memory, superimposing the image of the first one over a second stereogram resulting in a three-dimensional figure. However, in a previous study by Walker (1976), two subjects were successful at performing these tasks after hypnotic age regression. Spanos guessed that some of Walker's subjects, anticipating and hoping for positive outcome, may have researched the stereogram to learn the correct responses before the follow-up session.

Anxiety and Fears

As discussed, expectations and motivations regarding outcome may affect the results of hypnosis. Inevitably, anxiety and fears also play a role in the results of hypnosis. Anxiety can be a positive or negative influence related to the learner's expectations of the situation and of the hypnotic process. For example, a person who is highly anxious about hypnosis itself or the learning tasks may be either energized or frozen with fright. Thus, anxiety related to hypnosis may or may not be helpful. The following sequence may occur:

Anxiety leads to increased motivation,
Leading to greater effectiveness of hypnosis,
Leading to lessened anxiety,
Leading to improved performance in problem areas.

A second aspect of anxiety/fear reduction is related to educational improvement.

Stanley Krippner (1963) has written and commented on the effect of hypnosis on anxiety associated with learning and test-taking. For example, during hypnosis, a student was told to consider his future goals and the effect his academic record may have on these goals. The student was also told to disregard outside stimulation and distraction during a test. For students with high vocational goals and real concern for the future, Krippner found hypnosis effective in helping them decrease their anxiety and improve their retention and performance. Thus, the students were more able to attain their goals.

In Krippner's study with primary and secondary school aged children, he believed that tension/anxiety problems disabled some readers. Whether the anxiety was a cause or an effect of disablement was not important to Krippner; the important factor was that it was a roadblock to their reading abilities. For these students, hypnosis was used effectively to lower tension and promote muscle relaxation during reading through his suggestions that the students relax, stop worrying about reading, and think about how they would like to read better (Krippner, 1966).

Other researchers also evaluated the role of lessened anxiety to help learning. Eisle and Higgins (1962) showed that hypnosis had good results in decreasing test anxiety and improving study habits and concentration.

In a single case example, Lodato (1969), using hypnosis, helped a woman to overcome her anxiety and tension, which prevented her from successful completion of a civil service examination. Hypnosis relaxed her and also gave her an awareness of the psychological obstacle that was affecting her test-taking skills. (In this case, a rebellious attitude toward authority was the culprit.)

Mellenbruch (1964) worked with the panic experienced by some students before an examination. Such panic can cause blocking and confusion of knowledge. After ascertaining that these students studied adequately, Mellenbruch used hypnosis to help determine the cause of the panic behavior. More positive, less anxiety producing feelings were then used to replace the fear and tension associated with the examination. His results were positive; some students were able to take the examination without panic, and their grades improved.

In a case by Mordey (1965), a client's stage fright was eliminated by hypnosis to elicit appropriate behavior, with partial extinction of the associated anxiety. Although continuing to experience some anxiety, the client was able to cope with it and channel her energy in a more positive direction:

A 35-year-old woman with the lead role in an opera panicked and feared she would forget her lines. Several hypnotic sessions were required for this therapy to be successful. First, she was encouraged to recall a happy, confidence-producing event. She then was told to imagine attending the same opera with her lead role sung by an excellent artist. Then, she was told to assume the role and confidence of the star. This confidence and perfection of performance were reinforced until she could imagine herself completely confident and playing the role perfectly. Her stage fright was eliminated, and she performed with confidence.

Although this is just one specific case, the effect of hypnosis on alleviating anxiety is supported.

General Effects on Learning and Recall

What actual effect does hypnosis have on learning? What does it actually do to enhance learning? Unfortunately, as pointed out at the beginning of this chapter, there is no simple, definitive answer to this. By evaluating recall of a list of 12 trigrams, St. Jean (1980) found that verbal learning performance improvement of university students was the same in two separate studies regardless of such variables as hypnotic susceptibility, waking or hypnotic state, or time distortion suggestions. Barber and Calverly (1964) also showed that hypnotic time distortion did not help verbal learning. One study by the Harleys (1968) actually found that hypnosis had an inhibiting effect upon verbal learning.

White, Fox, and Harris (1940) studied the learning and memory of words. They found that hypnosis improved recall of important material such as poetry, although it was ineffective for the recall of nonsense syllables.

Hypnosis Versus Waking Suggestions

Fowler's (1961) experiments resulted in an interesting comparison of hypnotic versus waking suggestions. In 1958, he studied the potential for hypnosis to alleviate reading problems of students in a university educational psychology course. Included as suggestions given the students in a trance were the following:

Their memory had improved
Their concentration would improve
Their comprehension would increase
Learning is pleasurable

The results were that students reported improved concentration, memory, and reading speed. Unfortunately, there was no control group. In a second experiment, Fowler (1961) included a control group. His results were that the group given suggestions while in a trance had no greater improvement on test achievement than the group given the same suggestions while in a waking state. Thus, both groups were affected by suggestion, independent of whether it was made hypnotically or while they were awake.

Cole (1979) found that groups given hypnotic or waking suggestions related to course content on improving academic skills and the group exposed only to related class curriculum showed no difference in improving learning skills. All groups improved in reading, spelling, and so on, possibly owing just to nonhypnotic class discussion. Cole does offer a possible explanation for hypnosis not having the expected results. He felt this could be due to too short a treatment procedure or absence of individualized induction.

Cooper and London (1968) showed that recall related to learning was not enhanced by hypnosis as such. Having used 52 college students as subjects, they felt that the suggestions for improved memory and motivation to learn were the effective forces in improving performance. Students were tested for recall of information from a 513-word article on a rare chemical. Hypnotic instructions and waking instructions were given in a similar manner. The procedure involved testing the subjects' memory in a waking and an hypnotic state. Directions given during waking instructions included mobilizing all inner energy for concentration and blocking distractions. This method enables one to be completely alert and attentive. The main emphasis here is that one can accomplish better concentration without becoming hypnotized and, through waking suggestions, can also perform tasks such as remembering better. Thus, hypnosis was considered ineffective.

Effect of Hypnosis on Motor Skills

Arnold (1970) studied the effects of hypnosis itself on motor skills. He used 45 highly tranceable and 15 nontranceable students in his study of the enhancement of the fine motor skill of mirror tracing and the gross motor skill of ball bouncing. Nine daily practice sessions involving these motor skills were required. The result was that individuals at either end of the tranceable scale were not affected differently by suggestions given in the waking state or posthypnotically.

Note carefully, however, that these results showing similar influence of hypnosis and nonhypnotic suggestions do not imply that hypnosis is ineffective. Instead, they show that in some situations effects of waking suggestions, when presented properly, may not be distinguishable from the effects of hypnosis. These effects may be positive and improve the student's learning by dealing with anxiety, recall, concentration, study habits, or specific problems such as reading skills. Results of some studies, however, are questionable owing to their lack of control groups (Dhanens and Lundy, 1975). Uhr (1958), evaluating the effectiveness of hypnosis for learning, concludes that most relevant experiments concerning hypnosis are inconclusive. Current review of the available literature and data reaches the same conclusion, that is, that hypnosis helps learning in some cases and has no effect in others.

Hypnosis and Reading

What, then, are the implications for the use of hypnosis in our educational system? In which situations should hypnosis be attempted to help the student who has learning problems? What are realistic expectations of the results of hypnosis?

Consider first the potential benefits a student may receive from hypnosis in improving reading skills. A reading program using hypnosis can have several sessions using posthypnotic suggestion as a basis for further improvements, with a cumulative effect. Knudson's (1968) study with college students showed that an increase in rate and comprehension of reading can last at least 11 weeks. His findings were based on a study of 24 subjects given four hypnotic sessions and followed up in 11 weeks. Posthypnotic suggestions included ideas to quell anxiety and poor reading habits.

Mutke's (1967) experiment with 94 random subjects also showed positive results on reading skills. In his study, one group was hypnotized and the second group was not. His results showed benefits from "image rehearsal" with hypnosis in establishing faster reading and improved comprehension. During hypnosis, students rehearsed corrective techniques for their identified errors or failure. This "image rehearsal" was used to develop improved reading practices. Students were taught the use of autohypnosis to further enhance their study techniques.

Kliman and Goldberg (1962) measured hypnotic effects on reading skills of 10 college students. All were hypnotized without suggestion of relaxation or sleep. Low-level illumination was used to flash words on a screen. Candlepower required for recognition of the words was recorded. The greatest improvement in visual recognition of words that had required the most illumination occurred for the students while under hypnosis compared to their results during control waking states.

Holcomb (1970) also studied the effects of hypnosis on reading skills of seventh graders. His results were that reading comprehension increases were slight, and that reading rate increase was significant for the experimental hypnosis group. As mentioned previously, positive participant expectations may have influenced these results.

Krippner (1966) had results of improved reading and spelling skills. Forty-nine students enrolled in a summer reading clinic participated. Although he showed gains in reading performance up to 1 year, he also had performance losses down to 9 months. The average reading improvement was 4.7 months. The IQ range of the students was from a high of 120 down to 76. Hypnosis was used successfully by Krippner to aid their reaudiotorization and revisualization skills. Revisualize and reauditorize refer to the ability of the mind to re-see or re-hear a word. One client with reading problems and limited visual skills incorrectly recited 85% of the words from a word list. After posthypnotic suggestions that his eye muscles would relax and he would read better, his incorrect responses were reduced to 35%.

An experiment by Cole (1977, 1979) had less than positive results, but the nature of the group studied probably best explains these results. The study group consisted of 93 students from a class on improving academic skills. The students were randomly assigned to one of three groups: a control group, waking suggestions group, or hypnotic suggestions group. Neither hypnotic nor waking suggestions improved participants' reading and test-taking skills more than their class curriculum did itself. All three groups improved their basic academic skills about the same. Owing to the fact that the course in which these subjects were enrolled was based on teaching how to improve academic skills, the curriculum repeated for all groups much of the same information that the experimental groups received.

Wagenfeld and Carlson (1979) used a different approach to test the usefulness of hypnosis in alleviating reading difficulties. Hypnotically using ego-strengthening, age-regression, and time-progression techniques, an adult subject was able to use the reading skills he had attained as a child but was unable to use at the time he sought help. By altering his own self-concept, the subject became able to acknowledge these reading skills. Before this, the individual had a negative self-concept upon which hypnosis had a positive effect while helping his reading problems. Thus, for this client with reading problems, an improved self-concept dramatically improved his use of previously learned reading skills.

Alert Hypnosis

Alert trance is a technique encouraged by Oetting. Hypnosis usually involves relaxation and sleepiness. Yet it is traditionally accepted that the subject must have increased awareness to study and to learn, and this implies awakeness. Further, if the student has personal emotional problems, he may spend more time in introspection while performing autohypnosis, than in active studying. To deal with this, an approach avoiding relaxation and sleep suggestions is encouraged by Oetting (1964). The student is trained in self-induction of alert trance rather than hypnosis *per se*. Oetting does not present specific data but implies the effectiveness of this technique based on his experience using it.

Swiercinsky and Coe (1971) tried to use an alert-trance hypnotic induction as suggested by Oetting. They thus tried to induce their students without suggesting relaxation and sleep, and then studied the effects of alert hypnosis on reading comprehension. Using 58 undergraduate college students, they compared the effects of three conditions on increasing reading comprehension:

1. Alert hypnosis encouraging deep concentration, with improved recall suggested posthypnotically
2. Awake suggestions encouraging increased imagination and concentration
3. No instructions (control group)

All students read the selected material and were given a posttest of factual information. Their results showed that the groups had no significant differences in reading comprehension improvement. Also, similar performances by students with high hypnotizability and those with low hypnotizability occurred. Alert-trance induction was not more beneficial than waking suggestions or controls.

Effect of Hypnosis on Academic Skills

Learning Disabled and Hyperactive Children. Hypnosis can help improve one's reading/learning skills. However, hypnotic suggestions are not necessarily more beneficial than other techniques or conditions such as waking suggestions or alert trance. In some situations, hypnosis may even help hyperactive and learning disabled children. Huff (1980) found that hypnosis used with sixth- and seventh-grade learning-disabled children was not more effective than relaxation training or suggestion in improving reading skills. This contrasted with the findings of Ambrose (1961), who had found that hypnosis did help children with learning difficulties.

In another experiment by Illovsky and Fredman (1976), tape-recorded hypnotic suggestions were given to 48 hyperactive children aged 6 to 8 years. They were characterized by short attention spans, lowered frustration levels, and low motivation to learn. Suggestions were given on relaxation, coping with emotional difficulties, and improved learning motivation. At the end of the school year, 45 of the children functioned better in school. Some had less hyperactivity, and some had achieved average classroom performance. Note, however, that there was no control group.

Calculus. A unique educational usage of hypnosis was that by McCord and Sherrill (1961).

> An intelligent mathematics instructor was put into a deep hypnotic trance. It was suggested to him that upon awakening he would be given some calculus problems which he would be able to work out faster than he had ever done before. The point was to have the client use his existing knowledge and skills more efficiently. Upon awakening, the client completed calculus problems in 20 minutes; the same problems normally would have taken him 2 hours. He was amazed at what he had accomplished.

This brief experience shows the potential for hypnosis in furthering human intellectual functioning.

Recall. Learning involves the ability to remember information. Thus, studies have evaluated the effects of hypnosis on memory. Haggedorn (1970) found in her experiments that hypnosis improved recall of lecture material in the experimental group. She used 61 graduate students who were evenly divided into experimental (hypnotized) and control groups. During hypnosis, the experimental group was given suggestions about interest for and retention of the material to be learned. The control group received no suggestions.

Another approach to evaluating the effects of hypnosis on memory is through experiments on dream recall. Since memory is of essential importance in learning, the ability to recall a dream through hypnosis may be applicable to the general phenomena of recall as related to learning. Blum and co-workers (1971) elicited through hypnosis detailed recall of a dream experienced 2 years previously by one subject. Another subject, however, had minimal ability to recall his dream imagery after 2 years.

Shaul (1978) tested eyewitness recall of a film of a crime. Hypnosis with imagery produced accuracy of recall greater than that of either imagery alone or control. Sellars (1979) used a short prose paragraph, which was learned by 48 female students. One half of the students were highly susceptible to hypnosis and one half were of low susceptibility. The result was that hypnosis did not improve the subjects' ability to remember the paragraph.

Stager (1974) showed that subjects of high hypnotizability scored higher on learning and recall than other subjects. Subjects viewed a short film and were asked questions about it immediately and one week later. Some were hypnotized, and others maintained a waking condition during the viewing. Those subjects of high susceptibility who were hypnotized had the greatest accuracy scores.

Krippner (1963) also considered recall. Although photographic memory is neither typical nor encouraged as posthypnotic behavior, Krippner reported that some students hypnotically recalled every word they read the day before. Cohen's (1972) results from investigation of recall were that there was no significant difference in hypnotic versus nonhypnotic groups. He found that if the groups were chosen, motivated, and treated comparably except for induction, they performed relatively the same in tasks involving recall.

Shubat (1969) tested 48 college students for recall of a prose passage presented 24 hours earlier. Interestingly, she found that the relationship between experimenters and the subjects was the influential factor enhancing recall. Hypnosis with minimal relationship between experimenters and subjects did not enhance recall. Although hypnosis is sometimes seen as effective in encouraging recall, other forms of suggestion without hypnosis and other extraneous factors may have similar effects.

Generic recall is another form of recall to be examined. It refers to partial rather than total recall. It is best exemplified by what occurs when one recognizes a face at a party but cannot remember the person's name. Subjects considered hypnotizable have significantly more generic recall than nonhypnotizable subjects (Kihlstrom and Evans, 1978). Therefore, not only hypnosis itself, but also one's susceptibility to hypnosis can be related to a subject's recall.

As another example, Dhanens and Lundy (1975), found that the only subjects with improved memory were those with high susceptibility who were given hypnosis and motivation about contextual, meaningful rather than nonsense, material.

Creativity

Bowers and Bowers (1972) found that hypnotizability was related to creativity; the more susceptible a subject was, the more potential he had for imagination and creativity. Raikov (1976) studied creativity by telling his subjects in deep hypnosis that they were famous persons with special talent in drawing, music, chess, and so on. Subjects able to be deeply hypnotized demonstrated increased creativity, which continued into the waking state. Those capable of only mild hypnosis and the control groups showed no improvement. Note, we are talking about improvement, not about their actual performance.

Attention and Concentration

Hypnotizability itself has been found to have other benefits. Wallace, Knight, and Garrett (1976) concluded that subjects with greater hypnotizability have greater ability for maintaining attention. Increased attention allows greater concentration and, thus, improved potential for learning. Graham and Evans (1977) also found that those with increased hypnotizability were better able to distribute attention.

Two components of learning are attention and the ability to concentrate. The potential to improve one's ability to concentrate and use effective study habits through hypnotic suggestion has been studied (Krippner, 1971; Mellenbruch, 1964; Oetting, 1964; Summo and Rouke, 1965).

Krippner (1966, 1971) found that hypnotic suggestion helped elementary, secondary, and university students in improved study habits, improved test-taking attitudes, and increased academic motivation. Most students can enter a light trance, and this may be all that is necessary.

Krippner (1963) reports about one student who had such poor study habits that he consistently interrupted himself. These distractions included leaving his studies to open the window, get a drink, or to turn on the radio. His bad study habits were gradually replaced with improved behaviors through hypnotic suggestion to ignore the room temperature, his thirst, and the radio.

Hypnosis and Student Counseling

Mellenbruch (1964) found hypnosis beneficial in helping college students achieve higher grade-point averages. After successfully deeply hypnotizing his students, he would tell them how eager they were to learn and study, to concentrate despite distractions, and to complete assignments promptly. After two or three follow-up sessions, many of these students, formerly on probation, became "A" or "B" students. They experienced improvement in study habits through goal setting and more effective concentration. Two students who generally disliked a course were able to substitute a more positive approach and attitude, thus showing another form of positive change.

Summo and Rouke (1965) developed other hypnotic counseling techniques for helping college students develop better study and learning habits. They labeled students as feeling embarrassed or guilty owing to their poor grades and study habits. They stressed hypnotic relaxation methods to help the student identify the internal pressures that were the causative factors of their study or grade problems. Another factor that they helped the student identify, during counseling, as sometimes detrimental to academic achievement is overinvolvement in extracurricular activities. Summo and Rouke emphasize that they require the student to assume self-responsibility for studying. Through posthypnotic suggestion, they help the student to eliminate distractions, test anxiety, and fear, and to improve concentration, memory, and relaxation.

Hartman (1969) reports his use of group hypnotherapy clinics for students at Southern Illinois University. The individual clinics specialized in weight control, smoking control, relaxation, improved study concentration to lessen test anxiety, and assertiveness training. Weekly sessions lasted 4 to 8 weeks; relaxation and assertiveness training were ongoing. Students would seek admission to the clinics or were referred by their counselors. Individual reports from counselors and the clients themselves showed that many clients were helped effectively.

Qualifications for Hypnosis

Proponents of the use of hypnosis, such as Krippner, praise the results of hypnotic suggestions. Krippner reminds us that a form of group hypnosis is used in everyday interactions such as teachers relaxing students before a hard assignment or high school coaches using "pep" talks before a game (Krippner, 1971). He is also very specific about the qualifications required if a professional is to be successful with hypnosis in an educational atmosphere. These specifications include a thorough knowledge and understanding of hypnosis and educational psychology. Krippner (1977) believes that expertise through proper training is essential and recommends membership in a professional hypnosis society. Knight (1977) supports this with a strong recommendation that educators receive in-service education on proper uses of hypnosis. He also encourages colleges to offer some related courses on hypnosis.

Conclusion

Having reviewed many of the limited available studies of the function of hypnosis as a tool in learning and education, one may still be confused about the final verdict. Studies both support and negate the proposed usefulness of hypnosis in education.

Dale (1972) summarizes nine potential uses of hypnosis in education. These include improving memory and concentration, reducing anxiety, and increasing motivation. Krippner, however, summarizes by writing that hypnosis is accepted as productive and useful in improving learning, but it is not a panacea; it must be used along with other methods and techniques.

Although it cannot be guaranteed that hypnosis will help every individual with learning and academic skill problems, it is certainly worth consideration as a treatment modality.

Education and Hypnosislike Experiences

In his popular book *Psychocybernetics,* Maxwell Maltz (1960) states that we are all "hynotized" and must "dehypnotize" ourselves. He believed that all persons have uncritically accepted negative ideas or beliefs from others and have so often repeated negative ideas and beliefs to themselves that they now believe them. He presents one technique of a 30-minute undisturbed period of exercising the imagination on an imaginary television screen so that the viewer sees himself acting the way he hopes to become. A second psychocybernetic technique involves sitting in an easy chair, relaxing each part of the body, and getting past conscious control to bring forth goals. These methods seem to be hypnoticlike, and one might question if they are not indeed self-hypnosis.

Maltz had an interest in education, wanting to apply his technique to the education of young people. In his book *Psychocybernetics: Creative Living for Today,* Maltz (1970) writes that the Forsyth School in St. Louis used his principles of imagination for the successful education of young children.

The school probably came quite close to using self-hypnotic procedures as a part of their creative teaching techniques. Thus, some idea is given of the potential educational environment possible through the use of hypnosis. Few, if any, schools have ever used such methods over an extended and continuous period. The Forsyth School seems unique.

The academic and emotional growth of the school's children is a favorable indication that some hypnoticlike techniques can be safely included in a school's curriculum to promote student development.

Mary Dunbar, the founder of the Forsyth School, recently wrote the following:

> When Dr. Maltz and I met, he was so enthusiastic about the Forsyth School program that he became a member of our advisory board and invited me to join his board. He visited frequently and talked with the children whom he loved. His lectures always included anecdotes of their successes.
>
> Forsyth School, St. Louis, Mo. is a private pre-school and elementary school for children ages three through twelve. The original purpose of Forsyth School was to teach children to recognize their potential and to express it. We taught them how to use the power of mind by goal setting and visualization (imagineering). This continued for 18 years.
>
> We began each day by gathering together and singing such songs as: "I Feel Wonderful," "It's a Happy Day," and many others—often invented on the moment. Good reports were given by the children of their successes. A three-year-old might report that he had dressed himself. An older student might report his progress in Arithmetic.
>
> Then came "quiet time" when we all took time to choose our goal for the day, relaxed from our toes to our heads, and taking ourselves to our secret happiest place, imagined ourselves having accomplished the goal. We especially emphasized imagining the good feeling we would be having over our accomplishment. We saw it and FELT it.
>
> As a result of this "programming for success" (change of consciousness, self-hypnosis) and our use of proper learning materials and methods, we built on successes. Normal children became "gifted," achieving amazing scores on standardized tests at an early age. Learning disabled children overcame their problems and the least achievement was scoring average on standardized tests. In

1980, five from a graduating class (1974) of twelve, were National Merit Scholarship winners.

One summer, Dr. Ray Klauber joined us during a 4 week session for Jr. High and High School students who were failing in math and/or reading. They were defeated "school haters." We stressed to them that though they had failed, they were not their failures. We practiced meditation and visualization daily. All improved at least a year or two. One boy gained 4 years on the standard-ized tests.

Self-image improvement was noted in a few days. A light seemed to come to their eyes, posture was improved; and they came to school happily. They became friendly with each other and teachers.

Since this time, I have used Psycho-Cybernetics as assigned reading in classes for improvement of reading and study skills. Each session begins with deep meditation and repetition of the statement, "I read easily, speedily—and I comprehend what I read." Speed and comprehension has tripled for most students, and many can read 2000 words a minute with a 90% comprehension from practicing self-hypnosis.

This method of over-coming learning disabilities and accelerating learning should be tried in all schools. (Mary Dunbar, 1/9/81)

Reading

It has long been recognized that students with reading problems often have emotional problems (Whitty and Kopel, 1939). For years there has been spec-ulation about whether the reading problems or emotional problems came first and whether one caused the other (Ruddell, 1974). Witty (1949) found that 40% of those in his reading clinic had emotional problems. He could not discern which might have caused the other. The answer remains unresolved but is further com-plicated by recognition that genetic and neurological difficulties may cause a variety of learning disabilities (Filskov and Boll, 1981). Further, there seems to be different personality types related to reading difficulties (Strang, McCullough, and Traxler, 1967; Spache, 1964; Hall, Ribovich, and Ramig, 1979). One per-sonality type could be conceptualized as shy, anxious, withdrawn, and insecure. A second possible type is characterized as hyperactive, aggressive, and hostile.

The shy anxious child with reading problems can often be helped through hypnosis. This is especially true if diagnosis points to the problem having more of an emotional origin. Lack of such symptoms as low-score Wechsler subscales in arithmetic, digit span, and coding, which relate to reading disabilities (Kauf-man, 1979), leads to a better prognosis.

Children whose reading problems are of an emotional origin often seem quite discouraged and no longer try to improve. Asking such a child to tell you the first memories he has of reading can be helpful in removing reading blocks, especially if the process is repeated under hypnosis for further elaboration.

One boy's first memory of reading was of his mother trying to teach him to read, which he remembered as not being enjoyable. With hypnosis, he was further able to recall that his older sister was present, causing him to feel ashamed because she was making fun of his efforts. With counseling, he realized that his early efforts to read were discouraged by his own comparison with his sister. Further, he realized that her disparagement was her way of maintaining dominance over him. He recognized that he could make further efforts to become a better reader without fear of criticism even if these efforts were unsuccessful. The younger child is in a race to outperform the oldest, and problems result if he decides he is incapable of the task (Adler, 1964, 1969, 1979).

Poor reading can begin as a way for the child to get attention from his parents or teachers who mistakingly help him with many words. The child stops frequently for help, even pausing at words he knows. Training, including hypnosis, to continue sweeping movements of the eyes rather than stopping each time a difficult word is encountered is useful. Metaphors such as slipping the eyes across pages of ice can be given. The speed of sliding can be recalled by the child remembering the time he played on ice. Dramatization is effective. An example is instructing the child to go outside in winter where an ice slick may have developed, run onto it, and slide its full length. Afterwards, under hypnosis, he is told again that his reading pages are ice and that his eyes will slip quickly across them just as quickly as he slid on the ice.

The child who hesitates is often overprotected and is fearful of making mistakes (Adler, 1968). General assertiveness techniques can help children who hesitate, who are fearful, and who will not risk possible failure. Both direct suggestion, as well as metaphor and symbolization, can bring about a more courageous attitude. One boy under hypnosis spontaneously imagined himself as a lion chasing after the words. That day in oral reading, he read aloud. He said every word as well as he could, not waiting for his teacher's sympathetic clues of how to say them.

Some children hesitate because they learned that they had to be perfect and were criticized when not perfect. They are sometimes helped by making mistakes on words they know in order to learn that they can survive mistakes. Under hypnosis they can be told that they will play a game in which they purposely make an error in class, predetermined by the teacher, but unknown to the other children. Should the other children be critical of that error, he will not feel any embarrassment. With the teacher's help, the child who makes a planned error or two will often continue through his lesson without further error.

A developmental reading disorder is defined by the DSM III (APA, 1980) as a reading score and school reading performance significantly below that expected after consideration of the individual's schooling age and mental age. Visual dyslexia, while meeting these criteria, also implies symptoms such as letter reversal and inversion, visual sequencing difficulties, poor visual memory, and mistaking similar words.

Crasilneck and Hall (1975) find that three fourths of their child patients with dyslexia showed improvement through hypnotherapy. They gave the dyslexic child suggestions related to vision, memory, coordination capacity, and anxiety.

Many of the remediation exercises recommended by the teachers of reading-disabled students can be combined and improved by hypnotic techniques. For example, the technique for eye coordination by having the students follow a penlight in a dark room is an hypnoticlike technique that works better with induction techniques.

Children and adults who read well through the traditional teaching of reading can be helped to read faster by hypnotic techniques. It can be suggested that they see and comprehend a larger expanse of the print on each eye fixation. Induction techniques should include the subject imagining that he is on an elevator, descending smoothly and rapidly but with periodic stops. This same smooth dropping movement is then suggested as similar to the movement of the eyes. Movements of the throat, lips, or tongue slow the speed of reading (Moffett and Wagner, 1976). After subjects learn the descending eye movements, they can eliminate other body movements through methods that are given in Appendix 28-1. Further suggestions should be given that subjects will not hear themselves saying the words that they read and that each fixation will group more and more words into comprehensible thoughts.

Thus, hypnosis blends with counseling and teaching methods to help students who are capable readers who want to read faster or those who are learning disabled or are emotionally handicapped.

Test Anxiety

The fear of tests is prevalent at all educational levels. This is not surprising, since a paper and pencil tests is generally used many times each year to determine educational placement, eventually occupational acceptance and ultimately life-style.

Children consider tests ways of gaining or losing approval from parents and teachers and, thus, exaggerate their importance. For the most part, the purpose of testing should be to ensure that the majority of students in any learning situation have reasonably accomplished the goals of instruction. A second reason for testing has been to select students to enter and complete difficult schools and professional programs.

It is the second reason, the perception of being superior or inferior to others, that underlies most test anxiety. Superiority needs may be motivated by the student's fear of failure and insecurity of his true basic ability.

One way to help is through counterconditioning the anxiety of test taking, often involving hypnotic relaxation. While this is useful, the treatment is more complete if the individual understands why he is afraid of failures and, thus, wants to demonstrate superiority and self-aggrandizement. Generally, a combination of hypnotic and nonhypnotic exploration of previous life events will be helpful in pulling together past events.

A 14-year-old boy, who feared tests, explored under hypnosis early educational memories. He was able to recall situations such as his parents doing his homework. With further counseling, it was apparent that his parents were poor and lacked opportunity. They saw the boy as their way to achieve and were thus overly helpful. The boy, under further hypnosis, recalled his delight in receiving the grades of his parents' work, but remembered how insecure he felt in class each time he was tested without parental help. He feared the embarrassment of not scoring as well as his daily performance level, thus disappointing his parents. After careful appraisal of his aptitude and abilities, he came to re-evaluate himself as a truly capable student who was not likely to be outstanding. Hypnosis was then used to visualize himself in the classroom, performing at the level he recognized as his.

A teen-age girl of divorced parents was now living with her father. She was overly anxious of tests, although she was generally outgoing and seemingly without neuroticlike qualities. Her only explanation was that she did not think her father wanted her to do poorly. Under hypnosis she eventually recalled the shame she had felt when living with her mother. One day, she felt great embarrassment when other children teased her over her mother's promiscuous life-style. Further, she remembered that in a previous trial of living with the father she had been required to return to her mother shortly after his disapproval of her grades. With these revelations, counseling was continued to help her work through these problems. A conference was called with her father that resulted in an agreement that grades would not be the basis of living arrangement changes. These actions resulted in less test anxiety.

Here hypnosis was used to uncover important repressed events. In the case of the 14-year-old boy, no major event was uncovered, but numerous memories were uncovered that fit into the theoretical approach of individual psychology.

Milton Erickson (1980) has helped people, ranging from high school students through lawyers and doctors, to control their examination panic in order to pass quizzes, state bar, and medical board examinations. Using hypnosis, Erickson established a trance ranging from light to deep. He stated that he could help the individual, even though that individual's own ways had previously led to failures. The test taker was to attempt to pass with the least passing grade, avoid anticipating the test initially, read the entire examination and allocate proper time to answer each question. The method was effective for nearly all subjects, especially those who could experience deep trance.

Performance Anxiety

Younger school children frequently find themselves in classroom situations that focus the attention of the entire class upon them. Each child having to take a turn reading aloud, answering the arithmetic problem, or simply being called upon after raising his hand are examples of such situations. Children who are shy and lack confidence may be fearful in silence each time the teacher is choosing someone to recite, as well as becoming noticeably fearful those times that they are actually chosen and must answer. Performance anxiety, or stage fright, is frequently found in high school and college students. These students may be participants in vocal or instrumental music, dance, theater, public speaking, and so on.

They may be superior performers in empty studios. However, when performing with a peer or a younger person of greater ability, they may fill with tension and may make severe errors, receiving unfavorable comparison. This is especially true if others of importance or authority, such as their teacher, are present. Many fear criticism and try to escape their critics by perfectionism. Avoidance behavior, from the child who will not raise his hand to the professional who will not come out of seclusion, is common.

According to Adler (1979), stage fright might have as its purpose the appeal to others for help and sympathy. Sometimes stage fright actually exists in order to overcome a sense of inferiority with a superior attitude of what one could have accomplished if not afraid. Wolberg (1948), in an explanation not incompatible with the Adlerian family constellation concept, considers defeat by a competing sibling to be a cause of stage fright.

Hypnosis is of help in many problems of performance anxiety. Often it can be combined with other techniques for more assertive, risk-taking behavior. Shy children can be given direct suggestions that they will volunteer more frequently, seem more certain of their responses, and talk loudly enough. These suggestions work best if they are given as part of a school team effort. The counselor, while providing the child with insight, needs to encourage the child to respond. The teacher should be supportive and complimentary of the child's efforts, helping the child gain positive class recognition, while sparing the child any embarrassment. Further hypnosis can help the child construct imaginary classroom lessons. He can then imagine the children he admires being right and wrong in the answers they volunteer. He is also right and wrong in his mental volunteering. Counseling continues to encourage risk-taking responses while offering insight. The teacher gradually withdraws her preferential treatment. Many shy elementary children will make noticeable progress in a few weeks. However, it is good idea to continue a program well beyond this time and have semester reevaluation for several years.

Dance, theatre, music, and other performing arts students, in the author's experience, are often quite hypnotizable, having excellent use of their powers of imagination. Several techniques are useful to help them perform and overcome anxiety. First, they can self-hypnotize as they observe the performance of accomplished performers, thus strengthening the memory and impression of the observed performance. Later, in a light state of self-hypnosis, they can periodically replay the memories of these performances. They can then picture themselves side by side with the superior performer, each identical to the other. With further practice they no longer watch themselves perform but imagine themselves seeing through their own eyes performing with superior qualities. Once the student has had several successful hypnotic experiences he is more likely to succeed in carrying out hypnotic suggestions that the audience, teacher, or competition will seemingly disappear as they perform. Thus, they will not feel scrutinized as they perform and will no longer be as afraid of imperfection or mistakes.

The final played note, posture, or word that completes their performance can be learned as a signal to refocus their attention to include the audience, teacher or others in their awareness, while bringing complete awakening.

Sufficient safety precautions should be considered when making these suggestions. Hypnotherapy or psychotherapy for insight should also take place if the anxiety seems part of an anxiety disorder.

Separation Anxiety Disorder

The primary feature of separation anxiety as related to education, is the child's refusal to go to school. It often occurs at school entry and is not at all uncommon through the primary grades. A more severe form of the disorder may have its inception at puberty. Children who fear separation have generally developed too close of an attachment with an overprotective, overindulgent parent. Further, the child has a need for his parents' exaggerated recognition and caring. When faced with the school's efforts for independence and the loss of a sheltered favorite status, having now to participate on his own merits, he is fearful. Except for a minority of cases in which psychosis is present, a desensitization of the anxiety of separation is useful. The techniques of Wolpe (1958) or Kroger and Feltzer (1976) may involve hypnotizing the child, who then imagines scenes from his hierarchical list of fear-arousing activities.

Direct hypnotic suggestions of encouragement can be given with reassurance that all will be well both at home and at school upon the child's resuming school attendance. This can be combined with counseling techniques of encouragement and assertion. Issues such as jealousy over preschool siblings receiving their parents' attention can also be discussed. A method I have found helpful, should the child fear for one of his parent's safety, is visualizing on an imaginary television screen a day of school activity. This is done under hypnosis. Simultaneously, a small second television exists, on which the child can monitor the home activity of his parent, thus being assured of their safety. The child experiences the usual fear as he watches himself at school. However, with supportive hypnotic suggestions, the child's attention is called to the small imaginary television picture of his parent to bring about relaxation and reassurance. Further suggestions are made to young children that should the child become afraid while attending school, he can use the imaginary small television technique to reassure himself of the parent's safety.

Study Habits

Sometimes students have very improper techniques of study. They may begin early enough and devote enough time to studying, yet learn very poorly (Brown and Holtzman, 1967).

One such boy who played in a band kept his radio playing the whole time as he stared at his open book. When questioned, he made light of this or any distraction. Since no progress resulted from questioning, hypnosis was attempted. He was hypnotized, with his permission, and obtained some depth. Recalling his previous evening's study, he was surprised when all that he could remember was the music. He seemed completely unaware that his mind had been occupied with hearing the radio.

A school teacher was not doing well in her graduate studies owing to not remembering the material that she had read. She would study in bed until early in the morning. Since it was suspected that she was falling asleep, but she would not be convinced to sit up to study at a different location, she was instructed to set an hour timer, and each time it rang she was to do an alerting self-hypnosis. She reported that she could now study several hours without losing comprehension.

A boy who was anxious in junior high school when given study time to answer assigned questions would not read them thoroughly, but feverishly began writing his responses. Thus, he was requested to read the question thoroughly and to plan his outline. He was still too much in a hurry to do this. When hypnotized, he was helped to understand what was meant by relaxation. Then it was suggested that he could relax in class and that he was to do this through a technique of self-hypnosis, which would be taught to him. Upon awakening, he was taught a covert self-hypnosis technique, a yawn technique in which he would yawn, cover his mouth with one hand, let the other arm go up also to cover the mouth, and then continue up to brush the hair behind the ear. After being hypnotized a second time to reinforce the first suggestions, he was helped and his grades improved to approximate his ability.

Maintaining Class Interest

A concern of every teacher is gaining the learner's attention while minimizing distractions.

Adler (1954) discussed the concepts of attention and distraction in everyday life. He felt that attention in general was embedded in interest of the world. Unfortunately, if a learner sees no possibility of his successful participation in the world or any particular situation, his attention will lessen as he withdraws. Negative and oppositional qualities often accompany this withdrawal.

In one case, a 9-year-old boy was not doing his assignments at school nor his homework at night. He forgot his books and pencil and did not remember his assignments. At times he was a classroom clown, while at other times he displayed his temper when disciplined or pushed to do his work. His IQ was in the high average range. Evidence of a learning disability was not present nor had he improved in medical trials for the control of hyperactivity. He was diagnosed as having an oppositional disorder, a diagnosis often found with children having school difficulties. His parents met with his teachers to establish a system of daily home/school communications so the parents would know of his conduct and work completion. With some, but insufficient, improvement, hypnosis was now initiated. Since he was too oppositional to visualize himself changing as requested, the office puppets became the characters in his mental plays. More satisfied, he not only visualized the puppet family's interaction but began creating longer stories of a projective nature. A theme common to this type of child emerged. He felt a dominating pressure from his father to perform, which was resisted through alliance and manipulation of his mother. Further, he believed that he could not please his father nor could he ever win his father's approval. This was discussed in counseling. Hypnosis continued to elaborate and further recall examples of the home situation. Each time the theme repeated, he, in gamelike fashion, was told to make changes so that the father puppet became admiring and accepting of the child puppet. The father actually was instructed to make special efforts not to override his son's needs. The mother was asked to support her husband. The boy, gaining hope from the hypnotic encouragement, was more accepting of his parents' efforts. The parents, seemingly encouraged by the son's progress, continued to cooperate.

Changing the parents' behavior alone is not sufficient, as the child must be given a way, such as the hypnotic symbolization used here, to accept the parents' changes in behavior.

There are children who, based on the DSM III, would qualify for a diagnosis of an attention deficit disorder with hyperactivity symptoms, which would include inattention, not finishing their school work, not listening to their teacher, becoming easily distracted, and not concentrating on his school work. Self-hypnosis can be used to focus the attention of these children. The psychologist can hypnotize the child periodically, teaching him to re-enter the state as needed to focus, by counting from one to ten. The teacher, prior to an important lesson, can help the child to prepare for learning by counting. In fact, the whole class may be calmed and motivated were the members to shut their eyes and count from one to ten, visualizing an interesting aspect of the day's lesson to be learned.

Conduct—School Behavior

Rudolf Dreikurs (1968), a student of Alfred Adler, clarified the reasons that children misbehave by the purpose or goal of the misbehaving act. One such goal of misbehaving is the receiving of attention. This usually occurs when the child feels frustrated at home or school, believing that his efforts and contributions are not fully acceptable. Oftentimes he feels overshadowed by siblings, peers, or parents and, thus, seeks status through other's overaffection or other's noticing his attention-seeking behavior. The following case illustrates how hypnosis blends with but improves traditional school counseling practices.

The day a boy age 11 was seen in counseling, he had been sent to the school principal's office for sailing a paper airplane, stepping on a piece of chalk, and dropping the coats hung in the wardrobe. The boy had nearly daily incidents of an attention-seeking nature. It was generally known that he had a bright, well-behaved brother 2 years older. Investigation showed that both boys came home together after school. Their mother would review their school work and assignments. She would read the older brother's first, praising him as the younger listened. There was little praise for the younger, and his mother used the time to be certain that he would do the night's assignments. At supper, it was the father's turn to review the day's school lessons. Again, attention focused on the older. While the younger was not overly reprimanded for his lack-luster school performance, it was recommended that he should do as well as his brother.

The younger boy was placed in counseling to help him better understand his situation. Further, he was hypnotized and assured that things were changing for the better. He was told to be a detective and find any positive changes in the way others acted towards him. He was to forget this hypnosis session until, in a later hypnosis session, he was asked to remember.

The parents, teacher, and brother were instructed to give and share some waking suggestions. The mother was to alternate which child's homework she reviewed first. Upon reading each, she was to make positive statements only. The boys would then say something supportive to each other related to the school work. The father was to alternate the dinner talk to focus on both boys in such a way that positive statements were made to both boys. Either parent was to go to visit with each boy as he went to sleep and give some further positive thoughts related to the next day in school. The younger brother's behavior improved. Hypnotizing him a second time, he was asked if he made any discoveries as a "detective." He smiled saying, "Yes, my parents think I learn really great."

This boy was temporarily given the attention he needed while being encouraged by waking suggestions. As Dreikurs (1968) points out, we need to recognize the child's current level, not what he might do some day. We need to avoid conditional acceptance, "If you would just . . . ," or "It's good but . . . ," and find what we can simply praise. The suggestions or statements to the boy did just that. The ones told to the boys as they went to sleep may have had more of an hypnotic impact. The formal hypnosis had a gamelike but serious quality. It prepared the younger boy to expect something to change and that he, as a detective, would discover it and report back.

Vocational Problems

It is an educational function of the senior high school and college to help the maturing student decide upon his vocational objectives. Brief group and individual counseling along with interest inventories make up the usual approach. At times these methods are not sufficient. In planning their future, students may deny their real interests in order to please or displease significant others. Hypnosis can serve as an additional method of finding one's real choices. Further, it can help students imagine themselves in the future so that now they can make the decisions that lead to desired outcomes. Additional functions are the use of hypnotherapy to treat interwoven emotional–vocational problems, as well as problems of immaturity in which the developmental process of vocational selection is incomplete.

E. Ginzberg, S. Ginsberg, Axelrod, and Herma (1951) conceptualize vocational selection as a serial process. During the phase that they designate as the "interest phase," which usually begins in preadolescence, the child feels a need to begin his career direction. At this time, he is most interested in the self-pleasures to be derived through work. By the time the youngster reaches 15 or 16 years of age he should enter the "value stage," becoming more aware of work being a long-term service to society rather than just a means for self-pleasure. Ties might be drawn to Adler's writings that the neurotic individual does not grow to develop social interest. He cannot stand to be a subordinate nor place his needs second to that of his work. Such persons have a great difficulty finalizing vocational choice (Adler, 1969).

A 22-year-old senior in college entered counseling with the fear of anticipated graduation in the field of elementary education. She had chosen this field because she would be free all summer to travel and because of the early afternoon dismissals. Her concern was employability. The only job openings currently available in her field were rural, which conflicted with her urban, single-life pursuits. She did not want to continue graduate studies, move to the out-state areas, nor pursue a less costly life-style. Upon graduation she could no longer be assured of her parents' financial support. The client seemed somewhat immature, hedonistic, and self-concerned. Everything seemed to center on what would happen to her and how awful life could become. To ask her to "grow up" would have resulted in her discontinuing counseling. Instead she was taught self-hypnosis for relaxation. Once relaxing she had some relief from the situational stress, including less disturbed sleep. She showed less symptomatology and formed a closer working relationship for counseling. Eventually, she decided to take a temporary job in the city doing whatever she could until a teaching position was available. With the immediate decision resolved in a comfortable enough plan, she agreed to further treatment by hypnosis. Visualizing her anticipated teaching assignments during therapy, she imagined situations in which she helped children. She visualized these children growing up, and how, because of her help, they made positive decisions that helped others. In one session she symbolized herself as the trunk of a tree and her future students as the branches. In our last hypnotic session, she spontaneously projected herself forward and visualized herself standing before the PTA receiving her gold watch as the principal recited her accomplishments. Whether or not she would ever have the opportunity to teach, the client perceived herself moving from a less mature to a more mature level of vocational development. Through hypnosis she seemed to have passed through a self-centered stage to a level more suitable to an adult.

According to a Ginzberg and co-workers (1951) theory, a capacity stage exists between the interest and values stages. It is here that the adolescent begins to consider and evaluate his abilities and talents in formulating vocational choices. Sometimes his ability, talents, and developing skills are so pronounced as to mandate vocational implications. Musicians in particular will often be well advanced in learning their art by the time they have reached the vocational capacity stage. If they are especially talented and come from a home that recognizes and encourages this talent, they and their families may have already assumed the vocation of choice.

A 22-year-old, gifted, piano student felt anxious and depressed much of the time. He and his family had assumed that he would be a professional musician for as long as he could remember. He never dared to think of any other possibilities. When he entered counseling, he was making errors in practice that caused him to worry about the adequacy of his next public performance. In the course of treatment, he was hypnotized to bring about relaxation.

After several weeks in which relaxation seemed helpful, further hypnosis of an exploratory nature was provided to better understand why he was continuing to make errors and what purpose was served by the errors. In a few more sessions, he symbolized himself behind the piano strings which serve as the bars to a jail cell. His parents were the jail keepers. He began to pull apart the "bars" to escape, but his parents shouted, "No! You should be ashamed of yourself." He awakened crying, feeling very weak and generally helpless. His firm belief that he wanted to be a musician was shaken. Having never previously considered any career but music, he had little idea of what else he might want to pursue. He was not even sure he wanted to give up his interest in music. A compromise was reached that he would undertake vocational exploration and testing so that he could pursue a second field of his choice. Later he could decide which would be his profession and which would be his avocation.

The Strong Campbell Interest Inventory is one of the best available for college students. It generally reflects the expressed interests of its users. However, at times the student is unable to realize much interest in the jobs listed. The inventory's report sheet resembles a menu with many jobs in tabular form grouped together by the six interest themes (Holland, 1973).

A method similar to Erickson's (1980) can be used that the unconscious mind help select job possibilities that the client might enjoy but are not chosen because of the client's unrecognized conflict. The student who can reach a sufficient depth of hypnosis is told to underline the jobs listed on the Strong report sheet that he would like to pursue. Immediately upon exposure of the sheet, he should underline so quickly that he cannot think of his choices. After hypnosis, in counseling, he may reveal why he would or would not consider an underlined job. Frequently he will admit that some of the jobs underlined appeal to him but seem unacceptable to significant others or would make him appear inferior to a sibling. By counseling and providing information related to the jobs he finds interesting, the client often chooses a future based on his preferences.

Social Problems of College Students

Problems of a love and premarriage nature that arise among college-age students would be the ability to find or choose a member of the opposite sex. Because of cultural/historical factors that still operate in our colleges, the problem of having to seek seems more male related, while the problem of choosing seems more female related. Both problems distract the student from their studies and are capable of bringing about enough conflict that motivation to learn declines.

Meeting Women

A frequently expressed need of college males in college counseling centers is the courage to socially approach, meet, and date college women. Most of these men are initially functioning well in their studies and as a group seem undiscernable in appearance from the student body.

Generally, they have an exaggerated fear of rejection. Most will not approach a woman they find attractive, and if they do, they will not ask her out. The problem can become an exaggerated part of their thinking and may bring on or exacerbate further feeling of inadequacy. Eventually this may harm educational performances. By limiting treatment by hypnosis to those male students who are fairly well adjusted, success is often achieved. I give the men ego-strengthening suggestions from Harland and pep-talk-like encouragement suggestions, and help them visualize themselves successfully approaching women. Further help similar to a rational emotive therapy approach can be used, having the hynotized subject dispute his irrational belief that he could not survive any rejection. The previously stated hypnotic techniques are designed to give encouragement and courage, qualities demonstrated necessary by Adler for boys with love/marriage-type problems.

Choosing a Man

A relationship problem frequently encountered by women is the choosing between two men. Generally, the men are quite different, each presenting different qualities. If the conflict is of an "approach–approach" nature, a little counseling usually resolves the difficulty to one man's favor. If, however, there is an "approach–avoidance" conflict with each man, such as one is daring but undependable while the other is reliable but boring, the conflict can become serious. Such conflicts can lead to a reactive depression. Given time, the situation might self-correct as one or the other man finds a new interest. In their worst, these situations can go on for a year or more with neither man willing to withdraw. The woman, refusing to choose, becomes upset and depressed—sometimes leaving school to think things through. An hypnotic solution that has worked when rational decision making did not, was helping the ambivalent woman project herself into the future, going through many days of experiences with each suitor until a positive feeling to one or the other diminishes. Thinking of the person's aging while going through the future can give insight. An example is the woman who dropped her more handsome male friend in favor of the male with more mutual understanding after she had pictured both men as bald. Another woman did the opposite. Seeing herself as becoming ugly, she felt she needed the better looking man.

Appendix 28-1

Improving Reading Speed by Hypnosis

If, upon examination, it is found that the slow reader is moving his throat, lips, or tongue, he should be told that the fastest readers move only their eyes. With proper rapport and diagnosis of the reading difficulty, the therapist could move into hypnotic techniques.

After a relaxing hypnotic induction, slowly say: "Your mind reads by ideas—in an instant, your mind grasps complete ideas through your eyes, faster than anyone could say each word. Your eyes are faster than your throat, lips, or tongue. Saying each word prevents a slow reader from achieving a pace quicker than he can speak. Without moving your throat, lips, or tongue, the meaning of the words quickly leaps through your eyes into your mind. If you like, I will teach you a way you can prevent these movements while reading. Would you like to learn such a method? If your answer is yes, raise this finger [after you touch his right index fingers, wait for him to raise it] . . . Good!

"Now slowly raise the fingers of your left hand to your throat, that is, place your finger lightly about your Adam's apple [guide hands and fingers if necessary].

"Now imagine that there is no movement; try to further imagine that not only does the area you are touching not move but that you no longer feel it . . . It disappears. Signal me with your right finger when you have imagined away your throat. [Wait for the signal and give further suggestions if necessary] . . . Good!

"The same forgetting of your throat will take place when you read. Your throat will be relaxed and comfortable. It will be still, rather than making the words you read. Lower your hand to your lap when you have imagined this in order to receive the next suggestions . . . Good!

"Now slowly raise the fingers of your left hand to your lips, that is, place your fingers lightly on your lips [guide hand and fingers if necessary].

"Now imagine there is no movement, try to further imagine that not only does the area you are touching not move but that you no longer feel it . . . It disappears . . . Signal me with your finger when you have imagined away your lips. [Wait for the signal and give further suggestions if necessary] . . . Good!

"The same forgetting of your lips will take place when you read. Your lips will be relaxed and comfortable. They will be still rather than making the words you read.

"Without moving your throat or lips as you read, the printed words group together into ideas that quickly leap through your eyes into your mind.

"Lower your hand to your lap when you have imagined this in order to receive the next suggestion . . . Good!

"Now slowly raise your left hand to your mouth and place one finger lightly on your tongue. Now imagine there is no movement, try to further imagine that not only does the area you are touching not move but that you no longer feel it . . . It disappears.

"Signal me with your right-hand finger when you have imagined away your tongue. [Wait for the signal and give further suggestions if necessary] . . . Good!

"The same forgetting of your tongue will take place as you read. Your tongue will be relaxed and comfortable. It will be still rather than making the words as you read.

"Without moving your throat, lips, or tongue as you read, the printed words group together into ideas that quickly leap through your eyes into your mind.

"Lower your hand to your lap when you have imagined this in order to receive the next suggestion . . . Good!

"You have now learned to read without using your throat, lips, or tongue. However, as you read, you will lightly touch your throat, lips, and tongue so that you know they don't move. You will be further assured that they aren't moving as you touch them.

"You will make these movements from time to time until you are sure that you never move your throat, lips, or tongue while reading. You will make these movements without thinking about them so that you will continue to concentrate upon your reading.

"Think about everything I told you . . . When you believe that you can read as you learned today, open your eyes and be fully awake."

References

Adler A: Understanding Human Nature. Connecticut, Fawcett Publications, 1954

Adler A: Social Interest: A Challenge to Mankind. New York, Capricorn Books, 1964

Adler A: The Practice and Theory of Individualized Psychology. New York, Humanities Press, 1968

Adler A: The Science of Living. Ansbacher H (ed). Doubleday, 1969

Adler A, Ansbacher H, Ansbacher R (eds): Superiority and Social Interest. Norton, 1979

Ambrose G: Hypnotherapy with Children, 2nd ed. London, Staples, 1961

American Psychiatric Association: DSM III-Diagnostic Statistical Manual of Mental Disorders, 3rd ed. Washington, DC, 1980

Arnold JB: Relationship between hypnosis and learning of two selected motor skills. Dissertation Abstracts Internat 31(3-A):1053A, 1970

Barber TX, Calverly DS: Toward a theory of hypnotic behavior: An experimental study of hypnotic time distortion. Arch Gen Psychiatry 10:209, 1964

Blum G, Graef J, Hauenstein L, Passini F: Distinctive mental contexts in long term memory. Int J Clin Exp Hypn 9(3):117, 1971

Bower G, Monteiro K, Gilligan S: Emotional mood as a context for learning and recall. J Verbal Learn Verbal Behav 17(5):573, 1978

Bowers K, Bowers P: Hypnosis and creativity: A theoretical and empirical rapproachment. In From E, Shor R (eds): Hypnosis: Research Developments and Perspectives. Chicago, Aldine-Atherton, 1972

Brightbill R, Zamansky H: The effect of expectancy and frequency on the work recognition threshold. J Pers 36(4):564, 1968

Brown S, Holtsman W: Survey of Study Habits and Attitudes. New York, The Psychological Corp, 1967

Cohen D: An experimental investigation of hypnotic hypermnesia; the effects of hypnotic induction and regression suggestions on recall. Dissertation Abstracts Internat (University of Kentucky) 35(5-B):2339B, 1972

Cole R: Increasing reading and test-taking skills with hypnosis and suggestion. Dissertation Abstracts Internat (Texas A&M University) 37(8-A):4859, 1977

Cole R: The use of hypnosis in a course to increase academic and test-taking skills. Int J Clin Exp Hypn 27(1):21, 1979

Cooper L, London P: Reactivation of Memory by Hypnosis and Suggestion. Final Report. ERIC Document Resume, ED037796. Washington, DC, October 1968

Cooper L, London P: Reactivation of memory by hypnosis and suggestion: Brigham Young U. Int J Clin Exp Hypn 21(4):312, 1973

Crasilneck H, Hall J: Clinical Hypnosis: Principles and Applications. New York, Grune & Stratton, 1975

Dale R: Hypnosis and Education. ERIC Document Resume, ED-087-710, 1972

Dhanens T, Lundy R: Hypnotic and waking suggestions and recall. Int J Clin Exp Hypn 23(1):68, 1975

Dreikurs R: Psychology in the Classroom, 2nd ed. New York, Harper & Row, 1968

Eisle G, Higgins J: Hypnosis in education and moral problems. Am J Clin Hypn 4(4):259, 1962

Erickson M: In Rossi E (ed): The Collected Papers of Milton H. Erickson on Hypnosis, vol 4. New York, Halsted Press, 1980

Filskov S, Boll T: Handbook of Clinical Neuropsychology. New York, John Wiley & Sons, 1981

Fowler W: Hypnosis and learning. J Clin Exp Hypn 9:223, 1961

Ginzburg E, Ginsburg S, Axelrod S, Herma J: Occupational Choice: An Approach to a General Theory. New York, Columbia University Press, 1951

Graham C, Evans F: Hypnotizability and the development of waking attention. J Abnorm Psychol 86:631, 1977

Haggedorn J: The use of post-hypnotic suggestions on recall and amnesia to facilitate retention and to produce forgetting for previously learned materials in classroom situation. Dissertation Abstracts Internat (University of Tulsa) 30(10-A):4275, 1970

Hall M, Ribovich J, Ramig C: Reading and the Elementary School Child, 2nd ed. New York, D. Van Nostrand Company, 1979

Harley W Sr, Harley W Jr: The effect of hypnosis on paired associate learning. J Pers 36(6):331, 1968

Hartland J: Medical and Dental Hypnosis. London, Tindall and Cassell, 1966

Hartman B: Group hypnotherapy in a university counseling center. Am J Clin Hypn 12(1):169, 1969

Holcomb L: The effects of hypnosis on the reading remediation of seventh grade boys. Dissertation Abstracts Internat (University of Oregon) 31(5-A), 1970

Holland J: Make Vocational Choices: A Theory of Careers. New York, Prentice-Hall, 1973

Huff P: The use of hypnosis in remediating reading in children diagnosed learning disabled. Dissertation Abstracts Internat 40(8-A):4491, 1980

Illovsky J, Fredman N: Group suggestion in learning disabilities of primary grade children—a feasibility study. Int J Clin Exp Hypn 24(2):87, 1976

Kaufman A: Intelligence Testing with the WISC-R. New York, John Wiley & Sons, 1979

Kihlstrom J, Evans F: Generic recall during post-hypnotic amnesia. Bull Psychonomic Soc (Harvard University) 12(1):57, 1978

Kliman G, Goldberg E: Improved visual recognition during hypnosis. Arch Gen Psychiatry 7:155, 1962

Knight J: Hypnosis in educational programs: Its implications as an educational aid. Dissertation Abstracts Internat (University of Sarasota) ERIC Document, ED188072, 1977

Knudson R: A program for improving reading efficiency through the use of suggestion. Dissertation Abstracts Internat 29(1-B):359, 1968

Krippner S: Hypnosis and reading improvement among university students. Am J Clin Hypn 5(3):187, 1963

Krippner S: Hypnosis as verbal programming in educational therapy. Academic Therapy 7(1):35, 1971

Krippner S: Individual hypnosis, group hypnosis and the improvement of academic achievement. In Greenberg I (ed): Group Hypnotherapy and Hypnodrama. Washington, DC, Nelson-Hall, 1977

Krippner S: The use of hypnosis with elementary and secondary school children in a summer reading clinic. Am J Clin Hypn 8(4):261, 1966

Kroger W, Feltzer W: Hypnosis and Behavior Modification: Imagery Conditioning. Philadelphia, JB Lippincott, 1976

Lodato F: Hypnosis as an adjunct to test performance. Am J Clin Hypn 6:276, 1969

Maltz M: Creative Living For Today. New York, Pocket Books, 1970

Maltz M: Psycho-Cybernetics. New York, Prentice-Hall, 1960

McCord H, Sherrill C: A note on increased ability to do calculus post-hypnotically. Am J Clin Hypn 4(2):124, 1961

Mellenbruch P: Hypnosis in student counseling. Am J Clin Hypn 7(1):60, 1964

Moffett J, Wagner B: Student-Centered Language Arts and Reading K–13: A Handbook For Teachers. Boston, Houghton Mifflin, 1976

Mordey T: Conditioning of appropriate behavior to anxiety producing stimuli: Hypnotherapy of a stage fright case. Am J Clin Hypn 8(2):117, 1965

Mutke P: Increased reading comprehension through hypnosis. Am J Clin Hypn 9(4):262, 1967

Oetting E: Hypnosis and concentration in study. Am J Clin Hypn 7(2):148, 1964

Raikov V: The possibility of creativity in the active stage of hypnosis. Int J Clin Exp Hypn 24(3):258, 1976

Rapaport D: Emotions and Memory. Baltimore, Williams & Wilkins, 1942

Ruddell R: Reading Language Instruction: Innovative Practices. New Jersey, Prentice-Hall, 1974

St Jean R: Hypnotic time distortion and learning: Another look. J Abnorm Psychol 89(1):20, 1980

Sellars R: In search of hypnotic hypermnesia for contextual material under conditions to retroactive interference. Dissertation Abstracts Internat 40(3-B):1385, 1979

Shaul R: Eyewitness testimony and hypnotic hypermnesia. Dissertation Abstracts Internat 39(5-B):21, 1978

Shubat N: The influence of state and relationship of hypnotic recall of previously presented material: A test of hypnotic hypermnesia. Dissertation Abstracts Internat 30(2-B):855, 1969

Spache G: Toward Better Reading. Champaign, IL, Garrard, 1964

Spanos N, Ansaii F, Stam H: Hypnotic age regression and eidetic imagery: A failure to replicate. J Abnorm Psychol 88(1), 1979

Stager G: The effect of hypnosis on the learning and recall of visually presented material. Dissertation Abstracts Internat 35(6-B), 3075B, 1974

Strang R, McCullogh C, Traxler A: The Improvement of Reading, 4th ed. New York, McGraw-Hill, 1974

Summo A, Rouke F: The use of hypnosis in a college counseling service. Am J Clin Hypn 8(2):114, 1965

Swiercinsky D, Coe W: The effect of "alert" hypnosis and hypnotic responsiveness on reading comprehension. Int J Clin Exp Hypn 19(3):146, 1971

Uhr L: Learning under hypnosis: What do we know? What should we know? J Clin Exp Hypn 6:121, 1958

Wagenfeld J, Carlson W: Use of hypnosis in the alleviation of reading problems. Am J Clin Hypn 22(1):51, 1979

Walker N, Garrett J, Wallace B: Restoration of eidetic imagery via hypnotic age regression: A preliminary report. J Abnorm Psychol 85:335, 1976

Wallace W, Knight T, Garrett J: Hypnotic susceptibility and frequency reports to illusory stimuli. J Abnorm Psychol 85:558, 1976

White R, Fox G, Harris W: Hypnotic hypermnesia for recently learned material. J Abnorm Soc Psychol 35:88, 1940

Whitty P: Reading in Modern Education. Boston, DC Health, 1949

Witty P, Kopel D: Reading and the Educative Process. Boston, Ginn and Company, 1939

Wolberg L: Medical Hypnosis: The Principles of Hypnotherapy, vol 1. New York, Grune & Stratton, 1948

Wolpe J: Psychotherapy by Reciprocal Inhibition. Stanford, CA, Stanford University Press, 1958

29 Hypnosis and Religion

PETER A. CARICH

Religion provides another opportunity for a therapist to enter into the deep inner self of his patient. According to Dorman (1968), man encounters many life crises, which may be a means of Divine revelation. In most cases, patients experiencing problems with self-worth, self-confidence, low self-esteem, inferiority, and inadequacy, along with other disorders, are confused in their spirituality. Slowly, man becomes his own worst enemy and further deteriorates his self-worth. As man perceives his self-worth relative to his relationship with his world, he reacts to the world in a similar manner. For example, if he see only the negative deep within himself, he feels low about himself as he fits into the society that he is perceiving negatively. In the modality of hypnotic treatment, creativity must be used in order to fit the uniqueness of each patient and his frame of reference.

Types of Disorders Treatable

Man's particular religious or spiritual preference does play a part in this mode of treatment. Francuch (1981) stated that

> Yet, part of the human mind and man's self-concept, self-awareness, awareness of life, and man's life struggle is the issue of spiritual values, the question of God, the purpose and meaning of life, religion, mysticism, the occult, and preoccupation with unknown, incomprehensible, yet ever present within the realm of human premonitions, feelings, inner senses and inner states.

It is of grave importance that the therapist have an open mind and a thorough understanding of the patient's religious beliefs. Also, it is imperative that the therapist have a complete history of the patient so that the treatment consists of the gestalt of the individual person.

The following are some modes of treatment in which hypnosis may be used: imagery, behavioral modification, ego strengthening, relaxation, autohypnosis, **623** projective techniques, systematic desensitization, and reality therapy. Spirituality plays an important role in the segment or wedge of the circle of personality. Man frequently suppresses spirituality or on the other hand goes overboard with his expectations of self, thus creating ambivalence in belief and behavior. It is not necessary for the patient to be committed to organized religion to benefit from spiritual hypnotherapy.

Transitional Imagery—Spirituality

In view of the fact that man conditions himself to pay a price for his wrongdoings, psychophysiologic disorders, which are basically conversion-type disorders, impinge upon an organ of the body, thereby creating a physical disorder. According to Francuch

> If we proceed from the point when man started to transform, at the level of his interior mind, the continuous flowing of God's love and wisdom and of his good and truth into the opposite, when man decided that he did not want to reciprocate the Love and Wisdom of God, then we can see that all the things of logic and order around man in man were turned into the opposite. Love and Wisdom were turned into evil and falsity. Good and truth were turned into sin, badness, deception, untruth, and wrong, and charity and faith were turned into selfishness, self-love, love of worldly material, and earthly things into a perversion of love, and into ultimate denial, atheism, materialism, faithlessness and perversion of truth.

These physical disorders can be treated through spirituality. Menninger (1974) indicates that Judeo–Christian religion has influenced our society's thinking and value system through the mechanism of transference. The definition of transference in this case is the situation in which a person or group influences another person into behaviors that are contrary to their value or belief system, thereby creating ambivalence or incongruence. On the basis of man perceiving his wrongdoings, whether transferred or brought into focus by the Judeo–Christian value system, individual teachings of organized religion, or individual unrelated preferences, man must have an encounter with self in order to balance himself. Man can suppress his wrongdoings and create psychophysiologic disorders. Kroger (1977) stated "in all magical healing one must distinguish between faith-healing, carried out through the confidence of the healer in his secular power, and spiritual healing in which the healer may act as an intermediary in a spiritual process initiated by a deity." An important point stressed by Kroger is that physicians and other nonreligious healers will use suggestive procedures only after ruling out the presence of organic disease.

Stein (1968) stated that the Bible offers numerous examples of psychotherapeutic techniques such as directive, authoritarian, dynamic permissiveness, group psychotherapy, psychodrama, adjunctive music and dance therapy, hypnotherapy, occupational therapy, medical or herb therapy as a tranquilizer, psychoenergizer, and even alcoholism prevention. The Bible and religion can play an important role in therapeutic intervention.

I coined the term transitional imagery as a hierarchical process in systematic desensitization and further explored the idea of using transitional imagery as a method in systematic desensitization, but within a religious setting. I introduced scenes of imagery that were spiritual or religious in nature. The qualifying factor before using this method of hypnotherapy should be that the patient have a deep spiritual commitment and belief. In actuality, the power of God becomes a reality because of the basic belief that the patient already holds. The effects of prayer under hypnosis was also explored with the use of transitional imagery. In this modality, transitional imagery is the use of scenes, step-by-step, that are spiritual in nature, enhancing the patient in overcoming a difficulty of a fear-provoking belief. This is demonstrated in the following case.

The patient is a 29-year-old, white male with above average intelligence. He has been happily married for 3 years and has one child. The patient has been involved in the Charismatic Renewal for over two years. For a number of years, the patient has experienced severe migraine headaches. He was treated in the past by five different physicians to no avail. The last physician related the migraine headaches to allergies. I met the patient at a weekend retreat, and the patient was in the third day of his headache, which became so severe that he was pale and nauseous. Prior to treatment, he stated that nothing was bothering him emotionally. The patient was sitting in a comfortable chair with his spouse on one side and a nun on the other side, with hands laid upon him and praying silently. A relaxation-technique type of induction was used, including a countdown. These are typical of the ones found in *A Syllabus on Hypnosis and a Handbook of Therapeutic Suggestions*. The transitional imagery used was the seashore, as might have existed at the Sea of Galilee. The Lord was at a distance, and the patient had to walk toward Him and have an interpersonel relationship or encounter with Him. As the action began, the patient showed frustration and bewilderment through facial expressions. At this point, I assumed that the patient had encountered difficulty, and gave a new suggestion to overcome the difficulty or change the part of the imagery that was creating the block. He overcame the block, and he had his encounter with the Master. The patient was given about 15 minutes under hypnosis for the encounter and then aroused. Following the experience, the patient openly discussed this experience with me as his spouse and the nun remained silent. I explored the effects of his encounter, which was very positive and effective. I inquired about his deep frustration and bewilderment, which turned out to be due to his inability to overcome the treacherous rocks that kept him from having his encounter. I played a hunch, as we often do as therapists, that the rocks represented something from childhood. I asked the patient what kind of relationship he had with his father, and he started to say excellent but then paused and said nothing for 3 to 4 minutes. He then said, "Not very good." He later, however, stated that he felt inferior to his father because he could never match his father's ability or his father's expectations of him. The stones represented this inability to meet the supposed expectations of his father, and the Lord was a representation in symbol of his earthly father. The patient felt unworthy to experience the good coming from the father. He was inhibited and suppressed his resentment and inferiority toward his father. The pressure caused by the forces of inhibition was released in a psychosomatic disorder of migraine headaches. His condition improved, and the headache was totally dissipated in about 2 hours. This was an unusual therapy session in that it was a "one-shot deal" that lasted for over 2 hours. I saw the patient recently to improve ego strengthening and motivation. He stated that there were no further occurrences of any severe migraine headaches.

The therapist must be aware of nonverbal bodily signs and expressions, which are analyzed and then creatively integrated into the patient's awareness of his problems.

The phenomena of hypnosis, prayer, and transitional imagery appear to have a powerful effect as a healing source. Patients treated with this method have reacted in a positive way, and the effects have been astounding. According to Whitehall (1968)

> Religious experiences, both Eastern and Western, have changed lives for the better . . . Eastern religions and philosophies have placed greater emphasis on developing psycho-physical exercises to bring about character change. In the West, however, the belated discovery and exploration of the nature of various levels of consciousness through the disciplines of psychology and parapsychology tend to confirm the Eastern approach that we have spiritual resources that are real, do function, and can be consciously sought out and utilized.

Healing of Memories

Regression may be defined as an act of returning to some earlier level of existence. Possibly, all events that have taken place in our lives are recorded in the conscious or subconscious levels of the mind. As past hurts are experienced and stored in the conscious or subconscious levels of the mind, the past hurts continue to cause inner conflict without the person having awareness of these past experiences. These past hurts can be converted into physical and emotional pain, and this experience can be traumatic. Many psychosomatic illnesses can possibly be attributed to the past life's hurts which have thought to be forgotten but never reconciled within one's inner self. Memories recalled in deep hypnosis or in spiritual healing of memories may evoke great emotional responses.

Hypnotic age regression and spiritual healing of memories enable a person to relive past experiences with the five senses with which he originally experienced them. Under these conditions, the individual gains insight into his past hurts or positive episodes in his life. This enables the patient to deal more realistically and accurately with the present painful emotional, and sometimes physical, conditions. The following are some of these painful conditions: depression, anxiety, agitation, resentment, fear, negative psychodynamics, lack of confidence, reliance, acceptance of self, low self-esteem, sexual problems, faulty ideas or misconception of religious beliefs, destructive ideations, obsessions, and compulsions. As the person gains insight into the relationship between past hurts and present emotional experiences, a catharsis takes place. Catharsis becomes a reality upon awareness and understanding of the problem from a cognitive and feeling level through the re-experiencing of the traumatic or painful episodes of the past, thereby allowing resolution to take place.

Hypnotic regression takes the patient back to earlier life experiences. Kroger (1977) stated that in revivification, the hypnotized subject relives past events in his life and all memories thereafter up to the age at which the patient has been regressed. Cheek and LeCron (1968) stated that a "back to childhood experience" can be understood with an adult viewpoint. One must remember that under hypnosis and regression a patient is capable of fantasizing or being confused about the actual event.

Penance Syndrome

Klinkman (1965) stated that "the greatest human problems lie not in the area of conflicting emotions, but in the area of conflicting emotionally-charged attitudes—attitudes toward one's self and attitudes toward one's world."

Man exists in a world today that has undergone dramatic changes in moral and value systems. Fear and uncertainty prevails in a changing society, which creates stress and emotional disorders. Man in search of his own identity has created vast problems for himself as well as others with whom he is in conflict. The temptations are strong within the changing times, and man gives into his own impulsive desires. According to Kolesky (1980), psychologists have been reluctant to deal with the effects of sin. Even though all have sinned, we must not maintain the concept that sin is an inherent nature of a human being. Man supposedly is created in the image of God. Man chooses to do the very things that God tells him not to do. Jesus himself was human as well as Divine and was tempted the same as human beings are today. Man appears to have an inner weakness that causes him to act impulsively.

Historically, man has been plagued with giving in to his desires and temptations. This goes back to the time of Sodom and Gomorrah, in the Biblical Book of Genesis, when God destroyed the two cities because of the wickedness therein. Accounts vary in regard to the nature of this wickedness, but the general consensus related to the wrongdoings of man in the eyes of God. Man became so wreckless in his impulsive desires that he lost awareness that these ambivalent behaviors created a distance between himself and God. Through the ages, man has continued to plague himself with psychological problems because of his inability to control the direct expression of his behavior. The problems that man brings upon himself can be viewed as internal and external. The internal problems consist of those man brings upon himself through his own thinking and choice of behavior. The internal problems consist of such behaviors as greed, adultery, stealing, covetousness, or any violation according to one's own moral and value systems. The external forces are divined by the pressures created by the outside forces, which create a pattern of behavior that sometimes can be avoided, such as sexual deviance. Unavoidable pressures might include such things as unemployment, war, pollution, political corruption, storms, and so on. Some acts, such as pornography, can be both internal and external. As man indulges and becomes part of the system, he must deal with his conscience as the inner turmoil begins or becomes worse. The more the inner turmoil, when the so-called evil forces prevail, the further man becomes removed from his identity with God. The more an individual violates his own interpretation of right and wrong, the further the separation between man and his Supreme Being or super-natural force. According to Freud (1949), man frequently has a need to be ill; therefore, he behaves in a way that creates disharmony within himself. Man suffers with the agony of this disharmony. Freud referred to this ambivalence that develops in a person, when deviating from his own value system, as disharmony between the id, ego, and superego. According to my understanding, Freud, being one of the early writers in psychological concepts, was very pessimistic and critical in his intimate knowledge of human nature. His opinion of the bulk of mankind was very low. He felt that the irrational forces in man's nature were so strong that the rational forces had little chance of success against them. Most men are more comfortable living with their delusions and superstitions than with the truth, thus leaving a minority who are able to live a life of reason. Freud's pessimistic viewpoint is developed in his book *The Future of an Illusion.* To a great extent, society, which has been fashioned and developed by man, reflects man's irrational nature in dealing with the forces of illusions. As a consequence, each new generation develops the same illusions and adds more forces to them as a result of the corruption transferred through learning. Man is born into an irrational society, which perpetuates disharmony by continuously adding on new forces of irrationality. Man has difficulty freeing himself from these irrational forces and the influence of man on society and of society upon man. The more disharmony that develops in man, the greater is the conflict with inner self, resulting in further separation between man and God.

I agree with others that man is basically rational, socialized, forward-moving, and realistic (self-actualized). Antisocial emotions, such as jealousy and hostility, exist, but they are not spontaneous impulses that must be controlled. These impulses are reactions to the frustration of more basic impulses, which are love, belonging, and security. Man has an innate nature of being basically cooperative, and trustworthy, and when man is free from defensiveness, his reactions are positive. Man has the capacity to become self-regulatory, to balance his needs against each other and to move towards psychological adjustment (Patterson, 1966). Man must bring meaning into his life. Psychological disharmony also exists through man's evaluation of his action or behavior, which is a reflection of how he views himself.

Maslow's (1954) hierarchy of motivation suggested that man has a need to belong. It is my opinion that when man is in disharmony he does not belong to God or in the "Family of God." He is not in harmony with the supernatural forces. In the midst of corruption, man must depend on the basic idea that he can be forward moving.

When the forces of disharmony are prevailing, man has always sought a way to alleviate the pains of disharmony through a form of penance or cleansing. Even going back to 500 BC, a form of penance or cleansing was used by people who viewed a series of three tragedies, such as Oedipus Rex, Creon, and Antigone. The people would watch the series and identify their emotions by crying and wailing in agony, thereby alleviating their forces of disharmony (sin). There are many patients who live in a world of constant penance. They are paying a price for their wrongdoing or perceptions of wrongdoings and they never seem to be able to pay up in total. The prevailing force of this penance is most likely coming from their subconscious. As man becomes involved in the penance syndrome, and he begins looking down on himself, thereby triggering the internal self-destructive force. A desperate feeling of inferiority and of being unworthy of being loved develops and prevails. Loneliness sets in, and the person finds himself incapable of being loved or giving love. Frustration becomes a reality, and he becomes plagued with confusion. Hostility, with extreme agitation at self and others, prevails. Some hold these emotions inward, suppressing them, feeling anxiety, and generally being unable to function very well at an emotional level. Man becomes unhappy, and dissatisfied with self and others, and cannot experience interpersonal relationships. Projecting the blame for his difficulties onto others is common. Frequently, self-pity is used, and he becomes more bitter and resentful towards self and his environment. Some live a lifetime in the penance syndrome and are not capable of accepting any good that comes to them. Faulty perceptions become a reality, and they see their world in a contorted manner. They live in a world of emptiness, and life becomes worthless. Life becomes bleak and hopeless to the holders of the penance syndrome. Francuch (1981) stated, ". . . thus the evils and falsities and all the tragedies of mankind were created by man through this level by virtue of perverted correspondences."

A major question for the therapist is, "What can I do to help this person?" I have found the combination of hypnosis and spirituality to be a useful tool in aiding those in psychological distress. This distress usually comes from the patient's spiritual disharmony or general ambivalence. Man must first face the forces of disharmony and then work through reconciliation, between himself and God, so that complete emotional healing may take place. I help the patient realize the disharmony and then takes steps in relieving the anxiety and tension created by the revelation. The next step employed is the use of hypnosis in a religious framework. This is a form of desensitization, which frequently lowers the anxiety level once the suppressed situations and experiences are dealt with. One method is to use hypnosis as a relaxation technique, followed by the use of imagery in a religious sense. The imagery often consists of a religious scene in which the patient feels that he is actually with Christ or developing a deeper interpersonal relationship with God. For the Christian, Jesus is introduced into the imagery and for a Jewish person, God is used. Scenery in the imagery is suggested to be as realistic as possible in keeping with the time of Christ as we have learned from scripture readings.

Case A

The patient is a 35-year-old white female who suffers from severe anxiety attacks. She graduated from high school in 1962. She has a son 17 and a daughter 13. Her father died at age 48 from heart surgery. Her mother is age 56 and in good health. She has a brother, age 31 and a sister, age 21. She gets along well with her family. She had the first anxiety attack at work in January 1967 and then went to her family physician, who referred her for psychiatric treatment. She had eight ECT treatments during her first psychiatric hospitalization in 1967. She found that drinking provided her with an escape from the anxiety attacks and subsequently had a problem with alcohol for approximately 8 years. This patient has had over 200 anxiety attacks and many periods of depression lasting from 5 minutes to 3 days. A medical doctor treated her with hypnotherapy for 10 years. She was having trouble getting to his office, since her anxiety attacks often occurred while she was driving. She was referred to me for continued hypnotherapy. During the past 2 years, this patient has become very religious and has given up alcohol. She still has anxiety attacks. I used a relaxation technique for an induction and then incorporated spiritual imagery. The scene was the Sea of Galilee, where she encountered the Lord. She was to discuss her problem with Him and receive any benefits that He was to give her. This patient had a very positive experience, and the frequency of anxiety attacks decreased.

Case B

The patient is a 25-year-old nun who has not taken her final vows. She has a twin sister. Her father is age 49 and her mother is age 53. She was born with a severe eye problem. At age 6, she had eye surgery and her eye was completely removed. She also had a tonsillectomy at an early age. Her right ovary was also removed. She graduated from high school and worked for a while before entering the convent. She attended 1 year of college prior to the beginning of her religious life, and worked as a secretary for 3 years. This patient recently completed part of her pastoral care training and presently is working in a hospital doing pastoral care counseling. She has many problems that she is presently working through. The main problem is a confused relationship with her mother, whom she sees as being extremely overprotective to the point of interfering with her life. Her mother was not allowing her to experience life or to grow emotionally. She has hostile feelings because her mother always had her way about everything and totally ruled the house. She stated that her mother always made her feel inadequate by telling her she could not do things that most people do. She feels that she received very little encouragement. Her mother constantly interceded in situations in which the patient was in total control, for example, school and work. This created much embarrassment and extreme hostility in the patient. This situation has continued through the years. The patient feels that her mother has caused her to become an invalid. Severe feelings of inferiority, hostility, frustration, depression, lack of confidence, nervousness, and anxiety developed to the point that she was experiencing significant difficulty and functioning at a low emotional level.

The technique of hypnosis and spiritual imagery was used as a form of treatment to encourage peace, tranquility, and reconciliation.

Hypnosis, Spirituality, and Creativity

Menninger (1974) stated that hypnosis was used as a method of therapy to bring into awareness a patient's behavior:

> That one could be induced by suggestion to do or think what he did not realize he was doing or thinking; or even remember that he had done so, was a phenomenon which squarely challenged the prevalent ideas of responsibility.

The following example demonstrates a method of treatment in which hypnosis and spirituality are used as a modality of treatment of the earlier discussed disorders.

The session usually begins with deep relaxation, such as a combination of muscle relaxation, counting, and imagery. A deepening technique should also be used to reassure total relaxation.

The therapist begins by saying, "I would like to take you on a journey. It should be a delightful and revealing experience for you. Allow yourself now to trust me as I take you on this journey through the use of your imagination. Let us begin by imagining a beautiful wooded area, with multicolored trees with leaves turning color. There is a hillside nearby, and in the distance you can see the beauty of grazeland and farm animals. We are on a path walking towards the forest. Please notice the beauty that is around us; the trees, grass, wild flowers, pink, blue, and red; various kinds of birds flying around so gracefully. Notice the special beauty of the sun as it reflects warmth upon us and the wind gently blowing through the flowers and grass. How gently the blades of grass bend forward and backward. Delightful relaxation and peace is beginning to cover your body. A true appreciation and nearness of God the Father comes to us as we realize previous scriptual teachings that verify the beginning as found in Genesis 1:1–26, also verifying that the Father loves us."

> In the beginning, when God created the heavens and the earth, the earth was a formless wasteland. . . . Then God said, "Let there be light," and there was light. . . . God made the dome, and it separated the water above the dome, from the water below it. God called the dome "the sky," . . . Then God said, "Let the water under the sky be gathered into a single basin, so that the dry land may appear." . . . the water under the sky was gathered into its basin, and the dry land appeared. . . . Then God said, "Let the earth bring forth vegetation." . . . the earth brought forth every kind of plant that bears seed and every kind of fruit tree on earth that bears fruit with its seed in it. . . . Then God said: "Let there be lights in the dome of the sky, . . . to shed light upon the earth." . . . Then God said, "Let the water teem with an abundance of living creatures." . . .

"So now you can experience a closeness to God the Father as you experience the beauty of his creation. You have a feeling hovering over you signifying love from God the Father."

This first part indicates to the patient that he is lovable and is significant in the creation. An awareness of God the Father also comes into being—God is not aloof and far away but here and now in the immediate present.

"As we continue on our journey notice the trees are becoming more dense. We are beginning to pick up a scent like vanilla, sugar, candy, cookies, spices, and sweetness such as we might experience at Christmastime while all the baking is going on. We are coming near an unbelievable place that reminds us of our early childhood—fairytales and nursery rhymes. The delightful fragrance is upon us, and we are in a beautiful place with cookie houses, candy sidewalks, and gingerbread windmills. The roof tops are made from pink icing and some are made of blue. The hard candy fences are beautiful. We are experiencing such freedom here—free from fear, world problems, daily trivia, and our own emotional paths."

In Matthew 19:13–15, Jesus blesses the children:

> At one point children were brought to him so that he could place his hands on them in prayer. The disciples began to scold them, but Jesus said, "Let the children come to me. Do not hinder them. The kingdom of God belongs to such as these." And he laid his hands on their heads before he left that place.

The basic idea here is to lower the person's inhibitions to that of a child, thereby allowing the patient to experience the new positive forces reflected by the therapist. This will lower the resistance and override the inhibitions.

"We must leave this delightful place and continue our journey. As we continue down the path, we are coming through more dense forest. Notice we are at a fork in the path; if it is all right with you, let us take the path to the right. Nearby, just off the path, there is a large beautiful key, about eight inches long and gold. It is fancy and so beautiful; we should take it with us and keep it. We again are coming to a clearing. As we approach the top of a hillside, we notice a top of a steeple of a castle or palace. It is nearby but not in full view yet. As we reach the top of the hill, we now know and can see it is an old palace. As we are approaching this magnificent building, notice the enormous wooden door at the entrance. Naturally we are now wondering if our key will open this door. Sure enough, our key now opens that big door. We are entering a large room that has one whole wall consisting of a fireplace made of stone. There is a woodpile nearby, as if we are supposed to build a fire. The place is rather damp and gloomy. There is a beautiful carved table and old chairs in the room. This reminds us of stories we have read about knights during the days of King Arthur. I will light the fire so we can be more comfortable. Notice that there is something special about this fire—a special glow. This light from the fire gives a feeling of friendship, warmth, beauty, and a deep inner peace. How can a fire do that? This fire is now special—it is the light of the world—our Master coming to us in a special way."

In Isaiah 9:1-2:

> The people who walked in darkness have seen a great light; upon those who dwelled in the land of gloom—a light has shone. You have brought them abundant joy and great rejoicing.

"The light of the fire not only gives us warmth but also a closeness to the Master himself as we feel his presence, for He is the light of the world. Without light there is darkness. The darkness also represents all of your trials and tribulations. The Master comes to share with us wisdom and knowledge as we open ourselves to new learning. You have frequently shared with me that you feel useless and insignificant as a human being with nothing to offer. The first scripture that comes to mind is the Parable of the Sums of Money as found in Luke 19:11-27. Basically the scripture reflects the story based on talents that are given to us, and we must decide whether to allow the inhibitions to control us to the point of not allowing ourselves to use the talents that we are given." (A reflection of this parable is paraphrased as follows.)

> The Master summoned his servants and gave them each a sum of money and instructed them he was leaving for a period of time and they were to invest this money. Upon his return the servants were summoned and the first servant said, "Master, you gave me $5000 and I have $10,000 to return;" the second one said, "Master, you gave me $4000 and I have $8000 to return," and the Master was pleased. The third servant said, "Master, you gave me $3000 and I have $6000 to return," and the Master was pleased. The fourth servant was summoned and he said, "Master, you gave me $2000 and I have $4000 to return," and the Master was pleased. The fifth servant was summoned and he said, "Master, you gave me $1000 and I have $1000 to return," and the Master was displeased.

"You must now decide whether you will use your talents or allow your inhibitions to hold you back; therefore, out of fear you bury your talents like the fifth servant. Such problems as the following will cause us to bury our talents: inferiority, inadequacy, self-pity, depression, anxiety, resentment, fear, hostility and any self-imposed punishments.

"If you think that you don't have any talents, I would like to share this story with you. There was a court jester who came to a monastery and desired to become a monk. When asked what he could do, he said, 'I cannot read or write, but I tumble and juggle.' The head Abbot said, 'We can't use you here.' So he said, 'I can work,' and upon that he was accepted. Every evening, after finishing his work, he would go to the chapel. The other monks did not know of his whereabouts, and they became so curious that one evening they decided to follow him. They hid in the choir loft. He was standing in front of the statue of the Blessed Mother. He prayed as follows: 'I offer my tumbling and juggling to you Blessed Mother only to bring you joy and happiness, for this is all I have.' He proceeded to tumble and juggle. As the monks watched, a tear and a smile came from the statue. The significance of this story is that even though he could not read or write, he used the talent that he had, and, most of all, his talent was acceptable. You now can choose to use your talents and grow, or bury them as did the fifth servant, for now you realize that you do have some talents.

"Allow yourself now to be touched by this healing light. Let all your inhibitions melt away as you enable yourself to give love and receive love and from deep within yourself have complete awareness that you are lovable."

By now, catharsis is taking place, and most patients release their emotions and cry. The patient has the opportunity to experience love and affection and to have awareness that his inhibitions can be healed. Many variations of this treatment can be used. The inhibitions should be personal reflections on the needs of the patient.

"The amazing idea of your experience at the palace is that you can continue to come to this friendship fire and continue to learn from the greatest teacher of all, our Master Himself. Each time you visit this palace you will learn again and again. We must continue our journey, and as we leave, let us lock the door. Now, I am giving this beautiful key to you and you can come here whenever you feel it is necessary or have the desire to do so.

"Notice that we are approaching another wooded area with many different types of trees. Some of the trees are big. There are strong ones, a few are short, and there are a few peculiar looking ones. The tall ones represent our friends. Notice the number of friends we really have compared to the few peculiar trees that represent people that could hurt us. The rewards are so great with the big trees that we lose our fear and inhibitions in making new friendships and developing deeper interpersonal relationships. And as we continue our journey, we will soon be back where we began, and I will ask you to leave this journey until the next time." (Pause for 2 or 3 minutes to allow the patient to begin preparing for the alerting state.)

"I am going to count to five, and you will slowly come into complete alertness. When I say one, you again will *think* about opening your eyes. When I say two, again you will slowly begin to open your eyes; when I say three, you will have them half open; when I say four, you will have them three-fourths open; and when I say five, you will be completely alert, refreshed, and feel good about yourself. 1-2-3-4- and 5."

Summary

This chapter has included various ways of approaching hypnotherapy as a spiritual-religious modality of treatment. Transitional imagery, the use of imagery in a Biblical religious framework, was presented. Some of the disorders mentioned that are treatable with this modality include: reconciliation with self and past life's hurts, low self-worth, self-inflicted pain, ambivalence, arthritis, amenorrhea, fear, frigidity, migraine headaches, lack of motivation, sleep disorders, anxiety, depression, lack of self-confidence, and negative psychodynamics. Finally, a method of creativity in use of spiritual hypnotherapy was presented. The results of this mode of treatment have been excellent.

References

Cheek D, LeCron D: Clinical Hypnotherapy. New York, Grune & Stratton, 1968

Dorman JW Jr: The Exploration of Spiritual Resources. Spiritual Resources in Hypnosis, 1968

Francuch PD: Principle of Spiritual Hypnosis. California, Spiritual Advisory Press, 1981, p 30

Freud S: (1949) Beyond the Pleasure Principle. New York, Liverright, 1967

Freud S: An Outline of Psychoanalysis. Strachey J (trans): New York, WW Norton, 1969

Klinkman M: Religion and Hypnosis Meet. Minneapolis, American Society of Clinical Hypnosis, 1965, pp 37–43

Koleskey RL: Psychology From A Christian Perspective. Memphis, Tennessee, Parthenon Press, 1980

Kroger W: Clinical and Experimental Hypnosis. Philadelphia, JB Lippincott, 1977, pp 16–17

Linn D, Linn M: Healing Life's Hurts. New York, Paulist Press, 1978

Maslow A: Motivation and Personality. New York, Harper and Brothers, 1954

May R: Love and Will. New York, Dell, 1969

Menninger K: Whatever Became of Sin. New York, Hawthorn, 1974

The New American Bible (St. Joseph Edition). New York, Catholic Book Publishing, 1970

Patterson CH: Theories of Counseling and Psychotherapy. New York, Harper & Row, 1966

Powell J: Why Am I Afraid To Tell You Who I Am? Niles, IL, Argus Communications, 1969

Sanford A: The Healing Gifts of the Spirit. New York, AJ Holman, 1977

Stallman RW, Watters RE: The Creative Reader. New York, The Ronald Press, 1962

Stein C: The Exploration of Spiritual Resources. "Pastoral Psychology in the Bible." Presented at the 10th Annual Meeting of the American Society of Clinical Hypnosis, New York, 1968

A Syllabus on Hypnosis and A Handbook of Therapeutic Suggestions. Chicago, The American Society of Clinical Hypnosis—Education and Research Foundation, 1973

Whitehall D: The Exploration of Spiritual Resources. "To Set the Mind on the Spirit is Life and Peace," pp 6–8. Presented at the 10th Annual Meeting of the American Society of Clinical Hypnosis, New York, 1968

Wolpe J: The Practice of Behavior Therapy. New York, Pergamon Press, 1973

Index

Index

Page numbers in italics represent pages with figures; a *t* following a page number indicates tabular material.

Abandonment, fear of, in psychotic patients, 382–383
ABC process sequence, in depression, 434
ABCDE model of human functioning, 155–159, *156*
  awareness and, 160
  function of, 159
  in rational stage directed therapy, 169–173
  time and, 159–160
Abdominal cramps, in anorexia nervosa, 485
Academic skills, hypnosis and, 599–601
Accidents, hypnosis for, 228–229
  in dentistry, 342
Adaptive regression
  hypnotic induction and, 43–44
  in hypnoanalysis, 151
  hypnotic relationship and, 90
  hypnotic susceptibility and, in schizophrenics, 372
  patient's capacity for, assessment of, 47
  as theory of hypnosis, 394–397
Adler, theories of hypnotic relationship of, 86–87
Adolescents, hypnosis with, in medical setting, 181–182. *See also* Children; Students; Education
Affect
  in cognitive theory of depression, 435–438
  in Freudian theory, 433
  strangulated, in theory of hysteria, 11

Affect bridge, in psychotic patients, 390
Affective type, of psychopathology, treatment of, 440–441
Age, and hypnotic responsiveness, 192–194
Age progression, in hypnotherapy for anorexia nervosa, 491
Age regression, 249, 251
  in family therapy, 332
  healing power of, 626–627
  historical accuracy of, 502–505
  in hypnotherapy for anorexia nervosa, 489–490
  in hypnotherapy for anxiety, 467–469
  in hypnotic recall, 502–505
  in psychotic patient, verbalization of, 398–401
Agoraphobia, 355
Alcoholism, hypnosis for, 319–320
Alert trance, 599
Alexia, breathing exercises for, 37
Alateral sclerosis, hypnosis in, 290–291
Amnesia, relief of, vs. refreshing memory, in hypnotic recall, 510–512
Analgesia, in dentistry, hypnosis and, 341–342
Anesthesia
  chemical, hypnosis and, 216–217
  glove
    in anorexia nervosa, 485
    preparation for, 266
    technique of, 271–274
  hypnosis for, 211
  in dentistry, 341